This volume is one of a complete set of the OSU **Centennial Histories Series** placed in this library in observance of the 100th Anniversary of **Oklahoma State University.**

CENTENNIAL

1890 • 1990

# A History of
# Oklahoma State University
# Student Life and Services

CENTENNIAL HISTORIES SERIES

# Centennial Histories Series

## Committee

W. David Baird
LeRoy H. Fischer
B. Curtis Hamm
Harry Heath
Beulah Hirschlein
Vernon Parcher

Murl Rogers
J. L. Sanderson
Warren Shull
Milton Usry
Odell Walker
Eric I. Williams

Robert B. Kamm, Director
Carolyn Hanneman, Editor
Carol Hiner, Associate Editor

CENTENNIAL
1890 • 1990

# A History of
# Oklahoma State University
# Student Life and Services

by Patrick M. Murphy, Ed.D.

OKLAHOMA STATE UNIVERSITY / Stillwater

Published by Oklahoma State University
Centennial Histories Series, Stillwater, Oklahoma 74078

Library of Congress Cataloging-in-Publication Data

Murphy, Patrick M.
  A history of Oklahoma State University student life and services.

  (Centennial histories series)
  Bibliography: p.
  Includes index.
  1. Oklahoma State University—Students—History.
2. Oklahoma State University—History.
  I. Title.    II. Series.
  LD4297.M87   1988                    378.766'34                    88-25283
  ISBN 0-914956-34-5

# Contents

v

# Foreword

Education is a *people* enterprise. It is the purpose of education to help people *to be* and *to become* the best each is capable of being and becoming! Regrettably, some colleges and universities have lost sight of "the centrality of students" in education, as they have sought to build larger and more comprehensive campuses and as they have concentrated on becoming greater research facilities.

Since Oklahoma State University's earliest days (first known as Oklahoma A. and M. College) students have been, to a considerable degree, "objects of affection" of the faculty and staff. Although manifested to a greater degree during some time periods than during others, the fact is that Oklahoma State University has appropriately become known as a *caring* institution. Contrary to the quip that "campuses would be great places if it weren't for the students," the fact is that it's the presence of students which justifies the presence of faculty and staff and which makes campuses the exciting places of learning which they are!

In planning for *A History of Oklahoma State University Student Life and Services*, it was believed that the author should be someone who not only loves young people but also understands them. Dr. Patrick Murphy, director of University Counseling Services, was selected to write the book—a choice which has proved to be a very good one. Dr. Murphy does indeed love students; and, he understands them. One of the most poignant and charming revelations from his thorough and intensive study of college students through the century is the *unchanging basic nature* of young people. Despite living in quite different worlds, Oklahoma A. and M. students of the 1890s were essentially the same as Oklahoma State University students of the 1980s. Their hopes, dreams, and aspirations; their optimism and their resilience; their self-assurance; their desire to be "on their own"; their positive response to caring faculty and staff; their basic likeable nature—all these have been manifested by the students of Oklahoma A. and M. College and Oklahoma State University over the past 100 years.

The Centennial Histories Committee is grateful to Dr. Murphy for his insightful presentation. The committee is grateful to others who have shared in the production of this volume. Special appreciation is expressed to former OSU Vice President Richard Poole who gave creative leadership as the original coordinator of OSU's overall centennial observance, and who conceived the idea of a Centennial Histories Project. He and former President L. L. Boger have been most generous and supportive, as is new President John R. Campbell. Dr. Ralph Hamilton, director of Public Information Services; Gerald Eby, head of University Publications Services; Edward Pharr, manager of University Printing Services; Heather Lloyd, reference librarian; and their respective staffs have assisted generously.

Working closely with authors of the project have been the Centennial Histories Project editors; and, deep appreciation is expressed to each of them. Judy Buchholz served ably as editor early in the project. From August of 1984 through February of 1988, Ann Carlson contributed greatly to the project in establishing procedures which will make possible the continued production of high quality volumes. On March 1, 1988, Carolyn Hanneman became editor, bringing to the position her skills and experience as an assistant editor, assuring continued excellence of volumes. On March 21, 1988, Carol Hiner, with her considerable publications experience, became associate editor, adding further strength to the editing process. Also, Dick Gilpin's dust jacket art adds much to the series.

Appreciation is also expressed to Dr. Ronald Beer, OSU's vice president for student services, who provided enthusiastic support in the writing of the volume. Also, sincere thanks are due Mr. Dale Ross, since the fall of 1987, the executive director of the Centennial Coordinating Office, and a strong supporter of the Centennial Histories Project.

> Robert B. Kamm, Director
> Centennial Histories Project
> President Emeritus
> Oklahoma State University

December 1988

# Preface

For a number of months Vice President for Student Services Ronald S. Beer had been seeking nominations for an individual to author the OSU Centennial Histories volume on student services. As I sensed him to be near desperation in his search for a "recruit," either retired or currently employed, I decided that I had to make a decision. His anxiety and my intuition combined in October 1982 when I presented myself at his office door to "negotiate a deal." With more ambivalence and honest naivete than confidence, I cautiously offered myself as the writer he needed. From him I asked for an allowance of time (in the summer months) for the duration of the project.

To my relief Dr. Beer neither laughed nor continued his search for a draftee. Our agreement was struck. On December 29, 1982, Dr. Beer wrote to Dr. Robert B. Kamm, director of the Centennial Histories Project, designating me the "official" author of the student services centennial book. The letter was graciously embossed with "Given his exceptional skill to conceptualize what might best be contained in such a series, his outstanding writing ability, and long term avocational interest in history, I think he will do an outstanding job." Before this letter, and still today, I have always appreciated Vice President Beer's confidence in and support of me. I wish to thank him for the trust he had placed with me to complete this project, seemingly so long ago.

I am thankful that Dr. Kamm chose personally to serve as my liaison to the Centennial Coordinating Committee, thereby affording me the opportunity of receiving his guidance, suggestions, and infinite experiences. Throughout this project Dr. Kamm's counsel has been welcomed and appreciated. He is a wise and unconditionally caring individual.

Hopefully it is not too noticeable but the writing of *Student Life and Services* has taken me far afield from both my academic discipline and my professional activities as an administrator and helper of students. How little I knew at the beginning. No one had told me of the required months of solitude, the frequent misgivings caused by feeling overwhelmed, the very difficult decisions about what events and people to omit, and the agonizing over accuracy, phrases, and even single words. At times I was haunted at midnight. In the beginning I was concerned about having enough information to work with. As demonstrated by the length of the manuscript I quickly found that my real problem was that I had too little space. Perhaps it is obvious that this has not been an easy task for me. To all of those students and others, whose stories deserved mentioning in this history but are not, I apologize and singularly bear the regret of the omission.

To my benefit I have also learned some things along the way. I discovered that a biased history is inevitable unless one has the opportunity of presenting every side of an issue. I did not have this luxury. Additionally my personal experiences and observations gave a perspective which is reflected in the manuscript. Although I expended a great deal of energy attempting to write accurate history, I admit my prejudices and apologize if my chronicle offends or misrepresents anyone. During the course of this work I have frequently wondered how legitimate scholar-historians avoid these pitfalls.

From the earliest conception of this book I have wanted the focus to be on students—their needs, out-of-class activities, and changing values and behaviors—and the university's response, which in part evolved into student services. While capturing important history was one goal, I also wanted latitude to embellish the story with examples which cover the entire range of human emotions. If the reader at times laughs, sadly remembers, or can reexperience the intimacy, happiness, or the concern of some past moment in time, then my greatest expectations will have been met.

Many people have been wonderfully generous in the matter of sharing their time and expertise in the completion of this project. Foremost among these individuals is Dr. Kay Rohl Murphy. Kay was always the first to read the worst of my writing. Her roles as a capable professional educator in her own right, supportive spouse, parent to our children, and demanding reader and tough critic are deeply intertwined in every page of this text. A few words can never express how instrumental she has been to the successful completion of this huge undertaking. I will be forever grateful to Kay, as well as Tim and Kelli, for their patience, help, and humor through my good and not so good days.

To Victoria E. McLaurin, a capable associate and colleague in the University Counseling Services, fell the tedious task of transferring my often unreadable scribblings from yellow tablet sheets to the word processor. Beyond this time-consuming activity Vickie afforded invaluable help by pointing out errors and sentences that made no sense, as well as making critical comments. She did a magnificent job with all that I asked and more. I am very grateful to her.

The manuscript was primarily written from photocopies of original documents. While becoming somewhat "infamous" for the amount of work which I burdened the staff of the Edmon Low Library with, never once was a request returned to me late or with discourtesy. Although many library professionals graciously assisted, special thanks go to Heather M. Lloyd, Kathleen Bledsoe, Greg Hines, Kim Mosshart, Kelly Secrest, and Mary Helen Evans.

A deeply felt acknowledgement is also due those who voluntarily reviewed the manuscript draft and provided helpful feedback: Dr. Ronald S. Beer; Dr. W. Price Ewens, professor emeritus in the OSU College of Education, and Dr. Ewens' wife, Frances; King W. Cacy Jr., retired associate director of OSU Financial Aid; Dr. Frank McFarland, emeritus OSU dean of student affairs and professor in the College of Education; Ms. Zelma F. Patchin, emeritus OSU associate dean of student affairs and a most gracious human being; and Dr. William D. Pennington, dean of student services at Tulsa Junior College, despite his having a Ph.D. in history.

Ann Carlson freely gave me unlimited assistance and important moral support as editor of the Centennial Series through the formative writing stages. I am appreciative of her special brand of expertise and dependability. Carolyn Hanneman provided invaluable help first as a research associate and subsequently as editor through the production stages. Along with associate editor Carol Hiner all of these individuals have brought stability, efficiency, and direction to this otherwise maddening experience.

A special thank you to all of my colleagues in student services who have assisted. Although too many people to mention individually, a few of those who made special contributions are: Dr. Don Briggs and Robert L. Jamison in University Placement; Dr. Mary L. Frye, retired Colvin Center assistant director; Dr. Thomas M. Keys and Allen Reding of the Student Union; S. Kay Faught, University Counseling Services; and Winona Wilhm, administrative assistant at the OSU Hospital and Clinic. Martha L. Jordan ably served as interim director of the counseling services during my "writing absences." Pat Hofler, assistant vice president for student services, has a record of more than twenty years of helping me. On this project I especially wish to recognize his help with financial matters.

To my knowledge this book is the first written history anywhere which is specifically devoted to student services and the student extracurriculum at one university. Because of this, I considered it a very special opportunity, a chance to set precedent, and in a small way to make a permanent contribution to my profession and institution. Yet there were trade-offs. In 1987 I spent a solitary summer "holed-up" in a Student Union hotel room. The goal was to write five chapters in eight weeks. During this intense time my twelve-year-old daughter printed a sign on her computer for me with instructions to place it in a conspicuous place. In bold letters her sign said "Crazy Man's Room . . . Patrick M. Murphy." With a renewed sense of balance to my life I met my summer's goal. I hope that others, including Kelli, will into the next century think that my efforts were worthwhile.

Patrick M. Murphy, Director
University Counseling Services

December 1988

# A History of
# Oklahoma State University
# Student Life and Services

# 1 Foundations from Other Times and Places

The north central Oklahoma weather had been warm and murky. Although dark clouds had threatened rain throughout the day, the night promised to be very pleasant for the 2,600 Stillwater residents who made their way across the dry dirt streets and walks in late afternoon.[1]

Guests arrived at the College Building and immediately observed the decorative student-made corn and wheat wreaths that adorned the walls. A festive atmosphere was evident, and anticipation increased as the crowd gathered in the assembly hall. As the time moved closer to 8:30 P.M. on this Friday evening, June 15, 1894, every seat in the room was filled; every aisle was crowded with local citizens, students, parents, and other friends of the college. On the rostrum were seated Territorial Governor William C. Renfrow, the college regents, and, still further back, the few faculty members of the Oklahoma Agricultural and Mechanical College. Immediately in front of the rostrum was the orchestra, so necessary to such an occasion. The seats near the front of the large crowded room were occupied by the one hundred or so young people who comprised the student body. In the center and closest to the rostrum, obviously in the chairs of honor, was the junior class. Among these were the students who would be the college's first graduates in 1896.[2]

Following an introduction befitting the evening's importance, the Reverend R. B. Foster, D.D., pastor of Stillwater's Congregational Church, came to the podium to deliver the dedicatory address. In 1894, the first permanent building on the campus was called "The College Building"; later it would be widely known as Old Central. Constructed largely from local materials, the building was new and youthful on this June night. To some it was even beautiful. For many the College Build-

It was new and youthful. To some, it was even beautiful. For others, it exuded feelings of permanence and safety for Stillwater's land-grant college. Old Central basks in its dedicatory photograph in 1894.

ing represented the fulfillment of a dream, hopefully even the end of a struggle that began before the college's chartering on December 25, 1890. Although the college had been about its work of educating the youth of Oklahoma Territory for nearly three years, there was in this building, for perhaps the first time, a feeling of permanence and safety for Stillwater's college. Tonight, then, was an evening for pomp and ceremony.[3]

The Reverend Foster, a short man with grey hair and a beard, started his speech without a tremor in his voice. This was an evening of happiness, he said. This building was important to the college and the territory of Oklahoma. Continuing, Foster pointed out that in the past the nation had separated itself into privileged classes and masses. The classes were to be educated; the masses were to labor and remain uneducated. Foster then said "now, the agricultural college is founded on a totally different idea from that; its idea is to educate laboring men who will still continue to be laboring men after they are educated.

"Let it be distinctly understood that old prejudices die hard—that

Centennial Histories Series

we are the heirs of a thousand years and more of training, in which time manual labor has been looked down upon—that agricultural colleges have been established only during the present generation, and that we cannot be expected to yet have outgrown the feelings of contempt for the horny-handed sons of toil.

"But I insist that the ideal of the agricultural college," continued Foster, "is that labor is honorable, and that a man can be a gentleman and delve in the earth as well as though he spent his time poking among musty law books, or dealing out poisonous drugs, or preaching prosy sermons to a few drowsy people who wish he would say 'Amen'."[4]

Foster's speech ended, as did the third commencement of the Oklahoma A. and M. College. Although no one graduated, the College Building had been dedicated.

Noticeably and significantly the seats of honor at the dedication had been given to the students. These first students were, after all, mostly sons and daughters of uneducated laborer parents, who would become with clear conscience and pride, educated laborers. Oklahoma A. and M. College was a land-grant institution, and this quality would make these students unique. A different kind of student, facing a new kind of curriculum, had come to Stillwater. Eventually many would leave as citizens with a different contribution to make to the nation's development.

Reverend Foster, in the first public exercises ever held in the College Building, had clearly, if not simplistically, set the stage for what the Oklahoma A. and M. College would become—"a factor of great merit in training the youth of the land to become useful men and women."[5]

The College Building's very purpose for being built, its long years of service to the education of students from Oklahoma and other places around the world, and the dedication speech all focus attention on what is most important in institutions of higher education throughout the nation, both then and now. A visionary speech at this dedication of a campus building called to mind that the essential ingredient which differentiated colleges and universities from society's other contemporary institutions was the student. In many ways the very vitality and life of a college or university emanates from the student body. Without the student there is little need for a curriculum, teaching, or textbooks. Campus buildings and classrooms become unnecessary in the absence of people interested in learning. Exceptional teachers and researchers are great in large measure because of their ability to motivate students to learn. Administrators exert their professional energy to develop budgets, establish procedures, and plan new buildings to provide the means for students to secure an education—an education which considers the student's needs both in and out of the classroom.

A university does not exist without the students. Students are the paramount ingredient. No history of a university can be complete, nor accurately portrayed, without including the needs, interests, and concerns of this segment of the campus community. After all, at an institution of higher education, "students are our work."[6]

The history of the Oklahoma State University can be viewed more clearly by understanding the students who have come and gone. Their interests and behavior over the years are an open window on the past of the university. During a century of existence, insights about the university can be gleaned from understanding past student uses and misuses of the campus buildings, studying the changes in student rules and regulations, and describing former student enterprises and organizations. Likewise, student elections, student protests, and past prestigious awards won by students, help to explain current circumstances. Such events also mirror contemporary times on the campus, whatever date the event occurs. The story of students of the past sheds light on what the Oklahoma State University will become in its second century of service to the state, nation, and the world.

The fullest grasp of the history of students and the large variety of institutionalized services provided for students by the university is gained by looking beyond December 14, 1891, when Oklahoma A. and M. College welcomed the first students. The forces that would eventually mold student services and the students' environment were already long at work. Educational foundations, traceable to American colonial colleges, existed which help to explain the university of today. Not to re-trace these foundations would leave unexplained much of what was to evolve in later student collegiate life.

The uniquely American system of post-secondary education contributed and influenced the collegiate atmosphere at the college in Stillwater. The very model or example of what a college should become is traceable in the hundreds of years of trial and error, as well as the successes, in higher education. The unique blend of curriculum and extracurriculum, professor and student, urban and rural setting, public and private sector, and even national, state, and international events, all impact upon a college's development. This is true for all colleges and universities, for none exist in a vacuum.

Unquestionably Oklahoma State's history began with a view which dated back to the original colonies in seventeenth century America. Over the years, external influences, primarily state politics, became a major influence on the early development and growth of the college and student services. In addition to meddling political forces, the college's geographic location, transportation, funding, and rapid student enrollment would represent, among other problems, additional barriers.

Because Oklahoma A. and M. College was established later, it remains a relative youngster in the larger family of colleges and univer-

At the dedication of Old Central, the first permanent building on the Oklahoma State University campus, the chairs of honor were reserved for the students. In the center of this distinguished student body was the junior class, those students who would become the college's first graduates in 1896. Some time after the dedication, this class gathered at Old Central. Standing left to right are Ervin G. Lewis, Arthur W. Adams, Kate Neal, Alfred E. Jarrell, Emma Smith, James H. Adams, Oscar M. Morris, and Frank E. Duck. The two women did not graduate.

sities in the United States. In a sense, the college had the luxury of taking the best of what higher education had to offer and molding many traditions or practices into what was best suited to serve the people of the state of Oklahoma. Despite the college's humble beginning, what soon followed was a collegiate atmosphere, heavily influenced by students and their desire to be like students elsewhere. Student activities were not new; their roots were historically in other places.[7]

Student activities, when implemented, all had a special Oklahoma A. and M. quality, unique to the reality of the hard times and the college's struggling beginnings. The college had all it could do to provide an academic program for the student. Out of necessity, and perhaps eagerness, students undertook for themselves the development of their social, physical, and spiritual selves, often against the better judgment of the faculty.

At the outset of the American Revolution, wealthy English colonists in the New World were sending their sons, but not their daughters, to any one of nine colonial colleges. Harvard was the first of these earliest

New World colleges. By 1770 William and Mary, Yale, New Jersey, King's, Philadelphia, Rhode Island, Queens, and Dartmouth had all been founded. Each was established to re-create a portion of what was best in higher education then found in England. In the uncultured and recently colonized New World, these colleges sought to ensure a supply of trained clergy and a selectively educated people. The founding fathers understood the importance of establishing a class of educated citizens who could spell the difference between a progressive enduring society and ignorance and stagnation. Although education was not for everyone, there must be a trained clergy, educated schoolmasters, and business leadership among the growing colonial population.[8]

Conversely, for most of the early colonists a college education was generally unimportant and could certainly wait. This attitude continued to prevail through the next century as more and more Americans moved west to settle the readily available land. For the average citizen survival of the family was easily the first consideration in the earliest decades of the nation. It was the obligation, if not the duty, of the sons of the settlers to stay at home and farm the land. College was a luxury most families in 1776, and for decades to come, could ill afford for their children. The basic need to clear the land, grow food, and help provide the most elementary rudiments of survival was of paramount importance. The value of a college education and its contribution in finding an easier way to meet basic needs would wait until after the American Civil War.[9]

By 1862 the shaping of the nation had moved ahead rapidly. Although still evolving, the Constitution with its Bill of Rights had established a cornerstone for equal rights and opportunity for all citizens. The United States had survived every external test and was emerging in the world community as a respected, free and independent nation. The Louisiana Purchase in 1803, which included the eventual state of Oklahoma, had provided additional land for growth and expansion. The severest test yet of the strength of the democratic government, the Civil War, caused the face of the nation to change still further. Factories, railroads, and the ever increasing population helped to create an alliance of resources from east to west across the nation. The United States was rapidly becoming industrialized. Oklahoma was yet to be born, but the Civil War had begun to draw the people to the region, then known as Indian Territory.[10]

During the Civil War era, the U.S. Congress enacted the Morrill Federal Land-Grant College Act in 1862. Although the *New York Tribune* did not mention this legislation among the important accomplishments of the Congress, this apparently innocuous legislation would eventually do much to make vocational, practical, and technical education a legitimate function of many of the nation's colleges and universities.

For the first time in American history the idea of going to college was freed from the constraints of social and economic background. As simply a practical matter, the needs of the nation's development were demanding that the agricultural and industrial classes of the society have access to higher technological skills and more progressive ideas.[11]

The Morrill Act provided for the support of at least one college in every state where scientific and traditional studies could be taken along with studies of agriculture and the mechanical arts. According to the act, each state received either public lands or land script in the equivalent of 30,000 acres for each senator or representative under the apportionment of 1860. No single event did more to cause higher education to become popularized. Although each state implemented the provision of the Morrill Act differently, by 1961 sixty-nine American colleges were being supported by this legislation and the several acts that followed, including the Morrill Act of 1890 which provided for regular annual appropriations for the land-grant colleges from the federal government. By 1955, this whole new network in American higher education—the land-grant system—would enroll more than 20 percent of American college students.[12]

The promise of land and federal money, combined with the initiative of the citizens of Payne County in Oklahoma Territory, set into motion the chain of events necessary for the founding of Oklahoma's own agricultural and mechanical college. Accordingly, Oklahoma's land-grant college was established on December 25, 1890. This territorial enactment accepted the provisions of the Morrill Acts of 1862 and 1890, and in addition incorporated the Hatch Act of 1887.[13]

The Hatch Act, another important legislative initiative of the Congress, provided money for agricultural experiment stations. It served to foster extensive and far-reaching agricultural related research; but perhaps as importantly, the Hatch Act further reduced the skepticism held by large numbers of farm families toward colleges. The provisions of this act, in combination with the Morrill Acts, softened people's resistance to sending their sons and daughters to college. The benefits of college work could now be seen and applied to useful purposes.[14]

Payne County was perhaps seen as a satisfactory location by some in the territorial legislature, at least in part, for reasons rooted further back in higher education's history. Colleges and universities had generally been located away from the negative, if not immoral, influences of urban life. Given the agrarian background of the United States, it was perhaps not surprising that locating colleges in rural settings dated to the 1700s. For example, in 1789 North Carolina provided in the state college's charter that the institution not be situated within five miles of any location of governmental proceedings or where courts of law were to meet. Still later, Georgia's college trustees selected a hilltop in north-west Georgia, acquired a forested tract of land, and called it Athens. Today, Athens is the location of the campus of the University of Georgia. In Oklahoma small rural towns such as Alva, Goodwell, Norman, Tishomingo, and Miami were all granted charters for colleges. Tulsa and Oklahoma City—Oklahoma's population centers—were conspicuously overlooked.[15] Stillwater clearly met the criteria of offering a wholesome country atmosphere to students. Payne County was a proper environment in which to mold young, impressionable minds to essential values, work habits, and positive social and religious ethics.

Appropriate religious guidance, and therefore attention to the spiritual development of students, was a basic foundation, if not an integral part, of the earliest American colleges. Theological training was among the highest priorities of the colonial colleges. Despite time and a changing society, early campus religious societies flourished in the early 1800s. With an increasing secularism on the nation's campuses, religious societies faded in influence after the Civil War. By the time the Oklahoma A. and M. College was chartered, the former intensive religious fervor on most college campuses in the nation had subsided. Specific religious denominations were experiencing difficulty in achieving their mission because of the increasingly homogeneous character of the college students. Nonetheless, few educators or religious leaders believed that attention to the spiritual needs of students was any less important. What was needed was a new means to accomplish a very old, yet still important, priority.[16]

At the end of the nineteenth century, the college pastorate movement, or the assignment of clergymen to work exclusively with college students, was underway. Closer ties between campuses and community churches was encouraged and supported by college presidents. Despite the then remote principle of law separating church and state, on-campus religious clubs and organizations were actively encouraged and supported. College facilities were used for meetings, and faculty advisors were provided to these religious clubs. Many colleges, including the Oklahoma A. and M. College, established the long-standing traditions of prayer days or annual religious emphasis weeks. Finally, denominational religions on campus gave way to the more generic and broadbased Young Men's and Young Women's Christian Associations movement.[17]

By the time the first students of the Oklahoma A. and M. College started their classes, a vital extracurriculum had been added to the earlier formal curriculum in colleges throughout the United States. From earliest collegiate times, debating clubs or literary societies were the first student-organized extracurricular activities. Within a year after the students started classes at Oklahoma A. and M., literary societies were organized. Paralleling the national trend, interest in literary societies eventually gave way to the development of social fraternities and sororities. As at

A rancher tends his herd of cattle on the prairies north of Stillwater. Through the efforts of the Stillwater townspeople and the Stillwater delegation to the Oklahoma Territorial Legislative Assembly, this area became the "right" location for the Oklahoma A. and M. College. Few people could have imagined that this prairie would spawn this sprawling campus nearly a century later.

more mature, older colleges, the students at Oklahoma A. and M. College became involved in a student newspaper and humor magazine, theatre groups, extensive intramural competitions between classes, and social organizations based exclusively upon the student's interest or hobbies. What would become extracurriculum had been largely defined elsewhere by the time of the college's chartering.[18]

As student enrollment grew in both size and variety, new, perplexing problems began to face the college president and the faculty. How much time could the faculty spend in disciplining students?[19] Could the faculty be expected to chaperon every activity or serve as advisors at every student meeting? Who should supervise the increasing number of women students, since their problems were so different than the men? Parents, college trustees, and influential political and religious leaders expected responsible guidance of students. Perhaps the supervision of students' behavior, in all of its increasing forms, was an unreasonable expectation to place upon the faculty. Nonetheless, because they were the only possible choice, the burden had fallen largely to them.

Because these problems were not merely philosophical, a pressing need to solve them developed. As a result, specialized college employees, generally labeled "the administration," began to increase in numbers after the end of the Civil War. Initially these positions were a combination of teaching and administrative responsibilities. In the first half of the nineteenth century a college's administration was handled by a president, a treasurer, and an often less-than-full-time librarian. By the time of the turn of the century a new set of administrative titles was commonplace among the nation's colleges. By 1900 position titles such as registrar, dean of women, and dean of men were born of necessity and firmly blended into the network deemed essential to administer a college.[20]

Other administrative systems were also clearly developing by the time of the beginning of Oklahoma's land-grant college. On most rural campuses, and on some urban campuses too, the dormitory had become a fixture by 1890. Probably born of the practicality of providing room, and later, meals for the increasing numbers of young people desiring a college education, dormitories were initially controversial. Critics pointed out the liabilities of the same rules and regulations for all students. There was also the potential hazard of mixing students with different personalities. Dormitories caused a lack of exercise among students. Perhaps most importantly, the critics frequently asked if the expenditure of money for building and maintaining dormitories would not be better used elsewhere for other critical purposes.[21]

Advocates countered that within dormitories the wishes of parents and faculty could be better implemented for the well-being of students. Students would also learn the attributes of community living, common decency, and self-respect within the cloistered setting of a dormitory. On a more practical level, self-government and student supervision could be more easily achieved. For these and other reasons, the dormitory advocates prevailed. On-campus housing for students spread throughout the nation's colleges.[22]

The earliest students at the Oklahoma A. and M. College lived with their parents. When students began to arrive in Stillwater from some distance, rooming houses—sometimes with board provided—were offered by the local residents. Frequently more enterprising students, interested in frugality, organized their limited financial resources and formed their own boarding houses. Although effective in many ways, the faculty and administration soon saw that the inefficiencies outweighed the benefits.

Before World War I, the Oklahoma A. and M. College had constructed its first campus dormitory. No one could have foreseen that in the next seventy-five years the campus residence system would be recognized as one of the best in the United States. With the student housing, personnel became an added necessity.

Still other foundations for student services and the Oklahoma State University's extracurriculum pre-date its charter. Following the Civil War, industrialization and more modern farming methods developed rapidly. For practical reasons alone, the demand for more advanced knowledge in mechanical, technical, and agricultural training became essential. The nation's population was growing rapidly. As the American lifestyle grew a bit easier and as more specialized training continued to be required, attending college became increasingly more popular. It was no longer vital to the survival of the family to have children remain at home. Concurrently, good jobs, and therefore upward mobility, impelled young people to pursue higher education more frequently. Meanwhile, in the nation's colleges distinctions between professional and vocational education grew smaller. In response, career and vocational counselors were employed to assist college students in determining their academic major.

In the late 1800s other foundations for today's institutionalized student services were being laid. Increasing enrollments surfaced the problems of containing infectious diseases and the sometimes immediate need to treat other student maladies. These student health concerns led to the establishment of college infirmaries and the employment of college physicians, dentists, and nurses.[23]

The lack of interest on the part of students to participate in physical activities resulted in the organization of campus intramural and recreational programs. Although physical education classes remained a part of the required curriculum, the intramural program was designed to improve students' physical fitness and to occupy, in positive productive ways, their leisure hours. The colleges, of necessity, assigned faculty to part-time teaching and part-time intramural program supervision. Students, past and present, were involved heavily in campus intramural and recreational programs. Some student motives do not change over time. In intramural activities "the student motives are clear: they wanted some exercise and they wanted more fun."[24]

Still other professionals were hired to assist students and free the faculty for their academic pursuits. Specialists were employed to help students find part-time employment to offset their college expenses. Later coordinating and awarding scholarships were added to the duties. Financial aid officers, who in contemporary times are experts at administering multimillion dollar grant, scholarship, work-study, and on-campus job placement programs for students, were of necessity, if not quietly, made a commonplace part of the college administrative structure.[25]

Former student association directors, today called alumni directors, were appointed to help solidify the ties between graduate and alma mater. Likewise, student placement services were organized, and specialists helped acquaint graduating students with prospective employers. In addition, with an increasing number of students arriving to study in the United States from nations around the world the initial foundations for a specialist in foreign or international student advising followed.

After the Civil War the regulating functions for college student behavior were starting to shift from the faculty and administrators to the students themselves. Frederick Rudolph, in his history of the American college and university, concluded: "This movement toward greater

Although Oklahoma A. and M. College was a mere "child" among institutions of higher education when it was chartered in 1890, it soon began to grow and develop. Soon a vital curriculum and extracurriculum had embraced Oklahoma's land-grant institution. In this turn of the twentieth century photo, two nattily dressed coeds "take a spin" around the campus.

Centennial Histories Series

formal recognition of student responsibility was probably a response to the sudden massive growth of athletics, the tendency of many institutions to assume a posture treating their students as if they were grown-up, and a distinction on the part of the new professors with their Ph.D. degree and scholarly orientation to have anything to do with such trivial matters as discipline and the extracurriculum."[26]

With the many changes in the collegiate way, the classical curriculum of earlier years, and the abdication of the faculty for assuming responsibility for students other than in their classroom-related learning, new administrative systems were required if the void was to be filled. Into the vacuum came the college dean of students. The dean of students was the initial college employee designated to maintain the "human touch" between institution and college students. The dean was unable to do the job alone. A semblance of the concept of *in loco parentis*, or the college serving in place of the student's parents, needed to be maintained. A network of faculty advisors, counselors, and campus chaplains soon joined this new campus network which gave expression to caring about and supporting the student as a whole person.[27]

Somewhere in time colleges acknowledged that students learn both in and out of the classroom. As a result, colleges increasingly felt obligated to provide opportunities in the spiritual, emotional, and physical realms, in addition to the educational. Given the social context of the late nineteenth century, it reasonably followed that all learning required guidance and supervision. Where once a dedicated faculty served exclusively, a new group of professional educators with a specialty in student development and philosophy and interest in the total student came upon the American college scene.[28]

By the 1950s the college had organized a cluster of student services called Auxiliary Enterprises. Representing a process of evolution, this administrative organization acknowledged the concept of a student being treated as a unique person. This idea was by then firmly entrenched among American institutions of higher education. Today, the broad umbrella of student services at Oklahoma's largest land-grant university encompasses the University Counseling Services; the Colvin Center, which provides campus recreational and leisure activities; the University Hospital and Clinic; Residential Life Department; the Student Union; and the Department of Financial Aid. Representing millions of dollars in physical facilities and services for students, the Division of Student Services employs several hundred professional, technical, and support personnel. Each area of the division has a unique history. The thread that ties them together can be traced to pioneering deans of men and women, college dormitory matrons, and early YMCA secretaries. All have the common thread of recognizing students as complex individuals who learn both in and out of the classroom.[29]

A student services philosophy, perhaps even movement, predates Oklahoma A. and M. College. Commonly called the student personnel movement, major underpinnings are based on the important concept that if a student is admitted to study at a college or university then the institution accepts an obligation to provide essential services to enhance his or her chances for success. Again, it is a holistic view which recognizes that every student is a unique individual. The student personnel professional appreciates the fact that experiences within and outside the classroom provide opportunities for student learning. Typically knowledgeable in such disciplines as adolescent psychology, group dynamics, and principles of learning, these advocates of students are concerned with the interaction of the academic environment and the individual student. Often the success or failure of the student rests upon whether such interaction is positive or negative. Simply stated, the loss of any student, particularly if that loss could be averted, is a tragedy. Student personnel professionals, whether a counselor, financial aid administrator, or residence hall director, work long hours to enhance educational success and forestall tragedies.[30]

From the first days, the faculty of the Oklahoma A. and M. College toiled to help each student grow to his or her full potential. That tradition has carried on through time. Perhaps without knowing it, the college has continually incorporated the basic tenets of the personnel point-of-view. Today, more than ever, the Oklahoma State University provides programs and services which assume that a student is never locked to a fixed point in time or maturation; rather, the student is an individual developing to maturity and adulthood. The responsibility of the institution is to assist the student in moving from dependence to independence; from interest to responsibility and competence; from casual concern to involvement; and, from egocentricity to successful social and interactive behavior.[31]

As the Oklahoma State University celebrates its centennial year, the campus offers many services. The multimillion dollar investment in campus buildings, the availability of highly skilled, supportive student services professionals, and a large variety of programs, from orientation to placement, all say better than words that students are important. Although some students might disagree, contemporary students lack for little. They can choose to live in a modern air-conditioned residence hall and select from a variety of food plans tailored to meet different eating habits. Physical and mental health services are available. Campus entertainment and recreational opportunities exist daily. Hundreds of campus student organizations enhance the quality of campus life and provide leadership experiences. The Student Union is recognized as one of the most complete and best facilities of its kind in the nation. Yet Oklahoma State University would not be the same without its nationally honored Greek system. Systems to help students finance their education, such as Veteran's Village in post-World War II days and the Lew Wentz Service Scholarship program, have also made a measurable difference in the institution's history. Both serve as important examples and historical windows to the past.

To omit students and the services that have evolved to support their needs would be a serious oversight in understanding a university's past. While teaching, research, and extension will remain the broad purposes of the university, all land-grant institutions generally share this same mission. What makes a university different, perhaps gives each a unique personality, emanates from the faculty, students, and administrators. People's successes and failures, interests and concerns, and dreams and plans differentiate one college or university from another. The history of the Oklahoma State University is the story of all of the people who have come and gone—the students and the people who interact with them.

The last decade of the nineteenth century was the first decade in the life of the Oklahoma State University. The stage was set for the starting of a new land-grant college in Oklahoma. The history of the nation's colleges and universities was old but rich in foundations from which to build a great university. Colleges were acceptable vehicles for upward economic and social mobility. Educational opportunities were available to all, not just the wealthy and educated classes. The technological

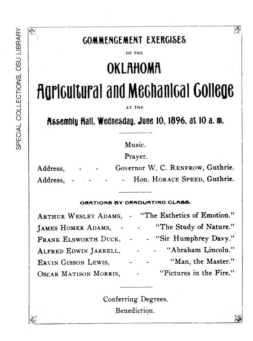

SPECIAL COLLECTIONS, OSU LIBRARY

COMMENCEMENT EXERCISES
OF THE
OKLAHOMA
Agricultural and Mechanical College
AT THE
Assembly Hall, Wednesday, June 10, 1896, at 10 a. m.

Music.
Prayer.
Address, - - Governor W. C. RENFROW, Guthrie.
Address, - - - - Hon. HORACE SPEED, Guthrie.

ORATIONS BY GRADUATING CLASS.

ARTHUR WESLEY ADAMS, - "The Esthetics of Emotion."
JAMES HOMER ADAMS, - - "The Study of Nature."
FRANK ELSWORTH DUCK, - - "Sir Humphrey Davy."
ALFRED EDWIN JARRELL, - - "Abraham Lincoln."
ERVIN GIBSON LEWIS, - - "Man, the Master."
OSCAR MATISON MORRIS, - "Pictures in the Fire."

Conferring Degrees.
Benediction.

revolution and an increasing trust in education had combined to require that the nation's colleges and universities offer both professional and vocational courses of study. By 1890 the nation was becoming far less reliant on hands and bodies to do the important work of the nation.[32]

In June 1894 Oklahoma A. and M. College students helped dedicate the first permanent campus building. Among the students present was Arthur W. Adams, the first to receive a diploma in 1896. Adams completed his degree in agriculture in four years. In later life he earned his livelihood as a real estate agent and accountant. Emma Smith, another member of the first class, left school before graduation when illness struck her family. Jessie O. Thatcher, who took five years to complete her degree with a major in science and literature, was the first woman graduate of the college. In her adult life she was a homemaker and a teacher.[33]

Many students had entered the college, but only some graduated. Not unlike students today, in this very first group of twelve young men and women, only six graduated in four years. Some would take longer to achieve their degree. Still others would not finish a degree program. While some students would choose a college major and directly apply what they had learned to their life's work, others began careers after graduation unrelated to their studies. Each of these first students had unique interests and aspirations, and each believed that the Oklahoma Agricultural and Mechanical College would permit them greater opportunity.

Yet, in the final analysis, perhaps it does not matter so much now whether the earliest students succeeded or failed. Within the context of passing time and the larger issues of life itself, every student, whether from the past, present, or even future, can rightly claim that they have been a part of the unique history of Oklahoma State University.

## Endnotes

1. *Stillwater Eagle-Gazette*, 21 June 1894, p. 1, 28 June 1894, p. 1.

2. Freeman E. Miller, "Exit the Bandit—Enter the College!" *Oklahoma A. and M. College Magazine*, vol. 1, no. 5 (January 1930), p. 24; *Stillwater Eagle-Gazette*, 21 June 1894, p. 1.

3. Miller, p. 4.

4. Miller, p. 24.

5. Miller, p. 4.

6. Oklahoma State University's third and current vice president for student services, Ronald S. Beer, frequently reminds faculty, campus visitors, and Division of Student Services staff that without students there is no purpose to the Oklahoma State University. In speeches and other contexts Beer often states that "students are our work" at the university.

7. Most of Oklahoma A. and M.'s earliest important student enterprises had their beginnings on other college campuses much earlier. For example, student literary societies began at Yale and date back to 1703. Influential campus student governments have their origins in post-Civil War colleges. The YMCA movement was well underway in 1875. Campus prayer days dated back to Yale University, the first being held in 1750.

8. The first college to admit women was Oberlin College in Ohio in 1837. Thus Oberlin was the first co-educational institution of higher learning in the United States. In 1839 the Georgia Female College in Macon was chartered as the nation's first college for women. Still later, in 1855 the University of Iowa was the first land-grant or state university to admit women. Frederick Rudolph, *The American College and University—A History* (New York, NY: Vintage Books, 1962), pp. 1-7.

9. Rudolph, p. 22.

10. Rudolph, pp. 240-263.

11. Rudolph, pp. 240-263.

12. Rudolph, pp. 241-263.

13. "The Development of the Oklahoma Agricultural and Mechanical College, 1940," p. 1, President's Papers, Special Collections, Edmon Low Library, Oklahoma State University, Stillwater, Oklahoma.

14. Rudolph, p. 261.

15. Dan S. Hobbs, "Oklahoma Demographics: Myths and Realities," speech, 2 May 1986, Stillwater, Oklahoma; Rudolph, pp. 92-93.

16. Rudolph, p. 79.

17. Rudolph, pp. 79, 459.

18. The first literary societies date to Yale in 1753. Shortly thereafter Princeton and Harvard added these rather intellectual organizations to their extracurriculum. Rudolph, pp. 144, 465.

19. From earliest days student disciplinary problems consumed large amounts of faculty time. In 1832-33 Dartmouth faculty met 68 times to consider student discipline cases. The University of North Carolina faculty decided 282 discipline cases in 1851. At the time North Carolina's student enrollment totaled 230 students. In general, faculty members served exclusively as student disciplinary tribunals on into the twentieth century.

20. Rudolph, p. 435.

21. Rudolph, p. 99.

22. Rudolph, p. 96.

23. Rudolph, p. 339.

24. "History of Student Personnel Services," p. 3, Student Services Collection, Special Collections, Edmon Low Library.

25. Rudolph, p. 388.

26. Rudolph, p. 431.

27. "History of Student Personnel Services," pp. 3-5; Rudolph, pp. 369, 459. In 1870, Harvard University appointed the first college dean of students. His responsibilities included discipline and the mechanics of enrollment, in addition to teaching. The president of Johns Hopkins University appointed the first "chief of faculty advisors" in 1889.

28. In 1837 Oberlin College, Ohio, opened its doors to women. Oberlin's President Finney observed "we will need a wise and pious matron with such lady assistants to keep up sufficient supervision." Horace Mann, of Antioch College, was even more skeptical about admitting women students. Mann said "the dangers of it [meaning the presence of women students] are terrible." The original lady matrons were the forerunners of the dean of women and a professional association called the Association of Women Deans and Counselors.

29. Rudolph, p. 460.

30. "History of Student Personnel Services," p. 1.

31. "History of Student Personnel Services," p. 1.

32. Rudolph, p. 485.

33. Alfred Edwin Jarrell, "The Founding of Oklahoma A. and M. College: A Memoir," *Chronicles of Oklahoma*, vol. 34, no. 3 (Autumn 1956), pp. 318-319; James Showalter, "Student Majors List," Memorandum to Centennial Book Authors, 27 August 1985.

# 2 Students in the Evening of the Nineteenth Century

As in many great enterprises, the beginning of Oklahoma A. and M. College was humble. Nearly one year after the college was chartered by the territorial government, the first students were welcomed on December 14, 1891. Organizing the college, finding the money and classroom space to open the doors, and hiring a faculty were only a few of the problems that had been surmounted.

The first college classroom was in Stillwater's Congregational Church, then located near Sixth and Duncan Streets. There was no campus and little money to carry on the struggling enterprise. Two hundred nearby bald prairie acres awaited future campus development.

The college could not be started without students. To solve this problem, forty-five students from the Stillwater public schools were recruited to enroll in a college preparatory school. In these times of survival it mattered little that the first students were neither college students nor academically ready to undertake the rigors of a college curriculum. Ready to greet the first students was the faculty. This pioneering group consisted of the president, the director of the Agricultural Experiment Station, and four faculty members.[1]

As the college's work began, Oklahoma itself was still a territory with a total population of just over 250,000 settlers, each with their own struggles to survive. Oklahoma's statehood would not come until November 16, 1907, nearly sixteen years later.

The location of the college in Stillwater involved the local citizens in political tradeoffs. Perhaps trickery and underhandedness could also be claimed by the citizens of neighboring towns. Of course, they were the losers in the negotiations needed to establish the land-grant institution within a specific town in Payne County.[2]

With history to be written, and much history already to build upon, the first students arrived to enter the Oklahoma A. and M. College's preparatory school. Promptly at 9:00 A.M., the students reported. Principal Edward F. Clark was in charge of registration. After the few minutes that it took to register the students, seats were assigned. As was practiced in any one-room country schoolhouse, the larger and taller students were assigned seats at the back of the room. Three or four small blackboards, mounted on rollers, were periodically moved about the room to take advantage of the best sunlight. Movable wooden partitions, about eight feet high and twelve feet in width, further helped to divide the classroom space. The college's first students brought their own textbooks with them. These were from their course of study in the public schools. The teaching methods in the college were similar to methods found in the public schools. Students not reciting were to study their lessons quietly.

The school year went by, and the students in the preparatory school faced their first serious challenge in May 1892. For almost a week students were administered a written examination. About twelve students passed these first comprehensive exams. In early June the fortunate twelve were selected as the first freshman class.[3] Oklahoma A. and M. College, with its first true college students, would begin to make its history when the fall term began.

The college freshmen returned for their first college classes in September 1892. The Congregational Church this time provided the college classrooms. Students who failed the May examinations were returned to college preparatory classes and moved to other buildings in Stillwater. The Congregational Church remained the campus for these first students during their freshman and sophomore years.

Oklahoma State University's students of a century ago, no doubt like students of today and tomorrow, longed for activities and social opportunities with other students. To fulfill the requirements of the student psyche, for time eternal, human contact primarily with other students has been a basic need. This need has historically been met outside the campus classrooms. While the relationship between teacher and student is central to learning, this relationship alone represents only a small part of what students, past and present, find to be important in higher education. Because the first students were people with basic human as well as student needs, they somehow knew, at least at an intuitive level, that a college education was more than what the first faculty could offer them. From the founding years of Oklahoma's land-grant college, the "magic" of class traditions and loyalties, societies and Greek organizations, athletics, and various agencies of entertainment would pull upon the interest of the student.[4]

Today's students enter the university with something in place to assist them in meeting every interest. It was not so at the Oklahoma A. and M. College in the 1890s. The earliest students were pioneers, in every sense of the word. Pioneers venture into unknown areas. They are innovators and discoverers. Pioneers blaze new trails and chart new directions. Through hard work and trial and error, pioneers make it easier for those who follow. The students of the first decade of the college, like the college itself, had few available resources. Intentionally or inadvertently, these pioneering students would help the college through hard times, certainly ensure a more pleasant "collegiate environment" for themselves, and build foundations upon which they could continue to prosper and also build further. In the years that followed many of the earliest graduates looked back at their undergraduate days and reflected upon their contributions with pride—sometimes, even in disbelief of what they and their classmates had accomplished.[5]

In 1951, Willa Adams Dusch, an 1899 graduate, reminisced about the origins and history of the Sigma Literary Society, one of the earliest

When the Oklahoma A. and M. College held its first classes on December 14, 1891, forty-five students, recruited from Stillwater's public schools, enrolled. These students were neither college students nor academically prepared to undertake the rigors of a college curriculum. Instead, they enrolled in a preparatory school. As this 1893-94 photograph of the senior preparatory class indicates, many of these first students were quite young!

and, at the time, most important of campus student organizations. Founded in 1893 this organization was more than a literary group. Dusch recalled that Maggie Hutto and Elsie Parker, the two students who conceived the idea of this literary society for both college men and women, had to secure faculty approval for their group. The students' desires for their own activities represent well the general purposes student activities serve even in contemporary times.[6]

Parker, in discussing the background of the Sigma, reflected: "I truly wish that I could say now that we two girls were imbued with a burning desire for culture and a high-minded literary goal. This, I am sure, would be dealing in pure fiction. Maggie Hutto and I were searching for the same thing that all youth are groping for throughout the ages; we wanted what was so very rare in those dead days—entertainment and social contacts. At that time, October 1893, I was a 'sage' of fourteen years, and Maggie was about two years my senior. All our activities were of our own making and we must be given credit for imagination even though we were short of years, experience, or judgment. In a literary society we could have self-expression and contacts. We directed our efforts to the realization of our project."[7]

Organizations, like colleges, begin humbly with high ideals and expectations, mixed with a bit of naivete blended in. Nowhere is this more evident than in student organizations. The Sigma Literary Society's founding illustrated this point. Frequently where there is student initiative there is commonly a reaction which equates to "checks and balances" within the campus community. Even in 1893 this was evident. Parker continued her memories of the founding of her organization: "Well do I remember my amazement when I learned that it was customary to consult the faculty regarding our venture. To me it seemed the 'old men' (some in late twenties or early thirties) were expecting a great deal. What possible interest could they have in what we wanted? Yes, of course, they might feel responsible for the building. Very well, we 'consented' to consult. We did."[8]

Parker then described one of the first encounters between student leaders and faculty at the two-year-old college. Out-of-class learning was the result. Controlling one's emotions, appearing humble, and making spontaneous response—all useful skills in life after college—were experienced by Parker. Continuing her recollections, she said: "We were seated along with President Barker in a row where the three of us were looking into the faces of the faculty sitting as a jury. Presently President Barker asked our purpose in being there. After a moment's pause, I, so recently chosen speaker, stated our desires to organize a literary society. I do not recall what President Barker's full remarks were, but they were brief. In fact, the dear man seemed to rely on his best chosen cough, or guttural throat-clearing sounds, which were an idiosyncracy of his,

The Sigma Literary Society was one of the most popular social organizations of the territorial college. Open to men and women, the society was responsible for the beginnings of the campus newspaper, the *Daily O'Collegian*. The Sigma Serenaders, a portion of the organization, gather in 1896. Standing left to right are Thomas J. Hartman, Cora Miltimore, Norris T. Gilbert, Willa Adams, George W. Bowers, and Minnie Dysart. Seated are Earl Myers and Jessie Thatcher.

never to be forgotten.

"I think we would have been dismissed at once had it not been for Professor Frank A. Waugh who seemed to think a little more was due the faculty. He may have been suffering for a little amusement himself. He requested me to give something of a detailed account of what we proposed to do. I acquitted myself as follows: Songs, readings, debate, and orations would be our regular mental diet. I was well pleased with my answer, but momentarily. Like a hawk ready to devour a mouse, he snapped, 'What kind of orations—original or standard?'

"Poor me!" Parker continued. "My temperature dropped with a dull thud. I never had heard of an oration being designated as 'standard.' Waugh knew, as I knew, I could not produce an oration if it were to save me from the gallows.

"It is said God looked after children and idiots. He came to my rescue. I divined if there were two kinds of the sauce we might as well have both. In a reassuring voice I said 'both'! Maggie, who had so recently placed me on the speakers bureau, gave a suppressed giggle.

I, in turn, gave her what I thought was a withering glance of disapproval."[9]

Parker then described the end of the meeting. "With more ominous sounds from President Barker we were dismissed with the remark that we would receive the decision of the faculty later. Out in the fresh air I felt saved."[10] After meeting the requirements of the faculty to draw up a set of rules to govern the organization, the Sigma Literary Society was founded with nine charter members on October 20, 1893.[11] Thus ended, at least for the time being, one of the earliest confrontations between faculty and students. Beyond the Sigma Literary Society itself, more pervasive issues also came to the surface. For years to come, philosophical principles, underpinnings for students and their out-of-class activities, were now becoming more concrete. Student rights, college rules and regulations, and the enduring concept of *in loco parentis* would now begin to grow along with the college itself.

In fact, the framework for the conduct of the college's students had been firmly laid, but not finished, nearly two years before students Parker and Hutto appeared before the faculty. When the college was just three months old, the first faculty meeting of record was held on March 17, 1892. Presiding at the faculty meeting was the college's first president, Robert J. Barker. Elected by the college's board of regents to the full title and rank of "President of the Faculty and Professor of Moral and Mental Science," Barker's title was perhaps ominous, yet fitting to the time and the board's view of the college's role in educating students. Fifty years later, Professor F. A. Waugh, in writing about Barker, characterized him as an honest, kind, and gracious individual who never received the credit that he deserved for his work. Nonetheless, Waugh also wrote that "the men who elected him to the presidency did not know what the job was and probably didn't care. Barker was a nice fellow and had been a school teacher; moreover, and much more important, a good Republican."[12] Barker remained as president until June 15, 1894. Importantly, he was the first of many early college presidents whose tenure was directly intertwined with territorial politics.

To the liability of the young college, quality of educational leadership seemed secondary to the political realities which would continue to plague the college's development for the next several decades. In 1892 six people constituted the entire faculty. Among them, Professor Waugh, with a new master's degree from Kansas State College, served for the next two years as professor of horticulture. J. C. Neal had been appointed the first director of the experiment station on August 14, 1891. Shortly thereafter Neal was made professor of natural sciences and served from the first year of Stillwater's college until his untimely death on December 22, 1895. A. C. Magruder was the first professor of agriculture and horticulture in the college. Magruder, who taught his first year at a salary of $41.66 per month, remained on the faculty until June of 1895. The Magruder medals for freshman oratory remain a part of his historical legacy to the Oklahoma State University.[13]

W. W. Hutto, professor of English literature and military tactics, and Edward F. Clark, professor of mathematics, also attended the first faculty meeting. Hutto and Clark, regrettably, further served to illustrate the negative pervasiveness of Oklahoma politics in 1892. At the fiftieth anniversary of the Oklahoma Agricultural and Mechanical College Professor Waugh wrote: "Hutto and Clark were alike in one point: Hutto had a brother whose political influence had landed him the job. Clark had a brother who was a prominent politician. Hutto's brother was a Republican; Clark's brother was a Democrat. Just then and there those classifications were vitally important. When the Democrats gained control, Hutto was the first man fired after President Barker. Clark stayed until the next change in politics. Then the Republicans got him."[14]

The last of the original faculty was George L. Holter, professor of chemistry. Holter, who was educated at Pennsylvania State University, was an exemplary teacher, a disciplinarian, and a man who required much from his students. A young man, he had the most experience in teaching college students. To Waugh, Holter "did more than anyone else, or all combined, to make a college out of our crude little community."[15]

With President Barker presiding and Professor Clark serving as secretary at their initial meeting, the first faculty undertook the deliberations required to approve their first ever agenda item—the rules relating to students! The original code of student conduct consisted of twenty-two rules. Although the students would not begin their studies for several months, the rules were written to assure that the students would be "trainees" and learners; the faculty would be in charge of the college. Rule eleven specifically stated "as obedience and subordination are essential to the purpose of the College, any student who shall disobey a legal command of the Pres [ident], Commandant, or any professor, or instructor, or other superior officer, or behave himself in a refractory, or disrespectful manner to the constituted authorities of the College shall be dismissed or less severely punished according to the nature of his offense."[16]

The very first rule, apparently reflecting two major issues of concern to the original faculty, covered firearms and deadly weapons, as well as a matriculation, or enrollment, pledge. It stated: "Each student— when he enters the College shall deliver to the President—all arms and deadly weapons of any description which may be in his possession, and shall subscribe, in a book, to be kept for that purpose (to) the following matriculation pledge: Being now about to enter as a student of the Agricultural and Mechanical College of Oklahoma I do hereby acknowledge my obligation and bind myself to obey all its laws and regulations and I pledge myself on honor that so long as I am a student of the College during term or while I remain at the College during vacation I will not have in my possession any deadly weapons except such arms as are furnished by the Military department, without the consent of the President or Faculty . . . ." The lengthy matriculation pledge continued by forbidding student involvement in secret societies or organizations, shouting or disrespect of others, and hazing or mistreatment of other students. Rule two, which directly reinforced rule one, stated: "Any student who shall willfully violate the foregoing 'Matriculation Pledge' shall be dismissed."[17]

The whole intent of the faculty in stressing deadly weapons remains a mystery. In later years Alfred Edwin Jarrell, one of the six college graduates in 1896, expressed his dilemma in understanding this particular rule when he wrote: "But none of the early students (so far as I know) ever claimed to be a gun man, or ever wore a six gun (with belt) and I know none of my class ever carried a six gun—or ever claimed to be

Students were required to wear uniforms during the first decade of the college. Cadets pose in their military attire in 1895. While women did not participate in military drill after the second year of the college's existence, they still wore uniforms. Emma Swope Dolde poses in appropriate dress in 1895.

an expert shot with one. I have seen samples of their shooting at various times, (pistol, rifle and shot-gun) and while some of it was good, none ever could be classed as expert." Although the first students could have brought weapons to campus, particularly given the time and location of the campus, there is no evidence that a western-type shootout, involving students or anyone else, ever occurred on or in proximity to the campus. Perhaps then, one might conclude, the college's first rule was effective. On the other hand, wearing sidearms invited trouble in Oklahoma Territory in the 1890s. Few citizens, at least in the Stillwater area, wore sidearms. It was far safer, if not simply practical, to go about one's business unarmed.[18]

The remaining twenty rules for college students were divided into sections covering student conduct, academic requirements, and administrative procedures. All misconduct was punishable under the college's basic code of military discipline, governed by a strict system of demerits. Under the codification of prohibitions for student's conduct was the restriction on the "use of any spirituous, or intoxicating liquors. Nor shall he upon any pretext visit any saloon or place of dissipation." Further, the students were required to attend morning chapel exercises, be courteous at all times, and "heartily cooperate with the faculty to secure the objects for which the college was established."[19]

The college's academic requirements mandated that the student present testimonials to his or her good character upon admission, maintain minimum grade requirements of 70 percent to avoid being declared deficient in a subject, and follow procedures for final examinations. Early administrative procedures required that students' grades be sent directly to parents or guardians at the end of each term, that students receive permission from the president before taking a leave of absence from the college, and that faculty meetings be closed meetings. Faculty votes were also to remain confidential, and no issues "connected with government or discipline of the College shall be debated by an officer in the . . . [presence] of any student."[20]

Two weeks after the original rules for students were passed, the faculty held their second meeting on April 1, 1892. College rules twenty-three through twenty-six were added to the original twenty-two. In these new rules it was mandated that all examinations would be written in ink on uniform size paper, that students should not be found upon the streets any evening except on weekend nights without the president's written permission, and that authorization was given to the president, assumedly by the faculty, to have discretionary powers in all cases of student discipline. When the faculty reconvened for their third meeting on October 11, 1892, it was moved and approved that rule twenty-four be changed. Assumedly, the faculty was discovering that governing the conduct of students was a complex, if not time-consuming task.[21]

The faculty's rules, being preliminarily finalized, were thereafter followed by the report of the committee on "merits and demerits." The committee, composed of Professors Holter, Clark, and Hutto, made their recommendation to the faculty in November 1892. The faculty discussed the suggestions by sections and then adopted the report in its entirety. Included was a provision to list all of the demerits received by a student during the term on his or her record, along with grades. Offenses worthy of demerits as well as the number of demerits assigned to each student breach of the rules lend insight into the Oklahoma A. and M. College environment in the early 1890s. Unexcused tardiness carried a penalty of two demerits. Unexcused absences from chapel garnered a student three demerits. "Wilfull violation of any college law carries with it twenty-five (25) demerits in addition to any other punishments given."[22]

Because these were the only specific offenses considered, wide latitude was left with the faculty for a case-by-case review and disposition. "All cases not provided for above shall be reported to the faculty for action." When a student accumulated one hundred demerits in a year, or forty in one term, the student was suspended from the college. Twenty-five demerits in a term, or fifty demerits earned at any time in the year resulted in the president's notifying the student's parents. Interestingly, the original faculty committee on "merits and demerits" made no mention on how students could earn any merits for their efforts. A new committee title, correctly reflected in the faculty minutes on the day that their report was approved, was the "Committee on 'Demerits'"[23]

Still other areas of student conduct remained for faculty oversight and intervention. In the faculty meeting of December 1, 1892, a date just two weeks short of the first anniversary of the arrival of the students, the problem of academic integrity on examinations was taken up. Prohibited were devices known to students as "cribs," "ponies," and "jacks." Students using any means to cheat would be sent from the room. The student would thereby become "conditioned" in the subject. After the incident was reported to the president, an emergency meeting of the faculty was scheduled within two days. The faculty could suspend the student for not less than one month and up to one year; students committing a second offense would be dismissed from the college. Nowhere in the faculty's record were there provisions which discussed the student's innocence, any right to appeal, or procedures to be followed in the event that a dismissed student might desire to be reinstated.[24]

The proceedings of the earliest faculty meetings included the various actions taken to codify the college's rules and regulations which governed students' behavior. These records, sometimes referred to as the "Minutes of the First Faculty" and the "Faculty Book," revealed that the faculty spent considerable amounts of time contending with student disciplinary cases during the formative years of the college. For example, student M. A. Gilbert's case was heard on December 5, 1892. Gilbert was charged with eating peanuts in his English class. Whether the mellowness that usually comes with the Christmas season had anything to do with it or not, Gilbert had the good fortune of a sympathetic faculty. Gilbert was required to write and read a letter of apology to Professor Hutto, the faculty member involved, within two days. Until this was done, he was suspended from the college. An original faculty motion to add twenty-five demerits to Gilbert's permanent record, however, was not approved.[25]

Not so fortunate were the students' cases heard in the first faculty meeting of 1893. Several disciplinary cases had apparently occurred toward the end of the fall term. Additional situations arose over the winter vacation. Nine students, all males, now awaited the results of the faculty's disposition of their circumstances. Using evidence provided by student testimony, the faculty took full opportunity to use their discretionary disciplinary latitude and the college's new demerit system. A. Campbell, charged with drunkenness during the holiday break from school, was given fifteen demerits. H. Bost was found guilty of taking part in two chicken roasts at Boomer Creek. Since one of the roasts occurred before Bost was a student, he was assigned a penalty of ten demerits. A. N. Caudell and A. Combs were given ten demerits and twenty demerits respectively, for participation in chicken roasts, and Jeff Smith, apparently a student leader, was given thirty-five demerits and a two-week suspension for involvement in three different illegal incidents of procurement and consumption of chickens from Stillwater stores.

H. Coffman was charged with a variety of breaches of the student rules. After he had apparently stolen oysters and chickens from local merchants, Coffman was penalized thirty demerits and suspended from college for two weeks. J. D. Murphy, who bought the crackers that were eaten with Coffman's oysters—but also helped eat the oysters—was given fifteen demerits. Finally, because R. Morse had been drunk with Campbell over winter break and also participated in the oyster-stealing incident, he received thirty-five demerits. All nine students were given a reproof, or expression of disapproval, by the faculty. Three additional students were reprimanded through a private word of caution by President Barker. Bost, Caudell, Combs, Coffman, and Smith were each required to pay fifty cents to a fund to reimburse the store owner for his stolen chickens. Thus the college's codified system of military discipline was implemented. The students themselves were not deterred in imbibing in intoxicating beverages, roasting chickens on Boomer Creek, or participating in other acts typical of their age, despite being clear violations of the faculty's "laws."[26]

Apparently Smith and Coffman's behavior in the chicken and oyster thefts from the local merchant remained troublesome. A strain in "town-gown" relationships was discussed by the faculty at their next meeting. Stillwater's City Council had turned over the two students for college disciplinary action. At their meeting Professor Magruder was elected to inform the members of the city council of the action taken against Smith and Coffman. In still another reaction to the problem of public relations, a motion was offered, but defeated, to send a representative of the college to see the editors of the city papers to ask them to refrain from publishing information of the "late troubles" caused by the students.[27] Given the nation's cornerstone doctrine of freedom of the press, it was not surprising that the motion to visit the newspaper editors was rejected. On the other hand, the college was still very young, it still had not moved to its campus or Old Central, and the winds of political concern about the college being moved from Stillwater still blew. Without thinking about the consequences, the students had not only strained the college's relationship with the citizens of Stillwater, they also caused adverse local, if not territory-wide, press. Understandably, the faculty had to be concerned about such a development.

Perhaps it was coincidence, but shortly thereafter still another set of "Laws Governing the Students in the A&M College" appeared in the faculty minutes. Unlike the earlier rules, article one—the introduction— was a straightforward plea for students to join with the faculty in the development of the institution. The first section of article one noted: "It is expected that students will be ladies and gentlemen in the highest sense; abstaining from all immorality, and observing the customs of good society. And in so much as the progress and prosperity of this institution largely depends upon its students, strict conformity to rules and regulations is injoined upon all." Article three was still more specific. A "mandatory" rule, it specifically prohibited students from loafing in public places or on the streets, going to bars, or using intoxicating liquor; it also set forth the conditions under which students could be absent from their homes on Monday through Thursday evenings.[28]

Near the end of 1893 the faculty's focus upon the students' conduct, both in and out of their classrooms, was beginning to cause them frustration. On October 6, Professor Neal reported that the freshman girls were petitioning the faculty for a release from their studies in agriculture. After a motion to ignore the students' petition failed, the subsequent motion to "deny" the petition was passed. In November, a motion was considered, but not passed, to read the rules and regulations of the college before the assembled students twice a month. That same month the faculty did pass a requirement that the "President be a committee of one to report at the next faculty meeting what rules and regulations

It might not be a "surrey with a fringe on top," but these young Oklahomans knew how to have a good time. The students of the 1890s were expected to observe "the customs of good society." These 1895 students not only knew how to interpret this rule but also how to choose appropriate attire for the social event. Standing left to right are Earl Myers, Thomas J. Hartman (later the first college alumnus to serve as a member of the original board of regents), and George Bowers. Seated in the carriage left to right are Cora Miltimore (the Oklahoma A. and M. College librarian from 1903 to 1914), Minnie Dysart, and Bertha Hutto.

we have on record for the government of the College and that at the same time he present his plan for remedying present evils in discipline.''[29] The problem of student rules and student discipline was not only increasingly annoying to the faculty, it persisted as a problem for years to come. For example, when Henry E. Alvord had been in his position for little over three months, the faculty decreed "all rules and regulations in force at present time rescinded and President Alvord appoint . . . a committee to prepare and present at a subsequent meeting such rules and regulations as he in his judgment might see fit.''[30]

In 1894 the Oklahoma Agricultural and Mechanical College had moved to its first permanent campus building, and the faculty had gone full circle on the rules and regulations which governed student behavior. While the faculty struggled with their domains of college control and influence, students had to cope with academic demands, meet their college expenses, and learn how to relate to one another. A student wrote a rather whimsical, but insightful, article for the *Oklahoma A. and M.*

*College Mirror*, which discussed his sophomore class and the problems of being a student in 1895. "Confidence in one's abilities insures success. This is mainly the reason for our being sophomores. Confidence in our abilities to hood-wink our worthy professors on examination day has served for more than one trying ordeal through which we would never otherwise pass. As it is we are a numerous class of four members, and unless the administration changes, there are great probabilities of an increase of minus two." The sophomore wondered where all of the nearly 100 students went that enrolled in the prior term. "A few have left this mundane sphere and gone to the celestial home above, or to the realms beneath the sea. Some have entered into the alluring fields of matrimony, there to cope with the real problems of life, compared with which the Pythagorean theorem appears axiomatic. Others, for some unknown reason, presumably want of confidence, have failed in their examinations, and may now be seen vainly striving to pass arithmetic in the freshman class again. But for the greatest number, however, come just long enough to find how little they knew and how much there was to learn, became discouraged, and returned to plowing corn or washing dishes."[31]

The lives of the Oklahoma A. and M. College students in this period mirrored, in many ways, the pioneering territory of which they were a part. They were poor, both in money to support their educational venture and in material things. Disputes sometimes ended in violence. They exerted extraordinary effort to foster a campus social environment. Due to family and personal reasons, these earliest students were frequently forced to discontinue their studies and leave the campus for a part of the academic year. Like the situation today, homesickness, discouragement, and the disciplinary code added to the toll of lost students. Infectious diseases, specifically smallpox and typhoid, further increased the student attrition rate. During this era the drop-out rate was high, and many students would come and go frequently. For these, and other reasons, it was not the best of times to be a student.[32]

Yet some would persist and overcome these deficiencies. Philip Reed Rulon, in his history of the Oklahoma State University, concluded: "Although it is impossible to pinpoint a specific date, the college campus eventually became a world unto itself. A community came into being which may be called the collegiate way. Pep rallies, modes of dress, dating customs, and many other things became institutionalized and prescribed certain forms of behavior." The collegiate way perhaps enhanced conformity and intellectual development among the students, while also providing a mechanism for dispensing classroom ideas to real life situations, but "the importance of these aspects of collegiate life should not be underestimated. It is entirely possible that peer group associations stimulated more behavioral change than anything else at the institution."[33]

With little doubt, foremost among student hardships was the constant need to earn enough money to pay college and living expenses. The cost for room, board, and personal necessities was always a larger burden than were the actual costs imposed upon the students by the college. A full page ad in an 1897 college newspaper noted: "The Oklahoma Agricultural and Mechanical College Endowed by the United States Government and Territory of Oklahoma; Tuition Free; No Fees of Any Kind."[34]

Near the midpoint of the 1890s the college catalog included the costs of attending the institution. Under the heading "inexpensive education" the prices were categorized: "Board and private rooms, $2.50 to $3.50 per week. Rooms furnished, $1.50 to $5.00 per month. Table board, $2.00 to $2.50 per week. Board in clubs, $1.50 to $2.00 per week."[35] The cost of books ranged from $6.00 to $10.00 per year, and students were encouraged to be frugal and purchase used or second-hand books whenever possible. It was predicted that textbooks would soon be available to students for free. To influence the prospective student further, the catalog also stated that the college was located in a beautiful and healthful location; the community had a population of 2,500 and a number of worthy organizations including a permanent temperance organization. The college could be reached by stage from either Orlando or Perry. In conclusion, the catalog stressed: "Many students have been able to pay the greater portion of their expenses while attending college here by work furnished on the Experiment Farm."[36]

The original faculty were apparently aware that the cost of education would be a large hurdle to surmount for their students. Student services, beyond the academic realm, were anticipated and implemented. For example, students enrolling for the 1894-95 school terms were encouraged, after taking the Santa Fe Railroad and then the stage to Stillwater, to "report at the president's office in the college building and [they] will receive information that will aid them materially in selecting board and rooms."[37] Likewise, Stillwater restaurant owners were sympathetic to the need for efficient ways to minimize the expenses for students. A newspaper ad of the Arcade Restaurant, located on North Main Street, informed students that "regular meals are 15 cents; special orders, 25 cents; oysters, game, and fish in season; 21 meals, $3.00. Special rates to students."[38] Although the special rates for students were never specified, a concern for student costs, and undoubtedly student business, was evident in the campus newspaper advertisement.

Not only did the students need employment to pay their expenses, the college, from its beginning, made work an integral part of the institution's philosophy and purpose. Under the academic label of practicum, students performed daily manual labor, much of which was paid.

The college avowed that "it is evident that the students must not, in acquiring a scientific education, lose either the ability or the disposition to labor on a farm."[39] To foster a taste for agriculture and manual labor all of the students, unless physically disabled, were required to work two hours each day, except Saturdays, on the college's farm or garden. In seasons when less labor was needed in the fields, students were assigned to work their two hours in the college's laboratories or shops. The two hours "while being instructive, is not paid for." Otherwise most students could work additional hours, at a rate depending on their ability, at a maximum of ten cents per hour.[40]

From the students' point of view concerning the economics of going to the Oklahoma A. and M. College, most worked at the college as field hands. However, as time passed and enrollment increased, the college did not have enough jobs to fill the demand. A process of screening and selecting the most able students for the positions caused stress. By 1899, campus positions were very competitive. The total budget for student wages during the year was $3,200.[41] During these times of general national depression, a student could live on $1.40 a week, if he or she were careful to avoid luxuries.[42]

Through it all many of the students remained amazingly motivated and sincerely appreciative of the opportunity to acquire a college education. R. Morton House, a 1903 graduate of the Oklahoma A. and M. College, stated: "Girls as well as boys 'worked their way through college' and it was an honorable undertaking."[43] Arriving on the campus as a freshman in 1899, House brought with him a new three-piece suit of clothes worth $7.00 and $62.50 in cash. During his four years of college, House lived in the same room at $2.00 a month and was able to obtain good meals for $3.50 a week. His income consisted of odd jobs on the campus at $.10 per hour, plus a guaranteed income of $10.00 a month for working as a janitor in Old Central.[44] After saving $150 from working on the wheat harvest in Kansas during the summer between his freshman and sophomore years, House returned to campus "with an ample supply of clothing, refreshed in body and mind, with more than twice as much money as when I started as a Freshman, with a job as janitor in the new Library, (Williams Hall) at $10.00 per month, without any financial worries, I knew I had earned half my way through college. I also knew that I could manage the next two summers to earn enough to carry me through my junior and senior years."[45]

Students found other work in Stillwater. Employment as store clerks, dishwashers, and maintenance men, in addition to whatever else would make money, was sought by many.[46] Norris T. Gilbert, an 1898 graduate, in later years reminisced about these early money problems for the student. One walked to school, if he or she were not one of the few who owned a bicycle. Also by today's standards students dressed poorly. He recalled that "we worked at odd jobs to earn money to buy our books. Everything was cheap. The Experiment Station supplied work for as many of the students as it could. Afternoons and Saturdays we worked at whatever it had to offer. We dug ditches, set out trees, plowed, cultivated, harvested. We painted fences and barns, hauled and scattered manure, and for it all we received ten cents per hour. At the end of the month, we got paid, whether we needed it or not, we were happy."[47] Gilbert perhaps captured the essence of the attitude of this generation of students as they struggled to balance academic goals with economic survival by reflecting that "they were a hardy set and if their homes were meager, they saw no imposing palaces of others to shame them."[48]

All of the original students of the preparatory program were from Stillwater and lived with their families. As the college enrollment increased with students from distances precluding commuting to the campus, Stillwater's citizens began to offer room and sometimes board. As the college student population grew still larger, the demand for housing soon outstripped the available space in the small community.

At the same time students seemed always to be looking for new and creative ways to economize. Near the end of the decade of the 1890s the college catalog acknowledged: "The college has no boarding department. Rooms can be obtained in private family homes. Many students board in clubs at reduced rates."[49] Students were required to arrange their own room and board. Although one student occupied the bell tower

No matter the era colleges have always had to be concerned about where and how students live. Constructed in 1899, the College Boarding Club was located on the site of present Crutchfield Hall. Privately owned by J. T. Land, the facility was open only to men. A resident paid $2 per week for room and board.

of Old Central for a period of time, most either rented rooms from local residents or participated in cooperative enterprises. These enterprises, where money and labor were pooled, offered room and board at below the going costs. The clubs were wholly run by the students as a business—the singular purpose of which was to save students money. The boarding clubs employed their own cooks, assistants, and waiters. College officials kept these student enterprises independent of the college's administrative control.[50]

The Slack Boarding Club was a popular venture. The college newspaper reported that the club was reducing the cost of boarding to less than $2 a week, while it was also a convenient place for eating meals. The success of the boarding clubs did not go unnoticed by the local business community. Entrepreneur J. T. Land constructed a boarding house a block east of the campus in the summer of 1899. Lauded by the student newspaper as a good investment for Mr. Land and a great benefit to the college, the College Boarding Club was simply a large plain building containing twenty-two rooms plus eating facilities. There can be no doubt that the housing was needed as all of the rooms were occupied by October. The students rented the building from Land and then organized the facility for their purposes. A cook was hired to prepare meals, and students were hired as busboys, dishwashers, and waiters. A steward was appointed to collect all of the money, manage the club, and maintain a budget. In addition to the steward, a president, vice-president, and secretary were elected by the forty-five members.[51]

In November the College Boarding Club had moved still further ahead in its organization. Rules about noise, or the college's first system of dormitory-type "quiet hours," had been put in place for certain nights of the week. This rule, plus others, was strictly enforced by the students themselves. In reporting on the club the campus newspaper even used the term "dormitory boys" in reference to the members. In truth, Mr. Land's enterprise had quickly taken on a dormitory-like atmosphere in its first three months of operation. It also was serving its primary purpose—students paid $2 per week for room and board.[52]

While students developed systems to sustain themselves financially and physically, the faculty directed itself to the mental tasks necessary for college students. The college's doors were originally open to any citizen of Oklahoma Territory between the ages of twelve and thirty, who could demonstrate an eighth grade level of academic preparation, provide evidence of "good moral character," and sign the matriculation pledge. Prospective students from outside the territory would also be admitted by meeting the requirements, in addition to paying a one-time $20 matriculation fee.[53] Originally the curriculum and class schedules were rigid. The 1896-97 College Catalogue described the curriculum: "Each student is expected to carry four studies, unless otherwise excused. With rare exception class exercises are held five times per week. Six to twelve hours of laboratory work are taken each week, except the freshmen year when the requirements are smaller."[54] Instruction was given by means of text and reference book, lecture courses, and extensive laboratory or field work.[55] In 1895 the faculty further prescribed that "each student of the Senior class, shall on or before the first day of May next preceding his graduation present an acceptable thesis of not less than three thousand (3,000) words and not more than five thousand (5,000) words, which shall be first submitted to the Professor in whose department its' subject matter falls."[56]

The senior thesis better assured the faculty that they would graduate future citizens capable of communicating in writing. The verbal skills, thought to be so necessary throughout life, were developed by the students over their four-year program through regular class recitations and ever present speech requirements. The capstone event was the senior oration given at commencement exercises. Usually before a large audience, often including members of the board of regents, the faculty, and state political dignitaries, each senior was required to address the assembly. In 1897, for example, senior George W. Bowers spoke on "The Drama of Life," Andrew N. Caudell selected "The Geological Features of Man's Origin," and Jessie Thatcher chose "The Dawning of the Twentieth Century."[57]

Junior, sophomore, and freshman orations were also required. In the annual exercises of the junior class in 1896, Thomas J. Hartman spoke on "Success and Failure," Clinton Morris selected "The Advancement of Chemistry," and Blanche Wise chose "Trifles." Three additional students also spoke at the exercises of the evening.[58] From earliest days oration was considered vitally important. In 1893, Professor A. C. Magruder offered a medal, later known as the Magruder medal, "for Merit in Declamation, Freshman Class." The first winner was Kate Neal, daughter of Professor Neal. In 1894 the Magruder medal was awarded to George W. Bowers. Changing the format in 1895, Magruder offered the prized award "For Best Oration, Junior Class." Arthur W. Adams received this award for his speech on "Electricity." Thus, in large part, "Magruder had provided an annual literary contest as part of commencement exercises."[59]

To accommodate the regimented class schedule, the verbal and written requirements, and the need for "hands-on" experiences, regular academic classes were held in the morning. Afternoons were set aside for laboratory work, practicum, and military drill. The academic calendar, nine months in length, was divided into three equal terms so that students who needed to return to their homes to help with family farm work could be accommodated. The influence of the students began to be felt in the curriculum by the mid-1890s. College elective courses reflecting a desire by the students for curricular flexibility surfaced in 1896.[60] Likewise, in 1895 the students convinced the faculty to adopt an honor system during examinations. With the system in place, the instructor would distribute an examination to the students and leave the room. Upon finishing the test, the unproctored examinee would write at the end of his or her paper, "I hereby certify on honor that I have neither received nor given assistance on this examination."[61]

Moral and religious development was also indirectly a part of each student's day. The college catalog assured the citizens of Oklahoma of a "symmetrical" development of body and mind. To carry out this responsibility "the College strives to build up its students in moral strength. While religious instruction is necessarily omitted from the course, moral and ethical obligations are given a fair and careful classroom study and religious exercises open each day's work. The College attempts, as much as lies within its power, to supply the support and encouragement which students might have in good homes."[62] The times themselves added impetus to the college's efforts in spiritual matters. The Darwinian controversy, considerable concern from the powerful National Grange about the general status of higher education in the South, and the early involvement of local churches and their ministers explained a part of this development. As a more direct example of the need for care, the Right Reverend Robert Brooks, the Episcopal bishop of Oklahoma, closely observed collegiate activities to be sure that the scientist teachers did not omit God while they sought the secrets of the universe.[63]

For personal and political reasons, chapel exercises were an important aspect of early institutional priorities. A. L. Sutherland, a freshman of 1896, wrote the faculty to be excused from compulsory attendance at chapel exercises on the basis of "conscientious scruples." Sutherland further protested that the Oklahoma Agricultural and Mechanical College was not a religious institution. In fact, he reasoned, the citizens of the United States and Oklahoma supported the institution, and it was open to all "without regard to their religious views." Sutherland summarized his case by stating, "My objection is to being compelled to attend such exercises." Without giving a reason, the faculty denied Sutherland's request to be excused from attending chapel.[64] Chapel exercises remained compulsory for all students as long as they were held.

The purposes which chapel exercises served did change with time. Chapel exercises had a wholly religious format until the students moved to Old Central, and coincidentally out of the borrowed classroom spaces in Stillwater's churches. In Old Central, chapel activities became more secular, always opening with a prayer but then incorporating campus announcements, faculty lectures, and still later a lecture series given by invited off-campus speakers. College President Angelo C. Scott was

During Oklahoma A. and M. College's early years, the institution strived to assure moral and religious development in the student body. In this rare photo taken in Old Central, students and faculty participate in chapel exercises.

so appalled by the students' English abilities that he often used chapel time to give lectures on grammar.[65]

Chapel eventually declined in importance, at least to the students. Frequent absences, tardiness, and pranks caused the faculty to hand out regular demerits for inappropriate behavior in chapel. Some of the earliest, if not infamous, pranks of students center around chapel exercises. On one occasion the chapel attendees arrived to be confronted by the physiology department's human skeleton sitting in the president's chair. At another time a cow was brought during the night to the room where chapel was to take place first thing next morning. The cow had been there long enough to cause that morning's exercise to be cancelled totally. Still another chapel dismissal was caused by a student who placed an offensive gas in the hot air shaft of the auditorium. At the time this student was thought to be a specialist in chemistry.[66]

Still another vital part of the original college curriculum was required military drill. Mandated by the Morrill Act of 1862, all land-grant colleges were to maintain military training in its curriculum. The Morrill Act obligated the federal government to provide equipment, instructors, and funds. The college quickly moved to meet its obligation. The earliest Oklahoma A. and M. College catalog described "tactics" and prescribed that "Military Science will be brought by lectures, supplemented by three hours drill per day." It then followed, since all students, male and female, were cadets, that "the discipline will be strictly military, with a system of merits and demerits that will accurately grade the standing of each student."[67] President Barker took the Morrill Act's meaning literally and thereby misinterpreted it to include a military requirement for women. Captain Lewis J. "Jeff" Darnell was to be in charge of the military department. Alfred E. Jarrell remembered Captain Darnell as he stood in a dust storm on an unimproved Stillwater street near the church where the college was organized. He wore his Civil War uniform with army belt, cap, and huge square-toed shoes that he used with great skill as he tried to teach a band of long-haired farm boys to execute "about face."[68]

Darnell was a tough old veteran and objected "with emphatic and vigorous language of the army type, to the inclusion of female students in his company. 'Ain't any sense in it, girls can't learn to be soldiers; ain't made for it', he declared, and stated further that he'd be 'gol darned' if he'd have anything to do with drilling girls." But President Barker responded: "This institution isn't yet permanently located. Other towns want it and are seeking every method they can to find vulnerability in my administration. If we neglect to comply with this law, there's no telling what might happen. We may lose this great gift to Stillwater and this community." Darnell, a local resident with some sympathy to the turbulent recent history of the college's founding, "reluctantly submitted and an order was issued for the first drill."[69]

Shortly thereafter, Professor Holter, the college professor of chemistry and physics, gave credibility to Captain Darnell's reservation about his department. Holter suggested a military drill scene in 1892: "Picture, if you can, a lot of girls in long dresses, in short dresses, in new dresses, having on their heads all shapes and sizes of hats and sunbonnets, and you have an idea, possibly, of the general appearance of the uniforms.

"While you are picturing just think of boys in long coats and short coats, long pantaloons and short ones, high-heeled shoes and low-heeled shoes, hats and caps of all descriptions, and you, possibly, have some idea of the uniform appearance of the boys.

"Now take this battalion of boys and battalion of girls, form them into a company, and drill them in an average Oklahoma April wind, and if the sight does not leave an impression in your memory, you are certainly puncture proof to all ordinary sights."[70]

For whatever reasons Captain Darnell's tenure was for the first year only. With experience the military department did improve. After the second year the females were dismissed from the ranks of cadets and were taught physical education. Shortly after the move to Old Central a cadet uniform was prescribed by the faculty. The students, not the government or the college, provided their own uniforms at a cost of $14.50. The manual of arms, formally practiced with shotguns, rifles, army muskets, broomsticks, or whatever the student could find to use, were replaced by discarded army rifles around 1895. There was no firing practice involving these "new" issued rifles, however. The college furnished four officers with swords and belts, one brass drum, two snare drums, one bugle, one large silk company flag, and one red silk sash. Despite the trials and tribulations, the cadets participated in the military portion of their curriculum with some enthusiasm. Student Lieutenant Norris Gilbert once gave an improper order to his troops that resulted in his being knocked to the ground and marched upon. On another occasion, an overzealous drummer beat his instrument during a parade with enough vigor to have the drum's moorings break loose. The instrument's head rolled rather unceremoniously past the corps and parade's spectators.[71]

The demerit system and student cadet participation was clearly explained in the *College Catalogue of 1894-1895*. The discipline of the college was described as semi-military, with authority vested through territorial law to the president and faculty for the government of the college. The commandant of cadets was charged with the responsibility for student conduct. An officer of the day was appointed from the roster of officers, and his duty was to have general supervision over the halls, stairs, and passage ways; to preserve order; and to report any infringements of college regulations. The commandant and president were jointly responsible for attending to all reports of delinquencies. Punishments were awarded according to the offense. Tardiness earned three demerits; absence resulted in a five-demerit penalty; and missing military drill meant an extra drill of four hours. The punishments were hierarchal. The first level included demerits, reprimands, and extra duty. With further disobedience or violation, the student could be arrested, confined to a room, or given a reduction of rank in the Cadet Corps. The third level of punishment was dismissal or suspension from the college. In extreme cases a student would be expelled from the college, never to be permitted to reenter.[72]

Yet the catalog affirmed: "This discipline is not severe, and does not deprive any student of the privileges ordinarily granted. It simply aids in creating and maintaining an 'Esprit de Corp' in stimulating pride in manners, in dress, in morals, and in securing prompt obedience to orders.

"The general morale of the student body is high. They are respectful, manly, obedient, and earnest in all their relations to the college."[73]

Due to the lack of suitable equipment, as well as difficulties in securing money and the appointment of a permanent army officer to take charge of the college's military department, the advent of modern military training was delayed until 1916. However, one enduring system did evolve from this period. The faculty's rules for student conduct had been transferred into an elaborate system of campus-wide military discipline. The demerit system, with its origins in the earliest faculty meetings, had been partially turned over to the students for implementation. Students, under the guise of their military rank in the Cadet Corps, were now observing and reporting student misconduct to the college's authorities. Through this era the rules were generally enforced, but in time became more lenient.

The military disciplinary system did have unforeseeable results, some of which were perhaps counterproductive. The system allowed little flexibility. In 1895 two brothers, who were Quakers, petitioned the faculty for permission to be excused from military drill. The faculty denied their request, and the students' parents withdrew the two brothers and a sister from the college. The system also unified students. The minutes of the faculty showed that accusations of drunkenness, petty thievery, and fighting could not be proven because the faculty was unable to find witnesses among the students who would substantiate the charges. The system drastically effected student attrition. An overview of the records of the disciplinary proceedings of the faculty in 1895-1896 revealed that between forty-five and fifty students were expelled from the college and preparatory school for misconduct under the military code.[74]

While the faculty was molding the campus academic and military environments, the students themselves were forging ahead with the creation of their collegiate environment. Social relationships, personal interests, and simple enjoyment—a way to break from the rather sterile rigors of the academic routine—were reasons enough for the students to take the initiative. Informal activities of the time included student picnics, athletic events, and a musical program. More formal student

From the founding days, students have forged ahead with activities affording social interaction. Both then and now watermelons have served as a staple food for many of these events. This 1899 watermelon feed features Carter Hanner, for whom Hanner Hall is named, seemingly choking on a watermelon seed.

enterprises, such as faculty-sponsored student receptions, a student newspaper, and literary societies, were also prominent in the decade of the 1890s. Throughout, the students seemed to keep a balance between the demands of their academic work and the realities of adolescence.

Sports competition was of the pick-up variety and very informal during the college's earliest years. To some students athletics were important. A. E. Jarrell remembered that in 1896 he did not go home for lunch so that he could participate in what he called townball, blackman, or a type of rugby football "when we were lucky enough to get a ball that would stay inflated or a baseball on which the cover was not entirely off."[75] Still in 1898 the faculty was forced to pass a rule which "moved that football and baseball be prohibited within 300 feet of the college buildings and that a committee be appointed to consider and provide for these games."[76]

The urgency of finding suitable fields was indicated by the fact that three weeks later the faculty approved a motion that "a tract west of college campus now occupied by cow pens" be designated the area for athletic activities.[77] Thus the first intramural playing field was established. Shortly thereafter, with a boost from Professors Lowery L. Lewis, John Fields, and Oscar M. Morris, who served as coaches and referees, contests in track and field between classes occurred. College spirit intensified when the first informal event later developed into competitions between other colleges in the territory. Intercollegiate athletics was not far away. Meantime, athletics were primarily concentrated in a day of football, sack races, foot races, potato races, and a tug-of-war on

Except for the annual athletics extravaganza held on Washington's Birthday, sports activities at Oklahoma A. and M. were informal and spontaneous in the early years. In this 1898 race, runners lunge for the finish line.

Washington's Birthday. Except for this gala annual event, sports on the campus remained mostly spontaneous, informal, and of the student's creation through the college's first decade.[78]

While athletics served to create excitement on the campus, so did oratorical contests. The students' interest and involvement in literary societies had fostered a part of this intense interest in debating and public speaking. Shortly after the first students arrived for classes, the Star Crescent Literary Society was organized in the first academic year. Formed for entertainment, few records remain to describe their activities. However, there was a debate held on the topic of women's suffrage, and the boys surprised the girls with a box supper as an entertainment for their last meeting of the year. For an unknown reason, the Star Crescent Society discontinued functioning. Regardless, student interest remained high, and an all-male literary society called the Webster Debating Society was organized the next year on October 16, 1893. The Websters strove to improve the members' debating abilities and general literature knowledge as well as to foster social development. On October 20, 1893, the Sigma Literary Society held its first meeting. The Sigmas served its members by improving their oratory and general literature knowledge and by promoting friendship.[79]

These early literary societies debated topics of interest then and now. Among the many questions that members attempted to resolve were whether capital punishment was justified, whether a student should choose his or her profession before entering college, and whether country life was better than city life. Not to be confused with today's Greek organizations, the two literary organizations were markedly different. However, they both competed for new members and campus prestige. As a result, feelings of animosity and competition intensified. At a rare joint meeting on December 4, 1896, months of insults and bickering flared into open conflict. A fist-fight resulted in several of the male students suffering bruises and lacerations. Despite attempts at reconciliation, matters continued to escalate. The Sigmas interrupted a Webster meeting by stealing their refreshments. In retaliation the Websters injected quinine and cayenne into a bushel of Sigma apples.[80]

As a result of the fight and subsequent events, the faculty intervened. Literary societies were abolished, and nine students were suspended from the college for three weeks. Most perplexing of all to the faculty was that the students of both societies refused to provide evidence or information about the events or students involved. The punishment, for those guilty and innocent, was the banning of the societies. Further, the faculty took steps to reassert authority. On November 6, 1897, the faculty passed and posted the following resolution: "TO WHOM IT MAY CONCERN: 1st—It is the sense of the Faculty that the students of this institution are under the control of the Faculty from the time they enter

College until their connection therewith is severed by withdrawal, suspension, expulsion, or graduation. 2nd—It is the further sense of the Faculty that no organization, Literary Society, or other body of students shall be permitted to hold meetings either in the College buildings or elsewhere without the special permission of the Faculty being first obtained. Any violation of this rule shall subject the students so offending to be disciplined in any such manner as the Faculty may determine."[81]

Shortly after this new ruling the faculty attended a meeting with eighteen students in the mathematics room of the College Building. The committee discovered the students believed the faculty was "hostile" to their forming literary societies. The new restriction limited participation. Further, the students expressed their view that "they have a right to meet as citizens and that they did meet as such. . . . No violation of the faculty has been intended on their part."[82] Students' assertiveness was beginning to be a factor on campus.

Despite the students' efforts to establish themselves, and even a willingness of the faculty to compromise by later permitting new literary societies, including the Omega Society and the Philomathean Society, the peak of literary societies was past. Clubs based upon academic subjects or disciplines became vogue and of more interest. The Chemistry Club was among the first of these organizations. Nonetheless, the literary societies had made a major mark on the institution. The students had been given an opportunity to extend their circle of friends and foster their collegiate atmosphere. No doubt the faculty became more sensitive to student needs and concerns. Still further, the literary societies had generated considerable positive recognition for the college.

Another legacy of the student literary societies, particularly of the Sigmas, was the beginnings of today's campus newspaper, the *Daily O'Collegian*. During their regular meetings the Sigmas read or passed handwritten news of the campus among the members. Subsequently, by using club dues, contributions, and money from advertising, the Sigmas published the *Oklahoma A. and M. College Mirror* in 1895. In the first issue editors Norris T. Gilbert and Samuel R. Querry wrote what they called a "Salutatory." It stated: "In launching our little boat on the great sea of journalism we do not expect to discover any new continents nor to reach impossible harbors. Our purpose is a modest one . . . first we desire to accomplish self-improvement; second, we wish to contribute something to the growth of the Oklahoma Agricultural and Mechanical College." They then appealed for the support of the students and friends of the institution while also promising to make "this little paper representative of the highest degree of Oklahoma's educational interests and her greatest educational institution."[83] Yearly subscriptions were fifty cents; one issue cost five cents.

The *Oklahoma A. and M. College Mirror* developed a regular format. It contained college and local news, advertising, educational information, news from other colleges, and biographical sketches of prominent people. The paper also provided an avenue for the students to learn about college life across the nation. As a part of a national system, the *College Mirror* was exchanged with newspaper editors in Arkansas, California, and Massachusetts, in addition to over one hundred other colleges and high schools.[84] The newspaper received generally favorable reviews by local editors and their student counterparts from across the country.

A lack of money and student apathy plagued the newspaper. Sensing the end to be near, the editors of the December 15, 1895, edition wrote: "The future of this paper seems to be somewhat of a problem. It may live and it may not. If the former, its size may be reduced; if the latter, this may be regarded as our formal good-by to our readers and friends."[85] In fact, the paper was not published in the next year, but it was resumed in September 1897. Financial problems persisted until the college organized its own department of printing late in the decade. Stability for the campus newspaper followed. With several name changes it has been continuously printed since 1897.

The *College Mirror* was a significant student activity because it served as a voice for both the college and the students. The paper was a source of practical advice. For example, the freshmen of 1898 were advised that their homesickness would pass when they delved into their college work. The freshmen were also admonished to be wary of the many college distractions, to take care in choosing their companions, to join the local churches, and, above all else, not to acquire the habit of loafing.[86] It provided campus news, sometimes with humor: "Murdered at the College laboratory, by the janitors, with aid of potassium cyanide, Sigma, the college cat. This beautiful and winsome cat will long be remembered by the young ladies."[87]

Impressively, the *College Mirror* consistently preached the attributes of the college itself. In an 1895 edition, students were informed that the new college catalogs were ready and that they should "send one to your friends where it will do the most good for the growth of the college."[88]

Perhaps most importantly, the newspaper lobbied on behalf of student interests. The budding editors were not shy, for example, about printing opinions on the college's academic programs and problems or state political matters. Early articles asked, "Should Examinations Be Abolished?" and "Am I Educated?" In 1898 the *College Mirror* suggested that it would always be a question "whether a few strong, well-equipped colleges will not do greater good than will a larger number, each with poorer facilities."[89] The students wrote this in reference to a rapidly growing number of colleges in Oklahoma.

In 1895 a small article concerning the admission of black students to Oklahoma's colleges, concluded with, "This disturbing question has not yet arisen here, but it is coming up for solution soon."[90] In still another issue a list of fifteen college needs including a library, department of domestic economy, and more laboratory space for the students was included. Stating that these needs were imperative, the paper suggested that the state was practicing a false economy and thereby had failed to meet what the students considered reasonable demands. Then the article directly attacked the political leadership of the territory by adding, "The last legislature was too parsimonious to appropriate $5,000 for this institution, but had plenty of money with which to pay political debts."[91] Whether helpful or not, it was clear very early that the newspaper would become a voice for the student, an advocate for the college, and an important vehicle of information to the campus community and citizens of Oklahoma.

While the curriculum, disciplinary systems, military drills, and necessity to work appeared to dictate that the students remain serious of purpose, there was little monotony. The students' extracurricular activities served to balance these first impressions. Then if the student's developing out-of-class social networks were not enough, there seemed to be regular spicing of campus life with humorous events, pranks, and

While the curriculum, disciplinary systems, and necessity to work seemed to dictate that students remain serious of purpose, there was still time for some fun. These two dapper gentlemen take some time from the books to strum a few bars.

planned diversions. As previously mentioned, one of the earliest and most frequent focal points of student mischief was chapel exercises. Faculty members and campus buildings were also the brunt of student misbehavior. However, most frequently, students vented their creativity at each other. Sometimes the pranksters would go too far, and demerits or other punishment would be given out by the faculty. As frequently, the perpetrators would never be caught.

Even the college president was not immune from the students' sense of what was funny. To illustrate, President Barker was a tobacco chewer outside of class and a gum chewer during class. After twenty-five students, probably led by Floyd J. Bolend, all agreed to chew gum one day in his class, Barker stopped chewing gum in class for about three months. On another occasion to celebrate Professor Holter's wedding, the students brought a small cannon to the front lawn of his home and fired it in salute. In the process much of the glass in Holter's home was broken. Before class began the next morning, Holter handed the boys the bill quoting the replacement costs. Class proceeded after the professor had his money in hand.[92]

Student drunkenness, shaving each other's heads, and stealing the slats from students' beds added other diversions to campus life. In one incident C. V. Jones placed an advertisement in the Stillwater Gazette in an effort to get his bed slats returned. The ad read, "Shoot our dogs and kill our cats, but bring, oh bring us back our slats."[93] Old Central once had a cow staked to the porch of its southeast entrance. Another time a buggy was moved, piece by piece, to that building's bell tower where it was found reassembled the next morning. Stillwater's wood-planked walks were set afire on more than one Halloween night by students who would steal, stack, and burn them for fun. Lesser offenses included stealing food from the home economics kitchens, as well as from local citizens.[94]

Humor not only described a specific incident, it also represented a state-of-mind that assured an atmosphere where work and play would co-exist. By precedent humor was clearly made a part of the college's foundation during the 1890s.

The maturing of the Oklahoma A. and M. College was well underway by 1900. The college was now ten years old. The decade had begun with classes being held in several of Stillwater's churches and in the city's court house. In 1893 the six million acres encompassing the Cherokee Outlet (located a short distance north of Stillwater) opened for settlement. On September 16, 1893, Oklahoma A. and M. College students joined 100,000 homesteaders for the land run which opened the area. The event seriously affected the college's entire academic year. The year 1894 brought the college stability largely because of the move to Old Central and the establishment of the college campus. Six students became the first graduates in 1896. In 1899 blacksmithing was still the primary engineering course. The height of the literary societies had come and gone. A campus newspaper had been established, and, primarily due to political patronage, the college was under the leadership of its fifth president, Angelo C. Scott. Graduates entering the teaching profession could look forward to working in a one-room schoolhouse at a salary of $25 to $40 a month, during a five- to eight-month school year. Yet the optimism on the Oklahoma Agricultural and Mechanical College campus was high at the turn of the century.[95]

There was ample reason for optimism. Great things, some obvious, some subtle, were happening. In 1900 three graduates were on the faculty. The college had grown from 45 preparatory school students to an enrollment of 219 students in 1898-99. More importantly, for the first time, the majority of students were college students. In 1899 the enrollment again rose to a record 270 students. Of the twenty-four total graduates by 1900, all but two were gainfully employed. The exceptions were two women who had established homes. A student government, the College Legislature Assembly, was underway. An alumni association was active, with Oscar Morris having been elected the first president in 1897. The first international student, Avedis G. Adjemian, enrolled in 1899.

As the decade of the 1890s was nearing the end, the Oklahoma A. and M. College was beginning to look and feel like a real college. A number of traditions had been established. The class of 1898 enjoy Arbor Day.

Four American Indian students had enrolled. Miss Ella Effie Hunter was hired as the first female faculty member in 1894. A new chemistry building had been completed, and two more academic buildings would be completed within two years. The Oklahoma Agricultural and Mechanical College was beginning to look and feel like a real college.[96]

As the decade of the 1890s was nearing its end, Jessie Thatcher became the first woman graduate of the Oklahoma Agricultural and Mechanical College and the first woman ever to receive a college degree in Oklahoma. Thatcher was a student leader during her undergraduate days and perhaps typified the students at the college in her era. Thatcher came to Oklahoma Territory from Iowa with her parents. After graduation, she married Henry A. Bost, also an Oklahoma A. and M. College student, and became a homemaker and parent. Her children and grandchildren were later students at Oklahoma State University. She also taught eighteen years in the public schools in Cleveland. Mrs. Bost died on February 14, 1963, at the age of 88. She remained interested in her university throughout her life and served as the second president of the OSU Alumni Association's Half-Century Club.[97]

In 1897 Thatcher had graduated from the Oklahoma Agricultural and Mechanical College, along with George W. Bowers and Andrew N. Caudell, as a part of the second graduating class. She was twenty-two years old. In the Assembly Hall of Old Central, Thatcher delivered her original oration as a part of the commencement exercises. Her speech was entitled "The Dawn of the Twentieth Century." Thatcher and her speech were both eloquent, as she delivered her oratory from her handwritten manuscript. She discussed the history of education for women, surveyed human progress through the nineteenth century, and ventured that the twentieth century would be a century of specialization. She also prophesied that the arriving new century would be a time when human knowledge would be condensed, made more accessible, and applied more easily. She called her time of graduation the evening of the nineteenth century and described the twilight of the century as being brighter than the morning. In conclusion she said: "In every field of art and science and literature, of human industry and human struggle, stand forth the mighty achievements of sincere and godly men, of brave and tender women. A few more days and we shall step across the threshold of your wondrous possibilities. God grant that we may be worthy of that century of greatness, and live up to the high level of our vast inheritance!"[98] Shortly thereafter Thatcher and her college entered the twentieth century, both to make contributions worthy of the future which she had predicted.

# Endnotes

1. Most of the original students in the territorial college were under fifteen years of age. As time passed the average age of the students increased. The May 1898 *Oklahoma A. and M. College Mirror* noted that by then the average age of the students when they entered the college or preparatory school was seventeen to thirty-five years. One-third of these students were younger than this age while 43 percent were older. "A 75-Year Heritage," *Oklahoma State Alumnus Magazine*, vol. 6, no. 7 (September-October 1965), p. 10.

2. Philip Reed Rulon, *Oklahoma State University—Since 1890* (Stillwater: Oklahoma State University Press, 1975), pp. 1-16. More information on the early history of Oklahoma State University is discussed in another volume of the Centennial Histories Series entitled *Oklahoma State University Historic Old Central* by LeRoy H. Fischer.

3. Alfred Edwin Jarrell, "The Founding of Oklahoma A. and M. College: A Memoir," *Chronicles of Oklahoma*, vol. 34, no. 3 (Autumn 1956), pp. 315-318.

4. Frederick Rudolph, *The American College and University: A History* (New York, NY: Vintage Books, 1962), p. 448.

5. A. E. Jarrell, J. H. Adams, and Jessie Thatcher Bost, among other past Oklahoma A. and M. students, in later years contributed letters and other memoirs of their being among the first college graduates. For example, Jarrell, as the last surviving member of the first graduating class, talked about his classmates before his death. Quoted in an article entitled "Now There Are None?" in the *Oklahoma State University Magazine*, vol. 2, no. 12 (June 1959), p. 13, he stated, "My classmates have all departed to the Indians' 'Happy Hunting Ground.' Collectively, they laid the foundation for a seat of higher learning that today not only trains the youth of our nation, but also the students of many nations."

6. Willa Adams Dusch, *The Sigma Literary Society, 1893-1897: A Chapter in the History of the Oklahoma A. and M. College*, edited by Berlin B. Chapman (Stillwater: Oklahoma A. and M. College, 1951), p. 3.

7. Dusch, p. 4.

8. Dusch, p. 4.

9. Dusch, pp. 4-5.

10. Dusch, p. 5.

11. Dusch, p. 5.

12. Berlin B. Chapman, "First Faculty Set Standards," *Oklahoma A. and M. College Magazine*, vol. 15, no. 5 (December 1943), p. 4.

13. Chapman, "The First Faculty Set Standards," pp. 4-12. Magruder later earned a medical degree at Tulane University and practiced medicine as an eye, ear, nose, and throat specialist in Colorado.

14. Chapman, "The First Faculty Set Standards," p. 12.

15. Chapman, "The First Faculty Set Standards," p. 13.

16. "Minutes of First Faculty, 1891-1899," p. 103, Special Collections, Edmon Low Library, Oklahoma State University, Stillwater, Oklahoma.

17. "Minutes of First Faculty," pp. 101-102.

18. Alfred Edwin Jarrell to Berlin B. Chapman, 16 July 1956, Berlin B. Chapman Collection, Special Collections, Edmon Low Library.

19. "Minutes of First Faculty," pp. 102-103.

20. "Minutes of First Faculty," pp. 103-104.

21. "Minutes of First Faculty," pp. 106, 110.

22. "Minutes of First Faculty," p. 120.

23. "Minutes of First Faculty," p. 120.

24. "Minutes of First Faculty," p. 123.

25. The term "Faculty Book" is used to describe the records of the earliest faculty meetings in an article appearing in the January 1937 issue of the *Oklahoma A. and M. College Magazine*. The Oklahoma State University's Edmon Low Library also has a verbatim typewritten copy of the faculty meeting records in the "Theodore Lowry Collection." The Lowry file is labeled "Minutes of First Faculty." In fact, this invaluable early record of the territorial college's earliest faculty proceedings are handwritten directly into a large pre-bound book of original blank pages. The meeting minutes start with a faculty meeting in March 1892 and continue to January 1900. The records, in themselves, are an interesting story. S. A. McReynolds, an Oklahoma A. and M. graduate of 1902, took it upon himself to keep the bound book, with the handwritten meeting minutes, rather than burn it with other trash as he had been ordered. This event occurred in 1902 when McReynolds, a student employee of the college, was cleaning the basement of Old Central. McReynolds secretly kept the book in his possession as he pursued his career in business and traveled the world. Always wanting to return it, McReynolds placed the "Faculty Book" back in the care of the college in 1935. See Helen Freudenberger, "Records and Reminiscences," *Oklahoma A. and M. College Magazine*, vol. 8, no. 4 (January 1937) pp. 5, 13, for the story of McReynold's historically important action. "Minutes of First Faculty," p. 125.

26. "Minutes of First Faculty," p. 129.

27. "Minutes of First Faculty," p. 129.

28. "Minutes of First Faculty," p. 129.

29. "Minutes of First Faculty," pp. 151-155.

30. "Minutes of First Faculty," p. 178.

31. *Oklahoma A. and M. College Mirror*, May 1895, p. 3.

32. Rulon, *Oklahoma State University—Since 1890*, pp. 96-97.

33. Rulon, *Oklahoma State University—Since 1890*, p. 99.

34. *Oklahoma A. and M. College Mirror*, 15 September 1897, p. 16.

35. *Oklahoma A. and M. College Catalogue, 1894-1895*, p. 33.

36. *Oklahoma A. and M. College Catalogue, 1894-1895*, p. 34.

37. *Oklahoma A. and M. College Catalogue, 1894-1895*, p. 7.

38. *Oklahoma A. and M. College Mirror*, 16 September 1895, p. 15.

39. *Oklahoma A. and M. College Catalogue, 1892-1893*, p. 12.

40. *Oklahoma A. and M. College Catalogue, 1892-1893*, p. 13.

41. Oklahoma A. and M. *College Paper*, 1 November 1899, p. 66.

42. H. E. Thompson, "1892—A. and M. College—1930," *Oklahoma A. and M. College Magazine*, vol. 1, no. 8 (April 1930), p. 4.

43. R. M. House, "Working Our Way Through College," *Chronicles of Oklahoma*, vol. 42, no. 2 (Summer 1964), p. 36.

44. House, p. 38.

45. House, p. 52. Also, Philip Reed Rulon, in his history of the Oklahoma State University, mentions the importance of the "rippling effect" on the attendance of the earliest college students in subsequent generations of Oklahoma State University students. R. M. House serves as an excellent example of Rulon's point. House, in addition to his first 1903 degree, earned two additional degrees at his alma mater. He had two sons who both graduated from OSU. These two children had six children of their own, two of whom earned degrees at OSU. There were four mothers in this genealogy. All four mothers were college graduates, and one of the mothers earned a degree from the Oklahoma A. and M. College. Clearly, at least in the House family, education bred education.

46. Alfred Edwin Jarrell to Berlin B. Chapman, 22 September 1957, Berlin B. Chapman Collection.

47. Record Book Committee, compiler, "Selections from the Record Book of the Oklahoma Agricultural and Mechanical College, 1891-1941. Compiled on the Occasion of the Fiftieth Anniversary of the Founding of the College," vol. 1, p. 75, Special Collections, Edmon Low Library.

48. Record Book Committee, compiler, vol. 1, p. 75.

49. *Oklahoma A. and M. College Catalogue, 1897-1898*, p. 4.

50. Rulon, *Oklahoma State University—Since 1890*, p. 97; *College Paper*, 1 October 1899, p. 61.

51. *Oklahoma A. and M. College Mirror*, 15 October 1897, p. 8; *College Paper*, 1 October 1899, p. 61, 15 June 1899, p. 41, 1 October 1899, p. 61.

52. *College Paper*, 1 November 1899, p. 75.

53. *Oklahoma A. and M. College Catalogue, 1892-1893*, pp. 11-12.

54. *Oklahoma A. and M. College Catalogue, 1896-1897*, p. 6.

55. *Oklahoma A. and M. College Catalogue, 1896-1897*, p. 6.

56. "Minutes of First Faculty," p. 218.

57. *Oklahoma A. and M. College Mirror*, 15 September 1897, p. 6.

58. Emma Swope Dolde, "Alumni Writes Impressions," *Oklahoma A. and M. College Magazine*, vol. 10, no. 1 (October 1938), p. 11.

59. Chapman, p. 4.

60. *Oklahoma A. and M. College Mirror*, 15 April 1896, p. 4.

61. Rulon, *Oklahoma State University—Since 1890*, pp. 84-86.

62. *Oklahoma A. and M. College Catalogue, 1894-1895*, p. 32.

63. Rulon, *Oklahoma State University—Since 1890*, p. 74.

64. "Minutes of First Faculty," p. 235.

65. Rulon, *Oklahoma State University—Since 1890*, p. 74.

66. Record Book Committee, compiler, vol. 1, p. 100.

67. *Oklahoma A. and M. College Catalogue, 1892-1893*, pp. 18-19.

68. Jarrell, "The Founding of Oklahoma A. and M. College," pp. 323-324.

69. Record Book Committee, compiler, vol. 2, p. 305.

70. Philip Reed Rulon, "The Campus Cadets: A History of Collegiate Military Training, 1891-1951," *Chronicles of Oklahoma*, vol. 52, no. 1 (Spring 1979), p. 68.

71. George W. Bowers, "Early Military Training," *Oklahoma A. and M. College Magazine*, vol. 1, no. 7 (March 1930), p. 4; Rulon, "The Campus Cadets," pp. 68-72.

72. *Oklahoma A. and M. College Catalogue, 1894-1895*, pp. 93-97.

73. *Oklahoma A. and M. College Catalogue, 1894-1895*, p. 97.

74. Bowers, p. 4; "Minutes of First Faculty," pp. 127-128, 207-271.

75. Alfred Edwin Jarrell to Berlin B. Chapman, December 1954, Berlin B. Chapman Collection.

76. "Minutes of First Faculty," p. 327.

77. "Minutes of First Faculty," p. 329.

78. A. C. Scott, *The Story of an Administration of the Oklahoma Agricultural and Mechanical College* ([Stillwater: Oklahoma Agricultural and Mechanical College, 1942]), p. 11; Record Book Committee, compiler, vol. 1, p. 41. Intercollegiate athletics at Oklahoma State University are discussed in another volume of the Centennial Histories Series entitled *A History of the Oklahoma State University Intercollegiate Athletics* by Doris Dellinger.

79. Scott, p. 11; Dusch, pp. 1-33.

80. Dusch, pp. 23-27.

81. "Minutes of First Faculty," p. 300.

82. "Minutes of First Faculty," p. 302.

83. *Oklahoma A. and M. College Mirror*, 15 May 1895, p. 1.

84. For a rather complete listing of the colleges and high schools that the student editors of the *Oklahoma A. and M. College Mirror* exchanged newspapers with see the *College Paper*, 1 February 1902, pp. 192-193, April 1902, p. 1.

85. *Oklahoma A. and M. College Mirror*, 15 December 1895, p. 1.

86. *Oklahoma A. and M. College Mirror*, April 1898, p. 5.

87. *Oklahoma A. and M. College Mirror*, 15 December 1895, p. 11.

88. *Oklahoma A. and M. College Mirror*, 16 September 1895, p. 16.

89. *Oklahoma A. and M. College Mirror*, January 1898, p. 3.

90. *Oklahoma A. and M. College Mirror*, May 1895, p. 1.

91. *Oklahoma A. and M. College Mirror*, 15 September 1897, p. 5.

92. Berlin B. Chapman, "President Robert Barker," manuscript, p. 4, R. J. Barker File, Berlin B. Chapman Collection; James K. Hastings, "Oklahoma Agricultural and Mechanical College and Old Central," *Chronicles of Oklahoma*, vol. 27, no. 1 (Spring 1950), p. 83.

93. Olin W. Jones, "Aggieland's First Collegiates," *Oklahoma A. and M. College Magazine*, vol. 1, no. 6 (February 1930), p. 4.

94. Jones, p. 4, 24; Record Book Committee, compiler, vol. 1, p. 109.

95. Arrell Morgan Gibson, *Oklahoma: A History of Five Centuries* (Norman: University of Oklahoma Press, 1981), pp. 180-181.

96. A. E. Jarrell, "A First Aggie Gives His 1950 Report," *Oklahoma A. and M. College Magazine*, vol. 22, no. 2 (October 1950), pp. 28-29; *College Paper*, September 1899, p. 1, 1 November 1899, p. 76, 1 December 1899, pp. 1-5; *Oklahoma A. and M. College Mirror*, 15 June 1896, p. 12, 15 September 1897, pp. 5-7, 15 November 1897, p. 8; *Stillwater NewsPress*, 31 August 1983, p. 6B.

97. "Jessie Thatcher Bost Honored," *Oklahoma A. and M. College Magazine*, vol. 17, no. 9 (June 1946), pp. 5-6; "Funeral Services Held For First Woman Graduate," *Oklahoma State Alumnus Magazine*, vol. 4, no. 4 (April 1963), p. 15; Henry G. Bennett, "Jessie Thatcher Bost—Symbol of Womanly Progress," 1946, Weldon Barnes Collection, Special Collections, Edmon Low Library; Jessie Thatcher Bost, "The Dawning of the Twentieth Century," *Oklahoma State University Outreach*, vol. 16, no. 6 (June-July 1975), pp. 16-17.

98. Bost, pp. 16-17.

# 3 Kindness Wins More With Students Than Severity

 

As the twentieth century began, most citizens of the United States were satisfied, if not content, with life. Aside from a rare financial crisis, not much had happened to disturb middle class America since the Civil War. Turn of the century times were good for the large majority of people. As most individuals saw it, there was no need for change. Yet social change did come. It was little wonder that few could have known about the events that were about to confuse, alter, and even upset their lifestyles after 1900.[1]

Some people did risk prophesying the future. For example, the *Literary Digest* predicted that the automobile, then called a horseless carriage, would never overtake the bicycle in popularity. Although taken to task for being irresponsible by *Popular Science Monthly*, the secretary of the Smithsonian Institute predicted that there would someday be flying machines able to travel at speeds and heights then inconceivable. However, no one was foreseeing the nation's involvement in a world war in just seventeen years. Nor was anyone forecasting that within two decades women would bob their hair and wear make-up and short skirts. Public displays of affection or frequenting a speakeasy were unimaginable.[2]

The winds of change were blowing, and the results would dramatically alter Victorian society. By 1900 the majority of states had enacted laws allowing women to retain their earnings and purchase and own property. Divorce had become easier to obtain. In 1901 President Theodore Roosevelt caused a national stir by inviting Booker T. Washington, a prominent black leader, to dine with him at the White House. That same year Andrew Carnegie retired from business and began to turn his fortune into the construction of more than 2,500 libraries, several concert halls, and the Carnegie Endowment for International Peace.[3]

The face of the nation was changed further because of the automobile—in 1900 fast becoming America's favorite toy. Despite a medical journal article that likened the effect of the speed of the horseless carriage to the addictions of alcohol and tobacco, the automobile would play a large part in making social mobility possible. Some were not happy about the invention. The *New York Times* predicted that the "terrible apparatus" was here to stay, then added, "Man loves the horse and he is not likely ever to love the automobile." Princeton University President Woodrow Wilson warned that this foolish and expensive automobile would likely cause the spread of socialist ideals.[4]

In 1909 the *Ladies Home Journal* warned people about the evils of buying on credit and using the installment plan. In 1911 Irving Berlin's "Alexander's Ragtime Band" caused a revolution in dance manners. The Turkey Trot, the Grizzly Bear, the Kangaroo Dip, and the Bunny Hug followed as new ragtime dances. Although the experts knew that the money would be spent foolishly, Henry Ford made newspaper headlines in 1914 when he raised the wages of his 13,000 automobile workers to a huge $5 for an eight-hour shift. America's conception of a fair wage was instantly changed with Ford's benevolence. By the time the

*1916 REDSKIN*

While there were warnings that that "terrible apparatus" would likely cause the spread of socialism, most admitted the automobile was here to stay. Maybe these campus "airmen" should have stuck with the horse!

United States entered World War I, "nice" girls were smoking and drinking in public. In a single generation America's manners and morals had changed forever.[5]

Colleges and universities soon joined the "peculiar madness of the time."[6] From the turn of the century and on into the 1920s, campuses shared the mood of the country. It was a time to elect campus beauty queens, most popular men and women, and the outstanding athlete. All were given campus recognition and suitable prizes. Students strove for experiences that were humanizing, yet emulating of "real life." Student social life began to center on dancing, motion pictures, the automobile, and the over consumption of tobacco and alcohol. Greek organizations, athletic teams, campus newspapers and magazines, and student government were all stabilized. Each became a permanent part of the scene in American higher education. Extracurricular activities were the vehicles for campus fellowship, character building, and well-roundedness for students in these days of post-Victorian-era America.[7]

Fads and fashion, as well as permanent social change, often took time to reach Oklahoma. From the student's point-of-view, it was good fortune that brought Angelo C. Scott to the presidency of the Oklahoma Agricultural and Mechanical College on July 1, 1899. Dr. Scott, like no other president before him, would involve himself in a supportive way with the students. Scott enjoyed students because they made him feel perpetually young. He believed that students deserved and should have a wholesome campus environment.[8]

In describing the Oklahoma Agricultural and Mechanical College around 1900, Dr. Scott wrote: "The College farm comprised 200 acres, of less than average fertility. The only buildings were Old Central; a tiny white building just east of Central used as a biological laboratory, a flimsy two-story residence where the director of the Experiment Station lived; and a small ramshackle barn. In the year preceding the beginning of my service on the faculty there were between 125 and 150 students, most of them in the preparatory department. The catalog of that year was a mere folder of four pages, not even containing the names of the students."[9]

Dr. Scott was an educator by training and by experience. He was also a scholar, having been the valedictorian of his graduating class at the University of Kansas in 1873. He had come to the Stillwater campus in January 1898 as the head of the Oklahoma A. and M. College's English department. By the time of his promotion to the presidency, students knew him as an excellent teacher and lecturer. Dr. Scott was not an agriculturist. He believed that a college education should not only be liberating and general but also force students to have a probing mind. Although his views on education were favored more by students than the general public, Scott went about the work of putting a curriculum in place which would prepare the college's graduates to participate actively in society. President Scott was instrumental in bringing about dramatic permanent change in the environment for students. Upon leaving the presidency Scott reflected "that kindness wins more with students than severity."[10] This was seemingly his guiding principle as he brought the land-grant college into the twentieth century.[11]

President Scott was by no means a liberal, nor was he a pushover for the students. To the contrary, he was an individual of strong principles and beliefs, an advocate of church, God, and life of high values, and an educator willing to act upon what he believed. For example, he believed in academic standards. In 1903 fifty students were not admitted to the Oklahoma A. and M. College because of academic deficiencies. This was the first time this had happened. Scott disdained the evils of gambling and alcohol; once he presented a ninety-page speech on temperance to a meeting of Stillwater's citizens. Perhaps pushing the bounds of propriety on this occasion, Scott accused the audience of inflicting an evil influence on his students. President Scott observed that the state's citizens generally saw the Oklahoma A. and M. College as a place for teaching farming and high school work. Scott attacked this perception through his speeches, a dramatic campus building program, and active involvement in state and national politics—all on behalf of his college. On campus and in the community he involved himself in athletics, a town band, Young Men's Christian Association (YMCA) and Young Women's Christian Association (YWCA), and several operettas.[12] The University of Kansas' alumni magazine later remembered Scott by stating: "He looks like an actor; he would like to have been a preacher; he has been an editor, a lawyer, and a politician; he is a teacher."[13]

Thus, with the winds of change blowing across the nation and a "student's president" in the chair of leadership on the prairie campus, Scott began the work of developing an institution to serve in the new century. In 1900 there were seventeen faculty members. The entrance requirements were competency in reading, writing, United States history, spelling, grammar, and arithmetic. Construction projects, large and small, would be part of campus life for years to come. Building materials were hauled from the railroad's freight depot to campus by wagon and team. The campus library, later named Williams Hall for Professor Benjamin Franklin Williams, was completed in 1900. Williams Hall was at times called the "castle of the plains" because of its spires and other architectural features. The Prairie Playhouse was added to Williams Hall in 1903. Total cost of this construction was $48,500.[14]

Other campus improvements of a smaller nature were also underway. The College Paper of October 1902 noted that a girl's toilet room was under construction in the basement of the library building, a large sewer system was being connected to all campus buildings to "effectu-

It's a lot more fun to sit on the back row. One never knows just who might take your picture? This young man seems a bit distracted from the 1911 graduation exercises.

ally drain the entire campus," and the "heating system is now complete and we can rest secure in the feeling that we shall be quite warm this winter."[15] Prior to this the college had erected sheds west of the granary to stable the horses which students rode to and from the college. The new tables for the library which had been completed by students Howard and Carl Pigg and John J. Brown confirmed that students were excellent carpenters. Some things remained to be done. For example, the driveway through campus had not been repaired, and due to heavy rains and mud, it was closed to all but light vehicles.

Students were not always helpful in matters related to campus improvements. A 1903 *College Paper* expressed displeasure when it related: "We have a few students who have not yet passed the 'mischievous small boy' stage. This is evidenced by the overturned piles of bricks and the stakes that were pulled up where our sidewalks are to be. We cannot see what satisfaction young men get from doing what small boys are past doing."[16] Despite this disruption, the campus' first sidewalks to the town were eventually completed.[17] Students were reminded that bicycle riding on sidewalks was against city law. "Besides making yourself liable to arrest and fine, you are endangering the life and limb of your fellow students," reprimanded the *College Paper*.[18]

Progress was also being made elsewhere on campus. With the erection of more and more buildings, a college fire department, with a newly purchased hose cart, a "goodly length of hose," and twenty strong student volunteers, had been formed. Regular practices by the firemen were common. Students continued to walk on the newly-seeded lawns despite repeated warnings. However, the physical plant facilities were growing; progress was generally underway.[19]

Oklahoma's statehood was achieved, and a constitution adopted in November 1907. With the Democrats coming to political power, every major college president, as well as faculty members, would be fired because their appointments had been made by Republican politicians. To satisfy himself, Scott initiated his own resignation before the political axe fell. Scott was the last of the territorial presidents. The last day of his tenure was June 30, 1908.[20]

President Scott had endeared himself to the students through his leadership and dedication on their behalf. Later when talking about his presidential years, the educator captured this mutual feeling when he said: "As I look back upon these years, I am bound to say that the greatest pleasure they brought to me, and the greatest pleasure the remembrance of them still brings to me, is the friendship of the students of the College. In the years since I have left the college this friendship has been shown to me in countless ways, and it is one of the joys of my life to meet the young men and women who were in a measure under my care during the nine years of my presidency."[21]

In his nine years of leadership, enrollment had grown to 497 students. The college now owned thousands of acres of land. The value of buildings and teaching equipment had risen from $40,000 to $300,000. A library, several new academic buildings, and the first campus residence halls had been constructed. And to Scott, most gratifying of all, was that he left campus among the cheers and wild support of the student body.[22]

With the growth of the campus physical facilities and student enroll-

During the administration of Angelo C. Scott, the Oklahoma A. and M. College strived for higher academic standards and more college-supported student activities. Many budding musicians had fun in the first college band, shown here around 1902.

ment, changes were also being made in the areas of academics and student conduct. Through the Scott era and then the presidency of J. H. Connell, from 1908 to 1914, the Oklahoma A. and M. College's academic and disciplinary environments were liberalized. Some changes occurred as a matter of practicality since the number of students precluded reasonable management of the formerly rigid academic system. Still other schemes were devised to accommodate what students wanted. In general, the notion of in loco parentis was still publicly stated. This was a necessity in Oklahoma. In reality, students were given increasing freedom to establish their organizations. The student newspaper and yearbook became deeply rooted. Student life was characterized by class unity and keen competition between classes. A true collegiate atmosphere developed. Unique traditions, such as the class fight and tug-of-war, were examples of events that were developed locally. Greek organizations and a student government organization, representing all students, served as viable illustrations of student systems brought to campus from the national scene.

The era from 1900 to the advent of the involvement of the United States in World War I was a time for student initiative, experimentation, and establishment. By 1917 the "collegiate environment" had grown so large that students were cautioned not to spread themselves "too thin" at the expense of their academic pursuits. Other students were accused of being apathetic. YMCA meetings were being cancelled or rescheduled because of competition with other events. For good or bad, these qualities are all a barometer of a campus "growing up."[23]

The faculty played a part in campus growth and change. Around 1901 the commencement oratory requirement was dropped, except for selected class representatives, because the graduating classes were becoming too large. For obvious reasons, students were pleased with this change. The rules for student conduct were recodified and made more realistic. However, the military quality of the rules remained. Students who withdrew from school without going through the required process were labeled "deserters." Students would rise and stand until given permission to retake their seats when their teacher, the college president, or any dignitary entered the classroom. If a student were convicted in a civil lawsuit, he or she would be automatically expelled. Any student found to be a habitual user of tobacco would be dismissed by the college. Attendance at chapel exercises remained a requirement.[24] The faculty reminded the students that "loafing, strolling, loitering or idling on [the] campus for social or similar purposes during study hours is strictly forbidden,"[25]

The demerit system became more flexible, and automatic penalties were no longer assessed violators. Further, a grade was now given each term for discipline. Students with eight or fewer demerits received an A. Those with sixty-four or more demerits in one term were assigned an F. Students now had a right to appeal an injustice against them, and they also had a right to petition against any grievance. Although hazing was rampant, it was a practice that could lead to suspension. If the faculty had strictly enforced the hazing rule, probably most freshmen and sophomores, plus a fair number of upperclassmen, would have been dismissed.[26]

While hazing was generally ignored, other disciplinary action was swift and final. The conduct of Velma Watt and B. C. Bullen was reported to the college's discipline committee. It was documented that the two students were seen together in the hammock at or near eleven o'clock at night on the front porch of Mr. West's house without his knowledge or approval. The discipline committee's findings to the faculty resulted in Watt's being suspended indefinitely. Bullen, a graduating senior, was awarded his degree but forbidden to participate in the upcoming graduation exercises. Justification for the faculty's action was that the students "on this occasion behaved in a manner as to expose themselves to unfavorable criticisms." There are other interesting facets to this disciplinary case. Bullen asked for and received a direct appeal before the faculty, but it is not known whether his efforts served to soften his pen-

While hazing incidents such as the paddle line were generally ignored, the faculty often resorted to swift and final disciplinary action in other cases. Still, problems persisted.

alty. Also, Bullen asked for a public discussion and vote in his presence. This request was flatly denied. In any case, Bullen had taken unusual latitudes with the faculty. Assertiveness with the faculty was risky business. No doubt his having already met graduation requirements played a part in Bullen's rare disciplinary scenario being played out.[27]

While the faculty continued to protect the interests of the college and attempted to modify the students' behavior through the disciplinary code, problems persisted. The *1906-1907 Catalogue* reported that "all examinations and tests are conducted under the honor system."[28] The students continued to be placed on their honor not to cheat and were required to sign the same pledge that first appeared eleven years earlier in 1895. The responsible faculty member was relieved of anything that "resembled watching or espionage." Violations of the code led to immediate dismissal. By 1908 the *Orange and Black* reported that there was difficulty in enforcing the college's honor system, and, in fact, it was of "little use."[29] Eight years later, in 1916, the *Orange and Black* again reported: "Very few exams, yes, very few, indeed, are given here but that some ride through nicely on a little white pony with ink markings."[30] The editorial then declared that cheating was far worse than two or three years before.

In analyzing the causes of cheating the student writer suggested: "Most of the students cheat because so few seem against it. Some cheat because its their nature to take something that does not belong to them. Others cheat because temptation is put in their way by the examiner leaving the room."[31] The editorial then proposed one remedy would be for the faculty member to do his duty by remaining in the examination room. Faculty members soon agreed. The student's honor system, like the dinosaur, had its peak, served its purpose, and became extinct shortly thereafter.

While the demise of the academic honor system was becoming evident, an enduring academic system to help students was being born. The growth of student enrollment necessitated an academic advisement system. The Oklahoma State University's first academic advisement organization was reported in the faculty meeting records of October 25, 1910.[32] The *1910-11 College Catalog* publicly explained the advisor-student relationship: "To bring about a close relationship between students and members of the faculty, and for the purpose of safeguarding every interest of the individual student, the college has adopted an 'advisory system' which applied to all students." All faculty members served as advisors to a small group of students that he or she would get to know personally. Advisors worked closely with parents and contacted them directly if any circumstances warranted such action. Further, "parents should not hesitate to write concerning matters that may have to do with the student's comfort and progress in their studies."[33]

The academic advisement system was implemented and apparently was effective. Perhaps to the chagrin of some of the faculty advisors, students were placing a heavy burden on them as the second semester of the 1916-17 academic year got underway. In fact it was reported that the advisors "have been wearing long faces trying to make out cards for dissatisfied students and undecided students."[34] Students complained that registration was done in too short a period of time. Many changed their course of study and transferred to different schools to pursue a new area of study. Students were anxious to get their last semester's grades, and extra clerical help had to be employed to deal with the flood of paperwork.

In the meantime, the 1862 Morrill Act mandate for military training in the nation's land-grant colleges was not ignored by academic planners at Oklahoma A. and M. College. It was suggested that L. L. Lewis, while serving as acting president in 1914, orchestrated the advent of modern military training. Confirmation of progress in the military program was found in the 1917 Redskin where it was reported that student attitudes had changed for the good, for problems had been corrected, and "no doubt the military department has made more progress in the last four years than any department in the college."[35] Some of the changes included exempting juniors and seniors from required participation, a changing of uniforms from a formerly uncomfortable and unattractive blue to regulation olive-drab, and moving the drill time from the heat of afternoons to the first hour of the morning. The military band had also greatly improved. The implementation of the Reserve Officers Training Corps in 1916 boosted cadet morale.[36]

By 1917, a Redskin writer reported that "the real genuine military man is now envied by the lowerclassmen, admired by the fair sex and petted by the faculty."[37] Military cadets now participated in full-scale

The air was filled with the sound of rapid firing. Shots whizzed by. The ground was soon covered with fallen warriors. The weekend sham battles, an integral part of campus military training for the student soldiers of the Oklahoma A. and M. College, were in session.

military maneuvers on weekends. These mock battles, or sham battles as they were called at the time, involved nearly everyone. The coeds provided support by performing quartermaster duties, preparing hot meals, repairing uniforms, and delivering supplies. The military campaigners would walk a mile or two from campus, build trenches and bulwarks, and do battle with each other, student against student, until their ranks would eventually thin from desertion, fake wounds, or plain weariness. The battle would be declared over, and the losers would buy the victors beer at Peck's or some other nearby student "watering hole." There, war stories would be told, wounds would quickly heal, and spirits were greatly uplifted.[38]

The cadets, despite their renewed and enthusiastic spirit, also continued to have problems. On one occasion Cadet H. H. Hancock appeared intoxicated at a class party in Morrill Hall and was indefinitely suspended. Another time Captain Judge ordered his company to double time. Soon the captain was left behind and became entangled in his sword. When he finally caught up with his unit, they had gone over, around, and under a barbed-wire fence. Blustering and panting, the captain insisted that he had given the command to halt. Each cadet was given five demerits for disobeying the order. On another occasion a cadet platoon opened their moving ranks on the campus sidewalk to allow Professor James W. Means to pass. This time the cadets were reprimanded for breaking ranks without an order.[39]

Despite these minor trials, the Cadet Corps had become a significant showpiece for the college. The cadet regiment held an annual parade during commencement week activities. In connection with the football contest with the University of Oklahoma, the cadet regiment boarded a special Santa Fe train in November 1915 to go to Oklahoma City. The witnessing audience was "pleasantly surprised" and "enthusiastic" as the 600 cadets marched up Broadway, led by the forty-piece military band. Governor R. L. Williams and his staff were among the dignitaries present. The campus newspaper reported that "the behavior of the cadets was beyond reproach and entirely in keeping with proper conduct of soldiers."[40]

Gone were the days when the Redskin's yearly calendar would have listings like "January 11—Drill—will it ever rain?" or "February 17—Rain!!! No Drill!!!"[41] Instead, by 1916, the commandant's report to the president stated: "At the present time military instruction is given to about 600 students three hours per week. Of this number over 50 students continue to take military training voluntarily and from this group nearly all of the cadet commissioned officers are chosen. The fact that after a minimum of two year's compulsory training such a large percentage of them continue the military training voluntarily, speaks for itself." The commandant then concluded his report by emphasizing that the spirit of the Cadet Corps was excellent, that the program received loyal support from the faculty, but that the program was handicapped by the fact that there was no armory. He observed that the "military department has become an important feature of the college."[42]

Campus athletics paralleled the growth of military training. Competition and class loyalty were powerful forces on the campus which found the greatest outlet in intercollegiate athletics, intramural sports, and recreation programs. In 1900 President Scott challenged the student body during chapel to prove their athletic prowess by participating in the Oklahoma Intercollegiate Athletic Association competition in Guthrie. In January 1900, the A. and M. Athletic Association was enthusiastically organized. Students and faculty scraped out a quarter-mile track in an alfalfa field. Faculty often served as volunteer coaches. The first local track meet on campus was held on April 22, 1900. The "rag tag" group of victors from the campus class competition, representing the very best that the Oklahoma A. and M. College could offer, went to Guthrie and won the territory-wide competition. The Douglas Cup, symbol of territorial supremacy and the winner's trophy, was returned to Stillwater. After two more straight wins in subsequent years, the Douglas Cup became the permanent possession of the Oklahoma A. and M. Tigers.[43]

Football quickly bubbled to the surface as the sport that was most intensely fought. The class of 1905 beat all other classes in the 1901 season. Olin W. Jones said that "games were played that made your teeth stand on edge, if your teeth survived the game." Jones, in talking about this 1905 team, recalled that "those were the days of class rivalry and bitter hatred, to the extent that many attempts at maiming were pulled during the games." Joe Thornberry lost four teeth in one game. Joe Houska died during this time as a result of a reported case of tonsillitis. The fact Houska was a target for one team and received a knee to his neck shortly before he died probably did not help. Heads were used, not for diagnosing plays, but as ramrods. "Since we didn't have intercollegiate sports," Jones recalled, "the honor of the class was important to us then as was the honor of the school, and our class fights were really fights. Even President Scott didn't dare to interfere much."[44]

Houska's death caused the faculty to suspend the playing of football on campus or out-of-town. An article in the *College Paper* in November 1902 reported that the senior class had decided no longer to take part in the football games between classes. Calling the game dangerous and a threat to life and limb, Lila Nelson, student writer, said: "I believe the senior class is setting a good example by refusing to play football and that the time will come when future senior classes will arise and 'call them blessed' for the stand they took in regard to the football curse."[45] Nelson's voice was but a small one in the wilderness, as football was reinstated after this brief setback.[46]

Campus athletics continued to grow. Class competitions and intramural programs were now supervised by the faculty. The Athletic Association sponsored seasonal competitions in baseball, tennis, basketball, and track. In 1901 the women improvised a court in the basement of the Library Building and played basketball. Favorite sports of coeds in 1910 were tennis and basketball. The women were also starting to play indoor baseball and field hockey. Male coaches for women's teams were discouraged because of two tendencies: men either overworked women because they lacked an understanding of their physical limits or they went to the opposite extreme by believing women could not play as well or as much as men and therefore allowed them to play as they pleased.[47]

Other trappings of a growing athletic system also developed. Peer pressure was building for student participation. In 1903 students were urged to pay their twenty-five cents dues and use the college gymnasium for their own health and body development. At that time only thirty male students were regularly frequenting the gymnasium. On another occasion, in 1907, some students printed their own tickets to save the ten cents admission charge to a basketball game. Nonetheless, plans for a new armory-gymnasium were in place in 1917. The *Orange and Black* described it as a place ''for gymnastic exercises, military instructions

Oh, to be able to lob a shot off the old backboard! These 1903 coeds not only had to play with improvised equipment, their playing field certainly was not a hardwood floor! Intramural programs suffered from meager facilities for years.

and drill, and for athletic events, but the contemplated building will be admirably fitted to fulfill the secondary mission of a college gymnasium, i.e., a center for large social gatherings."[48] This building, which still stands north of Morrill Hall, contained a shooting range and gun and ammunition rooms. The second floor provided offices for the military department and a large lecture room. The YMCA was given temporary quarters on the third floor. With the new armory-gymnasium the military and athletic programs would have the finest facilities in the state, as well as state of the art equipment.[49]

The academic complexities of the Oklahoma Agricultural and Mechanical College were growing in relationship to the size of the student enrollment and the scope and breadth of the curriculum. When each college class was small, all of the freshmen were scheduled to take the same class, in the same hour together. The academic work of the sophomore, junior, and senior classes was also self-contained, much like classes are scheduled today in Oklahoma's smallest high schools. With more students all of the earlier curricular simplicity changed. Students were now forced to contend with problems characterized by personal conflicts. Student life was becoming more difficult. Classes had to be scheduled. College academic majors had to be chosen.

The inevitable student dilemma of academics versus social, and in what balance, appeared for the first time as a major problem on the campus. In 1917 an *Orange and Black* editorial reminded students of their final semester examinations: "The automatic process of culling out the laggard and indifferent student—flunking out—is in vogue and is making its mark. The path is about the same width as of previous years. The majority of those falling into its dangers, as usual, are new students, but occasionally an old student falls into the mire." The editorial added: "The majority will be here with us again, but perhaps on probation."[50]

This problem, of course, was not unique to the Oklahoma A. and M. campus. Through the centuries each student has had to struggle with the question of how much time he or she will study. And not unlike today, students often ignored the advice offered to them on this perplexing problem. One newspaper article of the era suggested: "Keep awake and alive in the classroom . . . the easiest way in the world to get through college is by doing good honest classroom work and since the hour must be spent there in any event why not get help from your instructor. Any one who does not do so is a chump and there are many chumps in this college."[51]

A graduate of the Oklahoma A. and M. College wrote a helpful article to his former college classmates on "How to Study" in 1901. He reflected: "Take proper care of your body; keep clean, use soap less sparingly and more vigorously. Shield your eyes, and take every precaution possible to keep them in good, healthy condition. Use a shade on your lamp. Refrain from keeping late hours; it is not only annoying to others but it is very injurious to your health. Have regular habits, a time for everything. Never think of taking your work to bed with you. That is the place to rest, not to study. The burning of the midnight oil may seem to many a necessary evil, but the student who practices such, in the end, suffers from injurious effects."[52]

Nonetheless, students' interests, organizations, and other distractions were growing rapidly. The dilemma of studying was made more difficult by the mere thrill of being a student at a time when campus social life and student organizations proliferated. Stillwater's Alamo Theatre showed Mary Pickford in *Hearts Adrift*, a four-reel motion picture, at admissions ranging from ten to twenty cents. Comedian Charlie Chaplin's movie *Mistress of the Air* could be seen for five cents and ten cents. The Rooters' Club, a student pep organization, was voted the most popular student organization. Over a thousand students attended the new student's reception sponsored by several of Stillwater's churches. Although the effort failed, several hundred students petitioned to have final examinations abolished. The Philos Literary Society debated the same question.[53] The most hated academic requirement was the memorized freshman speech for "this is what makes anarchists of men and suffragettes of women. As for myself, I think that a few more months of it will force me to seek refuge for the remainder of my days in the Institute for Mental Cripples."[54]

At each year's commencement exercises there were ceremonies of "passage." The "Burning of the Troubles" and "Planting of the Ivy" were two of these developing traditions.[55] In this age of women's suffrage, a self-government organization for women was founded on campus. Since its suggestion "several problems have come to the minds of the founders, and with them the idea that the girls' organization would be the only proper jurisdiction."[56] The junior class annually hosted the gala Junior-Senior Banquet. Given the "feeling of enmity, those class rivalries were only natural," but this banquet stood out as the one campus tradition where an entire class gathered socially with another, without conflict, hard feelings, or injury.[57]

Nowhere was the intensity of class rivalry more visible than between the sophomore and freshman classes. In the developing campus social system, it was a sophomore's duty to "guide" the freshmen through their first year. Indoctrination to campus tradition was imperative. Likewise, it was important for a "frosh" to be humble and fully aware of the lowly position he or she held in the campus milieu. Conversely, it was the freshman class's duty to resist, fight, and generally sabotage the sophomore class's efforts. The rivalry between these classes annually, quite naturally, became very intense. Freshman rules of conduct were printed and issued by the sophomores. Pranks were carried out in this give-and-take between classes. The annual class fight and tug-of-war became deeply imbedded in the affairs of campus life.

A large poster printed by the class of 1909 sophomores proclaimed to the in-coming freshman: "We, the noble sophomores of the O.A.M.C. do hereby state and proclaim that the Ignoble and unsophisticated Freshman do, on the account of their weak and undeveloped mental facilities need the advice and guidance of the most learned Sophomores, and having admitted the superior mental capacity and strength of the class of 1909 have cosigned themselves to the guidance and protection of aforesaid Sophomores and have agreed to abide by the undersigned laws."[58] This preamble was then followed by the laws for freshmen. Typically prohibitions included: do not fail to wear the freshman beanie, or green cap; do not use "Lovers Lane" on College Avenue; do not fail to salute upperclassmen; and do not carry a cane or sprout a mustache (for these are left to "senior asses"). Further, a frosh was not to lead any college yells or songs, congregate in groups (especially in front of Peck's), sit in the first five rows of the Alamo or Camera Theatres, or smoke a pipe in public.[59]

The freshmen often responded to the sophomores' challenges. The class of 1910 printed their own poster and hung it about the campus and town. Their preamble proclaimed that it was their duty to throw off the "yoke of despotism," fight for their "inalienable and indisputable rights," and declare that certain "truths to be self evident." The first of these truths affirmed, "That all sophomores are born fools and that they were not endowed by their creator with brains nor are they as idiotic imbeciles entitled to any rights, respect or recognition by us—the Class of 1910."[60] The bonds of class unity grew rapidly as this banter between classes was carried out. The class of 1906 ended their declaration of independence from their sophomore antagonists: "And in support of our declaration, we mutually pledge to each other our lives, our chances of honorable graduation, and our sacred excellence in scholarship and deportment."[61]

As a class went about interspersing its academics with picnics, receptions, and other festivities, another class would plot to gain superiority. The *College Paper* in May 1903 pointed out that hair cuttings, cake stealing, and dunkings were common occurrences the past year. On one occasion, ammonia was thrown on a group of partying students. One participant later wrote, "If anyone wishes to know the painful effect of this, he should try the experiment himself, as no words can describe it. Suffice it to say that eyes were almost blinded and complexions ruined."[62] The hostilities sometimes caused ill feelings which lasted for years. Paul G. Crouse, reminiscing about a 1904 ice cream stealing episode nearly sixty years later, recalled the incident vividly, adding: "I SHALL NEVER FORGIVE THEM"![63] Crouse was referring to his class's

Rolling out of the north like an Oklahoma spring thunderstorm, the sophomores engaged the freshmen in battle at the old cottonwood tree outside of Old Central in the annual class fight. As spectators watched from the windows of the matriarch campus building, noses were bloodied, eyes were blackened, and clothes were torn—all in the name of campus bragging rights and class loyalty.

Oklahoma State University

protagonists—the sophomores.[64]

Once each year the ultimate test of superiority between classes was contested in a cottonwood tree west of Old Central where the freshmen would hang their class flag atop the tree and issue a challenge to the sophomores. The history of the class of 1920 documented a typical class fight: "The next event in line was the annual class fight on the afternoon of September 13th, which was the greatest struggle of its kind ever witnessed between two generations of Oklahoma A. and M. sons. We had our colors up at 1:30 P.M. sharp, and eager for revenge on the husky Sophs, who had been gathering behind the library for an hour. When they came, they came like a thunderstorm, rolling out of the north, the dust rolling from under their feet like dust from under the feet of a cattle stampede. After about two hours of hard fighting, the Sophs began to see their weakness and tried to carry off the green-painted boys one-by-one, but without avail, for they would soon break loose and come back to the scene of conflict. By 5:30 P.M. the green and white still floated in the tree top, which was the sign of the first notable victory won by the 1920 class."[65]

As hundreds of freshmen and sophomores battled, Old Central's windows were filled with spectators. Other observers would encircle the belligerents and the tree. The "no holds barred" contest would usually last for hours. Although concrete evidence is lacking, there were rumors of guns and brass knuckles sometimes playing a part in the warfare. A college newspaper article portrayed the typical class fight consequences: "The onslaught of the sophomores was made and received amid spirited war hoops and battlecries, and a moment later the battlesite was a scene of torn clothes and sweating and bleeding bodies—bruised knees, skinned elbows, bleeding noses, wild eyes and panting, mingled fearfully with the shouts, jeers and groans of both participants and non-participants."[66] Although hard to comprehend by some, the class fight purported to produce a feeling of community and loyalty, campus enthusiasm, and friendship.[67]

In 1907 the class tug-of-war was initiated as still another tradition which pitted the sophomores against the freshmen. Although far less violent than the class fight, the tug-of-war served the same purposes and was as intensely fought. A challenge was again issued. An equal number of men would stretch a rope across Theta Pond, then called the college pond, and the two adversarial class teams would await the firing of the starting gun. Under the watchful eye of a faculty referee, the teams would struggle. Sometimes after hours of pulling the losers would be dumped in the pond. The winners would leave as campus heroes after taking a piece of the rope home for a souvenir.[68]

After several years of tug-of-wars where there was a clear winner, disappointment occurred in September 1915. The campus paper declared: "The day was ideal, the water was cold, the crowd was large, and the only disappointment was that nobody got wet." On this day the two class teams of ten members struggled for two hours without making headway. Finally, the faculty judge called the contest off, declaring a draw. Disappointed, the on-lookers spontaneously grabbed the rope determined to get someone wet. Still another creative individual then cut the rope, causing bodies to fly backward in all directions. The fun for the day was finally over. Combatants and witnesses alike left the scene without fanfare.[69]

The Harvest Carnival in the fall and May Carnival in the spring were times of calm and celebration on the campus. The classes would temper their competitive hostilities and join together to participate in these major social activities. The Harvest Carnival, the forerunner of the annual homecoming weekend, began in 1913. Proceeds from the Harvest Carnival went to support the college annual, the *Redskin*. Each class nominated a Harvest Carnival queen candidate. In an all-college assembly the queen would be elected from among the candidates. On the day of the carnival the queen's coronation was held, a parade with floats followed, and in the evening a carnival was held. At the carnival the college boxers and wrestlers would accept all challenges—for a small price. Confetti, often still on the ground years later, was thrown in abundance. Chester Gould, a student and later the originator of the *Dick Tracy* cartoon strip, once set up a table to draw cartoons for those who would pay him a quarter. Every major campus organization had a money-making booth or activity, and a free motion picture was shown in the college auditorium. Football games became an added attraction. In 1916 the Harvest Carnival became the Tiger Roundup. Alumni and college friends flocked to the festivities.[70] Apple cider was sold by the Home Economics Society. The cider was always sold out, and "spirits" were always considerably lifted by the cider.

Another major attraction which caused a special excitement was the 1921 "Follies" production. On this occasion several young women caused a stir by baring their limbs in a showline dance routine. Stillwater's Ministerial Alliance was horrified and went to work to close the show. Although they were successful, by the time the tent flaps were closed at eleven o'clock most of the students had seen the censored production.[71]

Campus-wide excitement and participation recurred in the spring with the May Carnival. Started in 1909, the May Carnival, to the delight of college authorities, was held without confetti or paint. The May pole dances highlighted the afternoon and evening events. A parade through the campus and town and a carnival, again with booths, were part of the festivities. All other scheduled college events were suspended for this one special day of noise and laughter. The two deputy sheriffs that

The Harvest Carnival spawned the annual homecoming weekend. If campus fervor were not fueled after this 1916 parade, crowds could take part in the carnival or the football game. To be pelted with confetti, to sip cider at the Home Economics Society booth, to get an original cartoon from campus artist Chester Gould—those were the sights and sounds of autumn at Oklahoma A. and M. College.

were usually assigned to the event, in case of problems, were typically not needed. Prizes were given for the most attractive and most grotesque make-up in the parade. Stillwater's churches and businesses partici-pated, many selling food to the revelers. The May Carnival served to raise money to help student organizations pay their bills. The primary sponsors, the Women's Athletic Association and YWCA, cleared about $130 for their hard work in 1910. The May Carnival also marked the end of another college year for the students. Before long, final examina-tions would be upon them.[72]

The campus carnivals, class picnics, and even the class rivalries brought young men and women together. Naturally, romance among students followed. By 1910 a whole set of "norms," including places and behavior, had evolved which characterized the campus in Stillwater. The *1910 Redskin* called it the "course in campus." Subparts to this course of seventy or more years ago included "scheming, candy talk, campus strolling, winks in the library, and soirees in the hall." Com-pletion of the course is called matrimony, but few who start the course ever intend for it to go that far. The *Redskin* then suggested that the course in campus "is all practicum and its laboratories are the best filled out on the campus. No student should leave the institution without hav-ing been in the race for one or more of the *many valuable prizes* offered by this department.''[73] In 1916 Mr. Sunderland, the campus night watchman, reported seeing and hearing about many love affairs. About his job, he noted, "Nothing much happens, but I see quite a few couples spooning every evening."[74]

A good time in 1905 entailed "on Monday night we all went down to Emma's and had some ice-cream and some cake, two kinds, some coffee too and also some wafers. And we played cards some, and some played Flinch and some went away at 10 o'clock. I know not why but Carl took Gertrude home and then came back and took Hattie home. I guess everybody had a good time."[75] Nell Dent Bentley, a graduate of 1909, recalled that the steps at the rear entrance to the library were always shady and cool in the spring and summer and served the double purpose of benches and "courtin court."[76] At the time this area was not called "Lover's Lane," but rather "Lover's Porch." The students declared it a "resort for 'moon struck' youths and maids from town and college."[77] However, it was still a semi-Victorian era. To be caught meant demerits. Sometimes it even required a personal visit to the president's office. There the limit of demerits would be given, which would allow the offenders to remain in school provided they did not get any more.[78]

At least from the student's viewpoint, the increasingly romantic environment was enhanced by an ample mixing of dance and alcohol. The Payne County chapter of the Women's Christian Temperance Union did its part to stop the growing tide by placing books and pamphlets on alcohol and prohibition in the college library. In another effort, the Stillwater Ministerial Alliance wrote newly appointed college President J. W. Cantwell reminding him that the college buildings were built and paid for by the Christian people of the state. Since Christian people did not believe in dancing as a proper amusement, the students who wished to indulge in dancing should be asked to make their arrangements off-campus. The ministers then added: "In the past history of the college those intelligent and distinguished men who have been invited to address the students have invariably when referring to dancing warned the young people against it. Those physicians that have discussed sex hygiene before the young men have advised most emphatically against dancing. The recent lecture of Dr. Duke's was urgent in pointing out the evil effect liable to follow this practice."[79] These efforts were made in vain. Students continued to dance and consume intoxicating beverages.[80]

In fact the I.P.A. club was formed. After some investigative reporting the campus newspaper discovered the initials meant: "I Prize Ale." Lessons were offered on campus for those who wished to learn to dance. Dancing became the focus of class social activities. Student groups raised money by sponsoring dances. For example, on January 29, 1906, the Athletic Association cleared $60 to pay off a football debt. The 1916

Junior-Senior Banquet was a "howling success." The water was fine too. Molly drank fourteen glasses of water and she wasn't nervous either. "Romeo" got away with eleven; "Farmer" was pouring her drinks in the cuspidor. "Never did get lit, nayther." Next day, "three juniors and four seniors were seen on the campus. They had headaches." On another social evening, two students, Broemel and Gundy, gave an exhibition dance. As a result "pandemonium reigned for several minutes."[81] Through it all people had mixed feelings about these new student behaviors. For instance, the college janitor did not approve of dancing, but did like the extra money he earned when a college social club held its meetings.[82]

The dance craze continued in Stillwater and nationally. Locally the faculty developed the rules that they felt necessary to cope with the situation. The minutes for the September 1912 faculty meeting mandated that hereafter a form, in triplicate, would have to be submitted by at least two students in good standing, three days prior to any dance. The form must contain the name of the chaperon and all of the male students that would be attending. After the dance the same students would submit a report including the names of the women accompanying the men, the amount of money collected, and an itemized list of expenses. No student would be allowed to attend a dance more than once in two weeks. No dance could be held on a regular study night. Finally, all dances ended by midnight.[83] It is clear that neither the new rules nor the paperwork diminished the students' enthusiasm for dancing.

While dancing, dating, and general social life were on the rise, an equal popularity could be seen in the growth of other enduring campus extracurricular activities. The campus lyceum series grew and brought a variety of campus entertainment. In 1916 Eugene V. Debs, four-time Socialist candidate for United States President, spoke on campus. Admission was twenty-five cents. In the same year the Fidelio Grand Opera Company was still another lyceum presentation.

In addition to the *Orange and Black's* sarcastic warning to students whose motto was "Never let College studies interfere with your college education," by 1915 the college faculty set aside a common hour during the class day for all student meetings.[84] This endeavor was to decrease the amount of class and study time lost by students "cutting classes" to participate in the extracurriculum.[85]

Initiatives meeting the student's widest interests had once again preceded the faculty's response with the "activities hour." Although distracting to people studying above, a roller skating club met in the basement of the library. A folk dancing club, an A&M Cadet Rifle Club, which eventually became the national championship winning ROTC Rifle Team, and the Prohibition Society were all started. In 1916, an organization for those interested in flight, called the College Aeronautical Society, was formed. The following year Maude Cass was elected the president of the first enduring organization dedicated to the special interests of women. This women's organization existed into the 1970s and acquired the permanent name of the Association of Women Students (AWS).[86]

On a larger and more permanent scale, the student body approved a constitution for the Student Association on April 6, 1915. Although there had been several college councils prior to this date, none had been able to survive.[87] This new attempt to form a campus-wide student government provided for the association to be composed of the four classes. A Student Senate, composed of fifteen members, was empowered to legislate matters of student interest. The freshman class, due to the on-going belief of their immaturity, was not allowed representation in the senate. The Student Association was to "bring about a closer relationship between the Faculty, the Student Body, and the Board of Agriculture, to develop student government, and to recommend, maintain, and regulate the customs and traditions of the College."[88] The first executive officers and senators were elected on May 6, 1915. Campus politicking was heavy prior to the election, with a rumor prevalent that more than one vote was bought at Peck's, a popular student hangout.[89]

As the fall semester opened, the direct ancestor to the Oklahoma State University Student Government Association went into operation. President Cantwell installed the first officers on September 15, 1915. Joe L. Robinson became the first president of the Student Association. Fern Lowry took the oath of office as vice president, and Harry E. Johnson was sworn to the duties of the secretary and treasurer. Lowry, in her brief remarks before the student body, stated her support of Robinson, then added: "She did not know what she would do with fourteen boys, but that she would endeavor to hold up the girls rights even if she had to get a book of parliamentary rules and learn it."[90]

In October the Student Senate took its first ever legislative action. This legislation provided for the "Student Enterprise Ticket." For the one price of $14.30 students would be admitted to over forty campus events, including athletic competitions, oratorical contests, dramatic productions, and musical entertainments. In the second agenda item ever discussed by the Student Senate the "taking of green caps from freshmen by upperclassmen" was discussed. The senate decided to defer any formal decision but warned that if such behavior continued, action would be taken. The work of student government was now underway. Harry E. Johnson was elected the second president in the next election. Thirty men would serve as Student Association president before Bonnie E. Emerson became the first woman president of Oklahoma A. and M. College's Student Association in 1945.[91]

The Student Association became the major campus organization at the Oklahoma Agricultural and Mechanical College in just a few years. The campus newspaper, the *Orange and Black*, and the college annual, the *Redskin* (spelled as two words, *Red Skin*, in 1910), were brought under the association's supervision in 1917. Like the Student Association officers and the senators, the editors of each publication were placed in office in a campus-wide election.

Campus newspapers until 1909 usually had a short existence. Money and the need to print the newspapers off campus were two of the usual insurmountable problems. The *Orange and Black* which had succeeded the *College Paper* had a stormy beginning. Ray Lindsey credited editor Wilbur Lahman with stabilizing the paper during the 1908-09 year. The Philomathean Literary Society had started a movement to publish a paper the year before. Two editions of the *Orange and Black* were printed in April and May of the prior year. In 1908-09 the newspaper staff, like those before it, struggled to sell advertising and subscriptions. When a new edition was published, each individual took time off from regular duties at the paper and personally canvassed students, faculty, and local citizens to sell individual copies. When the students' enthusiasm and energy diminished and the work became discouraging, which was apparently often, Lahman's "untiring perseverance and smiling persistence, would cheer us up" and the work would continue. President Scott soon after established a college printing department. With printing costs reduced, the student newspaper was greatly aided and survival was assured.[92]

In the spring of 1909 the last issue of the *Orange and Black* was a "yearbook-like" publication called "The Retrospect." In offering some theory about why this larger, special *Orange and Black* edition was printed, it was suggested that an oversupply of bright orange paper needed to be used up so that new paper, more to the student editor's liking, could be ordered for the following year's edition.[93]

The first edition of the *Redskin* was published in 1910 in the living room of a house rented by a number of Delta Sigma fraternity men. Originally the yearbook was also called "The Retrospect," but the class of 1911, when questioned by the class of 1910, did not support the proposed name. Many preferred a name with some relationship to Indians and the state. "Rube" Allen, in talking to four other men while on their way to a laboratory class, spoke up and said, "Boys, how does 'The Red Skin' sound to you?" Quick agreement was reached among the five students; and W. E. Camp, 1910 editor, and J. S. Mayall, 1911 editor heartily endorsed the name "Red Skin" as the name of Oklahoma A. and M.'s annual.[94]

Camp, in the first *Redskin* edition wrote: "We not only expect to see the 'Red Skin' published each year in the future by the succeeding classes, but we expect a great improvement in each volume over its

1920 REDSKIN

OSU OUTREACH

One of the earliest *Redskin* and *Daily O'Collegian* cartoonists was Chester "Chet" Gould. From Pawnee, Gould drew impressions of student behavior as a prelude to achieving fame as creator of the cartoon strip, *Dick Tracy.*

predecessors."[95] The first volume, consisting of 216 pages, was distributed to subscribers in the spring of 1910. On the fiftieth anniversary of the *Redskin* in 1959, the yearbook had grown, certainly to Camp's satisfaction, to 618 pages and a weight of seven pounds.[96]

While the stars of the college student newspaper and annual were just rising above the horizon, the campus "Ys," the Young Men's Christian Association (YMCA) and the Young Women's Christian Association (YWCA) had been doing substantial good for the students and the campus. The "Y" movement was a national campus phenomenon. The college YMCA was first organized on April 13, 1900. The original elected officers were: W. S. Richards, president; G. W. Stiles, vice president; F. L. Rector, secretary; and W. T. Thornberry, treasurer. Rector would become president of the "Y" in 1902 and then attend medical school at George Washington University, graduating in 1907. Like so many college students who are influenced in their career interests by college experiences, Rector eventually had a distinguished public health career. Rector's humanitarian concerns lead him to positions with the U.S. Public Health Service and the American Society for the Control of Cancer, now the American Cancer Society. He also served as editor of the *Nation's Health,* a magazine for public interest.[97]

By 1917 the "Ys" had grown to become the most influential and helpful student organizations on campus. Although both "Ys" were student-run organizations, the college president served as the president of the YMCA advisory board. A 1915 freshman reported on the critical difference the "Y" had made for him by saying, "It was a Y.M.C.A. man who asked me to go to Sunday School and church; it was a Y.M.C.A. man who helped entertain we new students and helped us get acquainted; and it was a Y.M.C.A. man who helped me through the first few trying weeks of college life."[98] This student's experience was not atypical. Students, organized through the "Ys," would annually meet every new train bringing students to Stillwater, help them secure room and board, and furnish them the information they would need for a smooth transition to college life. The "Y" also published the "Student Handbook" and a "Student Directory." The "Y" provided rooms for quiet reading and study and a piano for singing. Sunday afternoon meetings included Bible study and speakers. It was not unusual for two-thirds of the student body to hold paid memberships in the YMCA and YWCA.[99]

The YMCA organized a labor bureau, where local citizens could arrange for the employment of students, and published a college calendar. Each fall the "Ys" would sponsor the annual college reception. Students would fill the reception room, porch, and lawn of the Women's Building. A vocal program, which included college songs, was incorporated. The college president would give a welcoming address to the students. In 1916 President Cantwell reminded the students that college life had three phases—the physical, mental, and spiritual. Without all three, Cantwell told the students, they could not be successes in life. The president suggested that the "Ys" were the source of the student's spiritual development. Cantwell continued: "This is the purpose of the great organizations that have entertained us tonight. I cannot too strongly recommend that every student join hands with these organizations and help them in their work for better things. The spiritual life, without which life cannot be as it should."[100]

Despite all of the good work, the "Ys" were handicapped by an inability to secure the employment of a full-time secretary. The students consistently worked and lobbied for such an appointment. They solicited private donations and requested that the Oklahoma State Board of Agriculture, the college's governing board, provide partial salary for a secretary. The board was reluctant, regularly replying that state money could not be used to employ a person in a position constituting religious work. Although the governing body allocated $800 for the secretary in 1915, a change of membership led to the board's rescinding the earlier decision. On several occasions students and faculty alike undertook private fund drives to raise the required salary. Finally, what was described as "one of the greatest events in the history of the college" did take place.[101] On February 24, 1917, W. W. Crutchfield, international

For many years the campus chapter of the Young Women's Christian Association was among the most influential groups at Oklahoma A. and M. College. The "Y" provided many services to help students make a smooth transition to college life. As evidenced from this glimpse of a reception at an annual convention in the early 1910s, the coeds enjoyed this fellowship.

secretary of the YMCA of the Southwest, announced to 1,300 assembled Oklahoma A. and M. students that enough money to hire a "Y" secretary had been raised. Generations of future students would be affected as the organizations' work would be stabilized and continued due to the hiring of a full-time "Y" secretary. Because Crutchfield had been active in the campaign, Crutchfield Hall was later named for him.[102]

Through the growing maze of more complex student social behavior and campus organizations, the debating clubs persisted. In 1910 one publication still maintained that "the two societies of perhaps greatest importance to the student body as a whole are the Philomathean and Omega Literary Societies."[103] Debate topics reflected the interests and concerns of the time. The Philos Society explored the topic of whether interscholastic and intercollegiate athletic contests as existed were desirable and worthy of the support they were given. The Omegas debated the question of whether women and men performing the same work should receive the same wages. In an intercollegiate debate considering whether every able-bodied male citizen should perform one continuous year of military service before reaching the age of twenty-five, the Oklahoma A. and M. team won, taking the affirmative in a contest with Colorado A. and M. (now Colorado State University).[104]

The three campus oratorical groups, the Alphas, Philos and Omegas, collectively organized the Oratorical Association. From debates among the three groups, Oklahoma A. and M. teams were selected to compete against teams from Kansas and Colorado. Despite success in such contests, strife between the three groups continued at home. The Philos had control of literary affairs during the early years of the association. The Omegas and Alphas had grown discontented with the Philos' administration. The subsequent dueling for supremacy through a series of face-to-face debates became as heatedly contested as were contests against outside opponents. In 1914 and 1915 the Omegans won the sceptor, symbol of conquest. However, the strife and ill feelings were renewed annually. The oratorical contests added to the vitality of campus life, and student interest in debate remained intense.[105]

On January 7, 1916, the twenty-fifth anniversary of the founding of the Oklahoma Agricultural and Mechanical College was celebrated. The large event included a band concert and banquet. Historical reviews were given by first graduate Arthur W. Adams, members of the First Territorial Legislature, Stillwater citizens of 1890, faculty members, President Cantwell, and others. It was a time to pause and appreciate, to honor and thank, and to thrill at the growth of the college. There were now fourteen brick and stone buildings where twenty-five years before there were none. Tuition was still free, and the college was offering academic degrees in seven divisions or schools. One-third of the student body was composed of young women. There were 110 teachers. The college was a member of the Southwest Intercollegiate Athletic Association and participated in seven sports, competing favorably with any college in the region. More than 1,000 students enrolled annually; graduating classes now numbered over 100 each year. The library had 24,000 bound and 100,000 unbound volumes. The main campus covered over 80 acres. Summed up, Oklahoma A. and M. College, after twenty-five years, was the largest educational institution in Oklahoma.[106]

Student life had certainly grown in a way rich in variety, opportunity, and tradition. Students then were like students now. "Red" Tarver had been a campus leader, class "clown," and foremost student cheerleader. Tarver was an expert sign painter and used this skill to pay his

Student life at Oklahoma A. and M. College grew in a way rich in variety, opportunity, and tradition. By the twenty-fifth anniversary of the college, numerous students—each with a unique story of their life on the Stillwater campus—had attended the institution. The officers of the Women's Athletic Association in 1915-16 included Fern Lowry (*front*), Beulah Mondy, Norma Brumbaugh, and Layla Selph (*left to right*). Lowry had been a campus leader during her time at college. A member of the YWCA as well as a foremost debater, she also served as vice president of the first Student Association. After graduation she planned to work as a foreign missionary.

college expenses. For Tarver academics never received his top priority. His academic dismissal made the front page of the *Orange and Black* in 1916. In contrast, Ed Gallagher, a freshman in 1908-09, surfaced as an outstanding athlete. He became the premier college wrestling coach in the nation and brought the college national recognition. Fern Lowry was active in student government, YWCA work, and the Women's Athletic Association. She aspired to work in foreign missionary service after graduation. Carl P. Blackwell was an athlete, public speaker, manager of the track team, associate editor of the *Orange and Black*, and a captain in the Cadet Corps. He later returned to his alma mater as the widely-respected director of the Agricultural Experiment Station from 1928 to 1936.[107]

Blackwell, Lowry, Gallagher and Tarver—students in the first twenty-five years of the history of the Oklahoma A. and M. College—were each unique, but all a part of a changing college campus. Their differences help to explain the growth and diversity of Oklahoma's land-grant college. These brief biographical synopses indicate variety in vocational choices; the availability of a number of sports in which to participate; and the presence of a campus government and newspaper—both vehicles for change by and for students— all of which pointed to the maturation of the college. Although students continued to experiment and innovate, the years of trial and error, hesitation and chance were giving way to a stable, mature campus ready to face the future.

# Endnotes

1. Mary Cable, *American Manners and Morals* (New York, NY: American Heritage Publishing, 1969), p. 337.

2. Cable, pp. 337, 339.

3. Cable, pp. 337-343.

4. Cable, p. 339.

5. Cable, pp. 337-344.

6. Frederick Rudolph, *The American College and University—A History* (New York, NY: Vintage Books, 1962), p. 454.

7. Rudolph, pp. 454, 464-465.

8. Philip Reed Rulon, "Angelo Cyrus Scott: Leader in Higher Education, Oklahoma Territory," *Chronicles of Oklahoma*, vol. 47, no. 1 (Spring 1969), pp. 494-503.

9. A. C. Scott, *The Story of an Administration of the Oklahoma Agricultural and Mechanical College* ([Stillwater: Oklahoma Agricultural and Mechanical College, 1942]), p. 7.

10. Philip Reed Rulon, *Oklahoma State University—Since 1890* (Stillwater: Oklahoma State University Press, 1975), p. 503.

11. Scott, pp. 13-19; Rulon, *Oklahoma State University—Since 1890*, pp. 497-503.

12. Rulon, *Oklahoma State University—Since 1890*, pp. 494-503.

13. Undated story from Kansas University Graduate Magazine on A. C. Scott, Angelo C. Scott Collection, Special Collections, Edmon Low Library, Oklahoma State University, Stillwater, Oklahoma.

14. Hays Cross, "Veterans View Five Decades," *Oklahoma A. and M. College Magazine*, vol. 12, no. 6 (March 1941), p. 4; "Brewer Recalls Other Aggie Building Boom," *Oklahoma A. and M. College Magazine*, vol. 20, no. 5 (February 1949), p. 19; Fred Knoblock, "Memories of Williams Hall," *Oklahoma State Alumnus Magazine*, vol. 10, no. 7 (September-October 1969), pp. 12-13. Williams Hall was torn down in 1969 to make room for the Seretean Center for the Performing Arts.

15. Oklahoma A. and M. *College Paper*, October 1902, p. 94.

16. *College Paper*, 28 January 1903, p. 187.

17. *College Paper*, 15 October 1903, 1 February 1900, p. 109.

18. *College Paper*, November 1904, p. 41.

19. "Faculty Minutes," 20 November 1909, Special Collections, Edmon Low Library; R. Morton House, "The Class of 1903 at Oklahoma A. and M. College," *Chronicles of Oklahoma*, vol. 44, no. 4 (Winter 1966-67), p. 392; *College Paper*, 1 April 1900, p. 21, 1 November 1900, p. 2, November 1904, p. 41; Oklahoma A. and M. College *Orange and Black*, 6 April 1917, p. 2. The admonishment to students about staying off the grass in the 1917 *Orange and Black* read: "The spring weather is beginning to bring out the green grass, and soon the campus will be a beautiful scene, excepting the places where students have 'cut' campus so much that there is no chance for the grass to grow and blot out the foolishness of their work . . . for a path is a disgrace to the campus; beauty is destroyed." This "battle" over grass had been going on for years, and would still continue for more years.

20. Scott, pp. 18-19; "Angelo C. Scott, Fifth President," *Oklahoma A. and M. College Magazine*, vol. 20, no. 6 (March 1949), pp. 18-20.

21. *1916 Redskin*, p. 222, Oklahoma A. and M. College Yearbook.

22. Scott, pp. 18-19; "Angelo C. Scott, Fifth President," pp. 18-20.

23. *Orange and Black*, 1 January 1916, p. 2. A student newspaper editorial in this paper served to illustrate the peer pressure to be involved in student activities. Entitled "Every Student Out For Something," the editor appealed to everyone to see their involvement as a "duty" to the college and other students.

24. "Faculty Minutes," November 1909, pp. 83-87. A letter dated 8 January 1917, in the President's Papers in Special Collections, Edmon Low Library, further discusses "deserters," and student Fountain Johnson, whose name had been posted on the college bulletin board as a deserter. Johnson had left campus on December 12 without arranging a legal absence. The letter goes on to attempt to clear up the missing student's financial records. Berlin B. Chapman, "Through Golden Years," *Oklahoma A. and M. College Magazine*, vol. 25, no. 4 (December 1953), p. 11.

25. "Faculty Minutes," 5 March 1914.

26. "Faculty Minutes," November 1909, pp. 86-87.

27. "Faculty Minutes," 15 May 1912, unnumbered pages.

28. *Oklahoma A. and M. College Catalog, 1906-1907*, p. 76.

29. *Oklahoma A. and M. College Catalog, 1906-1907*, p. 76; *Orange and Black*, May 1908, pp. 12-13.

30. *Orange and Black*, 17 January 1916, p. 2.

31. *Orange and Black*, 17 January 1916, p. 2.

32. "Faculty Minutes," 25 October 1910, p. 124. The faculty guidelines for academic advisors also emphasized the importance of being a "counselor" and helper to the students. At least one, if not more, meetings each month was "authorized." A letter was sent by the college to parents informing them of their daughter's or son's advisor by specific name. On campus, advisors were to monitor such things as student illness or absences. Any special problems were to be reported to the president. The guidelines reflect an advising system which was parent-like, yet the tenor of the wording seems to indicate a personalizing, nurturing, and supportive environment was sought by the documents writers.

33. *Oklahoma A. and M. College Catalog, 1910-1911*, p. 16. This catalog was the college's twenty-fifth anniversary edition.

34. *Orange and Black*, 27 January 1917, p. 1.

35. *1917 Redskin*, p. 151.

36. Philip Reed Rulon, "The Campus Cadets: A History of Collegiate Military Training, 1891-1951," *Chronicles of Oklahoma*, vol. 52, no. 1 (Spring 1979), p. 73; *1917 Redskin*, p. 151.

37. *1917 Redskin*, p. 151.

38. Rulon, "The Campus Cadets," p. 73; *1915 Redskin*, pp. 140-143.

39. "Faculty Minutes," 16 February 1910, p. 57; *College Paper*, March 1906, pp. 79-80.

40. *Orange and Black*, 29 November 1915, p. 1; Oklahoma A. and M. College *New Education*, 1 June 1913, p. 1.

41. *1911 Redskin*, pp. 187-188.

42. R. J. Davis to President James W. Cantwell, 23 November 1916, President's Papers.

43. House, pp. 392-394.

44. Olin W. Jones, "A Little Rough, Yes . . . ," *Oklahoma A. and M. College Magazine*, vol. 1, no. 7 (March 1930), p. 12.

45. *College Paper*, 28 November 1902, pp. 125-127.

46. House, p. 397.

47. *College Paper*, 1 March 1901, p. 142, 28 February 1903, p. 16; *New Education*, 1 April 1910, pp. 2-3.

48. *Orange and Black*, 14 May 1917, pp. 1, 3.

49. *College Paper*, 28 February 1903, p. 16, February 1907, p. 43; *Orange and Black*, 14 May 1917, pp. 1, 3.

50. *Orange and Black*, 20 January 1917, p. 2.

51. *College Paper*, 1 October 1900, p. 62.

52. *College Paper*, 1 February 1901, pp. 123-124.

53. *Orange and Black*, 13 December 1915, p. 3, 16 September 1916, p. 4, 1 February 1917, p. 3; *1912 Redskin*, p. 252.

54. *1914 Redskin*, p. 134.

55. *1915 Redskin*, p. 63.

56. *Orange and Black*, 4 April 1917, p. 2.

57. *1915 Redskin*, p. 63. In the "Burning of the Troubles" the graduating seniors would have a large bonfire on campus. Personal items, such as freshman beanies, classnotes, and other unwanted college memorabilia, would be tossed upon the fire to signify the end of the students' difficult academic careers. Also, each senior class would symbolically plant ivy next to campus buildings—thus, the graduation week tradition of "Planting of the Ivy." The ivy would be a memento of the class' presence.

58. "Reminiscences of Clarence S. Bassler," p. 3, Berlin B. Chapman Collection.

59. *1915 Redskin*, p. 318.

60. "Reminiscences of Clarence S. Bassler, p. 1.

61. *College Paper*, February 1906, p. 58.

62. "College Paper Discloses Class History," *Oklahoma A. and M. College Magazine*, vol. 1, no. 6 (February 1930), p. 27.

63. Paul G. Crouse to Berlin B. Chapman, 15 October 1966, Berlin B. Chapman Collection.

64. *College Paper*, April-May 1903, p. 59.

65. *1917 Redskin*, p. 81.

66. *Orange and Black*, 16 September 1916, p. 1; *1915 Redskin*, p. 146; *1917 Redskin*, p. 274; Jack Ray, "Is A. and M. Tradition Bound?" *Oklahoma A. and M. College Magazine*, vol. 10, no. 8 (May 1939), p. 3.

67. *Orange and Black*, 16 September 1916, p. 1.

68. *Orange and Black*, 30 September 1916, p. 1; *1915 Redskin*, p. 148.

69. *Orange and Black*, 4 October 1915, p. 1.

70. *Orange and Black*, 16 September 1916, p. 1, 30 September 1916, p. 1; Lawrence Thompson, "When Aggieland Was Fairyland," *Oklahoma A. and M. College Magazine*, vol. 1, no. 4 (December 1929), pp. 8, 26.

71. Thompson, p. 26.

72. *New Education*, 15 May 1910, p. 2; *Orange and Black*, 6 May 1916, p. 1; *1915 Redskin*, pp. 136-139.

73. *1910 Redskin*, unnumbered page.

74. *Orange and Black*, 4 July 1916, p. 4.

75. *College Paper*, January 1905, p. 65.

76. Nell Dent Bentley, "Thoughts on Visiting the Campus," *Oklahoma A. and M. College Magazine*, vol. 17, no. 4 (January 1945), p. 3.

77. *College Paper*, March 1903, p. 55.

78. Record Book Committee, compiler, "Selections from the Record Book of the Oklahoma Agricultural and Mechanical College, 1891-1941. Compiled on the Occasion of the Fiftieth Anniversary of the Founding of the College," vol. 1, p. 59, Special Collections, Edmon Low Library.

79. Stillwater Ministerial Alliance to J. W. Cantwell, [1916], President's Papers.

80. Stillwater Ministerial Alliance to J. W. Cantwell, [1916], President's Papers; *Orange and Black*, 23 September 1916, p. 1.

81. *1916 Redskin,* p. 375.

82. "'09 Class Plans Spring Reunion," *Oklahoma A. and M. College Magazine*, vol. 20, no. 4 (January 1949), p. 6; *Orange and Black*, 11 March 1916, p. 4, 31 May 1917, p. 2; *College Paper*, February 1906, p. 63, 1 October 1901, p. 113; *1916 Redskin*, p. 375.

83. "Faculty Minutes," 21 September 1912, p. 236.

84. *Orange and Black*, 19 December 1916, p. 2.

85. *Orange and Black*, 13 September 1915, p. 1, 19 February 1916, p. 4; *1916 Redskin*, p. 402.

86. *1916 Redskin*, p. 218; Barney Neal, "Aggieland's Rifle Teams!" *Oklahoma A. and M. College Magazine*, vol. 20, no. 6 (March 1949), p. 2; *Orange and Black*, 13 December 1915, p. 2, 13 November 1916, p. 3, 10 February 1917, p. 1, 27 January 1917, p. 1.

87. An earlier attempt at establishing a student government to represent all of the Oklahoma A. and M. College students is described on page 52 of the 6 December 1901 edition of the *College Paper*. This particular student government was modeled after the Oklahoma Territorial Legislature. The organization had two legislative "houses" and met weekly; and the paper noted that it "does valuable work." Also, a complete copy of the original Student Association Constitution can be found reprinted in the *Orange and Black*, 13 September 1915 edition, starting on page 1.

88. *1916 Redskin*, p. 254.

89. Bonnie E. Emerson, "Democracy in Action on Campus," *Oklahoma A. and M. College Magazine*, vol. 9, no. 9 (April 1944), p. 3; *1916 Redskin*, p. 379.

90. *Orange and Black*, 20 September 1915, p. 1.

91. *Orange and Black*, 11 September 1915, p. 1; Emerson, p. 3, 8, 9, 14.

92. *1916 Redskin*, pp. 217-220.

93. W. L. Lahman, "Orange and Black Had Stormy Start," *Oklahoma A. and M. College Magazine*, vol. 19, no. 1 (October 1947), p. 11; *Orange and Black*, May 1909, unnumbered page; *1916 Redskin*, p. 219. A copy of the Student Senate bill which mandated that the editors of the *Orange and Black* and *Redskin* would be chosen by a vote of the student body appears in the 17 February 1917 edition of the *Orange and Black* on page 1. This senate initiative was controversial and hotly debated among the students.

94. *1916 Redskin*, p. 213.

95. Gordon Hart, "Fifty Years of Yearbook Memories," *Oklahoma State University Magazine*, vol. 2, no. 2 (May 1959), p. 9.

96. Hart, pp. 8-11.

97. *College Paper*, 1 May 1900, p. 20, May 1902, p. 27; F. L. Rector, "Battle for Better Health," *Oklahoma A. and M. College Magazine*, vol. 28, no. 9 (May 1957), pp. 28-29.

98. *Orange and Black*, 8 November 1915, p. 1.

99. *Orange and Black*, May 1909, unnumbered page, 8 November 1915, p. 1; *1912 Redskin*, p. 287.

100. *Orange and Black*, 16 September 1916, p. 1; *1913 Redskin*, p. 180.

101. *Orange and Black*, 24 February 1917, p. 1.

102. *Orange and Black*, 24 February 1917, p. 1, 4 September 1915, p. 1, 2 December 1916, p. 1, 4 October 1915, p. 1.

103. *New Education*, 1 October 1910, p. 5.

104. *Orange and Black*, 9 December 1916, p. 4, 24 February 1917, p. 4; *1916 Redskin*, p. 258.

105. *1914 Redskin*, p. 156; *1916 Redskin*, p. 258.

106. *1916 Redskin*, p. 399; *1915 Redskin*, pp. 41-42; *Oklahoma A. and M. College Catalog, 1915*, p. ii; *Orange and Black*, May 1909, unnumbered page, 10 January 1916, p. 1, 20 May 1916, p. 1, 16 October 1916, p. 1.

107. *Orange and Black*, 4 March 1916, p. 2; *1911 Redskin*, p. 41; Kay Nettleton, "OSU's Third Decade: Victorian Innocence Ends With a World War," *Oklahoma State University Outreach*, vol. 54, no. 12 (December 1982), p. 3. Lake Carl Blackwell is named for Carl P. Blackwell, former student and Agricultural Experiment Station director.

# 4 Services and Deans For the Students

Student excitement and enthusiasm permeated the campus. The Oklahoma Agricultural and Mechanical College was alive with the work that was such a necessary part of the annual Harvest Carnival. Laughter and camaraderie prevailed, as students rushed to put the finishing touches on their parade floats and costumes. Students dressed as clowns, Indian maidens, and German peasants were seen in the large number of frantic revelers. The first event of this gala day, the parade, was forming in front of the Women's Building. The echoes from the sounds of the building of booths and bleachers could be heard. It was a little before noon, October 16, 1914.[1]

The mood of merriment was instantly shattered by the first scream of ''The Dorm's on Fire!'' The second tragedy in less than three months, a second major fire in a campus building, was developing. In August, Morrill Hall, located just west of the Women's Building, was gutted to a shell by a fire that was allowed to burn because of a two-month drought and an exhausted Stillwater water supply. In the Morrill Hall fire, valiant efforts had been made to save the college's earliest records. Nonetheless, the president's and registrar's offices had been lost, along with students' transcripts and other irreplaceable records. This time personal belongings would be destroyed; cherished items would be lost. Oklahoma A. and M.'s first campus dormitory for women was on fire.[2]

The smoke curled upward from the windows and roof vents. Out of the confusion of the moment students began to mobilize and move into action. Some rushed into the building to gather what valuables they could find. Tears were evident among some of the forty college women who called the Women's Building home. From open windows, belongings were tossed to the ground. Down the front steps came a piano, chairs, and beds, along with dressers, still filled with personal possessions. The appearance of the pandemonium was "grotesque-almost amusing."[3]

Within fifteen minutes the fire had engulfed the tar paper roof. Fortunately, the loss of the roof represented most of the $15,000 damage to the structure. Firefighters, including the campus student volunteer firemen, were able to contain the fire largely to the upper floors. A second major fire tragedy was averted. In a few hours, the forty women who lived in the Women's Building had new homes with Stillwater citizens. The Oklahoma State Board of Agriculture quickly moved to repair the building—this time using fireproof materials—and also finish the fourth floor. With the completion of the fourth floor the on-campus housing capacity for women would double to eighty students. Meantime, the Harvest Carnival was delayed only briefly by the near-tragedy of the day. With renewed vigor, the students went on to make the 1914 carnival a time of unrestrained fun, a day that was successful in every way.[4]

"The dorm's on fire!" Shortly before the annual Harvest Carnival of 1914, flames raced through the upper floors of the Women's Building. Students, many dressed in costumes for the carnival, rushed to save possessions and to aid the firefighters. Only briefly diverted from their social plans, the students rebounded and later attended the carnival and watched Oklahoma A. and M. defeat Henry Kendall College of Tulsa in football by a score of 13 to 6.

The chronology of the Women's Building fire illustrated the student quality of irrepressible resiliency. In a matter of hours the merriment of the Harvest Carnival was turned to discouragement. Then, as rapidly, the students rallied from their gloom with a renewed zeal toward their festivities. This irrepressible nature of college students, including their boundless energy and initiative, continued to grow in proportion to the Oklahoma A. and M. College's enrollment. Clearly, by the time of events such as the fall carnival and Women's Building fire, the student's zeal for student organizations, with the commensurate requirements to supervise and monitor their collective behavior, had grown to a major problem. Simply stated, the college student's out-of-class initiatives were becoming too much of a burden for the faculty, a president, and a part-time registrar. Like other institutions of higher education throughout the United States, this phenomenon was not unique to just one campus. A new administrative system, frequently called student services or student affairs, was becoming mandatory.

Paralleling this dilemma, students were requiring easily accessible, reasonably priced campus facilities, starting with the basics of room and board, in order to be attracted to a college. With the rare exception of a few urban institutions of higher education, the students of the early twentieth century were frequently basing their decisions on where to go to college on their evaluation of a total campus environment, rather than simply the quality of the education they would receive. The prospective student often would look for other students who had similar interests. Financial assistance, including the prospects of finding a job, athletics, and social activities all either encouraged or discouraged students in their decisions about enrolling. These factors, as well as many others prevalent in contemporary times, were also important with prospective student decision-makers decades ago.

Oklahoma State University's student services developed from these administrative quandaries and issues which included the irrepressible student, the need for physical facilities to support academic pursuits and a collegiate environment, and an increasingly overburdened faculty. The humble beginnings of student services dates to 1910 when the Women's Building and Crutchfield Hall, a residence for men, were constructed and opened as student dormitories, the first on-campus student housing. Where once the faculty and president had handled all matters pertaining to student life, now live-in matrons and housemothers supervised the students living in the "dorms." In 1916 the board of agriculture promoted Mrs. F. C. Kent, matron of the Women's Building for the previous two years, to the title and position of dean of women. Dean Kent's responsibilities encompassed the general welfare of all college women, including the residents of the Women's Building, sorority houses, and off-campus rooming facilities. It was imperative that the rule forbidding college men and women from living in the same building be absolutely enforced.[5]

Other than a college registrar, first hired as a part-time employee in 1903, and Mrs. Margaret Evans, who in 1910 was appointed part-time women's matron and first holder of the title dean of women, Oklahoma A. and M. had moved slowly in allocating scarce resources to non-academic objectives. Kent's dean of women's position was significant as the first professional position dedicated exclusively to the out-of-class interests of students.[6] The men of the college would wait until 1928, the year of Henry G. Bennett's appointment to the college presidency, to have an official dean of men acting on their behalf. At that time C. H. McElroy would formally be assigned the title of dean of men. Although McElroy was given the title in 1928, "Dean Mac" had carried the responsibilities earlier. The 1928 Redskin, in a full page titled "The Dean of Men," stated: "There being no official rank of Dean of Men resting upon his shoulders, Dean McElroy is looked upon by the men of the college as their advisor. To him they go when in need of advice; and from him they always receive that advice, given in a straightforward and kindly manner, glittering with the 'gowd' which rests in the soul of Dean 'Mac'."[7]

During the eighteen years starting with the building of the first campus residence halls and stretching up to the formal appointment of McElroy to the position of dean of men, the students would observe tremendous growth in the breadth of services afforded them by Oklahoma A. and M. College. Although the depth and quality of these services would take more time to develop, by 1928 the college employed a Young Men's Christian Association (YMCA) director, several live-in employees working in campus housing, a manager for student publications, and the two deans of students. A professional food service manager headed the campus cafeteria. Placement and alumni activities were also underway. A physician and nurse were hired to treat real or imagined student illnesses. Student employment and other forms of financial aid, including scholarships and loans, became large enough to warrant specialized attention. A college bookstore, with a manager, was operational. Campus intramural and recreational activities also had specialists working with a variety of athletic activities. Although the students loudly vocalized their support for a student union—a campus center for student government and activities—this would be deferred well into the long tenure of President Bennett. Except for the union, by 1928 every element of today's student services had been started. Although each service was put in place for the most pragmatic of reasons, all were adding to the efficiency, if not the quality, of the rapidly growing collegiate environment.

Although impossible to know for sure, Dean of Women Kent's duties

94

were numerous enough to give her little time to reflect on the future importance of her pioneering activities. Kent's office was located in the Women's Building, the social center of campus. The six-year-old Women's Building was built from a grandiose plan described in a 1910 edition of the *New Education*: "Let us not have a building useful for only a single purpose; but let us offer the young women who clamor for admittance to our college, a place in which they can live and move and have their being—in other words—a true home."[8] The Women's Building was futuristic in design; the residence hall philosophy of "living-learning," a concept in vogue in the 1960s and 1970s in higher education, was used fifty years before its time. The Women's Building also housed the Department of Domestic Science, the forerunner of the College of Home Economics. Dean Kent's responsibilities, coupled with the location of the Department of Domestic Science, resulted in the Women's Building's becoming a busy campus faculty-student social center.

The Women's Building had a women's gymnasium and a swimming pool, a visitor's gallery for receptions, a large dining room with an orchestra platform, and a kitchen "with an up-to-date steel range, large steam-jacketed kettles, coffee percolators, and other furnishings for rapid and satisfactory service" on its first floor. The second floor was an academic area for the home economics department and included a domestic science kitchen, serving and fitting rooms, a lecture room, and food laboratories. In addition, a large reception room for social entertainment and smaller rooms for entertaining guests and relatives were a part of the second floor. The third floor, and after the renovation caused by the Harvest Carnival day fire, the fourth floor, housed women students. The rooms were suite-style, each student having a private room with common study space for several students. The Women's Building also had a hospital room where the college physician would attend to the medical problems of the residents.[9]

The Boy's Dormitory, to the north of the Women's Building, was constructed at the same time and was less elaborate. Later renamed Crutchfield Hall, for William Walter Crutchfield, a former YMCA director, the men's residence hall did not have a kitchen or dining hall. Meals were eaten in the Women's Building. Interestingly, while the Women's Building was under the supervision of a matron-dean of women, Crutchfield was run by a committee on welfare, composed of student residents, and directed by a student, who was a senior cadet officer. The rules and organization of the building originated from the students. A housing committee of faculty gave final approval to any student initiatives. Although smaller than the Women's Building, Crutchfield contained all of the conveniences available at the time. Steam-heat, electricity, and showers were particularly highlighted in resident recruitment materials.[10]

Crutchfield and the Women's Building were the first dormitories erected in the state of Oklahoma with the use of legislatively appropriated money. Crutchfield housed 120 college men, who in 1910 paid $3 a month for their furnished room. In 1920 room rates had risen to $5 per month in both buildings. By 1928 the rent was $18 to $27 a semester, depending upon whether a resident had a roommate or not. Food in the dining hall was provided at cost; in 1913 the price was $3.25 per month, always payable in advance. By 1925 a la carte service had been started. Roast beef and cured boiled ham was priced at ten cents per serving; pie was five cents; cake six cents; vegetable soup and mashed potatoes cost five cents; coffee was five cents a cup; and milk cost four cents. An average dinner meal was estimated to cost twenty-one cents, lunch eighteen cents, and breakfast sixteen cents. Students could eat well each day for a total of fifty-five cents.[11]

There never seemed to be enough campus housing. Congested conditions caused by a high demand for on-campus housing was reported in the *Orange and Black* in 1923. In that year the Women's Building had a designed capacity for 98 women, but had 113 female residents. The lounges, then called sitting rooms, were poorly furnished, but they were used as dormitory rooms. College officials attempted to cope with the housing shortage. In 1917 a house was leased at 111 Knoblock Street and opened as a dormitory annex for twelve women. Two years later, a campus livestock pavilion, which had also been an army barracks and basketball court, was converted to a dormitory barracks for Student Army Training Corp scholarship students. As was typical for on-campus construction then, students were employed to do the work.[12]

The campus housing squeeze was somewhat abated when the Oklahoma Legislature authorized the Oklahoma A. and M. College to sell $300,000 worth of bonds to construct two buildings, one for men and one for women, in the spring of 1924. The bonds would be repaid in twenty-five years by charging the student residents of the new halls $7 per month room rent. Both buildings were of similar architectural design, three stories high, constructed of reinforced concrete and brick, and fireproofed to the degree that the technology of the times would allow. Both were built at a cost of $150,000. The singular difference in the two buildings was that the women had facilities for washing and ironing clothes. For whatever reasons, the men were allowed to find a different means to attend to their dirty garments. Both dormitories opened for student use in January 1926. Hanner Hall was named in honor of Captain Carter C. Hanner, a former student, who was killed on October 9, 1918, in France during World War I combat. The women's hall was named for the first woman graduate of the college, Jessie Thatcher.[13]

From the student's point-of-view these two buildings were appeal-

In 1926, two new dormitories opened on the Oklahoma A. and M. campus. Of similar architectural design and accommodations, Hanner Hall (for men) and Thatcher Hall (for women) eased the housing crunch. As the dedication photo (*upper*) of Hanner Hall indicates, the building was constructed of brick and stone and was three stories in height. The rooms of the new dormitories, as shown in Thatcher Hall (*lower*), featured Murphy in-a-door beds.

Oklahoma State University

ing. A 1926 *O'Collegian* article, written at the time the facilities were first opened, described the accommodations: "Rooms of the two buildings are spacious. One sees upon entering, two beds, folded and standing in closets, and in the middle of the floor a study table with two chairs. A porcelain wash basin is in one corner of the room, and another closet is conveniently located to care for the student's clothes. In the women's dormitory are dressers, with four drawers, two long and two smaller ones; each dresser has a large mirror. In the men's dormitory are chiffoniers, with four long drawers and two shorter ones. A white medicine case is placed over the wash basin, with a mirror in the door." The beds were spring-assisted Murphy in-a-door beds, that could be raised out of the way during the day. The study tables, with book racks in either end, and the chiffoniers were all made in the college shops by student employees. Large reception-reading rooms and the matron's rooms were located near the three doors which made up the main entrance.[14]

As the on-campus residence hall system developed, the need to provide food services grew in proportion. Not to discount the merits of campus food, the age-old problem of student opinion about the cafeterias has been present since these earliest days. For example, a *Redskin* wit noted in 1916, "The steak of the dorm is like the football team: it will defy man or beast."[15] However, this kind of comment was a minority viewpoint. More often, the student newspaper, at least, was appreciative, and even glowing, in its reviews of the beginnings of Oklahoma State University's food services. In 1916 the Women's Building dining room was serving up to 185 people per meal at an average cost of fifteen cents per meal. Food services also was employing twelve students, a cook, a baker, and a stewardess. Even then, food was served on a cooperative plan; all food was bought in quantity at the lowest bid. The *Orange and Black* declared the 1916 operation as one in which "the students get the best in the way of food for the least money possible."[16]

From 1911 to 1927 Ben Banks directed the college food services. "Big Ben," a large man with a deep voice, wore a two-gallon hat. At one time, Banks kept a menagerie of eight possums, a badger, a raccoon, and a coyote near the cafeteria. To relieve student anxiety about his plans for the animals, Banks assured those who ate at the cafeteria that only the possums would be used for a special future meal. The other animals were to be tamed as pets. Banks regularly met with students about their food preferences, served special meals in conjunction with important campus events, worked hard at instituting a food conservation program during World War I, and regularly changed his kitchen equipment and serving systems to maintain efficiency in cost and service.[17]

Banks brought the food program to some maturity. In 1911 a large cafeteria crowd numbered sixty students. Sixteen years later the cafeteria had been moved from the Women's Building into a building formerly used by civil engineering, west of Morrill Hall where the College of Business Administration Building now stands. Under Banks, three out of every five students, consuming between 200 to 250 pies and over 1500 meals daily, were being served. During a Farm Congress, "Big Ben" served 2,300 people in a two-hour period. Thirty to forty students were now employed by the college cafeteria.[18] Banks sounded like a food service director of today when he once said: "It is the purpose of the cafeteria to feed students as nearly at cost as possible. This allows many men and women to remain in college who otherwise could not do so because of finances."[19]

Cafeteria-style on-campus student food consumption had apparently caused problems which seemingly could not be solved. Banks regularly asked students to remember the rules of cafeteria etiquette such as avoiding loitering after meals so others could sit to eat and cleaning the tables and returning their food trays to the proper place. A 1917 campus newspaper article complained of cafeteria lines, the poor variety of food choices, the size of the portions of food, and the high cost of some menu items. During this period a faculty member reported in a cafeteria survey, taken over a two-week period, that the average male cafeteria customer took six minutes to eat a meal while a woman took one and one-half minutes longer. The quickest meal eaten took four minutes to consume and consisted of a doughnut, one piece of pie, and a glass of water.[20] The researcher concluded: "At this rate of chewing and swallowing food in another generation the people of the world will be toothless."[21]

To allow for a closer tie to the home economics food laboratory program, the Oklahoma A. and M. College food services was reorganized in 1927. At that time Banks was replaced as the manager of food services by Ina Pemberton, a professional cafeteria manager, formerly employed at a YMCA cafeteria in St. Louis.

With the new residence halls and food services, the students began to refine their residence hall environments. On November 10, 1911, the cadets in Crutchfield Hall submitted rules for hall governance for approval by the faculty. Study hours were from 7:30 to 10:30 P.M. each evening except Saturday and Sunday. On study nights all students were to be in their rooms by 7:30 P.M. Playing musical instruments and loud talking were not permitted during study hours; in fact, visiting during study hours was by special permission of the floor manager. Hall lights would be turned out at 10:30 P.M. Rooms would be inspected at 9:00 A.M. daily. Obscene language and the use of tobacco were prohibited in the building. Any rule could be changed by a two-thirds vote of the cadets living in the residence hall. Similar rules, always incorporating study hours and a fixed time for lights to be turned out, were developed for off-campus students and the other residence halls.[22]

A popular student hangout in the early 1920s was Dad McGrew's. Offering candy, cigarettes, desserts, and "DATES," Dad's was located just outside the gate to campus. But perhaps the most popular item on the menu was hamburgers, which, according to the *1921 Redskin*, "rattle in your stomach like a mule in a tin barn."

Sometimes students are irreverent. Residence halls rules received the brunt of some of this irreverence, even from earliest times. Marybelle Wheeler suggested her own "Dorm Commandments" in 1917. Wheeler's rule two was: "Thou shalt not dance in the hall or loiter, or call to him who walketh by, for the matron may see thee, and great will be the punishment thereof, for thou shalt be doomed to give up thy dates forever unto the third and fourth weeks." Rule six read: "Thou shalt not sleep two to a bed." Rule eight reminded Wheeler's friends: "Thou shalt not laugh at thy neighbor's clothes, for to do so is to cause war between roommates." The ninth commandment suggested: "Thou shalt refrain from applause when serenaders make sweet music under thy window."[23]

The *1912 Redskin* carried irreverences even further than Wheeler's commandments. Indicating that the date for implementation should be the year 20001 B.C., this listing of "Dorm Rules and Irregulations" suggested that upon deciding to come to the Oklahoma A. and M. College, one should notify the dean. A suitable chaperon met new students at the train. To care properly for rooms, students had to nail the window screens so that notes could not be passed nor escapes made during a fire. At all times shades were drawn closed. Students were advised that "the Dean of Women will always be a person who has successfully withstood the wiles and temptations of mankind. She is your natural guardian and will advise as to the proper handling of your affections and the refrigeration thereof." Still another rule proclaimed, if a female student

Centennial Histories Series

appeared in public twice in succession with the same date she had to report to the dean and tell her if she was engaged or not. The student's mother would be notified of the answer by the dean. The *Redskin* reminded hall residents that the dean was hurt more than the student by administering punishment, but because of justice, the punishment must be administered.[24]

Despite the fun involved with the banter about rules, a residence hall environment evolved. Students who lived in the halls were called "dorm rats" by the student media. A regular system for hosting "open house" where men and women visited each other's halls developed.[25] Incidents of controlling residents' behavior for the good of the "community" occurred. For example, one student who regularly used vulgar language was put through a ritualized "baptismal ceremony" in a Crutchfield Hall shower one night. The "baptized" student became "quiet, gentle, modest and unassuming . . . May he go on in the straight and narrow path he has chosen and become a worthy denizen of the Boys Dorm."[26]

Hall governments, called house councils, were formed by 1916, and a government, with similar purposes to the Residence Halls Association of today, was formed by 1925. This interhall group was called the Campus Club, and each hall selected three representatives to form a steering or coordinating group. No executive officers or chairpersons were

SPECIAL COLLECTIONS, OSU LIBRARY

A group of students gather for a quiet evening in the living room at Gardiner Hall. The one young man reassures that the evening would be incomplete without the "lilting airs" of the Victrola.

elected in deference to increasing the democracy of the organization. In one of the Campus Club's first actions, Swim's Hall, a social gathering place for students near campus, was rented for one hour each day for the exclusive use of hall residents.[27] The hall matrons served as chaperons, and one of the matrons thought that the plan would "be good training for boys and girls who have not had the advantage of social life before they entered college, and it will afford good wholesome entertainment."[28]

Hall governments busied themselves by buying such things as Victrola music players. Students, particularly men, were ordering out for food, usually hamburgers from businesses near campus. Students were regularly reminded not to cook in their rooms. Prizes, often a cake made by the campus food services, were given in contests for the cleanest and best decorated rooms. Under emergency conditions, for example during a 1919 rainstorm, a hall matron came to assist the residents. In this case, Mrs. Thornton suggested: "Girls, if you think you're going to get drowned, put up your umbrellas and sleep peacefully on."[29] But perhaps best of all, the 1929 Catalog discontinued using the word dormitories as a label for on-campus housing. Now they were called the college residence halls. The shift was inconsequential to the students. However, without doubt, it was another mark in favor of the residence hall and food systems.[30]

Students living off-campus had rules like on-campus residents requiring study hours from 7:30 P.M. to 10:30 P.M. Lights were to be turned off, and no snacks or refreshments to reduce late night hunger pains could be ordered after 10:30 P.M. After social events off-campus, students were required to return directly home. Violations brought demerits to the students, and for the landlords the penalty was the removal of their property from the college's approved housing list. Students were also prohibited from leaving Stillwater unless prior approval was officially secured for a visit to their home.[31]

As progress was made in campus housing and nutrition for students, a concurrent improvement appeared in the handling of student health problems. In the first quarter of the twentieth century, the campus was forced to deal with at least five life-threatening epidemics. In 1914 and 1916, and again in 1918, the Spanish flu was rampant among the student body. In 1900 the college was totally closed for three weeks due to the fear of the spread of smallpox. When smallpox again returned in 1928, over a thousand students volunteered for vaccinations. Scarlet fever and typhoid were other illnesses that persisted and demanded the concern of college officials.[32]

There can be no doubt that the student body lived on the edge of death during the era. College and Stillwater officials were often forced to take extraordinary efforts to combat the spread of the life-threatening plagues. On many occasions these efforts became extreme. During the 1928 smallpox epidemic a quarantined area was established in the Biology Building to contain the spread of the disease. In 1916 the Spanish flu caused the Stillwater Board of Health to prohibit any public social events. The movie theatres were also temporarily closed. Local churches cancelled Sunday services. Students pitched in to nurse and get sick trays from the cafeteria for their ailing classmates. At other times, the old home of the college president and the south wing of Crutchfield Hall were pressed into service as temporary hospitals. One particular siege of Spanish influenza lasted forty days. Throughout the time a red flag was hung near the entrances of quarantined areas to warn people to stay away.[33]

Regardless of these superhuman preventative efforts, students and faculty did die from contagious diseases and other illnesses. The college, despite financial constraints, realized that a medical service, devoted strictly to students, was necessary. In fairness, during the founding years, the college did have an informal agreement with several Stillwater physicians to treat students, and the college health education faculty worked with the health problems of students. However, these systems proved inadequate. Volunteer nurses, the lack of regular examinations and medical records, and the use of temporary medical facilities for patient care, all added to disaster when coping with the too frequent epidemics.[34] As a result, the 1920 Catalog advertised to prospective students and their parents: "The health of all students is a matter of chief concern to the officers of the A. and M. College."[35]

In 1909 the first college physicians were employed. Duncan Hyder Selph, a graduate of the University of Tennessee, and Laurence Albert Cleverdon, an alumnus of the University of Kansas, allowed the Oklahoma A. and M. College to publicly announce: "The College employs responsible physicians who attend all students without charge in cases of illness or injury incurred in line of duty."[36] Cleverdon and Selph maintained a general medical practice in Stillwater and worked part-time with the students until 1915. At that time, Charles Dudley Simmons became the full-time college physician, followed by I. G. Soutar. After the campus was without a physician for over a year, L. A. Mitchell was hired.[37]

The first administrative rules relating to the college's medical services appeared in the faculty minutes of July 13, 1910. These rules established a time for "sick calls," and in an emergency, treatment could be secured through the college president or commandant of cadets. Services were free. No student would be treated by the college physician if the injury or illness occurred because of the student's own misconduct. Any student on sick report ten times in a month would be referred by the physician to the discipline committee. The student could then possibly be forced to withdraw from school for missed work. Fifteen years later, in 1925, the students were required to report all illnesses promptly to the college physician and pay a health fee of $2.50 and also a charge of $1.00 per day if hospitalized.[38]

The 1923 Redskin was dedicated in part to "Doc" Simmons. Because of his insight into the medical system of the time, the student-written dedication noted: "Doc has withstood the storms of faculty disapproval in order that the students may be given that 'fair chance' to which they are entitled. Day after day and week after week this man of one pill for every ill has stood untiringly issuing furloughs to those who need sleep and are unable to attend classes. Although our 'lines' have been rather weak, he has nevertheless 'doubted us not' and the furloughs have been forthcoming. Many problems of the student body have been solved by these magic words, 'sign here'."[39]

Still another step in the name of progress was made in 1925 when the residence hall sick rooms were abandoned and an infirmary building was established in a one-story, five-room frame house at 407 College Avenue. The living room and dining rooms were used as the reception and treatment areas. One bedroom, with one bed, was used for hospitalization needs; another bedroom was for a nurse's quarters. The infirmary had one bathroom. A married couple assured twenty-four hour coverage, while the nurse also served as housekeeper, cook, and office assistant.[40]

Medical business soon became a comfortable part of campus life. Irene Campbell was the first patient admitted to the new College Avenue infirmary on October 27, 1925. Mrs. Grace Vickers, the college nurse, ran the infirmary. Twelve students a day saw Dr. Mitchell, and in September he saw 316 student patients. In the next month his patient-load jumped to 450 ailing visitors. A student newspaper editorial proclaimed, "The infirmary is for your welfare. Don't be afraid to go there."[41] President Bradford Knapp, in a letter inquiring about the reasons for the on-campus success of treating students with influenza, acknowledged that the college physician was quick to respond to student ills. However, he also suggested, "You know when the doctor is free or when the horse is free, there is plenty of riders."[42] Without directly stating it, the president had suggested that perhaps not all of the reported influenza cases were real. Students liked the service and were using it to maximum capacity. The public media had overplayed the severity of the campus epidemic. The correspondence was precipitated by state and campus publicity giving credit to the college's doctor for not losing a single student to the flu in his over 400 treated cases. In 1925 this was considered an unparalleled success. Interestingly, Dr. Mitchell administered chlorine gas as a cold cure.[43]

President Knapp proposed a permanent on-campus college hospital building at a cost of $25,000 in 1925 as a part of his campus master plan. A 1929 legislative appropriation of $125,000 allowed for the construction of a modern three-story infirmary on-campus. This structure, which opened in 1930, still stands on the campus and is in service as the Public Information Building.

Throughout this period frequent campus speakers and student opinion augmented the concern for student health. Dr. John W. Duke, state commissioner of health, spoke to male students on sexual hygiene. Sponsored by the federal government, Dr. Caroline Crossdale came from Philadelphia and gave a series of five lectures to college women on their particularly unique health problems. Dr. William H. Baily theorized that insanity, sunstroke, and baldness all were connected to going bareheaded in the sun. At one point, the college students themselves suggested that their problems with indigestion and dyspepsia were caused by the crowded and stressful class schedule demanded of them by the faculty. And finally, when Eva Parker was suddenly taken ill while attending her classes on April 18, 1904, and died later in the day, the attending physician attributed her death to "a disease of the brain, probably caused by overstudying."[44] The health service was well established by the time of a change in college presidents in 1928.[45]

Both college administrators and students shared the reality and problems caused by the fact that almost everything cost more money. The necessities of residence halls, food services, and health care all brought with them new budget dilemmas. Adding to the financial woes were the students' own action to impose a tax on themselves of $1.50 each semester for a subscription to the *O'Collegian*, $3.00 for the college annual, and a $4.50 per semester student activities fee. The perpetually nagging shortfall of state-appropriated funds had also necessitated a long list of incidental charges. By 1927 a $1 per semester library fee, a diploma fee of $3, and $1 each semester registration fee were being charged. Piano students were charged $15 a semester. Chemistry and geology students had a $1 per semester credit hour charge, plus a $3 breakage fee. College costs were rising. In 1908 the total cost for nine months of college was estimated at between $136 and $172. By 1926 costs for a similar nine-month academic year at Oklahoma A. and M. College had risen to between $300 and $450. In sixteen years the students were paying approximately 55 to 62 percent more for their education. Once again, a problem arose; how could college students be assisted in paying for their education. The solution was a broad based program of student financial aid.[46]

Students at Oklahoma A. and M. College still came from families with meager incomes. Little had changed about this since the college's founding. In 1915, 63 percent of the enrolled students worked, and 13 percent received no financial help from home. In 1927 nearly one-half of the student body was still required to work part- or full-time to pay for their college expenses. In 1925 a survey was mailed to 389 students who did not return to college for their sophomore year. The results confirmed that finances were a primary problem for the non-returning students. Of the 170 students who returned their questionnaires, 69 percent replied that the lack of finances was the primary reason for not continuing their enrollment.

Student frustration about costs was also surfacing directly. One student newspaper editorial pointed out that the ''A. and M. is widely known as a campus of working students. This is a fine reputation. It would be even finer if the campus was known as a campus of students working at the job of being students.''[47] It was true that the college provided work. In 1913 the college budget allocated $4,000 for on-campus student employment, excluding dining hall work. By 1925 the figure had grown to $12,500. However, this was not enough. The $12,500 was paid out to 130 students. Another 490 student applicants for campus positions were forced to look elsewhere for employment.[48]

Through the Depression years of the 1930s the problem of assisting the students in meeting their financial obligations required some unusual turns. In the meantime, by 1928 a substantial student financial aid program had been established at the institution. Where work and family assistance were once the only sources for financial help, the students now could secure loans, scholarships, and, for the neediest students, even fee waivers. Paying jobs were given to the neediest and most capable students. The competition for the positions was intense. Throughout this era, work-for-pay would remain the primary source of income for students. Nonetheless, a faculty employment committee and the YMCA and YWCA matched students needing work with off-campus employers. Available positions were now posted in a central location, and students could make one application for whatever jobs were available. The result was a first—a coordinated, centralized student employment service. Students still worked in the dairy barns and as janitors on the campus. In-town positions included working at the cafes, shining shoes, and being a stenographer. Regardless, most positions were secured through a newly streamlined student employment system.[49]

Student loan programs soon came into the campus student financial aid picture. In 1917 the Lahoma Club, composed of faculty women and wives of faculty members, established the Lahoma Club Loan Fund for junior and senior women. The money for the program was raised through the work of club members. Letters were written and mailed to citizens across Oklahoma to solicit contributions; and fund raising projects, including a concert by Rollin Pease (a popular baritone singer), were held in the Stillwater area. In addition to the Lahoma Club's loan program, within seven years there were ten other separately funded loan

Ponca City oilman-philanthropist Lew H. Wentz (*center*) made receiving a college degree easier for thousands of students through a series of financial bequests beginning in 1926. The Wentz loan program remained the principal source of student loan money until the 1950s and 1960s. Visiting with Mr. Wentz are Irene Rick and Dean of Agriculture W. L. Blizzard.

programs for Oklahoma A. and M. students. The Daughters of the American Revolution, the College Alumni Corporation, and Omicron Nu (home economics honorary society) were among the sponsors. Small in monetary terms, each loan program also restricted the applicant group; and each set specific eligibility requirements.[50]

A major turning point for student loan programs occurred on the campus in late June 1926 when the sum of all campus loan funds in existence totaled less than $10,000. Lew H. Wentz, Ponca City oilman-philanthropist, instantly and dramatically enhanced the loan programs by establishing the Lew Wentz Student Loan Fund with his gift of $50,000 to the Oklahoma A. and M. College. With net personal assets of $25 to $30 million, Wentz was known nationwide for his benevolence. An associate of Wentz once said, "Money has become an agency for him to make others happy."[51] Wentz's gift was heralded on the campus. President Knapp stated: "The student loan funds at the A. and M. College are exceedingly meager and so administered that the institution has very little to do with the loans and therefore it feels an inability to help worthy young men and women who apply to the institution for help . . . the A. and M. College, (is) under a very deep debt of gratitude to Mr. Wentz for his broadmindedness and far-seeing attitude toward the future of the state and for this splendid provision for promoting higher education and training of young men and women who will be of value in the solution of many problems of Oklahoma."[52]

The Wentz money was entrusted to the Lew Wentz Foundation, a structure for the supervision of the Wentz funds that exists today. Borrowers had to be enrolled for at least one year, a sophomore in standing, and earning part or all of their college expenses. The Wentz Foundation trustees gave careful, individual attention to each loan application. A justification of need and the student's academic and personal qualities were a part of the loan approval process. There is no doubt that Wentz's contribution was needed. By February of 1928 the original $50,000 had been totally loaned by the Wentz trustees, and no further applications for Wentz loans could be taken until the repayment of the loans began. In 1928 Wentz gave an additional $25,000 to the Oklahoma A. and M. College. With interest, his contribution now totaled $77,000. In two years over 225 students had received loans. A study of Wentz borrowers also showed that their grades improved after they received a loan. The Wentz loan program would remain the primary source of student loan money until the 1950s and 1960s when the advent of large federal and state financial aid programs reduced the demand.[53]

Scholarships afford the capable and qualified student the opportunity to study without repayment of the funds that have been awarded. Tragedy caused the advent of one of the earliest Oklahoma A. and M. scholarship programs. In October 1919, the son of Mr. and Mrs. Jacob Katz, proprietors of Stillwater's Katz Department Store, died at the age of sixteen while attending a Missouri military academy. In September of the following year, the Jerome Katz Memorial Scholarships—five $100 awards for needy students—were established as an annual program. In the same year, the state legislature initiated an ambitious program of scholarships for the study of practical agriculture. M. J. Otey, an Oklahoma A. and M. alumnus and the college financial secretary, established still another scholarship program shortly thereafter. The Oklahoma Bankers Association and the Cottonseed Crushers' Association of Oklahoma further increased the number of available scholarships. Combined with a formal and informal system in which certain fees could be waived for the financially poorest students, scholarships, limited as they were when compared to the need, further impacted the retention of financially strapped students. With a little good fortune, students who would have otherwise dropped out only a few years before had an increased chance of continuing their education due to the growing financial assistance options.[54]

Although decentralized and administratively haphazard, the essential elements of a modern financial aid program for students were largely established in 1928. Work, loans, scholarships, and fee waivers comprised a large part of the financial aid administration. Like most student work, the business of financial aid administration is a tough business. Students apparently always asked hard questions despite the best intentions of college authorities. For example, at one point an editorial series in the *O'Collegian* took the college to task on campus working conditions. Problems included the prevailing 1926 wage of twenty-five cents per hour and the fact that students working in the college cafeteria worked six to eight hours per day for meals and a "hole" of a room located above the cafeteria. Still another editorial considered borrowing to pay educational expenses a bad habit, one which could weaken initiative.[55] Certainly for a freshman or sophomore, the student writer proposed "borrowing any considerable sum to attend college seems folly."[56] This editorial elicited little response.

The college placement bureau, the name for the coordinated student employment service, came under the direction of E. E. Brewer, purchasing agent at the institution, by 1928. Brewer, at that time, stated that although each year it was possible to obtain employment for a greater number of students, "it is doubtful, however that the demand will ever equal the supply of student labor."[57] As Brewer was working with the employment of enrolled students, the placement of students who had graduated was similarly surfacing as a desired service. A faculty committee, appointed by President J. H. Connell at the suggestion of the Oklahoma State Board of Agriculture, was to "constitute a Board of Recommendation for promoting the best financial aid and professional interests of the graduates of this college."[58]

Five years later the Graduate Student Club proposed a teachers' placement bureau to Dean H. P. Patterson of the School of Education and President Knapp. The student newspaper supported the idea in an editorial which stated, "We can think of no other move which will give A. and M. College more favorable notice."[59] In the summer of 1925 the Schools of Education and Home Economics had each established a student placement bureau, and fifty students had secured fall teaching positions with the aid of this new service. A commentator of the time stated: "The bureaus are not complicated affairs, nor does their operation entail any considerable expense, but their effectiveness is nonetheless apparent."[60] Oklahoma State University's placement services evolved and grew, but remained a decentralized service with each college placing its own graduates until July 1960.[61]

A frequent initiative, one which would be an on-again, off-again source of frustration for students over the next thirty-five years, was a campus building for social events and student activities. The year before the campus was plunged into World War I, Student Association presidential candidate Harry E. Johnson stood before the student body and suggested as a campaign platform thought that the Alumni Association and the Student Senate should join together to raise money for a student union building. At the time of Johnson's proposal, college unions were being developed across the United States. At least students saw the concept as an essential part of a complete college environment. Despite this, Johnson's idea remained dormant.

Again, in 1920 and still another time, in 1926, student union proposals made the front page of the student newspaper. In 1927 plans went so far as to begin to raise $200,000 for the building of a campanile and student union as a war memorial on the site of Old Central, a condemned building. Student editorials were unconditionally supportive. "Complete the stadium . . . Build the Student Union" was a regular newspaper masthead for weeks.[62] The effort, like those before it, was doomed to failure. The continuity of this particular drive to build a student union was torpedoed by other incidents of Oklahoma politics, which disrupted the usual campus calm. This time, as was too frequently the case, President Knapp, one of the prime movers of the union plan, resigned. With his departure the building of a student union would again be deferred, this time for nearly a quarter of a century, until 1950.[63]

Some student services cannot wait for buildings, money, or wide support. The bookstore was started in a 7 by 11 foot room in the Library Building in 1906. The library later used the first bookstore's space as a closet. Because some members of the Stillwater business community complained that the bookstore on the campus offered unfair competition, it was moved to a 12 by 12 foot building near the east campus entrance on Knoblock Street.

O. T. Peck, an Oklahoma A. and M. alumnus who became interested in the sale of books and stationery when he was the student manager of the library's "storage space" operation, was also the manager-proprietor of the second bookstore. Peck, along with his brothers, C. P. Peck and H. L. Peck, remained in student-oriented enterprises in Stillwater until 1929. The Pecks' business eventually grew to a building, called Peck's Lodge or "Aggieville, the campus city," which contained twelve different shops and sixteen efficiency apartments for students. The Pecks were also loyal supporters of the college and student activities. For example, in 1919 the Peck brothers gave $20 to the *Orange and Black* to allow a newspaper reporter to cover the state legislature while it was in session. Peck's Lodge and the Peck brothers were closely intertwined with early campus life. In many ways student social life centered in "Aggieville"—their building was a landmark, a place to chat, dance, and eat.[64]

As one might expect when the college grew, the bookstore business

A popular watering hole, student haunt, and campus landmark, Peck's Lodge indeed deserved the nickname, "Aggieville, the campus city." Not only did it contain twelve different shops, it had sixteen second-floor efficiency apartments for students.

became more complicated. For example, in 1917 Peck Brother's College Store—"booksellers for A. and M."—requested a conference with President Cantwell to resolve the differences and problems that they were having with the instructors at the college. The Pecks were receiving the professors' textbook orders too late to have an adequate number on hand for the students to buy. Teachers also changed their textbooks without notifying the store, and some teachers had recommended that the students purchase their class supplies, supposedly less expensively, from other suppliers.

Bookstore problems persisted, and by 1928 the college itself had initiated its own bookstore in competition with Pecks. In this year, J. L. Gillum, manager of the new campus bookstore, reported that $20,000 had been spent by students on course texts. Of the 7,000 volumes sold at the start of the fall semester of 1928, one-fourth were used, or secondhand, books. Twelve students were employed in the store. The greatest quantity of books bought and resold were textbooks used in freshman English and chemistry. Textbooks in engineering and bacteriology were the highest priced books then required, costing $11 each. The bookstore manager pointed out that more store space was needed to serve the students adequately. This concern seemed to be one of those unsolvable problems, since the college textbook and school supply business continually grew in proportion to student enrollment. Subsequent years would validate this point.[65]

During the 1920s an increasingly sophisticated atmosphere enveloped the Oklahoma A. and M. campus. Because of the experiences of World War I and the period after, the student body had matured markedly. President Woodrow Wilson went before the Congress of the United States on April 2, 1917, and declared: "It is a fearful thing to lead this great, peaceful people into war, into the most terrible and disastrous of all wars, civilization itself seeming to be in the balance."[66] Four days later, on April 6, 1917, the Congress voted to enter the nation as a combatant in World War I. Shortly thereafter, the vitality and atmosphere on the Oklahoma A. and M. campus changed. By May 1917 a newspaper describing the campus noted "news has been scarce due to the fact the old place resembles a graveyard, since the boys have all gone to be soldiers."[67]

One year after the United States declaration of war, the Oklahoma A. and M. College was described as a place where "the percentage of girls is greater, and the student body as a whole is composed of younger class people. The social side of student life is minimized and the conservative, practical and productive side is emphasized."[68]

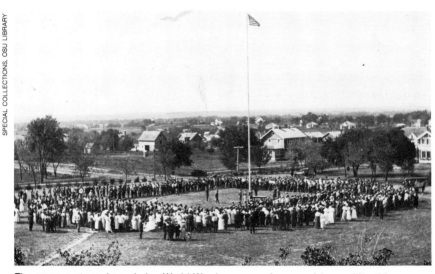

The campus atmosphere during World War I was one of purposefulness. After this campus swearing-in ceremony in September 1918, the Student Army Training Corps was established on campus. Studies were accelerated to provide officers for leadership roles in the military.

In a word, the student's attitude during the war years was purposeful. The YMCA and YWCA had raised $5,000 for the country's war relief fund. Students signed up to pledge themselves to the conservation of food. Faculty and students participated in buying Liberty Bonds. The "Student Friendship Fund," a relief fund for prisoners of war in Europe, was started by the women students. In reference to this program, a young woman said: "We are going to do any and every kind of work that is honorable. We can't fight for our country, but we can give of our time to help those who do fight."[69] To fulfill their pledges, students picked beans and donated their wages. Seeds and shells were saved; it took 600 peach seeds to make one gas mask.

Women students taught food economy, pledged to provide 500 Navy comfort sets (sleeveless jackets, mittens and scarfs), and entered Red Cross work. The faculty, being concerned about enrollment, wrote prospective students that the authorities would defer drafting young men until their studies were completed because of the value of the increased training of college graduates. The Adopt-A-Soldier program was organized by the *Orange and Black*. Students would select the name of an Oklahoma A. and M. serviceman and write him letters, or perhaps send an occasional gift. The *1918 Redskin* was dedicated to the students in the armed forces.[70]

Campus events, such as the annual May Festival, were cancelled, but the annual military ball was held. "Due to the uncertainty of the stay of the cadets in College . . . it will be a patriotic event and will serve as a sort of farewell to the boys expecting to take in the training camp at San Antonio."[71] On campus some debated whether athletics and commencement exercises should continue.[72] The 1917 spring campus election was uncommonly quiet. The newspaper reported: "No cigars were passed out, nor any political speeches made. The war question seemed to be absorbing the minds of students, for not over one-third of the legal voters cast their ballots."[73] In January 1918 the Student Senate was unable to meet because the call to arms had depleted the senate's elected members to the extent that a required quorum was impossible. Controversy from the outside came when the Oklahoma A. and M. president was compelled to respond to charges that the college band had been playing a German marching song and that a textbook used on campus praised the German Kaiser.[74]

Undoubtedly one of the more interesting aspects of the days of World War I on the campus was the OAMC Service Flag. The Girl's Student Association had been instrumental in making a flag of honor to acknowledge those students who served their country. The flag was a source of pride and taken to places and events around the state to remind audiences of the college's contribution to the war effort. The Service Flag was huge, 13½ by 28 feet in dimension. A four-inch white star and

The OAMC Service Flag was one of the most well-known campus projects of World War I. A flag of honor, its stars represented each student who served in the war. Although the original flag disappeared, the 1927 class memorial was a replacement flag. Raymond Hurst was the first Oklahoma A. and M. student to die in battle.

an individual name, representing one soldier, was painstakingly embroidered on the blue flag. If a student were killed, a smaller gold star was placed in the white star. The letters OAMC were spelled out by 693 stars.[75]

A campus mystery, which would never be solved, occurred in the fall of 1923. The Service Flag was reported missing. The disappearance of the flag, still a source of pride after four years, resulted in a massive search of the campus, as well as wide speculation. The consternation caused by the lost Service Flag was at least partially alleviated when the class of 1927 replaced the flag as a senior memorial project. The flag was duplicated at a cost of $500, was 28 feet by 20 feet in size, and took seven weeks of embroidery work to complete. This Service Flag was used only on state occasions and, when not in use, locked in a storage vault for protection.[76]

While patriotism in Oklahoma ran rampant, the realities of war would eventually be brought home to the campus. On February 16, 1918, Raymond Hurst became the first reported student to lose his life in World War I combat. Hurst was buried in Scotland alongside eleven other Oklahomans who had died when their American ship was torpedoed by the German navy.[77] This sober campus mood persisted in Stillwater until the first announcement of an armistice in Europe came. Pandemonium broke out. Although three days premature, on November 8, 1918, whistles blew, noise could be heard throughout town, and the "A&M campus went wild."[78]

As people calmed and grew more reflective, the college's war contribution was tallied. In addition to Hurst, thirty other students and former students had paid the ultimate price of war. Fifteen hundred sons and former sons, plus faculty, had served their country. Largely due to the required campus military program, over 700 men, or nearly half who served, had been officers in the military. Thirty-one had been decorated for heroism. The 1919 college annual was titled the *Victory Redskin*. In honor of the war's end and in anticipation of the homecoming of Oklahoma A. and M.'s students and faculty, a live campus Christmas tree was erected and decorated in December, thereby starting a long-standing Christmas tradition on the campus.[79]

From the purposeful campus atmosphere of World War I, the return to a more normal pattern of activity was quickly achieved. Campus pep organizations, such as the Peppers (a women's pep club), the Hellhounds, and the Ag-he Ruf-nex, were active. Other pep groups, like the Aggievators, were disbanded by the Student Senate because some of the members had been intoxicated at a football game in Enid. Charles Lindbergh flew his famous airplane over Stillwater in 1927. Carl Sandburg, former U.S. President William Howard Taft, and Lowell Thomas were among prominent speakers appearing on campus. A record student crowd watched the international debate between the Oklahoma A. and M. debaters and England's Cambridge University. Cecil B. DeMille, famous motion picture maker, and actor Aldolphe Menjou volunteered to judge who would be selected as *Redskin* beauties. Will Rogers, Oklahoma's famous son, also had the opportunity to judge this beauty contest. However, feeling the job to be out of his range, he declined. Student Beulah Snider completed a rigorous ordeal established by the Women's Athletic Association to earn the first "O" sweater ever given to a woman at the college.[80]

In 1921 an International Relations Club was established with the purpose of increasing world understanding among faculty and students. The club was primarily a scholastic endeavor, but social activities were often held. Students were not only maturing in their outlook, but they were also becoming less parochial. After one year of operating as the International Relations Club, the organization nationalized as the Cosmopolitan Club. The Association of Cosmopolitan Clubs had been founded at the University of Wisconsin in 1903. This organization purported to bring "about a better understanding between the students of the United States and foreign countries. This understanding [was] to be political, social, economic, and commercial."[81] Club membership requirements were rigorous. Prospective members had to fulfill specific pledgeship requirements, write a 2,000 word theme on a subject of an international nature, and have an 85 percent average in scholastic standing, among other criteria for acceptance. The Cosmopolitan Club had student members from Argentina, Guam, the Philippines, Canada, and Egypt by 1926.[82]

In 1928 the campus newspaper, since December 1, 1924, called the *O'Collegian*, had also become worldly, but in a different way than the Cosmopolitan Club. By a three to one majority, the student body had voted to support Student Senate Bill 1094, which required student subscriptions to the newspaper at enrollment time. With the newspaper's financial base nearly assured, it was given membership in the Associated Press. The *O'Collegian* was only the fifth college newspaper to gain membership in that association. Shortly after, Raymond Bivert, a junior from Luther, was hired as the paper's business manager. Bivert, indicating an interest in a one-year appointment, stayed with the paper until 1942, first as business manager, then later as general manager of student publications. Bivert is given credit for the continuity that eventually stabilized the paper and placed it in a sound financial position.[83]

At times, the *O'Collegian's* editorial policy was as troublesome to campus administrators as its financial ups and downs. To illustrate, after President Knapp worked during the fall semester of 1925 to influence the *O'Collegian* editor, Clarence Paden, to become more conservative in his editorial policies, a major confrontation developed in January 1926. Knapp had been receiving complaints from off-campus people who were concerned about the tone and policies of the newspaper. Knapp, a deeply religious man, believed the paper to be under the control of the publications committee, not the students. Paden's decision to continue on his course of editorial independence and Knapp's religious principles collided shortly after the second semester began. The specific issue that brought matters to a head was an editorial entitled "Youth's Revolt Against Moral Code." In this column Paden summarized a speech on social hygiene made at a national student leader meeting.[84]

The controversial piece suggested that modern transportation and communication technologies had freed students like no prior generation of young people. No longer did college age people have to apologize for such behavior as sexual relationships before marriage. This editorial constituted the last straw for Knapp. Although the students proclaimed his action censorship, the president prevailed. Paden resigned as the editor due to an "editorial policy clash" and transferred to the University of Missouri. The incident was smoothed over in time, students again returned to support Knapp's policy, but the stresses and strains caused by the philosophical issues of who makes student newspaper policy, editorial and otherwise, continued.[85]

Campus politics were intensely contested during the 1920s; the rise of the clandestine Theta Nu Epsilon (TNE), a secret fraternity, helped to turn many political races into bitter battles. The TNEs appeared at the Oklahoma A. and M. College in 1920, but were originally founded at Wesleyan University in 1870. The Stillwater chapter of this secret fraternity, for it forbade members from acknowledging their membership in it, quickly gained a reputation for ribald behavior and sub rosa control of campus politics. Twice during the 1920s and 1930s TNE was banned by college presidents. Nonetheless, TNE influence persisted on campus through their secret political activities, at various times infiltrating the Interfraternity Council, Panhellenic, Board of Publications, and the Student Senate. TNE membership was comprised of representatives of all campus social fraternities with the singular exception of Theta Beta Pi. The Betas consistently fought TNE influence. This adversarial relationship was explosive, leading to political unrest among the students and frequent local and state newspaper headlines.[86]

Ballot box stuffing, ''Anti T.N.E. Tickets'', and charges and countercharges were common characteristics of campus elections. In 1928, election wrongdoings were extreme enough that President Knapp was moved to write a front page editorial in the *Daily O'Collegian*. Knapp had proof that in the School of Agriculture election 297 votes had been cast—36 votes more than there were eligible voters. Knapp ended his essay with ''will you be patient and calm, and wait while we try to work this thing out so that right may prevail?''[87] The president's plea for calm was just another barometer of the intensity of students' political feelings at the time.[88]

SPECIAL COLLECTIONS, OSU LIBRARY

Campus politics were intensely contested in the 1920s. Ballot box stuffing and political haggling were common. The 1926-1927 Student Senate worked to combat the influence of the controversial Theta Nu Epsilon (TNE), a clandestine organization which contributed to the political unrest.

TNE exerted varying degrees of influence over campus politics, including the most prestigious and politically powerful student organizations, through the 1930s. In 1930, organized opposition to TNE appeared when the Betas allied themselves with campus independents, or non-fraternity men and women. Thereafter political power swung back and forth. TNE activity was rumored to exist on campus even to 1969. In retrospect, any damage or good caused by TNE is speculative. However, without question the TNE added color and interest to student life.[89]

In the 1970s Paul Miller, a student leader and TNE member, and still later a nationally-noted journalist and OSU benefactor, reminisced about the 1920s TNE era on campus. His insightful comments referred to Clarence H. Breedlove and Walker Stone, other TNEs. Miller wrote: "TNE is Theta Nu Epsilon, outlawed political-drinking fraternity to which all mentioned above belonged, and through which we ran the school. It included members of all fraternities except Beta Theta Pi—we finally took in one who seemed to be a decent guy however misled—and several nonfraternity men. Main elements were Kappa Sigma (Stone and myself), Phi Gamma Delta (Breedlove and others), and Sigma Nu. Half a dozen other fraternities were in. Meetings were sometimes in Otoe Pastures in a nearby valley with jugs of corn whiskey and of home-made wine to lubricate oratory."[90] Interestingly, Miller's anecdotal comments were written upon the occasion of his and Walker Stone's returning to the Oklahoma State University campus both to receive the Henry G. Bennett Award, the university's most prestigious recognition given for service to the institution and nation.

The *Daily O'Collegian's* editorial policies and Theta Nu Epsilon represent student struggles for identity and influence on the campus. Beyond specific issues, by the 1920s student life can be characterized as a time in which students pushed for campus independence. Oklahoma's land-grant college still cast a heavy cloud—the *in loco parentis* philosophy—over student social behavior. Students were required to have chaperons for all social events, including the commonly held class picnics at Yost Lake or trips to the river bluffs at Ripley. The first offense for alcohol abuse resulted in a student being warned and placed on probation. A second indiscretion with alcohol consumption led to immediate suspension.

Students discounted the importance of the college's demerit system. Rule number eleven which prohibited the social use of automobiles symbolized the students' lack of concern about the college's behavioral prohibitions.[91] To present a context, President Knapp justified the car ban rule in 1925. He said "prevention of immorality so prevalent over the entire country, due largely to the indiscriminate use of automobiles by the young," was one reason for the car ban. Secondly, "it is a noteworthy and important fact that students in institutions everywhere in the country who have their own automobiles are generally failures in their college work. The use of automobiles at the college invite failure and is a waste of the students time as well as a financial obligation to the parents."[92] Knapp's seemingly sound reasoning was widely ignored. From April 1924 to April 1925 eight students were suspended or expelled for the social use of an automobile. Another twenty-five men and women were placed on social probation for "joy" riding in unauthorized cars. The struggle to control the national car craze was made more difficult by Stillwater's entrepreneurs who were advertising cars for hire.[93] Ray M. Hull, one of the car leasers, advertised: "Driverless Livery, we will hire you a car by the hour or by the mile. Open and closed cars. Charges reasonable."[94]

Although the automobile was an important symbol of student behavior in the 1920s, efforts to become a "metropolitan" college could also be found elsewhere in campus life. By 1924, the "Howdy Spirit" had been born. Students were promoting the campus as cordial and hospitable, a place proud of traditions. Charlie Strack ate twenty bowls of oysters in record time. Knickers and the use of make-up by the coeds were fads of the day. The campus post office was handling an average of 125 bags of dirty laundry a day—all sent home to be washed and returned. The college women were surveyed on the question of whether they should continue their careers after marriage. Charles Darwin's theory of evolution had been hotly debated by the state legislature; Oklahoma A. and M. students seemed to take Darwin's ideas in stride. Further, the student newspaper began using the name Oklahoma State College to portray better what the institution really was.

Also a new college radio station was established. In 1928, Dr. J. C. Perrine, representing the American Telephone and Telegraph Company, came to the Oklahoma A. and M. campus to deliver a talk on the experimental device called the television. Soft drinks were working a financial hardship on students. On Wednesday nights Stillwater's ministers were teaching an elective class for college credit on religion. The traditional class fights had become extinct. A professionally done "How to Study" handbook was advertised for sale in the O'Collegian. The lack of paper towels in the campus lavatories received editorial note in the student newspaper. When the School of Home Economics started a course in social etiquette, the student newspaper predicted that it would become the most popular course in the college.[95]

The campus humor magazine enjoyed nationwide appeal during the Roaring Twenties. The Oklahoma A. and M. College joined in on this vehicle of expression, too. The Earthquake, an underground humor magazine, came and went in 1920 as a first effort. The A. and Emmer followed and was first published in 1922. This magazine's content, all local news, was written by students in the English and news-writing classes.[96] In college humor magazines little about college life remained sacred. In one edition of the *A. and Emmer*, "The Student's Twenty-Third Psalm" appeared:

"The college professor is my shepherd
and I am in dire want.
He preventeth me from lying down in
the bed which I renteth.
He leadeth me to distraction with his
exam questions.
He shaketh my resolution to get a
college degree.
He leadeth me to make a fool of myself,
before my enemies.
Yea, tho I burneth my light until the
landlady howleth.
I fear much evil, for he is against me."[97]

A permanent and successful humor magazine was finally established in 1924 with the advent of the *Aggievator*. Produced by the College Press Club, the magazine's first editor was Elmo Flynt. The *Aggievator* would appear "at irregular intervals, and under varying conditions."[98]

The *Aggievator* received national recognition in 1926 from *College Humor*, a nationally circulated publication and was invited into several associations relating to campus humor magazines shortly thereafter.[99] In the "Interscholastic Issue," the publication described itself as "absolutely not a serious publication although we do spend much time, paper and thought in uplift movements and reforms in aggieland."[100] In fact, the publication appeared on a quarterly basis, was advertised by local businesses, and was professional in appearance.

The *Aggievator* eventually became financially solvent and used materials from college humor magazines published throughout the country. The scope of the magazine's jokes varied widely. Regular columns, such as Pasture Piffles, appeared. Concerning the Student Senate the *Aggievator* suggested: "The best in amusements furnished the student body, regardless of expense."[101] Frequently on the fringe of appropriateness, another joke stated: "The owners of this dance hall reserve the right to refuse admission to any body they think proper."[102] In the "Prexy's Contribution," meaning President Knapp, the *Aggievator* printed: "The no car ruling will put all the students on an equal footing."[103] Concerning sororities the magazine recommended the following supplies: "One housemother—blind, deaf and dumb variety preferred; must be partially disabled. Several porches, numerous swings, cushions, et al. Two telephones, with a permanent busy signal attachment, so that the sisters will appear popular. One sister employed in

"Impressions of Oklahoma A. and M. College Campus By One Who Has Never Seen It"

the office of the dean of women. One accessible rear window or coal chute.''[104] The *Aggievator* used cartoons and caricatures liberally. The magazine was popular among students and remained so through the 1950s.

From the Stillwater boarding houses grew the first Oklahoma State University Greek social organizations. When the student body was small, every student knew every other student. They went to class together and worked together. When students also started to eat and live together in boarding houses, a logical outcome was social groups, which though informal, eventually acquired an identity through a name. ''Rites of passage'' and more organization, including soliciting and ''pledging'' new members, followed.

Delta Sigma, the first Greek social fraternity, was founded in 1908. Established by dancers and singers, this group rented a home as a chapter house at 124 Elm Street. In 1910 the Sigma Beta Chi chapter was founded. Four years later Phi Kappa Delta was founded by the political leaders of the class of 1917. They rented a house on Knoblock Street. In 1915 Gamma Zeta was started by men who disapproved of how the three other men's organizations were run. Dancing, playing cards, and smoking in their house at 318 West Street were forbidden. Composed largely of agricultural majors, the Gammas had twenty members in 1917, ran a boarding house cooperative, employed a matron for the supervision of members, and had a full-time cook.[105]

The first of the Oklahoma State University's sororities was Beta Phi, founded in 1912. In 1917 the group consisted of eight members and four pledges. The *Redskin* reported that the Betas were known for their beauty and good dancing. The Alpha Theta sorority was organized out of a Friday afternoon tea group in 1913. The Gamma Phis were organized one afternoon at a motion picture show by Vera Morgan, Ruth Evans, and Gladys Frieday. In response to the directions taken by earlier sororities, Delta Delta was started in the summer of 1916. Like Gamma Zeta fraternity, the Deltas were against smoking, drinking, dancing, and gambling.[106]

Although the Oklahoma State Board of Agriculture had banned such social organizations from 1908 to 1916, Greek societies had continued as secret underground clubs. When the United States entered World War I, the Oklahoma A. and M. College had four fraternities and four sororities coordinated by the Interfraternity Council and Panhellenic Council. None of these Greek groups had affiliated with a national fraternity or sorority by 1917.[107]

One of the more enduring and important student movements of the post-World War I campus era was the development of nationally-affiliated Greek social organizations. By order of the War Department, fraternity life had been suspended during the war years. The War Department believed that fraternity activities and military discipline were, by their very nature, incompatible. Any college with a Student Army Training Corp was required to defer further Greek life until the end of this "latest emergency."[108]

After the end of World War I, interest in Greek life grew rapidly. In 1919-1920, eleven national fraternities were installed on campus. Of these, eight were honorary and three were social organizations. Lambda Chi Alpha was the first to nationalize on September 16, 1917. In 1923 Delta Sigma, the first local Greek organization and the first to purchase a chapter house, nationalized as a chapter of Beta Theta Pi.[109]

Delta Delta became the first local sorority to affiliate nationally; its charter was granted on June 14, 1919, and the Nu chapter of Kappa Delta was installed on August 9, 1919. This oldest of local sororities was ahead of Pi Beta Phi's national chapter installation by only three days. Kappa Alpha Theta became the third national sorority on the campus September 6, 1919. Thus, in just over a month three sororities had achieved national affiliation. By 1927 the Oklahoma A. and M. College's Greek system would grow to nineteen nationally-affiliated chapters, including twelve fraternities and seven sororities. In addition there were three local Greek organizations, one of which was a sorority.[110]

Greek life had expanded to become a major subsystem of student life by 1928. In 1920 fraternity intramural competition was added to class and course leagues. Sigma Tau, with five wins and no losses, was champion of intramural basketball in the first Greek league. Those who lived in Greek houses were required to live by the same rules as other living groups in 1921. Two years later every house was mandated to hire a live-in housemother. The Interfraternity Council and Panhellenic grew in influence and prestige. Like all systems with assets and liabilities,

By the time Henry G. Bennett became president in 1928, the Greek system at Oklahoma A. and M. College was well established. Twelve fraternities and seven sororities were nationally-affiliated chapters. The Interfraternity Council and Panhellenic Council were important campus leadership organizations. Many of the Greek organizations had also built chapter houses. In 1927, Chi Omega occupied the house on the left while Kappa Alpha Theta resided in the house on the right.

trouble came in 1927. Nine of the nineteen Greek social groups failed to make grades equal to the all-college grade average and were prohibited from pledging new members. The Pi Phis had also been placed on social probation by the Panhellenic Council for violating rushing rules.[111] In this incident the fraternities threatened to hold a date boycott of all sororities until the Pi Phis were freed from being "chained to their new $20,000 chapter house."[112]

Hazing pledges to an extreme also became a part of the growing Greek environment. An *Orange and Black* article of 1923 explained: "'Hell Week' is just what the name implies for most. It comprises seven days of the most gruesome tasks which can be given to an individual. It means temporary loss of self-esteem, it means a loss of ego (which is so often present in abnormal quantities).

"Age-old stories of crimes committed, of brave acts, of Indian-like disdain of pain, all-night orgies; all these lend a fantastic charm to traditional ceremonies. Despite much criticism of the practices of old, nothing diminished this charm. What pledge would care to miss the ordeal?" This particular account of student hazing continued: "Women frats have their Hell Week too, they do not use all these methods to test their neophytes. But they do have lots of fun at the expense of the pledges."[113] Clearly sorority hazing was not as severe as in fraternities. Fraternity methods included visiting graveyards at night to get the next day's program from a particular tombstone, standing with cow, pail, and stool on a downtown street to learn the ways of farmers, and sweeping the streets of the city. Sometimes pledges counted the bricks in several blocks of these same Stillwater streets. Cats, live and decapitated, along with other kinds of animals, including rats, sparrows, and pigeons, were ordered returned by pledges to their houses. Failure in any task could lead to the application of a stick of oak. Hazing was not unique to the Oklahoma A. and M. Greek system, nor would the practice disappear easily, despite pressures to change.[114]

The flapper years were colorful, testing, and important. The Oklahoma A. and M. College had grown to some maturity, and students could boast of a student lifestyle similar to colleges across the nation. In 1928 the nation was one year from the crash of the stock market of October 29, 1929, and the start of world-wide depression. Accreditation problems were resolved, and institutions like Chicago University and Columbia accepted Oklahoma A. and M. College's degrees at face value. Over 1,200 freshmen and a total of 3,329 students would be studying on campus in the academic year 1928-29. Clarence H. McElroy would officially be made the dean of men and serve for nearly two decades in that position. Upon being named, "Dean Mac" said that his duties as dean of men would be infinite. Julia E. Stout also became dean of women in this year of administrative transition. Stout would serve as dean for twenty-two years, until 1950.[115]

After serving five years as president, Dr. Knapp left the campus on June 30, 1928, to assume the presidency at Auburn University in Alabama. Prior to coming to Stillwater, Knapp had been president of Iowa State University. After leaving Auburn, Knapp became the president of Texas Technological College in Lubbock. A man with exceptional leadership abilities, Knapp's departure, amid unfair charges against him, caused a statewide protest, as well as a groundswell of support on his behalf.[116]

Knapp once expressed that colleges were more than buildings and were really a composite soul of the people—students, faculty, and other employees. In a sense, Knapp left a part of his soul in Stillwater. Whitehurst Hall and a student newspaper, that was now being published daily, were a part of his legacy to the college. Further, students liked him immensely. They suggested that Knapp would be difficult if not impossible to replace. On June 1, 1928, the Oklahoma State Board of Agriculture met to appoint a successor to Knapp. No one could have known it at the time, but the board's appointment of Henry G. Bennett, the president of Southeastern State College in Durant, would bring to Stillwater an exceptional successor. Bennett began his presidency in late June 1928, at the handsome salary of $10,000 per year.[117]

It was prophetic, if not ironic, that a year before Dr. Bennett arrived to take up the toils presented by the office of president, a student editor of the *O'Collegian* printed a narrative on a utopian Stillwater college of the future. The writer described the dean of men and dean of women as doing full-time work in the service of students at this future school. Both deans, in turn, would be people well liked and long remembered by the students. How well the *O'Collegian* staffer could have been describing Stout and McElroy. Yet it was at least a year before each would take up their dean's responsibilities on the campus.

Even more interesting, the utopian college would be named Oklahoma State University. It would be a true university with the academic divisions called colleges. There would be new dormitories to the west side of the current campus, where Scott-Parker-Wentz, Kerr-Drummond, and Willham Residence Hall complexes now stand. In 1927 the writer described a giant football stadium on the campus, but it would not be the paramount structure. A beautiful new library, with a centered sparkling fountain, would be pleasing to the beholder. A garden area, perhaps around Theta Pond, would be in front of Whitehurst Hall. As well, there would be a sunken garden area around a community structure known as the Student Union Building. Offices for student government, a dance hall, a small auditorium, cafeterias, and lounging and reading rooms would be located in the Student Union.

In the utopian Oklahoma State University, students would regularly

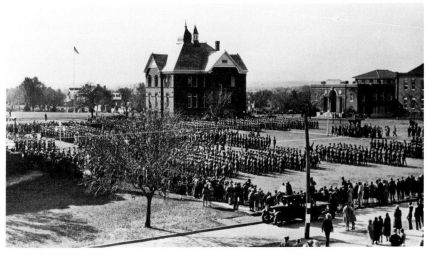

During the 1920s, Armistice Day (since 1954, known as Veteran's Day) annually combined with the military emphasis of the college in a huge ceremony and remembrance. This 1929 scene marks the eleventh anniversary of the November 11, 1918, armistice which ended World War I.

be asked by the college's administration to serve on the most important university committees. All outside political interference in the affairs of running the institution would be history. Importantly, there would no longer be class distinctions made among the students, except for the first few weeks when the freshmen would have a rigorous course of orientation. The course would teach the new students about precedents, traditions, and the importance of Oklahoma State University.[118] This rather remarkable prophet ended his thesis by writing: "Should a concentrated plan be brought forth and given publicity to the students and citizens of Oklahoma, it can be realized. Such an institution as pictured here— Oklahoma State University—is to be within the future; it is to be desired."[119]

Fifteen months later, Dr. Bennett arrived on campus. Eventually he developed a Twenty-Five Year Plan, which had incredible parallels to the futuristic university of the *O'Collegian* writers. At the last convocation of freshman week in 1928, President Bennett told the students: "The College believes in the essential worth whileness of every individual. We are determined to escape the tendency of mere mass education. We do not expect to know you as so many hundred freshmen or as so many seniors. We expect that in the case of every one of you that there will be at least one officer of the College who will know you personally and who will counsel with you as a friend whom he knows and understands."

Bennett continued: "On the other hand, the College hopes to create a community consciousness. We hope you will feel yourselves responsible members of this community, and will take part in all phases of its life, learn to do team work and acquire the art of social living." The president finished his speech by sharing his belief that the college itself stood for high moral character. Above all else, Bennett noted, "We are concerned first and foremost with the forming of those traits and habits which together constitute character. If we fail in this, all our learning is in vain."

Dr. Bennett then asked the freshmen and upperclassmen to take the following pledge: "I pledge, here and now, life long loyalty to the ideals of scholarship and character of the founders of this institution to the end that I may loyally serve the College, this commonwealth, and this nation!"[120] The convocation dismissed, President Bennett took up the role of educator. The students assumed their tasks as learners.[121]

A new chapter in the Oklahoma Agricultural and Mechanical College's history—one which would be more dynamic than any before it—was beginning to unfold. By now, the college could point with pride to many services developed especially for students. Whether in residence halls, food services, or health facilities, Oklahoma's largest land-grant college realized that an institution of higher education provides not only academic guidance, but other programs and accommodations as well. An air of maturity and sophistication had enveloped the campus. As the college was thrust into the throes of the Great Depression of the 1930s, it would become evident that the institution could handle the uncertainties with calm and assurance.

# Endnotes

1. *1915 Redskin*, p. 150, Oklahoma A. and M. College Yearbook; *Oklahoma A. and M. College Catalog, 1928-1929*, p. 24. In 1928, the Women's Building was renamed Gardiner Hall for Oklahoma A. and M.'s first home economics teacher, Maud Gardiner. Still later, the building was refurbished and renamed the Bartlett Center for the Studio Arts.

2. *1915 Redskin*, pp. 144, 150; Oklahoma A. and M. College *New Education*, 7 August 1914, p. 1.

3. *1915 Redskin*, p. 150.

4. *New Education*, 1 November 1914, p. 1; *1915 Redskin*, p. 150.

5. Oklahoma A. and M. College *Orange and Black*, 29 July 1916, p. 1.

6. *Oklahoma A. and M. College Catalogue, 1903-1904*, p. 6.

7. *1928 Redskin*, p. 26; "Deans of Students," Student Affairs File, Student Services Collection, Special Collections, Edmon Low Library, Oklahoma State University, Stillwater, Oklahoma.

8. *New Education*, 15 January 1910, p. 3.

9. *New Education*, 15 January 1910, p. 3.

10. *New Education*, September 1911, p. 1; "Career of Service," *Oklahoma A. and M. College Magazine*, vol. 22, no. 10 (June 1951), p. 42; *Oklahoma A. and M. College Catalog, 1927-1928*, p. 24.

11. *New Education*, September 1911, p. 1; *Oklahoma A. and M. College Catalog, 1929*, p. 25; *Oklahoma A. and M. College Catalogue, 1908-1909*, pp. 18-35; *Oklahoma A. and M. College Catalogue, 1913-1914*, p. 18; Oklahoma A. and M. College *O'Collegian*, 25 January 1925, p. 3.

12. *Orange and Black*, 8 February 1923, p. 2, 15 September 1917, p. 1, 14 September 1918, p. 1, 17 September 1919, p. 1.

13. *O'Collegian*, 24 April 1924, p. 1, 5 July 1925, p. 1, 5 January, 1926, p. 1; *Oklahoma A. and M. College Catalog, 1925-1926*, p. 10.

14. *O'Collegian*, 5 January 1926, p. 1.

15. *1916 Redskin*, p. 384.

16. *Orange and Black*, 18 July 1916, p. 3.

17. *O'Collegian*, 23 November 1924, p. 1, 25 January 1925, p. 1; *Orange and Black*, 10 November 1917, p. 1.

18. *O'Collegian,* 18 September 1925, p. 1, 25 January 1925, pp. 1-2, 3 April 1927, p. 1, 6 April 1927, p. 1; Mary Goddard, "It's . . . Older Than Oklahoma and Still in Daily Use," *Oklahoma A. and M. College Magazine*, vol. 23, no. 9 (May 1952), p. 4.

19. *O'Collegian*, 25 January 1925, p. 2.

20. *O'Collegian*, 17 April 1924, p. 3; *Orange and Black*, 29 September 1917, p. 2, 4 February 1920, p. 2, 17 November 1921, p. 1.

21. *Orange and Black*, 17 November 1921, p. 1.

22. "Faculty Minutes," 10 November 1911, p. 180, Special Collections, Edmon Low Library; *Orange and Black,* 9 June 1919, p. 1.

23. *Orange and Black*, 3 March 1917, p. 2.

24. *1912 Redskin*, p. 254.

25. *1916 Redskin*, p. 370; *Orange and Black*, 6 December 1915, p. 4.

26. *Orange and Black*, 10 February 1917, p. 3.

27. *O'Collegian*, 3 February 1926, p. 1.

28. *O'Collegian*, 27 September 1925, p. 3.

29. *Orange and Black*, 12 May 1919, p. 4.

30. *O'Collegian*, 27 September 1925, pp. 1, 3; "Mimeographed Stories, July 1 - November 1, 1927," Weldon Barnes Collection, Special Collections, Edmon Low Library; *1916 Redskin*, p. 387; *Orange and Black*, 12 February 1916, p. 4; Oklahoma A. and M. College *Daily O'Collegian*, 2 December 1927, p. 1; *Oklahoma A. and M. College Catalog, 1928-1929*, p. 24.

31. "Rules and Regulations, 1923-1928," and "House Rules for Rooming Houses," in Rules and Regulations, 1923-1928, President's Papers, Special Collections, Edmon Low Library.

32. *Orange and Black*, 16 November 1918, p. 3, 12 October 1916, p. 1; *1914 Redskin*, p. 221; Oklahoma A. and M. *College Paper*, 1 March 1900, p. 126; "Mimeographed Stories, January 1 - March 1, 1928," Weldon Barnes Collection; *O'Collegian*, 4 April 1925, p. 2, 9 March 1927, p. 1; *Daily O'Collegian*, 8 February 1928, p. 1.

33. *Daily O'Collegian*, 8 February 1928, p. 1; *Orange and Black*, 12 October 1916, pp. 1, 4.

34. *Orange and Black*, 2 November 1918, p. 2; *Oklahoma A. and M. College Catalogue, 1906-1907*, p. 72; Mary Louise Stout, "A History and Survey of the Health Services to the Student Body of the Oklahoma Agricultural and Mechanical College Over the Years 1928-1937 (Master of Science thesis, Oklahoma A. and M. College, 1938), p. 9.

35. *Oklahoma A. and M. College Catalogue, 1920-1921*, pp. 13-14.

36. *Oklahoma A. and M. College Catalogue, 1909-1910*, p. 15.

37. *Oklahoma A. and M. College Catalogue, 1914-1915*, pp. xii-xiii; *Oklahoma A. and M. College Catalogue, 1915-1916*, pp. xiii-xiv; *O'Collegian*, 4 June 1925, p. 2.

38. "Faculty Minutes," 13 July 1910, p. 111; *Oklahoma A. and M. College Catalogue, 1910-1911*, pp. 16-17; Stout, p. 10.

39. *1923 Redskin*, p. 289.

40. Stout, p. 10; *O'Collegian*, 30 September 1925, p. 3.

41. *O'Collegian*, 9 January 1926, p. 2.

42. M. T. Clark to Bradford Knapp, 4 March 1919, President's Papers.

43. *O'Collegian*, 28 September 1925, p. 1, 14 January 1925, p. 1, 14 November 1926, p. 1; M. T. Clark to Bradford Knapp, 4 March 1919, President's Papers; *Orange and Black*, 11 January 1919, p. 3.

44. *College Paper*, 1 April 1904, p. 8.

45. *Orange and Black*, 6 January 1917, p. 1, 28 April 1919, p. 1; *O'Collegian*, 10 September 1925, p. 2; *College Paper*, January 1905, p. 66.

46. *Oklahoma A. and M. College Catalogue, 1926-1927*, pp. 21-25; *Oklahoma A. and M. College Catalogue, 1908-1909*, pp. 36-37.

47. *O'Collegian*, 22 September 1927, p. 2.

48. *New Education*, 15 March 1915, p. 1, 15 October 1913, p. 3; *O'Collegian*, 4 December 1926, p. 2, 12 February 1925, p. 3, 10 December 1925, p. 4.

49. *New Education*, 1 April 1910, p. 2; *Oklahoma A. and M. College Catalog, 1926-1927*, p. 26; *O'Collegian*, 15 December 1917, p. 3.

50. *Orange and Black*, 10 February 1917, p. 1, 13 January 1917, p. 1, 20 April 1922, p. 1; *Oklahoma A. and M. College Catalog, 1926-1927*, pp. 27-29.

51. *1927 Redskin*, p. 208.

52. *O'Collegian*, 2 July 1926, pp. 1-2.

53. *Oklahoma A. and M. College Catalog, 1926-1927*, p. 27; *Daily O'Collegian*, 8 February 1928, p. 1; "Mimeographed Stories, October 8, 1928," Weldon Barnes Collection.

54. *Orange and Black*, 8 October 1919, p. 1, 29 March 1919, p. 1, 8 December 1921, p. 2, 3 November 1921, pp. 2-3, 28 September 1922, p. 1; *O'Collegian*, 14 June 1927, p. 2; *Oklahoma A. and M. College Catalogue, 1926-1927*, p. 29.

55. *O'Collegian*, 1 December 1926, p. 2, 3 December 1926, p. 2, 23 March 1926, p. 2.

56. *O'Collegian*, 23 March 1926, p. 2.

57. *Daily O'Collegian*, 19 December 1928, p. 1.

58. *New Education*, 15 February 1910, p. 2.

59. *O'Collegian*, 5 May 1925, p. 6.

60. *O'Collegian*, 19 July 1925, p. 4.

61. *O'Collegian*, 5 May 1925, pp. 1, 6, 19 July 1925, p. 4.

62. *Daily O'Collegian*, 1 April 1928, p. 2.

63. *Orange and Black*, 29 April 1926, p. 1; *O'Collegian*, 8 October 1926, pp. 1, 3, 5 July 1927, pp. 1, 4; *Daily O'Collegian*, 1 April 1928, p. 2; Cathy Criner, "Heart of Campus Celebrates 35th Anniversary," *Oklahoma State University Outreach*, vol. 57, no. 3 (Spring 1986), p. 12.

64. *1928 Redskin*, p. 401; *Orange and Black*, 6 May 1916, p. 3, 17 May 1919, p. 2; Kurt Gwartney, "Peck's Lodge: Remembered by Generations of OSU Alumni," *Oklahoma State University Outreach*, vol. 57, no. 2 (Winter 1985), pp. 16-17; "Peck's Lodge Early Part of Campus History," *Oklahoma State University Outreach*, vol. 15, no. 1 (January 1974), p. 7; Robert Jamieson, "A Brief History of University Placement at Oklahoma State University," manuscript, 7 June 1986, Student Services Collection. Peck's Lodge still stands, and the name "Peck's Lodge" can still be seen carved on the face of the building at the corner of Knoblock and University Streets.

65. "The College Store—Peck Bros.," 7 February 1917, pp. 1-2, President's Papers; "Mimeographed Stories, July - to November 1, 1927," Weldon Barnes Collection; *O'Collegian*, 24 September 1927, p. 1.

66. *New York Times*, 3 April 1917, p. 1.

67. *Orange and Black*, 19 May 1917, p. 2.

68. *Orange and Black*, 6 April 1918, p. 3.

69. *Orange and Black*, 27 October 1917, p. 1.

70. *Orange and Black*, 16 April 1917, p. 1, 23 April 1917, p. 1, 14 May 1917, p. 1, 21 July 1917, p. 1, 13 October 1917, p. 2, 27 October 1917, p. 1, 3 November 1917, p. 2, 17 November 1917, p. 1, 5 October 1918, p. 1; *1918 Redskin*, p. 2.

71. *Orange and Black*, 16 April 1917, p. 4.

72. *Orange and Black*, 16 April 1917, p. 2.

73. *Orange and Black*, 17 May 1917, p. 1.

74. United States Attorney to R. L. Williams, 23 January 1918, and C. D. Dudley to J. W. Cantwell, 26 January 1918, President's Papers; *Orange and Black*, 12 January 1918, p. 1.

75. *Orange and Black*, 4 May 1918, p. 1, 16 March 16, 1918, p. 1.

76. *O'Collegian*, 5 December 1925, p. 1, 15 September 1927, p. 1.

77. *Orange and Black*, 16 February 1918, p. 1.

78. *Orange and Black*, 8 November 1918, p. 1.

79. "World War I and A. and M. Service Flag," President's Papers; *Orange and Black*, 8 November 1918, p. 1, 21 December 1918, p. 1.

80. *Orange and Black*, 10 November 1921, p.1, 24 November 1921, p. 1, 26 February 1919, p. 1, 2 March 1922, p. 1, 9 November 1922, p. 1; *1927 Redskin*, p. 366; *Daily O'Collegian*, 1 December 1927, p. 1, 10 November 1927, p. 1, 19 January 1929, p. 1; *O'Collegian*, 5 April 1925, pp. 1-2, 4, 3 October 1925, p. 1, 7 November 1926, p. 1, 8 January 1927, p. 1, 1 October 1927, p. 1; *1923 Redskin*, p. 143.

81. *O'Collegian*, 22 January 1926, p. 1.

82. *Orange and Black*, 8 December 1921, p. 1; *O'Collegian*, 22 January 1926, pp. 1, 3; *1934 Redskin*, p. 249.

83. Vera Kathryn Stevens Anderson, "A History of the *Daily O'Collegian*, Student Newspaper of Oklahoma A. and M. College: 1924-1934" (Master of Science thesis, Oklahoma State University, 1975), pp. 18-26; *1927 Redskin*, p. 22.

84. *O'Collegian*, 14 October 1925, p. 1, 14 January 1927, p. 2, 16 February 1927, p. 1, 26 January 1927, p. 1; *1927 Redskin*, p. 222.

85. *1927 Redskin*, p. 222; *O'Collegian*, 26 January 1927, p. 1.

86. Anderson, pp. 151-161; *O'Collegian*, 14 April 1926, pp. 1, 3; "O'Collegian Articles, 1924-1928," 17 May 1926, pp. 1-2, President's Papers.

87. *Daily O'Collegian*, 21 April 1928, p. 1.

88. Anderson, pp. 151-161; *Daily O'Collegian*, 21 April 1928, p. 1, 19 April 1928, p. 1.

89. Anderson, p. 165; *Daily O'Collegian*, 3 September 1974, p. 12.

90. C. H. Breedlove to Walker Stone, 10 April 1972, Walker Stone to C. H. Breedlove, 22 April 1972, and anecdotal note by Paul Miller entitled, "To Any Who Read " [1972], Paul Miller Papers, Special Collections, Edmon Low Library.

91. *Orange and Black*, 24 November 1917, p. 2, 19 April 1923, p. 2.

92. *O'Collegian*, 28 September 1924, p. 2.

93. *"O'Collegian* Articles, Knapp, 1924-1928," 18 April 1925, pp. 1-5, President's Papers.

94. *O'Collegian*, 18 September 1924, p. 2.

95. *Daily O'Collegian*, 24 February 1928, p. 1, 22 March 1928, p. 2; *Orange and Black*, 22 February 1919, p. 2, 3 May 1919, p. 3, 14 September 1922, p. 1, 22 March 1923, pp. 1-4; "Religion, 1926-1927, Knapp," 9 August 1927, pp. 1-2, President's Papers; *O'Collegian*, 7 September 1924, p. 4, 11 April 1925, p. 1, 23 September 1925, p. 2, 26 September 1925, p. 1, 3 November 1925, p. 4.

96. *Orange and Black*, 13 May 1920, p. 1.

97. *Orange and Black*, 4 May 1922, p. 4.

98. *1927 Redskin*, p. 225; *O'Collegian*, 23 March 1924, p. 1.

99. *1927 Redskin*, pp. 224-225.

100. *Aggievator*, vol. 2 (May 1926), p. 4.

101. *Aggievator*, vol. 1, "Heifer Number" ([November] 1925), p. 4.

102. *Aggievator*, vol. 1, "Heifer Number," p. 3.

103. *Aggievator*, vol. 1, "Heifer Number," p. 19.

104. *Aggievator*, vol. 2, "Interscholastic Edition" (May 1926), p. 21.

105. *1917 Redskin*, p. 298; *1916 Redskin*, pp. 225-235; *Orange and Black*, 29 September 1916, p. 3, 8 September 1916, p. 3.

106. *1917 Redskin*, p. 299.

107. "Thirty Years Ago," *Oklahoma A. and M. College Magazine*, vol. 1, no. 6 (February 1930), p. 14; *1917 Redskin*, pp. 209, 227.

108. *Orange and Black*, 2 November 1918, p. 1.

109. *Orange and Black*, 27 May 1920, p. 1, 11 January 1923, p. 1, 22 September 1917, p. 1, 19 February 1920, p. 1; *1927 Redskin*, pp. 304-331.

110. *Orange and Black*, 29 October 1919, p. 3, 17 September 1919, p. 3, 10 September 1919, p. 1, 15 September 1921, p. 1.

111. *Orange and Black*, 19 March 1923, p. 1, 28 January 1920, p. 2, 29 September 1921, p. 2; "Mimeographed Stories, July 1 - November 1, 1927," Weldon Barnes Collection; *1927 Redskin*, p. 332.

112. *O'Collegian*, 19 February 1927, p. 1.

113. *Orange and Black*, 18 January 1923, p. 1.

114. *Orange and Black*, 18 January 1923, p. 1; *O'Collegian*, 28 January 1926, p. 2.

115. Theodore L. Agnew, "Survival, Stability, Maturity," *Oklahoma State Alumnus Magazine*, vol. 10, no. 5 (May 1969), pp. 16-18; "The Passing of an OSU Patriarch," *Oklahoma State Alumnus Magazine*, vol. 11, no. 5 (May 1970), p. 30; "Miss Julia E. Stout, Former Dean, Died," *Oklahoma State Alumnus Magazine*, vol. 10, no. 5 (May 1969), p. 28; J. W. Cantwell, "Annual Report," 31 December 1920, p. 370, President's Papers; *Oklahoma A. and M. College Catalogue, 1928-1929*, p. 370.

116. Philip Reed Rulon, *Oklahoma State University—Since 1890* (Stillwater: Oklahoma State University Press, 1975), pp. 181-198. Rulon's Chapter 7 is a fascinating account of Bradford Knapp's presidency at the Oklahoma A. and M. College. Knapp's administrative activities, his relationship with the student body, and his political troubles are detailed and give credibility to the man's considerable ability.

117. *Daily O'Collegian*, 18 March 1928, p. 2; Rulon, pp. 219-220; Kay Nettleton, "OSU's Fourth Decade: Adolescence During the 'Roaring 20s,'" *Oklahoma State University Outreach*, vol. 55, no. 2 (Winter 1983), p. 12.

118. *O'Collegian*, 20 May 1927, pp. 1-2.
119. *O'Collegian*, 20 May 1927, p. 2.
120. "Mimeographed Stories, September 20, 1928," p. 2, Weldon Barnes Collection.
121. *Daily O'Collegian*, 4 December 1928, p. 1.

# 5 A Pragmatic Adolescence

On the Oklahoma Agricultural and Mechanical College campus student interests and behavior seemed a world apart from the growing national economic crisis during the early Depression years of the 1930s. In the college newspaper, for example, little lament was given America's growing problems in the banking and business worlds. On November 1, 1929, shortly after the stock market crash, business students were playing a whimsical game, with fake portfolios of stock, in which they bought and sold imaginary companies. After two weeks, the campus investors of two undergraduate classes, Business Finance and Forecasting and Economics, had heavy financial losses. The classes concluded that playing the stock market, at least at that time, was a losing proposition. The whirlwind of the stock market catastrophe would eventually cause real bewilderment and somberness.[1]

In addition to the Great Depression, the 1930s are also marked by other important events. In 1933 the Eighteenth Amendment to the U.S. Constitution which called for prohibition was repealed. Newspaper headlines reported a plane crash in Alaska on August 15, 1935, in which Will Rogers, Oklahoma's beloved man of wit and wisdom, was killed. Toward the end of the decade, the movies would reach their all-time popularity. By that time eighty-five million Americans attended the "talkies" at least once a week. Reasonably stated, the students of the 1930s experienced a period of waiting—waiting to get an education, waiting sometimes to find a job, and waiting for better times before getting married.[2]

Franklin D. Roosevelt became the President of the United States in 1933. Although economic improvements were being made, depression was now worldwide. In America one person in four was out of work, while only one of thirty-three paid income taxes. Upstanding, hardworking citizens had to stand in bread lines to assure their survival. New technologies and a growing group of service industries (frozen foods, cellophane, electric appliances, and dry cleaners) presented increased leisure time. The new leisure and tight family budgets resulted in a tremendous popularity of books, magazines, radios, musical instruments, equipment for indoor and outdoor games, and motion pictures. A particularly appealing game for families short of cash was Monopoly, invented by a salesman left jobless by the Depression. Miniature golf, amateur photography, assisted by the newly available Kodachrome film in 18-exposure cartridges, and bowling became popular recreations. *Life* magazine began publication in 1936, followed a year later by *Look*. Both would help to redefine American lifestyles.[3]

In 1936 the average cost for a year at a state-supported college in the United States was about $400. As late as 1940, the Oklahoma A. and M. College was still offering a reasonably priced year of education for between $350 and $450. The going national wage was still between twenty-five and thirty cents an hour. Nevertheless, more than a million students, a new record, were getting a college education at the midpoint of the Depression era. At least two-thirds of the students supported themselves, to a certain degree, by working at lowly jobs.

A *Fortune* magazine survey indicated that college students were taking more courses in economics, history, and social sciences than their counterparts of the 1920s; that they read the papers more carefully; and that they knew much more about what was going on in the world. In this same *Fortune* report, about half of the men and even more of the women wanted to marry after graduation, and about half of these hoped they would have children of their own soon after. Forty percent of the females feared that homemaking would be boring and hoped somehow to combine a career with marriage. In contrast, 85 percent of the men were against this particular proposal. Both sexes placed a high priority on personal security. Whatever was permanent and secure in life was of far more interest to the students of 1936 than anything adventurous or radical. In these Depression years students, like their parents, believed if they worked hard and well they would prosper. If they failed to make good, it was their own fault. Yet this belief was severely shaken by the lack of reason or justice that was all around them.[4]

Closer to Stillwater, the 1930s were a time of advance and maturity at the Oklahoma A. and M. College. Resident student enrollment grew from 2,921 students in 1929 to 7,142 students in just twelve years. The rapid student growth in enrollment was temporarily ameliorated by the addition of eight new buildings, including four residence halls, two classroom buildings, a new infirmary, and a field house. Enrollment was such that the college no longer had to prepare high school age students to enter into a college-level course of study. The college's preparatory school, a part of the college since 1891, was discontinued in 1930.[5]

The Oklahoma State Board of Agriculture adopted a twenty-five year campus plan in 1930. The plan called for a maximum ten-minute walk between any classroom, incorporated a total of 150 parking spaces for cars on campus, and had the library as the focal point and hub of academic activity. When asked about the uniformity of campus building appearance, longtime university architect Philip A. Wilber once called the architectural style "Pseudo-collegiate- Georgian-Oklahoma-Bennett-Wilber-et. al. 1930-40-50-60."[6] The campus plan, originally designed for an expected seven thousand students to be enrolled by 1955, was preempted when the enrollment projection was reached fifteen years early. As a result, the marvelous vision of a long-range campus plan would be modified, time and time again. However, larger planning principles were maintained. Today's beautiful campus remains lasting testimony to an early vision of architectural harmony and long-range planning dating back more than half a century.[7]

The land-grant college movement was not started primarily by educators, but by people who wanted service that colleges in existence in the late 1800s did not give or did not want to give. Henry G. Bennett was an educator who would prove that he knew about the essential land-grant college ingredient of service, so often lacking at other colleges and universities. During his tenure as president from July 1928 to December 1951, Bennett would combine a solid sense of the future, charismatic leadership, and political common sense and maneuvering.[8]

In Bennett's first public speech in Stillwater, he pledged an administration free of politics, the appointment of faculty and other college officials on the basis of merit, a rapid growth in student enrollment, and a general rise in standards for the college. These were lofty ambitions. The Former Students Association, later the Alumni Association, simply wished Bennett a long tenure in office. Originally opposed to Bennett's appointment, the Former Students Association later reversed its opinion of the man and hoped that it would be able finally to disband "The Committee," a semi-permanent group whose function was to greet and welcome the seemingly everchanging Oklahoma A. and M. College president.[9]

A sympathetic humorist suggested that all Bennett had to do to maintain his new position was "lick O.U. on the gridiron and pin Iowa's wrestlers to the mat and then go to the International Livestock Show in Chicago and drag down a few blue ribbons, we will soon forget all about Bradford Knapp." The clever observer reminded Bennett that "as an educator you are a good politician . . . unless you are a good politician it won't be long until your tanned hide will be hung on the fence."[10]

With more advice than was probably necessary and with polite well wishes, President Bennett plowed into his work with determination and purpose. No doubt the term visionary aptly described Bennett's leadership style. Authoritarian, sensitive, and charismatic, Bennett could also have been labeled a benevolent dictator. He believed in consolidation of administrative power and circled himself with colleagues like Earle C. Albright, assistant to the president. Albright, a close Bennett advisor, served in the president's absence from campus and closely monitored the college's day-to-day internal functionings. Early nonacademic appointments were made to fellow church members or friends; Julia Stout replaced Blanche Freeman as dean of women, and R. J. Schull became the college physician. Stout and Schull were both from southeastern Oklahoma where Bennett had ably served as president of Southeastern State College in Durant prior to his move to Stillwater.[11]

Schiller Scroggs also came with Bennett from Durant. Scroggs was officially given the title of director of administrative research. Sometimes alluded to as the president's hatchet man, the *1940 Redskin* described Scroggs as a man who "provokes some to think, some to tears, some to hatred, some to reconsider, some to action, some to respect—

Henry G. Bennett, president of Oklahoma A. and M. College from 1928 to 1951, points with pride to the Twenty-Five Year Plan, a proposal for campus development. Called the college's "number one level-headed dreamer," Bennett combined a solid awareness of the future, charismatic leadership, and political common sense and maneuvering.

Centennial Histories Series

but whatever, he is a provocative man."[12] Regardless of these opinions, Scroggs ably served Bennett, and fit well the new president's needs for competence, contribution to larger goals, and action.

Haskell Pruett, the college business manager, provided an illustration of the early priority for efficiency of campus resources. In a general letter that he sent to all Oklahoma A. and M. faculty and employees, he curtly proclaimed in the first sentence: "Did it ever occur to you that thoughtlessness and carelessness in leaving [a] classroom or office without turning off the electric lights is costing you money personally, as shown by your low salary check?"[13] Although Pruett's point may be well taken, the tone and directness reflected Bennett's early efforts to reorder the college, consolidate his administrative organization, and take charge through people willing to implement his philosophy.[14]

By 1934 the Oklahoma A. and M. College had granted five thousand academic degrees. Fourteen presidents had served the institution. By then Bennett had held office longer than any other individual with the exception of Angelo C. Scott, who served for nine years. As testimony to the institutional growth, Bennett had signed 52 percent of the total five thousand degrees conferred during his short six years in the presidency. The college's alumni magazine acknowledged: "The phenomenal growth of the institution in recent years and the greatly increased number taking graduate work, together with the evident tendency toward stability of tenure and administration is gratifying. We hope that these indications of a great institution will continue."[15]

Bennett's credibility with the Former Students Association had obviously grown. Likewise, students were increasingly appreciative of the president's efforts on their behalf. When Bennett took office, townspeople were indignant and the faculty's morale was at low ebb. Eight years later the college had been steered "successfully through the most acute years of the depression until at length the dawn of recovery finds the institution with standards maintained, personnel strengthened, and spirit unbroken." Bennett was democratic and congenial—a person who had won the heart of the student body. No student was too small or insignificant to have access to the president's private office.[16]

President Bennett more than once proved his ability as a talented politician as well as his considerable knowledge about the subtleties of Oklahoma politics. In 1933 the college was in dire need of more residence hall space. Despite the Depression, Bennett undertook the task of securing federally-appropriated money. To avoid potential interference by Oklahoma Governor William H. Murray, Bennett recommended the building be named for Murray in recognition of his state leadership. Murray Hall opened the following year.[17]

Just three years later Bennett maneuvered through the quagmire of Oklahoma politics to solve another campus space problem. The state fire marshall had condemned the English and History and the Music and Arts Buildings. Bennett knew that a legislative appropriation of the nearly half-million dollars needed to replace the buildings was unlikely. Rarely a passive person in such situations, Bennett asked his board for permission to use tents as temporary replacements for the condemned buildings. With the permission and support of his superiors, Bennett ordered six tents, thirty by forty feet, and then erected them in the quadrangle behind Morrill Hall, in space normally used for intramural sports. Eighteen hundred students attended classes in the tents and, to add some clout to the showmanship, it was announced that the tents would be used until the condemned buildings could somehow be replaced. The tents were written about, with accompanying photographs, in the media throughout the state. At the peak of embarrassment, and without question growing political pressure, the legislature benevolently provided the funds for new classroom space.[18]

President Bennett was also an able on-campus administrator. At times he used his substantial political and diplomatic skills with students. Early in his presidency, students were in widespread rebellion against the compulsory military training program. When they threatened to go to the Oklahoma State Board of Agriculture and, if necessary, the governor, they received widespread coverage by the media. The rebellion was put down after a private meeting between Bennett and student leaders. Few details of the meeting were available; but afterward, required military training continued, and the students publicly thanked Bennett for his sympathy and courteous attention to their problems.[19]

The growth in student enrollment was the result of hard work. Bennett was an astute high school student recruiter, who would personally write potential students. With political aplomb, he used solid, psychologically persuasive approaches to entice prospective students. In a 1941 recruiting effort targeted at high school seniors, the president personally affixed his signature to a letter starting with "Dear Friend," which read in part: "Just what part you are to play in the great drama of human events you, of course, do not yet know. But you have a great deal more to say about what this part shall be than you perhaps imagine. You can make of yourself pretty much what you wish. To be sure, people have different talents, and one's environment helps or hinders in the choosing of courses; but place against this the number of people who fail to live up to their possibilities, who drift in the channel of their environment without much effort to swim, who give up, and you will see that determination, energy, vision, persistence, and integrity still count heavily for success. If this institution or any of its staff can be of service to you—can counsel you in making an education decision—we shall count it a privilege to do so. Please write us."[20] The thought-provoking, straightforward letter was then simply signed, "Henry G. Bennett, President." Certainly college students choose to attend a particular college or university for a combination of complex reasons. Nonetheless, in the year following this particular Bennett recruitment letter, there was another record setting enrollment of nearly two thousand students in the freshman class at the college.[21]

The Depression years would immediately require Bennett's staff to find unique, if not creative, ways to assist college students financially if the president's announced goals of continued growth in enrollment and service to people were to be achieved. Again, not to be deterred, Bennett, Schiller Scroggs, and A. Frank Martin, who in 1933 was appointed director of student employment, would play leadership roles for the college. The students themselves also became allies in finding ways for paying their college expenses. Ironically, the Depression, with the accompanying lack of jobs, had stimulated college enrollment throughout America. L. W. Burton, Oklahoma A. and M. College registrar, pointed out that people in Oklahoma were similarly more interested in attending college because of limited employment prospects.[22] Burton then added in a January 1930 *Daily O'Collegian* article that "despite the fact that the country was hard pressed for money this semester's enrollment in the college was the largest in the history of the school."[23]

In fact, although students were not discouraged from their desire to attend college throughout the Great Depression, changes in both lifestyles and student organizations were required. During the Depression years, students could be seen returning to Stillwater at the start of a new semester or after a vacation break in old dented cars filled with student passengers, canned food goods, vegetables, and sometimes even live poultry. The *Daily O'Collegian*, in cooperation with the YMCA, started an "anti-wolf campaign." An employment initiative, the "anti-wolf campaign" led to the forming of the "Window Cleaner's Association," "Floor Waxing Association," a "Car Washer's Association," and the "Gardener's Association." George Bullock, executive secretary of the YMCA could be called at work or at home, day or night, by any prospective employer of a student. No job was too small or difficult, and any employment request could be filled immediately.[24]

Student activities also felt the effects of the Depression. A significant student debate resulted when the Panhellenic Council decided that moderation in spending money on homecoming would be a prudent course of action for the festivities of 1931. Panhellenic's proposal recommended that only one parade float, representing all sorority chapters, be constructed. Likewise, rather than decorate the exteriors of the sorority houses as was the tradition, this money should be used for lunches, dinners, and other social activities for campus homecoming guests. A huge protest from other student organizations followed. Within two weeks the Panhellenic Council revised their earlier decision. Although no prizes would be given, homecoming, including all of the traditional trappings, was held. The Depression had other effects. Delta Zeta and Phi Omega Pi, two social sororities, were forced to abandon their chapter houses. Omega Kappa Nu, a prominent campus social fraternity, was forced to disband. The sororities remained otherwise active, but Kappa Nu's members were absorbed by other fraternities. Sigma Mu Sigma and Alpha Rho Chi also dissolved.[25]

Fraternities and sororities survived a severe threat to their system in 1931 when members of the Oklahoma Legislature proposed a law to tax chapter houses and property; the measure was defeated after stormy debate. When the crisis passed, chapter house construction and renovation was renewed. The Greek system stabilized, grew stronger, and continued to influence campus politics. The men's Panhellenic became the Interfraternity Council on April 25, 1934. Farm House was installed on campus on May 12, 1928. After ten years as a local chapter known as Chi Beta, Sigma Alpha Epsilon was installed on February 14, 1931. Also added in the 1930s were Phi Kappa Theta in 1937 and Phi Kappa Alpha in 1939. After surviving the worst of the Depression years and legislative threats, the Greek system remained stable through the 1930s. By 1941 there were five nationalized sororities and twelve fraternities on campus.[26]

Important events, one national in scope and a second, short-lived and local in origin, were the direct counterattack on the effects of Depression-caused money problems for college students. On the national front, President Franklin D. Roosevelt orchestrated the federally financed National Youth Administration (NYA) in 1935. This program represented the start of national direct financial assistance programs for students in institutions of higher education. With the stated purpose of increasing college enrollments, the NYA program funded jobs for part-time student employment. These positions were in addition to jobs that the college was already providing. Many students worked from twenty to thirty hours per week and could earn about $20 a month, an amount sufficient to pay for room and board. The program was effective, partly because it was administered by the college under A. Frank Martin. His selection of NYA-funded students was primarily based on need, then secondarily on the student's ability to do the work. From 1936 and for the next few years, the NYA program allocated roughly $60,000 a year to Oklahoma A. and M. College. By the spring of 1936 more than 400 Aggie students had been employed and paid by NYA dollars. The NYA program remained a valuable national financial aid program through the 1930s.[27]

On the local front, an extraordinary series of student employment opportunities was created under the broad title of the Student Self-Help Industries. The Student Self-Help Industries were publicly announced

During the Depression of the 1930s, Oklahoma A. and M. College created an extraordinary series of student employment opportunities under the title of Student Self-Help Industries. In the Quality Craft Hooked Rugs industry (*upper*), students worked with discarded hose, silk underclothing, and woolen materials to produce rugs that were later sold in department stores. The ceramics factory (*lower*) produced flower pots which were then sold in Oklahoma and adjoining states.

on the campus on September 13, 1929. Funded initially with a capital investment of $150,000 under the general direction of Schiller Scroggs, the self-help industries were projected to provide 500 part-time student jobs. Employed students were required to arrange their class schedules so that they could work a maximum of four hours in a solid block of time. In some industries students could choose to be paid on the basis of "piece of work," but most students earned from twenty-five to forty cents an hour. Student Self-Help Industries were nonprofit organizations, produced quality products for sale in the public marketplace, and were always dedicated to providing students a means to earn money for educational expenses.[28]

At the height of productivity, the college had established seven different Student Self-Help Industries. Bird Brand Brooms, produced at the campus broom factory, were sold from Louisiana to Minnesota. At peak production the broom factory employed 100 students. The college's art and needlework department directed the fortunes of the industry called Quality Craft Hooked Rugs. In this self-help industry, fifty students toiled with discarded hose, donated silk underclothing, and woolen materials to produce rugs, which incorporated colonial, Indian, and modernistic patterns. The rugs were sold in wholesale lots to department stores in Oklahoma City and Tulsa. Each rug took six to twelve hours of work and were usually eight foot square.[29]

Select Farm Products were produced at the student self-help farm near Perkins. Twenty students worked on 220 acres of land, of which 80 acres were planted in wheat, 40 acres were dedicated to truck farming, and 100 acres were planted in both cotton and oats. The farm also raised livestock. A fourth industry, the Duplicating Service, employed one full-time and two half-time students in operating multigraph and mimeograph equipment to provide duplicating services for the community and campus. The Cabinet Making Shop, utilizing $7,000 worth of woodworking machinery, produced furniture for use in campus buildings. In 1930 the shop-sponsored industry produced $2,500 worth of business and paid $1,400 of this amount for wages to twenty-five student employees. In this year the woodworking industry's output included twenty-three office desks, two mahogany typewriter desks, two walnut standard office desks, four mahogany hall trees, and eight laboratory tables, plus several made-to-order special wood pieces. A sixth Student Self-Help Industry was the Tiger Tavern, formerly the College Cafeteria. In 1930 the Tiger Tavern employed fifteen students who served 17,000 meals in the month of May alone at an average cost of twenty-nine cents per tray.[30]

The seventh of the self-help industries was the ceramics factory. Using an old ROTC barracks located on land currently occupied by the Student Union, thirty students were employed to operate a $1,200 flowerpot stamping machine and kilns heated to between 2,000 and 2,400 degrees Fahrenheit to bake the pots. Although the ceramics factory's capacity was larger, the greatest consumer demand for the flowerpots was 6,000 per day. Student employees of the factory drove trucks to deliver the pots to florists in southern Kansas, northern Texas, western Arkansas, southeastern Missouri, and Oklahoma. Later, the ceramics factory produced frogs, which were painted either black or green. The mouths of the ceramic frogs were useful for ashtrays, and their size made them a handy doorstop. About 750 frogs were produced between 1930 and 1932, but another specialty item, a ceramic duck, was produced only fifty times. Bird baths, although experimented with, were never produced on a large scale.[31]

The Depression had created the need for the ceramics factory and also caused its demise. In 1934 the price of flowerpots dipped so low that competition from other producers made further production marginal. The final blow came when a large number of the factory's creditors could not pay their bills. Stated in a capsule, the ceramics factory found that it was nearly impossible to collect payable accounts, especially overdue accounts, during a depression. On September 20, 1934, the ceramics factory venture was closed after nearly five years of operation. By then the broom factory and rug manufacturing operation had also closed. In total, the seven industries had at their peak employed slightly over 200 students. Less than one-fifth of the students who applied for positions in the seven industries received them. Regardless, those students who did work were able to continue their studies. On a grander scale, the Student Self-Help Industries were truly unique in their structure and purpose. They represented a noble and interesting effort to provide a means for students to pursue their academic goals in the midst of depression.[32]

In 1936 the Student Employment Bureau, headed by A. Frank Martin, was staffed by a full-time assistant to Martin, and eight part-time student employees. At the midpoint of the Depression era, the employment bureau placed over 1,200 students in positions through the self-help industries, NYA program, and in more typical jobs in academic departments and support services. The service also worked closely with local businesses and private homes to help still other students find a means to secure room or board or both, plus a financial income. Martin was charged with administering all of the requirements of the student employment program. Forms to be completed by students were developed and carefully reviewed. In every application for work three references were required: one from the student's high school principal or superintendent, a second from a responsible business person of the local community attesting to the applicant's need for financial aid, and lastly, a letter from a responsible citizen writing about the applicant's character and general standing in the community. Rigid rules set the minimum academic and work standards for students to maintain their positions. All of these activities, plus others, came under Martin's responsibility.[33]

When the demand for jobs increased in the 1930s, loans became a more acceptable and important way for students to help finance their attendance at college. The Lew Wentz loan program continued to grow, and in 1930, four years after Wentz's initial gift to the college, over $100,000 'had been loaned through this program. The average size of a loan was $230, and all borrowers had to be in part self-supporting. Yet problems arose in the student loan program. Improvements needed to be made in both accounting and collection procedures. An administrative attitude prevailed that the loaning and collecting of money was a part-time activity. This attitude caused inconsistency, decentralization, and inefficiency. One study suggested that a full-time financial aid administrator would do much to resolve the problems. This recommendation would be implemented, but not during this particular period of time.[34]

The student loan program, with its successes and problems, provided the additional benefit of being a subtle, but effective instructional tool. Students who received loans were asked to provide feedback on how the administration of the college's loan program could be improved. Arlie L. Tomlinson, a business major, freely stated: "I do believe that in all practicality in all cases of indebtedness that it is much easier to borrow than it is to repay . . . . I found it difficult to repay my loan as I had to buy furniture and other necessities to set up housekeeping." Myrel J. Greenshield's commented, "I suggest loans of a modest amount."[35] After their graduation in 1934 both students had evidently learned a good deal about loans and the fact that loans needed to be paid back.

While assisting the students financially remained an important priority throughout the Depression, other student services, though not as visible, also became firmly established. Probably unknowingly, President Bennett stated a concern of his as well as a philosophy for developing student services on the campus in a 1936 letter. Bennett acknowledged that on a growing campus where department heads and faculty must by necessity be concerned with curriculum and staff, it was important that there be people available who are interested in the student as a "human being rather than as a scholar."

The president observed that the students' personal problems seemed to be the same through all of the academic divisions of the college. "It is, therefore, sound for the college to employ a person primarily responsible for thinking about these problems . . . . Not having a trained psychiatrist, the deans of men and women must of necessity care for much of the mental hygiene work that needs to be done. It is my feeling that as the size of the institution grows and the danger of the individual losing his sense of individual worth and identity increases, special officers must be appointed to contact him for the institution, protect him against the feeling of being submerged in the mass, and devise activities which will promote the development of the well-rounded personality."

Bennett believed that the need to develop a program of student services, coordinated by the two deans of students, was a matter of "growth rather than a preconceived and formally launched plan." In fact, the deans' areas of responsibilities were growing by this time, and Bennett's evaluation of the developments in the student personnel programs at the college were "a step in the right direction, that it met a need, and

Clarence H. McElroy, the first dean of men at Oklahoma A. and M. College, had the unique ability to maintain authority, while being widely admired by both students and faculty. "Dean Mac" often referred to his dean of men's position as "Dean of the Wild Life." Shown on the left with the College Government Committee, McElroy strived for personal contact with students.

that the person selected for the work was of the right type."[36] The individuals who were of the "right type" were Julia E. Stout, dean of women, and Clarence H. McElroy, dean of men.

Dean McElroy was characterized as "always calm and always considerate and seldom severe, except on special occasions . . . . And none do dislike him, and all do honor him, and do try to stay out of his office."[37] With the second longest term of service at the college by 1940, McElroy, who had a degree in veterinary medicine, had served seven years as the dean of the School of Science and Literature (later the College of Arts and Sciences). He would later become dean of the School of Veterinary Medicine. McElroy was respected and liked by former students and others who knew him throughout Oklahoma.[38]

Each spring, when the warm weather caused young men and women to enjoy each other's company out-of-doors, McElroy would write letters to the students reminding them that the college's standards of morality would be enforced, and violators would be subject to disciplinary proceedings. Not only did Dean McElroy enforce all college rules, examine low grades, and approve off-campus rooming houses for male students, he was also the general supervisor of all student activities. Fraternity rush, Freshman Orientation Week, and service on the college classroom assignment committee, athletic council, and the college dean's council were among his multitudinal assignments.[39]

It was also McElroy's job to hear students' appeals for legal furloughs or leaves of absence prior to college vacations. Excused furloughs or absences were necessary to avoid double absences on class attendance records. To students requesting early leaves from campus, the dean's best suggestion seemed always to be, "If you must go, take your cuts."[40]

Thus if the student left early, the departure would be illegal, and the consequences would be theirs to carry.

As Dean McElroy's seniority at the college grew, he also became something of a historical philosopher on campus changes. Once, in reminiscing on the changing times, he reported that methods of teaching and grading papers had varied very little in over three decades of time. Neither had student interests and behavior changed. However, semantics had changed. Where a man "queened or fussed" his girl-friend, he now had dates. Where once the horse and buggy worried college officials, now the automobile was the problem. Yet the same old trails were being used for student hikes and class picnics. McElroy then added, with a delightful sense of humor, "only people with remarkable memories are able to get through this institution. In some departments the teacher says 'Tell us about what is on page 386,' if it's a daily recitation; if it's a test, it's 'Discuss chapter five,' or whatever chapter you are studying; if it's a final examination, you are merely asked to discuss the main features of the book, but they must be discussed fully."[41] As historian, student mentor, and loyal employee, McElroy established himself as the prototype of the dean of men. He had the unique ability to maintain authority, while being widely admired by both students and faculty.

Dean of Women Julia Stout was similarly effective with women students. A campus publication revealed: "She has quiet, simple taste in everything but hats. She likes her hats large like canopies and wild as the spring song of thrushes. But her hair, while awe-inspiring, is cut in a boyish bob, her face, only slightly rugose, has the blush of youth, despite her thirty years as teacher, advisor, and friend to younger women. She wears well-cut clothes of plain, solid colors, a small black onyx on the little finger, and glasses which demand respect."[42] Indeed, Stout went about her work much like McElroy. She was widely appreciated, although her duties were a broad mixing of pleasant and difficult. Some of her earliest ideas and initiatives would remain a part of the Oklahoma State University until contemporary times.[43]

One innovation of Stout's was especially noteworthy, as well as lasting. In 1936 the dean of women implemented a system of guidance and counseling support which was later copied at other colleges and universities. Murray Hall, a huge $450,000 five-story residence hall that housed over 400 women, including all freshmen, presented unique problems. Instead of employing full-time hostesses, usually matronly older women, in staffing the new campus residence hall, Stout employed graduate students on scholarships to work on a half-time basis. Their specific tasks were advising and tutoring students and supervising study hours in the hall. In addition to the six graduate women counselors, a head resident, Maud Latimer, and one undergraduate student proctor for each of the

The "dean of women's deans in Oklahoma," Julia E. Stout (*center*) was the first full-time dean of women at Oklahoma A. and M. College. A farsighted and innovative administrator, Dean Stout served as advisor to every campus women's organization. Shown with her very serious-looking staff of matrons in 1929, the dean and her assistants indeed invoked respect—if not fear!

building's eight wings were hired. An office assistant, responsible for student mail and the telephone switchboard, and five housekeepers, one for each floor, were also employed as additional staff. Finally, in an especially effective move, Vesta Etchinson, the YWCA secretary, lived in Murray Hall. Miss Etchinson advised freshman women and chaired the meetings of the hall counseling staff. Stout later added a theory course for residence hall staff employees as a requirement for working with the counseling positions.[44]

There can be little question that the educational principles incorporated into Stout's Murray Hall staffing scheme were sound. With many variations, her ideas are generally used in residence halls throughout the United States today. At Oklahoma State University, her system, although modified frequently, was implemented in other women's residence halls in addition to men's on-campus housing. Talented, upper-class undergraduate students are still hired to serve as resident or student assistants for every residence floor or wing. The theory class, a requirement of the job, is still taught for academic credit. The principle of close, personal contact with each hall student remains important. The roles of advisor, guide, and sometimes tutor, continue as important functions of the position. The assignment of one housekeeper per floor also remains as another legacy of Stout's innovations in Murray Hall.

Stout was farsighted. She was also a busy professional, always seemingly concerned for the individual student and her general welfare. At one time she served on eleven standing committees of the college, including the housing, social, and loan committees. She was in charge of sorority rush and women's financial aid, constituted primarily of off-campus job placements. Her office inspected and approved the women's living spaces in town, a minimum of two times each year. Stout served as advisor to every campus women's organization. If a campus dance or other activity included women students, the event had to have the prior approval of the dean of women. Stout personally spoke with each woman transfer student, either individually or in small groups, welcoming them and assessing their needs; and she talked individually with every graduating senior woman about her future plans. All students in her charge had a personnel card, which recorded honors, illness, and other anecdotal information.[45]

Like the dean of men's office, Stout's office could offer, in exceptional circumstances, furloughs for women students to leave campus without negative consequences. Stout would personally visit any student with a serious illness and incorporate her findings into a letter to the student's parents. Handwritten cards of congratulations were sent to women who received a special honor. Students with a failing course grade would see the dean about correcting their academic problems. Several times a semester Stout would directly inspect the women's restrooms on campus for cleanliness and any required maintenance that might be needed. In 1933 Stout implemented a program to select the outstanding senior women on campus on the same basis as a longstanding program for men. Achafoa, later Mortar Board, and a Stillwater chapter of the American Association of University Women were other important priorities of Dean Stout.[46] In concluding her 1928 annual report to the college president, Stout wrote, quite accurately, "the duties of the dean of women are so numerous and of such variation, as daily personal conferences concerning health, financial, employment and social problems, group conferences consisting of transfer, senior, and women's organizations, temporary committees, etc. that it seems futile to attempt to enumerate them."[47]

Deans of men and women have always been the brunt of stories by student observer-humorists. Dean Stout was no exception. The 1929 Redskin, under a title of "They Really Said It," purported that the dean had told the freshman women, "Now girls, never say soup when you are with a boy, because it puckers up your lips and makes them want to kiss you." Also, "How can you expect boys to resist you when you paint yourselves up like a stick of candy."[48]

Whether Stout did or did not say these things may never be known. What was known was that the dean of women was responsible for maintaining high moral standards among women students on the campus.[49] The students themselves suggested, "Her manifold duties rival, if not exceed, any other group of assignments on the campus in importance and hard work."[50]

Some characteristics of college students have markedly changed over the years, while others have not. One of those unchanging student qualities was the struggle to choose a college academic major that related to gainful employment. Testimony of early-day career confusion is found in a half-century-old study of freshman and senior students. With the usual limitations acknowledged in such a study, the researchers asked Oklahoma A. and M. students about their courses, career plans, and what services from the college would have assisted them in their efforts to choose an academic major and a suitable career. The findings were similar to results still found among students fifty years later. Over half of the senior student respondents had changed their academic major one or more times. Only one-fifth of the freshmen had done any investigation of their major before enrolling in it. About 40 percent of the freshmen admitted having no knowledge of the career field that they had chosen. Both the seniors and freshmen believed that the college needed a full-time career counselor to help them. The greatest mistakes made by the 1933 freshmen in starting their college careers were lack of attention to their personal work, failure to plan their work so as to avoid taking unnecessary subjects, and the lack of study.[51]

For pragmatic reasons, including the fact that student dissatisfaction with their academic major causes student attrition, a series of career-based activities were undertaken to assist Oklahoma A. and M. students. A 1930 college bulletin, *Vocational Guide*, was written and distributed to prospective high school students.[52] The preface, signed by President Bennett, said forthrightly: "The mission of this institution as a technological college is to aid the youth to find his work and to prepare him for it when he has decided on the career of his choice." Bennett then added in the final paragraph: "Aimlessness in education is a waste; and the chief criticism which can be brought against modern education is its aimlessness."[53] The high quality *Vocational Guide*, with a liberal number of pictures of campus buildings and academic deans, discussed college majors, the professional fields to which they led, and the salaries that could be obtained.[54]

By 1935 free, all-day vocational guidance conferences were regularly held on the campus for high school seniors. Mornings were devoted to a series of speakers who spoke about vocational and career opportunities at the Oklahoma A. and M. College, and in the afternoon small group and individual conferences were held. The high schoolers received various free literature detailing how the college's curricular offerings could meet their career aspirations.[55]

More sophistication was added when Freshman Days—a required orientation program for the incoming freshman class—was held before freshmen were permitted to enroll or begin class work. In the Freshman Days program the courses and training offered by each school were explained "in order that the new student may be enabled to enroll with a better and clearer understanding of the course which he selects." Additional orientation topics included tips on how to study effectively and stay physically healthy, lessons on a student's duties and responsibilities at the college, and information on specific procedures, such as how to complete registration.[56]

To help students choose a college major early and succeed academically, Elmer B. Roger was appointed college examiner and director of admissions. He and his staff examined high school and college transfer transcripts, administered compulsory English and psychological examinations and departmental placement tests, compiled the information, and signed and issued admissions cards to the entering students. The office also did on-going research on how and why students dropped out of school. Departmental grades were maintained, while college entrance scores were collected and compared with actual college grades, thereby attempting to measure student performance. This was in an effort to increase student retention. Dr. Roger's work was pioneering. Modern for the time, these retention studies took place more than half a century ago. As an outgrowth, the Bureau of Tests and Measurements was later established.[57]

Through the worst years of the Depression, campus construction came to a virtual standstill. However, by the midpoint of the 1930s vigorous student recruitment, financial aid programs, and the academic support system began to bring a payoff in bulging enrollments. The small campus and limited physical plant had to be enlarged to accommodate the growth. Given the general economic climate of the state and nation, the massive campus construction program between 1929 and 1941 is impressive, particularly during the five-year period starting in 1936. During this decade Bennett's leadership, the federal government's efforts to stimulate the nation's stagnant economy, and the requirement that students pay a larger share of the cost of their education combined to finance several huge campus structures, such as Murray and Willard Halls. Interestingly, most of the building projects were tied to improving out-of-class student services. Notably few gains were made in enlarging classroom, laboratory, or faculty office space. These parts of the academic environment would typically be a responsibility of the state. Throughout this period the Oklahoma Legislature remained generally passive to the academic needs created by the growing student enrollments in Stillwater.

The one exception had come in 1929. The legislature appropriated $125,000 for the construction and equipping of a college infirmary. No doubt the college's health services needed the hospital. In spite of the college's efforts to provide good health care, four students had died during the year. R. J. Shull, the college physician and primary advocate for an on-campus student hospital, was a busy individual. In the academic year ending in June 1929, Shull had treated 2,640 of the 2,917

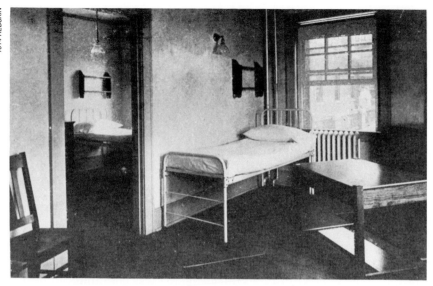

When the Women's Building opened in 1910, a separate room was set aside for a physician to attend to the medical needs of residents (*upper*). In 1925 residence hall sick rooms were abandoned, and health care was offered in a frame house off-campus. Thus, when the Oklahoma A. and M. College Infirmary opened in 1930 (*lower*), the college and students pointed with pride that now a "real" hospital existed on campus. Students could go to the infirmary for dental care and even have their tonsils removed.

enrolled students in his College Avenue cottage infirmary. One student had consulted the college doctor ninety different times. In one of the two semesters, Shull made 1,040 patient visits to students' rooms or residences. Shull had administered 40,000 doses of cold medicine, 20,000 aspirin tablets, and 11 gallons of cough syrup, in 2-ounce containers. After Shull treated 327 cases of flu in a month, he noted that with a true hospital the number could have been reduced by one-half simply because flu victims could have been isolated.[58]

The modern hospital opened for business in 1930. Several hundred fruit trees had been removed to make room for the structure on the then far west side of the campus. The Oklahoma A. and M. College Infirmary was a three-story brick building. The first floor had offices for physicians and a dentist, a reception room, dispensaries, examination rooms, laboratory and X-ray rooms, as well as a staff kitchen and dining room. The second floor was reserved for men students; it had a general office in the center, a ten-bed ward, private rooms, isolation wards, and shower rooms. The top floor was designated for women. The floor also contained an operating room and living quarters for the regular nurses and women's physician. The entire building was connected by an elevator—the first on campus and in Payne County. A special rear entrance was designed for emergency ambulance service. To add a touch of luxury, telephone service and radio connections were installed in patient rooms.[59]

In addition to Shull, Katherine Bergegrun was employed as the first women's physician. H. B. Sherrod became the college dentist. Sherrod's appointment was unique. Aside from colleges with a dental curriculum, the appointment of a full-time college dentist was both innovative and rare in American higher education. The physicians and dentist were supported by a staff of seven nurses and technicians.[60] In the spring of 1931 the *Redskin* proclaimed that "this year was the first when the student body did not have cause to fear the spread of contagious disease."[61]

With the infirmary's opening, a new brand of student health services began. Modern infrared projections were used to reduce muscle pain and soreness. Medical staff used an ultraviolet lamp to administer artificial sunbaths. In the first month, two students had their tonsils removed in the hospital's operating room. Dentist Sherrod saw twenty-five patients in one of his first weeks of activity. The student newspaper noted that "all swollen jaws from now on will be as a direct result of Beech Nut [chewing tobacco] and not tooth ache, if the rushing business of the college dentist, Dr. H. B. Sherrod, is an indication of the trend of student dental productivities." Dental services cost nothing extra as they were a part of the $2.50 medical fee paid by all students.[62]

The college health services were heavily used by the students. From a part-time physician and a graduate student nurse working in cramped quarters off-campus in 1928-1929, the infirmary staff grew to three full-time physicians, one dentist, eight nurses, three secretaries, one cook, and five janitors in just ten years. In the academic year 1936-1937, 1,560 students spent one or more days as a patient in the new hospital, an increase of 300 percent in just three years. It would take time to educate students to the importance of preventing sickness through proper care and hygiene.[63]

Down the street from the college infirmary, at the corner of College Avenue (now University) and Monroe Streets, Murray Hall opened in

Murray Hall, completed in 1935, brought opulence and gracious living for women at the Oklahoma A. and M. campus. Dean of Women Julia E. Stout first employed a system of guidance and counseling at this residence hall which was later used across the campus as well as at other colleges and universities. In looking at the desolate location of the building, it seems almost incongruous that the building today occupies one of the busiest corners (University and Monroe Streets) of the campus.

1935. Built with federal New Deal money, Murray was reportedly the largest single dormitory in the United States. Murray Hall was equipped with modern conveniences such as a buzzer system from the reception desk to individual student rooms, an elevator, regulation United States mailboxes, and two pay telephone booths on each floor. The reception area and adjoining guest parlors lent considerable dignity to the building. Soft-toned draperies and carpets, overstuffed furniture, a baby grand piano, and a grandfather clock brought a new level of opulence to student housing. Margaret West and Margaret Moorehead, representing the combined Gardiner and Thatcher Hall student governments, efficiently served as the hall's earliest student government presidents. Mrs. Maud Latimer was Murray's first staff hostess.[64]

With the opening of Murray and the completion of an adjacent 150-resident structure called North Hall in 1936, all freshmen and upperclass women were required to live in one of the two buildings. Both halls were known as Murray Hall until 1948 when North Hall was renamed North Murray Hall and became a separate entity with its own student government, social program, and staff. With the new housing for women, the Women's Building, renamed Gardiner Hall in 1928, was converted into an academic building. Hanner Hall continued as a male residence, and Thatcher Hall, originally built as housing for women, was renovated and occupied by men in 1935. Thatcher's residents soon became known as the "Thatcher Sissies."[65] Two different *Redskins* added to the "sissies" image by printing:

"Since the boys moved over to Thatcher Hall,
They've experienced a second Adam's fall,
Of course we can see a small connection
With their receiving this cast reflection
Thatcher Sissies

"But we can't decide why in all God's earth
This nomenclature should arouse such mirth,
It seems that in time the fun should wear off,
But the buffoons continue to sneer and scoff
At Thatcher Sissies

"Are we just too dense to get the point
Or is something wrong with the joint?
Oooh, yea - girls' and boys'
Dorms aren't built alike!"[66]

Two even larger residence halls, funded with federal Works Project Administration money, were constructed in 1939 and opened in 1940. Willard Hall, named for Frances E. Willard and lobbied for by the local and state chapters of Women's Christian Temperance Union, was built north of Theta Pond and across the street from Murray and North Murray to house 415 women students. Styled in modern Georgian architecture, the dormitory had a mix of Chinese and Colonial furnishings. With the opening of Willard Hall the west side of campus became the women's side. Margaret E. Smith was hostess, and Virginia Pope was assistant hostess. Wanda Lee Overmiller served as president during the first year Willard Hall opened.[67]

Students of the time, not unlike students of fifty years later, collected a variety of items to decorate and personalize their residence hall "homes." Mabel Converse collected pennants of all variety. Nina Wainwright lined her desk, window sill, and a table with plants. While Harmony Garner covered her room walls with dance programs, Ethel and Verndia Baker collected soap figures.[68]

Cordell Hall was reported to be an adaptation of a Harvard University residence hall and at the time of its 1940 construction was the largest college dormitory in the southwestern part of the nation. Named for Harry Cordell, longtime Oklahoma State Board of Agriculture member, this hall for 530 men was constructed, not accidentally, on the east side of campus immediately west of the football stadium.[69]

When a student journalist who wanted to find out about the new dorm called the hall's president, he received the following description over the telephone: "This is Pale McClain speaking. I am president of the new Cordell Hall, a home for five hundred and sixteen lovely col-

At the time of its construction in 1940, Cordell Hall was the largest college dormitory in the Southwest. At the left, Vernie Potts checks for a letter from home. On the right, Potts visits with Kate Massey, Cordell's first hostess.

lege boys. The living quarters for every two boys consists of a large room furnished with individual beds, desks, chairs, closets, drawers, and venetian blinds. The dining hall located in the basement of the dorm is headed by Miss Betty Stearns, dietician, who is aided by a staff of sixty-five people including part-time student waiters.

"The building is a four-story fire-proof brick structure built in a Southern Colonial design. A spacious living room furnished with leather upholstered chairs and combination piece divans along with three separate anterooms which include a club room, music room, and a library, all of which are furnished with selected period furniture, make an excellent recreation center and lounge for students and guests. Recreation rooms in the basement are available for the more strenuous forms of activity. Mrs. Kate Humphrey Massey, hostess, and Mrs. Stella Stone, assistant hostess, lend the necessary feminine touch.

"The residents of the hall make all their own laws and regulations through the cabinet, which is the legislative body of the dorm. There are twenty-one members on the cabinet. This includes a wing leader from each of the three wings and one floor leader from each floor of each wing.

"I stand before the boys as a shining example of the advantages of being an independent.

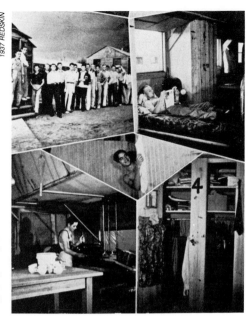

1937 REDSKIN

From 1937 to 1941, Aggie Hall provided "no frills" housing for many Oklahoma A. and M. College students. The men who resided here paid $15 per month for both room and board in the barracks-like facility.

"My pal and buddy, Bob Black, has been vice president during this year. I am the real leader of the bunch. What can I do for you this morning?"

"Nothing now," replied the reporter.[70]

In 1940 the college alumni magazine stated that the completion of Willard and Cordell Halls marked the completion of "a system of adequate housing facilities for the rapidly increasing enrollment at A&M College."[71] In fact, nearly two thousand student residence hall spaces had been built or renovated in just five years. Students were paying under $50 a month for room and board. Still less expensive college housing was available. Aggie Hall was located near the present location of University Apartments and consisted of six buildings which housed thirty men. Aggie Lodge, located on West Sixth Street, provided low cost housing for twenty women. Both residence areas served students from 1937 to 1941 at $15 a month for room and board. Murl Rogers, former OSU Alumni Association director, was just one of many students who was able to complete their education due to the low cost, "no frills" Aggie Hall and Aggie Lodge barracks.[72]

By the early 1940s all freshmen and sophomores were mandated to be in their residence halls by 8 P.M. every week night. In all of the residence halls students were asked, if not required, to be in their rooms from 8 to 10 P.M. on week nights for study hours. More generally, the

If a building could personify a "jack-of-all-trades," clearly this facility could fit the role. At different times this versatile building served as the blacksmith shop, a bookstore, an armory and gymnasium, a home for civil engineering, the campus placement center, and the college cafeteria. When it was finally razed to make room for the current College of Business Administration Building, this structure had become a base for the developing Division of Student Services.

rules covered everything from housing, to automobiles, to serenades. A permanent faculty social committee, sometimes flatly called a censure committee, functioned to review and approve all student plays, exhibitions, parades, and social events. The most unpopular rules were those which closed student events at 11:30 P.M.; curfew was at midnight regardless of whether a student lived in a Greek house, residence hall, or room off campus.[73]

In keeping with the theme of helping students regardless of their ability to pay for their education, the college offered room and board ranging from inexpensive to more expensive rooms with twenty cafeteria meals each week by the beginning of the 1940s. To enhance the room options for students the College Cafeteria, renamed the Tiger Tavern to recognize the Oklahoma A. and M. College Tiger athletic teams, was renovated and continued to serve meals for on-campus employees and guests, plus nearby resident students. Willard, Cordell, and Murray Halls were each built with a completely equipped cafeteria. The combined four on-campus cafeterias could serve 5,000 meals a day. In 1941 Daisy I. Purdy became the first director of the total food units system.[74]

Shortly after Purdy assumed her duties, she was quickly forced to deal with the typical problems encountered when running a food service for college students. Just three months after the start of the academic year a parent wrote President Bennett to express concerns about her son and the food in his residence hall cafeteria. This particular mother wrote: "It has been brought to our attention rather forcefully by our son and various other boys who are living in Cordell Hall, about the food being served there. The food that is served is good and a balanced diet it seems, but the boys are complaining about not having enough to eat."[75] Suggesting, in a kind way, that some action be taken, the mother pointed out that her son, a husky boy with a large appetite, had lost eighteen pounds, or three pounds a week, since the start of the school year. Whether this student's problem was resolved was not part of the record. However, with the growth in size and complexity of the college food units, pleasing all constituents would obviously become a very difficult, if not impossible, task.[76]

Other health-related problems also existed at the college. In 1928 the *Daily O'Collegian* editorialized: "One of the things which is found most lacking on the campus is intramural sports, as all inter-organization and other athletic events outside of varsity sports are called, every year, while this feature at A&M is losing its strength."[77] The following fall two important events happened that would markedly improve intramural programs on the campus.

In September 1929 Agnes Valerie Colvin would begin a significant forty-year professional career at the college when she was appointed to assist Flora May Ellis, director of physical education for women, with the women's athletic program. Coming to Stillwater with degrees earned from Alabama Women's College and Columbia University, the young Colvin would teach physical education classes and be in charge of women's intramural programs in hockey, soccer, basketball, indoor baseball, track, swimming, and tennis. Early in her career Colvin became a pioneer in forming the Oklahoma Athletic Federation for College Women, working to strengthen the college's Women's Athletic Association (WAA), and broadening the opportunities for female students to secure academic credit for participation in activity classes.[78]

At about the same time, T. M. Aycock, a coach in the college's athletic department, was appointed to head the newly-created Department of Intramural Athletics. A five-member administrative board and a constitution governed policies and rules for the new system. In the first year fraternity, dormitory, and specially selected leagues for off-campus students participated in events scheduled through the year in basketball, tennis, golf, cross country, horseshoes, wrestling, football, baseball, and track. Boxing also became a popular intramural sport by the mid-1930s, with large crowds attending the matches between student pugilists.[79]

Although now on firmer foundations, the separate intramural programs for men and women were administered and funded as secondary priorities within the larger athletic and academic departments. Despite Colvin's toiling, athletic facilities for women's intramural sports

A pioneer in women's athletics, Agnes Valerie Colvin served Oklahoma A. and M. College for forty years. Put in charge of women's intramural programs shortly after she arrived on campus in 1929, Miss Colvin diligently strived for improvements in facilities and equipment for sports.

remained under the control of the male-dominated athletic department. Even with the completion in 1939 of the 4-H Club and Student Activity Building, more commonly known as Gallagher Hall, the building was scheduled for classes in the morning and varsity athletics in the afternoons. As late as 1941 WAA events were scattered over campus—in Gardiner Hall, the men's gymnasium, a new gymnasium-dance studio in the basement of North Murray Hall, on playing fields west of North Murray and north of Gardiner Hall, and in bowling alleys in downtown Stillwater.[80]

Other issues, primarily having to do with an adequate budget for intramural programs, surfaced regularly. The student newspaper once publicly asked the intramural board to open their budget books for public review, and then added that if enough money was available, as proclaimed, how was it possible that "the crowds had to be scoured for an umpire; when rude boards had to be used for bases; when the game had to be delayed nearly an hour while suitable catching equipment was unearthed."[81]

On another occasion the newspaper called on leaders of the intramural programs to end intrafraternity football. After several serious injuries, the vigilant editor wrote: "Intrafraternity football steps beyond the mark in the list of clean, healthy, intramural competition. It has no place in college, where its teams are composed of young social lions unaccustomed to the terrific roughness incurred therein."[82]

The public relations-minded administration often distanced itself from the recurring fusses over campus intramural programs. However, unlike intramural programs, a much discussed and slowly started campus placement service was pushed as a viable, important activity.

Seeing the dual long-range gains from a service to assist graduates and former students in finding suitable career employment and cementing alumni organizational attachments to the college, President Bennett took an outline of a proposal for a placement service from the Former Students Association to the Oklahoma State Board of Agriculture. On June 1, 1929, the college Placement Service Bureau was formally established. The college agreed to pay a portion of the costs of the placement plan, with the remainder coming from the Former Students Association. Every college department could use the employment service, and it was free to Oklahoma A. and M. students and alumni. A. Frank Martin opened an office in the Whitehurst Building and served as director of the placement bureau and as secretary to the Former Students Association. A former superintendent of schools in Yale, Martin was an Oklahoma A. and M. graduate and former student leader.[83]

After a successful first year of placing over 250 graduating or former students, the placement bureau was separated from Former Students Association activities. With the separation, A. O. Martin became the first full-time director of placement services. The placement office now moved to Old Central. Through 1941, A. O. Martin had primarily developed a system for educational placement, but a general trend toward placements in business, engineering, and agriculture had also developed. Prior to 1941 the placement bureau assembled over two thousand individual placement files. Placement enrollees could take advantage of twenty-five employment areas. During the Depression the placement bureau served a critical need. To illustrate, in 1936, a turning year for the Depression, all but 5 percent of the college's graduates were able to secure gainful employment. At the time college officials declared the 95 percent placement record a new high for the state.[84]

Ralph Waldo Emerson once said: "Each age has its own follies, as its majority is made up of foolish young people."[85] Through the thirties the Oklahoma A. and M. students went about the campus enjoying social activities, seemingly undaunted by the growing array of change around them. Although never caught-up in some of the stronger, more extreme fads of other college campuses, the Oklahoma A. and M. students did frequently prove Emerson an accurate prognosticator. At the least, the Depression years proved some of the liveliest times in the entire history of Oklahoma's land-grant institution. Student social life and student activities during this time could be characterized as sometimes liberal and conservative, sometimes passive and aggressive, and often both serious and humorous. Just as the Depression itself brought uncertainty, student behavior could also be described as uncertain during these times.

At the start of the decade, both men and women students were consumed by several interesting fads. In 1929 yo-yos could be seen all over campus. Stillwater merchants reported yo-yo sales by the hundreds of dozens. One innovative student made a yo-yo by attaching two phono-graph records to a wooden spool. Still another student welded two metal disks to a short rod to construct his homemade yo-yo. Impromptu yo-yo endurance contests on campus spontaneously attracted large crowds. Still another fad, Coca-Cola, at five cents a drink, was more popular than Dr. Pepper. But neither soft drink was as favored as cherry cokes. The Oasis and Swim's—the two most popular student social refuges—were selling a combined total of 3,285 cokes a week in 1931. At the same time and oddly during the winter months, coeds received permission from the dean of women to enter the campus underground heat line tunnel to "sweat" off some excess weight.[86] About this fad, the superintendent of the college power plant reported, "Not a few hefty maidens have achieved a stylish like form by this method, preferring such physical discomfort to exercise."[87] Freshmen, in their omnipresent beanies, con-tinued to be well versed in campus traditions—especially to stay off campus grassy areas.

Old cars, painted and built to look their worst, with names such as "Question Mark," "Spirit of Aggieland," and "Castouts" were raced between Stillwater and Norman or Tulsa on football game days during the Flivver Derby races. In the 1929 race, it was reported that the "prizes are many, the rules are few" for the twenty-three flivver car entries. Cig-arette smoking was rampant, with Lucky Strikes outselling all other brands. An estimated 89,500 cigarettes were sold annually by the vari-ous stores near campus in 1931, despite the continuing prohibition against the use of all forms of tobacco on the campus itself. Chewing tobacco was also popular.[88] Noting that chewing tobacco could be a campus aid, the *Aggievator*, popular campus humor magazine, reported "what girl will slap her date's face if he is chewing tobacco. Chewing tobacco serves such great purposes as killing flies, putting out candles, curing warts, antiseptic [mouthwash], and dying shirts. No man should be without a chaw."[89]

During prohibition, city and county police raided student functions to look for illegal alcoholic beverages. Occasionally "bootleg" alcohol was found. The Young People's Branch of the Women's Christian Tem-perance Union (WCTU) was active on campus. Among students, opin-ion about prohibition was about evenly divided concerning strict or modified enforcement. Few students thought the law should be totally abandoned. For example, in one informal 1930 poll about prohibition, fewer than 10 percent of the students thought that the best course of action would be to repeal the Eighteenth Amendment which called for prohibition. In a more scientific study, most students were "mildly in favor of prohibition," with freshmen the strongest supporters of the law. Conversely, the assumedly more worldly juniors and seniors were much less in favor of the Eighteenth Amendment.[90]

Nearly every major campus organization sponsored a queen contest, usually as a fund raiser for their activities. Queen kidnappings were commonplace. Though kidnappings were all in fun, the consequences were severe if the kidnappers were caught. In the early thirties, four engineering students who took the Aggie queen from her campus room and held her captive for twenty-four hours were expelled. Eventually there were so many queen contests that there was something of a student revolt; the Women's Self Government Association started the movement by deciding to remain uninvolved with any queen race where money was to be raised.[91]

During the 1930s celebrities Jeanette McDonald and Will Rogers made personal appearances on the campus. Several long-term campus traditions began such as Religious Emphasis Week in 1928, and Varsity Revue and Parent's Weekend, both in 1929. Campus dances continued as quite popular attractions. The annual Military Ball for ROTC cadets and the St. Pat's dance for engineers annually drew huge crowds. Sadie Hawkins dances, where women asked men for dates, were also popular.

A chapter of Mortar Board, national women's honorary organization, was established on November 16, 1940, after a ten-year effort. Blue Key, a men's leadership honorary, was installed on May 18, 1932. An international student talent night, representing talent from ten different nations, was held in 1931. Ittanaha, an ancient Choctaw word meaning "The Council of the Redman," and forerunner to the Native American Student Association, was organized in 1928. In 1939 the name of the Women's Self Government Association was changed to the Association of Women Students (AWS). The name was changed to coincide with the national organization's name, but despite the name change the organization's purposes remained the same. Beyond influencing campus beauty queen contests, the AWS represented all of the enrolled female students in social and administrative matters. The AWS also sponsored campus social activities for women only—sometimes to the chagrin of the men—as well as campus speakers, who would represent women's issues on the still male-oriented and dominated Oklahoma A. and M. campus.[92]

Through much of the decade of the 1930s the student newspaper, by then called the *Daily O'Collegian*, worked to live up to its pledge to "be a palladium of independent and aggressive thinking, neither groveling at the feet of any tin gods or needlessly grinding any under an editorial heel."[93]

In its efforts the newspaper sometimes caused controversy. One noteworthy near-catastrophe occurred when the student writers openly criticized the college band not only for the type of music it was playing, but also because it played too softly at the football games. The newspaper flatly suggested that the band would not fulfill its proper function

Varsity Revue was born out of a *Daily O'Collegian* editorial which chastised the college band's performances at football games. As a result the campus Press Club and band members joined forces to raise money for the purchase of band uniforms. The 1930 rendition, dubbed "Hello World," played to a packed house. Wonder what a sombrero-sporting, banjo-playing musician sounded like!?!

until it became a pep band. Not surprisingly a huge controversy followed which received statewide and national press coverage. The college band went on strike and refused to appear at any game until they received a public apology from the *Daily O'Collegian*. The public apology, along with the announcement of a compromise to resolve the differences between the two important student groups, was printed in an editorial column shortly after the fuss started.[94]

Campus newspaper editorials often indicated trends of the times. Regarding the new talking motion pictures, the student newspaper criticized, "If its the ambition of Hollywood to subjugate the world, let the medium at least be an artistic one."[95] When the newspaper called on the citizens of Stillwater to repeal a law prohibiting showing movies on Sunday, a bitter fight erupted between students and church and civic leaders.[96]

Never shy to take on anything that was seen as an evil, the *Daily O'Collegian* of 1934 advocated changes in the educational system of the college. Modeling the University of Chicago, the students' ideas for reform advocated that the college's role in education was to provide the physical facilities and teachers. The students would then be left to choose for themselves how much of the system they would involve themselves with and when. The plan was based on a desire for more student independence and responsibility. In theory, the newspaper suggested, the 1934 system of unrelated courses and set schedules for study should be replaced by a healthier structure of comprehensive examinations, definite objectives for college courses, and voluntary class attendance.[97]

Ranging far and wide to serve students and "fix" campus problems, the *Daily O'Collegian* protested and suggested solutions frequently. Campus causes of the newspaper included the college collection of a host of incidental fees during registration, a ban on campus organization meetings after 7:20 P.M. during the school week, and the use of belts on freshmen by sophomores during the traditional hazing period at the start of a new academic year. The newspaper admitted having little success when it complained that the professors changed their course textbooks too often. The athletic department was disapproved for scheduling games with small state schools. Leaving no group unscathed, students were also frequently criticized for making "cow-paths" on campus lawns. More success was found in eventually taking a position of minimal newspaper coverage for campus queen contests, advocating that graduate students not be given a representative in the Student Senate, and campaigning to require fraternity and sorority houses to install locks on the doors of rooms. In the latter appeal, undoubtedly two burglaries in Greek houses at about the same time as the editorials on the importance of locked doors moved the *O'Collegian's* cause forward.[98]

With the rapid growth of buildings and enrollment college administrators sometimes failed to maintain efficiency. A 1936 *Redskin* poem presented the students' points-of-view, if not their frustrations, with some of the systems:

"Illumined faces, battered shins,
Mangled bodies, sickly grins,
Patient longing, shattered hopes,
Wiseacre sophomores, ignorant dopes,
Tortured martyrs, eager for knowledge,
Choked with red tape for this is college."[99]

Student registration procedures seemed to be a particular problem area where student anger and sarcasm regularly focused. Because all three major student publications took turns at criticizing or punning the method of registration, all students apparently could relate to the problem. As early as 1930 the *Daily O'Collegian's* managing editor, Ewing Jones, titled an editorial "Antiquated Method" and angrily wrote that "the fact cannot be disputed that the entire system of registration, as employed by the college for the past years, is antiquated, cumbersome, and unsuitable to progress. The ingenious brain that devised such an annoying labyrinth of incoherent red tape probably did not take into consideration the fact that it is possible for the college to expand . . . . It is high time for those in charge to seriously consider the adoption of a more sane type of enrollment."[100]

Because college registration was a nagging, ongoing headache at many institutions of higher education, the Oklahoma *Aggievator* suggested that it was important for students simply to "be tough. Soak your feet in salt water before retiring. The worst argument against being tough is that tough people don't go to Heaven, but don't worry about that. Why, up in Heaven Saint Peter makes you fill out so many registration slips and papers that enrolling here seems like writing your name on the back of a meal check. And you can't waive a thing up there, either. You have to subscribe to everything; take the harp, halo, nightgown and all."[101]

Not to be left out, the 1936 Redskin left among the memories for the graduating class the thought that by September 7, the students would have survived registration. To be graphic, the students were reminded that on that date "the battle started, and with the new efficiency methods installed by experts, headed by Science and Little Dean Scroggs, it was made possible for the lucky enrollees to complete enlistment in the minimum forty days and forty nights of standing at attention, with only 267 reported cases of collapse from fatigue, lack of exercise, insufficient food; 425 suffer from bunions, charley horses, gangrene, dropsy and palsy; 629 developments of delirium tremors, paranoia, manic depression, psychopathic constitutional inferiority, insomnia, slobbering insanity; 83 instances of sleeping sickness; and 2,749 victims of housemaid's knee."[102] Continuing, the student observer of registration procedures remarked: "Okla. A&M College is scattered over 3,597½ square miles of cobblestones when measured by a registering surveyor, especially a freshman registering surveyor, including retakes of familiar multibeaten paths which must be retrodden at least fifty times each for a complete enrollment."

Describing the required fees that the student enrollee would subscribe to before registration could be completed, it was explained that the general enrollment fee was one which "establishes good will between the student body and the administration, provides excellent means of making the college education scholarly and without diversion, creates necessity for writing home more often, stirs up propaganda about a stadium." The library fee "makes possible the purchase of books posterity may sometime have a chance to read, encourages students to run up fines." And the infirmary fee "finances redundancy of red pills, lamp treatments, and a corps of doctors and nurses." Not to be forgotten, the purpose of the miscellaneous fee was to "give prestige to fee slips and the college in general."[103] By the end of the 1930s students apparently had enough. In a student election, three proposed new mandatory fees were defeated. Over two-thirds of the voters rejected compulsory Daily O'Collegian, Redskin, and athletic ticket fees.[104]

As assuredly as no issue on campus was too small to tackle, the student writers were also frank in expressing their beliefs. Harry Long, editor of the Aggievator, brought national publicity to the college and a loud furor from the female students when he decreed that he believed that women lacked originality and had a poor sense of humor. Further, the *Aggievator* editor decreed that he did not want women to work on the comic magazine. Despite the turmoil caused by Long's views, women continued to write for the *Aggievator*. The publication grew and was mailed to all parts of the United States and even to some foreign countries. Long survived the campus uproar resulting from his controversial opinion and was offered a prestigious position as a writer at the RKO motion picture studies in Los Angeles by the editor of the nationally-circulated *College Humor Magazine*.[105]

As a further example of the frankness of the day, *Aggievator* editor Joe Knox noted that student journalists seemed compelled to write a swan song about their tenure of service. While refusing to write a memorial to his service as a journalist on the campus, Editor Knox did express the thought about college editors in general: "It has been a year since he was elected to the office of editor and he has forgotten that he was put into office probably not because of his outstanding ability in journalism but because his political connections were outstanding. And so, to the favored son who has been selected as Second Assistant Custodian of the Emergency Pencil Sharpener, at the grave risk of being labeled a dyspeptic and cynical misanthropic, we take this opportunity to say 'Nuts'."[106] Knox correctly reflected upon the times; student editorships were elected positions and heavily influenced by student political party affiliations.

The *Daily O'Collegian*, *Aggievator*, and *Redskin* were all periodically controversial in the name of student progress. Not to be outdone by the publications, other campus organizations also made their contributions to growth, as well as controversy. The Student Association remained the one organization to which all students belonged. The Student Senate continued as its governing body. Among the senate's responsibilities were the making of rules and regulations for the general student body, sponsoring the homecoming decoration contests, chartering all other student groups, and recommending students for appointment to college committees.[107]

Assumedly to reward student leaders, college officials turned the college over to the students once a year. The officers of the Student Association, Student Senate, and other major campus organizations were afforded the opportunity literally to run the college. This administrator-for-a-day activity was supposed to give student organization leaders insight, and one can assume some empathy, toward the heavily burdened college administrator. The students planned ahead. Obviously when this one day as college president arrived, for example, it would be efficient, if not useful. Interesting actions were taken. In 1939 the College Council, primarily composed of student leaders playing college deans, recommended that one day be set aside for a dance and picnic by each school of the college, that home economics majors be required to take a new

Psychology III course on personal orientation and preparation for marriage, and that a course in spelling be added to the general curriculum.[108] In the same year, Ben McCammon—acting college president—but during the rest of the year Student Association president, ordered: "Effective today, irrelevant of action taken by the State Legislature, all administrative, faculty, and student employees will receive a thirty-three and one-half per cent increase in salary."[109] Meantime, while the students resolved longtime problems, ranging from poor spelling to low salaries, the college administrators spent their day behind the scenes catching up on work, while perhaps simply enjoying the enterprise of the students.

The Young Men's Christian Association (YMCA) and the Young Women's Christian Association (YWCA) continued to serve students through their religious character building and service programs and activities. Like many student organizations, the YMCA and YWCA served all students and accomplished a great deal with only a core group of hard workers. The YMCA published the student directory and the freshman handbook. Both groups had programs to assist incoming freshmen. The "Ys" co-sponsored the Vital Topics Hour, a series of weekly discussions where faculty or Stillwater ministers discussed religion, philosophy, or personal problems. YMCA gospel teams presented programs in nearby towns. The YWCA further enriched college life by sponsoring a variety of discussion groups and a Bible study course. Both organizations co-sponsored the annual Religious Emphasis Week.[110]

The golden anniversary of the Oklahoma A. and M. College was scheduled for December 14, 1941. The fiftieth anniversary of the first student classes was to bring alumni and state notables to campus for a series of events, including dances, a play, open house, and the traditional Founders' Day banquet. President Bennett had been president for thirteen years and was beginning to earn a prominent reputation among educators throughout the nation. Bennett liked to refer to the Oklahoma A. and M. College as the "people's college." The campus Twenty-Five Year Plan was in place; there had been a period of rapid campus expansion, and plans were underway for several more buildings, including a student union. The war in Europe and the Far East presented a distant crisis to the nation, but in Stillwater in December of 1941 attention was directed to the college's past fifty years of service, as well as a future view for the next fifty years. No one could have known that the festivities would be abruptly sabotaged by the Japanese attack on Pearl Harbor on December 7, 1941, only a few days before the birthday festivities were to begin.[111]

The half-century birthday spanned three days of banquets, guest speakers, and ceremonies. In a speech to the assembled student body, President Bennett avoided commenting on the war, cautioning the stu-

On December 14, 1941, Oklahoma A. and M. College celebrated its golden anniversary. While the Japanese attack on Pearl Harbor only a few days earlier dampened the festivities, the college found time to pause to celebrate the past but to contemplate the future. President Henry G. Bennett stressed optimism and reassurance as the key themes for the birthday observance.

dents only to remain in college until called to the nation's service. Bennett's speech was optimistic; the students were reassured that the future would be better. The president then struck a theme that seemed to be a guiding belief. He told the students: "I believe in the unlimited perfectibility of man (physically, mentally, morally, and in other fields not yet approached)."[112]

The intense emotions and reactions caused by Pearl Harbor were captured forever in a chance occurrence involving the preparation for the college's fiftieth anniversary. Professor B. B. Chapman's history class of the fall of 1941 was preparing a two-volume history of the college's first five decades. As a part of the undertaking student leaders of the major campus organizations were asked to write letters to the Oklahoma A. and M. students of 1991. These letters were collected and compiled in the "Record Book." They contained brief student organization histories, statements about the activities on campus in 1941, and well wishes to the future students. Those who wrote after December 7, 1941, were apprehensive about the impending consequences of another world war upon their lives and the nation.[113]

Donald W. Shaklin, president of Hanner Residence Hall, wrote to the students of 1991: "When this letter is opened Carter C. Hanner may be a thing of the past. A victim of the progress of Oklahoma A&M, I hope however, that the type of student and their ideas will not be a thing of the past . . . . For today as I began writing the radio spoke of the Japanese attack upon our outposts in the Pacific Ocean. And now, after stopping for some hours to listen, I finish this letter with the radio telling of the reaction of a war crazy world to this new outbreak of war. As I am a reserve officer I shall soon be called to duty along with others of my friends.

"Among the students in this dormitory too young to have already registered for service there is growing talk of dropping out of school or joining up. That kind of stuff is typical of the stuff which has made the United States and Oklahoma A&M College into what they are today and will be in 1991.

"God willing, I shall be here in December 1991 to be a witness to Oklahoma A&M's progress."[114]

An unidentified student from the Pi Phi sorority soberly wrote: "This letter is being written tonight to those who will be filling our places fifty years hence. Had it been written only three nights sooner, various prominent aspects of the 1941 Pi Phi life which will here be mentioned surely would not be present. For three nights ago we were comparatively care-free, college girls—studying, dancing, quarreling with our boy friends or proclaiming his superbness to all our sisters. But tonight there is a shield of graveness over all our spirited ways. We are now women whose country is at war . . . . Already many of us are knitting for the boys in service, and plans are being laid for further work that we can do. Tonight our meeting was dismissed early so that we could listen to President Roosevelt deliver a message to the nation about our position in the world crisis."[115]

Jess Harris Jr. and David Murray, officers in Sigma Nu fraternity, were more succinct when they briefly pledged: "In this national emergency we gladly lend our lives and efforts so you of the future generation may enjoy that which college life affords."[116] Alpha Kappa Psi President Ed Clemens minced no words when he wrote for the "Record Book": "The students of Oklahoma A&M College and the people of the United States have now but one purpose in mind—to 'set' the Rising Sun and kick HELL out of Germany and Italy in order that you, the students of 1991, may enjoy the privileges and freedom of action that we have enjoyed."[117]

Martha Jean West, president of the YWCA further reflected the campus mood by reporting that the day after the bombing of Pearl Harbor "our student body sat in Gallagher Hall and listened to President Roosevelt as he asked Congress to declare war on Japan. It was a memorable occasion which was so filled with silent emotion that it cannot be described. We have not greeted this war with shouts of joy but rather with prayers on our lips. Our hope is that your world will not be at war."[118]

The gravity of the nation's situation in 1941 cannot be underestimated. Oklahoma's Secretary of State C. C. Childers, in his letter to the "Record Book," provided insight to the intensity of the time. Secretary Childers noted: "This letter is being written at the most momentous hour in the World's history. The entire world is engaged in war and all the children of men are in deep distress. A gigantic struggle to determine whether civilization shall perish and another dark age come upon the world, is taking place." Becoming less philosophical and returning to the students still half a century in the future, Childers then added: "This institution has filled a great place in the life of Oklahoma, and I predict that fifty years hence, long after the smoke of battle has cleared away, the A&M College at Stillwater, Oklahoma will stand forth and shine resplendently in the annals of time."[119]

The toughest days of the Depression having been weathered, the lively and optimistic mood of the campus in the late thirties was suddenly shattered with the new reality of World War II. Student concerns about college policies and procedures, campus politics, and, for many, college itself were largely placed aside. Not surprisingly, most campus problems became relatively unimportant within a matter of hours. Few people could doubt that everyone's life would be touched by the monumental war effort at hand. The day after Pearl Harbor students started volunteering for armed duty. Reserves were called to active duty. Within months Stillwater and the Oklahoma A. and M. College took on a military appearance. The face of the campus changed when tents and Quonset huts were erected for classroom space. Military uniforms could be seen everywhere. Shortages of commodities, normally taken for granted, became commonplace. Not unlike World War I, the focus of the Oklahoma A. and M. College turned toward the total support of the nation's war effort.[120]

# Endnotes

1. Mary Cable, *American Manners and Morals* (New York, NY: American Heritage Publishing, 1969), pp. 353-368; Oklahoma A. and M. College *Daily O'Collegian*, 1 November 1929, p. 1.

2. Joseph A. Stout Jr., "The Will Rogers Project," *Chronicles of Oklahoma*, vol. 51, no. 3 (Fall 1973), p. 356; Cable, pp. 354-356.

3. Cable, pp. 353-368.

4. Cable, pp. 353-368; *Oklahoma Agricultural and Mechanical College Catalog, 1939-1940*, p. 47.

5. John H. Kephart, "A Pictorial History of Oklahoma A. and M. College, 1891-1941" (Master of Science thesis, Oklahoma Agricultural and Mechanical College, 1942), p. 5; *Daily O'Collegian*, 24 September 1930, p. 1; *Oklahoma Agricultural and Mechanical College Catalog, April 1942*, p. 625.

6. Otis Wile, "Brick, Stone, Dreams, and Travail," *Oklahoma State Alumnus Magazine*, vol. 6, no. 1 (January 1965), p. 9.

7. Wile, pp. 6-11.

8. Philip Reed Rulon, *Oklahoma State University—Since 1890* (Stillwater: Oklahoma State University Press, 1975), pp. 219-238; *Daily O'Collegian*, 5 June 1928, p. 2, 30 June 1928, pp. 1-2.

9. *Daily O'Collegian*, 2 July 1928, pp. 1-2, 5 June 1928, pp. 1-2.

10. *Daily O'Collegian*, 30 June 1928, pp. 1, 4.

11. Rulon, pp. 225-228; *1941 Redskin*, pp. 98-99, Oklahoma A. and M. College Yearbook.

12. *1949 Redskin*, p. iii.

13. Haskell Pruett to A. and M. Faculty and Other Employees of the College, 11 December 1935, President's Papers, Special Collections, Edmon Low Library, Oklahoma State University, Stillwater, Oklahoma.

14. Rulon, pp. 225-228.

15. "Increased Numbers and Stability," *Oklahoma A. and M. College Magazine*, vol. 6, no. 1 (October 1934), p. 2.

16. *1935 Redskin*, p. 9.

17. Rulon, p. 245; "A. and M. To Have $450,000 Girls' Dormitory," *Oklahoma A. and M. College Magazine*, vol. 5, no. 7 (January 1934), p. 7; Dave Knox, "New Dormitory Under Construction," *Oklahoma A. and M. College Magazine*, vol. 5, no. 6 (March 1934), p. 5.

18. *1937 Redskin*, p. 191; "Tent City," *Oklahoma A. and M. College Magazine*, vol. 8, no. 9 (May 1937), p. 10; Rulon, p. 249.

19. *Daily O'Collegian*, 13 January 1931, p. 1, 24 February 1931, p. 1.

20. Henry G. Bennett to Dear Friend, 30 June 1941, President's Papers.

21. *Oklahoma Agricultural and Mechanical College Bulletin, April 1942*, p. 624.

22. *1936 Redskin*, p. 218; *Daily O'Collegian*, 14 January 1931, p. 1.

23. *Daily O'Collegian*, 12 January 1931, p. 1.

24. William Edward McFarland, "A History of Student Financial Assistance Programs at Oklahoma State University, 1891-1978, With An Emphasis on the Creation and Administration of the Lew Wentz Foundation" (Doctor of Philosophy dissertation, Oklahoma State University, 1979), p. 44; *Daily O'Collegian*, 13 October 1931, p. 1.

25. *Daily O'Collegian*, 28 October 1931, p. 1, 28 October 1931, p. 1, 4 November 1931, p. 1, 6 January 1932, pp. 1, 4, 28 January 1930, p. 1.

26. *Daily O'Collegian*, 15 February 1931, pp. 1, 3, 20 February 1931, p. 1, 6 March 1931, p. 1, 7 March 1931, p. 1, 8 April 1931, p. 1; *1939 Redskin*, pp. 240-241; *1929 Redskin*, p. 361; *Oklahoma Agricultural and Mechanical College Catalog, 1936-1937*, pp. 44-45.

27. McFarland, pp. 49-50; *1936 Redskin*, p. 218.

28. *Daily O'Collegian*, 13 September 1929, p. 3, 5 April 1930, p. 4; *1930 Redskin*, p. 403; Lawrence R. Thompson, "Poor Boy Gets A Break," *Oklahoma A. and M. College Magazine*, vol. 1, no. 1 (September 1929), p. 19.

29. *1930 Redskin*, p. 403; "Mimeographed Stories July 1, 1929 - September 30, 1929," Weldon Barnes Collection, Special Collections, Edmon Low Library; *Daily O'Collegian*, 27 June 1930, p. 1, 18 July 1930, p. 1; "Student Self-Help Industries, Art and Needlework Department," *Oklahoma A. and M. College Magazine*, vol. 1, no. 2 (October 1929), p. 2.

30. Thompson, p. 19; "Student Industries Are Enlarged," *Oklahoma A. and M. College Magazine*, vol. 1, no. 10 (Summer 1930), p. 7; *Daily O'Collegian*, 6 June 1930, pp. 1, 3; "Mimeographed Stories July 1 - September 30, 1929," 12 January 1930, Weldon Barnes Collection.

31. Robert E. Smith, "The Ceramics Factory at Oklahoma State University," *Chronicles of Oklahoma*, vol. 50, no. 2 (Summer 1972), pp. 205-218.

32. Smith, pp. 205-218; *Daily O'Collegian*, 5 April 1930, p. 4.

33. A. Frank Martin to Prospective Student Employees, [1936], and A. Frank Martin to Deans and Department Heads, 12 October 1938, in President's Papers; *1936 Redskin*, p. 218; *1930 Redskin*, p. 403.

34. "Loans Totaling $106,151 Made From Wentz Fund," *Oklahoma A. and M. College Magazine*, vol. 2, no. 3 (November 1930), p. 92; McFarland, p. 50.

35. "Financial Aid Papers," Student Services Collection, Special Collections, Edmon Low Library.

36. Henry G. Bennett to F. J. Findlay, 22 December 1936, President's Papers.

37. *1940 Redskin*, p. 22.

38. *1935 Redskin*, p. 14; Rulon, pp. 197, 227; *1940 Redskin*, p. 22.

39. *1940 Redskin*, p. 22; *1935 Redskin*, p. 14; *Daily O'Collegian*, 20 December 1929, p. 1.

40. *Daily O'Collegian*, 20 December 1929, p. 1.

41. *Daily O'Collegian*, 15 December 1928, p. 1.

42. *1940 Redskin*, p. 23.

43. *1935 Redskin*, p. 15; *1937 Redskin*, p. 33; Julia E. Stout to Henry G. Bennett, 22 June 1936, Student Services Collection.

44. Julia E. Stout to Henry G. Bennett, 22 June 1936, Student Services Collection; *Oklahoma Agricultural and Mechanical College Catalog, July 1938*, p. xxiii; *1936 Redskin*, pp. 254-255.

45. *1935 Redskin*, p. 15; *1937 Redskin*, p. 33; Julia E. Stout to Henry G. Bennett, 22 June 1936, and Julia E. Stout, "Report of the Department of the Dean of Women," 31 October 1930, pp. 1-8, in Student Services Collection.

46. *Daily O'Collegian*, 12 January 1930, p. 4; Julia E. Stout, "Report of the Department of Dean of Women," 31 October 1930, p. 2, and Julia E. Stout, "Achievements in the Department of the Dean of Women, 1928-1939," pp. 1-4, in Student Services Collection.

47. Julia E. Stout, "Achievements in the Department of the Dean of Women, 1928-1939," p. 4.

48. *1929 Redskin*, p. 399.

49. *1935 Redskin*, p. 15.

50. *1937 Redskin*, p. 33.

51. Ray Blanchard Azeltine, "Determining Factors of a College Education" (Master of Science thesis, Oklahoma Agricultural and Mechanical College, 1933), pp. 44-47.

52. *1936 Redskin*, p. 22; *Oklahoma Agricultural and Mechanical College Bulletin: Vocational Guide*, vol. 27, no. 9 (July 1930), pp. 1-62.

53. *Oklahoma Agricultural and Mechanical College Bulletin: Vocational Guide* (July 1930), p. 3.

54. *Oklahoma Agricultural and Mechanical College Bulletin: Vocational Guide* (July 1930), pp. 29-62.

55. "Vocational Guidance Conference To Be Held March 8," *Oklahoma A. and M. College Magazine*, vol. 6, no. 7 (March 1935), p. 6.

56. *Oklahoma Agricultural and Mechanical College Catalog, 1935-1936*, p. 35.

57. *1936 Redskin*, p. 22.

58. *O'Collegian*, 4 June 1929, p. 1.

59. Mary Louise Stout, "A History and Survey of the Health Services to the Student Body of the Oklahoma Agricultural and Mechanical College Over the Years 1928-1937" (Master of Science thesis, Oklahoma Agricultural and Mechanical College, 1938), pp. 10-11; "May First Marks Use of New College Infirmary," *Oklahoma A. and M. College Magazine*, vol. 1, no. 8 (April 1930), p. 9; *Daily O'Collegian*, 28 September 1929, p. 1.

60. "May First Marks Use of New College Infirmary," p. 9; *1931 Redskin*, p. 36; "Aching Tooth No Excuse," *Oklahoma A. and M. College Magazine*, vol. 2, no. 1 (September 1930), p. 11; *Daily O'Collegian*, 28 September 1930, p. 1.

61. *1931 Redskin*, p. 36.

62. *Daily O'Collegian*, 24 September 1930, p. 4.

63. Mary Louise Stout, pp. 16-30.

64. Dave Knox, "New Dormitory Under Construction," *Oklahoma A. and M. College Magazine*, vol. 5, no. 6 (March 1934), p. 5; *1936 Redskin*, p. 254.

65. *Daily O'Collegian*, 16 January 1929, p. 1; *1929 Redskin*, p. 213; *Oklahoma Agricultural and Mechanical College Bulletin, 1936-1937*, pp. 25-26.

66. *1936 Redskin*, p. 309; *1940 Redskin*, p. 230.

67. *1940 Redskin*, pp. 225-228; Frank Eyler, "A. and M. Students Well Housed," *Oklahoma A. and M. College Magazine*, vol. 11, no. 8 (May 1940), p. 7; "History of the Residence Halls," pp. 1-2, Office of the Dean of Women File, Student Services Collection; *Daily O'Collegian*, 13 December 1941, p. 4, and section 3, p. 2.

68. *Daily O'Collegian*, 13 December 1941, section 3, p. 3.

69. Eyler, p. 7.

70. *1940 Redskin*, pp. 234-235.

71. *Oklahoma Agricultural and Mechanical College Bulletin: Aggie Halls*, vol. 35, no. 7 (July 1938), pp. 1-4; *Stillwater NewsPress*, 25 May 1986, pp. 1, 5.

72. Eyler, p. 7; *Oklahoma Agricultural and Mechanical College Bulletin, July 1937*, pp. 26-27; *Stillwater NewsPress*, 25 May 1986, pp. 1, 5.

73. *Daily O'Collegian*, 13 December 1941, section 2, pp. 1, 5.

74. J. E. Hudgens to Henry G. Bennett, 1 November 1941, and Henry G. Bennett to J. E. Hudgens, 7 November 1941, President's Papers; Fountain Brower, "Tiger Tavern," *Oklahoma A. and M. College Magazine*, vol. 3, no. 2 (November 1931), p. 9.

75. J. E. Hudgens to Henry G. Bennett, 1 November 1941, President's Papers.

76. Daisy Purdy to Henry G. Bennett, [November 1941], and J. E. Hudgens to Henry G. Bennett, 1 November 1941, in President's Papers.

77. *Daily O'Collegian*, 26 September 1928, p. 2.

78. Sports for Women, "Mimeographed Stories July 1 - September 23, 1929," Weldon Barnes Collection; Sharon Mae Holmberg, "Valerie Colvin: Pioneer Physical Educator in Oklahoma," (Doctor of Education dissertation, Oklahoma State University, 1978), pp. 31-32; *Daily O'Collegian*, 15 September 1929, p. 3.

79. Department of Intramural Athletics, "Mimeographed Stories, October 1-30, 1929," Weldon Barnes Collection; *Daily O'Collegian*, 10 October 1929, p. 3; *1935 Redskin*, p. 218.

80. Record Book Committee, compiler, "Selections from the Record Book of the Oklahoma Agricultural and Mechanical College, 1891-1941. Compiled on the Occasion of the Fiftieth Anniversary of the Founding of the College," vol. 2, p. 218; Holmberg, pp. 34-35. In 1988 Gallagher Hall was re-dedicated as the Gallagher-Iba Arena.

81. *Daily O'Collegian*, 19 May 1931, p. 2.

82. *Daily O'Collegian*, 1 November 1930, p. 2.

83. *Daily O'Collegian*, 25 June 1929, p. 1, 7 June 1929, p. 1; *1931 Redskin*, p. 131; Mary Frye, "The Development of Leisure Services and Campus Recreation at Oklahoma State University," February 1986, p. 2, unpublished manuscript, Student Services Collection.

84. *Daily O'Collegian*, 13 June 1930, p. 1; *1936 Redskin*, p. 219; *1941 Redskin*, p. 100.

85. Cable, p. 377.

86. *Daily O'Collegian*, 19 September 1929, p. 1, 10 January 1931, pp. 1, 4, 12 April 1929, p. 1.

87. *Daily O'Collegian*, 12 April 1929, p. 1.

88. *Daily O'Collegian*, 21 November 1929, p. 1, 22 November 1929, p. 1, 26 November 1929, p. 1, 15 February 1931, p. 1, 31 March 1931, p. 1, 14 December 1941, section 3, p. 1.

89. *Oklahoma Aggievator*, no volume, "Pansy Number," (May 1933), p. 4.

90. *Daily O'Collegian*, 14 March 1929, p. 2, 18 January 1931, p. 3, 18 May 1930, p. 1; Margaret Louise Daniel, "The Social Attitudes of College Students" (Master of Science thesis, Oklahoma Agricultural and Mechanical College, 1933), p. 24.

91. *1941 Redskin*, p. 102; "Aggie Day-Queen Kidnapped; Four Expelled," *Oklahoma A. and M. College Magazine*, vol. 11, no. 9 (May 1931), p. 266; *Daily O'Collegian*, 25 September 1930, p. 2, 24 April 1931, p. 1, 22 September 1931, p. 1.

92. *1939 Redskin*, p. 56; "Organizations," 10 October 1929, pp. 1-2, and News Releases, 9 April 1929, 5 November 1929, and 12 November 1929, in Weldon Barnes Collection; *Daily O'Collegian*, 8 November 1929, p. 1, 6 February 1931, p. 1, 27 February 1931, p. 1, 5 May 1939, p. 4, 14 December 1941, section 3, p. 1; *1930 Redskin*, p. 146; "Mortar Board Installed," *Oklahoma A. and M. College Magazine*, vol. 12, no. 4 (January 1941), p. 6; *1941 Redskin*, p. 311; *1935 Redskin*, p. 115; "On the Campus," *Oklahoma A. and M. College Magazine*, vol. 2, no. 5 (January 1931), p. 150; *1941 Redskin*, p. 342; *1935 Redskin*, p. 24; *1949 Redskin*, p. 26.

93. *Daily O'Collegian*, 26 January 1932, p. 2.

94. *Daily O'Collegian*, 29 September 1929, p. 2, 2 October 1929, pp. 1-2, 4 October 1929, p. 2.

95. *Daily O'Collegian*, 17 February 1929, p. 2.

96. *Daily O'Collegian*, 16 October 1930, p. 2, 29 October 1930, p. 2, 11 December 1930, p. 6, 13 December 1930, p. 1; *1941 Redskin*, p. 102.

97. *1934 Redskin*, pp. 218-219.

98. *Daily O'Collegian*, 26 January 1932, p. 2.

99. *1936 Redskin*, p. 304.

100. *Daily O'Collegian*, 25 January 1939, p. 2.

101. "Editorial," *Oklahoma Aggievator*, no volume, "Pansy number" (May 1933), p. 4.

102. *1936 Redskin*, p. 304.

103. *1936 Redskin*, p. 305.

104. *Daily O'Collegian*, 11 May 1939, pp. 1, 3.

105. *1931 Redskin*, pp. 176-177; *1932 Redskin*, pp. 214-215.

106. "Aggievator," *Oklahoma Aggievator*, no volume, "Exam number" (May 1936), p. 1.

107. *1934 Redskin*, p. 24.

108. *Daily O'Collegian*, 21 April 1939, pp. 1, 4.

109. *Daily O'Collegian*, 21 April 1939, p. 1.

110. *1935 Redskin*, pp. 234-235; *Oklahoma Agricultural and Mechanical College Catalog, 1936-1937*, pp. 38-39.

111. Record Book Committee, compiler, vol. 1, Appendix B, pp. 1-5; *Oklahoma Agricultural and Mechanical College Catalog, 1940-1941*, p. 1; *1941 Redskin*, p. 2.

112. *Daily O'Collegian*, 16 December 1941, p. 1; "Fiftieth Anniversary Observed," *Oklahoma A. and M. College Magazine*, vol. 8, no. 4 (January 1942), pp. 2-3.

113. Record Book Committee, compiler, vol. 2, pp. 282-296.

114. Record Book Committee, compiler, vol. 2, pp. 282-296.

115. Record Book Committee, compiler, vol. 2, pp. 282-283.

116. Record Book Committee, compiler, vol. 2, p. 262.

117. Record Book Committee, compiler, vol. 2, p. 289.

118. Record Book Committee, compiler, vol. 2, p. 216.

119. Record Book Committee, compiler, vol. 2, pp. 275-276.

120. Carolyn Gonzales, "OSU's Sixth Decade: A World War Brings Sudden Maturity," *Oklahoma State University Outreach*, vol. 57, no. 2 (Winter 1985), pp. 2-6.

# 6 Ten Years in Pursuit of Unlimited Perfectibility

During the 1940s the Oklahoma A. and M. College would be consumed by war and then experience startling postwar growth; President Henry G. Bennett would seize every opportunity to move his college toward providing students new ways to achieve their own perfectibility. By 1951, Bennett's Twenty-Five Year Plan for the campus would be largely completed. The president himself would become the highly respected dean of the nation's land-grant college presidents. Nationally and internationally, Bennett would be proclaimed an educational missionary and a worker for world understanding and peace.

By the time of the onset of World War II, Stillwater boasted of paved highways leading in and out of the city, one weekly and two daily newspapers, and a new city hospital and library. Excluding students, Stillwater's population numbered about 11,000 citizens. Four theaters, three golf courses, and four lakes were enjoyed by students and residents. The quality of life was further enhanced by five city parks and playgrounds, encompassing fifty acres of land.[1]

Prior to the bombing of Pearl Harbor the Oklahoma A. and M. College had graduated 11,196 students and had grown in enrollment to over 6,000. The majority of students still required financial help to attend college. By 1941 the Lew Wentz Foundation had loaned 1,380 students $333,425 over its fifteen-year history. The college's business offices were using IBM machines for test scoring, registration, enrollment, and accounting. Sixty-eight percent of the sophomore class believed that the feminist movement had gone too far, and two months before the nation's entry into World War II, 95 percent of the students responding to a campus poll were against war on Japan or Germany. More specifically,

40 percent of the students favored doing no more than preparing against an invasion attempt on the United States.[2] Student John March suggested, "We should wait till war is absolutely inevitable."[3] March's inevitable came all too soon. As a result, the face and priorities of the college would be changed forever.

A December 1941 editorial in the *Daily O'Collegian* bore the headline: "Here We Go Again." The writer thoughtfully made the case that there was only one course of action, whether one had been a pacifist, non-interventionist, or activist. Japan had caused the nation to unite. The only possible response was to fight to a victory.[4] While the December editorial was reflective, two months later a second editorial titled "War and Education Don't Mix Very Well" appeared. Writer Sammy Batkin complained that the war had caused prices to rise, student income to drop, shortages to be taken for granted, and the rationing of essentials to be necessary. He continued that government financial aid had been cut sharply and "money meant for school buildings goes for armaments . . . paper meant for learning goes for fighting purposes." Although the current circumstances did not seem to make much sense to Batkin, he counseled himself and his peers that they must trust and accept for there was a promise that out of the chaos and hardship of war "will evolve a golden era of education free to all."[5]

The war would linger for four long years. The *A. and M. College Catalog* of April 1942 stated that the Oklahoma Agricultural and Mechanical College subscribed to the basic policy that an institution of its traditions, objectives, and nature should maintain high adaptability to current social needs. "The overwhelming social need of today is to win a decisive victory in the war that has been thrust upon us."[6] In words and action President Bennett moved the college in an all-out attempt to support the nation's war effort.

In the Pacific war zone Curtis J. Haldridge, graduate of 1940, became the first Aggie hero of World War II. Lieutenant Haldridge was awarded the Distinguished Flying Cross for valor after piloting his bomber in a successful attack which sank several Japanese vessels. Nicknamed "Red Dog" by students, Haldridge had taken his first flying lesson eight months before his heroic encounter with the Japanese Navy. This event occurred about one month into the war.[7]

On the campus, military requirements had been accepted with "negative resignation" before Pearl Harbor. Where once military activity was a fad and students complained about the "Bull" and griped about marching to Boomer Lake, a new seriousness set in. As described in the *Redskin* there was "no more yelling about being forced into something, no regrets that the rest of their education would be postponed, not much outward show of hurt of leaving 'here'—only one thing to do now. Preparation and training are necessary for the job ahead."[8]

During World War II, over 37,000 men and women trained on the Oklahoma A. and M. campus in twelve separate military programs. With a sense of purpose and duty to country, this group of WAVES (Women Appointed for Voluntary Emergency Service) march through the streets of Stillwater. The WAVES trained for various clerical jobs.

Along with the attitude change found in the ROTC program, everyone else's lifestyles were altered by World War II events. All men between the ages of eighteen and sixty-five were mandated to register for possible draft into the armed forces. Henry Clay Potts headed a committee which collected 15,000 pounds of scrap metal. The Young Women's Christian Association (YWCA) launched a campaign to collect nylon and silk hosiery to be used for parachutes and powder bags. Student organizations sponsoring dances used their profits for purchasing United States Savings Bonds. Nearly a thousand students signed up for the voluntary civilian draft, pledging to serve if needed in such units as the auxiliary police, demolition crew, and decontamination corps.[9]

Eventually the college's academic year was placed on an accelerated schedule of three semesters each year with shorter vacation breaks. The goal was to permit a student to graduate in three years, rather than the usual four. Students became more serious in their purpose. Fewer failing grades were recorded in the registrar's office during the war years. Conversations among students were as likely to be about the issues of the day as they would be about proms and dating. Significantly, enthusiasm for campus politics lessened considerably. Rationed rubber tires and gasoline for automobiles had an impact on students' comings and goings. Tents and Quonset huts erected for additional classroom space sprang up on campus. By the war's end 37,523 military women and men trainees, from twelve separate programs, came to the campus to receive at least a part of their preparation for military service.[10]

The Oklahoma A. and M. College students adapted to the military environment. By May 1942 every student eighteen years of age or older had to register for a sugar ration book. Four stamps secured one pound of the scarce commodity. At the same time the campus residence halls were being converted for use by military trainees. Plans were also developed to use the college's three largest halls—Willard, Cordell, and Murray—as military hospitals in the event of bombings. Within these buildings the civilian wounded of the Stillwater area would be cared for. Rules were established that gave military formations on campus and city streets the right-of-way over civilian automobile traffic. Failure to stop a car to permit a military unit to pass could lead to arrest.[11]

Before the end of the 1942-1943 school year it had been clear that there would soon not be enough men in any fraternity to maintain an organization, let alone pay the mortgages and other financial obligations of the chapters. In a stroke of genius, nine fraternities entered into a mutual agreement with the college. The college consented to use the fraternity houses for the duration of the war to house women students. This freed the on-campus residences for military trainees. The fraterni-

Campus coeds actively supported the World War II effort by contributing to scrap metal drives and purchasing savings bonds. These young women proudly hold pictures of some of the Oklahoma A. and M. students who were serving in the military.

ties also agreed to suspend chapter activities including all pledging. In exchange, the college would provide upkeep to the fraternity property and pay rent for the use of the chapter houses.[12]

In May 1943 the first six fraternities rented their houses to the college. Pi Kappa Alpha house was the first, and during the remainder of the war it was renamed Victory Hall No. 7. Pi Kappa Alpha had been installed in March 1939, had 150 members at the outbreak of the war, but three years later had only one active member still on campus. In a short time the Sigma Nu house was Victory Hall No. 5, and the Lambda Chi Alpha house was Victory Hall No. 9. Every other fraternity on campus suspended its programs by the start of the fall semester of 1943.[13]

Despite the changes and hardships, students generally supported the nation's war effort. Unlike students on campuses in other parts of the country, the Aggie students expressed a near unanimous belief that conscientious objectors should at least be assigned to a non-war task.[14] Three consecutive Redskins were dedicated to war-related themes. In 1942 the college annual was called the "American Issue," dedicated to "those who will carry the torch of humanity and replenish the flame of freedom and love."[15] The Aggies in the military were praised in the 1943 Redskin dedication, and the following year all on-campus Naval and Army trainees were honored.[16]

At the start of World War II the sale of marriage licenses increased dramatically in the Stillwater area. The availability of Coca-Cola syrup

By 1945, World War II had almost ended. Still, the bustling Campus Corner had a "military" look.

and bottled Coke, the students' favorite soft drink, fell by 50 percent. Nonetheless, typical-aged college students and military trainees seemed to blend together, prompting the *Daily O'Collegian* to suggest that the military types considered themselves "alumni" of the institution. This was perhaps not surprising since at the peak of activity some local residents believed that the college might be closed to civilians.[17]

Given the magnitude of the worldwide conflict, it is noteworthy that only 232 Oklahoma A. and M. College students and former students lost their lives. These students were among 6,017 former students and 113 faculty and staff who served in the military during the conflict. The college's War Records Committee, headed by Dean C. H. McElroy, reported that former Aggies served and fought from Pearl Harbor to Berlin, from Iceland to Iwo Jima. Former students received a total of 2,411 decorations, including 200 Purple Hearts, 164 Distinguished Flying Crosses, and 80 Silver Stars. Among the total were 905 foreign decorations. Of the 6,017 who served, an impressive 4,510 were officers. Outstanding military alumni, among others, were General Patrick J. Hurley, Brigadier General George P. Hays, and Rear Admiral Joseph J. Clark.[18]

As President Bennett had expected, World War II spawned new demands upon the college. Increased veteran's enrollment was felt by December 1944, when over 500 former G.I.s, many of them married, were in classes. Among other shortages, housing was a particular crisis. Subsequently, application was made to the Reconstruction Finance Corporation to secure money to build married student housing. By 1947 Oklahoma A. and M. had a veteran's housing complex valued at more

Although Veteran's Village never offered luxurious living, it did provide homes for returning G.I.s and their families. The feeling of community that pervaded the Village made residents quickly forget the lack of facilities. Whether a family lived in a hutment (*left*) or a trailer (*right*), most residents agreed that it is never too late to stop for a chat with neighbors.

than $4 million. In an effort to solve the immediate need for married family housing, the college purchased surplus temporary housing from the military. From Kansas, Texas, Louisiana, and Oklahoma came 178 trailers, 410 apartments, and 693 hutments. Still, 700 requests for such housing could not be filled by 1946.[19]

Early records indicated that John Adees of Elk City was the first to apply for space in the new veteran's housing complex. However, on January 28, 1946, Mr. and Mrs. Leonard West were the first residents. The Wests moved to a trailer at number 9 Osage. The housing complex, logically called Veteran's Village, soon became a rich and colorful chapter in the Oklahoma A. and M. College's history. By 1949, this new Oklahoma town sprang up in one square mile of former cow pasture, with 1,290 housing units and 5,000 residents jamming the area.[20]

In the Veteran's Village commissary, hamburger cost thirty-one cents a pound, a can of spaghetti and meatballs nineteen cents, and a pound of Polar Bear coffee thirty-one cents. The new complex eventually opened its own post office, a laundry, dispensary, fire station, recreation hall, and three nurseries for children. A mayor council form of government, with council members representing twenty-two Veteran's Village precincts, was organized on March 29, 1946. John Kelly was elected as the first mayor, and Clifton J. Byrd of Sallisaw served as vice mayor. Later Village mayors included Melvin Berger, Walter Skaggs, Robert J. Brown, and Willis J. Wheat. In the fall of 1946 Robert Kelley became the first fire chief. The J. W. Mooney Memorial Recreation Center, named for a former student and head of the Village maintenance department who passed away in 1948, was opened as an unnamed build-

1949 REDSKIN

SPECIAL COLLECTIONS, OSU LIBRARY

"Watch out for tattletale gray! No worry. I always use Super Suds at the Village Laundry." (*left*) While shopping with mom at the Village Commissary, (*right*) one young Village resident seems concerned that he might not get home with his oatmeal!

ing a year earlier. The college employed John A. Stevens as the Village manager in August 1946. Val J. Connell had preceded Stevens, but lasted only a short time in the job. The first of many babies born to residents was Mildred Lucille Bronker, who arrived on February 23, 1945. Mr. and Mrs. Gladden Bronker were the parents of the "Virginia Dare" of Veteran's Village.[21]

Although a planned community, conditions in the Village were initially primitive. Engineers, who served in the war, named west section streets for Pacific islands and east section streets with French names. Hastily constructed sewers would frequently stop up. Heavy rains would turn the Village's roads to mud. The unattractive and minimally functional hutments had half-inch plywood walls and no insulation. Leonard Soloman, who later retired as director of the Oklahoma Conservation Commission, reported that he once watered an ivy plant, left the plant two feet from his hutment stove, and awakened the following morning to find ice on his plant. The original Village fire truck was a handpumper on a four-wheel cart pulled by a tractor. Electricity to the Village was such that no irons or hot plates could be used except from 9 A.M. to 5 P.M. No light bulbs over forty watts were permitted. Kerosene for the heating stoves was supplied and stored in drums next to each dwelling. All electric refrigerators brought a fifty cents per month additional charge to the rent bill. Residents were warned that if they left the Village for an extended period during cold weather they were to cut off their water and drain all pipes and the hot water tanks.[22]

President Bennett took great pride in Veteran's Village. Politicians often visited the Village to speak in the Mooney Recreation Hall. Bennett himself frequently spoke about the project in the community and over the radio. With time the Village matured. At different junctures the veterans published two different newspapers, the *Home Base News* and the *Village Times*. Often because of adversity, sharing became a way of life among the residents. Wives who were going to classes or working depended on each other to help with child care, shopping, and laundry.[23]

Former OSU track coach Ralph Tate summed up this comradeship and mutual support when he said: "We were in the same boat, so we kind of paddled together. If an emergency came up there was always a place where you could turn."[24] The veterans and their families were a determined group. Often survivors of hasty marriages, sudden departures from home and friends, extensive travel, living in strange places, and raising children during a depression and a war, the Village's residents were willing to do whatever was necessary to complete a college degree.

The veterans became a major force on campus. A Collegiate Veterans Association was formed. A regular column called "G.I.'s, Gabs, and Leathernecks" appeared in the *Daily O'Collegian*. The vets participated in intramural programs, entered floats in the homecoming parade, and even chose their own homecoming queen. Less than two years after the war ended, the Oklahoma A. and M. College enrollment had grown to 11,882 students. About half were ex-service men. Forty-three "semi-permanent" Quonset style buildings were erected to serve as additional classrooms, laboratories, and offices. In the fall of 1946 one enrollment line extended several campus blocks and started forming at five o'clock in the morning. The term veteran did carry a negative connotation for some traditionally-aged undergraduates, but all in all the attitude on the campus was good will and contentment.[25]

For the Aggies who had been on the campus during the war, there was a thrill at being a part of a once again active and progressing institution. Oklahoma A. and M. athletic teams helped to excite and unify the growing heterogeneous student body. In 1945, within a three-month stretch, Aggie athletic teams won national championships in football, basketball, and wrestling. From 1945 through 1946 student athletes like Bob Fenimore, Bob Kurland, Neill Armstrong, Ralph Tate, and David Arndt helped to string together fifteen months of unprecedented sports achievements. These accomplishments included Cotton Bowl and Sugar Bowl wins, two consecutive national basketball titles, and a national wrestling championship. At the same time, in the truest meaning of the phrase student-athlete, Kurland, Fenimore, Tate, and Armstrong, among others, were elected by other students to significant campus leadership positions in the Student Association.[26]

By the mid-1940s students enrolled from every state in the nation and from many nations of the world. As a result student out-of-class activities grew and abounded in variety. The annual Howdy Dance, held at the start of each new academic year, drew overflow crowds. Every residence hall, sorority, and fraternity usually held two formal dances a year. Hayrides, picnics, and steak fries were popular in the fall and spring social schedule. More informal events included sock hops, house parties, scavenger hunts, and square dances. Tennis and golf were popular informal sports. The all-girl Coed Prom, with skits, costumes, and prizes, continued to be a major annual event, so large it was held in Gallagher Hall. Sadie Hawkins Week, where girls paid all bills, held the doors for men, and asked for dates continued its long tradition of forcing "backward" behavior.[27]

During this era Allied Arts programs were organized into an A and B grouping—a popular series and classical-variety series. In 1948 Fred Waring and his Pennsylvanians played to an audience of 8,000 people. A year later Woody Herman, Nat "King" Cole, Victor Borge, and Spike Jones, with his Musical Depreciation Review, played on campus. In 1950 Eddie Cantor and Duke Ellington were part of the Allied Arts menu. The following year the Ames Brothers appeared with Guy Lombardo and his Royal Canadians. A month after Lombardo was on campus, Louis Armstrong, with his jazz band of six members, including Jack Teagarden, Cozy Cole, and Earl Hines, played to an appreciative overflow crowd in the field house. Armstrong's concert ended abruptly when he realized that there was a 10:30 P.M. curfew for Aggie coeds.[28]

The singularly most important campus dance of each year was the annual Junior-Senior Prom. Tickets were sold to non-dancers for balcony viewing in Gallagher Hall's permanent seats. The basketball floor wore to the feet of between 1,700 and 2,200 couples each year. The turnout of students, both dancers and watchers, enjoyed the big band sounds of the likes of Harry James, Tommy Dorsey, and Sammy Kaye.[29]

The college could boast of several quality dance bands of its own. Probably the most noteworthy was the Varsitonians. Bob Convert, a trombonist, was the band's leader during this time, and the vocalist for the group was Alyce Reed. By 1950 the Varsitonians had been a part of campus life for eighteen years and were a source of gainful employment for its fifteen or more members. Playing throughout the Southwest, the band once had a nationally broadcast run of thirteen weeks on the Mutual Broadcasting radio network. Closer to home, the group played for the

In 1948 an Allied Arts program featured the big-band sounds of Fred Waring and his Pennsylvanians who played to an audience of 8,000 in the field house.

Centennial Histories Series

1949 and 1950 Varsity Revue shows, at Howdy Dances, and campus group-sponsored events. Other campus musical groups included the Sammy Robertson Orchestra and Jimmy Baker and the Collegians, once dubbed America's best college band by *Downbeat Magazine*.[30]

In addition to weekend movies shown on campus, local theaters included the new Leachman Theater, which opened on June 22, 1948, the Campus, Mecca, and Aggie. A drive-in theater south of town was being planned for 600 cars just as the Leachman opened for business. Motion pictures were an important social activity for the students. The stars of the time included Humphrey Bogart, John Wayne, Van Johnson, Betty Grable, and Dan Daily. Before and after the movie student hangouts included Ralph Jackson's Y-Hut, Tiger No. 3 (formerly Pearson's Drug), McCaffree's Campus Drug, and the Coffee Shop on Washington Street. Brock's Frat Shop was a Greek hangout. Other heavily frequented spots included Bud and Sue Andrews' Breadbasket and Van Horn's College Drug, located on Knoblock near Williams Hall, now the location of the Seretean Center and the Campus Fire Station.[31]

Through the late 1940s the students debated in the campus newspaper whether they would remain the Aggies or become the Cowboys. The *1950-51 Student Handbook* suggested: "The tradition of the term 'cowboy,' that is in the process of being established here, will connote those characteristics of the cowboy of the old west who exemplified such virtues as loyalty, courage, perseverance and chivalry."[32] Meanwhile other traditions such as freshman hazing continued; involuntary haircuts, wearing orange beanies, and greetings of "Howdy" were but part of the annual fun. High school and prep school letter sweaters and jackets were prohibited.[33]

Student spirit and national publicity peaked during the days of student walkouts or holidays. Dating to the Fenimore-Kurland so-called "golden era of sports," student walkouts were a student self-proclaimed "victory holiday demonstration." The unplanned student vacations were originally spontaneous. Later the student government attempted to plan the holidays in an effort to somehow control mob behavior. The walkouts always disrupted classes, frequently caused injury, and almost always damaged campus property. For students, the boycott of classes and rules was a source of fun, providing a means of letting off steam and showing school spirit. For administrators they were simply a headache. In October 1948 an aborted walkout caused $3,000 worth of damage to Murray Hall, and six students were expelled from school. At times fire hoses and Oklahoma Highway Patrol officers were brought to campus to reinforce normal security efforts. In one reported incident a college professor, after refusing to dismiss his class involved in taking an examination, was literally carried from his classroom—chair, papers, and all—and set down on the sidewalk outside his building. The teacher just remained there and returned to grading and recording his tests.[34]

Not everyone favored the walkouts. The G.I.s, largely older with different priorities, considered the walkouts an interruption which interfered with their education. In a 1951 walkout about 1,500 people, including the college band with their instruments, marched about the campus yelling, clanging cow bells, beating on tubs, and blowing horns. On this occasion a resulting newspaper article headline noted ''Faculty Stands Fast Against Walkout Mob.'' Nonetheless the walkouts remained a nagging problem to college officials and student leaders alike.[35]

Other major student problems of the time included student parking on campus and the price of having clothes commercially dry cleaned. The ''Aggie Baggie'' strike of Stillwater cleaning establishments—a movement for lowering cleaning prices—was backed by every major student organization. In 1948 the Cleaner's Association charged the effort was communist-backed.[36]

While parking, walkouts, and cleaning prices stirred emotions, the post-World War II threat of the Soviet Union's, buildup of nuclear weapons did not. Most students polled about the atomic bomb in 1949 confessed that they had not given it much thought.[37] World War II veteran and Cordell Hall head resident L. C. Thomas said: ''I don't think the Russians have the atomic bomb. The propaganda they do is just another attempt to upset the American people into playing into their hands.''[38] Joe Collier, a 1946 sophomore, simply philosophized: ''I think the best thing to do is to drop it, not the bomb, but the idea.''[39]

During the postwar years, rules and regulations continued to be implemented. Fraternities and sororities were prohibited from entertaining groups of men and women without special permission from the dean of students' office. Any social event with men and women present required chaperons, with a minimum of two married members of the faculty always included. Chaperons were informed by the Committee on Student Activities of their appointments and their responsibilities for student conduct, decorum, dress, and for closing dances or other student events. Student organizations were required to end their meetings by 7:20 P.M. Freshmen and sophomores missing any class were mandated to present their instructor a written, signed statement explaining their absence. In town, rooms could not be rented to both men and women in the same house. Any female student under the age of twenty-one had to reside in a residence hall or sorority house. Finally, women students wishing to leave Stillwater were required to have written permission from their parents. Still some years from equality of rules or equity between sexes, the rules generally tried to control the comings and goings of the coeds. At least in part, and not uncommon in higher education, the thinking was that if the women were in their halls or houses, the men would soon retreat to their own places of residence.[40]

Campus humor in the print media continued to appear four times a year in the form of the *Aggievator*. In 1949, editor Carl Meyerdirk, aided by associate editors Lee Carman and Bob Jacobson, published a Sadie Hawkins issue of the *Aggievator* during the annual campus backward week. This edition was purported to be the first *Aggievator* to appear on time in the near thirty-year history of the humor publication. In the same year the *Daily O'Collegian*, the active watchdog of campus events, accused the *Aggievator* staff of printing lewd and filthy jokes. Through it all the *Redskin* proclaimed that "the professional big-business atmosphere of the magazine" just seemed to hold one staffer, Pappy Baker, to his work. The log chains and bear traps also helped." By year's end no members of the *Aggievator* staff were hanged.[41] Probably for an *Aggievator* staffer these comments represented a compliment since nothing seemed sacred or safe from its often risque, controversial, and opinionated columns.

While the *Aggievator* made light of serious problems, the campus *Daily O'Collegian* was sometimes at the center of them. The newspaper was particularly good at prodding the Student Senate, the representative body of the Student Association. An editorial in 1950 stated that a senate meeting played the "same song, second verse," and was highlighted by acute boredom. Another time a headline proclaimed "Preliminary Senate Meeting Flops." Frequently the *O'Collegian* printed long lists of student needs that needed attention. With each of their agendas for action the *O'Collegian* asked publicly why the senate was not fulfilling its representative duties. For example, in the fall semester of 1950 the *O'Collegian* agitated for action on ten different problems, including insufficient heat in Bennett and Hanner Halls, an honor system to reduce campus examination cheating, a teacher evaluation system, and a growing problem of examination files in the Greek houses which put independent students at an academic disadvantage.[42]

A noteworthy academic year for the campus publications and the Student Association was 1944-1945. World War II had depleted the campus of male students. Those that remained could be correctly concerned about a call for duty in the service. As a result most major student leadership offices were ably filled by coeds. On the normally male-dominated Oklahoma A. and M. College campus this was a first in history. Georgia Ann Strickler became editor of the *Daily O'Collegian* and was assisted by Shirley Angle. Lou Wilson became editor of the *Aggievator*, and Edwyna Grant was assistant editor. Peggy Howard edited the college annual. For the first time since organization in 1915, Bonnie E. Emerson was elected president of the Student Association following a successive string of thirty male predecessors. Further coed opportunities resulted after the spring 1944 campus-wide elections. The traditionally male-dominated School of Agriculture elected Phyllis Bur-

During World War II coeds ably took up the campus leadership roles formerly dominated by male students. Bonnie E. Emerson (*left*) became the first woman to be elected president of the Student Association in 1943-44. In 1944-45 more history was made when Peggy Howard edited the *Redskin*, Lou Wilson oversaw the *Aggievator*, and Georgia Ann Strickler headed the *Daily O'Collegian*.

key to its senate seat. Peggy Howard set a precedent when she was elected secretary-treasurer of the Student Association.[43]

Particularly in the years following the war, campus elections were hotly contested; charges of mudslinging were more common than not. The Fraternity Party broadened its base of appeal and became the Representative Party. It annually contested the Independent Party, composed primarily of non-fraternity students. Elections were usually controlled and won by students who proclaimed Greek or non-Greek loyalties, were popular, and could use propaganda successfully. The secret and outlawed Theta Nu Epsilon, or TNE, also continued to contaminate and influence election results.[44]

Perhaps adding to campus political turmoil, Dean of Students R. R. Oglesby reported in 1951 that he had been aware of the existence of TNE on campus for several years. Oglesby had not felt a need to take official steps to suppress TNE activities and added: ''I think I have followed the activities of TNE very closely over the years and I can truthfully say that I feel the organization has never done anything with which I completely disagree.''[45] Oglesby's comments sent reverberations throughout the student leadership. Particularly noteworthy was the fact that there had been a requirement in place for years for candidates seeking office to sign an oath which declared their non-involvement with secret organi-

188                                                  Centennial Histories Series

zations, namely TNE. For some, TNE was likened to the Ku Klux Klan, a group which "causes amusement and perhaps harm."[46] The TNE influence, for good or bad, continued to be a force in campus politics in later years.

Despite many side issues, student apathy, and frequent editorial badgering, the Student Senate went about the work of representing the student body. A 1932 constitution was totally rewritten and approved by campus-wide vote in 1944. Rules for electioneering were enacted, including prohibiting the use of paint or paste on sidewalks or other property. Convicted violators were fined $10. The Junior-Senior Prom was a major student government-sponsored annual event. Pep clubs, distribution of athletic tickets for out-of-town events, and the improvement of on-campus intramural facilities were senate activities. Drives for later coed hours and better campus parking for students received a boost from various senates. Senators annually took responsibility for the homecoming parade and awards. The annual Campus Chest campaign, a parallel to the United Way drive of later years, was approved by the senate on May 10, 1948.[47]

Student walkouts, teacher evaluations, and the seemingly always controversial campus-wide elections were recycled themes for the Student Senate in the late 1940s. Another yearly plague was contending with the multitude of separate administrative fees, including a $2.50 registration fee, a $4.50 infirmary fee, and ten other independent charges. These issues in search of a solution and the variety of other senate activities seemed a bargain considering the student body was assessed only fifteen cents each semester for use by their Student Association.[48]

The 1940s was a colorful decade for campus politics. In the early years Gene Smelser, Leroy Floyd, and Bonnie Emerson carried the burdens of the demanding Student Association presidency. The 1947-48 senate president was Bennett Basore. Basore later became a distinguished OSU professor and administrator in the College of Engineering, Architecture and Technology and a friend and ally to subsequent generations of students. For each of these student leaders their position provided lifelong learning experiences. All gained the satisfaction that comes from the responsibilities of leadership and helping others. To the negative but still useful side, all learned to tolerate criticism.[49]

Because of the larger enrollment at the college after the war, campus facilities and corresponding human systems to support the new and returning students were needed. As early as September 1942 Bennett had told a general faculty meeting that his vision of the future Oklahoma A. and M. College would necessarily use the "residence halls, the gymnasium, the stadium, and the concert hall to develop the finest in students as we now hope to effect in our laboratories and lecture rooms." Continuing, Bennett suggested: "The role of guidance will become fundamental, knowledge will not be an end in itself."[50]

At the time of the speech to the faculty, the college's Auxiliary Enterprises were under the direction of W. J. Marshall, the business manager. His responsibilities included the profitability of the residence and dining halls, the college gasoline station, the Veteran's Village Commissary, and the concession stands in each of the residence halls. The bursar, accounting offices, internal auditor, and purchasing agent also reported to Marshall. In effect, all nonacademic business and financial matters eventually concerned the business manager.[51]

The student personnel program continued to be headed by Deans Julia E. Stout and Clarence H. McElroy until 1947. The deans were responsible for maintaining student records, student discipline, off-campus housing approval, student employment, including the Student Entertainers, and advising nearly a hundred international students. Each dean advised student organizations and assisted with freshman orientation programs. Both were accountable for residence hall staffing, including hosts, hostesses, and the student residence counselors. As time allowed, individual counseling with students occurred in the deans' offices. The annual religious week and men's and women's fraternity rush programs presented annual times of extra demanding work. Then, with each student victory holiday or walkout, the deans' energies were intensified, if not stretched, even further.[52]

Being a dean of men or women required the enforcing of rules clearly designed to maintain the traditions of in loco parentis, or the college assuming the role of parents. As a result, the rules on student conduct were specific, lengthy, and rigidly written. Something of a preface to the rules stated: "The conduct of the individual is an important indicator of character and future usefulness in life. It is therefore incumbent upon every student to maintain the highest standards of integrity, honesty and morality."[53] To assist the students in understanding this philosophical underpinning, ten pages of rules covering nearly all aspects of student life, with special attention given to freshmen, were made available.

In September 1948 O. K. Campbell assumed the newly created position of dean of students. Dr. McElroy transferred to full-time duties as dean of the School of Veterinary Medicine and thus ended nearly a quarter of a century of formal and informal service as the dean of men. McElroy estimated that he had helped 70,000 college students with their problems by the time of his appointment to head veterinary medicine. McElroy retired from the college in 1953. When he died at the age of eighty-three on March 7, 1970, the Oklahoma State Alumnus Magazine announced his death with the headline, "The Passing of an OSU Patriarch."[54]

Dean Stout had been "deaning" at Oklahoma A. and M. for twenty-three years. Called the "Dean of Women's Deans" in Oklahoma at the time of her retirement banquet on January 26, 1951, her legacy was further confirmed when it was announced the Women's Hall would be named Stout Hall in her honor. By 1951 Stout's total career in education spanned forty-one years.[55] President Bennett personally hosted Stout's banquet. He told her that "although you come from an old Quaker family, which doesn't believe in war, all of us here tonight consider you a good soldier.[56]

Dean Stout had become nationally recognized for her residence hall counselor program and her student assistant academic course taught through the School of Education. Locally, she was a leader in creating the Association of Women Students, a national chapter of Mortar Board, and the Grand Council (forerunner to the Women's Residence Hall Association, and still later, the Residence Halls Association). Stout was also active in the National Association of Women Deans and Counselors. She was given a special award by this group at their national convention in Chicago in March 1951. The sixth dean of women and first full-time dean of women in the college's history, she became dean emeritus officially on September 1, 1950. She retired on a pension of $150 a month and remained in Stillwater until her death on March 27, 1969, at the age of eighty-nine. Her final resting place was in her hometown of Cicero, Illinois.[57]

Succeeding Dean Stout in February 1951 was Zelma Florence Patchin. Dean Patchin came to the campus with a master's degree in home economics from Oklahoma A. and M. and a background in teaching home economics; she had considerable experience in student services, having served as a counselor under Dean Stout in Murray Hall.[58] Dean Patchin immediately impressed a *Daily O'Collegian* reporter, who wrote: "Charmingly feminine in spite of her extraordinary executive talents, the brown-haired, dark eyed new dean believes that 'most young women are very normal.'"[59] With this assumed vote of confidence, Patchin and another staff member, Estelle A. Hammond, joined Dean of Students R. R. Oglesby, who had succeeded Campbell in 1950, in the task of helping students. All turned their attention to the college's 200 student organizations and the students' behavior, as well as their misbehavior.[60]

The housing of students had become a complex business, which reflected a difficult balance between the student's right to privacy and the college's role of parent in absentia. In 1944 the enrollment of students and the subsequent demand for housing increased to the extent that a separate office for handling housing assignments on campus was organized. Ethel Prosser directed this new, and first distinct housing office. Miss Prosser served over thirty years in student housing. Starting in the office of the chief clerk, Prosser's career spanned the building and opening of eight residence hall structures in addition to Veteran's

Village, later family housing. Initially she was the person who assigned student rooms in the campus dorms.[61]

Miss Prosser's job was not easy. After the war Murray, Willard, and North Halls were the only on-campus residences for coeds. Fifteen hundred women were annually squeezed three and four into rooms designed for two students. Near the end of the war, North Hall was the first hall to reopen to regularly enrolled women students. With Gertrude Reed as hostess, the hall gained freedom from its annex status in 1948; now known as North Murray Hall the facility later housed male students, then graduate students, and still later was called the international dormitory because of the large number of international student occupants. The fortunate few students who lived in college housing paid between $160 and $180 each semester for a room and twenty meals a week, eaten in the campus cafeterias. Those perhaps less fortunate were assigned to Stadium Hall, a barracks-like accommodation for 120 men located on the north side of Lewis Stadium, or the West Sixth Dormitory, another barracks facility for 75 men in the 1500 block of Sixth Street. Oretoopa Halls, with oretoopa meaning "men of wisdom," was a small city of 320 Army tar paper-covered hutments located on West Tenth Street. Each hutment at Oretoopa housed four men each. This housing complex accommodated another 1,350 men. Still 5,000, mostly male, students simply fended on their own in off-campus apartments or rooms.[62]

In the spring and summer of 1947 a huge step toward resolving several campus problems was taken when the board of regents authorized the sale of $9,150,000 in self-liquidating bonds. In addition to a new campus power plant, an expansion to Lewis Stadium, the long-discussed Student Union, and Stout and Bennett Halls were to be built. Prosser proclaimed that all of the temporary housing would soon end. Prosser's supervisor, Edward L. Morrison, the director of campus residence halls, thanked the people of Stillwater for their assistance in alleviating the student housing crunch. Vacant Oretoopa hutments were sold at $150; all were gone by the fall of 1949. A large modern residence hall system would be in place by 1951 at the Oklahoma A. and M. College.[63]

Moving toward the modernization, Stout Hall was occupied in June 1949. Housing 460 women, the hall's first head resident was Gertrude Reed. In 1950, another large hall to house 1,100 men opened. Costing $4 million, Bennett Hall was dedicated to the president because he was a man "who has dreamed no little dreams" for the college. Bennett Hall was proclaimed the finest and largest building of its kind in the Southwest. The structure covered more ground acreage than any building yet built on campus; and if the entire length of the interior were walked, one would cover two and one-half miles of hallways and stairs. M. G. Orr, a former coordinator of veteran's services, worked as the first Ben-

Ethel Prosser (*left*) was a mainstay of single student housing administration for more than thirty years. Her career spanned the building and opening of eight residence halls including Bennett Hall (*right*). When this men's residence hall was opened in 1950, the structure covered more ground acreage than any building yet built on campus.

nett head resident. Mrs. Orr was hostess of the west wing, and Mr. and Mrs. Floyd McGlamery were host and hostess of the east wing.[64]

Students were pleased to have Bennett Hall, but comments also included, "Couldn't they build it further out," to "Man, that's a long way from the chemistry building." The campus paper suggested that the students should appreciate what they had, but also proposed, with tongue-in-cheek, that maybe a subway would soon be built. Until then, all Bennett residents were chided just to double up on their bicycles. Aside from the distance from classrooms another early Bennett flap broke out over whether a Theta-type pond would be built north of Bennett Hall. There was the question of whether the need for intramural playing fields would outweigh campus esthetics. The proposed $8,000 pond, surrounding an island with three connecting bridges, would be suitable for barbecues and student picnics. The conflict of interest caused petitions and Student Senate investigations. Eventually supporters of the pond, who were the vast majority of Bennett residents, lost their campaign.[65]

During the 1940s, many completed long tenures of service in student housing. Harriett McNabb, who left her position on September 1, 1942, had been the only hostess of Hanner Hall since the building opened in 1926. McNabb was also the first hostess of a men's dormitory at the college. By 1947 Maud Latimer had also compiled fifteen years and Eleanor Gassaway thirteen years, in a variety of dormitory hostess positions.[66] Student Gil Schneider once wrote a letter to the *O'Collegian* and reminded students that the dorm housemothers, or hostesses, were human beings deserving of thanks for jobs well done as contrasted to the common opinion which held that they were "a necessary evil, a person who is continually flicking the lights off and on [to chase men out of the women's dorm at curfew] and one who is always sticking her nose into other people's business."[67] The first professional residence hall staffer came to work in Willard Hall on September 1, 1951. Catherine Williams held her master's degree in counseling and guidance from Indiana University.

In 1951 the Grand Council, forerunner to the later Women's Residence Hall Association and the Residence Halls Association, was nine years old. Started as a group to coordinate women's dormitory student programs in the Victory Halls during World War II, the idea survived the war and was continued by the women. Thinking the Grand Council was a good idea, men formed the Independent Men's Residence Council (IMRC). The IMRC was organized, had its constitution approved by the Student Senate, and held its first joint meeting with the Grand Council in January 1948. George Geyor was the first IMRC president. Frank Rachel and Bill Bruton were president and vice president in 1951-52. Pioneer Grand Council student leaders included Margaret Bennett, Louizon Killingsworth, and Ruth Franklin. Franklin was president of the Grand Council at the historic initial joint meeting of the combined IMRC and Grand Council.[68]

New residence hall buildings, a professionally-trained staff, and organized student government all served as bench marks for a contemporary system of campus housing. Also, each hall resident now paid "house dues" of fifty cents at the beginning of each semester. An additional key to progress was the advent of a cost efficient, timely, and tastefully done food service. Henry Clay Potts became director of college food units on December 18, 1942. In his first year in the position Potts and his staff served over one million meals in five scattered campus food units. Potts had served ten years as director of short courses before he assumed his new position. A good organizer, a skill sorely needed by the food service, Potts became involved in working with food as an avocation. Eventually Potts became something of a legend, known nationally for his barbecue, chuck wagon, western atmosphere menus, and catered events. Unafraid of large groups, Potts' largest catered event was a barbecue for 17,000 convention-attending miners.[69]

Despite Potts' organization and fame, his problems were monumental. Until large cafeterias in Stout and Bennett Halls were functioning the food service director was faced with operating food units in temporary and old buildings. The problem was always too little space to feed too many people. For example, the College Cafeteria, which later became the Student Affairs Building, was located on the site of the current College of Business Administration Building. In 1947 the structure

After serving as director of campus short courses for ten years, Henry Clay Potts became director of food units in 1942. A good organizer, Potts had become interested in foods as an avocation. Truly the "barbecue king of Oklahoma," Potts enjoyed a national reputation for his catered barbecues and western atmosphere menus.

could seat 200 people at one time. Twelve hundred people were being fed in this facility each meal time. Another 900 students in the Oretoopa complex on Sixth Street were fed in a temporary military cafeteria built for war trainees. Once seated, students were fed three meals a day for the total cost of $1.07.[70]

A public relations article on Potts in the *Oklahoma A. and M. College Magazine* reassured the parents of current and prospective students that if their son or daughter were eating food planned by Potts and his staff they had nothing to fear. "Likely the kids are getting the best and most nutritious food that money can buy. They're getting it at reasonable rates too, at the Oklahoma A. and M. College dining units. Maestro Potts has seen to that!"[71]

Perhaps fortunately, not many students saw that article. No doubt if they had, they would have written the editor of the magazine, as well as the *Daily O'Collegian*. Typical of complaints is a letter of November 1949 in which thirty-four Cordell residents lamented "most of the time the food isn't fitt'n for human consumption . . . it seems that the old gripes about Cordell chow have to be reopened."[72] Another student described his breakfast as "one thin slice of fried mush with flakes of ham sparingly scattered through the mush, dry cereal, coffee, toast, and three cooked prunes."[73] Even the very modern Bennett Cafeteria was not immune. Dan Vincent signed his letter to the editor "Hungrily" after writing that one of his cafeteria friends recently told him that he had "fed better stuff than this to the pigs!"[74]

Whether the food served in the college food units was good or bad was a matter of individual opinion. What was certain was that in the 1940s opinions, both pro and con, were voiced. In a sense, the verbal complaints, as well as written sarcasm, merely reflected the nature of college students. Historically food services were always a target for student frustration, sometimes even a scapegoat for campus problems not nearly so emotional nor visible. Nonetheless, by 1951 the Oklahoma A. and M. College was housing 3,500 single men and women in eight residence halls, five of which had their own cafeterias. Each of the cafeterias was heavily used. All served a balanced menu at very reasonable prices. In relative terms, most students had few complaints. Potts had, at the least, turned long lines and a haphazard operation into a unified efficient system.

Still another important form of college-affiliated housing was dramatically impacted by the events of World War II. Like the dorm system, these residences also returned to recover fully after the war. In January 1946 three years of dormancy ended for the Greek system. With rules laid down by the college, rush and pledge programs were reinstated. Ray Adler, a member of Lambda Chi Alpha, became the president of the Interfraternity Council. Adler and his executive team of Sonny Williams (Kappa Alpha) and Hal Hazelrigg (Sigma Phi Epsilon) rewrote the Interfraternity Council constitution, focused little on social activities, and spent most of their time resolving unprecedented problems in reestablishing the fraternity system.[75]

George you're losing weight, are you eating at Cordell too?

We're a little crowded at the moment. I hope you won't mind doubling up for a semester or two.

In both the fraternities and sororities stability and growth followed. By 1947 Tau Kappa Epsilon, Phi Delta Theta, Theta Chi, and Alpha Tau Omega enlarged the numbers of fraternities to seventeen. Alpha Chi Omega and Kappa Kappa Gamma joined Alpha Delta Pi, Chi Omega, Delta Zeta, Kappa Alpha Theta, Kappa Delta, Pi Beta Phi, and Zeta Tau Alpha to form a thriving, influential sorority system. In 1951, the number of fraternities had grown to twenty, with the addition of chapters of Phi Kappa Tau, Delta Tau Delta, and Delta Chi.[76]

In the years 1950 and 1951 Alpha Gamma Rho, Kappa Kappa Gamma, Kappa Alpha, and FarmHouse all moved into modern new chapter houses. Other fraternities and sororities completed house expansion and renovation projects. Internally and externally the Greek system grew. Seeking better relationships between campus Greeks and independents, the first Greek Week was held in April 1951.[77] New Oklahoma A. and M. President Oliver S. Willham, in an open letter supporting the new experiment called Greek Week, stressed cooperation among campus living groups. Willham went on to acknowledge that fraternal groups "can contribute significantly to the development of character, personality, and behavior of students . . . the fraternities are to be commended for this latest move."[78]

At the time there was a need for a call for cooperation. The Greek system was a powerful force on campus, involving and often dominating everything from student politics to homecoming and intramural activities. Independents were called "barbarians" by some Greeks, while independents stereotyped the Greeks as rich elitists. Spring elections colored by propaganda, mudslinging, and wild accusations of all kinds caused bitter campus strife between Greeks and independents. Scorn, bitterness, and even hatred often permeated much of the campus each April as the Independent Party and the Greek-dominated Representative Party battled for political supremacy.[79] The first Greek Week was welcomed by the *Daily O'Collegian* as a positive step to "preserve good relations between Greeks and independents so that both groups can work together for the betterment of the campus as a whole."[80]

Although the 1,500 or so fraternity and sorority members constituted a small minority of the total 12,000 students, there can be no doubt that the system was an influential and appealing campus segment. College Avenue was now called "fraternity row." In the fall of 1950 there was a record setting Rush Week, Bid House, and Ribbon Dance. The Greek system welcomed 445 new pledges. Larger system interests were ably coordinated by the prestigious Interfraternity and Panhellenic Councils. Strong traditions, new chapters, a building boom in Greek houses, and postwar growth all assured a healthy future for campus Greeks. For decades to come it was assured that the Greek system would enrich campus life, give students a valuable housing and living alternative, and,

When a young man escorts a young lady to a dance, he must always wear a coat and tie! This student took the 1949 Phi Delt "half-formal" dance quite literally. Dances were a mainstay of Greek social life during the late 1940s and 1950s.

most importantly, provide chapter members lifelong friendships.[81]

Much like Greek social fraternities, campus intramural programs were also greatly influenced by World War II and its aftermath. During the war a money-conscious economy caused travel to be curtailed. An emphasis was placed on on-campus activities. Nowhere was a lack of money and a need for college-centered use of time by students more vivid or impacting than in intramural programs. Through the decade the theme of "making do with what you have" fell largely to women's intramural director Valerie Colvin, men's director Gordon Gilbert, and their student helpers. Physical education classes and intramural programs were scattered through five different buildings, including the new women's gymnasium-dance studio in the basement of North Murray Hall. Stillwater commercial enterprises hosted bowling and roller skating activities. The old gym's swimming pool, twenty yards in length and seven yards wide, served classes and a large aquatics club. Outdoor space was used wherever it was available. But matters worsened for intramural programs before they got better.[82]

In February 1946 Gilbert returned to the campus after a four-year stint in the Army. At the end of the next year another 6,000 former G.I.s had followed Gilbert to the campus. The increased enrollment caused intramural programs to reach new records in participation. The positive aspects became compounded when both temporary and permanent buildings were erected on playing fields formerly set aside for intramural play. Gilbert and Colvin were confronted with providing space for nearly twice as many participants as pre-war days on less than half the campus space.

Despite the limitations in space and money, somehow most students wishing to participate were given the opportunity. Some students even took part in as many as six sports a year. To provide the facilities, every conceivable space was used. One softball diamond incorporated a steep embankment and an outfield extending onto College Avenue. Another diamond found home base within fifty yards of President Bennett's office in Whitehurst Hall. In the 1946-1947 school year the men's intramural program was offering fifteen different competitive sports, while the women's program offered ten. Coed activities included golf, social and square dancing, swimming, archery, and fencing. Over 3,200 students, a record number, participated in the programs that year.[83]

A year later the men's program offered sixteen activities and grew to around 4,000 participants. Out of a total male enrollment of 5,300 at the college in 1950-1951, 2,452 were playing competitive and club intramural sports. Growth on the women's side was as rapid. The Women's Athletic Association started a broad program of regularly awarding "Os" to the most outstanding women athletes who met a rigid set of minimum criteria in 1944. The following year two women's basketball teams contested the all-college championships in Gallagher Hall. This was the first time in the building's history that a group of coeds had played a game in the male-dominated facility. At the same time, the campus paper editorially proposed that it was time that the women fielded a varsity team to compete intercollegiately. Flora May Ellis' Social Dance Club drew as many as 500 participants in the early 1950s. Colvin herself organized and directed Saturday night recreation for hundreds of students and faculty.[84]

The number of intramural participants, breadth of offerings, and stewardship of Colvin and Gilbert were obvious strengths. However, periodic cries of outrage and appeals by student leaders, directed at campus administrators for their lack of support for improved facilities for intramural programs, dampened the otherwise progressive efforts. One of the first volleys was fired in 1947 by the Student Senate when Senate President Bennett Basore wrote an open letter complaining of the leaking roof in the old gym and the extensive repairs needed on the campus tennis courts. On behalf of the health, physical education, and recreation program, Schiller Scroggs, the dean of the School of Arts and Sciences, replied that although intramural sports and recreation were a matter of sincere concern there simply was little or no money budgeted by the college for the maintenance of intramural sports.[85]

Two years later the situation had further deteriorated. Touch football teams were playing on shortened, rocky fields spread from the campus to Sixth Street. Twenty teams were not permitted to play a schedule because of a lack of playing fields. At one juncture there were twelve softball fields, but six more were needed. Nevertheless, the following year new building construction had further exasperated the shortage problem by reducing the number from twelve to four. Paralleling the softball field problem, hundreds of students were simply precluded from playing intramural basketball. Enough playing courts were impossible to find. Even then the few available courts were old and inadequate. A *Daily O'Collegian* editorial headline summarized: "Has Our Administration Forgotten Intramurals? Situation Is Desperate."[86]

There were times of hope. A faculty committee composed of Gilbert, Colvin, and Housing Director Morrison, plus a number of student leaders, including among others Les Metheny representing intramural programs, WAA President Freda Everett, and *O'Collegian* sports editor Bill Harman, submitted a report on the intramural program to President Bennett in 1949. The report called campus facilities inadequate. It also asked for immediate action.[87] The student newspaper responded to the report with "hang tough, you intramural athletes, we've got the best chance in the last ten years for help from the administration."[88]

Two months later the president moved ahead to avert an immediate crisis in intramural programs by designating additional campus space for softball fields. More importantly, a long-range plan appeared for the first time which included four locations on- and off-campus for the development of outdoor fields. Indoor play would be helped by a 115 by 180 foot covered floor space for three basketball courts, in addition to volleyball and other indoor sports. Any celebrating was short-lived as little progress was made on behalf of intramural programs. The new library was planned and built over another playing area. A paved parking lot near the stadium covered another intramural field. "Millions of dollars have been spent in the past five or more years toward making the A&M campus a more presentable campus—toward a goal which is, in short, a lure to potential students . . . but not one cent spent to keep them here once they've committed themselves. And not one cent spent for intramural sports facilities," blasted George McBride in the *Daily O'Collegian.*[89]

The intramural problem would not go away for twenty more long years. Until a final solution was found, Gordon and Colvin persisted with the pushes and pulls of larger institutional needs and the immediate desire to provide students a quality intramural program. As much as the students, Colvin and Gilbert did live with the limitations and still were able to move ahead toward better intramural activities and better times.

Unlike the campus intramural program the Student Health Service showed a marked contrast during the war years and after. Grace Vickers, superintendent of nurses, was an infirmary stabilizing force as she entered her third decade of tending to student injuries and illnesses. Regularly enrolled students, plus the Army and Navy trainees, kept the hospital staff busy day and night. For a $3.50 fee charged at enrollment time the facilities could accommodate fifty students in beds, provide modern X-rays, and offer the service of a dietitian and laboratory. College dentists, including at different times N. L. Hiniker, John G. Kelly, and Brandon White, took care of students' teeth for the cost of materials. Anywhere from two to six doctors, as many as twenty-six nurses, plus a variety of other employees, including receptionists and student assistants, also were paid from the enrollment fee in the "pay-its-own-way" health services.[90]

In 1942 Roxie A. Weber, with a medical degree from Johns Hopkins University, arrived on campus from a position at a college in upstate New York to begin a long and distinguished career of campus and com-

Roxie A. Weber (*center*) came to Oklahoma A. and M. College in 1942 and became the director of health services by 1950. An innovative physician, Dr. Weber advocated a campus wellness program—a proposal which finally came to fruition in the 1980s.

munity service. J. O. Thompson joined Weber in 1945 and took up the duties of director. Thompson and Weber were both planners and willing to speak out on behalf of student health. Two of Thompson's earliest actions included persuading the intramural program to eliminate playing eleven-man football in lieu of the six-man game. Another Thompson appeal, although not nearly as successful as the football declaration, was to reduce the number of students being thrown into Theta Pond under the banner of celebration. In both arenas Thompson's interest was to reduce the resulting injuries. Like Thompson, Weber's campaign was preventative in direction. She advocated annual voluntary physical examinations and a campus wellness program or preventative education which covered personal, community, and mental health. Weber's ideas were innovative; four decades later large numbers of experts would grasp her concepts and start to push preventative health care.[91]

The postwar enrollment boom caused the hospital to adjust and grow. A dispensary, staffed by a nurse, was established in Veteran's Village. Three Quonset huts, connected to the hospital by an overhead roof, provided forty-three additional beds for patients. Veterans' wives had their babies in the Stillwater Hospital, and then the mother and baby would transfer back to the campus hospital maternity ward until ready to return home. The college's maternity ward was originally on the main hospital's third floor, but in September 1947 it was moved to one of the adjoining Quonset hut annexes. Purported to be one of the few maternity ward operations on a college campus in the nation, the infirmary closed this part of its service to students in June 1948, after serving more than 600 G.I. wives. The fourteen-bed maternity ward lost money because the new mother could stay as long as she wished for the total hospital fee of $3 a day.[92]

In the month of September 1950, the infirmary was visited by 8,472 students. Of that number 3,700 received their required physical examination, while the remainder received medical care. A fourth floor expansion of the 1930 hospital building was planned as a part of the campus Twenty-Five Year Plan. Medications and dental service were still provided at cost.[93]

By 1950 Dr. Weber, who was the senior physician in years of service, had also become the director. Weber and Loraine Schmidt served as women's physicians. Men's physicians were J. O. Bruner, J. O. Thompson, R. R. Rigg, and Forest Olsen. The fee paid by students was now $4.50, and the total budget for the hospital operation was $135,000. This budget was a problem. Two physician vacancies had been open for over a year. Despite over a hundred replies to advertisements, none who were offered a position would accept because of low salaries.[94] Neither the public nor the students knew of the problem. According to the 1950 General Catalog, it "remained business as usual" when it proclaimed: "Good health is imperative if the student is to secure the best results from his college work. To this end the Student Health Service has been established."[95]

At the start of the 1950s the health service fee was one of dozens of miscellaneous assessments that a student could be charged. The amount of these fees depended on the student's enrollment and class decisions. Included as part of the maximum $48 general fee was a charge for registration, use of the library and Gallagher Hall, and a laboratory use fee. In addition, so called "occasional fees" included a $1 a day late registration charge, with a maximum of $3, and a class drop or add fee of $1; and for those who changed their major from one school to another, an assessment of $1 was made. Although the overall cost of a year's worth of general fees, room and board, books and supplies remained at a seemingly moderate $475 to $700 a year, students still lived on tight budgets. Work, loans, and scholarships continued to be important for many students to remain in school.[96]

Interestingly, World War II caused a decrease in the students' need for financial aid. Lower student enrollment, with students joining the military service or entering wartime industries, increased the amount of money in general circulation. War Department loans to students in defense-related accelerated programs in engineering, physics, and chemistry further reduced the demand on the college's financial aid programs. On-campus and community part-time jobs were easier to find.[97]

The lull for financial assistance programs ended with the rapid postwar enrollments. In the early 1950s the statement was made that "so many students do part-time work that sometimes those who do not work feel that they are in the minority."[98] The Student Employment Service cautioned students "not [to] plan to work unless you must have a job. Leave the available employment for those who are forced to earn part of their expenses."[99] With this caution, and a few simple rules, every student could file an application for part-time work at a centralized Student Employment Office for Women, under the direction of Associate Dean of Women Estelle Hammond, or at the YMCA Hut Student Employment Office for Men under T. N. Harris.[100]

From the fall of 1949 to the spring of 1950 over 6,000 students were employed with the assistance of Harris and Hammond. Over 1,000 women, representing about one-fourth of all enrolled coeds, and over 5,000 men, 2,016 of these in part-time jobs off campus, worked at every conceivable unskilled job to earn a part of their college costs. Noteworthy in more contemporary times, the available jobs were stereotypically divided. The women students filled positions as secretaries, stenographers, bookkeepers, receptionists, babysitters, telephone operators, or helpers in food units. Their male counterparts worked as janitors, manual laborers, and food services employees. Most jobs for women

"You mean I finally reached the end of this line—I only started at Perkins!" For decades standing in line has become almost a tradition at Oklahoma's land-grant college. These eager students are participating in the Freshman Orientation of 1946.

were on campus. A survey of the late 1940s also showed that the women averaged more hours of work each week than the men, but received less pay. A high-paying job brought $1.50 an hour. Nonetheless the women averaged forty-seven cents an hour while the men did slightly better at an average of fifty-one cents an hour.[101]

A unique source of student employment was provided by the Student Entertainment Bureau, later called Student Entertainers. In 1936 A. Frank Martin assumed responsibility for organizing students with the ability to entertain. Fifteen years later hundreds of talented students had earned money to help defray their expenses through participation in the amateur talent group. Meantime, the college was reaping the benefit of the bureau's public relations impact at campus conferences, in Oklahoma, and throughout the nation.[102]

Ranging in size over the years from 50 to 165 members, the 1951 Student Entertainer groups presented 374 programs before more than 70,000 people. Seemingly able to provide entertainment for every occasion, the student entertainers' talents ranged from a female ventriloquist to a girl's coronet trio, to quartets such as the Cowboys and the Gospel Singers, to the Little Symphony Orchestra and the Range Riders Western Orchestra. Former entertainers who later had distinguished careers at their alma mater included Kenneth McCollom, former dean of engineering; Vernon Parcher, a former head of civil engineering; and Max Mitchell, longtime head and professor of music.[103]

Loan money provided by the Serviceman's Readjustment Act allowed thousands of military veterans to enter college after the war. The consequence of the government's entry into the business of financially aiding veterans was obvious on the campus. Locally based loan programs remained relatively small in magnitude. Loans were offered by the Bureau of Indian Affairs under the 1931 Indian Appropriations Act, the Lew Wentz Foundation, and the Lahoma Club. For loan information non-veterans could write directly to the president's office. Prior to the war Lew Wentz Foundation loan requests regularly exceeded the number of dollars available, but from 1943 to 1946 the trustees only approved one or two loans each year. From 1946 to 1950 only sixty-six loans were granted. As the 1950s began, the federal government had substantially involved itself in student financial assistance. On-campus loan demand was small, and outright scholarship programs for undergraduate students numbered only thirteen. For students needing money, part-time work remained the primary source of earning their way through college.[104]

On June 9, 1949, Lew H. Wentz died. A stipulation in his will directed that 20 percent of the residue of his estate be given to the Oklahoma A. and M. College's Wentz Foundation. At the time no one knew of the magnitude of this bequest. In fact, Wentz had given more than $2 million to the foundation to support needy students. This gift, coupled with Wentz's bequest of twenty-three years earlier, permitted the trustees to manage the Wentz Foundation as a perpetual program of financial aid for outstanding students. Although perhaps not intended, Wentz's contribution also became a basis for a living memorial to his belief in returning his financial good fortune into opportunities for young people. With the advent of an economic recession, starting in 1957, the Wentz money again became a major campus source for student loans. Even later the Wentz Foundation would refocus the use of the bequest and establish the prestigious Wentz Scholar Program.[105]

With appropriate anticipation and fanfare, another source for student jobs was opened for business on September 9, 1950. After decades of efforts cut short, the Oklahoma Agricultural and Mechanical College could finally boast of the opening of a magnificent Student Union Building. Students of later years could never know about the years of dashed hopes, student mass meetings, and legislative lobbying that had preceded dozens of earlier efforts to build a home for on-campus student social life.[106]

Thirteen graduating classes before the Student Union became a reality, the *Daily O'Collegian* printed a front page article entitled, "Here's What A Student Union Building Is." This 1937 column was written in response to several student inquiries about what all the fuss was about for a student center of some kind. The newspaper stated that "the use of student union buildings varies on the principal campuses of the nation, 11 such buildings house student social, governmental, and recreational activities." Citing recommendations from the National Association of College Unions, the article related that the following elements were considered "essential for such a building: ballroom, student association offices, general lounge room, soda fountains, billiard room or bowling alley, smoking rooms, cafeteria or dining room and an information or employment bureau."

Cautioning that a facility providing more than the basic needs might not be possible at the Oklahoma A. and M. College, the *Daily O'Collegian* pointed out that if it were possible the paragon of student unions could also include alumni offices, art galleries, banquet rooms, barber and beauty shops, candy and other stores, hotel rooms, magazine and lounge rooms, music rooms, a theater, reception rooms, and even a shoe shining stand. This early view of what was possible concluded: "Although no one student building has all of these rooms, all of the activities listed are housed in some student union buildings."[107]

Thus this new building, with its unofficial opening marked by President Bennett's annual address to the faculty on September 9, was not only a magnificent achievement, it offered students a near ideal of what a student union could be. Nearly fourteen years after obtaining associate membership in the National Student Union Association, the work was richly rewarded. The Interfraternity and Panhellenic Councils' annual Ribbon Dance was held in the union on September 12, 1950, just three days after Bennett's speech to the faculty. This first major student event in the ballroom was attended by 1,500 students, who danced to the music of Jimmy Clayton's Varsitonians. A few nights later, the Student Senate sponsored the annual Howdy Dance. Charlie Keys' Collegians provided the music for this free, and first, all-campus event in the Student Union.[108]

On the same day that the Howdy Dance was scheduled, the Student Union's first advertisement appeared. Noting that the building was not yet complete, the ad suggested, "Whenever you see a friend, leave them with this saying, 'I'll meet you at the Union.'"[109] "I'll meet you at the Union" caught on. The students flocked to the new building to relax, study, meet new friends, and simply explore the huge structure.

The union's construction was finally made possible when the board of regents backed a special obligation bond issue which promised buyers that the union would pay for itself through student fees, building space rentals, and the sale of goods and services. Colonial Georgian architecture enclosed 223,700 square feet of space which ran 453 feet north to south and 209 feet to the east and west. Primary architects were Thomas Sorey, Alfred Hill, and Lee Sorey all of Oklahoma City and Philip A. Wilber, the college architect. General contractor was the Manhattan Construction Company of Muskogee. This most ambitious building project ever attempted at the college took two years to complete. Actual con-

"I'll meet you at the union!" Finally, after decades of agitation by students, the Student Union was under construction by 1948 (*upper*). By 1950 students were dancing in the Starlite Terrace on the "Waldorf Astoria of College Unions."

Oklahoma State University

207

struction cost was $2,432,345. According to the bond prospectus for the Student Union the total cost for the building, including heat and air-conditioning, plus equipment and furnishings was $3,860,000. Still later estimates, when the building was complete, increased the cost estimate to around $4.5 million.[110]

There is no doubt that the union was built as a community center or living room for the students. Not nearly as well known was that the visionary President Bennett had wanted the union to serve also as a conference center to support the college's mission in extension service. The union, a part of Bennett's 1928 long-range campus master plan, was, among other things, to be a source of statewide pride, without adding a great burden to the taxpayers. The union would meet both of these Bennett priorities when it opened to such adjectives as "lush, lavish, colossal, spectacular, and the 'Waldorf Astoria of College Unions.'" Two measures of the union's success included the fact that in its first five years over fifty tons of coffee had been brewed, and the food department was serving in excess of one million people annually.[111]

The original blueprints of the Student Union were started before World War II and were labeled "Students' Union." Architect Wilber himself emphasized that the design was to plan a "big education unit, not just a playhouse."[112] The union did become an educational and social center for the campus. Underneath one roof students and visitors could eat, buy clothing, and rent a $4.50 hotel room. Over two hundred rooms filled every function from beauty, to bowling, to buying books. Six dance floors, including the magnificent multipurpose grand ballroom, where 1,000 couples could be accommodated, encouraged students to continue dancing. A browsing room contained 1,000 books, magazines, and periodicals for readers on a break from studies. Five Stillwater businesses leased space to form a mini shopping mall. Peyton Glass and his son sold men's and women's casual wear. Creech's Sports and Gift Shop offered additional merchandise. One could buy a corsage at Reichman's Florist. A barber shop and shoe shine parlor, managed by Clifford Marrs and run by the Student Union, rounded out the convenient business outlets in the building.[113]

The French, Chinese, and Modern Lounges were furnished in steel, wood, and upholstered furniture supplied by leading manufacturers. The building's period rooms incorporated imported antiques from Middle Europe, England, France, and the Far East as a part of their decor. The building's 21 meeting rooms could seat 3,000 people simultaneously and ranged in size from a capacity of 40 to over 1,200. Dining rooms named the Dean, President's and Mural, the Starlite Fountain, and the Frontier Room Cafeteria handled five to eight major parties at one time. Shortly after becoming fully functional the union was serving students and guests 35,000 meals in the cafeteria, 8,000 meals in the coffee shop,

700 meals in the private dining areas, and 5,000 lunches, banquets, and teas in the dining parlors and lounges each month.[114]

Within the rooms, emphasis was placed on the students' use of the facilities. Students rapidly found ways to express themselves in the splendid building in studying, dancing, recreating, visiting, or just plain relaxing. Student organization meetings alone often numbered over 100 a week, bringing 5,000 and more to the union for this reason alone. Undoubtedly one reason for making student use a success was the Student Union Advisory Board, later the Student Union Activities Board (SUAB). Chosen by the union director, the first board meeting was held in Dr. Bennett's office where he proclaimed, "It is your building."[115] Nineteen student leaders, from every major student organization on campus, attended the historic meeting. Called pioneers for their early work, the group influenced major union policy from the opening of the building. Various rooms were named by this group. The SUAB met weekly and was headed by Student Association President Gale McArthur. Helen Harry, J. L. Morton, and Don Tucker chaired important committees during these early formative days.[116]

With policies and procedures largely complete, the Student Union Advisory Board moved into the student activities programming business the following year. Ivan Griffith presided over the steering committee that implemented the first Student Union Activities Fair on October 19, 1951. While Cathy Temple was crowned Fairest of the Fair, Alpha Chi Omega won a trophy for the best booth. David Leonard served as Fair Clown. Boyd Baker, SUAB president, proclaimed the event a success and predicted larger events in the future. The SUAB Fair, in fact, continued to current times.[117]

No enterprise as large as the Student Union could remain afloat very long without capable professionals. President Bennett named Chester A. Tibbetts the Student Union's first director. Tibbetts served from May 20, 1950, through June 1, 1953. After his appointment Tibbetts quickly learned that the union would be his to run. This message became even clearer when after he recounted his multitude of problems to the president, Dr. Bennett stopped him and said: "Mr. Tibbetts, I hear you but let me tell you this. If I could settle all your problems by pushing various buttons, I would not need you." With new motivation, the director hired a staff and made the union operational within thirty days.[118]

Joining Tibbetts' union management team was Vesta Etchinson as social director. Reed Andre, a 1942 Cornell graduate in hotel management, assumed duties as food manager. Arthur Taylor, with a degree from Michigan State and hotel management experience, became resident manager of the Union Club, the building's eighty-three room hotel. Abe L. Hesser, a charter member of the student board, was completing his degree in hotel and restaurant administration and worked as Tibbetts' part-time assistant. Hesser would become the union's second director. Other key staff included Joe Robinson, chief of maintenance; Craig Hampton, assistant director; and John Gillum, bookstore manager. By January 1951 the union employed 293 people, including 109 part-time student workers.[119]

Tibbetts and his staff ran into problems which included paying an annual $263,000 debt service on the bonds and trying to bring profitable harmony to the varying demands of the academic and business communities. Additional issues were caused by students.[120] Ten days after the building opened O'Collegian editor Bruce Johnson wrote: "To the gentleman who was found one day swinging a hanging chandelier back and forth with a happy expression upon his little face, a spoiled bunch of bananas. To the 200 pound kids that love to push every dadgum button in the self-operating elevators before retiring, out! Go find a doorbell to lean on."[121] There were other problems, too. Probably because the building was so opulent, students initially did not come to the union. Later necking, courting, or petting particularly plagued the union supervisors.[122] Seemingly an issue not easily solved, Tibbetts finally informally decreed "as long as they had one foot on the rug, they should not be disturbed."

Prior to the Student Union's opening, students usually held their many formal events in the Greek houses or in hotels in Oklahoma City or Tulsa. This business was needed in the union, and similar conditions and services had to be provided. Oklahoma was a "dry" state. A union philosophy, perhaps described as pragmatic, evolved which allowed students—secretly and certainly unofficially—to bring liquor into the building. Tibbetts later reflected: "This was part of life. It was rather interesting to see the number of bottles that would be hidden in the folds of the red velvet drapes in the ballroom after a student party."[123]

The many attractive features of the union caused additional problems. One O'Collegian editorial headline decreed: "Save the Union!" The editorial explained to students that both souvenir hunting and stealing from the building cost all students. There can be no doubt that missing equipment was a problem. Fifteen months after the doors were opened, replacement costs totaled $3,979. Missing equipment, including 78 dozen dinner knives engraved with OAMC on the handle, totalled 7,952 pieces. Signs with raised letters which cost $15 to $20 to replace were favorite collector items. Brass lamps located outside the union frequently had their bases and rings removed. Stainless steel serving dishes, ash trays, and huge amounts of plastic ware also vanished. A system for replacing lost, broken, or stolen items was implemented.[124]

Two years after the union was completed, the classes of 1950 and 1951 presented the first television set to the facility. Louis Prima and his band was the inaugural venture of the union into sponsoring big

By 1951, students could find another excuse for not studying—television had come to campus. Students gather around the set in the Student Union. This set had been provided by the classes of 1950 and 1951.

name entertainment. The student lounges were the most popular aspect of the building according to a student survey. This survey also found that the students were using the facility and that the building had become an integral part of campus life.[125] The researcher, Lynn McCalmont, a business senior, concluded: "Time will improve the Union, and until then the students will continue using it and using the school-wide phrase, 'Meet me at the Union'!"[126]

Fifteen months after the union opened, President Bennett lost his life in a plane crash in Iran on December 22, 1951. On leave of absence after twenty-three years as president of the Oklahoma A. and M. College, Bennett was serving as administrator of President Harry Truman's Point Four Program. World-wide tributes followed the news. Bennett left a living memorial through his campus building program, his educational and administrative style, and with, as a student said, his being the college's "number one level-headed dreamer."[127] "The Doctor," a common title for Bennett among colleagues, and Mrs. Bennett were paid last respects by 8,000 people on January 11, 1952, in Gallagher Hall.[128]

In many respects Bennett's death marked the end of an unmatched era. In his last speech on campus Bennett had predicted that in the future more and more international students would be seeking an education at Oklahoma A. and M. Earlier he had made speeches to his students on the awesome potential of atomic power and its potential misuse. He feared the rising influence of the Soviet Union and consistently advocated world peace and brotherhood. Through more earthly vision his college had grown to a campus physical plant valued over $50 million. The Auxiliary Enterprises and student activities budget had grown to over $3.5 million annually.[129]

The last ten years of Dr. Bennett's tenure were particularly important. World War II had prompted a sharp decline in the number of male students. As happened at many other institutions in America, the phenomenon spawned greatly expanded opportunities for curriculum and leadership choices for women. Women took over traditionally male roles on the campus and did them well. After the war, record enrollment increases were fueled by the G.I. Bill. Although campuses returned to male domination, things would never again be the same for women. Additionally, students were enrolled from every state and forty-four foreign countries. By 1949 ethnic minority groups were also asserting their rights to equal educational access. These changing student demographics, to say nothing of irreversible political forces, planted the seeds for the college's emergence as an international institution of higher education.[130]

Despite the rapid growth and sure tide of changes to come, Karleen Anderson DeBlaker, class of 1952, wrote an essay eight years after her graduation entitled ''What Is Oklahoma State University?'' Two particular paragraphs, of which Bennett no doubt would have approved, portrayed the busy, busy days of the 1940s and early 1950s. DeBlaker warmly wrote of her fond memories and stated that her alma mater ''is the wild scramble to get classes sectioned—before a better system was established. It is the first 'Howdy Dance' and a walk home across campus, 'rush week' with its squeals of happiness and its disappointments, and a coke and dance 'up at Brooks.' Oklahoma State is a torchlight parade and pep rally, the flash of the orange and black as the band plays 'Ride Em Cowboys' at homecoming, and the waving arms of thousands singing 'OAMC.'

''Oklahoma State is the cold water of the swimming pool in the old gym, the steaming heat of quonset hut classrooms, the tarpaper shacks of Oretoopa, and Vet Village. It is a fraternity dance at Edgewood, Guy Lombardo at an Allied Arts program, and a bench by beautiful Theta Pond. Oklahoma State is a line in front of a movie, a picnic at Yost, and a wooden gun on the shoulder of a boy walking between classes. It is the 'O'Colly,' a voice calling 'Mary Smith, 306' in a dormitory hall, coffee at the Union, and a goodnight kiss on the steps of Murray.''

DeBlaker's beautiful prose, representing student memories for a lifetime, also included that Oklahoma A. and M. College meant that ''it is also a man and his wife on a flight in the Far East—red roses at a memorial service in Gallagher Hall—and a chapel."[131] This is a fitting testimony to a period in time, a college, and a man all so seemingly inseparable.

# Endnotes

1. Oklahoma A. and M. College *Daily O'Collegian*, 13 December 1941, p. 6.

2. *Daily O'Collegian*, 13 December 1941, section 3, pp. 2, 4, section 2, p. 4; "Values: How Do the Classes of 1943 and 1978 Compare?" *Oklahoma State University Outreach*, vol. 19, no. 3 (June-July 1978), p. 7; *Daily O'Collegian*, 28 October 1941, p. 1.

3. *Daily O'Collegian*, 28 October 1941, p. 1.

4. *Daily O'Collegian*, 9 December 1941, p. 2.

5. *Daily O'Collegian*, 28 February, 1942, p. 2.

6. *Oklahoma Agricultural and Mechanical College, 1941-1942 General Catalog*, pp. iii-iv.

7. *Daily O'Collegian*, 10 January 1942, p. 1.

8. *1943 Redskin*, p. 292, Oklahoma A. and M. College Yearbook.

9. *Daily O'Collegian*, 3 October 1942, p. 1, 2 February 1943, p. 1, 19 December 1941, p. 1, 6 March 1942, p. 1.

10. *Daily O'Collegian*, 2 October 1942, p. 1, 24 March 1943, p. 1; Carolyn Gonzales, "OSU's Sixth Decade: A World War Brings Sudden Maturity," *Oklahoma State University Outreach*, vol. 57, no. 2 (Winter 1985), pp. 4, 6; "Contributions of the Oklahoma A. and M. College to the State and Nation in World War II," pp. 2-3, Weldon Barnes Collection, Special Collections, Edmon Low Library, Oklahoma State University, Stillwater, Oklahoma.

11. *Daily O'Collegian*, 2 May 1942, p. 1, 5 May 1942, p. 1, 20 November 1942, p. 1, 15 May 1942, p. 1, 16 June 1942, p. 2.

12. *1945 Redskin*, pp. 186-187; "Fraternities, World War II," 1942 File, Henry G. Bennett to Leland F. Leland, 28 September 1943, and Henry G. Bennett to J. Russell Easton, 2 August 1943, in President's Papers, Special Collections, Edmon Low Library.

13. *1944 Redskin*, pp. 170-184; *1945 Redskin*, pp. 186-187.

14. *Daily O'Collegian*, 9 December 1941, pp. 1-2.

15. *1942 Redskin*, p. 7.

16. *1943 Redskin*, p. 5; *1944 Redskin*, unnumbered page and p. 61.

17. *Daily O'Collegian*, 28 February 1942, p. 1, 19 March 1942, p. 2; Philip Reed Rulon, "The Campus Cadets: A History of Collegiate Military Training, 1891-1951," *Chronicles of Oklahoma*, vol. 52, no. 1 (Spring 1979), pp. 82-83.

18. Rulon, pp. 81-84; *Daily O'Collegian*, 8 March 1946, p. 1; "War Dead," pp. 1-4 and "A. and M. War Contributions," pp. 1-2, in Weldon Barnes Collection.

19. Rulon, p. 87; *Daily O'Collegian*, 28 November 1945, p. 1, 21 December 1945, p. 1; Chester J. Frazier, "Veterans Village Comes of Age," *Oklahoma A. and M. College Magazine*, vol. 20, no. 1 (October 1948), pp. 4-5.

20. "Outline of the History of the Village," manuscript, 1949-1951 File, President's Papers; Frazier, p. 4; Carolyn Gonzales, p. 8.

21. Frazier, pp. 4-5; Rulon, p. 87; Oklahoma A. and M. College *Village Times*, 5 November 1946, p. 2; "Veterans Village Commissary Specials," 1949-1951 File, President's Papers; Oklahoma A. and M. College *Home Base News*, 17 November 1947, p. 1; *1949 Redskin*, p. 167; *Daily O'Collegian*, 8 March 1946, p. 1.

22. *Village Times*, 25 October 1946, p. 2, 14 March 1950, p. 1, 5 November 1946. p. 2; *Daily O'Collegian*, 25 June 1948, p. 1; "Temporary Regulations for the Village," pp. 1-5, 1949-1951 File, and "Veterans Village Terms and Conditions of Occupancy and General Information," pp. 2-11, in President's Papers; Frazier, pp. 4-5.

23. Rulon, pp. 88-89; *Home Base News*, 27 November 1947, p. 1; Nester Gonzales, "Not A Sacrifice, But A Privilege," *Oklahoma State University Outreach*, vol. 54, no. 1 (September 1982), pp. 10-11.

24. Nestor Gonzales, p. 11.

25. *Daily O'Collegian*, 6 February 1946, p. 2, 23 March 1945, p. 4, 16 February 1945, p. 2; Oklahoma A. and M. College *Name Me*, 6 November 1947, p. 1, President's Papers; "The Next Twenty Years," Faculty Address September 1947, p. 2, and "Enrollments, 1945-1948," p. 2, Report to the Higher Regents, in the Weldon Barnes Collection; *Oklahoma Agricultural and Mechanical College Bulletin, May 1947*, p. 11; Mary Jo Botkin, "School Opens With Rush and Lines," *Oklahoma A. and M. College Magazine*, vol. 18, no. 1 (October 1946), pp. 3-4.

26. *Daily O'Collegian*, 29 March 1946, p. 3; Carolyn Gonzales, p. 8; *1946 Redskin*, p. 183.

27. Evanell Johnson, "Fun After Class," *Oklahoma A. and M. College Magazine*, vol. 21, no. 7 (March 1950), pp. 44-45; *Daily O'Collegian*, 19 October 1945, p. 1, 23 February 1945, p. 1.

28. *Daily O'Collegian*, 17 November 1948, p. 1, 29 November 1949, p. 1, 1 November 1949, p. 1, 7 October 1949, p. 1, 20 April 1950, p. 1, 14 February 1950, p. 3, 17 February 1951, p. 3, 15 March 1951, p. 8.

29. *Daily O'Collegian*, 22 April 1947, p. 1, 25 April 1959, p. 3, 4 April 1948, p. 4.

30. *1950 Redskin*, p. 529; *1947 Redskin*, pp. 383, 343.

31. "Formal Opening—The Leachman," 1948, pp. 1-9, Weldon Barnes Collection; *Daily O'Collegian*, 13 September 1944, p. 8, 23 May 1950, p. 3, 19 May 1950, p. 3, 12 May 1950, p. 12, 26 April 1950, p. 8, 28 April 1950, p. 4, 4 May 1950, p. 8, 27 April 1950, p. 8.

32. *1950-1951 Oklahoma A. and M. College Students' Handbook*, p. 13.

33. *1950-1951 Oklahoma A. and M. College Students' Handbook*, p. 10; *Daily O'Collegian*, 11 May 1945, p. 1, 3 October 1945, p. 2.

34. *Daily O'Collegian*, 9 March 1951, p. 1, 5 January 1945, p. 1; Guy R. Donnell, "Ah! . . . That Was Life," *Oklahoma State University Outreach*, vol. 17, no. 2 (March 1976), p. 12.

35. Donnell, p. 12; *Daily O'Collegian*, 10 March 1951, pp. 1, 10.

36. *Daily O'Collegian*, 25 May 1950, p. 2, 10 December 1948, p. 2.

37. *Daily O'Collegian*, 30 September 1949, p. 11.

38. *Daily O'Collegian*, 30 September 1949, pp. 1, 10.

39. *Daily O'Collegian*, 6 July 1946, p. 2.

40. *1951 Aggie Angles*, pp. 60-70, Oklahoma A. and M. College Student Handbook.

41. *1949 Redskin*, pp. 202-203.

42. *Daily O'Collegian*, 11 November 1950, p. 2, 18 September 1951, p. 2, 10 November 1950, p. 2.

43. *1945 Redskin*, pp. 165-167; Bonnie E. Emerson, "Democracy In Action," *Oklahoma A. and M. College Magazine*, vol. 16, no. 9 (April 1944), pp. 3, 8-9, 14; *Daily O'Collegian*, 21 April 1944, p. 1.

44. Emerson, p. 8; *Daily O'Collegian*, 4 April 1951, p. 1.

45. *Daily O'Collegian*, 12 April 1951, p. 1.

46. Emerson, p. 8.

47. *Daily O'Collegian*, 12 May 1944, p. 1, 31 March 1942, p. 1, 11 May 1948, p. 1; *1948 Redskin*, pp. 460-461; Emerson, pp. 3, 8.

48. *Daily O'Collegian*, 4 October 1947, p. 1; "Student Senate," manuscript, 1942-1945 File, President's Papers; Emerson, p. 14; *1948 Redskin*, p. 460.

49. Emerson, p. 14; *1948 Redskin*, p. 460.

50. *Daily O'Collegian*, 10 September 1942, p. 11.

51. "Organizational Report of the OAMC," manuscript, May 1951, pp. 32-34, Oliver S. Willham Collection, Special Collections, Edmon Low Library.

52. "Organizational Report of the OAMC," pp. 35-37.

53. *1951 Aggie Angles*, p. 60.

54. *Daily O'Collegian*, 17 September 1948, p. 1, 22 November 1947, p. 4, 23 September 1950, p. 1; "The Passing of an OSU Patriarch," *Oklahoma State Alumnus Magazine*, vol. 11, no. 5 (May 1970), p. 30.

55. "Dean Julia Stout, 1928," 1950 File, President's Papers; *1950 Redskin*, p. 55; *Daily O'Collegian*, 19 January 1951, p. 4.

56. *Daily O'Collegian*, 1 February 1951, p. 4.

57. "Dean Julia Stout, 1928," pp. 1-3; *Daily O'Collegian*, 22 March 1951, p. 2, 20 January 1951, p. 8; "Personnel Action for Julia A. Stout," Student Services Collection, Special Collections, Edmon Low Library; "Miss Julia E. Stout, Former Dean, Dies," *Oklahoma State Alumnus Magazine*, vol. 10, no. 5 (May 1969), p. 28.

58. "Dean Julia Stout, 1928," p. 3; *Daily O'Collegian*, 2 February 1951, p. 8, 21 September 1950, pp. 1, 6, 22 September 1950, p. 2, 26 September 1950, p. 11.

59. *Daily O'Collegian*, 2 February 1951, p. 8.

60. *Daily O'Collegian*, 21 September 1950, pp. 1, 6; "Personnel Action for Zelma F. Patchin," 1 July 1975, Student Services Collection.

61. "Career of Services," *Oklahoma A. and M. College Magazine*, vol. 22, no. 10 (June 1951), pp. 42-43; *Daily O'Collegian*, 23 July 1946, p. 1.

62. *Oklahoma Agricultural and Mechanical College Bulletin, 1944-1945*, pp. 43-48; *Oklahoma Agricultural and Mechanical College General Catalog, 1948-1949*, pp. 25-27; "1947 A. and M. Statistics," 20 August 1947, Weldon Barnes Collection; *Daily O'Collegian*, 24 September 1946, p. 2, 23 February 1950, p. 3, 10 January 1950, p. 10, 18 September 1951, pp. 1, 10, 21 July 1944, p. 1, 25 February 1947, p. 1; "History of the Residence Halls," p. 2, Office of the Dean of Women File, Student Services Collection.

63. *Daily O'Collegian*, 10 June 1947, p. 1, 10 January 1950, p. 10, 23 February 1950, p. 3.

64. *Daily O'Collegian*, 17 December 1949, pp. 1, 6, 22 July 1949, p. 7, 10 June 1949, p. 1, 6 October 1950, p. 4.

65. *Daily O'Collegian*, 1 April 1950, p. 2, 18 November 1950, p. 1, 11 November 1950, p. 3, 22 November 1950, pp. 1, 6, 30 November 1950, p. 1.

66. *Daily O'Collegian*, 19 June 1942, p. 2, 25 November 1927, p. 4.

67. *Daily O'Collegian*, 29 March 1949, p. 2.

68. *Daily O'Collegian*, 19 September 1951, p. 7, 13 December 1947, p. 1, 10 January 1948, p. 1, 8 January 1948, p. 1, 11 October 1951, p. 3, 17 January 1948, p. 4; *1946 Redskin*, p. 140.

69. "Terms For Occupancy of Oklahoma Agricultural and Mechanical College Residence Halls, 1948-1949," p. 1, Weldon Barnes Collection; "The Army and Navy Must Eat," *Oklahoma A. and M. College Magazine*, vol. 15, no. 4 (November 1943), p. 5; *Daily O'Collegian*, 8 December 1943, p. 1, 23 June 1944, p. 1; Richard M. Caldwell, "College Town Barbecue Baron," pp. 1-4, manuscript, 1936 File, President's Papers.

70. "Potts Sets A Good Table," *Oklahoma A. and M. College Magazine*, vol. 19, no. 2 (November 1947), p. 7; *Daily O'Collegian*, 22 November 1950, p. 8, 9 September 1947, p. 1.

71. "Potts Sets A Good Table," p. 7.

72. *Daily O'Collegian*, 4 November 1949, p. 2.

73. *Daily O'Collegian*, 14 October 1947, p. 2.

74. *Daily O'Collegian*, 17 February 1950, p. 2.

75. *Daily O'Collegian*, 8 May 1945, p. 2, 14 December 1945, p. 1, 23 January 1946, p. 4; *1946 Redskin*, p. 113.

76. Don Looper, "News Of The Campus," *Oklahoma A. and M. College Magazine*, vol. 19, no. 1 (October 1947), p. 18; *1947 Redskin*, pp. 197-242; *Daily O'Collegian*, 21 January 1947, pp. 2, 4, 24 May 1947, p. 4, 22 September 1948, p. 4, 19 February 1948, p. 4, 7 October 1948, p. 4.

77. *Daily O'Collegian*, 18 January 1950, p. 7, 20 September 1950, p. 7, 31 October 1950, p. 7, 28 February 1951, p. 7, 9 March 1951, p. 1, 31 March 1951, pp. 1, 6.

78. *Daily O'Collegian*, 31 March 1951, p. 1.

79. *Daily O'Collegian*, 29 March 1951, pp. 1, 6, 31 March 1951, pp. 1-2.

80. *Daily O'Collegian*, 31 March, 1951, p. 2.

81. "Fraternities Offer Social Opportunity," *Oklahoma A. and M. College Magazine*, vol. 22, no. 6 (February 1951), p. 15; "1947 A. and M. Statistics," 1947, p. 1, Memorandum to Elizabeth Stubler, Weldon Barnes Collection.

82. Sharon Mae Holmberg, "Valerie Colvin: Pioneer Physical Educator in Oklahoma" (Doctor of Education dissertation, Oklahoma State University, 1978), pp. 43-44; *Daily O'Collegian*, 8 November 1947, p. 5; "The Intramural Program," *Oklahoma A. and M. College Magazine*, vol. 18, no. 9 (June 1947), p. 10.

83. "The Intramural Program," p. 10.

84. *Daily O'Collegian*, 8 June 1948, p. 3, 15 November 1951, p. 9, 9 May 1946, p. 3, 14 March 1945, p. 2; Holmberg, p. 43.

85. *Daily O'Collegian*, 30 September 1947, p. 1.

86. *Daily O'Collegian*, 14 January 1949, p. 2.

87. *Daily O'Collegian*, 19 February 1949, p. 1, 24 January 1949, p. 2.

88. *Daily O'Collegian*, 24 January 1949, p. 2.

89. *Daily O'Collegian*, 22 March 1950, p. 2.

90. *Daily O'Collegian*, 16 December 1942, p. 1, 26 March 1943, p. 1, 14 October 1943, p. 1, 16 June 1950, p. 9, 13 November 1947, p. 1.

91. *Daily O'Collegian*, 19 October 1950, p. 7, 27 April 1946, p. 3, 9 April 1946, p. 1, 12 September 1945, p. 4.

92. Don Looper, "Aggieviews," *Oklahoma A. and M. College Magazine*, vol. 18, no. 1 (October 1946), p. 5; *Daily O'Collegian*, 21 June 1946, p. 1, 8 March 1947, pp. 1-2, 16 July 1946, p. 1, 15 January 1948, p. 1, 29 June 1948, p. 1.

93. *Daily O'Collegian*, 12 October 1950, p. 3, 13 November 1947, p. 2, 16 June 1950, p. 9.

94. *Daily O'Collegian*, 19 October 1950, p. 7, 16 June 1950, p. 9; A. and M. Health Services Director to Henry G. Bennett, 3 December 1948, Bennett Correspondence File, President's Papers.

95. *Oklahoma Agricultural and Mechanical College Catalog, 1950-1951*, p. 56.

96. *Oklahoma Agricultural and Mechanical College Catalog, 1950-1951*, pp. 47-48.

97. *Daily O'Collegian*, 22 September 1942, p. 1; William Edward McFarland, "A History of Student Financial Assistance Programs at Oklahoma State University, 1891-1978, With An Emphasis on the Creation and Administration of the Lew Wentz Foundation" (Doctor of Philosophy dissertation, Oklahoma State University, 1979), p. 59.

98. "Land of Opportunity for Working Students," *Oklahoma A. and M. College Magazine*, vol. 23, no. 7 (March 1952), p. 5.

99. "Your Student Employment Service," *Oklahoma Agricultural and Mechanical College Bulletin*, vol. 47, no. 16 (15 August 1950), unnumbered.

100. "Land of Opportunity for Working Students," p. 5; "Your Student Employment Service," unnumbered; *Daily O'Collegian*, 21 January 1950, p. 3.

101. *Daily O'Collegian*, 22 September 1950, p. 8, 17 February 1949, p. 8; "Your Student Employment Office," unnumbered; "Land of Opportunity for Working Students," p. 5.

102. *Daily O'Collegian*, 18 September 1941, p. 1, 15 September 1940, p. 1, 29 November 1951, p. 3, 21 May 1939, p. 4.

103. *Daily O'Collegian*, 29 November 1951, p. 3; A. Frank Martin, "Yesterday's Entertainers—Today," *Oklahoma A. and M. College Magazine*, vol. 16, no. 8 (March 1944), pp. 3, 8, 9, 13.

104. *Oklahoma Agricultural and Mechanical College Catalog, 1950-1951*, pp. 51-55; McFarland, p. 59.

105. McFarland, pp. 65-70.

106. "Student Union Opens," *Oklahoma A. and M. College Magazine*, vol. 22, no. 2 (October 1950), p. 5; A students' building on the Oklahoma A. and M. campus pre-dates the Depression of the 1920s. Major pushes for the construction began in 1941. Over the years a number of unsuccessful bills to fund a building were introduced in the Oklahoma Legislature. In September 1938 President Bennett asked for $450,000 in grant money from the federal Public Works Administration. This application was returned without being acted upon because of a lack of evidence that Oklahoma would be willing to provide matching funds for the project. For further reading of this facet of the Student Union's history see "Student Union Talk," *Oklahoma A. and M. College Magazine*, vol. 8, no. 4 (October 1936), pp. 3-4. *1937 Redskin*, p. 36; E. W. Clark to Henry G. Bennett, 9 September 1939, and H. A. Gray to Henry G. Bennett, 10 November 1938, Bennett Correspondence File, President's Papers.

107. *Daily O'Collegian*, 6 January 1937, p. 1.

108. *Daily O'Collegian*, 15 December 1936, p. 1, 14 September 1950, p. 1; "Student Union Opens," p. 5.

109. *Daily O'Collegian*, 14 September 1950, p. 13.

110. "Description of the Students' Union Building—Oklahoma A. & M College," [1948], Weldon Barnes Collection; "Student Union Building Revenue Bonds, Series 1948," 1 July 1948, President's Papers; Chester A. Tibbetts, "Silver Anniversary at the Student Union," manuscript, 1 February 1976, Student Services Collection.

111. Allen B. Reding, "Student Union Twenty-Five Year Presentation," 14 February 1976, pp. 1-2, Student Services Collection.

112. *Daily O'Collegian*, 13 January 1948, p. 2.

113. *Daily O'Collegian*, 14 September 1950, pp. 14, 16, 18-20.

114. *The Student Union* (1951-1952), publicity booklet, Student Union File, Student Services Collection.

115. *Daily O'Collegian*, 13 May 1950, p. 11.

116. "Alumni Mecca . . . Student Union," *Oklahoma A. and M. College Magazine*, vol. 22, no. 6 (February 1951), pp. 12-14; *Daily O'Collegian*, 27 September 1950, p. 1; *1951 Redskin*, pp. 4-5. In addition to those mentioned in the chapter text, other charter members of the Student Union Advisory Board were Bob Lemon, Bill Long, Emmalyn DeShong, Ross Conrad, King Gibson, Arlen McNeil, George Allison, Charles R. Graham, Mary Prichard, Betty Fox, Peggy Lawyer, Marjorie Blackburn, Abe L. Hesser, Richard Von Drehle, Doris Pitcher, and Bruce Johnson.

117. *Daily O'Collegian*, 26 September 1951, p. 1, 23 October 1951, p. 3.

118. Tibbetts, pp. 1-2.

119. *Daily O'Collegian,* 4 November 1950, p. 7, 28 July 1950, p. 1, 17 October 1950, p. 8, 20 May 1950, pp. 1, 6, 5 October 1950, pp. 1, 6, 21 July 1950, pp. 1, 6, 18 January 1951, p. 12; Abe L. Hesser, "The Oklahoma State University Student Union," manuscript, pp. 1-5, Student Services Collection.

120. Hesser, p. 4.

121. *Daily O'Collegian*, 20 September 1950, p. 2.

122. Author's personal communication with J. Lewie Sanderson, 8 January 1988; *Daily O'Collegian*, 23 February 1951, p. 1.

123. Tibbetts, p. 3.

124. *Daily O'Collegian*, 18 December 1951, pp. 2-3, 17 February 1951, p. 2, 16 March 1951, pp. 3, 10.

125. *Daily O'Collegian*, 22 June 1951, pp. 1, 10, 27 September 1950, pp. 1, 3, 29 September 1950, p. 1, 10 December 1950, p. 8.

126. *Daily O'Collegian*, 19 June 1950, p. 8.

127. *Daily O'Collegian*, 3 January 1952, p. 2.

128. *Daily O'Collegian*, 11 January 1952, pp. 1, 10.

129. "He Carries A Torch for A. and M.," *Oklahoma A. and M. College Magazine*, vol. 23, no. 6 (February 1952), p. 32; "Basic Hope for Peace," *Oklahoma A. and M. College Magazine*, vol. 23, no. 6 (February 1952), p. 34; "Your Great Adventure," pp. 10-15, 1945, manuscript, Weldon Barnes Collection; "Agricultural and Mechanical College Financial Report," *Oklahoma Agricultural and Mechanical College Bulletin Series*, 30 June 1952, p. 35, President's Papers.

130. *Daily O'Collegian*, 22 December 1949, p. 6.

131. Karleen Anderson DeBlaker, "What Is Oklahoma State University," p. 1, undated manuscript, Student Services Collection; *Daily O'Collegian*, 22 October 1960, p. 2.

# 7 Student Services Befitting A University

It is a truism that civilization itself depends upon the transmission of knowledge from one generation of young people to the next. Societies depend upon each new generation to accept and employ what it learns. As a result, the burdens falling to a university are great. Civilization is never more than a generation away from ignorance.

Given this basic principle of national prosperity, it is easy to understand why taxpayers, college authorities, and even parents, find college students such an enigma—puzzling, ambiguous and, at times, even inexplicable. College students can be compassionate, helpful, and funny. They can also be cruel, destructive, and discourteous. While a certain student event might bring state-wide pride and national acclaim, another situation, occurring only days later, could bring embarrassment, legislative denunciations, and a flood of angry letters to the college president.

On the last day of June 1966, Oliver S. Willham retired from the presidency of the Oklahoma State University. Appointed president on January 17, 1952, President Willham ended a long and difficult fourteen years of dealing with perplexing problems, often involving the most enigmatic students yet to be seen on the campus. A modest and humane man, with a knack for remembering names, Dr. Willham was the first Oklahoma A. and M. graduate to hold the position of president. His retirement also marked another milestone. This president was the first not to be fired, resign, or die while in the position.[1]

In the beginning the Oklahoma Agricultural and Mechanical College students welcomed Dr. Willham's promotion from the position of executive vice president. The new president had a proven record of caring about students. The *Daily O'Collegian*, while acknowledging that "Willham Faces Mammoth Job," editorialized: "We believe that Dr. Willham will direct A&M College to new recognition and improvements with the same practical, sincere, and unassuming manner which has led him to his present position."[2] At the time of his appointment no one could know that over the next fourteen years this loyal Aggie campus veteran would face unprecedented problems and challenges.

Some of the issues that President Willham would be facing during the 1950s and early 1960s were simply characteristic of the times. The nation as a whole was experiencing a time largely without deprivation. College students were called apathetic. Others suggested that student indifference to larger problems was simply a reflection of the character of the entire nation. People were tired, if not lethargic, after the colossal effort required to win World War II. The Korean conflict never would be called a war. Although warnings appeared in the campus newspaper as early as 1955, Vietnam was still many years away. Other problems were so large, so impersonal and remote, that people mostly repressed them. The threat of a nuclear holocaust or communism, to say nothing of desegregation and all of its implications, seemed remote, perhaps even too perplexing to worry about. Even more difficult to imagine were the early 1960s events on the campuses of the University of California at Berkeley and Columbia University and subsequent protests by college students throughout the nation against "the establishment."[3]

The 1950s was a time when John Dewey's "progressive education" seemed to reach full flower. Students increasingly assumed that they knew more than their teachers and often did not hesitate to tell them. Student governments not only governed students but gave suggestions to presidents and deans, sometimes in the form of ultimatums. Like some students of today, great effort would be taken to enroll in classes already full; then later the same student would drop the course. Students complained about the food in the campus dining halls, while consuming their third helping. Others would drive their car to the Student Union, two blocks away, knowing full well the adjacent parking lots to the union were always full at that time and always had been full over their entire four-year stint as students.

President Willham moved to the presidency promising to continue the college's goal of providing "an educational opportunity for every boy and girl in Oklahoma who wants to receive higher education."[4] He assumed oversight of a campus physical plant valued at nearly $41 million and an on-campus enrollment of 8,000 students. Compared to other land-grant colleges, the Oklahoma A. and M. College ranked eleventh in the nation in total student registrations, second in the number of students enrolled in agriculture and home economics, and fifteenth in the total number of all degrees conferred. A campus centerpiece, the Edmon Low Library, was nearing completion. Education for Oklahoma's sons and daughters was still financially within reach, being a bargain at a near national low of $550 to $700 for a year of study.[5]

On the surface Dr. Willham appeared to have a solid base upon which he could continue to build. However, significant events, some known and others inconceivable, immediately surfaced. The transition from Henry G. Bennett to a new president would be anything but smooth. A low salary scale for faculty and problems with the administration of the college's athletic program resulted in the North Central Association of Colleges and Secondary Schools announcing that it would recommend dropping the Oklahoma A. and M. College from their list of accredited schools on July 1, 1953. The news rocked the state and campus; some students talked of withdrawing if accreditation was lost. One week before the deadline, on June 26, the North Central Association withdrew the discrediting notice. Promises from Dr. Willham to correct the problems, plus a special $825,000 appropriation from the Oklahoma Legislature, averted disaster.[6]

Other problems faced the institution and were inherited by the new president. The postwar prediction of an enrollment drop-off of about 10 percent never happened. To compound the difficulty the "baby boomers" began to arrive on campus by the end of Willham's years in office. By 1966 the student enrollment had nearly doubled to over 15,000 students. As a result the college president was forced constantly to express the need for a "merely adequate" budget.[7] For example, in 1955 Dr. Willham stated: "Oklahoma A&M College is in the predicament of having too many students for the number of faculty employed. This situation, alarming now, is likely to become dangerously acute as enrollments increase, unless added funds are provided for resident instruction."[8] Through his fourteen-year presidency the same issues continually resurfaced—replace "temporary" buildings, develop faculty salary programs, increase student fees, and build ample facilities to house and educate the growing student body.[9]

Oklahoma's taxpayers and government leaders, as usual, largely remained passive to the college's appeals for reasonable funding. In contrast, these same groups became publicly outraged when the Aggies staged a property-damaging student holiday, or worse, a panty raid on a women's residence hall. After a May 1955 panty raid which caused $1,200 damage, twenty-four men and women were disciplined, including two student expulsions and eight suspensions.[10] Illustrating another consequence of the raid, a citizen from Mountain View wrote President Willham stating: "It is my opinion, that if you cannot maintain enough order in the school, so that such decent and self respecting students as yet exist, do not have to submit to so called panty raids by the bums and hoodlums that are enrolled as students, then you should resign. A man would be a fool indeed to send a girl to college in such a filthy place as the A&M College.''[11]

Despite a strict prohibition and stern public warnings, there was another campus disturbance in 1959—a "victory" walkout involving approximately 3,000 students. Again, in 1962, thousands participated in what was called a riot. Thirty-one students, including nine expulsions and twelve suspensions, were disciplined after havoc broke out in the Murray, Stout, and Willard Hall campus living areas. Interestingly, nine of the punished students were females, each charged with inciting and encouraging the men to enter their living areas.[12]

Both students and administrators grew increasingly perplexed—and frustrated—with each of these public relations catastrophes. Student Anne Larason's editorial on the riot situation pointed out that the May 1962 events "resulted in extensive property damage to the dormitories, the severe disciplining of several OSU students, and worldwide unfavorable publicity for the University.''[13]

Among administrators, Abe L. Hesser, the director of the Student Union, university housing, and food service, wrote the dean of student affairs a stinging sixteen-point letter covering the things needing correction to prevent further student disturbances. Along with questioning unclear lines of authority and the efficiency of student discipline, Hesser suggested that the Oklahoma Highway Patrol or even the National Guard should be called to bring order, since students held little respect for local police. Providing some insight to the possible dynamics at work, Hesser then theorized: "I think some concern should be given to the fact that the students I have talked to indicate that approximately six to twelve athletes . . . actually started the disturbance and left as soon as it got underway . . . . They had planned all semester to lead a panty raid on the dorm. I might also add that there were a number of girls who encouraged this by wearing scanty clothing, leaving their lights on, and actively encouraging the boys to come on in.''[14] There can be little doubt that the Aggie students' panty raids compounded the institution's problems.

Another complication, in which the college fared better, was the period of transition involving the integration of black students. The United States Supreme Court's controversial, but landmark, decision nullifying the concept of "separate but equal" was handed down on May 17, 1954. The Student Senate had passed an official resolution more than a year earlier, in March 1953, declaring, in part: "We, the Student Senate, look forward to the day when racial equality shall be a reality on our campus. Further, we wish to express our approval of all constructive measures to this end.''[15] The vote on the senate resolution was 7 to 3. Segregation, with all of its complexity, was deeply rooted in the Oklahoma culture.[16]

Although Sapulpa graduate student Nancy Davis broke the segregation barrier by enrolling for a master's degree in home economics in 1949, in spite of the dean's lack of support, it was not until September 1954 that the *Daily O'Collegian*, was able to print an editorial headlined "A&M Welcomes State's First Negro Freshman." Two black men and one black woman had enrolled as freshmen. They were the first undergraduates ever to be permitted to do so. Previously, undergraduate students could enroll at the Oklahoma A. and M. College only if the courses they needed were unavailable at Langston University. While President Willham saw little change in policy as necessary because of the court's decision, he did draw the line at assigning a black student and a white student as roommates in college housing. However, despite public proclamations, black students would encounter racism, and the problems would remain to contemporary times.[17]

In a 1955 poll taken by Oklahoma A. and M. psychology professor Herman M. Case, which randomly sampled 3 percent of the student body, the findings demonstrated that the majority of the students would have trouble accepting black students in their social groups, college dances, and residences. The student respondents were more tolerant of black students in academics, athletics, and student government. Professor Case was not surprised with these findings as the Aggie students of 1955 were "people who have had discrimination drummed into them literally from the day they were born."[18]

In 1951 Johnny Bright, an outstanding football player from Drake University, was seriously injured in a game in Stillwater. The incident was reported in *Time* and *Life* magazines and boded that there would be integration problems. In 1960 racial problems continued when Josh White attempted to secure the office of president in the Oklahoma Young Democrats. To the positive side of the mixed ledger, Samuel Howard was named a *Redskin* Congratulate in 1961, and the first black fraternity at OSU, Alpha Phi Alpha, was installed in April 15, 1958. Lee Ward, a Stillwater school principal, served as advisor to Alpha Phi Alpha at the time of colonization. Donald Brown, Archie Harris, and Orlando Hazley, along with Howard, held early leadership positions in the chapter.[19]

Cars and campus parking remained a continuing problem through the 1950s and early 1960s. In 1951 the first campus parking permits were issued to restrict faculty and student parking to certain lots. At the time, OSU Security Chief Tillman I. Bocock reported "the traffic problem got out of hand because students would try and drive from one class to the next to avoid walking. Traffic was so heavy it's a wonder some one didn't get killed."[20] Meanwhile, the student response was "parking lots have been scientifically placed so that students must walk at least two miles to class each day." Noting that Abraham Lincoln walked four miles a day to school and then became president, an Aggie should then obvi-

Although transportation to campus remained a problem for many, students could whet their appetites before setting out on their long journeys back to their cars by stopping at the Y Hut. Operated by Ralph and Velma Jackson, the cafe was located just east of the Classroom Building. The Jacksons, both blind, were an inspiration to the campus community.

ously someday become vice-president since every alumnus would have covered half of Lincoln's distance each day. Forty percent of the student body was driving a car on campus and around Stillwater by 1962. The problem was proclaimed perennial. Suggestions to limit who could bring automobiles to campus were heard, but no solution was or has been found.[21]

While lenient about automobiles, the rules governing general student conduct remained traditional and restrictive. No undergraduates could live in apartments or other unsupervised housing without official college approval. Women's hours improved in 1962 when changes were made to permit freshman and sophomore coeds 10:30 P.M. hours on weeknights, regardless of their grades. All women could stay out until 1:00 A.M. on Friday and Saturday evenings. Students were still required to provide a written excuse to their instructor the first class following an absence. Alcoholic beverages were prohibited everywhere on campus and at all student organization events held off-campus. Punishments for violation of the prohibitions on alcohol consumption were severe. Nonetheless in 1961-62 the Student Conduct Committee heard 134 discipline cases. Of these, about one-half involved alcohol rules violations. Guilty students were always placed on "alcohol probation," and some were dismissed from school. If the event occurred in a residence hall, the students were generally moved to another building.[22]

After a one semester trial period, Saturday classes were re-instituted; students returned to a five and one-half day school week. Administrators argued shorter school weeks resulted in lowered grade averages, more student absences, and a noticeably empty library on the weekends. In the later days of Dr. Willham's administration 7:30 A.M. classes were started in order to utilize crowded campus classroom space better. While the college fine-tuned the academic schedule, students agitated for a dead week, a period of moratorium from routine homework and examinations the week before final examinations. They also debated what form final examination week should take.[23]

A peak year for President Willham and his institution was 1957. The Oklahoma Agricultural and Mechanical College, after sixty-seven years of existence, officially became the Oklahoma State University of Agriculture and Applied Science on July 1. Throwing out tradition, an opinion poll showed that students favored the name change by a two to one margin.[24] Among the students, though, there were objections and strong feelings. John E. James urged: "I think the name of Oklahoma Agriculture and Mechanical College is an excellent name. The change needed is for some unsatisfied people to move elsewhere."[25] Another student, Jim Goodhue, favored a name change, but wanted to avoid any possible confusion with the sister institution in Norman. Goodhue advocated a name like Great Plains University, North American University, or Atomic University, to assure some true identity for his college.[26] Despite the minority opposition and creative advocates, most students, like Esta Lee Barnes of Stillwater, simply thought: "We have a university's qualifications and we should be recognized as such."[27]

The OSU name change was followed by other adjustments. In the same week that Oklahoma Governor Raymond Gary signed the bill into law changing the college's name, the Big Seven Conference added OSU to membership to form the Big Eight. On May 18, 1957, the college newspaper blasted a headline across page one: "OSU Finally Admitted to Big 7 Conference."[28] Within months, 1949 graduate Robert L. McCulloh had completed the words and music to the *Alma Mater*, and Frank "Pistol Pete" Eaton rode in the 1957 homecoming parade spurring support for his caricature sketch to become a permanent tradition. Eaton, a legend in his own lifetime on the Aggie campus, had been informally the mascot since 1923. In 1958 Charley Lester, agriculture sophomore from Clinton, appeared as the first Pistol Pete in the annual homecoming events. The following year Bill Smith, Ardmore sophomore, weighted his body with the now famous, oversized, papier-mache head of Pistol Pete. Pistol Pete subsequently continued as another common OSU image.[29]

As committees of students, faculty, and administrators blessed new songs and mascots to fit the new university mystique, student traditions and activities persisted. Like always, some changed, some grew, and others entered oblivion. General guidance for new students appeared in *Aggie Angles*, the student handbook. Under "Table Tips" student couples were told that "unless asked direct questions by the waiter, the lady expresses her wishes only to her date." Likewise, "toothpicks are

Frank B. "Pistol Pete" Eaton served as the model for OSU's mascot. Often entertaining students with tales of the Old West, songs, and fiddle playing, he was sure to attract a crowd with his legendary fast draw. But even Eaton had an occasional bad day—once he drew and shot a hole in the baseboard of the Student Union's Varsity Room.

as out of place in public as toothbrushes, so avoid their use."[30] In a section titled "Between Classes," *Aggie Angle's* readers were asked to remember "that no matter how comfortable the divans in the Union are, they are not objects upon which you assume the horizontal position— dirty feet and all. Sleep vertically and gracefully."[31] The walkway between the Student Union and Theta Pond was proclaimed "Howdy Lane." When passing, everyone was to greet each other with "Howdy, Aggie." Students were asked, if not compelled, to continue the frenzied waving of their arms at athletic events. Finally, everyone was invited—although there was usually no room to sit down—to join in the popular coffee hour in the Student Union's Sun Room.[32]

A student club or organization existed to match nearly every interest. Among nearly 200 student-led groups were the Slowpokes, a student automobile club; the Aggie Barbell Club; and the Double "O" Club, an organization for disabled students. Historically student organizations have existed to meet the needs and interests of members, whether those interests were social, educational, or simply to add another credit to a resume. A plague for serious student group leaders, then and now, was the question of how to involve more students. Variety and opportunity simply does not attract participation. OSU undergraduates were no exception. In 1958, for example, only about 25 percent of the students belonged to one of the organizations. Within the larger analysis, it did help that many belonged, and substantially contributed, to three or more organizations. A detracting force was the fact that while many students held memberships in organizations, they participated and contributed negligibly.[33]

What did cause student participation was a nationally prominent speaker or entertainment event. Former President of the United States Harry S. Truman and World War I Congressional Medal of Honor winner combat pilot Eddie Rickenbacker both drew large audiences in 1957 and 1962, respectively. In 1963 the Allied Arts program celebrated its fortieth anniversary. Under the directorship of P. Terry Martin and starting in 1947, Max Mitchell, the A and B series offered a setup unique in the country. The students supported the programs, but this was not surprising given the menu of entertainment offered through the years.[34]

In 1953 students could purchase a ticket for a dollar to see Henry Fonda and Lloyd Nolan act in *The Caine Mutiny Courtmartial*. Fred Waring and the Pennsylvanians as well as Arthur Fiedler and the Boston Pops each made two different appearances in Gallagher Hall during the 1950s and early 1960s. Van Cliburn and Peter Nero displayed their classical talents during this time. Jazz concerts were performed by Count Basie and Ella Fitzgerald, backed up by Gene Krupa and Dizzy Gillespie. Under the auspices of Allied Arts the ever popular big band sounds of Benny Goodman, Jimmy Dorsey, Glenn Miller, and Duke Ellington came to campus.[35]

A long string of outstanding comedians further balanced the program offerings of Martin, Mitchell, and other campus organization sponsors. Victor Borge and George Gobel performed in the early fifties. A decade later Bob Hope and the Smothers Brothers packed overflow crowds into Gallagher.[36] After riotous renditions of such classic folk songs as "Cabbage" and "Since My Canary Died," the student audience delighted to hear the Smothers Brothers declare their pleasure in visiting "the great city of excitement, Stillwater, America—city of sin."[37] Hope, not to be upstaged by Tom and Dick Smothers, answered the questions about how old he was by replying, "Jack Benny is 39 and I'm 10 years younger than he."[38] Hope appeared on campus in 1962 and 1963.

Each year other name entertainment came to campus for the Junior-Senior Prom. The Student Senate and other interest groups debated back and forth whether corsages should be bought for this huge annual event. More simply stated, the question was: were they a financial hardship on the men? Eventually, corsages and Gallagher Hall, traditional site for the prom, were abandoned. In 1956 the prom moved to the Student

Thanks for the Memory!!!
Overflow crowds at Gallagher
Hall enjoyed performances by
entertainer Bob Hope in 1962
and 1963.

Union, where the second and third floors were closed to everyone but ticket holders; and Les Brown and his "Band of Renown" combined for a successful change of tradition. Other proms featured the Four Freshmen, the Les Elgart Orchestra, Ray Anthony, and Woody Herman. For $3.50 a couple, thousands of students crowded this event year after year.[39]

While the Junior-Senior Prom remained a yearly campus highlight, other student activities also endured. But like many student enterprises, some activities had more success than others. Attempts to recognize excellence in student leadership and scholarship failed. In the late 1950s a Student Senate Achievement Day was annually held before being voted out of existence due to a lack of participation and interest. An Association of Women Students-sponsored Scholarship Emphasis Week did not fair much better, even when one of the days was pushed as a time to "take a date to the library." Still another week focused on Oklahoma's heritage. Western Week, a Block and Bridle-sponsored event, required every student to dress western. Students violating the western dress code were jailed by student deputies. An oversized pair of jeans hung in front of the Student Union to add appropriate symbolism. Like Achievement Day and Scholarship Emphasis Week, Western Week folded after several years. Westernism somehow became confused with rowdyism. A Brahma bull ended up inside the union in 1958. Campus property damage and fear of mob violence added to Western Week's demise. The May 24,

1960, edition of the *Daily O'Collegian* commemorated the passing of Western Week with the headline: "In Memoriam."[40] Finally, Sadie Hawkins Week, one of the longest running of traditional weeks on campus, began to lose spirit and enthusiasm among students. The situation had become so bad that one male student complained, "In fact, it's much too safe out on campus for Sadie Hawkins Week."[41]

The phenomena of campus queens dated to 1911, and queen coronations made the transition from the Oklahoma A. and M. to OSU years.[42] A 1960 student editorial proclaimed, "Oklahoma State undoubtedly has more queens than all of medieval Europe ever thought of." In reality, it did seem to the writer that "every group, lodge, order, tribe, political party, non-political party, club and fraternity has a queen."[43] Thirty-seven queens were chosen to different titles in the 1953-54 school year. Hundreds more coeds served as attendants, ladies-in-waiting, or runners-up. Through the fall of 1955 twenty-three additional women were named to positions of campus royalty. Perhaps, one of the most successful of these was Delois Faulkner, a native of Sallisaw. Miss Faulkner was chosen queen of the American Royal Livestock Show in Kansas City and then was named 1955 Maid of Cotton.[44]

Campus beauty queen contests were governed by rules set forth by the Association of Women Students (AWS). Conflicts of interest and purpose collided when the AWS banned any queen contestants from appearing in public or photographs in bathing suits, shorts (including Bermuda shorts), or toreador pants. Violations resulted in the candidate being declared ineligible. This particular rule was denounced by an agitated group of students, including a minority of females, as old-fashioned and ridiculous.[45] Many male students were against the rule and simply stated it "was doing the girls (and us) an injustice." On the other side of the issue, another student, perhaps aware of larger concerns, reflected: "It is a good ruling because it stops all those cheesecake photographs published in the state newspapers."[46]

Regardless, the rule stood as declared. Support from the administration, particularly the dean of women, stood firmly on the side of the AWS. Despite the furor over queen contest rules, the AWS served as the primary advocate of coed interests on campus. A futuristic conference held in 1956 by the AWS brought speakers to campus who focused on the theme "Women as Winners." In two- or three-year cycles the AWS agitated, always through established channels, for liberalized hours for women. By current standards, the 1950s AWS was a conservative organization. Allowing for the nature of the campus, the organization's social events, including "kampus klues," an orientation program for women, and Mom's Weekend, encouraged support among women. Speakers focused upon women student pride. In general, the AWS gently pushed for women's equality, perhaps, at times, unknowingly. Yet the organization did move the male-dominated campus toward accepting women on an equal basis. Among others, some of the AWS presidents of the time were Luanne Mohler, Grace Hays, and Connie Staff.[47]

As the AWS lobbied for women, other Aggie student enterprises continued to mature. In 1959 the thirtieth annual Varsity Revue, "Kontinental Kapers," played before a full house each of three evenings. Hundreds of students were annually involved in the production, set construction, music, and dancing in the now near-professional campus extravaganza. Doris Wuestenburg became almost synonymous with Varsity Revue after dancing in shows for five years. The technology of motion pictures permitted 50,000 people to see the 1957 Varsity Revue production. Competition among contending student acts was always intense. No professional help was allowed. Any profits were returned to the sponsoring organizations, Theta Sigma Phi and Sigma Delta Chi, women's and men's journalism fraternities, for scholarships.[48]

In 1954 the *Daily O'Collegian*, under the editorship of Neil Goble, began its sixtieth year of continuous publication. Only the year before a student writer concluded that for decades the *"O'Colly* has tried to keep students off the grass, attend class and convocations, show school spirit and support worthwhile activities."[49] Over one hundred students received practical experience in journalism by doing every facet of work needed to produce a newspaper five days a week. Through the Willham years the *O'Colly* remained at the center of campus storms, prodding a "do-little" Student Senate, complaining about the need to pave oceans of campus mud, supporting causes such as more state appropriations, and endorsing student political candidates. By 1959 the tabloid-sized companion to morning campus coffee drinkers could lay claim to being the newspaper with the largest circulation in Payne County. Pete Schneider, Janice Crook, and Al Sylvester had charge of a daily press run of 9,500 copies a day, and the 1,710,000 total *Daily O'Collegians* distributed over the course of the academic year.[50]

In 1959 the *Redskin*, the OSU yearbook, held its golden anniversary. Eighteen of the fifty former editors returned to their campus to share stories and compare notes. By the time of the reunion of editors the *Redskin* had amassed an enviable record of six "All-American" ratings, including a string of four consecutive such ratings running from 1952 to 1956. The "All American" rating was a superior score, the highest collegiate rating given in nationwide competition by the Associated Collegiate Press. Bob Kietzman and Glen Lemon edited "All-American" *Redskins* in 1954 and 1955. Additional *Redskin* editors of the period included Terry Lerd (1952), Richard Hays (1957), Boyd Chambers (1958), and Gordon Hart (1959).[51] Charley Wieman, 1956 editor, ended his "All-American" annual with the reflection: "The editors and staffs of other yearbooks on other campuses, and we of the *Redskin*, are all members

In 1959, the *Redskin* had its golden anniversary. Attending the celebration were eighteen of the fifty former editors. James S. Mayall, 1911 editor and assistant editor of the 1910 edition, is greeted by Gordon Hart, 1959 editor. Looking on (*left to right*) are B. L. Wertz, 1921 editor; Elbert Pace, 1923 editor; Russell Scrivner, 1916 editor; and Richard Hays, 1957 editor.

of a brotherhood of very tired people."[52]

While the stars of the *Redskin* and the *Daily O'Collegian* rose in the late fifties, the *Aggievator*, student humor magazine, was suspended and then permanently forced out of business, after thirty-seven years of irregular publication. The 1920s had given the nation vaudeville, burlesque shows, and campus humor publications. Frankly, the *Aggievator* was never a favorite publication of OSU administrators, since institutional irreverence, questionable taste, and censorship problems seemed to be continuing annoyances. Later years of financial problems, and a drop in general student interest gave the institution an opportunity, if not a reason, to review the further need for any campus humor magazine.[53] After all, despite its long tradition dating to 1921 "from the standpoint of supervisors and the University administration, the *Aggievator* has frequently, if not generally, been regarded as a publication of dubious value and advisability."

A committee of faculty and students compiled a lengthy report on the campus humor magazine during the 1957-1958 academic year. A part of the report included a poll of OSU students with the results unclear. Support for the *Aggievator* and its tradition in history surfaced when one student respondent volunteered: "In years past it was one of the best published and my parents and their friends couldn't wait to read it. It was very good publicity—showed we could be broad-minded." Another student noted: "The *Aggievator* added to an otherwise dull existence here at the University." Perhaps sarcastically, a student supporter flatly rationalized: "We need something for the President to be shocked about."

*Aggievator* detractors also came forward. One student affirmed: "We can do without degrading literature—and spend our time on the academic phases." Another suggested: "It is neither humorous or a magazine." One student, generally representing most of the negative opinions, offered that the *Aggievator* "had degenerated into a lewd and often violent type even below 'pulp' magazines on the newsstands."

After analysis and study, the humor magazine committee recommended "discontinuance of the *Aggievator* with real regret, realizing the significant role the magazine has played in the history of publications on the Oklahoma State University campus and the justifiable attachment that many persons have for it."[54] The *Aggievator* was shortly thereafter ordered into history. Last of a long line of *Aggievator* editors were Jim Thomas (1954), Norman Moore (1955), and Gary Doze (1956). Interestingly, Moore later returned to OSU to serve as the director of the Student Union and OSU's second vice president for student services.[55]

With the *Aggievator*'s passing some of the campus did miss, at least

SPECIAL COLLECTIONS, OSU LIBRARY

Have you seen that last issue of the *Aggievator*!?! Journalism student Don Terrell finds that the campus humor magazine can be quite an eye-opener!

until the next generation of students arrived, the urging to "take a chance on your reputation and buy a copy of the mealy, moth-eaten *Aggievator* which is still only two bits . . . ." Go ahead and ask, "Where can I get a feelthy magapine."[56]

A likely balance to the sometimes avant-garde *Aggievator* themes was provided by the campus Young Men's Christian Association (YMCA) and Young Women's Christian Association (YWCA). Although less influential than in earlier years, both organizations stood among the oldest at OSU. In 1955 the YMCA reached its fifty-fifth anniversary. A year later, in 1956, the YWCA became fifty years old. Both groups continued their work in promoting Christian leadership and ideas. Never organizations to shun controversial topics, in a single year the YWCA sponsored discussion groups on race relations, communism, and world hunger.[57]

Both groups' major annual event was Religious Emphasis Week (REW). Joining with other student groups in co-sponsoring REW, the "Ys" would annually bring in twelve or more nationally known speakers to conduct convocations, seminars, fireside chats, and personal conferences. A conservative estimate of the attendees at various activities scheduled for Religious Emphasis Week 1953 was 10,000. Generally religious activities, including REW, were valued by the administration. The institution gave active support by providing facilities in the old president's residence, then called the "White House," a religious life coordinator, and a budget partially derived from student directory sales. In 1953 Sam Botkin, an ordained Congregational minister, worked with the students as YMCA director and as an assistant to the dean of students.[58]

Religious Emphasis Week was a source of pride, both on- and off-campus. Similarly, recognition and more acclaim came to OSU in some unexpected ways in the 1950s and early 1960s. Twelve million television viewers saw Norman E. Gray, James W. Gentry, David E. Lawson, and Patricia Jo Pender appear on General Electric's "College Bowl" on December 11, 1960. The OSU team defeated Boston College on the weekly show; Allen Ludden moderated the battle of "varsity scholars."[59]

Other recognition for OSU came in a different form. In 1958 the OSU Flying Aggies was a decade-old student club. Starting with just twelve members, the ten-year-old Flying Aggies had been dominating intercollegiate flying competitions for eight years, winning the national championship five times. With their success, membership had grown to about two hundred. An additional benefit, in this same stretch of time, was that a thousand pilots had been taught their skills at OSU. Hoyt Walkup, club founder and longtime manager of the Stillwater Airport, had pioneered a tradition of winning and pride, as strong as any on the entire campus.[60]

During the early Willham years on the Stillwater campus, moustache wax was rediscovered and used effectively in stiffening crew-cut style haircuts. Slang such as "hacked"(meaning angry), "rack" (a bed), and beer bust (a party) came into vogue. Two-thirds of the student body had access to a television set and watched an average of three hours a week. Favorite programs included "Dragnet," "The Jackie Gleason Show," and "Batman." In 1954 pink and purple shirts, ties, and socks were favored by men. In the same year "the bop," a new dance fad, was banned in the Student Union. A few years later the twist fared better. While there was concern about the dancer's knees and ankles, the dean of women did say that she was not going to learn how to do the twist herself. Meanwhile, two Aggie male students were arrested for wearing Bermuda shorts. The arresting Stillwater officers charged the students with "indecent, immoral, and foolish" exposure of their legs.[61]

Students discussed and perpetuated longstanding activities through the Willham era. Cheating continued to be an issue that would not be solved—or go away. Dumping liquid soap detergent in the library fountain became a near annual event. Campus speakers and panels discussed student morals and whether sex education should be taught in Okla-

"Do this paper over - How do you expect me to give you a grade on a paper that isn't neat?"

Centennial Histories Series

homa's public schools. Students continued to toss each other into Theta Pond upon being "pinned," engaged, or announced as "going steady." In 1954 this activity got out-of-hand when a hundred students ended up in one campus fountain or another and in Theta's muddy water. Three injured coeds also landed in the campus hospital. Through these years the card game bridge was the largest participatory recreational activity on campus.[62]

While traditional behavior continued through Dr. Willham's tenure, there were also other notable imported trends. In 1958 the hula hoop was a rage among Aggies. By 1961 students had read twelve years of *Little Man On Campus*, starring the rumpled, often put-down student Worthal and Professor Snarf, the teacher who hassled undergraduate students at every opportunity. In 1963, elephant jokes occupied the students: "Do you know why elephants have red eyes? So they can hide in strawberry patches. Do you know how you can tell there is an elephant in your bathtub? Open its mouth and see if it smells like peanuts." In 1955 students were publicly clamoring for a big name Allied Arts program, specifically a new rock-and-roll group like Bill Haley and the Comets. Nearly ten years later the Beatles were beginning to make their mark in the music world.[63] Oklahoma State students generally liked the Beatles. However Ginger Durham thought: "The Beatles are to music as a coloring book is to art." Ron Osterhout flatly stated: "I wouldn't let my daughter marry one of them." Susan Schuler summarized: "I think their hair is too long, but they sound goooood! They look like the three stooges."[64]

The history of students and their out-of-class activities was chronicled through the 1940s, 1950s, and early 1960s by Haskell Pruett. "Doc," as he was known to thousands of students over his nearly quarter century of photographing student life and activities, could be recognized by his beaver top hat. An instructor of photography, Pruett and his shutterbug assistants would sometimes attend and take photographs at as many as thirteen dances in a single weekend. Pruett's photographic prowess was legendary; he once estimated that only one picture in five hundred turned out badly. "Doc's" hobby and recreation—his photographing of student events—permitted thousands of students over the years to retain cherished memories. Pruett retired in the summer of 1962, leaving behind an accurate record of campus events—a pictorial history of twenty-five years of student activities, which would increase in value with time.[65]

Functions such as the annual Howdy Dance, Junior-Senior Prom, and homecoming were photographed by Pruett. Each of these three major events, plus the Outstanding Speaker Program and the Senior Career Day, an event bringing high school seniors to campus, were all paid for by an activities fee of twenty-five cents each semester. The total dollars

The "Sultan of the Shutterbugs," Haskell "Doc" Pruett chronicled the out-of-class activities of students from the 1940s through the early 1960s in his photographs. Assisted by his wife, Agnes, Dr. Pruett assured that the cherished memories of by-gone days will live forever.

collected, $6,000 a year, comprised the budget of the Student Senate. The senate was the sponsoring organization for many events and the primary voice of the student body at OSU.[66]

Late in Dr. Willham's presidency he was asked what role student government should play in campus life. His reply stressed that issues involving academic affairs and general university policy were not the primary domains of student organizations. These were of concern to deans and vice presidents, and duplication resulted when students were involved. Student government should focus upon student life, Dr. Willham continued, where students could assess the desires and opinions of the entire student body. Thus, President Willham expressed his ideal of university governance. Naturally, the reality, and what the Student Senate thought, varied greatly from the president's expectation.[67]

To illustrate this discrepancy, in a two-year period from 1960 through 1962, the elected representatives of the students studied, recommended, and debated student loans, town housing, and the athletic cabinet. Additionally, the senate's interests led to action on campus traffic problems, dormitory telephones, or the lack of them, and a new plan for taking final examinations. The need for a foreign student advisor, a teacher evaluation program, and changes in the Allied Arts series also came under senator scrutiny. Not surprisingly, Dr. Willham's limited definition of student life as the domain of undergraduate leadership groups was broadly interpreted by students.[68] Thus, President Willham sometimes had to go before the board of regents when the students had overstepped their authority. But the president reasoned this happened because "students must have freedom if they are to learn how to use it, and you're going to have some problems now and then."[69]

Over time it became obvious that student government was run by an active, interested, but very small minority of the total students. As in larger society, elections were often won by a few votes cast by a small number of interested constituents. These problems were persistent at OSU. To use the jargon of the fifties, many students, maybe the majority of them, thought that their government was "Mickey Mouse," incompetent, and even irresponsible. There was little wonder then that many elections on the campus saw voter turnouts of 30 percent or less.[70] As

Although there was indifference to campus politics by the majority of students in the 1950s, organizations such as the Student Senate and Association of Women Students (AWS) continued to strive for improvements at the university. Here Barbara Autry, president of the AWS, and Tom Tate, president of the Student Senate, look over some campus plans with President Oliver S. Willham.

one disgusted student stated: "Popularity rules the polls and status seekers rule the Senate."[71]

In fairness, if not to present a sense of balance, the Student Senate provided valuable service despite the vocal detractors and the silent indifference of the vast majority of other students. Very real issues, such as student walkouts, the illegal consumption of alcoholic beverages at student functions, and housing discrimination in Stillwater, directed at both black and international students, were moved toward an improved chance for resolution by the senate's persistence. Theta Nu Epsilon, or TNE, that nagging secret political fraternity, was kept at bay by senate vigilance as this perplexing problem resurfaced in 1952, 1956, and again in 1962. The senate annually allocated a part of its budget to positive causes, such as Religious Emphasis Week, the General Electric "College Bowl" team, and homecoming. It was clearly from Student Senate initiatives, rooted in the 1950s, that the university developed "dead week," a teacher evaluation program, an annual audit of all on-campus student organization treasuries, and a specific office to serve the very unique needs of the thousands and thousands of international students who have studied at OSU over the years.[72]

For some student leaders their college experiences sparked a life-long interest in participating in the larger political arena. In 1959 and 1960 two students met in hotly contested political races to reinforce the notion that college politics can lead to political careers. In 1959 Colcord sophomore Dan Draper defeated agriculture major Wesley Watkins to win the office of Student Association vice president. In 1960 Watkins reversed the earlier outcome, when he defeated Draper and became the president of the Student Association. Draper eventually became an attorney and speaker of the Oklahoma House of Representatives. Watkins spent ten years on the OSU campus working as an assistant registrar and taking graduate work before moving to Washington as a member of the United States Congress. Continuing the phenomenon, two years after Watkins and Draper faced off at OSU, Henry Bellmon, a 1942 graduate, made political history when he was elected the first Republican governor of the state of Oklahoma.[73]

Whenever Student Association election ballots were being counted, often into the early morning hours, or students took to the streets for a walkout or panty raid, again at awkward hours, the dean of students or someone from student affairs was there. Additionally, Howdy Dances had to be chaperoned, student meetings advised, and individual students regularly needed disciplining or guidance. These responsibilities fell to the out-of-class and "odd-hours" university employees called student personnel staff. This work obviously grew more difficult with bulging student enrollments and new buildings, especially the Student Union and several new undergraduate residence halls. The size of the university would require, simply for the sake of efficiency and improved service to students, that these fragmented and decentralized auxiliary enterprises be coordinated as related offices and administered as a total system with common goals.

Whether purposefully or simply by chance, one of President Willham's first major acts was to direct a move toward the consolidation of campus student services. It was clear that something needed to be done. The 1953 North Central Association's threat to drop Oklahoma A. and M. College from the list of accredited institutions could, to a degree, be laid to what the campus visiting team found in their study of student services. Compared to fifty other doctoral degree granting institutions, the college ranked at or below the majority of other institutions in orientation, counseling programs, extracurricular activities, financial aid, and health services; in addition, the institution ranked well below three-quarters of the other universities in general student personnel administration. The North Central Association considered each area an institutional weakness.[74]

The North Central report was focused on institutional problems of priority and timing, not people. The "Student Personnel Point-of-View," the 1937 cornerstone document on student services in higher education, had been in existence for nearly two decades. The accreditation report merely pointed out the importance of student services and, through comparison with other major institutions, emphasized that Oklahoma A. and M. College was lagging behind. Certainly part of the blame rested with the ever-nagging problem of too few dollars to accomplish all that was important. Regardless of the causes, the student affairs program needed this boost. The North Central Association report represented a mixed blessing—unfortunate because it made public a negative rating but fortunate because it represented a catalyst to move forward. In the long run this momentary crisis was a pivotal event in the history of student services. Positive action quickly followed.

On December 19, 1952, President Willham sent a memorandum to faculty which announced that Edward L. Morrison, who had been director of campus residence halls for four years, had been appointed director of Auxiliary Enterprises, effective December 1. Morrison's promotion was the first chapter in the development of the eventual Office of the Vice President for Student Services. Morrison was to coordinate all college housing, including the residence halls for single students, the College Courts, Veteran's Village, the Student Union, all food units, a myriad of other pay-their-own-way non-academic support services, and the program at Lake Carl Blackwell. The operations placed under the new director were valued at more than $15 million.[75] The reason given for creating Auxiliary Enterprises was to "bring about greater efficiency and economy of operations by synchronizing, coordinating and consolidating these auxiliary units for better over-all administration."[76]

Morrison had received both his bachelor's and master's degrees as an Aggie student. While an undergraduate he was a three-year football letterman from 1922-1924, was a member of the Student Senate, and served as president of Sigma Phi Epsilon. Before returning to his alma mater he had been president of Panhandle A. and M. College at Goodwell for eight years.[77]

Joining Morrison on the central Auxiliary Enterprises management team was Raymond Garrett, who was the director's assistant and also responsible for campus concessions and commissaries, Dean McGlamery, Meta Rakey, and Pat Hofler. Each toiled with auditing and accounting functions. McGlamery and Hofler both remained at OSU for more than three decades. Hofler earned his way to the position of assistant vice president for student services. More importantly than being a wizard at dealing with dollars, Hofler became a personal, helpful friend to thousands of students.[78]

Morrison died of a heart attack on October 14, 1961, while serving in his eighth year as the first director of Auxiliary Enterprises. The death precipitated an evaluation of the future of Auxiliary Enterprises. At the president's invitation, Abe L. Hesser, director of the Student Union, recommended to the president that the position be elevated to that of vice president for business affairs, and that all campus service enterprises be channeled through one individual. No mention was made in the proposal as to whether the position would administer non-business or non-academic functions, specifically intramural programs, student activities, or student employment.[79]

After considering the alternatives, President Willham opted for a second proposal which was offered by Vice President for Academic Affairs Robert MacVicar. The airport, publishing and printing, and other functions clearly of service to the institution, not individuals, would be assigned to various line officers of the business office. The vice president for academic affairs would relinquish further responsibilities relating to student personnel programs; thus the dean of student affairs would assume broad new responsibility. In reorganizing, the MacVicar plan proposed that with Auxiliary Enterprises "it should be clearly stressed that they are not commercial ventures but rather service facilities needful to the creation of an environment suitable for study and learning— both in the formal areas of the curriculum and in the informal areas of the extra-curriculum."[80]

Basically, MacVicar's idea was to separate facility management from student life functions. A month after the academic vice president's memo was written, Student Union Director Hesser added the business management side of the housing and food units. As MacVicar recommended, the student personnel program in the residence halls continued to be administered by the dean of student affairs. In retrospect, the splitting of these functions was awkward, sometimes leading to confusion, ill feelings, and conflicts of accountability and territory. Adding to the problems, subordinates had two supervisors. Hesser and Dean of Student Affairs Frank E. McFarland had vast differences in philosophies, education, and professional experiences. At best, the variances in the two men's perspectives caused an uneasy relationship.[81]

A colleague of Hesser's in the Association of College Unions-International described him as "a great business man, but a poor manager of people."[82] These qualities and the conflicting interests of priorities can be illustrated by a 1962 memorandum from Director Hesser to the staff in the dean of student's area. Hesser, looking for more revenue from the canteens and concessions in the residence halls, asked about the longstanding policy of closing the snack areas from 8:00 P.M. to 10:30 P.M., the time for required quiet hours for study. In asking his question Hesser stated: "I think you can readily see that to close up during a period when students are most likely to purchase items from the concessions and canteen is poor management."

This memorandum asked the dean to reconsider the entire concept of quiet hours. The reason, according to Hesser, was "our residence halls are competing with apartments and rooming houses all over Stillwater who have no regulations of this type, and to enforce such strict regulations as quiet hours, places our residence halls in a very poor position."[83] No mention was made that historically all classifications of students, freshman to senior, had better grades, and therefore a higher graduation rate, than students living off campus. The conflict of efficient business management and enhancing student academic achievement, both essential and worthy goals, seemed to swing back and forth, with dominance usually depending upon student enrollment and the philosophy of the people in charge at the time.

Beyond the confusion caused by the struggle to discover the best administrative setup for student services, there can be little doubt that Hesser left an enduring mark on the beautiful, yet functional, Oklahoma State campus. Several Hesser-proposed and constructed buildings, including all of the high rise residence halls, continue to provide functional service to students and campus visitors. Hesser's business sense, facility management, and financial expertise (including paying for needed expansion without taxpayer's money), immeasurably aided OSU to grow through years of institutionally tight budgets in the 1950s and early 1960s.

Shortly after Hesser became the director of the Student Union on May 26, 1953, the building, originally claimed to be too big, was already crowded. A count of people entering the union's first floor in 1956 indicated that between 12,000 and 14,000 individuals entered the building each day. At this time, the Student Union was open eighteen hours a day, 365 days a year. Hesser proposed a major addition to the union in order to centralize services and offer more programs. Dedicated in December 1963, a five-story addition to the northeast side of the original union added 86,000 square feet of new space at a bonded cost of $2.25 million. In the expansion, offices were provided for the dean of student affairs, the Alumni Association, and the OSU Development Foundation. An escalator connected floors containing a new bookstore, a theater seating 600, offices for student government, and a fourth floor conference area, highlighted by three "Harvard" case study classrooms, each seating about 100 people.[84]

Joining Hesser in running the "Waldorf Astoria of Unions," so huge and complex as to rate as one of the top five unions in the nation, were a number of creative and capable people. From 1952 to 1958 Bill J. Varney toiled as assistant director. In 1958 Varney left OSU to become the director of the union at the University of Arizona. Vesta Etchinson remained the union's social director from 1950 to 1957; and upon her retirement she was replaced by Bettye Stratton. Both women worked with student programs, including scheduling, advising, and helping students in any possible way. Winsel Bilyeu worked as the manager of the Union Club, the union's hotel, from August 1955 and later became an assistant director. Norman Moore returned to his alma mater in 1959, later became the union's director, and still later, the OSU vice president for student services. Others playing pioneering roles in the union's early years included Bob Leake, Joe Robinson, Lucille Lovelady, Vi Shiever, Kitty Grantham, Emil Jafek, and John L. Gillum.[85]

Gillum was particularly noteworthy. Typical of many OSU employees who first came to campus as a student, Gillum spent his entire work life in service to the institution. The union's bookstore manager, he retired in June 1961 after forty years. A Minco native, with time out to serve in World War I, Gillum took ten years to complete a degree. He graduated in 1921, which was the same year that the college opened the first on-campus bookstore. Already employed in the finance office, Gillum was asked to order books for the proposed bookstore enterprise. He was next given the task of receiving the books. Without really realizing it he was eased into his life's career—running the bookstore for four decades as the first and only manager.[86]

Much of the union's popularity can be attributed to the building's student advisors and the Student Union Activities Board (SUAB). Organized before the union construction was completed, the SUAB has served as a policy-making and programming arm of the union since 1951. Involved students functioned as volunteer staff, organized from an executive board, with elected officers. The central governing SUAB then was subdivided into major subcommittees responsible for important func-

Regardless of the trials and tribulations of being a student, one could always relax with some good conversation and a cup of coffee at the Student Union.

tions such as publicity, social events, union exhibitions, and public relations. Annual SUAB events included the Union Fair, the Howdy Dance, casino parties, and starting in 1956 the former student government-sponsored Junior-Senior Prom. Art exhibits, bowling tournaments, bridge lessons, and sports forums were additional, but typical, SUAB activities. The SUAB assisted in hosting campus guests such as Emperor Haile Selassie of Ethiopia in 1954 and former President Harry S. Truman.[87]

The SUAB committees were a popular vehicle for student involvement, partly because there were enough jobs for everyone who volunteered. Not surprisingly, because so many students were involved, the office of SUAB president quickly became a prestigious and influential position. Unlike many other student leadership roles on campus this presidency was earned. Students normally would toil in a committee, rise through the ranks by demonstrating leadership ability, and ultimately, be elected to the presidency by their SUAB peers—a compliment of the highest kind, since popularity played only a small part in the decision.

Earliest SUAB presidents were Boyd "Pappy" Baker (1951-52), Rob Whiteaker (1952-53), and Ron Wright (1953-54). Through the mid-1950s the SUAB became well established under the leadership of people like Jim Pallard, Al Havenstrite, and Byron Behring. In 1960-61 Winston Shindell carried the responsibility, sparking a lifelong interest in union work. In the 1970s Shindell became director of OSU's Student Union and eventually became the director at the nation's largest student union on the campus of Indiana University. John McCabe and Mike Fenton became SUAB presidents just prior to the union's major expansion project. Linda Jones (1959-60), Judy Talmage (1961-62), and Diana Wilp (1964-65) each added a female perspective to the SUAB presidency during the early union years.[88] Each of these students, in turn, ably fulfilled the SUAB's purpose: "To see that obligations of the Union to students are fulfilled."[89]

Through the Willham years most things with the union went well. But there were also problems. After the popular student browsing room—a room to relax and read popular periodicals—was closed and turned over to the Alumni Association in 1953, there were loud student protests and an obituary in the *Daily O'Collegian*. Pigeons, or rather their droppings, caused costly damage to the building in 1956, and any reasonable idea on how to get rid of the birds was gratefully considered. In 1957 a heavy rain caused $3,000 worth of brick facing to fall from the building. Two years later rain again was a villain, this time flooding the basement and damaging nearly a thousand dollars worth of stored textbooks.[90]

The event of 1963 was a Union Club robbery. Two nervous, but heavily armed, men fired two shots while robbing the hotel's desk clerk, Jim Michael, of $39.75. Ironically, just a few hours before the robbery the local Police Benevolence Association had sponsored a charity show in another part of the building. Stillwater Police Chief Ralph L. White later conjectured that the bandits were after his department's show proceeds, which were earmarked for youth activities.[91]

Despite the temporary setbacks, national recognition came to the Student Union and Directors Tibbetts and Hesser. Representatives from eighty-nine colleges and universities came to the Student Union for the Association of Student Unions-International's (ASU-I) twenty-ninth annual national convention in April 1952. The 300 union professionals at the conference complimented everything from the decor of the building's lounges to the extensiveness of the games' room. These visitors were experts, and their praise confirmed what the staff, and others, had thought; the honors, however, did not end there. Exactly ten years later, Hesser was elected to the presidency of the ASU-I, according him national recognition for his work in the field of student unions and bringing the campus new prestige.[92]

As Hesser was serving his term as ASU-I president in 1962-63, a critical need for more on-campus student housing, for married and single students, consumed more and more of his time. The addition of university housing and food service to his title was no blessing in disguise for him. But perhaps the fact that Hesser, the builder, was there at the time was fortunate for the institution. In retrospect, the addition of Bennett and Stout Halls in the late 1940s had made Hesser's predecessors job easy by comparison. By the mid-1950s seven residences, three for women and four for men, housed 3,300 single students. Things were so good that a 1954 study of what later would become Big Eight institutions by a University of Kansas researcher revealed: "Oklahoma A&M not only has more permanent, top-quality student housing in use, but also has the lowest board and room cost for the 9-month term."[93] The same study indicated that Oklahoma A. and M. ranked second in facilities for married students, with 600 units available.[94]

Reading between the lines, the information also showed that a housing crisis was on the horizon. Oklahoma A. and M. College was only one of two schools in the survey with no housing units planned or under construction. Rapidly increasing enrollments and the critical mandated-by-rule requirement to house all undergraduate coeds on campus soon caused the possible problem to become reality. Starting in 1959 an image prevailed statewide that Oklahoma State had a housing shortage. For obvious reasons, the rumor was played down by university officials, but, in fact, only by moving married students out of on-campus apartments and converting existing basement lounge areas to living quarters were new students accommodated. Due to the housing shortage rumor, some high school seniors began sending in room applications more than a year in advance. Even worse, 207 fewer freshmen enrolled in 1961 than in 1960 despite 1,208 more prospective OSU students being available after high school graduation.[95]

Residence hall construction began in earnest. Anticipating a trend, university architect Philip A. Wilber predicted: "Taller residence halls seem destined to become a part of the Oklahoma State University campus. Reasons for this trend are both economy in structures and ability to locate larger numbers of students near the campus center, saving on walking time between residences and classes."[96]

In 1962 two five-story student residences, Halls A and B, were occupied. Two years later a ten-story women's residence was finished, forming a triplex connected by a common separate cafeteria, with seating for 1,000. The three buildings brought 1,039 new room spaces into the total campus residence system. In 1965 Governor Henry Bellmon joined other guests and dignitaries in dedicating the first air-conditioned residence halls, plus a cluster of new campus apartments for undergraduate single women. At the dedication ceremony, the buildings forming the triplex were named for Angelo C. Scott, Oklahoma A. and M. College president in territorial days, Comanche Chief Quanah Parker, and Ponca City oilman Lew Wentz. Additionally, the apartments were named for Ben Brumley, who was the first World War II veteran to die while living in Veteran's Village. Interestingly, Brumley Apartments soon became the most popular single women's residence on-campus.[97]

Anticipating an enrollment of nearly 20,000 students by 1970, another $24 million worth of student housing was in the planning stages a year after the Scott-Parker-Wentz Complex and Brumley Apartments dedication. Henry P. Iba Hall, a residence for 240 student-athletes, Kerr-Drummond Complex, and the Oliver S. Willham Complex were all added to Stillwater's skyline between 1966 and 1968. Iba Hall was named for longtime coach and athletic director, Henry P. Iba. Kerr Hall, a twelve-story tower, was named for U.S. Senator Robert S. Kerr of Ada. Frederick "Gent" Drummond, a Hominy alumnus of the class of 1909 and former chairperson of the OSU Board of Regents, was honored for forty-eight years of continuous service to the institution in the naming of the second twelve-story building. Of course, the Willham Complex was named for the former university president.[98]

As the tall residence halls were being built, the situation in married student housing also improved. OSU was unusual in that the campus student population consistently reflected a high percentage of married students. In 1958 a twenty-seven campus study showed that 30 percent of OSU's students were married, placing the institution second highest among the surveyed schools. In response, between 1957 and 1965 four separate apartment complex construction projects, providing over 800 new apartments, were financed through borrowed federal money and completed. Meantime, the business community, in its vigilance both

Rapidly increasing enrollments plus the requirement to house all undergraduate coeds in campus housing led to a massive building effort in the early 1960s. Instead of the "rambling" residence halls like Bennett, the new student housing consisted of several high-rise structures.

to help students and make some money, were rapidly building competitive off-campus apartments. Forty North and The Patio Club apartments were under construction in 1965.[99]

Whether married or single, students in 1965 were still getting a housing bargain. Undergraduate students paid the lowest room and board rates of the Big Eight schools. Depending on the selected hall and meal plan, rates ranged between $580 and $770 a year for room and board. Campus married student apartments with two bedrooms rented for $85 a month. At the end of this phenomenal time of building campus housing, 60 percent of the entire student body was taking advantage of the economical opportunity to live in either single and married student residences or in campus-affiliated sorority or fraternity houses.[100]

Perhaps like no other segment of a university community, catering to student food tastes brings the greatest rewards—and most problems.[101] Some of the food services problems were classic. For example, in 1952 the Bennett Hall cafeteria was awarded a plaque by *Institutions Magazine* for high achievement in quantity feeding. At roughly the same time a mother, writing to the Stout Hall dietitian—of course with a carbon copy to President Willham—stated: "I am convinced that the food is being carelessly selected and prepared and that those in charge are not too concerned about its edibility."[102] About the food service in general, a student wrote that by a decent meal—which he was not getting for his money—he meant "one in which the meat is relatively warm and not composed of mostly spam, bread, and cereal and one in which the dessert has a degree of freshness, not staleness."[103]

Innovations in food service came with the advent of a popular a la carte food service plan in Bennett and Willard Halls in 1957. Electric popcorn poppers and coffee pots, although illegal, brought further innovation that permitted everything from steaks to soup to be prepared in a student's room. Interestingly, in the same year a la carte service was introduced, a survey of students showed that about one-third of the hall residents owned either a popcorn popper or coffee pot, or both. However, the popcorn poppers were preferred. Their versatility allowed one to make spaghetti, hot tamales, and chili.[104] By 1960 the residence hall students holding a food contract were fed on about $1.25 a day. The campus food service operation had grown parallel to the housing construction, and at $1.25 a day per student the food service budget was tight. As a result, some students complained and innovated, but most generally lived through the experience of residence hall cafeteria eating with few problems.

Henry Clay Potts retired as the director of college food units on July 1, 1961, after serving the institution in several capacities for thirty-three years. An undergraduate classmate of President Willham, Potts' reputation as "barbecue king" had made him one of the best known charac-

Meal time at a typical residence hall cafeteria sometimes evokes looks of seriousness that might connote ''food for thought.'' Oh well, these connoisseurs of Aggie cuisine can always grab a hamburger later at the snack bar (*lower*) such as this one in Cordell.

ters on the OSU campus. Serving as assistant director and working closely with Potts in the food service operation was Mary C. Barnes. Other notable food unit employees included Naomi Oleta Pattillo, Gladys Beyer, and Audris Rife.[105]

Not unlike earlier times, residence hall rules afforded students the opportunity to protest, legislate, and further test their ingenuity. In the early fifties "visitation," the right to visit a student of the opposite sex in his or her room, began its prolonged history as a nagging headache for OSU administrators, and upon occasion, even the board of regents. At this time most women students saw little reason or need for visitation privileges. Conversely, most men supported the idea. Summing up the traditional stand, one male student commented: "Staid morals are a thing of the past. If the girls want the boyfriends in the dorm then they should be the ones to make the decisions."[106]

Students protested the hall telephones cutting off at 8:00 P.M. for study hours. Required evening curfews, still set for women only, were likened to the coeds' being in prison.[107] Robert B. Canfield, concerned about how the men were being watched with suspicion by women's residence hall staff, complained: "This gives you a funny feeling, to say the least, when they treat you like a sex-maniac walking in a house of saints."[108] A dress code in the Cordell cafeteria which outlawed shorts caused seven protesters to appear for dinner wearing dinner jackets, ties, and Bermuda shorts. For their efforts they received a mixed round of cheers and boos from their fellow Cordell residents. When Walter Boyles, one of the protesters, was asked if it would not be more civilized to wear something more appropriate, he replied, "Oklahoma is not civilized, it is cloddy."[109] The Cordell demonstration was a light-hearted protest, but in the next decade the puritan-like residence halls' rules would be severely tested, with student demonstrations, lawsuits, and escalated activism.

Much of the foundation for the later push to change the constraints for undergraduates was being laid by the evolving residence hall student government system. The Grand Council, which became the Women's Residence Hall Association (WRHA) in 1963, was formed in June 1943 to coordinate the social activities of the campus World War II Victory Halls. The Independent Men's Residence Hall Council (IMRHC), initially formed in the late forties, became the Men's Residence Hall Association (MRHA) in the early 1960s and coordinated intramural and social programs. Like the larger housing system, the interests of men and women were perceived to be different enough to warrant separation. Yet as early as 1950 the groups were holding an annual joint meeting.[110]

As the size of the residence hall system grew, the prestige and influence of the governing groups spread. Each group had a position in the Student Senate. The president of the Grand Council automatically became a member of the Association for Women Students. Both groups gave awards to the halls with the highest cumulative grade point average and held an annual honors banquet. Initially, their purpose was to coordinate. With time their focus turned toward representing all residence hall students' needs to housing administrators. In 1961 the OSU housing governments hosted, under chairperson Jan Fleming, the eighth annual Association of College and University Residence Halls (ACURH) conference. A forerunner to today's National Association of College and University Residence Halls Association, ACURH was the premier national student-based group of its kind. And, in 1965, the groups sponsored the first Residence Hall Week, an annual event still carried on to spotlight residence hall living.[111]

Early IMRHC presidents included: Jack Castleman (1953), Dwight Griggs (1954), and Bob Hamm (1955). Hamm later became a professor of marketing at OSU. Other presidents included Herman Van Bebber, Mark Ferguson, Myron Simons, and Al Evans. After the organization became the MRHA, Bob Ewing, Bill Lackey, Ron Shirley, and Gene Benson served in leadership roles. The Grand Council chose Mary Ann Wiemer and Betty Hefley to presidencies in the early 1950s. Later Grand Council presidents included Larita Gibbs, Carolyn Boyer, Sandra Hadwiger, and Joy Chase. Joyce Gray was Grand Council president when the group's name was changed to Women's Residence Hall Association in 1963.[112]

As the size and shape of the campus residence hall system changed in anticipation of future growth, so did the OSU Greek social organizations. Two new sororities, Gamma Phi Beta, installed on February 8, 1958, and Delta Delta Delta (Tri Delt), chartered at OSU on November 12, 1962, brought the number of national sororities to eleven during the 1951-1966 era. The fraternity system grew when Delta Upsilon was installed at OSU on April 24, 1960. The number of fraternities increased to twenty-three with the chartering of Phi Gamma Delta (the Fijis) on November 10, 1962, and Triangle on October 20, 1963.[113]

Along with the five new nationals, the Greek system moved along with a huge construction and renovation program. In 1952 OSU's fraternity row was moving westward, with a half million dollar expansion plan. Kappa Sigma's Frank Lloyd Wright-style house was occupied in the fall of 1956. Pi Kappa Alpha built at 1512 West Third. The Pi Kappa Alpha house opened in January 1955, and an $85,000 addition was completed in 1962. Phi Delta Theta and Sigma Alpha Epsilon also opened new houses in the mid-fifties. On October 16, 1955, Alpha Delta Pi won a homecoming float trophy and two days later moved into their southern colonial-style sorority home at 1309 West University. In February 1956 Acacia completed a $150,000 "L-shaped" chapter house at University and Garfield. Six new houses had been completed and occupied in less than three years.[114]

Additional fraternity and sorority house building, including enlargements of already existing houses, began in another flurry of construction in 1959. The Zeta Tau Alphas returned to their chapter house at 1001 University after a $110,000 remodeling in March. The Delta Chis purchased the Kappa Delta house at 703 W. University and moved in the spring of 1959. Meantime the Kappa Delta sorority women waited in Hanner Hall for the completion of their new $300,000 home at the corner of Third and Cleveland. When the Kappa Deltas left their old house, they moved from the first sorority house built for that purpose at Oklahoma State University.[115]

Phi Kappa Tau, Pi Beta Phi, Gamma Phi Beta, and Delta Tau Delta were living in new chapter houses in 1962. Two years later, Alpha Chi Omega moved into their $260,000 mixed contemporary and traditional chapter house at 223 South Garfield. Also, in 1964, Chi Omega completed a $200,000 remodeling of their house, the fourth remodeling since the house was built in 1928. Concurrently, a $70,000 south wing was under construction at the Alpha Gamma Rho fraternity house. Phi Delta Theta had begun the fall semester of 1963 in a new residence at 224 South Monroe.[116]

Amidst the sawdust and bricks, undergraduate men and women, supported by a cast of noteworthy advisors, led the OSU Greek system to national recognition, the establishment of lasting traditions, and, maybe more importantly, enduring memories. By 1966 the coordinated system of the Panhellenic Council and Interfraternity Council (IFC) had passed its sixty-fifth birthday, having started with Lambda Chi Alpha's nationalizing in 1909. The Sigma Nu Frontier Ball, the Phi Delta Theta Half-Formal dance, and Kappa Sigma's lavish Mardi gras ball, were all traditions in their own right. "Pinning" and being thrown into Theta Pond by ones "brothers" remained both customary and controversial.[117]

By 1950 the Sigma Chi-Frank Lewis oak tree had survived disease and grown to a height of sixty feet. A member of the Sigma Chi fraternity, Lewis won a gold medal at the 1936 Olympics held in Berlin, Germany. Adolph Hitler, the German dictator, had presented an oak seedling from the Black Forest to each gold-medal-winning athlete. The tree still stands.

Through the years Dean of Women Zelma Patchin and Assistant Dean of Men Darrel K. Troxel, a native of Yale, served as near legends-in-their-own-time advisors of the respective systems. "Trox," as Troxel was warmly called by fraternity men, began to advise the Interfraternity Council formally in 1953. A 1956 *Daily O'Collegian* editorial reflected: "What Connie Mack and Grantland Rice were to their respective fields, baseball and sports writing—Darrel Troxel is to the A&M fraternity system."[118] A bachelor, Troxel was counselor, friend, and parent-in-absentia to thousands of students, both Greek and non-Greek. Patchin, although more formal in style than Troxel, was respected and as influential in sorority activities.[119]

Along with Patchin and Troxel, other individuals aided the Greek system in its growth to new heights. In 1956 H. H. "Rosie" Flinn, a longtime admissions office employee, died. Since 1925 Flinn had assisted in the initiation of 550 Sigma Nu members. After thirty-eight consecutive years as hostess of Sigma Alpha Epsilon, Katherine Condon Woods retired as "Dean of American Greek Housemothers" in 1961. This honorary title was bestowed upon "Mom Woods" by virtue of her having served one chapter longer than any other housemother in the nation. Mrs. Woods passed away on July 4, 1988, at the age of ninety-seven. Two years earlier on her birthday, she was honored with a reception at the chapter house, and the day was officially proclaimed "Katherine C. 'Mom' Woods Day" in Stillwater. Flinn and Woods were just two of many who have helped Greek students in a variety of supportive roles over the years.[120]

At the beginning of 1950, FarmHouse fraternity received summa cum laude honors from the National Fraternity Conference for its scholarship. Between 1950 and 1966 FarmHouse was recognized a dozen more times; in 1965-1966 it had the highest academic average of any fraternity chapter in the nation. FarmHouse's longstanding academic prowess was already well known on the OSU campus. This national prestige only enhanced the mystique and remained something of a tradition. Rarely did any chapter but FarmHouse win the annual OSU Greek scholarship trophy.[121]

Life for the Greek system and its membership, to be sure, was not always rosy. Racism, segregation, charges of elitism, problems with pledge sneaks (which were banned from crossing state lines in 1955), Hell Week, and hazing, all reflected some of the downside. Yet, there can be little doubt that the total fraternity system, for both men and women, added to OSU's ability to cater to a variety of student needs and helped attract students to the campus. In 1961 and 1962 the IFC was awarded the National Interfraternity Conference's "Iron Man" trophy, symbolic of America's leading fraternity system. The achievement was unprecedented. The "Undergraduate Interfraternity Conference Award," a 5-foot, 480-pound trophy, had never before been given to one institution in consecutive years. At the time only the University of Michigan and Ohio State University had won the honor more than once.[122]

Not to be outdistanced by their male counterparts, in the same years of 1961 and 1962, OSU's Panhellenic captured consecutive second place "Fraternity Month Awards." Comparable to the "Iron Man" for frater-

252

In 1961 and 1962 the Interfraternity Council was awarded the National Interfraternity Conference's "Iron Man" trophy, symbolic of America's leading fraternity system. Assistant Dean of Men Darrel K. "Trox" Troxel and Interfraternity Council President Don Timberlake admire the trophy. Troxel had advised the Interfraternity Council since 1953.

nities, the sorority award was given on much the same basis, including service to campus and community, special programs and scholastic standing. The combined four awards in two years represented an unparalleled time for OSU Greek life and established goals that would be difficult for others to repeat. Serving as IFC presidents during the "Iron Man" years were Jim Butts (1961) and Don Timberlake (1962). Bill Adams, Don McFarren, C. J. Rothlisberger, Roger Webb, and Rem Slattery were other leaders of the IFC during the unprecedented two years.[123]

Increases in enrollment, student activities, and Greek and on-campus housing caused a reactive growth, as contrasted to a planned response, in the university's student life administrative areas. Primary among those areas was the Office of the Dean of Students, which in 1961 was renamed the Division of Student Affairs.[124] The *Faculty Handbook* described the total work of the student dean's office as "general supervision of those relationships between the University and the student that fall outside the curriculum."[125]

In truth, in 1959 twenty-one substantial programs were administered by student affairs. All on- and off-campus housing personnel programs, student employment, loans, scholarships, and the advisement of student organizations fell among the responsibilities. General counseling, discipline, new student orientation, and student records added to the assigned tasks. Student addresses, withdrawals, and military deferment requests were routed through a student dean. Of lesser importance, but still essential, were the publishing of the student directory and student handbook and the coordinating of a campus tour service. Every student activity, from dances to serenades, was registered and approved by this office. In effect, if a faculty member did not know what to do about a student's request or problem, then the dean of student's office was contacted.[126]

Because of the increasing services provided by student affairs, it became clear that the division needed new offices as well as to be more centralized. In December 1964 student affairs vacated the Student Affairs Building to permit its demolition for a new home for the College of Business Administration. The old structure, constructed in 1906, had served many purposes. Alumni could date their undergraduate days by the name then given the old structure—Student Affairs Building, Old Cafeteria, Old Bookstore, YWCA headquarters, Agriculture Building, or Civil Engineering Building. Nevertheless, after a year without permanent offices, the Division of Student Affairs moved to modern space in the new wing of the Student Union. For the first time in the university's long history, student affairs was together under the same roof when OSU opened the new academic year in the fall of 1965.[127]

The dean of men's office had become the dean of students office in 1948. O. K. Campbell held the new title for the first two years. R. R. Oglesby then served until 1954 when he became the dean of students at Florida State University. J. N. Baker replaced Oglesby and was named the first dean of student affairs in 1955; he remained until 1961 when he became the president of Eastern Oklahoma A. and M. College at Wilburton.[128]

On July 1, 1961, Frank E. McFarland, the director of student personnel in the College of Arts and Sciences, became the new dean of student affairs. Born in Fort Towson, McFarland held an undergraduate degree with honors from Baylor University and the master's and the doctorate from Columbia University. Dean McFarland was also a licensed psychologist and had prior administrative responsibilities at Texas A. and M. University. Although unassuming, perhaps even quiet in his style, McFarland brought a wealth of experience to his work. In subsequent years it would fall to McFarland to volley back and forth with Abe Hesser, the director of the Student Union, university housing, and food units, about the proper balance between facilities, finances, and supportive personnel programs for students.[129]

McFarland and the other deans before him were ably assisted by a number of assistants. Sam Botkins and Troxel held early positions as assistant deans. With the name change to student affairs, James M. Miller was appointed dean of men in 1955. King Cacy Jr. was hired in 1956 to assist a growing number of student organizations. Three years later Cacy assumed the title of director of student activities. T. N. Harris, who

Hobart native, Zelma F. Patchin (*left*) succeeded Julia E. Stout as dean of women in 1951, a position she held until 1969 when she became associate dean of students. Her accommodating ability to bend with the needs and whims of the students made her a popular campus figure.

was responsible for student employment, loans, and withdrawals, was replaced by Moselle W. Stallings in 1958. Bill Powers helped with counseling and off-campus housing. Ashley Alexander Sr. continued the Student Entertainment Bureau after the organization's founder, A. Frank Martin, retired as director in 1956.[130]

Dean of Women Zelma F. Patchin began to report to the dean of student affairs at the time that Miller became dean of men. Although the title had been dropped seven years earlier, in 1955 the dean of men's position was reinstituted with Miller. Subsequently both Miller and Patchin reported to the dean of student affairs. Because of the departmental changes and the president's desire for fewer people to report directly to him, for the first time in the college's history, the office of dean of women was no longer an independent department. Thereafter, the men's and women's student personnel programs would be similar, but separated by male and female interests; and both reported to the same person, the dean of student affairs.[131]

Dean Patchin, the Hobart native who succeeded Julia E. Stout in 1951, was dean of women throughout the Willham presidency. Her assistant deans included Estelle Hammond, who retired in 1954 after nineteen years in the dean of women's office. Julia Lee Stephens, who had been Young Women's Christian Association executive secretary, moved into the slot created by Hammond's retirement. Maxine C. Adamson Harber, a Nowata native, served on Patchin's staff in a variety of roles from 1956 to 1962. While Patchin had overall responsibilities, Harber worked with the women's residence halls and Stephens assisted students in employment, off-campus housing, and loans. Helen Thacker Hill replaced Harber in 1962.[132]

As the student body became larger and more heterogeneous, increasing numbers of students suffered from the consequences of student overload and stress. As early as 1944 a faculty committee on the "Improvement of the Regular College Program" had recommended to the president that a formalized student counseling department be established to "assist in the areas of vocations, social life, and individual and public health." The suggested service, called "Office of College Counselor," would have carried no disciplinary functions, employed professional counselors unburdened by administrative tasks, and stressed the view that the institution was a whole system, not a series of divisions and departments.[133]

The faculty's recommendations lay dormant. In 1942 Roxie A. Weber of the Oklahoma A. and M. College Infirmary appealed for a psychiatric service. But the sometimes severe personal problems of the students continued. Some help arrived in 1946 when Harry K. Brobst, a psychology department faculty member, started the Bureau of Tests and Measurements. He also took a leadership role in the student affairs-directed summer orientation and enrollment program for incoming students. Perhaps as an outgrowth of Brobst's summer testing and counseling of new students, or just because the need for specialized help with student mental health problems persisted, the Division of Student Affairs established the University Counseling Services in January 1958. The new service was oriented toward helping students cope with career indecision and problems with their study habits. It was a meager start, for the first employee was borrowed. King Cacy, the initial counseling service head, transferred from his position as an assistant dean of student affairs to start the counseling services. Cacy served only briefly. In just a few more months he would become the first director of student activities. Nevertheless, in less than two years Cacy held three different student services positions, two of which were precedent setting.[134]

In the fall of 1959 Royal H. Bowers replaced Cacy. Before Bowers left in 1963 to become the dean of instruction at Panhandle A. and M., he had added two part-time counseling employees—Robert J. Dollar and Tama Ruth Luther—to his small program. Owen L. Caskey followed Bowers as director of counseling.[135] The long-needed service came under the dean of student affairs and was advertised formally in the student handbook. More informally, Director Bowers suggested in the campus newspaper: "Any student with a dilemma, whether he be curious, or on the brink of a scholastic disaster, is urged to visit the office."[136] With both Bowers and Caskey having a professional background in student mental health, the University Counseling Services began to stabilize and find permanence under the student affairs umbrella.

The 1950s were the initial Cold War years, and the world's super power nations spent billions on armaments. The Soviet Union's 1957 launching of *Sputnik*, the first satellite to orbit the earth, caused free world concern about technological superiority. The launch proved to be a blessing in disguise for college students in the United States. The United States Congress enacted the National Defense Education Act (NDEA) in August 1958. The NDEA was a milestone, marking the earliest involvement of the national government in the large scale funding of repayable financial assistance for students. The NDEA provided reasonable loans and graduate fellowships for the study of math, science, modern foreign language, engineering, and public school teaching, all areas vital to the nation's defense interests. The NDEA loans were sought by students throughout the nation. At OSU 666 students were awarded $314,362 in NDEA loans just two years after the act became law.[137]

Prior to the NDEA the campus financial aid programs remained decentralized and inefficient, at least for students. In 1955 progress was made when Raymond E. Bivert was made director of student loans. Bivert initially awarded loan money from the Lew Wentz and Howard and Robert Allen Foundations, then later added the NDEA program. When Bivert became director of loans, there were 8,000 students on the campus. Yet, there were a total of only 140 scholarships available, mostly for freshmen. Scholarships were awarded primarily by the academic colleges, with some coordinating assistance from the dean of student affairs office. Student jobs, still the main means for helping to pay expenses, remained separated into men's and women's programs and were administered by two assistant deans of students. By 1955 it was estimated that 48 percent of the student body, about 4,000 students, were working at part-time jobs, on- and off-campus. The average income for working students was $45 a month. At the same time, one of every six students was receiving some form of other financial assistance, either through grants, loans, or scholarships.[138]

The groundwork for major improvements to the fragmented financial assistance program started in 1960. In March of that year the Lew Wentz board successfully petitioned the courts to amend the provisions of the Wentz trust. In addition to gaining approval for some administrative changes, resulting in a more flexible program of Wentz loans, the Lew Wentz Service Scholarship program was established. This scholarship afforded excellent students valuable work experiences, and continues as a prestigious scholarship for upperclass undergraduates. In the initial year, the Wentz Service Scholarship was awarded to fifty-eight students, who received a total of $7,600. The program has since grown, along with the general administration of financial aid, to reward hundreds of recipients for academic excellence.[139]

As frequently happens, the next step in the name of progress was attempted by the students through the Student Senate. In 1964 the senate's "Financial Aid Director Bill" was taken up by the OSU Academic Council. By then Bivert was handling 4,000 loan applications each year. Scholarships continued to be awarded haphazardly; and student jobs remained in high demand, but separated by sex, and largely left to student initiative and leg work. The "Director Bill" asked that all student aid, jobs, loans, and scholarships be placed in one office in student affairs, with one designated person in charge. The students' recommendation was discussed in Academic Council in four consecutive monthly meetings, from May to August, and then was referred to a committee for further study. The committee was chaired by Dean of Student Affairs McFarland. There the good idea died of inactivity because of a lack of consensus among academic deans or some other reason.[140]

Substantial help for the students' suggestion came two years later when representatives of the United States Department of Health, Education and Welfare conducted an on-campus audit of the financial aid program. The visit proved that with federal money comes new oversight and, to a degree, a loss of control. The 1966 audit found OSU's decentralized student aid program substantially lacking, specifically in how the government's money was administered. At the time of the audit, the campus financial aid system was under the direction of Mr. Bivert who reported directly to President Willham. The Department of Financial Aid was established in March 1968 within the Division of Student Affairs under Dean McFarland. In subsequent years major nagging problems would continue in financial aid, some of them caused by huge amounts of federal bureaucracy and paperwork, and others the result of institutional and departmental self-defeatism. However, for the students the new organization represented major progress.[141]

Like financial aid programs, the University Placement Services struggled to find identity and, more importantly, a long-range purpose, during the institution's transition from a college to a university. Unlike financial aid, prior to 1958 the placement service anchored only briefly within student affairs, found the marriage wanting, then moved on to find another location from which to serve graduates. A dilemma arose in 1958 upon the retirement of A. O. Martin, who had served twenty-eight years as placement bureau director. The placement bureau and the Former Students Association, later the Alumni Association, had been started at OSU in 1929 by A. Frank Martin, who had been the director of the combined operation for two months. George McElroy followed A. Frank Martin and served only one year. On June 1, 1930, A. O. Martin became the head of alumni and placement services.[142]

Placement services was a free service intended to bring prospective employers and employees together. Ultimately and as importantly it was further hoped the fledgling service would also gain supportive alumni and public sector constituents for the institution. The joint responsibilities became unwieldy. On December 1, 1954, Martin retired as the executive of the Former Students Association and became the first full-time head of placement services. At this time the service was centralized, with the exception of an active placement function in engineering. When Martin retired, the primarily one man operation had placed over 10,000 graduates and was maintaining 8,000 sets of student placement credentials in office files. When Martin departed in 1958, he was praised for his long years of service and dedication to OSU. He had also gained national respect among his off-campus colleagues.[143]

Knowing that Martin's departure was close at hand, a year-long study of campus placement operations was undertaken by the Academic Council. Questions concerning who would be served by the functions of campus placement as well as whether it should be a centralized or a college-based service were taken up by the study group. The committees did not resolve the problems, but the institution did do what was recommended. The College of Education established a solid teacher placement service under Gerald T. Stubbs. Each of the other colleges coordinated their own campus interviews and student placements. The plan designated student affairs as the university contact point for general placement inquiries. From 1958 to 1960 M. W. Stallings, the assistant dean of men, took care of prospective employer requests too broad for a specific college to handle, such as civil service. As a result the university chose to discontinue the role of a placement director, leaving the important service to the varying interests of each respective college.[144]

Although well intended, the decentralized placement office configuration worked poorly. Four months after the new plan had begun, those students particularly close to graduation labeled the situation deplorable and accused the university of being unconcerned. The students in need of help found that most of the schools or departments had only token assistance or, worse, no placement program available at all. In summarizing, a November 1958 Daily O'Collegian editorial stated: "Recently, the university converted what used to be an all-campus employment service into a placement bureau for education students, leaving the majority without aid in locating work upon graduation."[145] In the following months the complaints continued, but not just from students. Influential employers, who sometimes supported the institution with money and in other ways, soon joined in the chorus to return to a centralized office with a director who was visible and available for assistance.

The change came on July 1, 1960, when longtime Oklahoma public

Over the years, student services has been graced with many dedicated employees. John Gillum (*left*) served as the bookstore manager for forty years. A member of the class of 1921, Gillum spent his entire career in the service of his alma mater. Hal N. Buchanan (*right*) served as director of University Placement Services for eighteen years. Under his direction, the placement office became more professionalized.

school administrator, Hal N. Buchanan, a native of Valiant, assumed the duties of director in the reconstituted University Placement Services. With offices in the Student Union, Buchanan reported directly to President Willham. His charge was to serve as a placement "clearing-house," to serve directly by placing teachers, and to coordinate all placement services, including those remaining in the schools. In 1966 Marian Dark was hired as assistant director. Buchanan would remain as director for eighteen years. Under his directorship placement services for arts and sciences and home economics, along with education, were provided graduating students and alumni. New services were added, and the University Placement Services became professionalized.[146]

On the same day that Placement Director Buchanan took up his work, Donald L. Cooper began his first day as the director of Student Health Services. Cooper succeeded Roxie A. Weber. In a warm letter, Weber had announced her retirement to President Willham by reflecting on an earlier conversation she had had with Dr. Willham, in which they had discussed the problems of their retired friends. At that time Dr. Weber promised to retire at her designated time, and thus she wrote Willham: "I promised you that you would not have to tell me when it was time to go. According to a letter from the Secretary of the Teachers Retirement Fund the date is June 30, 1960. I have enjoyed my years of work on the campus and will miss the associations, but I plan to keep my promise."[147] Dr. Weber, a graduate of Johns Hopkins University Medical School, ended an eighteen-year career at OSU, having been the health services director since 1949.[148]

Grace Vickers, supervisor of nurses, also resigned her position at the infirmary in 1960 to take a position at the Spafford Children's Hospital in Jerusalem. Vickers started her work in 1926 in the original bungalow used as the student infirmary. She had done every job conceivable, from writing for free medical samples from pharmaceutical companies to helping to administer a meager health services budget.[149]

In addition to Vickers and Weber, additional 1960 retirees included physicians Dorothea Curnow and Robert Ragland Rigg. Other physicians attending to the real and imagined ills of the students during Weber's directorship included Joseph O. Thomson, Ethelyn J. C. Anderson, Brandon A. White, Jacob Oliver Burner, Leon C. Freed, and Abbott C. Scott. Replacing the retirees and joining Cooper at the health services in 1960 were medical doctors George B. Schlesinger, S. Victor Yeakel, and Jeanne B. Johnson.[150]

The energetic, talkative Cooper, who had a medical degree from the University of Kansas and prior experience at the Kansas State University student health services, hit the OSU campus on the run. Within his initial month as director, Cooper changed the name of the infirmary to University Hospital and Clinic. With the name change Cooper desired improved prestige and a better psychological effect on student patients. The effort would not be easy.[151] Sarcastically, two Murray Hall residents asked that the "new" hospital stop waking up student patients to administer sleeping pills. In an editorial to the campus newspaper, they hoped "the infirmary wins its battle to become 'hospital' in the minds of the students . . . [but added] there is no excuse for rudeness."[152]

Next the new physician-director tried to convince the students that being the lowest rate payer is not always the best. Health services had not received an increase in student fees in fourteen years. At $6.50 a semester per student, which was the lowest in the Big Eight, the students were getting less of a health service than they deserved. In addition, the university did not contribute to this budget. Money for this service, or the lack of it, would plague Cooper throughout the next two decades. In Oklahoma, like elsewhere, people taxed themselves cautiously, and students were no different.[153]

Cooper continued to push for what he saw as a comprehensive student health service. In 1961 his efforts updated and improved the voluntary student health insurance program, one that had been started in 1955. The Cooper-directed hospital stopped issuing medical excuses to students who missed classes in 1963.[154] Wanting to encourage responsibility on the part of students, Cooper called the old system of issued excuses "juvenile and filled with much difficulty in terms of proper use."[155] In the following year a part-time psychiatric consultation program, started

**D.L. COOPER M.D.**

Donald L. Cooper became the director of Student Health Services in 1960. Literally hitting the Oklahoma State University campus on the run, Dr. Cooper strived to improve the image of campus health facilities and called for a comprehensive student health service.

in 1955, was transformed when Harvey W. Anderson, a psychiatrist, joined the medical staff full-time. By 1966 Dr. Cooper met one trend of the day head-on, when he publicly affirmed that in the foreseeable future only married women would be issued birth control pills through the campus health services.[156]

The young physician came to campus with more than one goal in mind. Besides changing the campus hospital's name and image and hopefully student attitudes about the health service, Cooper carried a longtime interest in sports medicine with him. For "Doc" Cooper his avocation with athletic injury prevention and treatment brought him, and OSU, national recognition. Meanwhile, Cooper focused his interest on cleaning up the rough play in the campus intramural leagues. In setting his goal and clarifying the problem, Cooper stated that one of his "primary concerns on the campus will be the prevention of injuries to students as a result of intramural sports, which, according to one survey, are in second place at Oklahoma State in causes of lost school time to college students, common colds being in the number one spot."[157]

Achieving this goal would be difficult, too. Through the 1950s and early 1960s intramural playing fields and courts continued to be stretched. Part of Cooper's problem began with the crowded conditions for play, and the rough surfaces that participant ankles and knees pounded. Except on weekends, practice areas were scarce. Spectator seating hardly existed. Nonetheless, students played in ever larger numbers. By 1964 the men were offered fourteen different intramural activities from which to choose. Out of a total enrollment of 7,834 men, 3,308 participated. These figures reflected an impressive 42 percent involvement in men's intramural activities. On the women's side of things, eleven sports were offered, and one-quarter of the enrolled females were active in one or more intramural or recreational activities.[158]

As measured by student interest, the intramural and recreational programs continued to have solid leadership from dedicated professionals. In 1954 Valerie Colvin succeeded Flora May Ellis as the chairperson of the women's division of the Department of Health, Physical Education, and Recreation. Colvin's responsibilities were eventually assumed by Ada Van Whitley, who in 1961 became advisor to the Women's Athletic Association (WAA). The WAA was eventually called the Women's Recreation Association, and it was the sponsoring organization for women's intramural programs. Whitley's counterpart for the men's program continued to be the greatly respected Gordon B. Gilbert, who by 1964 had been the men's intramural director for twenty-five years. Gilbert reported to Jim Kevin, head of campus recreational, leisure, and intramural programs.[159]

The intramural program not only provided students a positive outlet for their competitive nature, but it also provided beneficial physical activity, companionship, and planned recreational opportunities. The program's motto was "sports activity, not for the spectator, but for 100 percent participation in some activity for all students."[160] To reach this lofty goal something would have to be done to provide more students the opportunity. Facilities and fields needed to be available. Finally, Albin P. Warner—a man to get the job done—arrived on campus in 1962 to head the Department of Health, Physical Education, and Recreation.[161]

The university had previously discussed the need for a stand-alone swimming pool, projected for the high rise residence halls' area. Certainly knowing the needs, and with a suspicion that the time could be right, Warner took his appeal directly to the OSU Student Senate. This group had been vocalizing the need for improved intramural resources for years. In February 1963, Warner asked for their support of an already circulating student petition for a new recreational and swimming pool complex. He told the senators that the undertaking could minimally cost $250,000, but an all-purpose complex might require $2,000,000. The ball moved forward rapidly. In April a senate resolution supporting the project was on President Willham's desk, pointing out that 3,500 student petition signers also wanted a new facility. On May 7, 1965, a campus referendum passed three to one, with 2,670 students voting to

Because of the continued interest in physical education as a major as well as the popularity of intramural programs, it became obvious that better facilities were needed. In the spring of 1965, students approved an additional fee to help construct such a structure. The Colvin Physical Education Center opened in 1969.

tax themselves a $2 fee each semester, to go to $4 when the building was opened, to pay for a portion of the construction cost.[162]

With the tremendous support of the students, including the unprecedented willingness to assess themselves a fee, the administration moved ahead with plans to build a physical education and recreational building. In March 1966 the board of regents approved the projected $1.9 million facility as one of twelve other construction projects totaling $12.5 million. Architects brought ideas to reality, estimating that the one block by one-half block, 127,000 square foot building, designed to support both academic and recreational programs, would serve a campus of 25,000 students. The ultramodern structure was delayed when federal money was slow in getting approved, but in October 1966 it was announced that construction would begin in the following spring.[163]

Completed and furnished at a total expense of $3.3 million, the facility opened in 1969. Fifty-two percent of the cost was born by the self-imposed student tax. Ironically, Director Colvin worked only six months in the new building before her retirement. A new era for OSU physical education, intramural, and recreational programs would begin as she was departing. Appropriately, the new building, representing an end to four decades of extraordinary service often in the poorest of circumstances, was named the Colvin Physical Education Center, in honor of the forty-year educator and intramural program leader. More importantly, the facility's name seemed unquestionably fitting to generations of Colvin's former students and colleagues.[164]

The Colvin Center was begun under President Willham and completed and opened under a new president, Robert B. Kamm. Dr. Willham's June 1966 retirement ended fourteen stressful years as OSU president. Undoubtedly, Willham left his position believing that he had done all that he could to move the institution forward. Like his predecessors, Willham would have to trust that what had been successful in the past would continue to be so. Yet from his own experience, he probably also knew that the future would bring another set of new problems. Regardless, the reins of leadership, with all of the burdens and joys, passed from Dr. Willham to Dr. Kamm on July 1, 1966.

The Willham years were momentous, not only rich in campus activity but in events national and international. The campus had started to grow vertically, with high rise construction. Single classes of 200 or more students were being taught with the use of overhead projectors, and "mass instruction" became common. The years evoked the entire range of human emotions among students. The dilemmas of life, including sorrow, hope, and joy, were in evidence. In the single year of 1957 the Salk vaccine, so promising in the fight to eradicate polio, was easily available on campus, and the OSU Interfraternity Council spearheaded a massive immunization drive among the student body. In contrast, the campus also faced real life when T. N. Harris, an assistant dean of men and the first student member of OSU's Student Entertainers, lost his life in an automobile collision while returning with five coeds from a student entertainer engagement at Vinita High School. Undergraduate Jean Hawkins was also killed. Yet life must go forward. A month after the tragic automobile accident a giant Christmas tree was placed in front of the library, and the inaugural, but now traditional, all-campus tree lighting ceremony ushered in the holiday season.[165]

Additional ambiguity was thrust upon the students in the early 1960s when the campus preparedness plan against nuclear attack was publicly announced. The plans were complete with designated bomb shelters and tips for survival in the event of a nuclear holocaust.[166] At the time communism was "the single word on the Oklahoma State University campus that has the power to bring students en masse out of their ordinary apathetic state long enough to prompt a little discussion."[167] The campus debate and the real threat posed by communism escalated in October and November of 1962 with the events which unfolded in the Cuban missile crisis.[168]

As demonstrated by the Soviet Union's withdrawal of their missiles from Cuban soil, some world problems could be resolved. Meantime, the seeds of others were being sown. On November 22, 1963, the course of history changed when President John F. Kennedy was assassinated. Three days after President Kennedy's death, 5,000 solemn-faced students

On November 25, 1963, thousands of students gathered on the library lawn for a memorial service for President John F. Kennedy.

gathered at the library mall to participate in a memorial tribute.[169] A weary President Willham asked the somber crowd to "reflect seriously upon what each can do as an individual to prevent such tragedies in the future."[170] Like the nation, the OSU campus was stunned for weeks thereafter, groping to find some meaning in the events in Dallas.

Vice President Lyndon B. Johnson assumed the presidency. In 1964 American ships, off the coast of Vietnam, were fired upon by gunboats from North Vietnam. Dr. Martin Luther King Jr., in the center of the war for black and human rights, received the Nobel Peace Prize. Nikita Khrushchev fell from Soviet leadership and was replaced by Leonid I. Brezhnev and Aleksei Kosygin.

On the campus, the Student Senate had embroiled itself in controversy by considering, often heatedly, affiliation with the National Student Association (NSA). In some quarters the NSA was considered a subversive, if not communist plot, whose purpose was to undermine the government.[171] Sensing the winds of change the Reverend Van D. Spurgeon, a campus minister and president of the OSU Association of University Ministers was correctly predicting that the "decade of the 1960s will not see students passive or apathetic, but active and concerned, and in the forefront of not only University, but also national life."[172]

When Dr. Willham left his office for the last time, students were again fretting about being drafted into the armed services, to fight in the increasingly controversial war in Vietnam. An activist group was seeking a charter for a chapter of Students for a Democratic Society, an organization widely identified with national campus unrest. By now a clear pattern of campus disruptions, marked by demands, sit-ins, and violence, was becoming entrenched at colleges and universities. More turbulent days subsequently followed at OSU and elsewhere.[173]

Through the decade of the 1950s and the first half of the 1960s, students had shown their capacity for affection, enjoyment, and fun; for fear, mourning, and sadness; and for mischief, as well as scholarly achievement. As administrators and faculty coped to stay abreast, a subtle, but huge transition was made. No longer could students be worried about as a single entity such as a group, a class, or even a generation. The institution had grown too large, the students too divergent. The people working alongside the students, particularly those in student personnel-related services, of necessity, learned to worry increasingly about them as individuals. The institution would have to come to grips with the idea that they were all different. For some, this discovery would be profound. However, in the years that followed, the new president would frequently remind everyone who joined the academic community of this insight—no matter how large OSU is, the fundamental underpinning is "Emphasis People."[174]

## Endnotes

1. Warren E. Shull, "A University Without Peer," *Oklahoma State Alumnus Magazine*, vol. 7, no. 2 (February 1966), pp. 8-13; Oklahoma A. and M. College *Daily O'Collegian*, 19 January 1952, pp. 1, 6, 9 May 1953, p. 8.

2. *Daily O'Collegian*, 19 January 1952, p. 2.

3. *Daily O'Collegian*, 25 September 1953, p. 2, 14 May 1955, p. 2, 14 October 1958, p. 3, 8 December 1964, p. 1.

4. *Daily O'Collegian*, 19 January 1952, p. 1.

5. Jack Castleman, "Historical 1953 at A. and M.," *Oklahoma A. and M. College Magazine*, vol. 25, no. 5 (January 1954), pp. 5-7; "Facts and Figures, A and M Style," *Oklahoma A. and M. College Magazine*, vol. 24, no. 1 (September 1952), p. 10; Raymond Girod, "It's Your Move Now," *Oklahoma A. and M. College Magazine*, vol. 24, no. 6 (February 1953), pp. 26-27.

6. *Daily O'Collegian*, 7 April 1953, pp. 1, 2, 6, 25 April 1953, pp. 1, 6, 31 March 1953, p. 2; Shull, p. 10.

7. Shull, p. 10.

8. Shull, p. 11.

9. *Daily O'Collegian*, 7 February 1957, p. 1, 25 February 1959, pp. 1, 3, 31 January 1959, pp. 1, 6; *1959 Redskin*, p. 458, Oklahoma State University Yearbook.

10. *Daily O'Collegian*, 18 May 1955, pp. 1, 6.

11. Clyde Lee to Oliver S. Willham, 28 May 1955, Oliver S. Willham Collection, Special Collections, Edmon Low Library, Oklahoma State University, Stillwater, Oklahoma.

12. "Revision of Policy Statements on Holidays and Disorderly Assemblies," 30 March 1959, p. 1, Board of Regents Files, Special Collections, Edmon Low Library; Zelma Patchin to Frank McFarland, 28 May 1962, Oliver S. Willham Collection; "Disciplinary Cases, 1961-1962," 1 November 1962, pp. 1-15, Faculty Council Records, Special Collections, Edmon Low Library; *Daily O'Collegian*, 17 March, 1959, p. 1, 18 March 1959, pp. 1, 6, 18 November 1959, pp. 1, 6, 10 May 1962, p. 1, 12 June 1962, pp. 1, 10, 6 July 1962, pp. 1, 10.

13. *Daily O'Collegian*, 14 September 1962, p. 2.

14. Abe L. Hesser to Frank McFarland, 30 May 1962, Oliver S. Willham Collection.

15. *Daily O'Collegian*, 25 March 1953, p. 2.

16. *Daily O'Collegian*, 27 March 1953, p. 11.

17. *Stillwater NewsPress*, 16 November 1986, p. 3C; *Daily O'Collegian*, 16 July 1954, pp. 1, 6, 16 September 1954, p. 2, 10 June 1955, pp. 1, 6, 24 June 1955, p. 2, 12 November 1986, pp. 1-2.

18. *Daily O'Collegian*, 24 June 1955, p. 2.

19. *1961 Redskin*, p. 63; *1959 Redskin*, p. 302; *Daily O'Collegian*, 5 April 1960, p. 1, 28 March 1958, p. 7, 8 March 1958, p. 1.

20. *Daily O'Collegian*, 16 June 1953, p. 3.

21. *Daily O'Collegian*, 12 November 1957, p. 2, 5 October 1962, p. 2.

22. "Orientation Program," Fall 1952, pp. 1-4, Student Services Collection, Special Collections, Edmon Low Library; *1952-1953 Aggie Angles*, p. 87, Oklahoma A. and M. College Student Handbook; "Statement of Policy Re Use of Alcoholic Beverages on Oklahoma State University Campus," 13 January 1962, pp. 1-2, Board of Regents Files; "Annual Report of the Student Conduct Committee," 10 June 1957, p. 1, 24 May 1958, pp. 1-2, 29 May 1959, pp. 1-2, 1 November 1962, pp. 1-11, Faculty Council Records; *Daily O'Collegian*, 27 April 1962, p. 1.

23. "Press Release on Stolen Final Examinations," January 1956, p. 1, Weldon Barnes Collection, Special Collections, Edmon Low Library; *Daily O'Collegian*, 5 March 1953, p. 1, 18 September 1953, p. 2, 17 November 1964, p. 1, 15 May 1954, p. 2, 1 August 1962, p. 2, 14 February 1958, p. 1.

24. "Name of Oklahoma A. & M. Changed to Oklahoma State University," *Oklahoma A. and M. College Magazine*, vol. 28, no. 10 (June 1957), p. 5; *Daily O'Collegian*, 17 May 1957, p. 1, 7 June 1957, p. 1, 14 March 1957, p. 1.

25. *Daily O'Collegian*, 17 July 1956, p. 4.

26. *Daily O'Collegian*, 1 March 1957, p. 2.

27. *Daily O'Collegian*, 28 February 1957, p. 1.

28. *Daily O'Collegian*, 18 May 1957, p. 1.

29. *1958 Redskin*, pp. 141, 554; *Daily O'Collegian*, 20 December 1957, p. 8, 18 December 1963, p. 1, 4 November 1958, p. 1, 24 October 1959, p. 5. According to the OSU Athletic Gift Office, Alan Leech served briefly as the first Pistol Pete in 1958. He was followed by Charles F. Lester, Bill F. Smith, Curtis Manley, Pete Fay, Mark J. Sullivan, Joe Sullivan, Phil Glasgow, Mitch Dobson, Steve Costello, Bill Johnson, Dale Clark (alternate), Bill Ransdell, Ned Kessler (alternate), Richard Forshee (alternate), Gary Bridwell, Joe Elsener, William E. Beckman (alternate), Tom Bennett, Mark Whitlaw, John Michael Entz, Rick Dillard, Wendell Hicks (alternate), Dwain Gibson, Larry McAlister (alternate), Scott Kirtley, Kelly Green, Kurt Carter, Don Giles (alternate), Shane LaDuke, Rob Reynolds, Jesse Lancaster (alternate), David Treece, Rick Wilson, Scott Petty, Scott Noble, Lance Millis, Jack Franks, John Price and Matt Ketchum.

30. *1953-1954 Aggie Angles*, p. 50.

31. *1953-1954 Aggie Angles*, p. 53.

32. *Daily O'Collegian*, 5 June 1953, p. 8.

33. *1956-1957 Aggie Angles*, pp. 18-20; *Daily O'Collegian*, 25 April 1958, p. 2.

34. *Daily O'Collegian*, 2 March 1957, pp. 1, 6, 16 January 1962, p. 1, 23 September 1952, pp. 1, 6, 6 August 1963, p. 8, 2 May 1953, p. 1.

35. *Daily O'Collegian*, 2 April 1955, p. 3, 31 March 1955, p. 1, 3 November 1966, p. 1, 10 March 1953, p. 8, 29 January 1959, p. 1, 6 August 1963, p. 8, 18 November 1964, p. 1, 27 September 1960, p. 1, 14 October 1955, p. 1, 31 October 1958, p. 1, 7 January 1953, p. 1, 14 January 1953, p. 2, 3 May 1958, p. 1, 10 March 1956, p. 1.

36. *Daily O'Collegian*, 12 February 1953, p. 1, 17 March 1954, p. 1; *1964 Redskin*, p. 270.

37. *Daily O'Collegian*, 21 February 1964, p. 12.

38. *Daily O'Collegian*, 26 January 1962, p. 1.

39. *1956 Redskin*, p. 154; *Daily O'Collegian*, 15 March 1955, p. 1, 21 April 1959, p. 1, 18 May 1960, p. 1, 29 March 1952, p. 1, 17 January 1956, p. 1, 28 March 1952, p. 1.

40. *Daily O'Collegian*, 5 December 1956, p. 1, 8 January 1959, p. 1, 7 October 1958, p. 1, 7 November 1958, p. 1, 11 November 1958, p. 1, 22 March 1952, pp. 1, 9, 22 April 1955, p. 1, 20 April 1956, p. 1, 12 April 1958, p. 2, 24 March 1960, p. 1.

41. *Daily O'Collegian*, 20 November 1958, p. 9.

42. *Daily O'Collegian*, 21 October 1961, p. 1.

43. *Daily O'Collegian*, 2 November 1960, p. 2.

44. *Daily O'Collegian*, 21 May 1954, p. 1, 28 January 1955, p. 7.

45. *Daily O'Collegian*, 16 October 1956, p. 1, 13 October 1956, p. 4.

46. *Daily O'Collegian*, 16 October 1956, p. 1.

47. *Daily O'Collegian*, 24 March 1956, p. 1, 10 April 1958, p. 1, 10 January 1958, p. 1, 20 December 1963, p. 2, 9 September 1958, p. 1, 23 April 1966, p. 1, 20 March 1952, p. 1, 25 October 1957, p. 12, 11 February 1966, p. 4.

48. "Kontinental Kapers," *Oklahoma State University Magazine*, vol. 2, no. 8 (February 1959), p. 30; Bob Rives, "It Is 'Strictly Academic'," *Oklahoma A. and M. College Magazine*, vol. 26, no. 7 (March 1955), pp. 20-21; *Daily O'Collegian*, 13 March 1959, p. 1, 12 February 1959, p. 6.

49. *Daily O'Collegian*, 12 November 1959, p. 2, 13 November 1953, p. 2.

50. *1955 Redskin*, pp. 278-279; *1959 Redskin*, p. 108.

51. *1959 Redskin*, pp. 4-5; *1956 Redskin*, p. 579; *Daily O'Collegian*, 9 October 1956, p. 1.

52. *1956 Redskin*, p. 579.

53. Cecil B. Williams to Board of Student Publications, Oklahoma State University, 28 June 1958, President's Papers, Special Collections, Edmon Low Library; *Daily O'Collegian*, 23 May 1957, p. 1.

54. Cecil B. Williams to Board of Student Publications, 28 June 1958, President's Papers.

55. *1954 Redskin*, p. 190; *1955 Redskin*, p. 280; *1956 Redskin*, p. 96.

56. *Daily O'Collegian*, 23 March 1954, p. 1.

57. *Daily O'Collegian*, 15 December 1955, p. 5, 4 February 1956, p. 6, 17 October 1961, p. 1.

58. "Student Religious Life at A and M," *Oklahoma A. and M. College Magazine*, vol. 25, no. 3 (November 1953), pp. 16-17.

59. "Envoys of Academic Excellence," *Oklahoma State Alumnus Magazine*, vol. 2, no. 2 (February 1961), pp. 10-12; *Daily O'Collegian*, 29 November 1960, p. 1.

60. *Daily O'Collegian*, 18 December 1958, p. 8.

61. *Daily O'Collegian*, 18 September 1956, p. 4, 9 March 1956, p. 5, 24 November 1954, p. 6, 27 October 1954, p. 2, 23 September 1954, p. 1, 25 October 1961, p. 1, 16 April 1955, p. 1.

62. *Daily O'Collegian*, 4 December 1952, p. 2, 22 April 1958, p. 8, 10 March 1954, p. 1, 15 May 1954, p. 1, 18 September 1953, p. 1.

63. *Daily O'Collegian*, 16 October 1958, p. 8, 3 October 1961, p. 2, 30 July 1963, p. 2, 10 October 1955, p. 4.

64. *Daily O'Collegian*, 2 February 1964, p. 1.

65. *Daily O'Collegian*, 12 September 1956, p. 1, 22 May 1962, p. 9.

66. *Daily O'Collegian*, 24 April 1963, p. 2, 22 September 1955, p. 2, 18 February 1953, p. 2.

67. *Daily O'Collegian*, 30 April 1963, p. 1.

68. *Daily O'Collegian*, 9 January 1963, p. 2.

69. *Daily O'Collegian*, 7 April 1959, pp. 1, 6.

70. *Daily O'Collegian*, 23 April 1963, p. 1, 30 April 1955, p. 1.

71. *Daily O'Collegian*, 23 April 1963, p. 1.

72. *Daily O'Collegian*, 20 February 1959, pp. 1, 6, 8 May 1964, p. 1, 22 February 1952, p. 1, 29 April 1952, p. 2, 9 May 1952, p. 1, 4 April 1956, p. 4, 22 March 1956, p. 4, 22 May 1962, pp. 1, 10, 25 May 1962, p. 2.

73. Kay Nettleton, "Wes Watkins," *Oklahoma State University Outreach*, vol. 53, no. 3 (April 1982), p. 29; *Daily O'Collegian*, 1 May 1959, pp. 1, 6, 13 April 1960, p. 1, 8 November 1962, pp. 1, 10.

74. "North Central Association Report," *Oklahoma A. and M. College Magazine*, vol. 24, no. 9 (May 1953), pp. 24-26.

75. Oliver S. Willham to Staff Members, 19 December 1952, Oliver S. Willham Collection; "Auxiliary Enterprises at Oklahoma A. and M.," *Oklahoma A. and M. College Magazine*, vol. 25, no. 2 (October 1953), pp. 8-9; *Daily O'Collegian*, 19 December 1952, p. 1.

76. "Auxiliary Enterprises at Oklahoma A. and M.," p. 9.

77. "Auxiliary Enterprises at Oklahoma A. and M.," p. 9; "Ed Morrison Dies from Heart Attack," *Oklahoma State Alumnus Magazine*, vol. 2, no. 10 (November 1961), p. 18.

78. "Auxiliary Enterprises at Oklahoma A. and M.," p. 9.

79. "Ed Morrison Dies from Heart Attack," p. 18; Abe L. Hesser to Oliver S. Willham, 19 October 1961, Oliver S. Willham Collection.

80. Robert MacVicar to Oliver S. Willham, 24 October 1961, Oliver S. Willham Collection.

81. Robert MacVicar to Oliver S. Willham, 24 October 1961, Oliver S. Willham Collection; *Daily O'Collegian*, 21 November 1961, p. 8.

82. Author's personal communication with Floyd I. Brewer, May 1967.

83. Abe L. Hesser to Zelma Patchin, James Miller and Maxine Adamson, 19 June 1962, Student Services Collection.

84. Abe L. Hesser, "Oklahoma State University Student Union," speech, 1 February 1976, and Allen B. Reding, "Twenty-Five Year Tape Presentation of the Student Union," 14 February 1976, in Student Services Collection; *Daily O'Collegian*, 17 September 1960, p. 1, 15 January 1963, p. 1, 14 September 1962, pp. 1, 6; "The 'Catching Up' Process," *Oklahoma State Alumnus Magazine*, vol. 4, no. 3 (March 1963), pp. 42-43.

85. Bill J. Varney to Winston G. Shindell, 28 January 1972, Student Services Collection; Hesser, "Oklahoma State University Student Union;" *Daily O'Collegian*, 4 July 1958, p. 1, 2 August 1957, p. 1, 16 October 1957, p. 7, 11 September 1958, pp. 1, 6, 25 February 1956, p. 8, 20 September 1957, p. 8, 15 September 1959, p. 3, 7 August 1959, p. 6.

86. "No Substitute for Work," *Oklahoma A. and M. College Magazine*, vol. 25, no. 4 (December 1953), pp. 6-8; *Daily O'Collegian*, 20 January 1961, p. 3, 7 January 1954, pp. 3, 10, 29 June 1956, pp. 1, 6.

87. *1955 Redskin*, p. 222; *Daily O'Collegian*, 26 October 1962, p. 1, 18 April 1962, p. 12, 1 February 1963, p. 1, 22 June 1954, p. 5.

88. *Daily O'Collegian*, 9 May 1952, p. 1, 17 June 1952, p. 8, 6 May 1958, p. 8, 6 October 1954, p. 4, 3 May 1957, p. 1, 2 May 1958, p. 1, 17 April 1959, p. 1, 5 May 1960, p. 5, 3 May 1961, p. 1, 27 April 1962, p. 12, 18 April 1963, p. 12, 16 April 1964, p. 1; *1955 Redskin*, p. 69.

89. *1953 Redskin*, p. 407.

90. *Daily O'Collegian*, 7 October 1953, p. 2, 2 October 1953, p. 2, 15 October 1953, p. 1, 16 October 1953, p. 1, 8 February 1956, p. 4, 21 May 1957, p. 1, 16 October 1953, p. 1, 8 February 1956, p. 4, 21 May 1957, p. 1, 16 October 1953, p. 1, 8 January 1956, p. 4, 21 May 1957, p. 1, 23 May 1957, p. 1, 28 July 1959, p. 1.

91. *Daily O'Collegian*, 7 February 1963, p. 1.

92. "Abe Hesser Accepts IACU Presidency," *Oklahoma State Alumnus Magazine*, vol. 3, no. 5 (May 1962), p. 28; *Daily O'Collegian*, 25 April 1952, p. 8.

93. "Modern Student Housing," *Oklahoma A. and M. College Magazine*, vol. 26, no. 7 (March 1955), pp. 10-11.

94. "Modern Student Housing," p. 10; Abe L. Hesser to Oliver S. Willham, 31 July 1963, Oliver Willham Collection.

95. "Modern Student Housing," p. 10; Abe L. Hesser to Oliver S. Willham, 31 July 1963, Oliver S. Willham Collection; *Daily O'Collegian*, 28 September 1961, p. 1.

96. "Multipurpose, Year-round Housing," *Oklahoma State Alumnus Magazine*, vol. 3, no. 2 (February 1962), p. 7.

97. *1963 Redskin*, pp. 136-137; *Daily O'Collegian*, 2 August 1963, pp. 1, 6, 13 September 1962, p. 1, 14 June 1963, pp. 1, 6, 21 April 1964, p. 1, 23 September 1965, p. 1.

98. *Daily O'Collegian*, 29 March 1966, pp. 1, 2, 23 July 1965, p. 1, 29 October 1966, p. 4, 21 September 1965, pp. 1, 12, 16 December 1965, p. 7, 24 May 1967, p. 10, 26 May 1967, p. 3.

99. *Daily O'Collegian*, 15 May 1958, pp. 1, 14, 3 January 1957, p. 1, 14 July 1964, pp. 1-2, 1 April 1965, p. 3, 23 July 1965, p. 4.

100. "Rate Sheets for Men and Women Living in Residence Halls and Apartments School Year 1964-1965," 1 June 1964, pp. 1-4, Student Services Collection; *Daily O'Collegian*, 16 December 1965, p. 1, 1 April 1965, p. 3.

101. *Daily O'Collegian*, 15 March 1960, p. 1, 3 June 1959, p. 8.

102. R. E. Giddens to Mrs. Scott, 14 February 1952, Oliver S. Willham Collection.

103. *Daily O'Collegian*, 17 December 1959, p. 2.

104. *Daily O'Collegian,* 2 May 1956, p. 1, 20 December 1956, p. 7, 4 April 1957, pp. 12, 14.

105. *Oklahoma A. and M. College Bulletin* (10 June 1957), p. 14; *Daily O'Collegian*, 11 July 1961, pp. 1, 6.

106. *Daily O'Collegian*, 14 May 1954, p. 12.

107. *Daily O'Collegian*, 30 April 1964, p. 2, 7 May 1957, p. 2, 8 May 1957, p. 2.

108. *Daily O'Collegian*, 13 May 1954, p. 2.

109. *Daily O'Collegian*, 25 March 1960, p. 1.

110. *Daily O'Collegian*, 9 January 1959, p. 8, 11 December 1963, p. 7, 4 May 1955, p. 3.

111. *Daily O'Collegian*, 12 November 1953, p. 7, 28 April 1961, p. 1, 9 April 1966, p. 1.

112. *Daily O'Collegian*, 22 October 1953, p. 1, 4 November 1954, p. 1, 10 March 1955, p. 1, 26 October 1955, p. 1, 17 May 1956, p. 1, 15 April 1959, pp. 1, 6, 21 January 1960, p. 1, 10 May 1963, p. 1, 29 September 1960, p. 1, 23 April 1966, p. 4, 6 November 1952, p. 3, 22 April 1952, p. 7, 2 March 1953, p. 12, 15 March 1956, p. 1, 14 December 1957, p. 1, 14 January 1960, p. 1, 8 January 1963, p. 8.

113. *1961 Redskin*, p. 385; *1963 Redskin*, pp. 206, 232; Interfraternity and Panhellenic Councils, *Greek Life At OSU* (April 1987), pp. 1-2, brochure, and Jenny Sumner, editor, "Rush 1987—Picture Yourself Greek," OSU Panhellenic Council, (May 1987) pp. 1-40, Pledge Book, in Student Services Collection; *Daily O'Collegian*, 11 February 1958, p. 8, 5 February 1958, p. 1, 23 April 1960, p. 1, 21 April 1961, p. 1, 25 May 1961, p. 8, 10 November 1962, p. 1, 19 April 1963, pp. 1, 10, 9 October 1963, pp. 1, 6.

114. *1956 Redskin*, p. 47; *Daily O'Collegian*, 22 July 1952, p. 8, 8 January 1955, p. 3, 6 July 1962, p. 9, 17 November 1954, p. 7, 18 November 1954, p. 4, 4 February 1956, p. 5.

115. *Daily O'Collegian*, 19 February 1959, p. 8, 22 September 1959, p. 12, 4 April 1960, p. 1; *1960 Redskin*, pp. 112, 162; *1961 Redskin*, p. 363.

116. *1964 Redskin*, p. 336; *Daily O'Collegian*, 17 July 1962, p. 8, 6 October 1961, p. 6, 13 July 1962, p. 12, 20 July 1962, p. 7, 24 July 1962, p. 8, 22 September 1964, p. 7, 19 June 1964, p. 5.

117. *Daily O'Collegian*, 18 February 1955, p. 4, 16 February 1955, p. 3.

118. *Daily O'Collegian*, 8 May 1956, p. 4.

119. *Daily O'Collegian*, 9 June 1959, p. 8, 12 January 1963, p. 7.

120. *Daily O'Collegian*, 21 January 1956, p. 4, 22 February 1956, p. 3, 3 November 1961, p. 4; *Stillwater NewsPress*, 5 July 1988, p. 2.

121. *1957 Redskin*, p. 264; *Daily O'Collegian*, 16 May 1963, p. 12, 30 April 1958, p. 1, 25 September 1958, pp. 1, 6, 5 November 1966, p. 1, 8 November 1966, p. 1.

122. "The Nation's Outstanding IFC," *Oklahoma State Alumnus Magazine*, vol. 3, no. 5 (May 1962), p. 13; "The 'Iron Man' Trophy is Again Awarded to OSU," *Oklahoma State Alumnus Magazine*, vol. 4, no. 1 (January 1963), p. 11; *Daily O'Collegian*, 4 February 1955, p. 1, 23 February 1956, p. 4, 14 November 1964, p. 1, 2 December 1961, p. 1, 4 December 1962, p. 1.

123. *1962 Redskin*, p. 68; *Daily O'Collegian*, 10 January 1962, p. 1, 4 December 1962, p. 1.

124. *Daily O'Collegian*, 24 June 1955, p. 1.

125. *Oklahoma State University Faculty Handbook*, January 1960, p. 26, Faculty Council Records.

126. *Official Student Handbook of Oklahoma State University: Oklahoma State University Bulletin* (15 July 1959), p. 8.

127. *Daily O'Collegian*, 15 July 1952, p. 3, 12 January 1965, p. 1, 14 September 1965, p. 3.

128. *1953 Redskin*, p. 46; *Daily O'Collegian*, 9 July 1954, p. 1, 13 July 1954, p. 1, 5 October 1955, p. 3, 4 April 1961, pp. 1-2.

129. "Meet the New Dean of Students," *Oklahoma State Alumnus Magazine*, vol. 2, no. 8 (September 1961), p. 42; *Daily O'Collegian*, 6 June 1961, p. 1, 17 September 1959, p. 8.

130. *Daily O'Collegian*, 28 July 1953, p. 8, 11 February 1955, p. 1, 31 January 1958, p. 1, 3 November 1959, p. 1, 12 June 1956, p. 2, 24 January 1956, p. 1, 19 June 1956, p. 1.

131. "Deans of Women at Oklahoma State" [1951], Student Services Collection.

132. "Maxine Adamson Harber," August 1972, p. 1, press release, and "Division of Student Affairs Personnel" [1961], pp. 1-2, in Student Services Collection; *Daily O'Collegian*, 26 May 1954, p. 8, 9 September 1958, p. 8, 12 September 1962, p. 1.

133. H. F. Murphy to Henry G. Bennett, 21 July 1944, Weldon Barnes Collection.

134. Jim Reynolds, "Tests Help Solve Problems," *Oklahoma A. and M. College Magazine*, vol. 19, no. 6 (March 1948), pp. 2-3; *Daily O'Collegian*, 2 February 1956, p. 1, 14 June 1957, p. 1, 25 September 1958, p. 1, 31 January 1958, p. 8.

135. "Caskey Heads OSU Counseling Services," *Oklahoma State Alumnus Magazine*, vol. 4, no. 11 (December 1963), p. 19; *Daily O'Collegian*, 17 September 1959, p. 1, 31 January 1962, p. 5, 21 September 1963, p. 8.

136. *Daily O'Collegian*, 31 January 1962, p. 5.

137. William Edward McFarland, "A History of Student Financial Assistance Programs at Oklahoma State University, 1891-1878, With An Emphasis on the Creation and Administration of the Lew Wentz Foundation" (Doctor of Philosophy dissertation, Oklahoma State University, 1979), pp. 70-95; "National Defense Student Loan Report," 30 June 1961, p. 1, Oliver S. Willham Collection.

138. McFarland, p. 74; Murl Rogers, "An Outstanding Scholarship Program," *Oklahoma A. and M. College Magazine*, vol. 26, no. 12 (August 1955), p. 29; *Daily O'Collegian*, 10 October 1956, p. 7, 4 April 1959, p. 1, 7 January 1960, p. 1.

139. McFarland, pp. 87-90; *Daily O'Collegian*, 5 January 1961, p. 1.

140. Academic Council Meeting Minutes, 16 May 1964, p. 2, 12 June 1964, p. 3, 1 July 1964, p. 2, 1 August 1964, p. 2, Faculty Council Records.

141. McFarland, pp. 95-96.

142. "OSU Placement Bureau Director Retires," *Oklahoma State University Magazine*, vol. 2, no. 6 (December 1958), p. 20; *Daily O'Collegian*, 22 September 1955, p. 7.

143. *Daily O'Collegian*, 22 June 1954, p. 3, 16 November 1954, p. 7; "OSU Placement Bureau Director Retires," p. 20.

144. Robert Jamison, "A Brief History of University Placement Services at Oklahoma State University," 7 June 1986, p. 1, manuscript, Student Services Collection; *Daily O'Collegian*, 21 October 1958, p. 1.

145. *Daily O'Collegian*, 12 November 1958, p. 2.

146. Jamison, p. 1; *Daily O'Collegian*, 4 February 1960, p. 1, 26 October 1961, p. 1.

147. Roxie A. Weber to Oliver S. Willham, 5 February 1960, Oliver S. Willham Collection.

148. *Daily O'Collegian*, 27 April 1960, p. 1, 9 November 1954, p. 5.

149. *Daily O'Collegian*, 12 May 1964, p. 1.

150. *Oklahoma A. and M. Bulletin* (15 October 1952), p. 16; *Oklahoma A. and M. Bulletin* (20 November 1955) pp. 10, 12; *Oklahoma A. and M. Bulletin* (10 June 1957), pp. 12-13; *Daily O'Collegian*, 4 November 1954, p. 8, 15 September 1960, p. 1, 17 November 1960, p. 8, 12 April 1960, p. 7.

151. "Behind the Change in Name," *Oklahoma State Alumnus Magazine*, vol. 2, no. 4 (March 1961), pp. 5-7; *Daily O'Collegian*, 26 July 1960, p. 1.

152. *Daily O'Collegian*, 13 December 1960, p. 2.

153. *Daily O'Collegian*, 17 November 1960, pp. 1, 7.

154. *Daily O'Collegian*, 3 March 1955, p. 1, 19 March 1955, p. 1, 14 September 1961, p. 1, 30 January 1963, p. 1.

155. *Daily O'Collegian*, 30 January 1963, p. 1.

156. *Daily O'Collegian*, 25 September 1958, p. 1, 10 October 1959, p. 1, 15 October 1964, p. 12, 26 April 1966, p. 1.

157. *Daily O'Collegian*, 29 April 1960, p. 8.

158. "Humorous, Healthy, and Exciting," *Oklahoma State Alumnus Magazine*, vol. 5, no. 10 (November 1964), pp. 12-13; *Daily O'Collegian*, 13 November 1964, p. 8.

159. "Humorous, Healthy, and Exciting," pp. 12-13; Sharon Mae Holmberg, "Valerie Colvin: Pioneer Physical Educator in Oklahoma" (Doctor of Education dissertation, Oklahoma State University, 1978), p. 44; Mary Frye, "The Development of Leisure Services and Campus Recreation at Oklahoma State University," 10 February 1986, pp. 1-2, manuscript, Student Services Collection.

160. *1956-1957 Aggie Angles*, pp. 54-60; *1963 Redskin*, p. 290.

161. Frye, p. 1.

162. *Daily O'Collegian*, 21 February 1963, p. 1, 7 March 1963, p. 2, 26 April 1963, pp. 1, 10, 21 June 1971, p. 4.

163. *Daily O'Collegian*, 29 March 1966, p. 4, 7 April 1966, p. 4, 21 June 1966, p. 4, 14 October 1966, p. 2, 28 October 1966, pp. 1, 9.

164. Frye, p. 2; "OSU's New Physical Education Center," *Oklahoma State Alumnus Magazine*, vol. 9, no. 2 (February 1968), p. 2; Holmberg, pp. 48-49, 96.

165. "Seeking a Solution for Mass Education," *Oklahoma State Alumnus Magazine*, vol. 3, no. 5 (May 1962), p. 15; *Daily O'Collegian*, 20 February 1957, p. 1, 23 November 1957, pp. 1, 6, 11 December 1957, p. 1.

166. *Daily O'Collegian*, 29 September 1961, p. 1, 15 December 1961, pp. 1, 3.

167. *Daily O'Collegian*, 23 May 1961, p. 2.

168. *Daily O'Collegian*, 24 October 1962, pp. 1, 10, 26 October 1962, pp. 1, 10, 3 November 1962, pp. 1, 10.

169. *1964 Redskin*, p. 280; "In Memoriam," *Oklahoma State Alumnus Magazine*, vol. 5, no. 1 (January 1964), p. 6; *Daily O'Collegian*, 23 November 1963, pp. 1, 6, 8.

170. *Daily O'Collegian*, 26 November 1963, p. 8.

171. *Daily O'Collegian*, 4 December 1962, p. 2, 6 December 1962, p. 1.

172. Jerry Powell, "The Student," *Oklahoma State Alumnus Magazine*, vol. 3, no. 4 (April 1962), p. 29.

173. *Daily O'Collegian*, 30 March 1966, p. 1, 19 October 1966, pp. 1, 8, 4 December 1962, p. 2, 8 April 1966, p. 1, 15 October 1966, p. 8.

174. "Emphasis People," was a theme and motto used by Dr. Robert B. Kamm through many of his years as OSU president. Particularly in the early 1970s the phrase had common understanding, appearing on lapel buttons, T-shirts, and in campus publications. President Kamm often used the "Emphasis People" phrase in public talks before groups of students, staff and parents.

# 8 Those Agitating, Aggravating Students Leave a Legacy

Student activism dates to the very first colleges and universities. One great educator became so upset with what he called the outrageous and disgraceful behavior of the students at his college that he quit his teaching position in disgust. The college was at Carthage, the year was A.D. 383, and the infuriated professor was St. Augustine. Proof enough, for thousands of years college students have periodically tried the emotions of their mentors, even the patience of a saint.

One of those times occurred in the 1960s and early 1970s. Not since 1848, a year of student-led revolution in Europe, had so many groups of students tried so hard to restructure their colleges, their countries, or the world itself. The protest movement was worldwide by 1968 and unforeseen by educators, who only a few years earlier had criticized young people for their inactivity and silence. Students, moved by the issues of the day, went from alienation toward involved political activism. At the height of activity, students demonstrated for change in twenty different countries. In one three-month period more than three dozen universities were temporarily closed in various countries including the United States, Italy, Spain, Mexico, and Ethiopia.[1]

The worldwide trend of student interest in social and institutional change began in the United States, partly as a result of demands for more participation in campus decisions. It was enhanced by two larger, very emotional, issues. The first was civil rights. In the early 1960s young people learned that they could influence legislation through a show of power—behavior called civil disobedience. Taking lessons from what they experienced and saw, tactics such as sit-ins, marches, and even violence became weapons for change. The second issue was the war in

Vietnam, a conflict that many considered untenable and immoral; it was a highly personal issue for many students because of the draft.

An obvious reason for the students getting so much attention was that there were so many of them. In just over a decade college enrollments had grown from over two and one-half million to seven million. The larger student bodies made for larger problems. However, among the millions enrolled in America's institutions of higher education, the vast majority were never militant. Most were even appalled by the behavior of the extremists. According to estimates, only 1 to 2 percent of the students were ever highly committed agitators advocating change at any price. Another 5 to 10 percent were activists who were willing to demonstrate, although as Oklahoma State University would learn, the numbers could go much higher when a sensitive and specific issue was contested. Throughout, most students were not apathetic, but they remained more interested in their courses than the causes.[2]

Despite the differences of nationality or cause, student activists around the world had similarities. Live pictures of protests carried by television taught global strategy. Among other heroes, Martin Luther King Jr., Stokely Carmichael, and Robert Kennedy were widely respected. California Professor Herbert Marcuse argued that individuals were being smothered and manipulated by big governments and business. As such, individuals were obligated to oppose them. Literature by Marcuse, along with C. Wright Mills, Norman Mailer, and Paul Goodman, was read by this generation of students. The "Establishment" became the general target. The first specific thing to change was the university. As the activists saw it, the university was a training agency for the status quo. According to the students, the university should be a moving force for social reform. In the larger view, lines were drawn and a worldwide struggle developed. The differences between giving advice and taking control, being a part of the political process or dropping out, and advocating reasoned dissent as opposed to intolerance were all difficult lessons which followed.

In the United States, the students tended to be children of tolerant parents. Challenged by their elders to think for themselves, the students of the 1960s largely came from prosperous families, who were used to having their grievances acted upon promptly. The most active of the students clustered at universities that tolerated dissent, such as the University of California at Berkeley, the University of Wisconsin, and Columbia University. As a general rule, compulsory attendance at classes was on the decline, and there was more time to march for civil rights or to help political candidates. The activists were often liberal arts majors, oriented to philosophy, the humanities, and the social sciences, but not yet committed to a career. Fewer students than ever before now worked their way through college.[3]

The problems became so pervasive that President Lyndon Baines Johnson appointed a blue ribbon commission to study and recommend a course of action on campus disruption. In 1970 the President's Commission on Campus Unrest issued a lengthy report. The experts found that the roots of the dissension traced to the troubles of national life, including the slowness in resolving the issues of war and race. While placing a premium on First Amendment guaranteed free speech, the findings supported, as a function of a university, the value of dissent and peaceful protest. In contrast, violence and disorder, the antithesis of the democratic process, could not be tolerated. For their part, the universities of the nation needed to increase the participation of students in the formation of policy, reorganize or decentralize to make possible a more humane system of governance, and correct the many defects which had helped to fuel campus unrest.[4]

The academic year 1965-66 was Oklahoma State University's seventy-fifth anniversary year. In the spring the board of regents chose Robert B. Kamm as the institution's president. A man with a genuine smile and warmth toward everyone, Dr. Kamm assumed his new position on July 1, 1966. The new president had eighteen years of professional experience, including seven years as the dean of students at Drake University and three years as the head of the freshman division and student personnel services at Texas A. and M. University. At OSU the new president had been the dean of the College of Arts and Sciences and the vice president for academic affairs. President Kamm brought with him a wealth of understanding student behavior and needs. His creden-

During the late 1960s and early 1970s, campus unrest was common across the United States. At OSU there was certain media-attracting clamorings, but President Robert B. Kamm used patience and carefully considered judgements to guide the institution through potentially dangerous times. To the president, education is a people enterprise and through his efforts the student environment did become less repressive.

tials in student services-related interests included affiliation with the American Psychological Association Division of Counseling Psychology and a term as president of the American College Personnel Association, one of the two largest national professional organizations for student personnel professionals in higher education.[5]

Throughout his tenure as president, Dr. Kamm would use his formal and informal experiences to temper and guide the institution's direction. At the time of his designation as president, Dr. Kamm made an important promise—that there would be no lessening of the importance of agriculture at the university.[6] His administrative dreams included achieving an atmosphere where "freedom would flourish," where there could be a "great sense of community," and where there would be a "great academic breakthrough."[7] Student leaders were told that their function was to act as a watchdog for student welfare, and that "real leadership is not a question of power or force, but a quality of love, persuasion, and reasoning."[8] For the next decade President Kamm modeled his comments to students about leadership while attempting to balance his diverse goals into a unified land-grant mission. The work would not be easy.

President Kamm's tasks were complicated by the demands of his board of regents, a body consistently seeing its role as mirroring the wishes of parents and taxpayers and the influences of Oklahoma's environment. Jenkin Lloyd Jones, editor and publisher of the usually conservative *Tulsa Tribune*, perhaps illustrated the difficult quagmire that the Oklahoma State University president functioned in when he wrote: "President Kamm must find his way across treacherous ground. On the right there is the morass of over-control, of intellectual tumidity, of subservience to noisy religions and patriotic groups who are suspicious of any examination of traditional mores. And on the left is the quicksand of formless freedom, where the campus is turned over to the beats, the free-lovers, the Reds, the evangelical atheists and those who seek identity in witless commotion."[9]

As President Kamm undertook his tasks, no one could have predicted the series of issues, the protests, or the results that would unfold over the next years. The February 1966 North Central Association accreditation team of visiting educators found OSU's student organization leaders giving "a favorable impression of themselves through their able and responsible handling of problems, their anticipation of them, their support of and by the University administration, and their interest in constructive conditions for learning, service, and activities." The accreditation report was a mixed review which described the general campus atmosphere as one where the visitor has "the impression of a quiet, unexcited, but capable student body seeking to do the job for which its members come to OSU."[10]

Despite appearances the demographics of the student body had been changing, and with it some of the seeds of discontent were planted. As the presidential transition from Willham to Kamm occurred, 4 percent, or approximately 600 hundred students were international. Another 6 percent came from outside of Oklahoma's borders. Nearly half of the students were from central city or metropolitan areas, while less than one-quarter of the students came from rural or farm backgrounds. In comparison to the national average, more of OSU's students came from higher income families, and fewer came from households with very low incomes. Although many still chose majors in agriculture, engineering, and professional fields, increasing numbers came to the university as undecided majors and enrolled in liberal arts curricula. These trends mirrored those in colleges throughout the nation. The student body had quietly become a more liberal, less tolerant, and increasingly cosmopolitan entity.[11]

Oklahoma State University Student Association President Tom Lucas thought that the student body was better informed. Unlike prior generations of apathetic students, his contemporaries needed to be listened to and heard. Lucas thought that administrators should become less repressive and fearful of all student movements. Lucas, assumedly reflecting his own experiences, continued by suggesting that "most rules and regulations in today's colleges were formulated in the 1930s and although some of these still apply, the rules of the 1930s do not fit the 1960s." In general, administrators needed to "accept change as a positive value," concluded the Student Association president.[12] Dean of Student Affairs Frank McFarland echoed Lucas' remarks in a 1965 Academic Council meeting when he told the group of top administrators that to deter campus disruption the council needed to encourage closer contact between staff and students, to review the rules governing students and, as the university grew larger, to work to maintain a "small college" atmosphere where students and faculty have opportunities to work together, know each other, and be able to discuss issues and concerns freely.[13]

McFarland's concept of a closely knit campus would be difficult to achieve. In the fall of 1967 on-campus enrollment had grown to 16,546 students. By the fall semester of 1977 the on-campus student body numbered 21,852. During President Kamm's years the university experienced rapid growth and unprecedented turmoil among the students. But the institution did mature and grow stronger as a result.[14]

A *Faculty Handbook* of the time summarized: "In a period of more than unusual unrest on American campuses during the middle and late 1960s, the Oklahoma State University remained a stable campus where those qualities of freedom and responsible dissent which are so essential to a creative and productive institution were preserved and enhanced."[15]

Truly, some students became frustrated, even bitter, as each issue unfolded. In discussing events through 1970 one particularly agitated student would say: "All means of peaceful social change have been tried at OSU—students have petitioned, marched, held meetings, begged, pleaded, demanded and sued. Though the act of violence would only result in negative reaction, it is the only step left."[16] Outgoing student body president Louis Bullock appealed directly to the board of regents, but in a more restrained way. After four years of various leadership roles in campus government, Bullock reflected that the student leaders that he served with shared an ambition for a greater university "but for all the skill, dedication and determination, these students lost." Bullock continued, "They were beaten by the university they sought to improve."[17]

In reality, the university simply "came of age."[18] It remained open. Despite periods of extreme tension, there was no violence or damage of consequence to people or property. On the other hand, neither did the students lose. Old rules governing student conduct were updated and liberalized. The age-old issue of free speech was debated, and new respect resulted. Black students boycotted and demanded and were heard. Through it all—this richest chapter of student activism in OSU's history—many students learned there was much to be gained by working actively for change within the existing system.

The students enrolled in the decade starting in 1966 would experience a time of campus, national, and world events unlike any before or since. Emotions would rise and fall as on a roller coaster. Some students did drop out. But most would persist. In retrospect each would remember and have an opinion about the cast of leaders who played a part in the continual unfolding of one event or issue after another. In 1967 Student Senate President Bob Swaffar talked about a new political awareness among students. Suggesting that this political awareness would be directed at the institution's rules governing students, Swaffar matter-of-factly said: "Rules are established to protect the majority against a minority. However, if these rules become outmoded, it is up to the majority to change them." Perhaps aware of the historic pattern of change coming slowly in universities generally, he continued: "These changes will not come about quickly or easily—it often takes a vocal minority to act as a catalyst in promoting these changes. The question is, should a majority always need a minority voice to spin it into action?"[19]

President Kamm predicted that campus unrest would be a part of the campus scene for years to come. Affirming that there would be no tolerance for violence or destruction at Oklahoma State, Dr. Kamm stated that students must have the right to raise questions. This process was a necessary part of a college environment. President Kamm then summarized: "Oklahoma State University is in the process of change—as are other major universities—because society is changing."[20] Regrettably, Dr. Kamm's truism was not wholly believed. Complicated problems were made more difficult by outside groups with influence and power. Reminiscent of the institution's founding decades, legislators, newspaper editors, preachers, and governors, although undoubtedly well intentioned, added additional pressure with vehement demands to straighten out the students.

But for the first time ever, a few student leaders were ready to refuse to be intimidated. Given this atmosphere it was not long before the first

*1967 REDSKIN*

In the spring of 1967, a crowd gathered on the library lawn to protest a number of administrative actions, especially the campus speaker's policy.

clouds of controversy came over the campus. Ironically, planners of the traditional Religious Emphasis Week invited theologian Thomas J. Altizer to speak. Altizer was the author of the book, *Radical Theology and the Death of God*. Noting that the university's constituencies and the legislature would not support Altizer's appearance, Dr. Kamm disapproved the invitation and asked the committee to withdraw it. The seemingly inconsequential request occurred during the new president's initial semester in office.[21]

The fall semester was filled with debate and accusation. The *Daily O'Collegian* was generally sympathetic to President Kamm, at one point stating editorially: "For the past seven days it has been rather interesting and experiencing to watch one of the more controversial issues in OSU's history unfold and travel full circle." After an initial stage of shocked indignation, the debaters moved to censorship. Still the writer observed: "Its about time we got back to the issue, rather than personal vendettas. How can any responsible student deny the responsibility of our president to make decisions by comparing his authority (even remotely) with Communist and totalitarian governments?"[22] For its attempted reasoning the *O'Collegian* itself came under fire. Noting that students and faculty had fulfilled their responsibilities by causing pressure on the administration, graduate student Alan C. Bullen accused the paper of becoming a "voice of the administration."[23]

Fuel was added to the flames in January when the board of regents issued a lengthy resolution in support of President Kamm. The Oklahoma State University chapter of the American Association of University Professors (AAUP) joined the controversy and endorsed the campus speaker's policy. Oklahoma Governor Dewey Bartlett pledged his support to President Kamm. The Oklahoma Legislature passed a resolution commending OSU's president for banning participation in student demonstrations and protests by faculty and students.[24]

As the Oklahoma Senate debated their resolve to support OSU's position, Senate President Pro Tempore Clem McSpadden said that college faculty members "should have more to do than carrying picket signs around and hollering about academic freedom."[25] McSpadden was referring to the faculty of the sociology department, where the controversies had mostly centered concerning professor interests in the speaker's debate. Other factors not considered, within two months, nine of ten sociology department professors, and many of their graduate students, would resign "due to the fact that the academic climate on the campus had become intolerable by mid-spring."[26] For these professors and others the issues had grown from prohibiting a specific speaker to an issue of academic freedom.

A significant number of the students joined an alliance with the most active faculty members. On March 9, 1967, approximately 400 students gathered in front of the library to hear a number of faculty and student orators. Speakers decried administrative actions on a growing list of student complaints. A spokesperson affirmed: "Long have we been told by the administration who we may hear speak on campus, where and how we shall live, and who we may entertain in our apartments. Is this the function of a university? Many students do not think it is. If you believe changes are needed, support the student rights movement which has recently begun on the O.S.U. campus. Support the student movement for student freedom."[27]

In an unusual front page editorial the *Daily O'Collegian* concluded that it was "A Time for Action." The campus newspaper noted: "There are enough dissatisfied student and faculty members to cause the administration to take notice. Secondly, the students do have firm ground to launch a reform movement."[28] Although President Kamm was supportive of the students' rights to express their views in an orderly fashion so long as such protests did not interfere with "the regular educational program of the campus," his opinion differed concerning faculty. He stated: "There is a belief on the part of many that, although student protest meetings might be acceptable, faculty members (including graduate assistants) should not use such meetings to air their grievances. I agree with this position."[29]

As more highly publicized actions and reactions to the academic freedom problem took place, the Student Senate undertook the writing of

1969 REDSKIN

During the 1960s, students became more actively involved in campus issues. The war in Vietnam, freedom of speech, and *in loco parentis* were sure to garner a debate.

a Student Bill of Rights. Pushed by Senator David Harris, but opposed as the wrong approach by Student Association President Bob Bird, the controversial measure eventually died with the spring Student Association presidential election defeat of Harris by Tom Lucas. However, the thirteen-point Student Bill of Rights was passed in the senate on two separate votes before it died. It remained important as a gauge of what concerned the students in leadership positions at the time.[30]

Among the articles of the 1967 Student Bill of Rights was a non-discrimination clause opening the university and all chartered organizations to everyone without regard to "race, color, national origin, religious creed, or political beliefs."[31] Other articles proclaimed that students twenty-one years of age or older should be allowed to live where they pleased and be able to participate freely in off-campus activities, as other citizens could, so long as they did not claim to represent Oklahoma State University officially. The bill of rights mandated the elimination of "double jeopardy" disciplinary actions by both campus authorities and civil legal systems and required a disciplinary code guaranteeing students due process. On campus every student had a right to peaceful assembly, to join in unions or collective bargain actions, to petition for changes of curriculum, policy and faculty, and to invite and listen to speakers presenting topics of their choice. Although the bill was never adopted, various sections of the articles would become a part of later group campaigns for increased freedom of choice for students. In the Student Bill of Rights the format and approach were the issues; the ideas would later prove to be solid.[32]

By May the students put their issues aside and focused their energies toward final examinations. President Kamm wrote a reflective letter to OSU faculty and staff which pointed out that during his first year "there have been some problems, to be sure. For example, there's been a bit of discussion about the subject of academic freedom."[33] Dr. Kamm again ascribed to his personal belief in academic freedom, discussed the apparently perpetual problem of an inadequate OSU budget, listed a significant number of accomplishments, and ended by sincerely thanking people for their efforts. Meantime, the OSU Faculty Council reaffirmed its confidence in the new president. While the AAUP directed attention to an internal struggle about becoming an "activist organization," the board of regents were reassured that the campus was calming.[34] A "time for healing was at hand."[35]

The "healing" prognosis was premature. The following fall semester Dr. Timothy Leary, best known at the time as an advocate of the psychedelic drug LSD, was banned from speaking on campus. This time the board of regents took a direct hand in turning away Leary's invitation to campus by the Student Association Forum Committee. In making the decision the board appeared to ignore some elements of its own speaker's policy. The controversial speaker had been approved by forum committee advisor Margaret Brooks, a popular faculty member who headed the university honors program. The members of the regents felt strongly about Leary and questioned Dr. Kamm vigorously. One regent even suggested that every speaker should receive board approval.[36]

On the second day of the two-day board of regents meeting on November 4, 1967, the board followed-up its Leary decision by reaffirming the 1964 approved "Guides For Assemblies and Convocations." The regents then moved to make the speaker's policy more specific. In effect, any potential speaker who advocated lawlessness or disregard for the law, changing laws by other than peaceful means, or the forceful overthrow of government would hereafter be prohibited from speaking on campus. Campus reaction was swift and widespread.[37]

The *Daily O'Collegian* in an editorial titled "Arbitrary, Arbitrary" suggested that Leary was not worth fighting for "but the principle of students being free to hear what he stood for as an element of thinking outside of our academic island very definitely is."[38] The day after the regents acted, an emergency meeting of the Student Senate was held. A resolution was passed objecting to the apparent policy change.[39] The senate also called the action arbitrary and stated: "The recent limitations of speakers imposed by the OSU Board of Regents is a violation of the purpose of a university as well as being in direct opposition to the Board of Regents definitions of a university and speaker policy . . . ."[40] On the third day, President Kamm wrote to faculty and staff. His letter acknowledged that the board's action could be upsetting to some, but appealed for calm. Dr. Kamm reassured that the board was cognizant of the importance of freedom of ideas as an essential component of a university.[41]

As in the year earlier, a cycle, but with new variations, began anew. Citing such reasons as a delay in her approval as Student Senate advisor and administrative pressure, Dr. Brooks resigned her position at the university. Thirty-two of thirty-five senators signed an open letter to the student body expressing their regret and concern about Brooks' resignation. The letter also pointed out that within a twelve-month period fifteen doctoral-level faculty members had resigned their positions. Subsequently scores of other letters filled the pages of the student newspaper. Most supported Brooks, academic freedom, and student rights. A poll conducted by the Student Association indicated that 80 percent of the respondents believed that Leary should have been permitted to speak on campus. Ninety percent indicated that students were capable of judging controversial material for themselves.[42]

Panhellenic Senator Lynn Roney introduced—and the senate passed—a bill calling for a meeting of all students in front of the library.[43] Five to six thousand assembled people gave Senate President Swaffar a standing ovation when he told the crowd that a "university's primary responsibility is to the academic community" and not "various other publics." The meeting was tempered with restraint. Student Association President Lucas gave the audience five action alternatives, including talking to parents and college officials, writing letters to hometown newspapers and friends, and supporting the Student Senate.[44] Several months later one student reflected on the massive meeting and wrote: "Academic freedom once again was the cause for which we had to take a stand . . . . Organized and calm we listened to student leaders voice grievances and then we went our separate ways—to return to the classrooms, to social life, and to a maze of extracurricular activities that play major roles in our life at OSU."[45]

Perhaps as a matter of a show of force or out of a need to assert itself in an area which it could control, the Student Senate moved to join the National Student Association (NSA). The NSA was a controversial, leftist-oriented affiliation of college and university students. Although NSA membership was voted down in 1962, 4,500 students voted and narrowly approved joining in April 1968. Shortly before the NSA vote an opinion poll showed that students still were feeling strongly about the speaker's guidelines with 3,418 against and 924 in favor. Concurrently, "cries of patriotism" rang through the Oklahoma House of Representatives chambers as a bill banning controversial speakers from using facilities of state-supported colleges and universities passed despite an attorney general's ruling that such a bill would be declared unconstitutional.[46]

Through the spring semester of 1968 the guidelines for speakers stirred continuing controversy. Civil rights leader and Congress of Racial Equality (CORE) organizer James Farmer was permitted to speak. The Student Senate responded by asking "how"—given that Farmer had spent time in a Mississippi jail after being arrested in a CORE freedom ride. Two weeks later pacifist priest Philip Berrigan was moved off-campus after a number of incidents, including a bomb threat, occurred. Adding attention to Berrigan's visit was his recent federal conviction for mutilating government property, specifically pouring blood on draft records.[47]

Events of April compounded when Student Senate leaders Ken Dahms and Bill Streck sent highly respected Harvard economist John Kenneth Galbraith a letter and packet of materials describing the academic freedom controversy.[48] By return telegram, directed to the Student Association, Galbraith cancelled his appearance and said: "On reflection I have decided to yield to the pleas of your student leaders . . . and will not 'give a measure of sanction to the pompous idiocy' of the Board of Regents speakers guidelines." Galbraith's sponsors, the Great Issues Committee, had been working for a year on his appear-

A "screaming" collage of campus headlines elicts just some of the sights and sounds of the 1969-70 school year.

ance. The committee reacted in outrage. The *Daily O'Collegian* noted that perhaps unknowingly the former ambassador to India had initiated an effective strategy—"a cultural boycott"—that could be suggested to other proposed guests.[49]

The events of April, May, and June 1968 were numerous and newsworthy. Time slowed as news of the assassinations of Dr. Martin Luther King Jr. and Senator Robert F. Kennedy permeated the campus. On these two occasions differences were set aside as nearly everyone— students, faculty, and staff—mourned and expressed their disbelief. The death of both men reminded that "the Great Society" was not yet great. Within a few months campus flags were hung at half mast; silent marches were held in tribute. Despite the continuing differences, the academic family mindfully paused to reflect that violence was never a solution.[50]

A moratorium on the prolonged speaker's policy flap was reached when the Faculty Council offered a compromise policy. President Kamm established an advisory, coordinating, and confirming committee composed of faculty, students, an academic dean, and the dean of students. The committee's charge was to remain mindful of law and regent's policy, yet set conditions upon which speakers could appear. For their part, the regents established a committee of their members to study the Faculty Council's plan.[51] In June 1968 the regents revised their guidelines for speakers and allowed each of the campuses under their jurisdiction the latitude to "establish procedures to insure that each campus has a well balanced, educationally sound speakers program consistent with the laws of our state and nation."[52] Doug Caves, the Student Association president, and other campus leaders called the new guidelines a "vote of confidence" in OSU's faculty and students.[53]

Problems with off-campus speakers surfaced again the following May. Meantime, the students were content with the new policy on speakers and moved to other concerns. In September 1968 they questioned the administration's failure to consult students in the appointment of a new vice president for auxiliary and student services. In October the Student Senate refused to comply with the president's policy of requesting more student nominees than there were positions to be filled on various university committees. The month of November brought several nationally-known figures to campus for "Sexpo '68," a three-day symposium sponsored by the Association of Women Students and the Student Association.[54] Some of the speakers caused President Kamm to declare: "Although willing to hear other points of view, the university's position in matters of sex and sex education continues in the Judeo-Christian tradition, a position which also has been presented by various speakers from both on and off campus in recent days."[55]

"Sexpo '68" had received considerable publicity in the state media, and with it, off-campus criticism increased. Nonetheless, the president's well-intended, widely distributed reassurance stirred the hornet's nest. Unfavorable letters about the president's statement appeared in the student newspaper. The O'Collegian proclaimed that the "university president is suffering from a severe case of foot-in-mouth disease—a virus that tends to permeate the entire administration at times."[56] The Student Senate, continuing something of a pattern, voted 26 to 2 in opposition to the president's press release. Senator Delmer Boyles summarized with "the university has no right to state a position regarding such personal matters as sex, sex education and religion of OSU students."[57] Unfortunately the media hype and oversensitivity by students clouded an otherwise excellent program. After thousands of students participated, jamming every session, Stillwater religious leader Rev. James Struthers, among others, looked back and reflected: "The whole affair was really great . . . I thought the young people approached it in probably a more mature manner than many of their parents might."[58]

Over the next months it was as if the OSU campus was in the eye of a passing hurricane. During the respite the campus and nation applauded the *Apollo XI* lunar landing. On July 20, 1969, Neil A. Armstrong took humankind's first step on the moon, while a worldwide audience watched on television. For a few weeks troubles were set aside. OSU's long affiliation with NASA evoked special pride. The historic moon landing was needed. It was a rare positive event about which people could unite in these days of national division and unrest.[59] The relatively calm campus then experienced strong weather anew in the late fall of 1969.

For years discontent had been brewing among a number of minority student groups including women, international, Indian, and black students. Black students were the first among these groups to vent their frustrations through overt action. By 1969 there were 325 black students in a student body of 18,000. These students believed there was discrimination in grading practices, financial aid administration, and in the lack of general sensitivity to their unique culture and needs. There had been, at least from their perspective, little positive action taken to hire black faculty and counselors and in revising the curriculum to contemporary times. A number of incidents of physical and mental assaults and abuse intensified concerns. Speakers like Dick Gregory brought focus to the lives of Dr. King and Malcolm X and gave meaning to the nation's racial upheaval which had started in the Watts area of Los Angeles in 1963.[60]

Eight proposals submitted by black students in March 1969 to improve their situation became twelve demands as events escalated in November. The drive, spearheaded by the Oklahoma State Afro-American Society, led to an intense meeting of student leaders and administrators on November 14.[61] Nimrod Chapel, speaking for the students, left the meeting and stated: "There seems to be a very different view as to what the university feels it has implemented, and what, in fact, the black students have seen implemented."[62] Among the list of demands were a black male and female counselor, an increase in black faculty, a black studies program, and improved tutoring services. More difficult and extreme elements were a residence hall named after a noted black person, a lounge in the Student Union with Afro-American decor, and the hiring of a black advisor to the OSU president.[63]

As a "means of communication" fifty to sixty students entered the Edmon Low Library on the evening of November 20. An estimated 5,000 books were taken from the shelves and scattered in stairwells, chairs, elevators, and elsewhere. The raid on the library cost little in damage, but the disruption of normal library operations lasted several days. Five black students were placed on continuing conduct probation, meaning that any further violation of regulations could lead to their suspension from the university. After an appeal, the original sentences were reduced with two of the students receiving a reprimand, and the other three being placed on conduct probation until the end of the spring semester.[64]

Through the spring semester of 1970 the library episode faded, and the Residence Halls Association (RHA) gave birth to the next major flare-up. A moderate but liberalized open house policy was approved by the RHA Assembly and forwarded through channels for approval in February. The idea to modify the visitation rules governing the 7,000 undergraduate students who were living in the on-campus housing system had started back in October. A committee of students, housing officials, and administrators had toiled with the plan's formulation. Upon student approval, Housing Director Lynn Jackson publicly said, "I feel sure this is one bill we can approve."[65] In effect, the plan to permit guests of the opposite sex into the hall residents' rooms required advance publicity, a specified number of proctors, guest registration, approval by the residents of a hall of an overall structure for open houses, and limited hours.[66]

The prearranged agreement to approve the modified policy quickly came apart in early March when the vice president for student and auxiliary services held a meeting of housing staff and student leaders. Claiming parent and student feedback, reports of immorality, and drinking during open house as reasons, the vice president added the requirements that any acceptable plan would have to include open room doors during open house and specifically limited hours during which an open house could be held. The students responded to these events with anger and antagonism. Fifteen residence hall presidents refused to comply with the administration's request to open the doors during open houses. The Student Senate passed a resolution to support the RHA cause. An appeal to Dr. Kamm was rejected. The controversy ended squarely in the laps of the OSU Board of Regents.[67]

On April 11, 1970, RHA President Thomas "Zack" Cooper made an impassioned direct appeal to the regents on behalf of the students. The students were turned down on a vote of 9 to 0. June Tyhurst, writing for the editors and editorial board of the campus newspaper, summarized: "Open doors, closed minds, arbitrary decision, willing acquiescence to external opinion—these have been characteristics of the administration's position on student involvement. These are not characteristics of the high ideals which a university environment should hold."[68]

The following week about 1,100 students came to the library lawn to hear outgoing RHA President Cooper give a "State of the RHA" address. Muldrow student Elizabeth West, another longtime RHA leader, threw her letter of acceptance to OSU's graduate school in the trash, went to study elsewhere, and became a licensed social worker and successful attorney in Chicago. New Yorker Paul Kuznekoff, the incoming

1970-71 RHA president, vowed not to make the open house policy a special issue of his term and to use valid channels for change, if at all possible.[69]

As they accepted the open house-closed door loss and returned to academics, startling news from Kent State University arrived. On May 4, 1970, Ohio National Guardsmen had shot and killed four students on the campus commons. Another meeting was held on the OSU library lawn. About 600 students including "cowboys, ivy-league types, long hairs, and coeds in mini-skirts and bell-bottom pants made up the colorful crowd."[70] *Stillwater NewsPress* managing editor Lee Bell angered many in the academic community by printing his personal reaction to the events of Kent State. Bell wrote: "It isn't that I feel so happy over the fact that the students were killed, but the fact that someone had the guts to do what has to be done to put an end to this damn nonsense that has been going on."[71] Among other speakers, Professor Clarence Cunningham asked the assembly to have compassion for Bell's lapse

On May 4, 1970, Ohio National Guardsmen shot and killed four students on the campus of Kent State University. A few days later, OSU students held a vigil outside the ROTC practice field to protest the shootings as well as the escalating war in Southeast Asia.

in being human and suggested, "We can have neither physical or intellectual violence and still be human."[72]

When the crowd dispersed from the Kent State memorial service, some were given handbills reminding them that the next day there would be a silent "vigil" near the ROTC drill field. Because ROTC was a class and the drill field a classroom, university officials warned that interruptions would lead to the arrest of any disrupters. Meanwhile, the leaflets urged nonviolence and stated that the rally's purpose was to protest "the slaughter at Kent State, the invasion of Cambodia, aggression toward Laos and resumption of bombing in North Vietnam."[73] Others leaving the memorial activities headed to hear the results of the closed door meeting of the Oklahoma State speaker's committee. Would Yippie leader and Chicago Seven member Abbie Hoffman be permitted to speak on campus or not? A crowd of 300 students heard that Hoffman, convicted in February on federal charges of conspiracy to start a riot at the 1968 Democratic National Convention, would be prohibited from using campus facilities for a speech.[74]

With the decision, an old nemesis—the regent's speaker's policy—resurfaced. This time the speaker's flap would be played out in a more sophisticated way. Hoffman's appearance was delayed until after the Student Association went to federal court to secure an injunction against OSU. The students asked the court to prohibit university officials from invoking the Oklahoma law, called the "Speaker Ban Bill," upon which the regent's policy was based. The suit claimed that the law was an infringement on the students' rights under the First and Fourteenth Amendments of the Constitution, resulting in a limitation of free expression and speech. The Student Senate unanimously endorsed the court suit plan. Shortly thereafter, twelve students, including Lou Bullock and Randy Hopkins, the president and vice-president of the Student Association, Cooper and Kuznekoff from the RHA, Student Senators Beverly Oldham and Joe Hodges, and various others, like Floyd Duesler, P. Joe Armstrong, and Gary Stith, decided to pursue the cause. A minimum of $1,500 had to be raised in the expensive venture; $18,000 might ultimately be needed. Obviously, university-collected and controlled money would not be available.[75]

Over the summer months the university and students filed the necessary legal documents in the speaker's lawsuit and scrambled to prepare for the court battle. In July the regents approved a clarification statement on campus disruption which insisted upon the dismissal of any student found guilty of interfering with regular educational programs. The Oklahoma Legislature, assumedly to reinforce university administrators, had worked on a bill on campus rioting. Within the dean of student affairs area, step-by-step procedures for reacting to "sit-in's" and "anticipated disturbances" were put in place. In a three-page letter to

Oklahoma Governor Bartlett, OSU Vice President for Student and Auxiliary Services Abe L. Hesser reassured the anxious official that the media had blown two or three minor incidents out of proportion, giving far more credibility to racial minorities than they deserved.[76] Hesser ended his letter with: "We are not so naive as to say, 'it cannot happen here.' If it does, it will be in spite of our best efforts and not because we abdicated our responsibility as administrators of one of the nation's outstanding educational institutions."[77]

On September 14, 1970, President Kamm wrote a reassuring letter to every parent of an OSU student. The parents were told that any student participating in destructive or disruptive activities would be dismissed. They were asked to "counsel" their children on not becoming an "innocent bystander" in a serious incident—a possible reference to the Kent State incident. In conclusion, the president stated that the students were not expected to run the university. "The opportunity to go to college these days continues to be a privilege, not a right," Dr. Kamm reminded.[78] As the letter softly spelled out university policy to parents and students, it also noted that OSU had been able to avoid major upheaval and that the president, without saying it, aimed to do everything within his power to keep the record that way.

To reinforce this intention the *Stillwater NewsPress* and *Daily Oklahoman* ran news articles headlined "There's No Place at OSU for Militants." The media coverage, letters, and verbal volleys escalated feelings and polarized people. The *Enid Morning Star* and *Tulsa Daily World* published editorials on the "speaker ban law" and the students' use of the courts to resolve the issues.[79] The student plaintiffs were threatened and intimidated. An angry OSU administrator wrote Kuznekoff, the RHA president, "your immaturity and lack of judgment is very evident from your presumptuous letters . . . ."[80] Bullock, the immediate past-president of the Student Association, received one letter from an upset alumnus who threatened, "Get off your little pedestal before some of us knock you off—and I mean it."[81] Attorneys threatened other attorneys. Additional lawsuits would be brought if the university did not stop trying to influence the students who were parties to the speaker's ban case improperly.[82]

Through the ensuing months events took different turns. One of those turns was the regents approval of a new speaker's policy which was based on a policy drafted by a three-judge federal court in Mississippi. The substitute policy was made official in December 1970, before the students' suit was heard in court. In the strangest twist of fate, Hoffman was approved to speak on campus under these new policy guidelines. Hoffman drew 2,500 students to Gallagher Hall on April 28, 1971.[83]

In reaction to Hoffman's appearance, President Kamm said: "At a time when we are giving much attention to the physical environment,

The OSU speaker's policy created considerable controversy, especially when the OSU Board of Regents tried to prohibit those who advocated lawlessness or the forceful overthrow of government from appearances. Some of the notable social activists who did speak included from the left: Abbie Hoffman, Dick Gregory, and Jerry Rubin.

I would propose that we also give attention to pollution relating to those things which are spoken."[84] When Stephen Jones, the students' attorney wrote new Student Association President Harry Birdwell about his charges, he stated: "The plain truth of the matter is that the law suit was too interesting and I had too much fun to charge anybody any legal fee. Therefore, you may consider the question of the fee resolved."[85] Some of the students assured a second test of the new policy by bringing Jerry Rubin, a co-defendant of Hoffman's in the Chicago conspiracy, to campus in May 1972. Rubin's sponsors were the Student Association Forum Committee, the Interfraternity Council, and the Residence Halls Association.[86]

The speaker's policy took some of the time of university administrators in the 1970-71 academic year, but not all of it. Undergraduate women represented by the Association of Women Students (AWS) began another assault for change in the fall semester. In September 1970 AWS President Cheryl Reid and Vice Presidents Dana Beck and Margie Bell issued the "AWS Statement of Concerns." Referencing the various civil rights enactments of the federal law, the statement "strongly urged" a "policy of equalization between men and women concerning rules and regulations" and the "elimination of all discriminatory practices which relegate women to second class status."[87] The specific targets of the women's campaign were the historic rules governing required housing hours for women and a compulsory policy on where they could live. Both dated to the first residence halls on campus for women. Men had generally been free to come and go and live where they chose.[88]

To be sure, the rules governing women's hours in residence halls and other requirements had been liberalized through the 1960s. But the fact that the rules were so different for the two sexes never went away. For housing professionals, occupancy rates and in loco parentis concerns were also at issue. Additionally, "biological rhythms" had historically confused matters—that is, when the women go to their campus homes, the men, with little else left to do, would also return to their places of residence. As a result, persistent recommendations, particularly from the Women's Residence Halls Association, brought some progress, albeit ever so slowly.[89]

Not unlike the Residence Halls Association open house-closed door controversy, frustration had grown with administrative resistance. The AWS declaration for equal treatment in the rules code drew widespread support. Ardoth Hassler, RHA vice president for women, spearheaded a resolution, which was unanimously approved by the RHA Assembly, to support the AWS drive for women's rights. Sixteen living groups, the Panhellenic Council, and the Student Senate adopted similar resolutions.[90] The institution's response was, "There will be no further liberalization of these hours or policies in the foreseeable future."[91] Cognizant of the Student Association lawsuit, the AWS threatened a similar tactic. By February a protest meeting on the library lawn started with 500 people and ended with 2,000 in the Student Union Ballroom.[92] Looking at the problem in another way, a faculty member stated: "What we find is a large number of people being treated as if they were little children for part of each day. The rest of the day we are expecting them to perform their classwork in an adult manner."[93]

In March the residence hall living and hour requirements came to a head and quickly ended. Four Willham Hall coeds filed a lawsuit independent of the AWS, charging that the contested OSU regulations were discriminatory, arbitrary, capricious, and based upon sexual differences. Less than a week later the board of regents approved regulations that caused the suit to become moot. Starting in the fall of 1971 all unmarried men and women freshman and sophomore students under the age of twenty-one would be required to live in university housing. They would also all have the same hours too—midnights Sunday through Thursdays and 1:30 A.M. Friday and Saturday. In now typical fashion, there was a small, short-lived "sit-in" at the Student Union offices of the board of regents, and 450 irritated students heard a number of speakers vent their annoyance on the library lawn. The RHA Assembly was admonished to continue to push for "progressive action."[94]

Of all the campus crises during the turbulent 1970-71 year, including the speaker's policy, open house rules, and the discrimination of women, the most tense and potentially explosive started to unfold in the late evening of November 12, 1970. Exactly one year to the month after the library raid by black students, three black women were verbally harassed as they drove through a group of Acacia fraternity men who were drinking. The men had allowed their annual "Night on the Nile" party to go astray. The frightened women returned to their residence hall. After reporting the obscenity-filled incident to friends, a group of students returned to the original point of confrontation. A number of subsequent actions between black and white students escalated events, but in brief, three other black women were shot and injured by BB gun pellets fired at them from a window in the Delta Tau Delta fraternity house. More frightening, a loaded 30-06 rifle was taken from a man in the Pi Kappa Phi house later the same evening.[95]

The university's response to the incident was swift and forceful. Three men, two who fired the BB guns and the student with the high-powered rifle, were suspended the next day. Criminal charges were filed against two of the men by the district attorney.[96] The dean of students issued a public statement stating: "The University cannot and will not tolerate actions of this kind . . . physical violence, mental abuse and other evidence of vicious hate or unreasoned action is abhorred by all parts of the University community."[97] On November 16, President Kamm wrote an open letter to OSU students, faculty, and staff appealing for courtesy, affection, and friendship. A separate letter was sent to fraternities, sororities, and residence halls to remind the undergraduates that there were clear prohibitions against firearms and weapons on campus.[98] The three fraternities issued a joint statement of apology saying, "We are deeply sorry that the incidents happened."[99]

The racist incident of one night was seen as only one, although frightening, event in a continuing series of prejudiced-based happenings. However, it was the one incident that brought the campus black community together. After several long meetings on how to respond, anywhere from 225 to 300 black students left Stillwater on November 14, "until assurances could be made that OSU was no longer an armed campus."[100]

The black students boycotted the campus and their classes for ten days. During the period they moved to six different locations. Sanctuary and safety were found, among other places, first at Camp Redlands on Lake Carl Blackwell, at St. John's Church and the Walnut Cultural Center in Oklahoma City, and then back in Stillwater with members of the black community. Along their route they petitioned Governor Bartlett, to no avail, and received nurturance from the singing group Fifth Dimension. Many of the students' parents, the Afro-American Society, OSU Professor Earl Mitchell, state civil rights leader Clara Luper, and State Senator E. Melvin Porter were other sources of encouragement for the purposeful students.[101]

Early in the boycott a list of fifteen concerns were drafted by student leaders and presented to the administration. After the original demands

In the late 1960s, OSU black students called for improvements on the campus not only to assure equal opportunity but also to increase awareness of black culture.

were submitted, four black student-athletes joined the boycott and were suspended from the basketball team. A sixteenth item, the players' reinstatement to the team, was then added to the original list. Eventually negotiations got underway which involved Afro-American Society President Alonzo Batson, Mitchell, President Kamm, and a number of others. With President Kamm's reassurances after he personally visited the boycotting students' sanctuary, the walk-out officially ended on November 23 with a promise of more meetings.[102] Near the end of the days of general tension, a group of ten students placed a funeral wreath at the door of the president's office. With this symbolic act came the comment that the wreath "signifies to black students at OSU that the administration is dead—we can only hope for a rebirth."[103]

The entire campus, in one form or another, had paid a price as the boycott ended. Through it all, those with the strongest beliefs—the boycotting students—paid the heaviest toll. Ronald Lee Johnson, in his summary of these historic and eventful days, perhaps stated it best. Johnson wrote: "Once back on campus, they went their respective ways and tried to salvage the rest of the semester. Some were unsuccessful and left school the following semester. Some continued, to no avail, to get the basketball players reinstated. Others pressed for more positive action from administration, while some completely withdrew into themselves and retreated into a world of escapism."[104] Perhaps Bob Buck, John Robinson, Jerry Redo, and Kenneth Jackson, the four student-athletes who were dropped from the basketball team, made the most difficult decisions of all since they had the most to lose. In a sense, the four exemplify how deeply the commitment ran toward the principles involved in the 1970 student boycott.[105]

A year after the black student boycott ended, some of the demands had received positive action. Others had not and would not be implemented. There had also been important permanent gains for black students which went beyond the specific written list of concerns.[106] For the first time the boycott "united a substantial number of blacks on a common interest and forced them to work for improvements in a consistent and organized manner."[107] There can be no doubt that the students' action raised the level of awareness and focus of everyone, including students, faculty, and staff, on the degree of racism on campus.

In student services Howard Shipp joined previously-hired Thelma Cook as a response to the on-going appeal by black students for counseling assistance. A native of Muskogee, the man warmly referred to as "Shipp" was himself a product of Oklahoma's segregated public and higher education systems. Over a long tenure of service at OSU, Dr. Shipp became a highly respected leader in minority-related issues both at OSU and state-wide. Finally, as another positive action, in 1971 the institution hired Glenn Johnson as the first black professional in the Department of Financial Aid.[108]

On the first anniversary of the black student boycott, James Dossett, president of the Afro-American Society, and a group of other students went to the library lawn to rally and "pay tribute" to the monumental events of the prior year.[109] In one way or another subsequent groups of OSU students would pause on the boycott's anniversary to memorialize the protest. More importantly, later students would reflect on the tension-filled ten-day period with admiration, respect, and solemnness. The boycott served to remind students of the fear, risk, and other discomforts that the 200 or so pioneering students chose to take upon themselves in the cause of eliminating racism. Since prejudice, in all of its forms and general inequity, does not end with a single event, the boycott would be a continual reminder to each new group of students, black and white, of their significant OSU "roots" and the work that would be theirs to continue.

While the black student boycott likely represented the most volatile single event of President Kamm's era, the Vietnam War had the most longevity. No less explosive than other campus issues among students, the strong position taken by groups of students on the war remained a persistent danger. The ROTC drill field demonstration on May 7, 1970, the day after the library lawn Kent State memorial, served to exemplify

Following the black student boycott in 1970, the university's administration moved to meet some of the students' demands. As one of these positive moves, Dr. Howard Shipp joined University Counseling Services. Shipp is well known for his work on minority-related issues.

the kind of tension created by the war. Between 900 to 1,000 anti-war protesters and "anti-protester protesters" appeared for a planned peaceful rally. The ROTC drill area was roped off, and campus police promised to arrest any unauthorized person who entered the cordoned-off area. In addition, for safety reasons, the ROTC exercises had been moved from the regular drill area to the practice football field, disappointing anti-war leader Richard Fossey of Anadarko.

Anti-war demonstrators spent much of the two-hour vigil singing songs with two fingers held high to symbolize "peace." Pro-war forces made it clear that they considered the anti-war students "un-American." Meantime, the ROTC students went about their routine with a chanting of "Hup 2-3-4." At one point, during the singing of "America, the Beautiful," participants "asked the cowboys present to please take off their hats. Only half of the cowboys joined the singing and took their hats off." Some students raised American flags while adversaries held signs which could have easily incited the massive crowd. Verbal abuse and taunting gestures compounded matters. The polarization of students increased with time. Be it fate or luck, the ROTC drill ended before matters got out of hand. The demonstration ended peacefully, but the potential for physical violence had permeated the activity.[110]

Between 1965 and 1973 the Vietnam War intermittently became the primary target of student attention. The *Daily O'Collegian's* editorials were generally favorable to the war effort. In fact, the typical student was also sympathetic; although many did not particularly like the government's overall policy, they also believed that since American soldiers were there it was the citizenry's obligation to be supportive. Three thousand signatures were collected in 1969 in an open letter to President Richard M. Nixon supporting his stand in Vietnam. For the university's part, ROTC had been made a voluntary program in 1965. By 1970 a session at the summer freshman orientation clinics had been changed from discussing ROTC programs to talking about "military obligations." At the time, the Selective Service law was widely protested. Students objecting to the war were risking their U.S. citizenship by moving to Canada, declaring themselves conscientious objectors, and, in the extreme, publicly burning their draft cards and choosing jail terms over military service.[111]

Keeping the Vietnam issue alive was a small but active chapter of Students for a Democratic Society (SDS), a sympathetic group of campus-affiliated Stillwater clergy, on-going debate among knowledgeable faculty members, and a string of nationally prominent leader-figures who came to campus to discuss politics and war. With all of their varying opinions, the academic community heard speeches by Arizona Senator Barry Goldwater, Vice President of the United States Hubert H. Humphrey, Georgia legislator and civil rights leader Julian Bond, and Oklahoma Senator Fred R. Harris.[112]

Throughout the Vietnam War years, Oklahoma State's students debated and philosophized. Unlike other major universities, and to their credit, they were able to avoid the physical violence and destruction of property that marked this divisive period in the nation's history. The controversial war, which took over 50,000 American lives and cost billions of dollars, ended with the signing of a cease-fire document. In January 1973 the *Daily O'Collegian* proclaimed, "Gee, that was a long war."[113] Through the spring American troops were withdrawn from the small nation in southeast Asia and returned home.

As the war in Vietnam calmed and finally ended, the nation turned to healing its own wounds. But Vietnam, so unlike any other military involvement before it or since, presented such unique complexities that the return to health would be long in coming. There was little of the usual national outpouring for the veterans—they were neither heroes nor victors. In large segments of society Vietnam was treated as a bad dream, best just to be forgotten. Something would have to be done for the thousands of young people—many in jails or in other countries—who had taken a stand against the war. Parents and their children would have to try and reunite after their differences over the conflict became irreconcilable. Typically, millions of average people paused to think, seek some meaning from this latest war, and, at least mentally, make the transition from war to peace.

One OSU student was particularly poignant as he attempted to bridge the gap and draw meaning for himself from the war years on the Asian peninsula and the subsequent repercussions in the United States. In 1975 microbiology junior Richard B. Smith wrote an open letter in which he stated: "I don't know how anyone else feels, but the surrender of South Vietnam is a bitter sadness for me." Thoughtfully, Smith asked every American to reflect on all that transpired, including remembering "the graft and corruption of the Saigon government, terrorist bombings, massive drug addiction, tiger cages, lying politicians, draft resistance, demonstrations, political trials, a whole generation of alienated youth, My Lai massacre, SDS, Chicago Seven, Kent State, secret unauthorized bombings of Cambodia, Hanoi Hilton, POW's, B-52 raids, smart bombs and anti-personnel weapons—the most treacherous and deadly things yet conceived by mankind, thousands of burned and maimed children?" Moving to his own lesson and conclusion, Smith then suggested that the United States was a "nation of people of all temperaments and values and very short on perfection." Humbled by Vietnam, the insightful student concluded: "We may begin to look inside ourselves for the answers. After all, it is the world's only hope for peace."[114]

The Oklahoma State University campus provided the final major public platform for the man who orchestrated the United States withdrawal from Vietnam, President Richard M. Nixon. Coincidentally his appearance afforded the grist for the last public student protest during Dr. Kamm's presidency. The Watergate-embroiled President spoke before a huge crowd of 32,000 respectful people to highlight the university's seventy-ninth commencement on May 11, 1974. It marked the first time that a President of the United States had spoken at OSU while still holding office. A small group of students, calling themselves TAPES—Today's Americans Protesting Executive Secrecy—peacefully protested outside the stadium. Despite Watergate, the speaker was the President of the United States, and the aura of that office carried the evening. The night at Oklahoma State was also a morale booster for the politically-troubled President who would resign his office a few months later.[115]

In 1976 the Oklahoma Legislature rejected the Equal Rights Amendment for the third time. Gerald R. Ford had replaced Nixon as President, and three of the former President's closest advisors, including a secretary of state, were in jail in the aftermath of the Watergate conspiracy. Vietnam and Cambodia had fallen to communist regimes, and in March Dr. Kamm announced his resignation as president of Oklahoma State University, effective February 1, 1977. The fifty-seven year old administrator would step down from the presidency after serving ten years and seven months in the "pressure-packed" position. History would reflect that President Kamm served during a span of time unprecedented in the amount of student upheaval on the nation's college and university campuses, including Oklahoma State University.[116]

It is sometimes regretful, if not unfortunate, that young people are

In 1974 Watergate-embroiled President Richard Nixon spoke at OSU's commencement. Although most were honored by the incumbent President's visit, TAPES (Today's Americans Protesting Executive Secrecy) peacefully protested.

on campus as undergraduates only a short time before moving on to larger goals. Their brief experiences, whether in a one-year leadership position or a four-year academic program, afford a limited evaluation of campus changes. Likewise, an objective perspective of the people who assist students in achieving their priorities is often weakened by the near at hand feelings of frustration, anger, and even rejection. The seemingly unmoving milieu of campus committees and the inevitable "channels"—that infamous network of university decision-making called "the bureaucracy"—further confound accurate analysis. President Kamm's decade of service graphically illustrated the notion that as the years pass, emotions lessen, and the meaning of specific events becomes clearer.

In Oklahoma State's case time-tempered hindsight showed that in the late 1960s and early 1970s the "lot" for students changed dramatically and for the better. Students entered the period as serfs in the academic kingdom and exited with substantial gains in their rights as citizens. Archaic rules and regulations were modernized. Student government's influence in institutional governance increased. Many student recommendations were contemplated, approved, and implemented without conflict or fanfare. Among these were the abandoning of the code on "public display of affection (PDA)," due process procedures for student disciplinary cases, and rules governing the search of student rooms by police or institutional employees. Obvious gains were also made in the equalization of rules governing men and women and in heightened sensitivity toward the culturally-based needs of minority students. There was increased understanding that a student's room is a home-away-from-home, a place where friends should be allowed to visit. All of the changes, to the benefit of students, were unparalleled, cumulatively more than in all prior decades combined. More remarkably, they were achieved without substantial disruptions or damage to the campus or its people.[117]

As in most human endeavors, enough complexity was involved to make it difficult to know what cause and effect relationships existed during this noisy period. Whether because of or despite the students' activism, including the emotional appeals and petitions, vocal demonstrations on the well-worn library lawn, boycotts, lawsuits, and other media-attracting clamorings, the fact remained that Dr. Kamm was the president when the students' environment became substantially less repressive and more humane. His role in the history of the era was substantial. On a campus located in a conservative state with little tolerance for disobedience and unpatriotic causes, President Kamm, with patience and carefully considered judgments, guided the institution safely through potentially disastrous times. In Ohio, for example, a public student protest combined with overzealous politicians to bring about the insanity at Kent State.

Always a visible and enthusiastic man, President Kamm's surprise resignation announcement spread across campus. Students and faculty reacted with shock and disbelief. Supportive comments of respect and praise were widespread. Emphasizing that he was not retiring but just returning to teaching and other work for the university, Dr. Kamm stressed that after three decades of continuous work as an administrator in higher education, he and his wife, Maxine, "are looking forward to being free of the tremendous burdens 'of the presidency.'" He would miss only some parts of the position, but one aspect of the presidency that a void would be felt in was "the identification with the students."[118]

Regent Armon Bost, along with complimenting the near ex-president, observed that the gray-haired Dr. Kamm started in his position with "coal black hair."[119] There was little doubt that the years' events had taken their physical toll. But perhaps there was also consolation to be found. The sometimes agitating, aggravating students—those young people that the president would miss—would miss him too. "An individual that's more concerned with students' needs will be hard to come by," reflected RHA President Phil Wright.[120] "Kamm's tenure as president can only be described with praise . . . ," noted *O'Collegian* editor Floyd Stanley.[121]

The *1977 Redskin* was warm with praise and straightforward in dedicating a section of the annual to the Kamms. Speaking of Dr. and Mrs. Kamm as the team that they were, the writers said: "We are proud of their hospitality and endless energy. Together the Kamms are strong and positive; their zest for life set a friendly atmosphere on the OSU campus." Then, capturing the essence of the man's executive style, the students printed a poem titled "Together!" The first lines fittingly read: "Ho, brother, it's the hand clasp and the good word and the smile. That does the most and helps the most to make the world worthwhile!"[122]

## Endnotes

1. "Why Those Students Are Protesting," *Time*, vol. 91, no. 18 (3 May 1968), pp. 24-25.

2. "Why Those Students Are Protesting," pp. 24-25.

3. "Why Those Students Are Protesting," p. 25.

4. "Major Recommendations From the President's Commission On Campus Unrest," September 1970, pp. 1-3, Student Services Collection, Special Collections, Edmon Low Library, Oklahoma State University, Stillwater, Oklahoma.

5. *1966 Redskin*, pp. 3, 47, Oklahoma State University Yearbook; *1975 Redskin*, p. 46; Oklahoma State University *Daily O'Collegian*, 1 July 1966, pp. 1-2, 17 June 1958, pp. 1, 6, 15 February 1966, p. 1; "Robert B. Kamm " [February 1966], pp. 1-2, press release, Weldon Barnes Collection, Special Collections, Edmon Low Library.

6. *Daily O'Collegian*, 1 July 1966, p. 1.

7. *Daily O'Collegian*, 22 October 1966, p. 1.

8. *Daily O'Collegian*, 14 October 1965, p. 1.

9. *Tulsa Tribune*, 16 March 1967, p. 56.

10. "Kudos and Criticism," *Oklahoma State Alumnus Magazine*, vol. 7, no. 7 (September-October 1966), p. 28.

11. "Analysis of Culture, Student Body Profile, and Institutional Climate" [1965-1966], pp. 1-3, Weldon Barnes Collection.

12. *Daily O'Collegian*, 6 November 1970, p. 3.

13. Academic Council Minutes, 10 April 1965, pp. 2-3, Faculty Council Records, Special Collections, Edmon Low Library.

14. "Campus Briefs," *Oklahoma State Alumnus Magazine*, vol. 8, no. 9 (December 1967), p. 4; Student Affairs Department Heads Meeting Minutes, 15 September 1977, p. 1, Student Services Collection.

15. *Oklahoma State University Faculty Handbook, September 1973*, p. 6.

16. *Daily O'Collegian*, 6 November 1970, p. 1.

17. *Daily O'Collegian*, 9 February 1971, p. 6.

18. *Oklahoma State University Faculty Handbook, September 1973*, p. 6.

19. Pete Schneider, "Student Leaders Seek Larger Role," *Oklahoma State Alumnus Magazine*, vol. 8, no. 7 (September-October 1967), p. 13.

20. *Daily O'Collegian*, 3 December 1968, p. 5.

21. *Daily O'Collegian*, 14 December 1966, pp. 1, 8.

22. *Daily O'Collegian*, 20 December 1966, p. 4.

23. *Daily O'Collegian*, 6 January 1967, p. 4.

24. *Daily O'Collegian*, 10 January 1967, pp. 5, 7, 25 February 1967, pp. 1, 8, 18 March 1967, p. 4, 22 March 1967, p. 1, 21 March 1967, pp. 1, 6.

25. *Daily O'Collegian*, 22 March 1967, p. 1.

26. *Daily O'Collegian*, 16 May 1967, pp. 1, 7.

27. Robert Cordin, "Student Rights Meeting," March 1967, Campus flyer, Weldon Barnes Collection.

28. *Daily O'Collegian*, 9 March 1967, p. 1.

29. Robert B. Kamm, "Kamm List Views," 14 March 1967, press release, Weldon Barnes Collection.

30. *Daily O'Collegian*, 17 March 1967, pp. 1, 7, 18 February 1967, p. 4, 7 April 1967, p. 1, 5 April 1967, p. 1, 15 March 1967, p. 1, 15 April 1967, p. 1.

31. David Harris, "Student Bill of Rights," 8 February 1967, p. 1, Student Senate Bill, Weldon Barnes Collection.

32. Harris, "Student Bill of Rights," pp. 1-2; *Daily O'Collegian*, 5 April 1967, p. 1, 7 April 1967, p. 1, 15 April 1967, p. 4.

33. Robert B. Kamm to OSU Faculty and Staff, 3 May 1967, p. 1, Weldon Barnes Collection.

34. Robert B. Kamm to OSU Faculty and Staff, 3 May 1967, pp. 1-2, and "Faculty Council Statement Supporting President Kamm," May 1967, p. 1, in Weldon Barnes Collection; *Daily O'Collegian*, 10 May 1967, p. 1, 13 May 1967, p. 1.

35. *Daily O'Collegian*, 13 May 1967, p. 1.

36. *Daily O'Collegian*, 4 November 1967, pp. 1, 4, 7 November 1967, pp. 1, 12, 3 November 1967, p. 1.

37. Robert B. Kamm to OSU Faculty, 6 November 1967, p. 1, Faculty Council Records; *Daily O'Collegian*, 7 November 1967, pp. 1, 7.

38. *Daily O'Collegian*, 7 November 1967, p. 4.

39. *Daily O'Collegian*, 7 November 1967, p. 1.

40. Robert C. Swaffar, "Senate Resolution 24-A," 5 November 1967, p. 1, Faculty Council Records.

41. Robert B. Kamm to OSU Faculty, 6 November 1967, p. 1, Faculty Council Records.

42. *Daily O'Collegian*, 3 November 1967, p. 1, 4 November 1967, pp. 1, 4, 4 November 1967, pp. 1-2, 16 December 1967, p. 1, 16 January 1968, p. 4.

43. *Daily O'Collegian*, 7 November 1967, p. 1.

44. *Daily O'Collegian*, 9 November 1967, p. 1.

45. *1968 Redskin*, p. 29.

46. *Daily O'Collegian*, 1 March 1968, p. 1, 16 March 1968, p. 1, 9 July 1968, p. 2, 17 April 1968, p. 1, 18 April 1968, p. 2, 10 April 1968, p. 1.

47. *Daily O'Collegian*, 8 February 1968, p. 1, 16 April 1968, p. 1, 30 April 1968, p. 1, 24 April 1968, p. 1, 1 May 1968, p. 1.

48. *Daily O'Collegian*, 4 April 1968, p. 1, 3 April 1968, p. 1.

49. *Daily O'Collegian*, 2 April 1968, p. 1.

50. *Daily O'Collegian*, 6 April 1968, pp. 1, 4, 9 April 1968, pp. 1-2, 7 June 1968, p. 2, 11 June 1968, p. 2.

51. *Daily O'Collegian*, 15 May 1968, p. 1, 14 May 1968, p. 1.

52. *Daily O'Collegian*, 18 June 1968, p. 1, 25 June 1968, p. 4.

53. *Daily O'Collegian*, 21 June 1968, p. 1.

54. *Daily O'Collegian*, 18 September 1968, p. 1, 19 September 1968, p. 1, 11 October 1968, p. 1, 25 September 1968, p. 1, 28 June 1968, p. 1.

55. "Sexpo '68," *Oklahoma State Alumnus Magazine*, vol. 10, no. 1 (February 1969), p. 4; *Daily O'Collegian*, 21 November 1968, p. 1.

56. *Daily O'Collegian*, 22 November 1968, p. 4.

57. *Daily O'Collegian*, 22 November 1968, p. 1.

58. "Sexpo '68," p. 4.

59. "Apollo 11," *Oklahoma State Alumnus Magazine*, vol. 10, no. 8 (November 1969), p. 9.

60. Ronald Lee Johnson, "Black Student Attitudes: A Study in Alienation At Oklahoma State University" (Master of Science thesis, Oklahoma State University, 1975), pp. 4-5; *Daily O'Collegian*, 19 September 1968, pp. 1, 6, 24 September 1968, p. 2, 28 September 1968, p. 2.

61. *Daily O'Collegian*, 15 November 1969, p. 1, 19 January 1969, p. 1; "Black Student Demands, 1969-1970 " [November 1969], pp. 1-5, Student Services Collection.

62. *Daily O'Collegian*, 15 November 1969, p. 1.

63. Robert B. Kamm to Nimrod Chapel, 18 November 1969, Faculty Council Records.

64. Roscoe Rouse to Robert G. Schmalfeld, 24 November 1969, Roscoe Rouse, "A Report of the Afro-American Society Invasion of the Library on November 20, 1969," 24 November 1969, pp. 1-2, and Harry K. Brobst to Nimrod Chapel, 26 January 1970, in Student Services Collection; *Daily O'Collegian*, 4 December 1969, p. 1, 10 January 1970, p. 1, 3 February 1970, p. 1.

65. *Daily O'Collegian*, 5 February 1970, p. 1.

66. Residence Halls Association, "Open House Policy Appeal to the Board of Regents," 11 April 1970, pp. 1-6, Student Services Collection.

67. Abe L. Hesser to Residence Halls Staff and Student Leaders, 19 March 1970, and Residence Halls Association, "Open House Policy Appeal to the Board of Regents," 11 April 1970, pp. 6-8, Student Services Collection; *Daily O'Collegian*, 31 March 1970, p. 1, 19 March 1970, p. 1, 2 April 1970, p. 1, 10 April 1970, p. 1.

68. *Daily O'Collegian*, 15 April 1970, p. 1.

69. *Daily O'Collegian*, 17 April 1970, p. 1, 2 May 1970, p. 7. Thomas "Zack" Cooper went on to the presidency of the National Association of College and University Residence Halls and subsequently to become a successful Stillwater businessman. He continues today to support the RHA through scholarship money and other contributions.

70. *Daily O'Collegian*, 7 May 1970, p. 11.

71. *Stillwater NewsPress*, 5 May 1970, p. 2; *Daily O'Collegian*, 7 May 1970, p. 4.

72. *Daily O'Collegian*, 7 May 1970, pp. 1, 11.

73. *Daily O'Collegian*, 7 May 1970, p. 11.

74. *Daily O'Collegian*, 1 May 1970, p. 1, 7 May 1970, pp. 1, 11, 12 May 1970, p. 1.

75. *Stillwater NewsPress*, 28 August 1970, p. 1; Stephen Jones to Harry Birdwell, 7 June 1971, Student Services Collection; *Daily O'Collegian*, 14 May 1970, p. 1, 1 September 1970, p. 3, 25 September 1970, p. 1, 8 September 1970, pp. 1, 7, 8 May 1970, pp. 1, 4, 3 July 1970, pp. 1, 6.

76. OSU Board of Regents, "Emergency Disciplinary Procedures in Cases of Disruptions to the University's Educational Process," 11 July 1970, pp. 129-131, Board of Regents Files, Special Collections, Edmon Low Library; "The Changing University Scene," *Oklahoma State Alumnus Magazine*, vol. 11, no. 7 (September-October 1970), pp. 4, 8; *Daily O'Collegian*, 14 July 1970, p. 1, 18 March 1969, p. 1; Division of Student Affairs, "Procedures To Be Followed In the Event of a 'Sit-In'," 4 March 1969, pp. 1-2, Division of Student Affairs, "Pre-Disturbance Procedures," [1969], pp. 1-2, and Abe L. Hesser to Dewey Bartlett, 30 July 1970, Student Services Collection.

77. Abe L. Hesser to Dewey Bartlett, 30 July 1970, Student Services Collection.

78. Robert B. Kamm to OSU Parents, 14 September 1970, Faculty Council Records; *Daily O'Collegian*, 17 September 1970, p. 1.

79. Oklahoma City *Daily Oklahoman*, 1 September 1970, p. 13; *Stillwater NewsPress*, 31 August 1970, p. 1; *Daily O'Collegian*, 26 September 1970, p. 2.

80. Abe L. Hesser to Paul Kuznekoff, 1 September 1970, Student Services Collection.

81. *Daily O'Collegian*, 16 March 1971, p. 4.

82. Stephen Jones to W. Howard O'Bryan and E. Moses Frye, 3 November 1970, Student Services Collection.

83. "Speakers Policy Is Amended," *Oklahoma State Alumnus Magazine*, vol. 12, no. 2 (February 1971), pp. 13-14; *Daily O'Collegian*, 15 December 1970, p. 1, 24 April 1971, p. 1, 29 April 1971, p. 1.

84. "Abbie Hoffman's Appearance," *Oklahoma State Alumnus Magazine*, vol. 12, no. 6 (June-July 1971), p. 12; *Daily O'Collegian*, 29 April 1971, p. 1.

85. Stephen Jones to Harry Birdwell, 7 June 1971, Student Services Collection.

86. *Daily O'Collegian*, 26 April 1972, p. 1, 4 May 1972, pp. 1, 9.

87. "AWS Statement of Concern," Residence Halls Association Annual Report, 13 April 1971, Attachment II, p. 1, Student Services Collection; *Daily O'Collegian*, 1 October 1970, p. 1.

88. "AWS Statement of Concern," 13 April 1971, p. 1; *Daily O'Collegian*, 3 October 1970, p. 4.

89. *Daily O'Collegian*, 15 December 1967, p. 3, 7 March 1968, pp. 1, 8, 9 October 1970, p. 1, 9 March 1968, p. 2, 22 March 1968, p. 1.

90. *Daily O'Collegian*, 9 October 1970, p. 1, 19 February 1971, p. 4.

91. *Daily O'Collegian*, 19 February 1971, p. 4.

92. *Daily O'Collegian*, 16 October 1970, p. 1, 19 February 1971, p. 4.

93. *Daily O'Collegian*, 25 February 1971, p. 4.

94. OSU Board of Regents, "Revision of Single Student Housing Regulations," 5-6 March 1971, pp. 183-184, Board of Regents Files; *Daily O'Collegian*, 3 March 1971, p. 1, 9 March 1971, p. 1, 11 March 1971, pp. 1, 3, 16 March 1971, p. 1.

95. Shaila Aery to Zelma Patchin, 16 November 1970, Zelma Patchin, "Incident Notes," 13 November 1970, pp. 1-2, and Earl Mitchell and Earl Van Eaton, Transcript of Student Testimony, 13 November 1970, pp. 1-8, Student Services Collection; *Daily O'Collegian*, 17 November 1970, pp. 1-2.

96. *Daily O'Collegian*, 14 November 1970, pp. 1, 3.

97. *Daily O'Collegian*, 14 November 1970, p. 1.

98. Robert B. Kamm to OSU Students, Faculty and Staff, 16 November 1970, and Norman F. Moore to All Fraternities, Sororities and Residence Halls, 18 November 1970, in Student Services Collection.

99. *Daily O'Collegian*, 14 November 1970, p. 3.

100. *Daily O'Collegian*, 17 November 1970, p. 1.

101. Johnson, pp. 10-12; *Daily O'Collegian*, 17 November 1970, p. 2.

102. Johnson, pp. 8-11; *Daily O'Collegian*, 18 November 1970, p. 1, 19 November 1970, p. 1, 21 November 1970, p. 1; Robert B. Kamm, *They're No. One!: A People-Oriented Approach to Higher Education Administration* (Oklahoma City, OK: Western Heritage Books, 1980), p. 58.

103. *Daily O'Collegian*, 20 November 1970, p. 1.

104. Johnson, p. 12.

105. *Daily O'Collegian*, 18 November 1970, p. 1.

106. *Daily O'Collegian*, 24 November 1970, p. 1, 16 December 1971, pp. 1, 8.

107. Johnson, p. 13.

108. Johnson, pp. 13, 25-26; *Daily O'Collegian*, 15 June 1971, p. 7, 16 December 1971, p. 8, 29 October 1971, p. 9.

109. *Daily O'Collegian*, 13 November 1971, p. 1.

110. *Daily O'Collegian*, 8 May 1970, pp. 1, 4.

111. *Daily O'Collegian*, 28 October 1965, p. 2, 20 October 1965, p. 2, 2 July 1965, p. 1, 21 October 1969, p. 1, 23 November 1968, p. 1; Student Affairs Department Heads Meeting Minutes, 14 May 1970, p. 1, Student Services Collection.

112. "They Host Political Personalities," *Oklahoma State Alumnus Magazine*, vol. 8, no. 5 (May 1967), pp. 12-13; "Focus on Vietnam," *Oklahoma State Alumnus Magazine*, vol. 7, no. 4 (April 1966), pp. 9-12; *Daily O'Collegian*, 4 March 1967, pp. 1, 4, 15 October 1968, p. 3, 29 October 1968, p. 12, 23 October 1968, p. 3, 15 October 1969, p. 1, 22 February 1967, p. 1, 23 February 1967, pp. 1-2, 13 April 1967, p. 1, 14 March 1967, pp. 1, 7, 16 October 1969, pp. 1, 6.

113. *Daily O'Collegian*, 25 January 1973, p. 4.

114. *Daily O'Collegian*, 1 May 1975, p. 6.

115. Jo F. Dorris to Robert G. Schmalfeld, 2 May 1974, Student Services Collection; "Historic 79th Commencement," *Oklahoma State University Outreach*, vol. 15, no. 6 (June-July 1974), p. 3; *1975 Redskin*, p. 12; *Daily O'Collegian*, 26 April 1974, p. 1, 7 May 1974, p. 5, 24 April 1974, p. 2, 2 May 1974, p. 1, 11 May 1974, p. 1.

116. *1975 Redskin*, p. 281; *1976 Redskin*, p. 23; *Daily O'Collegian*, 27 March 1976, pp. 1, 5.

117. *Daily O'Collegian*, 6 November 1968, p. 2, 5 December 1968, p. 2, 9 October 1969, p. 8, 16 January 1973, p. 1, 11 April 1972, pp. 1, 9, 14 April 1972, p. 1, 17 April 1973, p. 1, 20 December 1973, p. 1; Administrative—Student Committee to Study the Mass Separation of the Sexes on the OSU Campus, "Campus Housing Report to the Board of Regents," 11 March 1972, pp. 1-5, and Norman F. Moore to Tony Warner, 18 April 1972, Student Services Collection; OSU Board of Regents, "Revision of Housing Requirements to Eliminate On-Campus Living Requirements for Sophomores," 10-11 March 1972, p. 228, Board of Regents Files.

118. *Daily O'Collegian*, 1 February 1977, pp. 1, 5.

119. *Daily O'Collegian*, 27 March 1976, p. 1.

120. *Daily O'Collegian*, 27 March 1976, p. 5.

121. *Daily O'Collegian*, 27 March 1976, p. 4.

122. *1977 Redskin*, p. 45.

# 9 Years of Consolidation And Hard Work

Prior to 1966 the present structure of Oklahoma State's student services was detectable, but fragmented. Largely due to the lack of adequate funding, Oklahoma's land-grant institution had historically been forced to institute out-of-class services for students primarily after a problem became so large that it could no longer be ignored. Rarely, if ever, did the institution have the luxury of anticipating a problem and proactively putting in place a mechanism or person to solve it. Even more uncommon was the time when dollars were allotted simply because it was the "right" thing to do, or because it would enhance the student's environment. Such decisions, although perhaps based upon sound principles, constituted "frills!"

In the decade roughly framed by the presidency of Robert B. Kamm, money to run OSU remained in short supply. However, between 1966 and 1977 scattered student personnel people and services were consolidated and brought together in a singular administrative entity. With the changes, more efficient use of human and fiscal resources followed. Awareness also caused greater understanding of the importance of the activities of the newly clustered organization. Students and faculty benefited from a more visible and accessible student personnel network. Allowing for subsequent modifications, the Division of Student Services was born and moved to the status of an equal partner in the institution's larger mission, under the guidance of the president.[1]

Two themes gave important parameters to the consolidation and changes in student services during President Kamm's tenure as chief executive officer. The first represented the larger influences of the state of Oklahoma and espoused a continuation of the age-old concept of *in loco parentis*. Despite national trends to the contrary, in May 1965 the Faculty Council's Student Affairs Committee reconfirmed that the "university stands in the parent's place and has moral and legal responsibilities for the health and welfare of each student."[2] While assuring that there would be a continuing place for people working with the extracurriculum, the affirmation reinforced a philosophy that had proven difficult to implement and was largely rejected by students who advocated that they were adults. Further, through the next two decades the principle of *in loco parentis* was a continuing source of confrontation between students, administrators, and faculty.

The second theme was found within the expectations and beliefs of a new president. Dr. Kamm affirmed that the primary role of "counseling and of student personnel work generally in the educational process is that of a *supportive* role to the academic."[3] The president could cite his own professional record as a student personnel administrator and noted his keen interest and concern with out-of-class student behavior. Without qualification he stated that there was a place for specifically prepared student personnel professionals since they are "essential to a strong program" performing "certain services which no one else can provide."[4]

However, student services programs do not replace a caring faculty nor are they more important in helping students. There should be limitations and good communication among student personnel offices. Foremost, all of the institution works in the service of helping students reach their academic goals. Student personnel services should be short-term

STILLWATER NEWSPRESS

President and Mrs. Robert B. Kamm greet students at the annual ice cream social. With a background in student personnel administration, President Kamm had a keen interest and concern for out-of-class student behavior.

Centennial Histories Series

and helpful. Not that earlier presidents had not cared, but to the benefit of students this time OSU had a president who intimately understood the student personnel profession, had definite ideas about what should be, and placed priority on their importance.[5]

When the new president took up his responsibilities, he continued the process of decentralization of authority, an undertaking started fifteen years earlier by President Oliver S. Willham. But thirty separate agencies and divisions still reported to Dr. Kamm. Within eight months of his July 1, 1966, starting date the chief executive decentralized the administration of OSU still further. Four vice presidents—one each for academic affairs, research, extension, and business and finance—would carry a considerable part of the load. Noticeably absent in the new configuration was a vice president for student services. The dean of student affairs and the directors of health and placement services would, for the present, continue to report directly to the president. Auxiliary Enterprises, including the Student Union, the business aspects of married and single student housing, food services, and maintenance, would be accountable to the vice president for business and finance. With the absence of a vice president for student services the misunderstandings and authority problems, both *de facto* and *de jure*, between Auxiliary Enterprises and the Division of Student Affairs, would continue for a time.[6]

The right time to correct the longstanding need for a clearly designated leader for extracurricular student programs and related auxiliary services came two years later when the OSU Board of Regents promoted Abe L. Hesser, the incumbent director of Auxiliary Enterprises, to the newly created position of vice president for student and auxiliary services at its September 18, 1968, meeting. With the promotion and new title, Hesser directed Auxiliary Enterprises, health services, some nonacademic aspects of the Colvin Physical Education Center, and student affairs. Within student affairs were the deans of men and women, student activities, financial aid, counseling services, and the Allied Arts program. With the board's action Vice President Hesser assumed direction of $50 million in physical property and some 2,000 employees. The seventeen-year OSU administrator undertook his responsibilities in earnest.[7]

Although a mild controversy arose following Vice President Hesser's promotion, few questioned the need or appropriateness of the position. Accordingly, plans were made to move ahead. An announcement was made on October 23, 1970, that Pat Hofler was being promoted to the position of assistant vice president for student and auxiliary services. Hofler, a personable twenty-year business and financial expert at OSU, became "the trouble shooter and informal man-behind-the-scenes in Student Services."[8] In December 1973 the offices of the vice president

Abe L. Hesser, OSU's first vice president for student services, examines an architect's depiction of the Chi Omega clock, a popular campus landmark. The "Chi O" clock, located between the Student Union and Classroom Building, was a gift to the university commemorating the sorority chapter's golden anniversary.

moved from the Student Union to Whitehurst, thus bringing all of OSU's senior administrators in close proximity to the president's office.[9]

A man who seldom avoided confrontation, minced words, or tolerated much deviation from policy or rules, Hesser remained in the vice president's role for a little more than two years. He toiled in tough times. Among other issues the undergraduates were persistent in pushing for student activity fee control and modifications. Student activity dollars were no small matter; since 1968 students were paying $807,000 to support seventeen different, largely university-prescribed campus activities. Other "flaps" developed about women's equality, open house-closed doors policies in the campus residence halls, room search and seizure procedures, and residence hall hours. For whatever reasons, Hesser started a nine-month leave of absence in November 1970. Private enterprise was to his liking, and OSU's pioneer vice president for student services resigned in June 1971.[10] President Kamm, in acknowledging Hesser's departure, noted: "He has been a valued member of the OSU family and has contributed much to OSU's becoming the fine university it is."[11]

When Hesser left on leave of absence in November, Norman F. Moore added the title "acting" vice president for student and auxiliary services to his position as director of the OSU Student Union. After Hesser's formal resignation and a national search to find the top person for the vacancy, Moore was recommended. On August 1, 1971, Moore became the second vice president for student services. At the same time the term "auxiliary" was dropped from his title since the extra word merely explained how most of the division was funded.[12]

Like his predecessor, Moore was an OSU graduate. The native of Pawnee had no doubt been "toughened" for his new position by a tour as editor of OSU's humor magazine, the *Aggievator*, during his undergraduate years. The experience likely groomed his warm sense of humor and his ability to deal with criticism. In addition to ten years of intermittent professional work in the Student Union, his philosophy was broadened by a stint as dean of men and manager of the student center at Rio College in Ohio and union positions at the University of Houston and the University of Wisconsin-Whitewater. Moore's administrative style was low profile, even-keeled, and effective.[13]

In the new vice president's first five years, three enduring programs, all of which coincided with the president's views on student personnel services, evolved. The Alpha program, a freshman and transfer student orientation program, began in 1973. Held the four days before the beginning of fall semester classes, Alpha has made a difference in some student's persistence. The program afforded new students the opportunity to feel welcomed, become familiar with new surroundings, and make new friends. In June 1975 the Office of Freshman Programs and Services (FPS) started under the leadership of Shaila Aery. FPS was jointly sponsored by the vice presidents for academic affairs and student services. Academically underprepared and low achieving students were assisted by the new and needed program. A natural adjunct to FPS was the Career Assistance/Learning Lab, or CALL Center, located in the basement of Murray Hall. Opened for the use of all students in the fall of 1976, CALL Center users could receive free tutoring, help with their study habits or reading skills, or information on OSU's academic majors or career opportunities. In all, the CALL Center provided seven different coordinated services all with the singular purpose of enhancing academic success.[14]

While taking direct creative initiative in organizing programs in support of academics, Vice President Moore also quietly stabilized and ordered student services. Under him was a group of talented capable student development professionals. They seized the latitude that Moore allowed to move ahead in the service of students. By the mid-1970s student services would be composed of eight divisions: the Colvin Physical Education Center, Single Student Housing, Married Student Housing and Student Services Maintenance, University Food Services, Division of Student Affairs, Student Union, the University Hospital and Clinic, and Freshman Programs and Services. Located within the Division of Student Affairs were the dean of student affairs and a staff of assistant deans, University Counseling Services, Department of Financial Aid,

Norman F. Moore, OSU's second vice president for student services used creative initiative in organizing programs in support of academics. In 1976 (*left to right*) Vice President Moore joins President Robert B. Kamm, Student Union Activities Board President Vaughn Vennerburg, and Student Union Director Winston Shindell in celebrating the twenty-fifth birthday of the Student Union.

Department of Special Services, Department of Student Activities, and Student Entertainers.[15] When a problem occurred between students and administration, student affairs became involved.

Student affairs personnel continued to be concerned with students' records and their release to outside agencies, the recodification of students' rules and regulations, chaperones at student social functions, and proper attire for women in the library. The activism of students added special flavor, and the division assumed responsibility for scheduling the library lawn for meetings, chartering student organizations, receiving petitions, and responding to sit-ins and boycotts. Student affairs was also concerned with each off-campus speaker's controversy. Despite a rule prohibiting such behavior, near mob-size snowball fights between Greeks and independents were certain to bring out the "deans corps."[16]

Student personnel administrators quickly learned to be prepared for the unique and unexpected. Such was the case in the spring of 1974 when Oklahoma State University became a leader in an infamous national campus fad—streaking! For the next decade and more, this "rite of spring" happened on the Thursday night before spring break.

The *1975 Redskin* observed: "Collegians began zipping across campus clad only in tennis shoes, followed closely by baffled safety and security men. Despite the administration's threats of suspension, the bare activities continued. With spring fever in high pitch, 5,000 students packed the 'strip' while the carefree nudists adorned roof tops and paraded through the streets. In typical cowboy fashion, the streakers rode the Sirloin Stockade bull down Washington Street and sailed into Theta Pond. Proceeding to use the floating bull as a diving board, the pond turned into a nudist swimming resort in a matter of minutes. Alas, the unusual happenings subsided as the campus cleared for spring break.''[17]

Some students thought that streaking was a great release for tension and boredom. The district attorney promised to jail anyone caught and charge them with ''outrage of public decency.'' Bad weather was never a deterrent as 3,000 people turned out in 1976 in a minus 20 degree wind chill. Despite the threat of a tornado, thousands of people again appeared the next year. Local police agencies pooled their ingenuity. A large truck was parked at the end of Washington Street and used as a ''booking station'' to ease the processing of arrested drunks and streakers. The creative students worked on topping each other—one streaker appeared wearing only a football helmet, another drove a motorcycle, and still others danced atop a roof in a chorus line. There was always property damage to stores—$1,400 worth in 1974 alone—and danger of injury from thrown glass beer bottles, fireworks, and the crush of a massive crowd. University officials, police, and others finally became resigned to the fact that streaker's night simply had to run its own course to oblivion. Meantime, apprehended student streakers were sometimes suspended and always placed on probation by the dean of student affairs office.[18]

*STILLWATER NEWSPRESS*

In 1974, OSU became a leader and a ''style'' setter in the national fad of streaking. Although a boon to the economy of the Washington Street bars, the craze also strained town/gown relations due to property damage, as evidenced when the Sirloin Stockade bull was sailed into Theta Pond.

Taken in perspective, the quasi-traditional streaker's night was a time of year when thousands waited in anticipation for people, male and female, young and old, to run nude through public places. Perhaps it was merely "spring fever" in another form. It was certainly an outlet after a long winter, a last chance to "party" with friends before leaving campus for a week, and, for the vast majority, simply a break from the routines of day-to-day college drudgery. However, for the more observant, streaker's night did showcase the pervasiveness of another real and significant problem. The amount of alcohol abuse and marijuana smoking by the huge crowd was alarming.

In the late sixties and early seventies the consumption of alcohol and the use of illegal drugs by students became severe enough to become a public issue. There is no question that OSU students have always consumed beer and liquor. Many will recall the "long standing tale on the Oklahoma State campus that purports that the ratio of beer consumed per student in Stillwater was more than anywhere else in the United States." Although consumption figures were not available to confirm the rumor, the fact remained that businesses stayed open only so long as a profit was made. In 1974 there were twelve beer establishments within three blocks of one another on Washington Street's "strip." Seven more rimmed the campus, with Knoblock Street's popularity growing. Ten additional taverns were inside the city limits, and grocery and convenience stores magnified the problem. One beer distributor summarized by offering that his sales were high "compared to lots of places and if something like who drinks the most is measurable, we'd be in the running."[19]

OSU was neither any better nor worse than other colleges and universities. The problem of the misuse of alcohol and other drugs had basically grown out of control almost everywhere, and university officials were being forced to respond to it. The Division of Student Affairs at OSU largely led the small counterattack. Counterbalancing the problem was difficult because the issues permeated through large segments of the student body. A 1972 survey of 3,800 residence hall students revealed alcohol, tobacco, and marijuana to be the most commonly used drugs. Nearly one in four students consumed alcohol weekly. Seventeen percent of the student respondents reported weekly smoking of "pot" while over one-third had tried marijuana at least once. Over one-quarter of the undergraduates smoked cigarettes regularly. The one-time use of an amphetamine or psychedelic was reported by more than 10 percent of this surveyed group.[20]

The report on the students' drug-related behavior was turned over to the university administrators with the conclusion that there was "a drug problem in the dorms."[21] A 1975 investigative student newspaper article written by Mike Ward flatly conjectured: "A student looking for almost any drug need not go further than another floor in his or her residence hall in an operation that has been almost matter-of-fact.''[22] In the five-year period from 1967 to 1972, front page headlines appeared in the *O'Collegian* at least once a year announcing a major drug raid by local police. An overview of these random articles revealed that fifty-three students were "busted." Most were charged with a felony. The majority were between eighteen and twenty-two years of age. In lieu of formal charges, seven were permitted to leave OSU "voluntarily." All of their lives were changed, in some way, by illegal drugs.[23]

The tragedy of drug abuse, including alcohol, by so many young people resulted in a variety of responses. One group of students lobbied and petitioned the Oklahoma Legislature for the legalization of marijuana.[24] Vice President Hesser took a police-like stance by wanting anyone arrested for selling drugs expelled, or at least suspended; he believed "that we must act now or expect a drug wave on campus that is impossible to control."[25] A short-lived Drug Analysis Center was funded by the Student Association. Realizing that illegal substances were used and that adulterated drugs were common and sometimes fatal, the program offered a confidential method of checking the contents of a drug. The OSU Board of Regents stopped the effort on legal and proprietary grounds. The Division of Student Affairs tried an education strategy. A drug education program, which spanned three days and incorporated national authorities as keynote speakers, was held on campus in April 1970.[26]

Through 1976 and beyond, it was concluded that educating students to the appropriate use of alcohol and other substances remained the best alternative. At OSU this task largely fell to the student services sector, and more specifically, student affairs. Substantial inroads would be hard to achieve, yet the consequences of avoiding the problem would be even more catastrophic. By the late 1960s it was widely acknowledged that the campus, as well as the nation, had a major drug problem. Drugs remain a national tragedy that demands a national response. However, neither OSU nor the country have yet "come of age" in the so-called "war on drugs."

After serving as the dean of student affairs for seven years, Dr. Frank E. McFarland transferred to the College of Education on September 1, 1968. The transfer stirred some controversy among students, but the respected dean chose to explain his motivation as simply a desire to teach. The Student Senate recognized McFarland by establishing the "Dean Frank McFarland Award." Dating to September 1968, this annual award has been given to an OSU administrator that the Student Association proclaims to be "outstanding."[27]

On October 1, 1968, Robert G. Schmalfeld replaced McFarland as the dean of student affairs. Schmalfeld continued to hold the position through the decade of the seventies. With a B.A. degree from Knox College and an M.A. from Northwestern University, Schmalfeld came to OSU after working in various student personnel positions at the University of Arizona, Heidelberg College in Ohio, and Lea College in Minnesota. Under Schmalfeld the separation of programs by sexes through the offices of dean of men and women ended when these titles and functions were assigned to the now associate deans. In 1972 the Department of Special Services was started to assist ethnic minority, physically disabled, and academically underprepared students. An interdepartmental effort to teach students leadership and group process skills was initiated, and in 1972 over 425 student leaders had participated in a weekend-long workshop under the direction of Patrick M. Murphy, Rex T. Finnegan, Thomas M. Keys, Howard Shipp Jr., Kent Sampson, and Winston G. Shindell.[28]

Under McFarland and Schmalfeld the Department of Student Activities became an area with considerable responsibility. Before 1966 one individual held the position of student activities director and was responsible for the coordination of nearly 250 student organizations and the publication of the *Student Handbook* and the *Student-Faculty Directory*. After the transfer of the campus Allied Arts program to student activities on June 30, 1969, a full-time concert manager brought the departmental staff to a total of three professionals. While continuing to sponsor traditional activities, such as Howdy Week and the President's Honor Roll Banquet, a major shift took place when the departmental philosophy took on a program development emphasis. Under this philosophy the staff stopped planning for students and started teaching and provid-

By the late 1960s, it had become obvious that OSU had a problem of drug and alcohol abuse. The counterattack on this growing campus problem was led by the Division of Student Affairs which stressed proper education as the most effective weapon. Some of the members of the division in the mid-1970s were (*left to right*) Terry Henderson, Jan Carlson, Patrick Murphy, Robert B. Clark, David Henderson, and Robert G. Schmalfeld.

ing services so that the student groups could accomplish goals for them-selves. This not only gave greater autonomy to student groups, but also represented a major moving away from traditionally heavy paternalism. Involved as directors of student activities during this time were Winston G. Shindell, who replaced King Cacy in 1966; Jo F. Dorris, who served from 1972 to 1975; and Jan M. Carlson, who has served since 1975.[29]

The change in style within student activities which cut away the "doing" for students occurred partially because it was no longer possible to operate as though OSU was still a small family. But a paradox existed. To succeed, no matter how small or large the university, some students still need an environment which affords the family-like qualities of an understanding ear, some sound advice, and an opportunity to talk about problems. In 1968 a conservative estimate held a minimum of 10 percent of the undergraduates had personal problems severe enough to warrant the assistance of a professional. Thus, within student affairs the University Counseling Services grew from a department of two and one-half full-time equivalent staff members, with one doctoral level member, in 1966 to six and one-half position equivalents, with four doctorate degree holders, by 1976.[30]

Counseling services offered assistance with personal problems, sleeplessness, depression, loneliness, and fear. Additional emphasis was placed on helping students with career decisions, academic concerns, organization of study habits, and use of time. In 1976 nearly 5 percent of the 20,490 resident students utilized one or more of the counseling services programs.[31]

The counseling services personnel worked hard at being friendly, helpful, and available. To add visibility, from 1967 to 1971 counselors left their Student Union offices one or more days each week to consult with students in other offices located in the larger residence halls. More enduring was an early 1970s push to become a proactive service—providing programs that were preventative. Rape awareness seminars, career exploration groups, and training programs for residence hall student assistants and Greek housemothers were included in this service.[32]

The University Counseling Services had two directors during this period. Charles E. Larsen served from 1965 to 1970. These were formidable years in which a balance of services and a niche within the larger university evolved. On August 1, 1970, a humorous and dedicated member of Larsen's staff, Rex T. Finnegan, was promoted to the directorship after Larsen resigned to move to South Dakota State University. Finnegan was able to justify a growth in the department. It was also under him that a balance between proactive and reactive services became established. When Finnegan was promoted, Patrick M. Murphy and Terry H. Henderson joined the counseling department. Howard Shipp

Jr. was recruited to the counseling services staff in 1971. Finnegan, Shipp, Henderson, and Murphy, who in 1971 became assistant director, would work with OSU students in the department into the 1980s.[33]

The four longtime counseling staffers combined efforts to bring strength and comradeship to the counseling services. More importantly, their often stress-inducing work, sometimes involving life threatening events such as a student attempt at suicide or a drug overdose, in time brought a degree of wider respect for the service from the campus and Stillwater community. At OSU, students "flocked" to the service. This was not only testimony to university counseling's importance and growth but also to the students themselves for their awareness and early action to seek help with their "very human" problems.

With all things being relative, the growth in the counseling services can only be labeled as meager when compared to the Department of Financial Aid. Robert B. Clark became the director of a singular department responsible for student financial assistance programs in March 1968. Rather than a long-planned decision, the move to departmentalize was precipitated by a federal government audit which mandated that OSU take better care of the taxpayers money. The timing was providential.[34] In April 1968 this department moved to Hanner Hall and organized into a single organization handling student loans, grants, scholarships, college work-study, and other student employment.

Between 1965 and 1976 student financial aid programs grew at an unprecedented rate. Where once college was seen as a privilege rather than a right, the pendulum had swung sufficiently to open the doors of higher education to millions of bright youngsters, who would have been previously excluded, primarily due to economics—the poor, ethnic minorities, and the disabled. The civil rights movement, President Lyndon B. Johnson's "Great Society" initiatives, extension of the G.I. Bill to returning Vietnam veterans, and a high unemployment rate in the early 1970s factored into an increasing role for government to assist students financially.

Inflation compounded the problems as the cost of educating the nation's youth grew dramatically. But at OSU a year of college remained a bargain. In 1970-1971 a student paid an average of $1,900 for a year's tuition, fees, room and board, and incidental expenses. Although the dollar amount had risen to $2,700 by 1977-1978, OSU's total expenses for a year of school remained relatively low compared to national averages.[35]

But even for Oklahoma State students' parents, college expenses constituted a hardship. The 1976 College Entrance Examination Board's (CEEB) annual national survey of high school seniors documented that three-fourths of the nation's families could not afford to pay the full cost of their children's freshman year of study. The average middle class

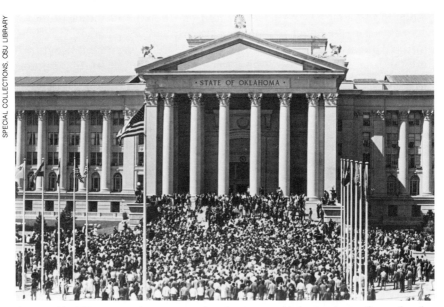

By the mid-1960s more and more young Americans were able to acquire a college education because of the growth of student financial aid programs. With the growth of the OSU student body, the need for more out-of-class services became paramount. Thus, in 1967 several hundred students turned out at the Oklahoma State Capitol to protest a multimillion-dollar budget reduction for higher education.

American household, in reality, could contribute $1,170. Interpreted for an OSU student, from a family with an average annual income in 1976, an additional $1,600 in financial assistance would be necessary to assure that the bills would be paid during the 1976-1977 academic year.[36]

The CEEB data painted an even gloomier picture for low socio-economic groups, particularly ethnic minorities. While the problems of college costs would be difficult without financial assistance for average income families, they were insurmountable for low income groups. A 1976 black high school graduate could reasonably expect $100 in parental help. Students of Puerto Rican or Hispanic descent fared little better at about $200. American Indian parents, again as an average, could contribute $570 from their income toward their child's college costs.[37]

In pursuit of the democratic ideal of equal access and full opportunity for all citizens, national and state governments rushed to solve the problems. Oklahoma State's total available aid for students rose from $1,400,000 in 1964-1965 to $4,650,000 in 1974-1975. During the 1975-1976 year the entire university received a total amount of $17,108,684 for its many projects. Of that amount, $3,122,054, or 18 percent of the total, was dedicated to the financial aid programs for students. In the same 1975-1976 academic year, 5,617 individual students were awarded assistance through the Department of Financial Aid. Two-thirds of the available money came from federal government programs. In total, financial aid was responsible for thirty-five separate programs with a value of $11 million by the time of the nation's two hundredth birthday.[38]

Given the phenomenal growth it is hard to imagine that many members of Congress, as well as experts on higher education, believed that students would not borrow money to secure an education. But students borrowed, worked, and competed for scholarships; grants, loans, and hourly wages became the norm. The federal college work-study program was started at OSU with thirty-five student participants on March 9, 1965, under the direction of a popular Aggie, James R. Fleming. In 1973 the Basic Educational Opportunity Grant (BEOG) program was established.[39] Within five years the BEOG enactment became "the most significant grant fund ever created by the federal government."[40] The Oklahoma State Regents for Higher Education administered the Oklahoma Student Loan Program. Begun in 1975, the Oklahoma program added additional financial aid loan dollars.[41]

Still more money for OSU student loans came from the Janice and J. I. Gibson Foundation and the Shepherd Foundation. Both foundations were chartered to administer sizeable private contributions. To illustrate, two Oklahoma City sisters, Lottie and Edith Shepherd, donated nearly $300,000 to an OSU student loan fund between December 1971 and 1978. Between 1972 and 1978 the Shepherd Foundation provided 590 students $450,000 in insured loans. The value of private contributions, such as provided by the Lew Wentz, Gibson, and Shepherd Foundations, should not be underestimated. During this "boom" period in financial assistance programs, each foundation provided additional options, flexibility, and balance to the so-called business of "packaging" aid.[42]

In many respects the Department of Financial Aid "grew up" between 1968 and 1976. Certainly problems still existed. Delinquency rates for collecting student loans remained high, although a drop from 48 percent to 38 percent showed improvement. Computerization of the complex tasks involved in financial aid administration was sorely needed; OSU was the last of the Big Eight institutions to move in that direction. Check disbursement and collections needed to be removed from other functions. Salaries for staff were low, no doubt contributing to a high employee turnover rate in the department. Frequent "cranky," angry, or upset students, the cramped quarters in Hanner Hall, and a high volume of human traffic did little for the staff's mental or physical health.[43]

Nonetheless, by 1975 the Department of Financial Aid had grown to include seven professional financial aid staff members, nineteen clerical employees, and twenty part-time students. In addition to Director Clark, longtime "jack-of-many-positions" and "firsts" in student services, King W. Cacy Jr. functioned as associate director. Pioneer financial aid administrator Raymond Bivert retired before the days of whirlwind growth in the department, going on to countless civic and volunteer leadership roles in Stillwater. The period ended on a dark note for the campus when Jim Fleming died from a heart attack on April 16, 1975. Fleming, an OSU horticulture graduate and faculty member, was attending a financial aid meeting in Tulsa at the time he was stricken.[44]

Fleming's untimely death saddened the many, many people who knew him. Yet, in hindsight, his death presented important insight into the business of student financial aid administration. Fleming entered the increasingly complex financial aid profession quite by accident in 1964 at a time when it behooved the institution to take advantage of a new federal program. Starting with fewer than three dozen work-study students, Fleming eventually became the program's director, learning as he went about the quagmire of federal regulations and paperwork. Over the next decade he witnessed huge increases in the program's dollar volume and student participation. But Fleming had not been unusual.

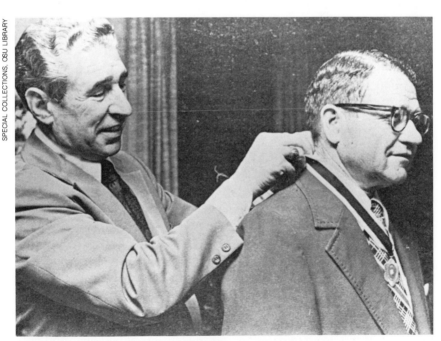

A financial aid administrator by accident, James Fleming directed the university's work-study program for over ten years. In 1975, Fleming (*right*) received the Distinguished Service Award of Phi Eta Sigma national scholastic society from President Robert B. Kamm.

Until the 1980s few people consciously chose to become student financial aid "experts." Most entered the area by chance, the majority left because of the demands of the work, and even fewer simply retired after many years of service in the area.

In September 1962 the part-time position of international student advisor was placed under the umbrella of the Division of Student Affairs. At the time similarities existed between the campus financial aid programs and the services provided international students. In the early formative years of the university both had suffered from neglect. What was done to help students was accomplished through the labor of part-time or volunteer people. In general, services were scattered, unorganized, and given low priority. Frequently, matters critically important to a student's ability to remain at the institution were left to the student's initiative to resolve.

Improvements in services for internationals had been needed and were a long time in coming. Oklahoma State University's involvement in international education predated the 1920s when the first international enrolled at Oklahoma A. and M. However, an international view on campus emerged when President Harry S. Truman appointed OSU President Henry G. Bennett as the first administrator of Point Four, the forerunner to the Agency for International Development. A myriad of technical assistance contracts with nations around the globe followed.

As a natural consequence, prospective students began to learn about OSU and its educational offerings. An increasing number of students from foreign lands began to enroll at Oklahoma's land-grant university. The trend started slowly; from the mid-thirties to early fifties an estimated 2,000 internationals had cumulatively been enrolled. But during the quarter-century from 1951 to 1976, yearly registration numbers grew from fewer than 75 to more than 1,000 students, representing over 70 different nations. With continued growth into the 1980s, OSU would eventually rank within the top ten institutions in the United States for international student enrollment. The actual numbers would level off at nearly 2,000, which translated to the reality that during the 1980s over 10 percent of the total student body were internationals.[45]

Despite infrequent proclamations of how the students from other lands "enriched" the campus, most Americans spent their time "sitting around waiting for them to become 'Americanized'."[46] Meantime, the international students all too frequently experienced what other minority groups experienced—misunderstanding, discrimination in housing and stores, racism, and few friendships with Americans. Compounding matters was the loneliness of being tens of thousands of miles from family and loved ones, as well as the barriers of language and culture. Then and now, being a student studying in a foreign land was many times more difficult than most people could appreciate.[47]

Prior to the establishment of an actual office for international student advisement, there were a few notable exceptions to an otherwise bleak system of help for international students. The International Relations Club (IRC) was chartered by the Student Senate in 1929 "for the high purpose of furthering international understanding."[48] The organization was open to everyone. Forbidden by the IRC's constitution from pushing a political ideology, the group sought better world relations. At times the student organization was one of the largest and most active on campus. After World War II the IRC was recognized nationally for its programs, and in 1951 and 1955 OSU supplied two national presidents to the larger organization with which the local club affiliated. The IRC ran a speaker's program. In past years the club brought Pearl Buck and Eva Curie to campus. Members assisted new international students by meeting them, providing campus tours, and helping them to adjust socially. Later faculty advisors to the IRC included R. R. Oglesby, Darrel K. Troxel, and Kenneth Ricker.[49]

Complementing the IRC was the OSU Community Hospitality Committee, a voluntary organization. In 1952 President Willham asked Mrs. Alfred Levin, wife of an OSU history professor, to organize a committee to help international students. This original committee had the

To further international understanding remained the goal of the International Relations Club. This organization as well as the Community Hospitality Committee strived to help international students adjust to life in America.

unlikely name of the "Integration" Committee. The purpose of the committee was "to make certain that foreign students get into American homes, to see that they learn something about the American community, to get their own idea of what makes America function and to see that they are happy while they are in the United States."[50] Subsequently, "Mama" Levin became a well-known personality at OSU, especially among the international students. She took her chairperson's job seriously, changed the name from Integration to Community Hospitality Committee, and established an entire series of helpful services, some of which continue today.[51]

Mrs. Levin was never paid for her work, despite working eight to five every weekday in her student affairs office.[52] At one point she explained: "There isn't a time of day in the week when these students can't call me to ask for whatever they want to have done."[53] Not only was Mrs. Levin and her committee of largely faculty wives not paid a salary, there was never a budget provided for their programs. Not one to be stopped by limitations, by 1960 the hospitality committee sponsored the "Home Town Day"—a day consisting of a luncheon, visits to on- and off-campus buildings, and an evening meal and night's relaxation with a Stillwater family. Regular Y-Hut coffees, Thanksgiving and Christmas break housing, and an orientation luncheon and program for new students were also initiatives of the voluntary organization.

The committee developed many longstanding events, including the still-running International Student Talent show, which dates to 1953; an international exhibition, where foods, culture, and attire were displayed; international dinners, where students from various nations prepared their favorite native dishes for sharing with others; and a speaker's bureau, which coordinated civic clubs and organization requests for a speaker on topics suited to international students. From the beginning, the Community Hospitality Committee affiliated with the International Institute for Education, a national organization.[54]

Despite the efforts of the Community Hospitality Committee and the International Relations Club, there remained critical gaps. Assistance was still needed with the U.S. Immigration and Naturalization Service, contact with embassies and consulates, help with money problems, campus employment, and a relationship with the student's sponsoring agencies. Problems relating to these matters were often complex, needed delicate handling, and were critical to a student's legal status in the country as well as their ability to meet their financial obligations. The advisement of international students was a specialized field. As long as OSU was willing to rely on volunteers and students, the institution fell short in meeting the obligation assumed by becoming a leading educational institution for internationals.

In 1960 the Student Senate began a discussion on the need for a full-time international student advisor. By March 1962 the senate and international student organizations—representing students from the Philippines, Iraq, India, Pakistan, China, Iran, and Africa—had approved a recommendation supporting the idea of a specialist advisor. By September 1962, an existing position largely responsible for the academic advisement of internationals and headed by Glenn B. Hawkins, the retiring department head in political science, was transferred to the Division of Student Affairs. Ted Kalivoda was hired one-half time as OSU international student advisor and one-half time assistant professor of Spanish. Kalivoda was well qualified; he came to OSU from Louisiana State University where he had directed international programs five years. He had also served with the U.S. Information Agency in Lima, Peru, and had received two awards from the National Association for Foreign Student Affairs.[55]

In 1963 Kalivoda reorganized the Community Hospitality Committee, and his office assumed some of what the committee had previously carried as duties. In 1967 the position of international student advisor became full-time. By 1969 the Office of International Student Advisement had grown to one full-time advisor, one and one-half time equivalent clerical employees, and one to two part-time graduate assistants. The "gaps" were gradually being filled; a two-day orientation program for internationals was being provided, and a campus-wide referral network was in place. Some permanency came to the advisor's position when Oklahoma native and OSU alumnus W. Douglas Wilson was employed from 1970 to 1976.[56]

When Wilson moved to another position at the University of Kentucky, he offered that the largest remaining problem for the near one thousand international students was their joining the "mainstream" of campus social life. Both the students and advisor pushed for additional staff as enrollments had more than doubled during Wilson's tenure alone.[57] The personable Wilson had also experienced enough to suggest that to "fill Oklahoma State University's commitment to international education, I would recommend the establishment of a Department of International Services."[58] Wilson's proposal remained dormant. But the staffing pattern was improved. Charles Aanenson assumed the international student advisor's role the following fall. A second professional, Richard Andrews, was employed as his assistant.[59]

Something of a "capstone" event was the building and opening of the International Mall, located north of the Edmon Low Library. Interestingly, the idea for the mall dated to a 1965 campus visit of past U.S. Presidential aide and prominent political analyst Bill Moyer. Moyer had suggested that the area "be made into an International Mall, honoring Henry Bennett's Point Four program."[60] The project was completed without a specific budget. After several years of part-time work the gravel parking lot for 200 cars was converted to a usable campus centerpiece. In May 1972 nineteen flags, representing seventeen nations of OSU's international students, the Stars and Stripes, and the flag of the state of Oklahoma, were raised, according to protocol, in a public ceremony.[61]

Adding to the mall's informal atmosphere was a monument of the dove of peace, atop a globe of the terrestrial earth. The 230-pound monument in white Cherokee marble was financed through donations from international students exclusively and coordinated by the International Student Association (ISA). Shehzad Shadig, a doctoral student in education, and his wife Parveen, both natives of Pakistan, presented the idea to the ISA, where it received unanimous approval. Mr. Shadig also drew the sketch from which the "symbol of international peace" was made.[62]

About his concept Shadig said: "The idea was to present the University with something that would be a source of inspiration for all international students who have, or, in the future, will come to Oklahoma

A lasting symbol of the value and richness brought to the OSU campus through the presence of international students is the monument of the dove of peace atop the world. Financed exclusively by international students, the marble structure is a prominent feature of the International Mall. Shehzad Shadiq (*right*), who designed the monument, views it with W. Douglas Wilson, international advisor, while Parveen Shadiq looks on.

State University for higher education . . . . We also wanted to leave a permanent symbol which would express identity and the presence of international students on the campus.''[63] The monument, born of the appreciation that the international students felt toward their alma mater, was placed on a pre-stressed ten-foot concrete pedestal in the International Mall and formally presented to the university on May 12, 1971. The gift serves as a lasting symbol of the mutual value and richness brought to the campus by the continuing presence of students from throughout the world.

Another historical reordering of the Division of Student Affairs in the period between 1966 and 1977 developed out of the cumbersome, sometimes stormy, relationship between the director of Auxiliary Enterprises and the dean of student affairs. From the time the earliest residence halls were built on campus, the personnel and programming aspects belonged to the assistant deans of men and women, both of whom were accountable to the dean of students. Budgets, maintenance, food services, and other business functions eventually came under the supervision of Auxiliary Enterprises. After lengthy discussion on-going problems were resolved with a new administrative organization for Single Student Housing. A single director of housing would be responsible for both facets, personnel and business. Under the director would be an assistant director for women's halls and a second assistant director for men's halls. Their former titles of assistant deans were dropped. In effect, with the changes, the way was paved for improved efficiency and the eventual demise of student affairs' day-to-day involvement in student housing. The changes were implemented on June 1, 1966.[64]

Lewis F. Wolfe became the first director of Single Student Housing. Stanley Hicks and Heather Meacham took on the duties of assistant directors in the new organization. Student activities' advising within the residence halls during these years led to the development of a coeducational residence hall government. The merging of the women's and men's Residence Halls Association into a single organization eventually developed into an additional central staff position with the title of program director. Patrick M. Murphy was employed in that position at its inception in 1968.[65]

Due to poor health Wolfe requested a transfer, and on August 1, 1970, the respected W. Lynn Jackson was promoted from assistant director to director of Single Student Housing. In 1972 Kent Sampson became the assistant director for programs, Murphy's former position, renamed, and with it, RHA advisor. By 1976 Phyllis Schroeder, assistant to the director for student relations, David Stoddart, area coordinator, and Ken Shell, custodial supervisor, helped to compose the central housing organization. Jackson, Sampson, Schroeder, Stoddart, and Shell continued to bring quality to the housing program, each in their own areas of exper-

Residence halls are well worn through heavy student use and even infrequent abuse. Over the years, many dedicated professionals have worked to insure that on-campus housing provides students a pleasant "home-away-from-home." Included in this group of Single Student Housing staff are (*front row, left to right*) Kent Sampson, Phyllis Schroeder, and Cathy Furlong; (*back row, left to right*) Dave Stoddart, Joe Awis, and Lynn Jackson.

tise, through the next decade.[66]

In 1977 Single Student Housing was generating $7.25 million in room and board revenue and could house, in normal circumstances, 6,855 students in 13 buildings. For twenty meals a week in an air-conditioned room typically housing two people, students paid $1,158 for the two-semester academic year. In 1973 there was short-lived concern about a reduction in occupancy rate, but by 1976 things had returned to a more normal "too many students with a housing contract for the available space." Things were termed "critical" in 1976 after floor lounges, basement rooms, and even the vacated old hospital were forced into service through the early part of the fall semester.[67]

Residence halls are buildings that are well worn through heavy student use, even infrequent abuse, and are never stagnant. They either decay or get refurbished. Some outlive their original usefulness and become uneconomical to operate. New facilities are built, and others undergo major renovation. And then, over time, student tastes and needs change.

There was no escaping this phenomena at OSU either. In 1968 Thatcher Hall was taken out of the housing system, and in 1973 it was refurbished as a home for the Army and Air Force ROTC programs. In the fall of 1971 Vice President Moore announced that North Murray Hall would be phased out of service as a residence hall. In 1974 several departments of the College of Education occupied North Murray. Floyd Hoelting, the assistant director for men, and Vice President Moore were nonrespectfully "hung in effigy" after a 1972 proposal to convert Murray Hall to married student apartments was made public. Factors involving money and efficiency, rather than the students' protest, gave Murray continued life—but only for a few more years. Finally, Bennett Hall, an eighteen-year-old bastion for men, was converted into a coeducational complex, after a major renovation project spanning eight months during 1967-1968. The result of a student-suggested plan in the fall of 1969, 550 women moved to Bennett Complex to share common eating and lounge space with 550 men.[68]

Food service goes hand-in-hand with residence hall systems. Historically, OSU has elected to operate its own food system, whereas many colleges and universities contract their food programs to private contractors or vendors. Like the residence hall system, on-campus food services had markedly changed over the years. In the 1977-1978 academic year University Food Services employed a central management staff of 17 as well as 232 full-time and 370 part-time, mostly student, workers on the serving lines and in the kitchens and dish rooms. The multimillion dollar service was operating seven residence hall cafeterias, a hospital kitchen, central butcher and meat processing plant, a central bakery, warehouse, and five areas of food services in the Student Union. Meal service contracts were held by 6,500 students. In the Student Union approximately 1.5 million customers were being served annually. Additionally, special events, such as the Alpha picnic and homecoming, were catered regularly. With the exception of Cordell, each residence hall had a snack bar run by food services.[69]

In 1976 Joe Blair, with nearly twenty years of increasing responsibilities in food services, was the director of the huge operation. Always dedicated to the principle of service to students, in the fall of 1976 Blair was awarded one of eight prestigious silver plate awards as "College and University Food Service Operator of the Year " by the International Food Manufacturers Association. In 1974-1975 Blair held a term as president of the National Association of College and University Food Service, an organization which he helped found. At Blair's urging and under his direction, the $3.5 million University Food Services Center on Farm Road was constructed and opened in November 1969.[70]

Oleta Patillo, assistant director, and Judy Quisenberry, administrative assistant, continued long tenures in Blair's food services central management group. In addition, through these years hundreds of loyal employees constantly attempted to get the most from the least costly foods and explain the answer to the infamous student question about "what's in the mystery meat." Two of the more dedicated were Grace Newbold, who in 1970 had accumulated a quarter century of service, and Mary Barnes, a twenty-four year employee in food services, who retired in 1971.[71]

The combination of student initiative and support from Single Student Housing and University Food Services brought the 1976-1977 National Association of College and University Residence Halls (NACURH) award as "outstanding in the nation" to Oklahoma State University. The coveted award from NACURH, a student association, capped an accelerated period starting with an April 15, 1969, vote of all residence hall students to merge separate male and female student government organizations into a single Residence Halls Association. In just eight years the RHA became one of the strongest and most influential organizations on campus.[72]

Thomas "Zack" Cooper, an agricultural economics major from Stroud, was the RHA "founding father" president during 1969-1970. Tony Warner served in the office in 1971-1972. His experiences in student government helped to launch him into a student personnel-residence halls career path. In 1976-1977 energetic Kathy Butler was the first woman to hold the RHA presidency. The next year, athletic Mark Myles, a black student, toiled in the demanding volunteer position. Tom Hanson set precedent by serving two terms from 1971 to 1973.[73]

Through these years the RHA wrestled with recommendations to liberalize the codes of conduct governing residents of the halls, sponsored "pop" entertainment events for the campus, established the annual Residence Hall Week, and usually worked well with housing administrators. The RHA focused on system-wide concerns and supported individual residence hall initiatives. At each annual RHA banquet dozens of awards were handed out for hall scholarship, outstanding cultural programming, and intramural championships. Meanwhile, the individual halls continued to have their own proud traditions. Those on campus would know about "Murray America," the Willard women rating men from zero to ten on flash cards at the library fountain, and the famous Cordell "Pumpkin Chorus." Vitality, pride and activity permeated the residence hall system. As NACURH acknowledged, it was "outstanding."[74]

The scenario was different for married students. Always more serious in their purpose of getting an education, short on cash, and less able to participate in the fullness of campus life, most of them worked and had children to raise. The university helped some ease their burdens by continuing to build reasonably priced, convenient, no "frills" hous-

"Hey, catch that guy with the blue backpack. He certainly rates a TEN!" Each year a rite of campus tradition occurred when the women of Willard Hall rated unsuspecting males as they passed in front of the library.

ing. In 1967 Veteran's Village was rapidly disappearing; from a 1,300 living unit "city" built after World War II, only 114 apartments remained. In its place appeared 710 brick, two-bedroom, furnished housing units. By 1977 Married Student Housing and Student Services Maintenance was responsible for 820 total apartments generating annual revenues of over $1.2 million. For $170 a month, the primarily graduate student renter lived in air-conditioned, all-bills-paid comfort, enhanced by a carpeted living room. A few Village apartments remained for those on very low budgets and rented at between $73 to $93 per month.[75]

After twenty-two years as director of Married Student Housing and Student Services Maintenance, John A. Stevens retired in June 1967. Richard M. Williams, a 1941 Oklahoma A. and M. graduate and a twenty-year Air Force veteran, retired with the rank of lieutenant colonel, assumed Stevens' position. The Hydro native made the directorship a second career, moving the program forward from July 1, 1967, to his retirement in the mid-1980s. Longtime associates of Williams included Emil Jafek and Rex Demaree, in Student Services Maintenance, and Clyde West, administrative assistant in Married Student Housing.[76]

Like every aspect of student services, the Student Union experienced the kind of changes and growth that pressed the staff to keep pace. In December 1965 the east wing on the north side of the original union was dedicated, providing an expanded bookstore, theater, a home for the Division of Student Affairs, offices for University Placement Services, and additional conference and meeting space. In 1970 a one million dollar three-level parking garage for 600 vehicles was constructed adjacent to the Student Union Hotel. By 1977 total union revenue surpassed $5 million, yet paying off the self-liquidating bonds and other financial obligations of the massive enterprise taxed the budget-balancing process.[77]

Aside from finances and expansion, the numbers relating to the breadth of service and volume of people in the Student Union were in themselves staggering. In 1975-1976 alone, 3,194 meetings were scheduled, along with 376 conferences, which attracted 65,000 off-campus visitors. Placement services reserved 1,071 union interview rooms in which outside companies talked with prospective student employees. The Student Union Activities Board's (SUAB) programming budget had grown to $35,000. The union's check cashing service handled over 128,000 checks, valued at over $2.5 million. Including food services customers, a conservative estimate was that in the single year of 1975-1976 over 2.25 million people had entered the union. However, after all of the activity, only $50,000 remained as revenue after expenses.[78]

Although the Student Union was never intended to be a nonprofit organization, it was annually as close to breaking even as an accountant could tolerate. But from the beginning, the union had been designated as a service enterprise for the campus community. This philosophy, to boggle the minds of ordinary business entrepreneurs, presented a difficult tightrope for Student Union directors to walk both then and now. Those directors from 1966-1977 who were constrained from making "too much money in deference to educational service" were Abe L. Hesser; Gerald E. Ruttman, July 1967 to May 1969; Norman F. Moore, June 1969 to July 1971; and Winston G. Shindell, former SUAB president and student activities director, who transferred from the position of director of student activities on September 1, 1971.[79]

On February 14, 1976, over 250 dignitaries, former students, and staff of the Student Union came together to celebrate a quarter century of union achievements and memories. Tony O'Bryan, the union's food services coordinator, and his staff baked a cake of four tiers from 450 pounds of cake batter. The union's first twenty-five year employee, J. V. "Mac" McReynolds, was recognized with an award. Many other longtime union employees attended the silver anniversary activities which spanned a full week. In 1976, 170 full-time employees worked in the union, and some with seniority were Assistant Director for Programs Allen Reding; Bookstore Manager Bill Hunter and his associate Thelma Olmstead; Barbara Contardi, M. M. "Bud" Andrews, and Chris Tinker in food services; Alice Richardson and Naomi Stephens in the business segment; and Winsel Bilyeu, Paul Kinnamon, and George Harrison in the hotel

In 1976, J. V. "Mac" McReynolds was honored as the first twenty-five year employee of the Student Union at the building's silver anniversary gala.

and operations areas.[80]

Since the union has virtually been viewed as "a lot of peoples" building, it has been a party to more than a few differences of opinion. Complaints about "no place to sit," inoperable escalators, and broken front doors, to needs a "pub" or pizza parlor, plus more parking—preferably without meters—have been perpetual topics among undergraduates.[81] Concerning beer in the union, the vice president for student services wrote the union director a two-sentence memorandum which flatly stated "that the serving of beer in the Student Union is out of the question."[82] This memorandum was dated June 1970. Pizza parlors and other private vending operations for the union have been periodically discussed, without action, for nearly twenty years. On a lesser plane, the union's parking garage started falling apart shortly after its completion and remains a nagging problem. And Aunt Molly's coffee house continued a long run in the union, having started in 1971.[83]

The decades of the sixties and seventies saw the expansion of the campus primarily to the west and north. Most of that growth was oriented toward student services. Married and Single Student Housing, the Colvin Center, and the University Food Services Center had helped to fill the area. The westward movement continued when a new hospital and

In 1976, a new Student Health Center opened. At this time the hospital's staff consisted of eight physicians, fifteen nurses, and two lab technicians.

clinic was opened on Farm Road, just east of Iba Hall, in June 1976. Completed at a cost of $2 million, the Student Health Center was made possible when the Student Senate overwhelmingly approved it and a required increase in student health fees in April 1971. In replacing the forty-four year old original hospital, Health Services Director Donald L. Cooper had fulfilled a sixteen-year ambition. As Dr. Cooper explained for years, a 1929 building for a campus of 3,000 eventually falls short when there are over 20,000 students averaging more than three visits each in a year's time.[84]

Assisting Cooper in the complex building project was Assistant Director Robert C. Tout and Administrative Assistant Frances Jackson. Tout would eventually take the position of director of health services at Kansas State University. Jackson remained with the operation for another decade, retiring in the mid-1980s. In 1976 the hospital's staff consisted of eight doctors, fifteen nurses, and two lab technicians. Mary Montague, another of those loyal employees, retired in 1972 after twenty years of nursing students.[85]

A division of the Bi-State Mental Health Association, headquartered in Ponca City, opened a campus clinic in 1968 and was housed in the Student Health Center in 1976. Two of the longer-tenured staff were psychiatrist Dale Maxwell and psychologist Larry Fulgenzi.[86]

Shortly before the Student Senate voted to support the new hospital's construction, those on campus who knew her were saddened by the news of the death of Roxie A. Weber. The former student physician, assistant director, and finally director of the OSU Hospital and Clinic, who had lived an active life—twenty-two years in the service of OSU students—passed away in November 1970.[87] A friend would share the thought that, "It is not often that one can say that a seventy-six year old person died an untimely death."[88] The pint-sized physician had always been a pioneer-of-sorts and a crusader, involving herself in women's issues before such causes became prevalent or popular. When Weber died, it was suggested that the new campus hospital be named to honor her. Although nothing came of this idea, Stillwater's modern housing complex for senior citizens was named the Roxie A. Weber Plaza. This came in recognition of Dr. Weber's post-retirement campaigns for low-cost housing and housing for the elderly in Stillwater— causes which she vigorously supported until the time of her final illness.

Just to the west of the hospital, the seven-year-old Colvin Physical Education Center had not been able to quench the decades' old campus thirst for recreation and leisure programs. In the six months following the Colvin Center's opening on January 27, 1969, the monthly average of building users was over 25,000. The 6,000 lockers for students and faculty were nearly filled within three and one-half weeks after the building opened. Open recreation users numbered 4,500 a day. By 1976-1977 the men's, women's, and mixed co-recreation intramural programs involved 16,000 participants out of a campus population of about 22,000 students.[89]

More westward expansion resulted. In 1974 Charles Schelsky, assistant director for facilities, announced a long-range plan for lighted tennis courts, intramural playing fields, a new "general activity" annex, and additional grass playing areas. Within two years the first phase of the expansion, additional intramural fields, was complete. Then in February 1979 the Colvin Center Annex was opened. The building's

In 1974, George Oberle (*left*) became the head of the Department of Health, Physical Education, and Recreation. Oberle promoted expansion plans for the Colvin Center Annex (*right*) as well as additional playing fields.

interior was completed on the basis of a student survey of what was most needed. The one million dollar student-fee-financed addition to the campus recreation complex included four multipurpose basketball-size courts, a jogging track, eight racquetball courts, an adjacent outdoor exercise course, and four more outdoor basketball courts. The annex was dedicated to open recreation, 360 days a year. Under terms of the student fee increase vote, classes and intercollegiate athletics could not be scheduled in the new facility.[90]

Leadership for campus recreation, leisure, and intramural programs during this period passed from Jim Kevin to Albin P. Warner, who arrived on campus in 1962 to spearhead the drive to build the Colvin Center. After Dr. Warner's sudden death at age fifty on September 29, 1973, George Oberle became the head of the Department of Health, Physical Education, and Recreation in the summer of 1974. Oberle supported Title IX, federal legislation which emphasized athletic opportunities for women, and promoted the expansion plans for the Colvin Annex and additional playing fields. Oberle continued as the department head into OSU's Centennial Decade.[91]

Policy formulation and major responsibility for the Colvin Center-based programs fell to Mary Frye, assistant director for programs, and Schelsky, who in 1974-1975 served as president of the National Intramural Association. After nearly thirty-three years as director of men's intramural programs, Gordon Gilbert retired at the end of the 1972-1973 academic year. Kent Bunker, an OSU Colvin staffer from 1970-1971, took up where Mr. Gilbert left off, continuing the strong program as chair of the intramural department. Ada Van Whitley assisted Bunker, shaping and expanding the intramural opportunities for women, as she had been doing since 1961. Joining the Colvin Center's management team, among others, were David Peshke, sports clubs and co-recreational director, and Sid Gonsoulin, recreation director.[92]

With a capable cadre of professionals and eighty additional employees, the Colvin Center complex, showcasing the new buildings and outdoor facilities, was by 1976 providing programs on a scale second to no other place in the country. The "Huck Finn" Saturday morning program for youngsters was well established. Sixteen sports clubs, covering interests from cricket to scuba diving, were consolidated, and more clubs were being formed. Twenty to twenty-five games a night were scheduled on thirteen playing fields during the fall touch football season—all in an effort to accommodate 57 percent of undergraduate male students as players. Women's intramural flag football was growing even faster than men's play; in 1974 forty-two women's teams boasted nearly one thousand females on team rosters. In 1976-1977 three thousand students played on "co-rec" teams, including their own football divisions. Campus intramural programs and recreation had reached a "golden" era, with facilities finally available to match the interest. A "booming" rate of participation naturally followed.[93]

On the south side of campus, just across University Avenue and only a few blocks from the Colvin Center, the Greek fraternities and sororities experienced neither "boom" nor "bust." Rather, the years between 1966 and 1977 were characterized by steady growth and subtle, but important, change. In 1972 there was a serious proposal to merge the Interfraternity Council (IFC) and Panhellenic Council into a single Greek government, but sorority alumnae torpedoed the initiative. Spring Sing, held in conjunction with Mom's Weekend, became an established tradition after being introduced in 1965. Longtime hazing activities, particularly among fraternities, the opening of chapters to minority student membership, and the curtailment of heavy drinking  represented topics of local concern that were influenced and pushed by national Greek organizations.[94]

Several of the Greek social organizations celebrated their semi-centennial anniversary on the Oklahoma State campus. Lambda Chi

*1968 REDSKIN*

Over the years, the campus Greek organizations have actively supported many community programs including holiday parties for needy children and assistance for the elderly. These men of Lambda Chi Alpha fraternity show their chapter's success in the Christmas Food Drive.

Alpha reached this milestone in 1966-1967. Among sororities, Kappa Delta, Kappa Alpha Theta, and Pi Beta Phi, along with fraternity Sigma Phi Epsilon, celebrated a golden anniversary in 1969. The Chi Omega clock tower, located between the Classroom Building and the Student Union, represented a gift to the university from members and alumnae celebrating that chapter's fiftieth anniversary. The twelve foot "Chi O" clock cost about $10,000 and was dedicated on April 18, 1970. Other golden anniversary Greek groups through 1978 included Sigma Nu (1970), Kappa Sigma (1970), Alpha Gamma Rho (1971), Delta Zeta (1972), Sigma Chi (1972), Beta Theta Pi (1973), Acacia (1973), Zeta Tau Alpha (1973), Alpha Delta Pi (1977), and FarmHouse (1978).[95]

On the "not so evident" side of OSU Greek life, the traditionally conservative system had changed over those first fifty years. Not all, but most chapters had loosened or dropped their dress codes. Jeans could be worn to classes. For women, hats were no longer required in church services, earrings were no longer prohibited, dancing partners could be held closer than twelve inches, and men could pick up their dates—comfortable in the knowledge that they could go someplace together in a car. Greek-independent mixing was easier, since the stereotype of "being Greek" was played down. "Dry" or non-drinking pledge programs became common.[96]

Other marks of a strong and stable system included Kappa Delta sorority and Sigma Phi Epsilon fraternity initiating their one thousandth members in 1965 and 1966, respectively. New houses were built by Delta Delta Delta at 1506 West Third in 1965 and Alpha Xi Delta at 1415 West Third in 1971. At the national Panhellenic conference in New Orleans in 1967, OSU Panhellenic President Melinda Hanraty accepted the award for "outstanding sorority system." A year later the IFC won the national scholarship award, recognizing the nation's best academic program among fraternity systems.[97]

Often Greek chapters rode a thin line between success and failure. Money, pledges, supportive alumni, involved advisors, and attractive houses and programs, all mixed to make the successful formula. Consequently, over time, chapters are founded and lost. In the years between 1931 and 1977 the Greeks experienced impressive growth. Alpha Chi Omega and Kappa Kappa Gamma became chartered sororities in 1947. Gamma Phi Beta (1957), Delta Delta Delta (1962), Delta Sigma Theta (1971), and Alpha Kappa Alpha (1973) further strengthened the women's system.

Fraternity chapters increased by three in the 1930s with the addition of Sigma Alpha Epsilon (1931), Phi Kappa Theta (1937), and Pi Kappa Alpha (1939). World War II then preempted further growth. Between 1946 and 1971 the fraternity system more than doubled in size. In this twenty-five year period, OSU fraternity charters were granted to

Phi Delta Theta (1946), Alpha Tau Omega (1947), Delta Chi (1948), Phi Kappa Tau (1949), Delta Tau Delta (1949), Delta Upsilon (1960), Phi Gamma Delta (1962), Triangle (1964), Alpha Phi Alpha (1966), Phi Kappa Psi (1967), Pi Kappa Phi (1970), Beta Sigma Psi (1970), and Kappa Alpha Psi (1971).[98]

To illustrate the sometimes delicate balance between success and failure, the then 1973 IFC president, and current Oklahoma City psychologist, Herman Jones explained the failure of the Kappa Alpha fraternity as the result of a "too tough" pledge program and a chapter house too far removed from the mainstream of Greek life.[99]

Sometimes lost to history was the fact that black Greek brotherhood and sisterhood organizations, first founded at predominantly black institutions of higher education, date to the nineteenth century. The civil rights movement and the opening of Oklahoma's formerly for "whites only" colleges and universities gave impetus to the establishment of traditionally black sororities and fraternities at Oklahoma State University. Pioneering in the effort to afford undergraduates an opportunity to experience the rich tradition of a black fraternity was Alpha Phi Alpha. Chartered at OSU on January 29, 1966, the chapter's president was Wardell Hollis. By 1973 a total of five predominantly black chapters had been added to the campus Greek system. Following the Alphas as fraternities were Beta Sigma Psi, chartered November 21, 1970, and in May 1971, Kappa Alpha Psi. The Kappa chapter at OSU was the 145th, dating from a single founding chapter at Indiana State University in 1911.[100]

The initial black sorority was Delta Sigma Theta, chartered at OSU on May 2, 1971. The latest chapter among 340 sororities in three countries, the Delta's origins date to Howard University, in Washington, D.C., and a founding date of 1913. Del City native Leila Seldon was the first president. A little more than two years later, a chapter of Alpha Kappa Alpha was chartered on October 28, 1973. Donnetta Henry served as president during the installation. Patrice Latimer, the first black and one of only a few women to serve as OSU Student Association president, was recognized as "Outstanding Black Woman on Campus" by the founding group of women.[101]

Before and since the 1976-1977 academic year the best of the twenty-three OSU fraternity and fourteen sorority chapters could highlight their year by receiving the coveted Troxel Award as the outstanding fraternity or the Zelma Patchin Award as the best of all sororities. Both people who lent their names to these marks of achievement were longtime Division of Student Affairs staffers who committed much of their professional and personal lives to the ideals of Greek life.[102]

Dean of Men, and later Associate Dean of Students, Darrel K. Troxel left OSU for a combination dean of students and political science teaching position at Pan American University, Edinberg, Texas, in 1970.

Before departing, the well-known man called "Trox" enriched the fraternity system for nearly two decades as general overseer and advisor to the IFC. Troxel was an early advocate of "Greek Week," equal opportunity for ethnic and cultural minorities, and a national figure in Greek circles. Troxel died in 1986 while still at Pan American.[103]

Associate Dean of Students Zelma F. Patchin retired on June 30, 1975, bringing to a close a near twenty-five year career of working with students at OSU. From 1951 to 1969 Dean Patchin held the title dean of women. With affirmative action, women's equality, and regulations from the Department of Health, Education, and Welfare, plus a bit of advocacy on her own part, she assumed responsibilities for both men and women's programs. The 1966 initiative of the Association of Women Students (AWS) to start a freshman women's leadership organization—Patchin Panel—represented still another measure of the esteem people had for this special dean.[104]

After retiring, Dean-emeritus Patchin traveled extensively, but remained OSU-active by volunteering to teach English as a second language to family members of international students. As Linda Welch, a student writer for the 1975 Redskin, discovered: "It might be serenity, it might be poise, but it's definitely unique and it generates . . .There's something very special about Zelma Patchin. It's an almost magical quality that you sense the first time you meet her but can never really define."[105]

Dean Patchin demonstrated that she was resilient and able to change with the demands of different times. Throughout her tenure she was responsible for the health of the sorority system. Near her retirement Dean Patchin pointed with pride to such programs as "Women Do Dare" and "Women's Symposium," a program on contemporary women's issues. The 1964 initiative to present the Panhellenic's Patchin Award for "greatest contribution to the campus" simply made formal what Dean Patchin advocated daily in her long and illustrious professional life at Oklahoma State.[106]

Dean Patchin's accommodating ability to bend with the needs and whims of the students was fortunate, for her last decade of work was especially taxing in its diversity. In part, the early 1970s might be labeled as years given to the rise of women and minority students. In stronger than ever tones, questions were raised about the usefulness of traditional student government. The origins of the election of class officers dated to the earliest years of Oklahoma A. and M. College, but in 1970 these offices were abolished due to a lack of purpose. The spring Student Association elections of 1972 saw Tom Bennett and Larry Holmes opposed by Doug Allen and Ron Frye for the top posts. Allen and Frye ran on a platform to abolish student government. Bennett and Holmes won, but by a mere one hundred votes. The Association of Women Students (AWS) President Kay Young showed fortitude when she placed her belief that the AWS no longer had a purpose on a campus-wide ballot. Young was proved correct when the AWS was ordered disbanded by the organization's undergraduate constituency in November of 1972.[107]

The passing of the election of class officers, the AWS, and, except for the narrowness of a few votes, the Student Association itself, represented a statement about the times. On a large campus, interests and energies tend toward specific groups or causes. Then some students could care less about any organization, which perhaps gave rise to the Stout Hall Apathy Club. One spokesperson for this club stated their goal as "we have no goals in the Apathy Club, because if we live up to our goals, we will be doing more than any other organization on campus . . . we will do nothing, then when we do something it will surpass our goals." The club's first speakers were professors because "they notice student apathy in class every day and they are sympathetic to the Apathy Club."[108] The Apathy Club, perhaps not surprisingly, also passed into history, due to a lack of interest.

But in fairness the outdated and unappreciated organizations did leave behind programs that perpetuate in time. Patchin Panel and Mom's Day, dating to April 1965, were both legacies of the AWS. The university retreated from the business of supervising and inspecting off-campus housing in 1967. The Student Association filled in a part of the gap for "renter's rights" by sponsoring the Renter's Association in 1976 and a Consumer's Action Council. In 1975 the association established a free legal advice service, a program still used by students. The Student Association, with a name change to Student Government Association (SGA), chartered the Off-Campus Student Association in 1977. A student co-operative, organized to provide discount goods and services, was tried and short-lived in the early seventies.[109]

Reflecting the larger society, 1975 served as a barometer measuring how women had entered the mainstream of student life. The demise of the AWS represented the trend. Women no longer found their own organization necessary. Their voice had grown through other groups, including RHA, SGA, the college councils, and in a multitude of special interest organizations. The campus was moving toward having chairpersons, rather than just chairmen. From 1971 to 1975 there were four consecutive female *Redskin* editors-in-chief. In the same period three coeds held the job of editor of the *Daily O'Collegian*. In 1975 Alice Moreland Duff became the first-ever single director of Varsity Revue. Women were regularly gaining the top student government positions, winning the popular vote on the still predominately male campus. Patrice Latimer had been elected Student Association president in 1973, and Kathy Butler was the 1976 RHA president.[110]

It was the late 1960s and early 1970s that gave rise to a number of important minority student organizations. These groups paralleled the movement of women toward campus equity, in part gaining momentum from the larger changing social order. Each was born from a need to raise campus awareness. A desire to celebrate and emphasize a cultural or ethnic heritage, or a role in society, provided additional impetus. All had as common purposes some high goals, including fellowship, personal and group pride, advocacy, and education of the majority population. Although similar organizations had been attempted earlier, such as the 1954 Double O Club for physically disabled students and the Ittanaha Club, an on-again off-again chartered vehicle for American Indian student interests dating to the 1920s, all had failed to maintain continuity. As a consequence, another commonality existed in that each of them became an enduring student organization after 1967.[111]

The Afro-American Society was officially chartered at Oklahoma State University on January 31, 1968. Glen Shoate, a Bartlesville native, was president. At the time of its chartering, the Afro-American Society took on responsibilities as the governing body for black students and for providing social, academic, and cultural programs. In cooperation with the Black Heritage Commission, the Afro-American Society co-sponsored the first OSU Black Heritage Week in February 1968. Among others, Willie Battiste played on important role in establishing the campus tradition. The initial Black Heritage Week was dedicated to Langston poet Melvin Tolson. Black Heritage Week also provided a platform for "Burnin' Black," a chorus that has subsequently distinguished itself with many performances over the years. Oklahoma civil rights leaders Clara Luper, Tulsa Senator Curtis Lawson, and Oklahoma City Senator E. Melvin Porter were speakers.[112]

Black Heritage Week 1969 was chaired by Haskell graduate student Margaret Williams. The campus-wide awareness program included a painting exhibit in the rotunda of the Student Union theater by Langston University art professor Wallace Owens and a day of eating "soul" food in the residence hall and Student Union cafeterias. The week-long celebration of black culture and history was purported to be the first extended Black Heritage Week on any college or university campus in the state. Since then the neglected heritage of America's black citizens continues as a key theme with each passing year's program. As for the Afro-American Society, its strength continued to grow, additional activities developed, and the traumatic 1969 and 1970 campus events eventually enhanced the group's influence and credibility.[113]

Since Pistol Pete is the mascot of Oklahoma State, many students, over the long history of the university, have felt like "Indians in Cowboy Country." In a very real sense, if the student was an American Indian, he or she could understand the dilemmas inherent in that phrase.

Although students of American Indian heritage had participated in the Ittanaha Club for years, the organization enjoyed a rekindled interest in the early 1970s. The now Native American Student Association strived to serve as a voice for Indian students as well as enrich campus life with an Indian Heritage Week.

But help was forthcoming. With funding from the Bureau of Indian Affairs, Blanche Wahnee, a counselor of Indian ancestry, was hired in the fall of 1972. On September 13, 1972, the Ittanaha Club officially changed its name to Native American Student Association (NASA). With this combination of events, plus the support of faculty members such as Donald N. Brown of the sociology department and Margaret F. Nelson of the English department, renewed strength came to campus American Indian students. Likewise, interest and vigor were rekindled in the floundering student organization.[114]

Despite Oklahoma having the largest Indian population in the United States, in 1972-1973 less than 1 percent of the total OSU student enrollment, or about 150 students, were of Indian descent. These students, no less than those before them, experienced the negative effects of stereotyping, overt racism, and subtle discrimination, both on- and off-campus. Discriminatory terms like "chief," "Tonto," and "Pocahontas" were all too frequently heard. Detracting from their search for an identity on campus was a lack of Indian faculty and staff. Campus jobs were difficult to find, particularly for many men who wore their hair traditionally. Nearly all of the students at OSU were on grants-in-aid from the Bureau of Indian Affairs. The students feared retaliation from the bureau if they asserted themselves, even for rights that other students had and took for granted.[115]

Just before the reconstituted Native American Student Association was organized, Anthony Thompson, from Wright City, said, "We don't want to be militant; we just want to survive."[116] Bill Tohee, Debbie Yates, Eddie Wilson, and Carol Chapman played early leadership roles.[117] The Native American Student Association quickly became "an active force within the campus community and a spokesman for Indian students enrolled in the University." Over one thousand visitors turned out in March 1972 for the initial NASA-sponsored Indian Heritage Week, including a pow-wow. The following fall, a second pow-wow attracted another thousand people. In April 1973 the second heritage week was held. The event continued to enrich campus life annually. The Native American Student Association's influence also spread to themes political, attitudinal, and helpful. Changes did come, albeit too slowly. Central to any progress was the Indian student's new organization.[118]

Although stability would be delayed until the early 1980s, the next group to assert its heritage and needs were the Hispanic students—students with ancestry pertaining to Spain and its language, people, and culture. The Hispanic students received support and comfort in their beginning efforts from psychology minority graduate program advisor, and still later Harvard Law School graduate, Gloria Valencia-Weber. Early student leaders included Steve Taylor, Viola Madrid, Mark Taylor, and Raquel Martinez.[119]

The Chicano Community Association became a chartered student organization in January 1977. The chartering sought to bring together people of Hispanic heritage to "promote an awareness and appreciation of the Chicano culture within the total multicultural society."[120] Visibility came slowly to the group. However, with more students and faculty, the now Hispanic Student Association began to accomplish similar global purposes as other ethnic minority organizations by the early 1980s. An awareness week, financial and educational assistance programs for their students, and advocacy for equality, representation, and solving their problems were all important issues.

In the spring of 1979 a small, but enthusiastic group of students, with varying degrees of physical disability, printed a T-shirt for their awareness week which prominently displayed their theme "The Last Minority Group." The week, like other awareness weeks, was planned to teach others to be aware of their attitudes, beliefs, and stereotypes regarding an otherwise capable segment of the campus community. The sponsoring organization was the Handicapped Student Organization. The seeds for the organization were planted in spring 1977, and the organization achieved chartered status the following year.

As early as 1968 OSU was beginning to provide some campus access for students who happened to have physical disabilities. However, Section 504 of the Federal Rehabilitation Act of 1973, which mandated inclusion of otherwise qualified handicapped people into every government-funded program, created additional pressure for institutions to provide accessibility to programs and facilities. With this legal initiative, increasing numbers of disabled collegians appeared on university campuses nationwide to secure a higher education.[121]

It was within this climate that the students joined together under the banner of the Handicapped Student Organization. Student group advisement came from George Hardin, counselor with the Oklahoma Department of Rehabilitative Services, and Patrick M. Murphy, an individual who knew little about physical disabilities, but who received a good education from the students.

Breaking the early ground in the late 1960s were students J. A. ''Tweed'' McNaughton and Sue Oxford. Leaders during the periods of later growth included Rusty Miller, Darrell Smith, Roger Chambers, Martin McCormick, Pamela Dollarhide, Jeff Jamison, and Launa Houston. These students, plus too many others to name, influenced the university's substantial effort to accommodate these previously excluded stu-

By the late 1960s, OSU was beginning to provide programs and facilities to assist students with physical disabilities. George Hardin (*right*) a longtime counselor with the Oklahoma Department of Rehabilitative Services, visits with Jerry Halstead. Halstead and many other students over the years have worked with university administrators to make the campus more accessible for the disabled.

dents. But since the aesthetically pleasant campus for the able-bodied presented a nightmare for people in wheelchairs or with visual problems, much remained to be done. The Handicapped Student Organization, subsequently renamed the Association for Concerns of Disabled Collegians, with Smith, Houston, Betty and Jerry Halstead, and Chad Coy as primary movers, continued to work enthusiastically with university administrators to modify the campus over the next decade.[122]

The early to mid-1980s was a time at OSU when students from a variety of on-campus sub-groups organized themselves and asked for social justice and equal opportunity. To a degree, they were heard and accommodated, and progress resulted. Nonetheless the great majority of students remained focused on simply being a "typical" student. By 1975 "No Smoking" signs were being installed all over campus. Students from the era will perhaps remember the 1971 rock festival crowd of 6,000 at Louis O'Haver's farm, featuring the Nitty Gritty Dirt Band; the heyday of Insane Liberation, an improvisational theater troupe; or the 1973 first issue of *Cow Chips*, another campus humor magazine that stirred confrontation with administrators. In 1975 the Student Union's nickel jukeboxes were replaced by two-plays-for-a-quarter machines. Gum went from five cents to fifteen cents a pack, and Hostess Twinkies doubled in price. Many more students would have noticed these kind of changes![123]

Despite claims of promoting ecology, easing finances, or insuring good health, the basic reason for a bicycle on campus remained—it sure beats walking!

In the early 1970s students especially liked the *Daily O'Collegian* editorial cartoons, letters to the editor, editorials, campus news-in-brief, and news about policies, administration, and combinations of that sometimes volatile mixture. Least liked in the newspaper were the crossword puzzles and news about fine arts, sports, and campus and city government.[124]

Ecology, finances, and preventative health issues gained favor as general topics of interest. A series of annual "Earth Weeks" and "Health Weeks" and a boom in the number of bicycles, with accompanying bike paths and bicycle racks, came to campus. Unleaded gasoline and automobile pollution devices drove up prices, but held promise in the struggle to save the environment.[125] Bev Oldham, *O'Colly* co-editor, generalized that "only beer and sex arouse the student body."[126] In a public service article listing fifty ways to have fun at OSU, fun lovers were encouraged to choose to go through orientation a second time, refuse to graduate, ask for second helpings in a campus cafeteria, or join a fraternity, sorority, or best, join both.[127]

On June 15, 1977, President Lawrence L. Boger, the institution's next chief administrator, took up the reins of leadership. Vietnam and Watergate had been replaced in the newspapers by news of an inflationary

As these coeds clearly exhibit, the era of equal opportunity in the labor force had become an integral part of their future career plans and goals.

economy. By then a period of incredible social upheaval had settled. During the years of Dr. Kamm's presidency, authority had been challenged and traditions shattered. Nationally and in Stillwater, women left their home for jobs, money, and a better life for themselves and their families. Sex and drugs had both become open issues. The existence of a moral code of conduct and God's very existence had been challenged during the era.[128]

On college and university campuses, students had protested, sat-in, and destroyed property. In the furor, lives had been lost. The established authority of administrators, faculty, and student personnel workers had been eroded. The legal system became a forum in which to resolve campus differences, and as a result educational wisdom and common standards were lessened. For many the privilege and honor of a higher education became a right, if not an expectation.

Throughout, the Oklahoma State University fared far better than most. There was little reason for lamenting or looking back. The eleven years from 1966 to 1977 were, in many ways, undeniably fruitful for students and student services. Buildings, programs, and rules had all been restructured to the betterment of everyone. Although there had been painful stress-causing problems, Dr. Kamm could take pride in knowing that each had been resolved without interruption to the institution's larger priorities. The new president would not see a yellow brick road, nor would he have to worry about simply putting old wine in new bottles. Despite everything, within student services and elsewhere, there was still work to be done and the opportunity to do it.

# Endnotes

1. Shortly after Robert B. Kamm became OSU president, several hundred students went to Oklahoma City to lobby against a $23 million reduction in the proposed Oklahoma State Regents for Higher Education budget. President Kamm met with the students just before their departure. He admonished them to be courteous, then added, "We need more dollars to do a better job. Follow through. Don't stop the effort today." See Oklahoma State University *Daily O'Collegian*, 27 April 1967, pp. 1, 8.

2. Troy Dorris, "Report and Resolution on Student Housing," Faculty Council Student Affairs Committee, 11 May 1965, p. 1, Faculty Council Records, Special Collections, Edmon Low Library, Oklahoma State University, Stillwater, Oklahoma.

3. Robert B. Kamm, "The Faculty and Guidance" [1955], p. 3, speech, Faculty Council Records.

4. Kamm, "The Faculty and Guidance, p. 5.

5. Kamm, "The Faculty and Guidance," pp. 6, 13.

6. "Two New Vice Presidents," 7 February 1967, p. 1, press release, Weldon Barnes Collection, Special Collections, Edmon Low Library; Edward C. Burris, "Report of the Ad Hoc Committee on Auxiliary Enterprises," 12 December 1967, pp. 1-5, Faculty Council Records.

7. Larry Snipes, "Abe Hesser—An Interview," *Oklahoma State Alumnus Magazine*, vol. 10, no. 3 (March 1969), p. 10; *Daily O'Collegian*, 12 September 1968, p. 3.

8. "Duties are Many and Varied," *Oklahoma State Alumnus Magazine*, vol. 13, no. 2 (February 1972), p. 8.

9. *Daily O'Collegian*, 9 October 1968, p. 1, 8 October 1968, p. 1, 10 October 1968, pp. 1, 4, 12 October 1968, p. 1, 17 January 1973, p. 9; Abe L. Hesser to Division Heads, 23 October 1970, Student Services Collection, Special Collections, Edmon Low Library.

10. Snipes, p. 10; "Addenda," *Faculty News*, vol. 17, no. 17 (20 November 1970), unnumbered page, OSU faculty and staff newsletter; *Daily O'Collegian*, 12 July 1968, p. 1, 8 October 1970, p. 1, 17 October 1970, p. 1, 18 June 1971, p. 1.

11. *Daily O'Collegian*, 18 June 1971, p. 1.

12. "Some Recent Appointments," *Oklahoma State Alumnus Magazine*, vol. 12, no. 8 (November 1971), p. 13; *Daily O'Collegian*, 27 July 1971, p. 1.

13. *Daily O'Collegian*, 27 July 1971, p. 1, 6 May 1969, p. 1.

14. "Alpha '73 Helping Students," *Oklahoma State Alumnus Magazine*, vol. 14, no. 9 (December 1973), pp. 12-13; "New Students Are Introduced to University Activity," *Oklahoma State University Outreach*, vol. 15, no. 8 (November 1974), pp. 8-9; *Daily O'Collegian*, 28 August 1973, p. 3, 24 July 1975, p. 7, 13 April 1977, p. 2; Barbara Jean Layman, "Perceptions of College Environment at Oklahoma State University By Incoming Freshman Students" (Doctor of Education dissertation, Oklahoma State University, 1975), p. 63; "Freshman Programs and Services 1977-1978," *Student Services Planning Book* (Summer 1978), pp. 1-2, Student Services Collection; "Discussion of Proposal for Freshman Programs," Administrators Council Meeting Minutes, 20 March 1975, pp. 4-5, Faculty Council Records; "CALL Center," *Oklahoma State University Outreach*, vol. 18, no. 1 (January-February 1977), pp. 12-13.

15. *1974-1975 Oklahoma State University Student Handbook*, pp. 24-34.

16. Robert G. Schmalfeld and Lynn Jackson to Head Residents and Fraternity and Sorority Presidents, 13 December 1971, Robert G. Schmalfeld to Division of Student Affairs Staff, "Guidelines For Release of Confidential Information from Student Personnel Records," 4 May 1970, and Robert G. Schmalfeld to Abe L. Hesser, 13 April 1970, in Student Services Collection; *Daily O'Collegian*, 18 March 1970, p. 1, 17 June 1969, p. 1, 19 November 1965, p. 1.

17. *1975 Redskin*, p. 478, Oklahoma State University Yearbook.

18. *Daily O'Collegian*, 8 March 1974, pp. 1-2, 6 March 1974, pp. 1, 3, 7 March 1974, pp. 1, 4, 20 March 1974, pp. 1, 4, 27 February 1975, p. 1, 7 March 1975, p. 1, 25 February 1976, p. 1, 28 February 1976, p. 1, 10 March 1977, p. 2, 11 March 1977, p. 1.

19. *Daily O'Collegian*, 31 July 1974, p. 3.

20. *Daily O'Collegian*, 11 May 1972, p. 1, 22 September 1972, p. 8.

21. *Daily O'Collegian*, 22 September 1972, p. 8.

22. *Daily O'Collegian*, 14 November 1975, p. 1.

23. *Daily O'Collegian*, 28 November 1967, p. 1, 15 November 1968, p. 1, 9 October 1968, p. 1, 30 September 1969, p. 1, 25 April 1972, pp. 1-2.

24. Jo F. Dorris to Robert G. Schmalfeld, 1 October 1973, Student Services Collection.

25. Abe L. Hesser to Bob Schmalfeld, 20 March 1970, Student Services Collection.

26. Department of Student Activities to Deans, Directors, and Department Heads, 18 March 1970, Student Services Collection; *Daily O'Collegian*, 3 February 1977, p. 4, 8 February 1977, p. 4.

27. "Dean of Student Affairs," *Oklahoma State Alumnus Magazine*, vol. 10, no. 2 (February 1969), p. 28; *Daily O'Collegian*, 23 July 1968, p. 1, 13 September 1968, p. 1.

28. "Dean of Student Affairs," p. 28; Robert B. Clark, "Ten Year Progress Report for Department of Financial Aids 1965-1975," 13 May 1975, p. 1, Robert G. Schmalfeld to Pat Hofler, 13 May 1975, Patrick M. Murphy to Robert G. Schmalfeld, 1 December 1972, King Cacy to Robert G. Schmalfeld, 21 November 1972, and Terry H. Henderson, "Special Services Program," July 1972, program proposal, pp. 1-3, in Student Services Collection; *Daily O'Collegian*, 13 September 1968, p. 7, 14 January 1969, p. 1.

29. Jo F. Dorris, "Student Activities 1974-1975," 13 May 1975, pp. 1-3, Winston G. Shindell, "Year End Report for Student Activities," July 1969, p. 2, and Rex T. Finnegan to Robert G. Schmalfeld, 22 April 1975, in Student Services Collection; *Daily O'Collegian*, 29 September 1966, p. 16; "Student Activities Director," *Oklahoma State Alumnus Magazine*, vol. 13, no. 2 (February 1972), p. 9.

30. "Problems, Problems, Problems!" *Oklahoma State Alumnus Magazine*, vol. 9, no. 4 (April 1968), p. 13.

31. Rex T. Finnegan to Robert G. Schmalfeld, 22 April 1975, and Rex T. Finnegan, "University Counseling Services 1975-1976 Annual Report," p. 3, in Student Services Collection.

32. Patrick M. Murphy, "University Counseling Services Fuzzies Outreach," September 1977, pp. 1-3, campus flyer, Student Services Collection; *Daily O'Collegian*, 5 December 1967, p. 9.

33. "Larsen Appointed Director of OSU Counseling Services," *Oklahoma State Alumnus Magazine*, vol. 6, no. 7 (September-October 1965), p. 61; Minutes, Student Affairs Department Heads Meeting, 30 April 1970, p. 1, 11 June 1970, p. 1, Student Services Collection; *Daily O'Collegian*, 27 July 1965, p. 1, 22 September 1970, p. 1, 15 February 1973, p. 2.

34. William Edward McFarland, "A History of Student Financial Assistance Programs at Oklahoma State University, 1891-1978, With An Emphasis on the Creation and Administration of the Lew Wentz Foundation" (Doctor of Philosophy dissertation, Oklahoma State University, 1979), pp. 95-96; Robert B. Clark to Robert G. Schmalfeld, 13 May 1975, Robert B. Clark, "Philosophy of Department of Financial Aids," July 1976, p. 2, and Jo Dorris to Robert B. Clark and Robert G. Schmalfeld, "Financial Aid Study Report," 28 November 1976, pp. 1-2, in Student Services Collection.

35. McFarland, p. 108.

36. Jo Dorris to Robert B. Clark and Robert G. Schmalfeld, "Financial Aid Study Report," 28 November 1976, p. 1, Student Services Collection.

37. Jo Dorris to Robert B. Clark and Robert G. Schmalfeld, "Financial Aid Study Report," 28 November 1976, p. 1, Student Services Collection.

38. Robert B. Clark to Robert G. Schmalfeld, 13 May 1975, and Jo Dorris to Robert B. Clark and Robert G. Schmalfeld, "Financial Aid Study Report," 28 November 1976, pp. 1-15, in Student Services Collection; *Daily O'Collegian*, 23 June 1972, p. 1.

39. McFarland, pp. 129, 144-145; *Daily O'Collegian*, 23 February 1973, p. 7.

40. McFarland, p. 145.

41. McFarland, p. 144.

42. "Plaque Honors Shepherd Sisters," *Oklahoma State University Outreach*, vol. 16, no. 4 (April 1975), p. 34; Robert B. Clark to Robert G. Schmalfeld, 13 May 1975, Student Services Collection; McFarland, p. 138.

43. Jo Dorris to Robert B. Clark and Robert G. Schmalfeld, "Financial Aid Study Report," 28 November 1976, p. 15, Student Services Collection.

44. "Financial Aids: Helping Pay the Bills," *Oklahoma State University Outreach*, vol. 16, no. 4 (April 1975), pp. 22-23; "James R. Fleming Dies in Tulsa," *Oklahoma State University Outreach*, vol. 16, no. 5 (May 1975), p. 22.

45. Jerry Leon Gill, "Oklahoma State University and the Great Adventure in International Education, 1951-1976" (Doctor of Philosophy dissertation, Oklahoma State University, 1976), pp. iii, 6; "Educational Crossroads of Many Languages," *Oklahoma State University Magazine*, vol. 1, no. 5 (November 1957), p. 29.

46. *Daily O'Collegian*, 7 December 1960, p. 2.

47. W. Douglas Wilson, "Social Relationships of International Students Attending Oklahoma State University" (Doctor of Education dissertation, Oklahoma State University, 1975), pp. 4-5, 16, 57-64; *Daily O'Collegian*, 24 September 1952, p. 2, 2 October 1952, p. 2, 19 April 1968, p. 1, 11 November 1966, p. 4, 16 December 1966, p. 4, 14 October 1958, p. 2, 10 December 1974, p. 6, 31 August 1974, p. 1.

48. Darrel K. Troxel to J. R. Vandegrift, 30 May 1952, President's Papers, Special Collections, Edmon Low Library.

49. Darrel K. Troxel to J. R. Vandegrift, 30 May 1952, President's Papers; "Educational Crossroads of Many Languages," pp. 28-29.

50. *Daily O'Collegian*, 22 April 1960, p. 12.

51. *Daily O'Collegian*, 22 April 1960, p. 12, 12 January 1962, p. 8.

52. Leo V. Blakley, "Report of the Student Committee of the Faculty Council," 30 November 1962, p. 2, Faculty Council Records.

53. *Daily O'Collegian*, 22 April 1960, p. 12.

54. *Daily O'Collegian*, 22 April 1960, p. 12, 12 January 1962, p. 8, 7 January 1956, p. 4, 15 November 1958, p. 1; Blakley, "Report of the Student Committee of the Faculty Council," p. 2.

55. *Daily O'Collegian*, 10 March 1960, pp. 1, 6, 22 March 1962, pp. 1, 3, 17 March 1962, p. 1, 12 September 1962, pp. 1, 6.

56. David Henderson to Robert G. Schmalfeld, Office of the Associate Dean of Student Affairs 1965-1975, 13 May 1975, Student Services Collection; "To Help Them Adapt," *Oklahoma State Alumnus Magazine*, vol. 5, no. 9 (October 1964), p. 16; Ted Kalivoda to Faculty and Staff, "Office of International Student Advisement and International Students," [Fall 1963], pp. 1-2, Faculty Council Records.

57. *Daily O'Collegian*, 20 April 1976, p. 5, 30 April 1976, p. 4.

58. Doug Wilson to Robert G. Schmalfeld, 20 December 1973, Student Services Collection.

59. *Daily O'Collegian*, 7 September 1976, p. 8.

60. *Daily O'Collegian*, 9 June 1967, p. 7.

61. *Daily O'Collegian*, 16 June 1972, p. 8, 7 April 1970, p. 1; "Flags Fly Over International Mall," *Oklahoma State Alumnus Magazine*, vol. 13, no. 8 (November 1972), p. 26; "The International Mall," *Oklahoma State Alumnus Magazine*, vol. 9, no. 8 (November 1968), p. 5.

62. "International Appreciation," *Oklahoma State Alumnus Magazine*, vol. 12, no. 3 (March 1971), p. 5; *Daily O'Collegian*, 27 January 1971, p. 5.

63. "International Appreciation," p. 5.

64. Robert B. Kamm to Abe L. Hesser, 7 September 1965, and Abe L. Hesser, Frank McFarland, J. Lewis Sanderson and Robert B. Kamm to Oliver S. Willham, 2 December 1965, in Student Services Collection.

65. Abe L. Hesser and Frank E. McFarland to Whom It May Concern, 24 May 1966, and Abe L. Hesser to Lewis Wolfe, 19 February 1968, in Student Services Collection; *Daily O'Collegian*, 7 June 1966, p. 11.

66. *1975-1976 Oklahoma State University Student-Faculty Directory*, p. 14; *Daily O'Collegian*, 14 July 1970, p. 6.

67. "Single Student Housing 1977-1978," Spring 1977, pp. 1-2, and "Student Services Budget for 1977-1978, Residence Halls and Dining Halls," 11 February 1977, pp. 1-2, in Student Services Collection; *Daily O'Collegian*, 8 February 1973, p. 1, 7 September 1976, p. 1, 26 August 1975, pp. 1, 17.

68. *Daily O'Collegian*, 24 February 1968, p. 1, 13 March 1973, p. 5, 22 October 1971, p. 1, 11 September 1973, p. 3, 18 April 1972, pp. 1, 3, 31 October 1968, p. 3, 11 September 1969, p. 1.

69. "Joe Blair," *Oklahoma State University Outreach*, vol. 18, no. 1 (January-February 1977), pp. 6-7; Joe Blair, "University Food Services, 1977-1978" [Summer 1977], pp. 1-2, Student Services Collection.

70. "Joe Blair—He Feeds Thousands," *Oklahoma State University Outreach*, vol. 14, no. 9 (December 1973), pp. 6-8; "Joe Blair," pp. 6-7; *Daily O'Collegian*, 6 October 1971, p. 11, 5 October 1972, p. 1.

71. *Daily O'Collegian*, 5 November 1970, p. 2, 21 January 1971, p. 6, 10 April 1975, p. 11.

72. "1976-1977 Annual Report," Oklahoma State University Residence Halls Association, May 1977, pp. 1-2, Student Services Collection; *Daily O'Collegian*, 15 April 1969, p. 3.

73. Kent Sampson, "RHA Presidents," p. 1, listing of RHA presidents 1968 to 1987, Student Services Collection; *Daily O'Collegian*, 7 April 1976, p. 1, 8 October 1976, p. 1.

74. *Daily O'Collegian*, 31 October 1967, p. 2, 31 October 1968, p. 1; *1973 Redskin*, p. 368.

75. Donald Neal Cook, "A Comparative and Descriptive Study of Married Students at Oklahoma State University" (Doctor of Education dissertation, Oklahoma State University, 1970), pp. 117-119; Richard M. Williams, "Division of Married Student Housing and Maintenance, 1977-1978 " [Summer 1977], pp. 1, 4-5, Student Services Collection; *Daily O'Collegian*, 7 October 1967, p. 7.

76. *Daily O'Collegian*, 7 October 1967, p. 7, 23 June 1967, p. 1, 27 June 1967, p. 5; *1975-1976 Oklahoma State University Student-Faculty Directory*, p. 12.

77. Allen Reding, "25-Year Tape Presentation—Student Union," 14 February 1976, pp. 2-3, script for audio-visual presentation, and Winston Shindell, "Student Union," July 1977, pp. 1-3, in Student Services Collection.

78. Shindell, "Student Union," pp. 1-2.

79. *Daily O'Collegian*, 23 February 1966, pp. 1, 5, 6 May 1969, p. 1, 17 June 1969, p. 5, 10 September 1971, p. 1; "The Union: Introducing New Director, New Features," *Oklahoma State Alumnus Magazine*, vol. 10, no. 9 (December 1969), pp. 12-14.

80. "Celebration of 25 Years of Service to OSU," *Oklahoma State University Outreach*, vol. 17, no. 1 (January 1976), pp. 18-19; *Daily O'Collegian*, 7 February 1976, pp. 1, 5, 12 January 1976, p. 1, 13 February 1976, p. 6.

81. *Daily O'Collegian*, 8 January 1977, p. 4, 20 January 1977, p. 1.

82. Abe L. Hesser to Norman F. Moore, 22 June 1970, Student Services Collection.

83. *Daily O'Collegian*, 8 May 1970, p. 6, 19 June 1970, p. 3, 23 October 1971, p. 2, 28 January 1977, p. 5.

84. "New Student Health Center," *Oklahoma State Alumnus Magazine*, vol. 14, no. 6 (June-July 1973), p. 12; "Ground Breaking for Health Center," *Oklahoma State University Outreach*, vol. 15, no. 9 (December 1974), p. 14; *Daily O'Collegian*, 9 November 1971, p. 1, 8 June 1976, p. 1, 30 August 1976, p. 7.

85. *Daily O'Collegian*, 8 June 1976, p. 1, 9 June 1972, p. 5, 22 June 1976, p. 6.

86. *Daily O'Collegian*, 27 June 1969, p. 4, 22 June 1976, p. 6.

87. *Daily O'Collegian*, 4 December 1971, p. 7, 13 December 1971, p. 4.

88. *Daily O'Collegian*, 13 December 1971, p. 4.

89. "Colvin Physical Education Center Semi-Annual Report," July 1969, p. 1, and "Colvin Physical Education Center, 1977-1978," July 1977, pp. 1-3, in Student Services Collection.

90. Mary Frye, "The Development of Leisure Services/Campus Recreation," 10 February 1986, p. 6, unpublished manuscript, Student Services Collection; *Daily O'Collegian*, 20 November 1974, p. 6, 16 April 1976, p. 8.

91. "Albin P. Warner, Head of HPER Department, Dies," *Oklahoma State Alumnus Magazine*, vol. 14, no. 8 (November 1973), p. 26; Frye, "The Development of Leisure Services/Campus Recreation," pp. 1-2; *Daily O'Collegian*, 2 July 1974, p. 9.

92. Frye, "The Development of Leisure Services/Campus Recreation," pp. 2-5; *Daily O'Collegian*, 13 April 1974, p. 5, 20 April 1973, p. 3, 20 September 1973, p. 7, 14 September 1974, p. 4, 4 September 1973, p. 9, 6 November 1975, p. 11; "Schelsky is NIA President-Elect," *Oklahoma State Alumnus Magazine*, vol. 14, no. 5 (May 1973), p. 11.

93. Frye, "The Development of Leisure Services/Campus Recreation," pp. 2-3; *Daily O'Collegian*, 6 November 1975, p. 11, 14 September 1974, p. 4.

94. *Daily O'Collegian*, 13 April 1972, p. 2, 21 April 1972, pp. 1, 5, 14 July 1972, p. 1, 24 April 1973, p. 11, 18 November 1965, p. 2, 30 October 1973, pp. 1, 4; Robert G. Schmalfeld to Pat Hofler, 13 May 1975, Student Services Collection.

95. "Kappa Delta's Celebrate 50th Anniversary," *Oklahoma State Alumnus Magazine*, vol. 10, no. 5 (May 1969), p. 31; "Sorority's Gift Keeps Time for Campus," *Oklahoma State Alumnus Magazine*, vol. 11, no. 6 (September-October 1970), p. 27; "Chi Omega's Give Clock to Campus," *Oklahoma State Alumnus Magazine*, vol. 11, no. 3 (March 1970), p. 19; *1967 Redskin*, p. 352; *1970 Redskin*, p. 429; *1973 Redskin*, p. 275; *1974 Redskin*, pp. 274, 348; *Daily O'Collegian*, 9 February 1967, p. 11, 5 March 1970, p. 1, 1 April 1971, p. 7, 15 October 1971, p. 7; *Stillwater NewsPress*, 19 August 1970, p. 7.

96. *Daily O'Collegian*, 8 September 1973, p. 2.

97. *1966 Redskin*, p. 336; *1967 Redskin*, p. 372; *1968 Redskin*, p. 298; *Daily O'Collegian*, 24 September 1965, p. 3, 30 September 1971, p. 7, 7 November 1967, p. 9; "Office of the Associate Dean of Student Affairs, Ten Year Summary, 1965-1975," May 1975, pp. 1-2, Student Services Collection.

98. "Office of the Associate Dean of Student Affairs, Ten Year Summary, 1965-1975," p. 2, Student Services Collection; *1966 Redskin*, p. 372; *1967 Redskin*, p. 382; *1968 Redskin*, p. 372; *Daily O'Collegian*, 21 September 1965, p. 8, 21 October 1970, p. 3, 21 November 1967, p. 7, 17 April 1970, p. 3, 2 May 1988, p. 9.

99. *Daily O'Collegian*, 2 February 1973, p. 8, 2 May 1988, p. 9.

100. *1966 Redskin*, p. 303; *1970 Redskin*, pp. 288-300; *1972 Redskin*, p. 263.

101. "New Sorority Chapter is Chartered," *Oklahoma State Alumnus Magazine*, vol. 12, no. 6 (June-July 1971), p. 27; *1972 Redskin*, p. 248; *1974 Redskin*, p. 282; *Daily O'Collegian*, 13 May 1971, p. 1, 3 November 1973, p. 2, 1 March 1974, p. 3.

102. *1976-1977 Oklahoma State University Student-Faculty Directory*, p. 178.

103. *Daily O'Collegian*, 14 July 1970, p. 6, 20 April 1976, p. 1, 29 April 1976, p. 3.

104. *1975 Redskin*, p. 242; "Zelma Patchin Retires After 24 Years on OSU Faculty," *Oklahoma State Alumnus Magazine*, vol. 16, no. 6 (June-July 1975), p. 22; *Daily O'Collegian*, 21 April 1966, p. 8.

105. *1975 Redskin*, p. 242.

106. *Daily O'Collegian*, 12 November 1963, p. 1.

107. *1970 Redskin*, p. 471; *1975 Redskin*, p. 96; *Daily O'Collegian*, 24 February 1972, p. 7, 19 December 1967, p. 1, 10 November 1972, p. 1, 14 November 1972, p. 1, 11 November 1972, p. 1, 3 March 1973, p. 1.

108. *Daily O'Collegian*, 11 November 1976, p. 6.

109. Abe L. Hesser to Robert B. Kamm, 14 August 1969, and "AWS Mom's Day" [Spring 1968], campus flyer, p. 1, in Student Services Collection; *1976 Redskin*, p. 27; *Daily O'Collegian*, 9 March 1965, p. 8, 21 April 1967, p. 1, 30 August 1976, p. 1,10 March 1977, p. 6, 30 August 1976, p. 2, 6 October 1972, p. 1, 21 November 1972, p. 4, 4 October 1975, p. 1.

110. *1975 Redskin*, p. 283; *Daily O'Collegian*, 15 November 1973, p. 1.

111. "Chartered Organizations," Department of Student Activities, 10 March 1967, pp. 1-12, Weldon Barnes Collection; *Daily O'Collegian*, 21 September 1954, p. 8.

112. "1967-1968 Chartered Organizations," Department of Student Activities, May 1968, p. 7, Student Services Collection; *1974-1975 Oklahoma State University Student Handbook*, p. 44; *Daily O'Collegian*, 2 February 1968, p. 1, 9 February 1968, p. 1, 12 February 1974, p. 12, 15 February 1968, p. 1.

113. "OSU's Black Heritage Week," *Oklahoma State Alumnus Magazine*, vol. 10, no. 4 (April 1969), pp. 42-43.

114. "Student Organizations, Constitution Changes, or Name Changes, 1972-1973," Department of Student Activities, June 1973, Appendix 3, and Donald N. Brown, "An Emerging Native American Studies Program at Oklahoma State University," April 1973, paper presented at 32nd Annual Meeting, Society for Applied Anthropology, Tucson, Arizona, pp. 1, 3-4, in Student Services Collection; *Daily O'Collegian*, 27 September 1972, p. 11, 30 September 1972, p. 8.

115. Jo F. Dorris, "Ittanaha American Indian Club," 29 February 1972, p. 1, Student Services Collection; *Daily O'Collegian*, 9 March 1972, pp. 1, 12.

116. *Daily O'Collegian*, 9 March 1972, p. 12.

117. Dorris, "Ittanaha American Indian Club," p. 1; *Daily O'Collegian*, 10 April 1973, p. 15, 4 April 1974, p. 7.

118. Brown, p. 4.

119. *Daily O'Collegian*, 30 November 1976, p. 7, 30 March 1977, p. 10.

120. *Daily O'Collegian*, 30 March 1977, p. 10.

121. "Concern for Handicapped Students," *Oklahoma State Alumnus Magazine*, vol. 9, no. 8 (November 1968), p. 14; Patrick M. Murphy, "Handicapped Students At Oklahoma State," *Handicapped Student Handbook* (Stillwater: Oklahoma State University, August 1982), p. 3; *Daily O'Collegian*, 18 October 1968, p. 2.

122. Minutes, Handicapped Student Organization, 3 September 1980, pp. 1-2, and Patrick M. Murphy, "Handicapped Student Organization Membership," November 1979, pp. 1-2, Student Services Collection; *Daily O'Collegian*, 18 October 1968, p. 2, 2 September 1980, p. 1.

123. Robert B. Kamm to Faculty and Staff, 28 November 1966, Board of Regents Files, Special Collection, Edmon Low Library; *Daily O'Collegian*, 5 September 1975, p. 9, 5 May 1974, p. 2, 6 May 1972, p. 8, 6 February 1973, p. 1; *1975 Redskin*, pp. 438-439.

124. Roger Ranch Klock, "A Profile Analysis of Reader Interest in the Daily O'Collegian" (Master of Science thesis, Oklahoma State University, 1975), p. 33.

125. *1975 Redskin*, p. 438; *Daily O'Collegian*, 21 April 1972, pp. 1, 5, 26 January 1974, p. 1; "Changing Mode of Transportation," *Oklahoma State Alumnus Magazine*, vol. 13, no. 1 (January 1972), p. 3.

126. *Daily O'Collegian*, 8 October 1971, p. 2.

127. *Daily O'Collegian*, 14 September 1968, p. 7.

128. Ralph Hamilton, "Lawrence Boger Is Named OSU President," *Oklahoma State University Outreach*, vol. 18, no. 3 (June-July 1977), pp. 3-4.

# 10 Events Too Recent To Be History

In 1985 Oklahoma State University reached the midpoint of the institution's Centennial Decade. At age 95, the university was still a relative youngster among the nation's 3,300 colleges and universities. Of this number, a few over two thousand were either four-year colleges or universities, many sharing similar priorities, problems, and missions.

In reality colleges and universities had become complex big businesses, employing thousands of people, costing billions of dollars, and educating millions—over twelve million in 1985 alone. They had generally grown in complexity because their product was still in demand. Between 1978 and 1985 the public's belief that a college education was "very important" had nearly doubled, from 36 percent to 64 percent.

The largest challenges for college and university presidents were finances, maintaining student enrollment, student retention, and increasing the quality of undergraduate academic programs. The word "quality" became a catchword among academic-types, and, in addition to strengthening courses, people using the word "quality" usually had several other goals in mind. Representing problems with a nationwide theme, institutions wrestled with the internal issues of improving by "restoring the liberal arts to a more central place in the curriculum, raising entrance requirements as well as standards for promotion and graduation, and amid fresh concerns, finding a way to do all of those things without closing the doors to capable but underprepared students, including members of minority groups."

At least part of the push to resolve these problems tied to a group of new forces which were causing external pressures. Federal and state governments, as well as taxpaying parents of students, were demanding evidence that universities and colleges were worth what they cost. In 1985 state governments were paying roughly one-third of the $100 billion being spent on higher education. Students living on campus were handing over an average of more than $5,300 a year to public four-year institutions for room, board, tuition, and other essential expenses. Additional pressure came with demands for more public accountability, competition among institutions for students and dollars, and new possibilities for partnerships with industry and government. Further, in the background there was a perpetual anxiety that President Ronald Reagan's drive to manage the national debt and his tax reform efforts would severely penalize campuses. Top university administrators would find little consolation in the fact that these same demands for accountability and proof of excellence had also seized the spotlight in many foreign countries.[1]

Despite Oklahoma State's rightful claim of being a "special place," it was still a university with many characteristics more similar than different when compared with other land-grant and multipurpose universities. Because of this it was not immune to the ups and downs of national trends. If anything, problems seemed to be magnified due to Oklahoma's historically turbulent connections between government, politics, and taxes and their relationship to education. From the late 1970s to the late 1980s, Oklahoma State was asked to evaluate, change, or defend its admissions criteria; retention rates, especially for minority students; policies on tuition and fees; and accounting for state and privately given money. Internally, not unlike other institutions, general education requirements and student attrition received priority attention. The number of classes taught by teachers with a rank of assistant professor or higher declined, while those taught by part-time faculty increased over 40 percent.[2] Despite increases in funding between 1977 and 1983 Oklahoma continued to have the "most poorly funded system of higher education in America."[3] In combination, these variables came together as a scenario for the times which perhaps required that OSU do more, get better, and do both with less.

On November 16, 1982, the state of Oklahoma celebrated its seventy-fifth anniversary, culminating a year of Diamond Jubilee events. Just over the horizon was a period of economic disaster for the proud state. Even the economists could not fully appreciate the magnitude of the impact of a disastrous simultaneous plunge in the oil and agricultural markets. Few citizens of Oklahoma were left untouched. As when a stone is thrown into a pond, the ripples of the economic downturn moved outward, and more and more businesses and jobs were lost. The sad reality for Oklahoma's higher education was that the earlier economic improvements of the late 1970s and early 1980s disappeared. Subsequently the financial problems for Oklahoma State University became staggering.

The magnitude of the severe economic downturn then became compounded. To understand fully the observer must consider that with few rare exceptions the lack of money to educate the state's citizenry adequately had really accrued through decades of underfunding. Oklahoma has historically resisted coming to grips with the true costs of higher education.[4] One result was that through much of the 1980s independent and government-appointed higher education commissions, study groups, administrators, and students joined together to try to sell state leaders on the idea that "excellent universities are essential to the future of all of Oklahoma."[5]

Although money does not in itself assure success, it is nearly impossible to be successful in higher education, or in any complex venture, without a good financial base. It logically follows that during a time of especially scarce resources, including several consecutive years of budget reductions, that a mark of an excellent administrator includes managing the institution with considerably more ingenuity and efficiency than is usually required and that is generally recognized. During this difficult period, a time when remaining optimistic and forward-looking was particularly essential, Lawrence L. Boger carried the burdens of the presidency of the Oklahoma State University. President Boger described

President Lawrence L. Boger enjoys a few minutes with students. Although Dr. Boger had to contend with the problems associated with Oklahoma's failing economy, he approached his job with optimism and called for growth and development in spite of the odds.

himself as an optimist, planner, and a determined man with an ability for administering budgets and appropriating needs.[6] Obviously unable to appreciate the events of the next years fully, in one of Dr. Boger's earliest public statements he personified his qualities to persist in difficulty with: "I like to see things happen. I have no ambition to preside over a dead, dying or stagnant institution or set of programs anywhere. I'm a firm believer that even in tough times there can be growth and development of a certain kind . . . . The tougher the times, the more selective you have to be, but it's still not impossible."[7]

President Boger assumed his duties as OSU's chief executive on June 15 and was officially installed as OSU's president at summer commencement exercises six weeks later on July 28, 1977. The summer of 1987 marked a decade of continuous service for the institution's president, yet perhaps fittingly, brought little fanfare since Dr. Boger's traits also included a preference for hard work, generally out of the limelight. After ten years he had shown aplomb. He had been required to call upon all of his self-described personal abilities to stretch a budget, to plan, and, as importantly as anything else, to be selective in facilitating a positive response to changing institutional needs.[8] History will perhaps document the era as a period where emphasis was "placed on maintenance rather than building."[9] It was also another time when one more OSU president would say, "OSU's biggest problem is inadequate financial resources."[10]

But under any circumstances, good or bad, OSU's presidency was a huge job. Because the position is clouded under the veil called education—and a university president is first and foremost viewed as an educator—in the private sector this position would equate to a niche akin to a top corporate executive. Located like a city within another city of 40,000 residents, OSU "maintained" a student enrollment of about 20,000 on its Stillwater campus, a teaching staff of over 1,000, and 1,500 additional employees in other positions. By 1985 Dr. Boger's responsibilities included managing an annual budget of over $200 million, including $16 million in tuition and fees paid by students and $24 million returned to students by way of financial aid programs. Oklahoma State and its president managed 22,000 acres of land.[11]

Continuing the analogy of being a city, OSU's top executive indicated: "We have our own roads, our own sewers, a motor pool and aviation equipment. We're in the laundry business and the fire protection business . . . ."[12] By 1987 OSU was also in the satellite telecommunications business and the telephone business. Meantime the institution continued in the entertainment arena, as illustrated by OSU's ranking among the top ten in NCAA Division I athletic programs' overall rankings. From necessity Oklahoma State was also the operator of a state of the art computer network.[13] In the 1980s the full force of the high technology information age struck campus. Staying abreast of the rapid changes taxed both human and fiscal resources.

However, old attributes, still basic to a progressive city, had to be continued. Renting functional rooms and apartments, providing thousands of meals each day, and maintaining a reasonable study and work environment represented basics. The campus-city maintained a professional security department administered by director of OSU Security Everett H. Eaton. Laws were enacted and appeared in OSU's "Policies and Procedures Letters" or, in the case of students, the "Statement of Student Rights and Responsibilities." Judicial "due process" was afforded through a series of committees and, for students, the Student Conduct Office. Physicians, counselors, psychologists, and experts on nutrition and exercise provided for the physical and mental health of residents. The bursar's office, directed by C. David Curtis, would accept a credit card for paying bills, and in combination with the Department of Financial Aid, exhibited many features of a modern bank. In the 1980s the "city" of OSU provided services as good or better than many other cities. But these were not frills, simply an effort to provide an environment where learning is enhanced.

In the long run the benefactor of all of the work and complexity that makes a university successful is the world's community of nations. In

SPECIAL COLLECTIONS, OSU LIBRARY

This is the "city"—Oklahoma State University. By the institution's centennial decade of the 1980s, the university was providing services that assured an environment where learning was enhanced.

the short run, the people who are called students—the individuals who come to a university to study, read, write, and do research, as well as socialize—also gain, benefit, and leave, hopefully to contribute to larger progress. One symbol of the experience and knowledge achieved at a university is the receiving of a degree. Shortly after Dr. Boger became OSU's president, the institution passed the 100,000 mark in graduates receiving a bachelor's, master's, doctorate, professional, or associate's degree. In the spring of 1987 alone 3,163 students declared their candidacy for graduation.

Another measure which gauges a university's contribution to the progress of society is whether earlier graduates encourage their children to return to their alma mater. Edward W. Means apparently never received a degree, but he did attend Oklahoma A. and M. in 1898. Eighty-five years later James Means Jr. was enrolled in business management as a fourth generation student from his family. His dad, James Sr. graduated with a bachelor's degree in 1962.[14] "I have always wanted to come here . . . ," said James Jr. "Heck, I was raised OSU this and OSU that."[15]

The 1983 fourth generation student likely thought differently than his dad and certainly had different ambitions and beliefs than his grandfather Frank Means, a 1925 Depression-era student. In fact and generally, the students of the late 1970s and 1980s were very different than their more socially-conscious predecessors of ten years earlier, those students who were so central to widespread socio-political protests and upheaval. The students during President Boger's tenure had been described as quiescent and conservative. Almost 60 percent of the traditional eighteen to twenty-four year old college age population had voted for President Reagan. The majority were not yet born or were very young in 1967. Thurgood Marshall's appointment as the first black on the United States Supreme Court, the Beatles' album release of "Sgt. Pepper's Lonely Hearts Club Band," the assassinations of Martin Luther King Jr., John F. Kennedy, and Robert F. Kennedy, the anti-war protests and slain students at Kent State, as well as the Watergate hearings, were events that the average freshman remembered little or nothing about.[16]

Values and attitudes had swung dramatically to a new direction. The students of the 1980s were individualistic and oriented to career, practicality, and economic success as opposed to interests in liberal causes, ideas, and societal injustices.[17] Charles K. Edgley, a professor in the OSU sociology department, summarized his observations: "The message of the 80s is if you can't save society, save yourself. It's dangerous to get involved." Edgley continued: "We are living in a time in which class consciousness is evident and stronger than ever, and money is the ultimate in individualistic character."[18] Another commentary suggested to college students that "success was the idol of the 80s."[19] From his professorial perspective Edgley risked a comparison. His insightful reflections included: "I would like to bring back the 60s without the bombs and physical hurt that went with it . . . . Today, I have to go to extraordinary lengths to make students really learn . . . . In the 60s, students were already tuned in to education and issues."[20]

While true that the 1980s university students were different, they should not be indicted for their behavior. Larger world problems had not been solved and probably had grown worse. By 1979 students had grown pessimistic, and they worried about crime and violence, future energy scarcities, environmental pollution, hunger, poverty, and the nation's economy.[21] A 1985 *Redskin* essay graphically portrayed what it was like to be a child of the nuclear age. When nuclear stockpiles had grown to the equivalent of four and one-half tons of TNT for every individual on the planet, student writer Carmen Vee suggested: "It's ironic that all of the planning, living and growing can be destroyed by an irrational government or a simple miscalculation." OSU senior Dave Watkins represented an entire generation of young people when he offered that he did not consciously think about a nuclear disaster. "Even if I thought about it, there's nothing I can do. Besides, if there was a war, I wouldn't want to live," Watkins commented.[22]

As a result of these and other issues, including intense competition for grades and credentials to assure a well-paid career after graduation, a generation was spawned which was deeply troubled about the state of the nation but quite optimistic about achieving personal goals and expectations. Compared to their counterparts of the 1960s, students were quieter, less conspicuous in dress and behavior, and less given to excesses. Although nine out of ten freshmen in 1979 believed that during the next five years things would get worse for the nation, they thought that their own lives would improve. As a further consequence, volunteerism and altruism—the quality to show concern for the welfare of others—lessened.

By 1985 all of these factors were dramatically portrayed in the student's orientation toward "pre-professional" careers, where "marketable" skills were sought in their selection of courses and less tolerance was shown for classes where students were asked to simply "learn to love learning." The most sought-after careers by the nation's 1985 freshmen were: business executive (11.9 percent); engineer (10.4 percent); computer programmer or analyst (6.1 percent); accountant or actuary (6.0 percent); and lawyer or judge (4.1 percent). Least popular careers were: minister or priest and school counselor (both 0.2 percent); homemaker (0.1 percent); statistician (0.1 percent); and school principal or superintendent (0.0 percent).[23]

Adding to the issues for students was the widely held feeling that higher education had become more a test of persistence in one's ability

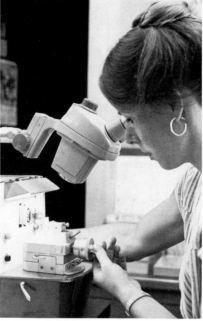

By the 1980s, college students were more oriented toward career and future goals. With success the idol of the times it was perhaps not surprising that students worked hard not only on their curriculum but the extracurriculum as well.

to survive a large bureaucracy. OSU student Bon Bick Bennett complained: "It seems the least of anyone's worries is whether he truly understands what is being taught, and whether he can apply it, but rather the emphasis is on passing the system, and obtaining a degree."[24] A part of this ferment could be laid at the feet of the institutions which were "still reexamining some of the dramatic changes that were made in the 1960s and 1970s—a time when enrollments were exploding and, it is widely acknowledged, standards were sagging."[25] Another factor was the changing demographics among students. A new kind of teaching was being demanded. Across the United States in 1985, 43 percent of all students were twenty-five years old or older, bringing to the classroom maturity and experiences from work and life that were unprecedented. Forty-five percent attended part-time classes while continuing in careers and parenting roles. Still in 1985, nearly half of all students lived within fifty miles of the institutions in which they had enrolled. This new kind of student body required new services and adjustments.[26]

Oklahoma State University also had to respond to this national phenomenon of the changing characteristics of students. At OSU in 1982 the fastest growing group of students were aged thirty to thirty-nine. Between 1976 and 1981 undergraduate enrollees in the eighteen- and nineteen-year-old categories dropped 13 percent. A survey of OSU returning students showed that the majority were women with two years of earlier college credit. These female returnees primarily lived in Stillwater, and most were raising children as well as taking classes. By 1987 nearly four out of ten OSU undergraduate students were taking more than the traditional four years to complete their degree. Nearly 10 percent of the students were internationals, many of these the very best and brightest students that ninety-two different countries from around the world could send to the U.S. to secure an education. The highest number of OSU degrees were being granted in management, marketing, accounting, journalism, and electrical engineering.[27] In general, it was clear that by 1986 "the age of the student body is increasing; there is a decreasing percentage of our students under twenty-two and an increasing percentage of them over twenty-two."[28]

Through the decade of Dr. Boger's presidency, adjustments were made to attract and respond to this changing group of learners. Participation in the University Center at Tulsa (UCT), a consortium program to bring OSU degree programs to adult learners in an urban setting, served as just one example. Other issues, in which some influence could be brought or issues for which the institution had direct responsibility, were continuing and complex in their nature. Some of these were the hiring of minority faculty, replacing those teachers who were finding more attractive opportunities elsewhere, halting the trend of decreas-

In the long run, the benefactor of all of the work and complexity that makes a university successful is the world's community of nations. By the early 1980s, ten percent of OSU's students had come to study from over seventy different nations.

ing student enrollment, improving academic assistance services, and preserving, maintaining, and changing campus facilities for current and future uses. Activities of the president and other key administrators that were no less important, but harder to assess, were coping with employee morale problems. These were in part caused by few salary increases; deep cuts in maintenance budgets, whereby available basics such as telephones, paper, and professional travel became scarce; and reductions in the general work force, leaving behind for those who remained even more responsibility. These were not the best of years. Nor were they the worst. Each segment of the campus community seemed to find their own ways to adjust and await better days.

Generally the students, as had every generation before them, worked to both graduate and fund at least a part of their education. As time was available they adjusted, coped, relaxed, and reduced their problems through participating in a multitude of time-tested and "faddish" diversions. As has always been the case with traditionally-aged undergraduates, some of their behavior was harmful, dishonorable, or self-defeating. Terms such as bulimia and anorexia, both forms of eating disorders, became a part of common vocabulary. Cheating, veiled in modern terminology such as academic integrity or dishonesty, was a national issue. At OSU a 1978 study reported widespread campus cheating. Freshmen and sophomores, perhaps because of the self-imposed pressures for high grades, learned to cheat early, believed that cheating was inevitable, and observed that those that did not cheat were in the minority. "Hackers," individuals who steal and use long-distance telephone codes, by 1987 were costing communications companies a half billion dollars a year. OSU had more than a few "hackers" among its numbers.[29]

In 1986 Oklahoma State University received the dubious honor of being named the number one party college among Big Eight institutions and received the overall rank of nineteenth in the nation. Whether *Playboy* magazine's subjective ranking was justified was mere speculation. Nonetheless, partying and alcohol consumption continued as an important way for students to socialize. In 1983 Oklahoma's drinking age was raised to twenty-one, thereby joining a national trend. Despite the law change the abuse of alcohol remained the major drug problem of young people. The concern was not reduced by the knowledge that alcohol consumption rates continued out-of-control in collegiate environments throughout the United States.

Yet, there were some positive signs. National Greek organizations had adopted "dry rush" policies, and OSU had followed suit. Campuses endorsed rules encouraging "moderation" and "compliance with applicable laws." Student organizations were urged to provide nonalcoholic alternatives at social functions. Recipes for nonalcoholic drinks became widely available. Boost Alcohol Consciousness Concerning the Health of University Students (BACCHUS), a national group that promoted responsibility in drinking, had an active chapter at OSU by 1981, the first such chapter in the state. Annually BACCHUS, the Panhellenic Council, the Interfraternity Council, the Residence Halls Association, and the Student Government Association banned together to sponsor participation in "National Collegiate Alcohol Awareness Week." In 1985 this week long educational activity won a national award from the National Association of Student Personnel Administrators as an exemplary program. Still further to the positive side, Stillwater's police agencies were reporting reduced use of illegal street drugs as compared to earlier years.[30]

By 1986 the infamous streaker's night had died. Public discussion occurred in the same year about whether Washington Street, the host area to the former pre-spring break ritual, was itself dead. More enduring was the Hideaway, first opened in 1963 by Richard Dermer and Mike Quirk; the popular student hangout and pizzeria sold over one thousand pizzas on a given Saturday night. Eskimo Joe's, with its logo and apparel growing in recognition far beyond the borders of Oklahoma, continued as a popular student haunt. By Eskimo Joe's tenth birthday in 1985, the bar had sold over 100,000 T-shirts. For those who preferred eating to drinking as a social activity, Stillwater offered The Ancestor, Bobo's Mexican Restaurante, and The Late Show, to represent only a few of the more enduring restaurants to which students took parents and dates. During the late 1970s and early 1980s fast food restaurants had opened in a flurry, and by 1980 there were thirteen pizza restaurants alone. For sweets, frozen yogurt became popular. For clothes, Bates Bros. downtown and Sam Bates' Campus Shop remained popular with students after more than forty years.[31]

For most students a pair of tennis shoes, jeans, and a T-shirt, imprinted with a logo, slogan, or message, was everyday campus attire.[32] Freshmen of 1985 were admonished to avoid looking their role by buying a backpack, to be "carried over one shoulder, never both shoulders unless bicycling is the preferred mode of transportation."[33] This was sound advice since for reasons of cost, convenience, and physical health, bicycles and roller skates gained in popularity. For that matter the general physical fitness explosion reached campus, and joggers and serious runners joined many others doing aerobics, weight training, swimming, and other activities to bring the numbers of people interested in regular exercise into the thousands. Mechanical bull riding, "frisbee golf," and "hacky sack" were popular among those inclined toward more moderate activity. For health and general cleanliness reasons, smokeless tobacco was banned from campus in 1986.[34]

A review of the students' interests during the era would be incomplete without mentioning games and television programs. By 1982 electronic video games were a $5 billion business in the United States. The games, befitting the computer age, had gradually replaced foosball and manual pinball in popularity with each new generation of increasingly complex and sophisticated mini-computers. In board games Trivial Pursuit and Stillwater-born Pente, originated by OSU student Gary Gabrel, kept students from their studies by the hours. Additional diversions from the books were lost to the nighttime soap operas "Dallas" and "Knots Landing." During the daytime, fans gathered around big-screen television sets in the residence hall cafeterias to watch unending sagas on "All My Children" or "One Life to Live." The most avid student "soap" fans went so far as to arrange their class schedules carefully thus assuring no conflicts with their favorite programs. "M.A.S.H." ended in 1983, to the disappointment of many students, but Bennett Hall residents marked the occasion with a "Last M.A.S.H. Bash" party. Another visual entertainment, the *Rocky Horror Picture Show*, recycled through campus with each Halloween, resulted in student participation in the film, audiences in costumes, and "weird" behavior.[35]

A driving force of student social behavior for the entire twentieth century has involved their relationships with one another, including dating, love, sex, and simply friendships. In the 1980s their relationships took many twists, some humorous, others which were flatly scary. Perhaps contributing to the change was the liberalized standards of everyday television and motion pictures. In the fifties and sixties young people

In 1982, OSU students flocked to Allie Reynolds Stadium not to watch a baseball game but to participate in the "Cowboy Kiss Off." Setting a *Guinness* record for numbers of participants engaged in a three-minute kiss, most agreed any resulting chapped lips were certainly worth it!

viewed shows in which father knew best, girls took second place to football, and married couples slept in separate beds. By 1980 all of that had changed. The new sex appeal market brought in a pattern of raising money for charitable causes by renting a student as a bed tucker, massage giver, goodnight kisser, or slave—in short, to do nearly any bidding. Dancing, including the early eighties popular disco and country styles, remained widely appealing but punk rock, something described by some as decadent, rose in popularity too. In 1982, 1,460 couples filled OSU's Reynold's Stadium to attempt to set a new kissing record for the *Guinness Book of World Records.*[36]

In the same year that the *Guinness* record was set, over two hundred OSU coeds signed up to become a prospective model for *Playboy* magazine, far exceeding *Playboy's* expectation. A degree of equity among sexes was exhibited when 400 slightly inebriated women packed a Washington Street nightclub to watch a male striptease show in 1984. Students generally believed cohabitation between a male and female was permissible, so long as no children were involved. These were also days of a push for "gay rights"; by 1981, 80 percent of the nation's universities recognized at least one homosexual student organization. It was a time of casual views about sex, relationships, and love. Some even called the time a sexual revolution. The revolution also spawned a June 1982 sexual harassment policy at OSU, educational programs on what constituted date rape, and support networks for people who were sexually assaulted. In the paradoxes of their relationships the students seemed to be proving themselves, testing ideas, values and concepts, experimenting, and perhaps even wanting to find their own definition of love.[37]

The scene changed somewhat from 1984 to 1988. Among people under twenty-five years of age, aside from the common cold, the most common infectious diseases in the United States were sexually transmitted. The advent of Acquired Immune Deficiency Syndrome, or AIDS, dramatically added impetus to the need to change the relationship scene, although for many observers this happened all too slowly. AIDS was a killer, and there was still much to learn about it. Campus AIDS or infectious disease guidelines came into existence nationwide; and at OSU this happened in the fall of 1986. The sexual revolution had slowed partially because of AIDS. Some students grew more cautious about casual intimacy.[38] The trend began to return to "long-term dating relationships and the age old idea of marriage."[39] AIDS had caused a panic among the nation's citizens and a medical epidemic. The 1987 Oklahoma Legislature enacted a law mandating AIDS education in the state's public schools. The Surgeon General of the United States advocated "safe sex." By the early spring of 1987 college newspapers, including the *Daily O'Collegian*, started accepting condom advertisements for publication. The following fall OSU planned its first campus-wide AIDS education week.[40]

Paralleling the dramatic changes in student relationships were the political and world events that each generation must react to anew. In 1979 the campus responded to the Iranian hostage crisis, the debate over the Equal Rights Amendment, and the Oklahoma Black Fox nuclear facility. After the Soviet Union invaded Afghanistan the following year, the United States boycotted the summer Olympics in Moscow. By 1985 aid to the Contra forces in Nicaragua was growing as a topic of debate. Two years later the Iranian-Contra arms-for-prisoners scheme was publicly aired; as Congress probed for illegalities, millions watched on television. Again in 1985 "Live Aid," a monumental effort to combat world hunger, was held. Also, Michael Jackson and Lionel Richie formed USA for Africa and produced the famine relief record, "We Are The World." The world and nation were stunned and thrown into grief by the explosion of the space shuttle *Challenger* in 1986. Throughout the 1980s students at OSU and elsewhere pushed for institutional divestment of investments in South Africa because of its policies of apartheid. Like the students of the 1960s, and despite the generalizations about them as a group, some students still became politically and socially active when an issue stirred deep emotions.[41]

But through these years students rarely vented their emotions. Instead, they generally enjoyed the campus environment and went about the business of securing an education. A January 1985 poll of a representative sample of OSU students, which used the American College

Shades of the 1960s protest era reappeared on the OSU campus in the late 1970s. Now rather than the war in Vietnam or civil rights, students debated numerous issues including political prisoners and the Equal Rights Amendment. This group of students protested the establishment of the Black Fox nuclear facility.

Testing (ACT) Student Opinion Survey, compared the respondents' viewpoints with college and university enrollees from across the nation. Oklahoma State's students generally were more satisfied with the university and the faculty's attitude toward them than their counterparts nationally. The mix of undergraduate and graduate students felt that OSU's greatest strengths were the variety of course offerings and available majors to select from, the institution's solid academic reputation, and the quality of the faculty and staff on campus. The opinion survey taken in preparation for a North Central Association reaccreditation review revealed that OSU students were not satisfied with the amount of financial aid, class size, academic advisement, and the total cost to attend the institution.[42]

With respect to the extracurriculum the ACT Opinion Survey showed that the students were appreciative, supportive, and "very satisfied with recreational facilities, the Student Union, opportunity to participate in student activities, athletic facilities, safety and security on campus, and other such university community services."[43] To some these findings were unexpected, perhaps even surprising. Between 1977 and 1985 no area within the whole university had changed as much as these. Although these transformations often occurred in a visible and distressing way, they were attempted with the hopes of improving economy, efficiency, and outcomes for a changing student body. Of course, most of these changes fell within the domain of the Office of the Vice President for Student Services.

At the time of the preparation for the North Central Association reaccreditation visit and through 1987, student services was still largely responsible for meeting the out-of-class needs of a diverse student body by providing a comprehensive system of co-curricular services. The thread that tied units together within student services was the concept of "student development." This was something of a national catchword for the 1980s among student personnel professionals. Student development had evolved into something of a theory and practitioner base for understanding student behavior. From this base of understanding, student services continued to strive to maintain an integral partnership in the institution's primary mission—the education of people.[44]

As Oklahoma State moved toward its centennial birthday, student services was one of five major administrative units, each headed by a vice president who reported directly to President Boger. As late as 1979 there were nine major student personnel units within student services, but eight years later only six would remain. Those units that evolved from this period of the most substantial organizational changes in the entire history of student services were: the University Counseling Services; Department of Financial Aid; Leisure Services; Residential Life Department; Student Health Services; and the Student Union. Lost through consolidation into the Residential Life Department were Single Student Housing, Married Student Housing and Student Services Maintenance, and University Food Services. The Division of Student Affairs was totally reorganized, and the name was lost to posterity. In the administrative reordering of the large division of six sub-units, all were headed by a director who reported to the vice president.[45]

By 1979 more than half of the money needed to construct some ninety major buildings at OSU had been raised through the selling of bonds. These various bond issues totaled $60 million. While constructing buildings based on the promise to repay the indebtedness through user fees was a good economic measure for taxpayers and legislators, the system could be a nightmare, particularly in bad financial times. Hit hardest are fee-paying students, their parents, and the administrators who are responsible for keeping the institution's promises to repay the bond buyers.[46]

The majority of these bond issues were used to provide students so-called "auxiliary" services, including the residence halls and family housing, the Colvin Center and Annex, the OSU Hospital and Clinic, and the Student Union. In 1985, 95 percent of the student services' budget of $27.5 million came from primarily student-user payments. The 1980s, that time at OSU when student enrollment leveled and part-time students increased, the state economy faired poorly, and energy and overhead costs soared. It would be a period remembered as an unhappy time of juggling budgets, careful forecasting, and increasing efficiency, sometimes by cutting people and facilities in student services. Those earlier years of keeping prices the lowest possible would come back to haunt administrators. Badly needed repairs, routine maintenance, and new equipment to help future students would all wait. Neither the students nor OSU, especially student services, had extra money to spend. The monumental efforts to pay the obligations of student services, whether they were repaying bonds, providing meals, or paying the salaries of a capable group of employees, went on behind the scenes. What the students saw was more likely reflected in their opinions in the North Central Association self-study report. What they hopefully really experienced was a "caring environment."[47]

On July 1, 1979, Vice President for Student Services Norman F. Moore left the position that he held since 1970 to take up a similar responsibility as vice chancellor for student services at the University of Missouri-Columbia. While a national search for Moore's replacement was conducted, Assistant Vice President Pat Hofler, the man who since the 1950s worked "with any student who comes in the door with a problem," served as interim vice president. When the vice presidential search ended, the first non-OSU alumnus to hold the position hit the campus running on January 7, 1980. Ronald S. Beer, a man with a vibrant per-

Ronald S. Beer (*right*), OSU's third vice president for student services, confers with Pat Hofler, the assistant vice president for student services. Both of these student services' administrators continually stressed the importance of addressing the unique needs of each student.

sonality and a love for students, was selected from 250 applicants. Holding the Ph.D. from Kent State University in Ohio, the new vice president left the position of vice chancellor for educational and student activities at the University of Nebraska-Omaha to come to Oklahoma State.[48] Dr. Beer constantly stressed: "Every student is a unique person, each with individual needs, and they need to be respected in that manner."[49] The vice president also affirmed: "We don't want to give students the run-around . . . we don't want students to think they are being forced through a bureaucratic structure."[50]

In just a few years Vice President Beer had compiled an unmatched record of giving to others, both on campus and in Stillwater. Aside from professional activities with the National Association of Student Personnel Administrators, Dr. Beer was active in the Boy Scouts of America and chaired the Stillwater Task Force on Substance Abuse, a committee of city and campus leaders to study and recommend measures for a counter assault on the use and misuse of alcohol and other drugs. In another year he served as board president of both the Stillwater YMCA and Chamber of Commerce, substantial positions even when held one at a time.[51]

OSU students quickly grew to admire him. In 1981 the Student Government Association awarded Vice President Beer the annual Frank E. McFarland Award for being OSU's "outstanding administrator who performed above and beyond the call of duty."[52] Very special student recognition followed in 1987 when OSU's Mortar Board chapter presented him an honorary membership. The action was only the eighth honorary membership awarded since the chapter's founding in 1930. Le Ann Page, Mortar Board president, reflected: "The nomination was our chapter's way of expressing our appreciation for his contribution to OSU and the Stillwater community . . . . Dr. Beer has been there for students at every turn."[53]

Knowing fully the longstanding prohibition against alcoholic beverages on campus the vice president, with tongue-in-cheek, would sometimes use as a mark of his administration "at least there's Beer on campus." In truth that was not one of his priorities. But there were other things to continue and plenty of problems to tackle. Programs coordinated in the vice president's office and carried out by all student services units continued. The fall 1987 Alpha orientation program was the fourteenth consecutive edition. The chairperson role for this massive undertaking annually rotated but in recent years was a responsibility of Nancy R. Childress and Sandra L. Bird, both assistants to the vice president.

President Robert B. Kamm's President's Leadership Council (PLC) continued to flourish through Dr. Boger's years and was a responsibility falling to Dr. Beer.[54] The prestigious President's Leadership Council celebrated two decades of longevity in 1987. Throughout, the organization still maintained its original purposes of providing scholarships and leadership education to about one hundred of the "top high school leader-scholars selected from graduating classes throughout the State of Oklahoma."[55] In 1986 over $70,000 was awarded the "centennial class of PLC'ers." Traditionally this group prided itself in being among the very best of Oklahoma's young scholar-leaders. Not surprisingly, many eventually moved to influential campus leadership positions. In time the President's Leadership Council became a springboard from which members became physicians, attorneys, career military officers, and politicians. Jan M. Carlson, coordinator of student activities, and Patrick M. Murphy, director of OSU's counseling center, among others, facilitated the PLC program through the period.[56]

More than either of his two predecessors, Vice President Beer's administrative style placed a premium on direct contact with student leaders. He would frequently hold weekly meetings with the top executives of the Student Government Association (SGA), Residence Halls Association (RHA), Off-Campus Student Association, ethnic minority student organizations, and leaders from Greek societies. A monthly meeting with the presidents of over twenty student governing bodies also filled a part of his busy schedule. In these meetings problems and plans were discussed, and communication was enhanced. Perhaps the most persistent troublesome issue among students was the matter of student activity fees—those special assessments paid by students to continue their extracurriculum. According to the 1985 North Central Association research on student opinion, campus-wide dissatisfaction with these charges was well above the national average.[57] "Most likely," the self-study reported, "students are not aware of the uses for the fees and simply respond negatively to any fee added to tuition."[58]

Among student leaders the amount of the allocation of student activity fee money to the intercollegiate athletic program and how and who decided how the money was generally distributed seemed to be general irritants. However, with students paying nearly $7 a credit hour for facility and activity enterprises, the total amount simply seemed too much. Difficulties continued despite efforts to make students aware of the purpose and importance of the fees. Not surprisingly students always had trouble understanding the relationship between facilities that they enjoy and wear out from heavy use and the fact that someone must pay for replacing them.[59]

Shortly after arriving at Oklahoma State University, Vice President Beer observed that problems existed in student services. Further, he gave the opinion "some of our services should be tied in with academics."[60] It would take some time to attend to these matters since many of them involved longstanding precedents and traditions and, even more difficult, capable people who had for many years worked hard in the service of OSU students. As in any large organization, territorial boundaries and differing personalities, with divergent points of view, complicated matters.

Merely because of professionalism and an "OK from the boss," the affiliations between student services and a variety of academically-related activities increased during this period. Martha L. Jordan orchestrated the teaching of ten or more semester sections of a course titled World of Work, a career development course for lower division students taught under the auspices of the Department of Applied Behavioral Studies in Education (ABSED). Leadership Development was taught within ABSED by Jan M. Carlson and Nora L. Pugh. The longstanding resident assistant training course, renamed after student assistants were retitled resident assistants, continued and was taught by B. Kent Sampson, Phyllis L. Schroeder, and other housing professionals. Elaine P. Burgess, coordinator of International Student Services, developed and taught a course, International Studies Seminar, in the College of Arts and Sciences. Howard Shipp and the Minority Programs and Services staff played a continuing role in Multi-Cultural Counseling, a graduate course for aspiring professional counselors. Through the Colleges of Arts and Sciences and Education, Lisa L. Grubbs offered an academic skills development course titled Survey of Study Habits and Attitudes.[61]

A longtime relationship between the College of Home Economics and University Food Services endured as dietetic internships were supervised, and food services staff taught. Most professionals in leisure sciences, located in the Colvin Center, taught subjects from activities to management of leisure programs. Every area of student services offered student personnel or counseling practicum or internship opportunities for graduate students. Rex T. Finnegan, Thomas M. Keys, Patrick M. Murphy, and Pete G. Coser, along with the vice president himself, represented only a few of those who held adjunct faculty appointments. These ties permitted supervising graduate students, serving on graduate student committees, and periodically teaching courses. In 1985 student services and ABSED combined financial resources to employ an individual to facilitate mutual development of the student personnel program. Marcia M. Dickman was the first appointee. Through the years, in addition to ABSED, working relationships with higher education, psychology, the marriage and family counseling program, and every academic college were either improved or developed.[62]

While moving student services to a closer partnership with academics primarily took time, other priorities needed immediate attention. For many reasons by the late 1970s the Division of Student Affairs had become vestigial, seen by at least some of the university as self-serving, largely invested within itself, and uncooperative. To be sure these indictments were directed at the leaders. Subordinates attempted to continue their responsibilities and did so to a remarkable degree despite the issues that surrounded them. Resolution began in September 1978 when Vice President Moore announced that the Department of Student Activities would be transferred from the responsibilities of the dean of student affairs and be placed under the Student Union and its director.[63]

Rex T. Finnegan, longtime counseling services director, took a leave-of-absence and within the year of his return to campus decided to step down from his post. Conflicts in philosophy, priorities, and feelings of little support from the dean had worn on him. In frustration he chose to return to a senior clinical counseling position rather than continue the hassles of administration, at least in that environment. Ironically, these events unfolded at the very time when the International Association of Counseling Services, Inc., an international association group for public and private agencies, granted Finnegan's service full accreditation. OSU's program was the first agency in the state to achieve this recognition. The two-year process, including a site visit by outside professionals, validated the capabilities of the counseling services. Nevertheless, eight-year assistant director Patrick M. Murphy was promoted to the director's position, after a national search, on July 1, 1979. At the time of the change the Department of Special Services, later refocused and renamed Minority Programs and Services, became a component part of the University Counseling Services.[64]

These events, and a myriad of other problems, came to a climax in the spring of 1981. Vice President Beer utilized an outside consultant's report as leverage to move ahead. The report cited certain deficiencies in the operations of the Office of the Dean of Student Affairs and the Department of Financial Aid. Subsequently, Robert B. Clark and Robert G. Schmalfeld relinquished their positions as director of financial aid and dean of student affairs respectively. In fairness, Clark and Schmalfeld, both thirteen-year veterans, had performed ably in many ways. Clark, as the first director, had professionalized the financial aid area. Few of his on-campus contemporaries fully comprehended the magnitude of the problems with which he had coped. Schmalfeld, among other things, had crusaded for equal opportunities for women and minorities long before each became campus-wide concerns.[65]

The almost routine computer interruptions, frustrating delays in issuing student checks, and long lines in financial aid became the responsibility of Charles W. Bruce. Coming to OSU in the spring of 1982, Dr. Bruce had been the financial aid director at De Paul University. Over the next four years changes were substantial in the areas of personnel, equipment, and administrative organization. "On-line" computer processing was added to the department's "tools." Interdepartmental cooperation improved. The problems lessened, but the heavy workload

In 1982, Charles W. Bruce became the director of the Department of Financial Aid. Despite increased use of the computer by departmental staff, the heavy workload continues with over half of the student body receiving some type of financial aid.

continued with the office averaging 9,000 financial statements and 60,000 pieces of documentation a year by 1985. All of this had to do with over half of the student body receiving some form of the total $24 million distributed from federal, state, and private student financial aid programs. King Cacy and Gary J. Garaffolo served as associate directors of financial aid during these hectic years.[66]

The ripples of change affected both financial aid and the counseling services. Each department's directors reported to the vice president after the reorganization. The title "dean" and all of its derivatives was set aside for the exclusive use of academic units. The dismantled Division of Student Affairs was reconstituted under Dr. Murphy. Through reorganization the University Counseling Services became a broad-based helping organization of coordinated areas incorporating the Personal Counseling Unit, including career and study skills development; Minority Programs and Services; the Student Conduct Office; Disabled

Student Services; and the International Student Advisement Office, in 1985 renamed International Student Services. Administrative coordinators of the units in the mid-1980s were Pamela A. Miller, Personal Counseling Unit; Martha L. Jordan, assistant director and coordinator of career programs; Elaine P. Burgess, International Student Services; Howard Shipp Jr., Minority Programs and Services; and Manuel D. Bustamante, OSU's first Hispanic counselor, Disabled Student Services.[67]

But the most obvious, far-reaching and dramatic changes within student services started to unfold in the spring of 1984. Richard M. Williams, director of Married Student Housing and Student Services Maintenance, and W. Lynn Jackson, director of Single Student Housing, each announced plans to retire. Both men were respected and had capably handled their large areas of responsibility. Jackson was a fourteen-year division head while Williams held his position a total of seventeen years. After twenty years in the military service before coming to OSU, Williams planned a third career in raising quality sheep on his ranch south of Stillwater. Frances Jackson, veteran administrative assistant in the OSU Hospital and Clinic, retired and joined her husband at their long-planned home in the state of Washington. Mr. Jackson, a 1980 Southwest Association of College and University Housing Officers Distinguished Service Award recipient, was paid a heartfelt tribute by RHA's leaders in their 1984-1985 *Floor President's Manual*. In it, the dedication read: "Lynn Jackson, whose tenure at OSU has been marked by a strong emphasis on student involvement in decision making as well as continued growth within the system will be retiring . . . . It is with respect, admiration and love that we dedicate this manual to the man who has helped make it all possible."[68]

On November 21, 1984, Vice President Beer announced the consolidation of Single Student Housing, Married Student Housing and Student Services Maintenance, and University Food Services into the Residential Life Department. Stating that improved economy was a primary reason for the changes, Dr. Beer also added that he wished to be removed as "mediator for the three groups."[69] In July 1985 Robert W. Huss moved from his former assistant director of housing job at the University of Georgia to head the new department. Within two years the Residential Life Department's head residents became part-time graduate student residence hall directors; student assistants were retitled resident assistants, a label more common nationally; and the residence halls were divided into "east" and "west" zones, each headed by an assistant director who lived off-campus. This model was adopted from a similar one used at the University of Georgia. Married Student Housing was renamed University Apartments, and efforts were pushed to make the life of residents easier by doing more than providing apartments. Child care and play areas for children, a newsletter, sometimes in the native

In 1985, Robert W. Huss became the first director of the newly formed Residential Life Department. As a part of the restructuring of this aspect of student services, programs were implemented regarding child care, play areas, and self-improvement courses for residents of University Apartments, the former Married Student Housing (*right*).

language of international residents, and educational programs covering meal preparations to parenting were introduced.[70]

In the new structure Dr. Huss was responsible to the vice president. Phyllis Schroeder was assistant director for administrative services. Assistant directors for residence halls-east and residence halls-west were Kent Sampson and Tim Luckadoo, respectively. Another assistant director, David E. Stoddart, made the inroads to refocus University Apartments. Joe Blair continued as director of food services. Judy Quisenberry, Blair's longtime food services associate, assumed the title of assistant director for personnel. James R. (Rex) Demaree became an assistant director for construction and renovation. The Residential Life Department moved its central offices from the Student Union to Iba Hall in 1986 thereby completing the transition to a "new look" for the reorganized division.[71]

The tasks facing the Residential Life Department seemed monumental. In 1987 the area had a one million dollar deficit. Whereas in 1981 occupancy rates in the residence halls were at 110 percent, a vacancy rate of 10 percent existed in 1987. Students had left on-campus housing at an annual rate of 300 despite plenty of publicity about off-campus dwellers paying $975 more each year. No doubt many factors caused the problem. Room and board rates increased from $821 a semester for an air-conditioned room to $1,187 a semester between 1981 and 1986. To combat the predictable problems, Cordell, Murray, Willard, and a section of Bennett Complex had been taken out of the system for housing students. The changes reduced the number of available spaces from 7,200 to 4,700. But utilities were consuming 43 percent of the total operating budget. With each room and board rate increase a huge proportion was dedicated to simply covering these costs. A declining enrollment of lower division students accounted for another aspect of the terrible dilemma.[72]

Even creativity did not solve the red ink problem. Residents could eat in any cafeteria in any hall and choose from a zero meal plan to twenty meals a week and three eating contract options in between. Some halls designated separate floors for men and women in the same building. There were also special interest floors where students in honors programs, fine arts, or foreign languages could join together on the basis of a common motivation. More identity for smaller groups was sought as floor units tagged their living areas with unique names. "Oak Tree Country Club," "John Wayne" house, and "Gehrig" house were some of the formal and informal labels.[73]

Throughout the crisis the Residence Halls Association and other students helped or offered their opinions. In general, students would focus their concerns on the mandatory requirements for freshmen to live in the halls, the alcohol prohibition, a lack of privacy, the desire for cable television, and the cost. While these were common, a more universal on-going problem prevailed. The decades old issue of men and women visiting in the same room loomed overhead like a black cloud. Still called visitation, in March 1987 the RHA and SGA again took a twenty-four hour visitation policy to the board of regents. Once again the proposal was turned down. However the board did promise to study some other proposals that were suggested by the students. The ideas that would be given study were a pizza parlor with delivery service, a laundromat, and an improved vending operation.[74]

Through management and planning, substantial effort was made to halt the exodus of residence hall students and the dollar deficits. Since all of OSU's residence halls were self-sustaining, a balance between room and board rates and decreasing occupancy had to be considered. The oldest halls were closed to reduce the total budget and the costs to individual residents. In the spring of 1983 Cordell Hall was closed at the age of forty-four. To illustrate the struggle that housing administrators faced—always in the midst of student protests about a hall closing—Cordell's continued use would have caused a $700,000 deficit in 1984-1985 and a rate increase for every resident in the system of $105. But because housing officials cared about people, these decisions were always difficult. Students have great attachments to their residences.[75] When Cordell closed, political science senior Susan C. Stallings wrote: "The laundries may flood, people may get locked out of their rooms, the food may not be so great, and the buzzers may sometimes stick, but we would not have Cordell any other way . . . Cordell has been a big part of my life. I may be leaving here but I'll never forget her. And neither will anyone else who has had the privilege to live here."[76]

For the same reasons that Cordell Hall became a liability and despite student appeals to reconsider, Murray and Willard Halls were proposed to close the following year. Willard residents took their case to the OSU Board of Regents and won a one-year reprieve. Murray was closed at the end of the 1984 spring semester, and Willard was closed to further occupancy by the fall of 1986. In closing Willard the housing system had saved over a million dollars in renovation costs—$600,000 to purchase a mandated fire sprinkler system, $500,000 to renovate the outdated cafeteria, and $30,000 to replace electrical wiring. In the spring the annual "I Love Willard" week took on extra meaning. RHA and SGA joined Willard's residents to bid a sad goodbye to the tradition-rich old hall. But outdated residence halls never really die. Cordell, Murray, and Willard would be turned over to academics—Willard being projected as a "student services" building.[77]

Other halls were refocused in purpose or modified to attract prospective residents. To appeal to some of the university's graduate students, a growing population who by 1985 made up over 16 percent of the total enrollment, Iba Hall was transformed from a home for athletes to a graduate student hall. The 1984 shift changed Iba Hall's purpose after seventeen years of ties to intercollegiate athletics. Students with severe physical disabilities, many of whom were previously excluded from higher education, were helped with a 1985 Drummond Hall renovation. Extensive modifications of the first floor permitted the start of an attendant care program providing twenty-four hour assistance for students needing help with the most basic needs. This widely praised program was the first of its type in Oklahoma.

In 1987 a $3 million renovation of Bennett Hall, converting one wing into eighty to one hundred apartments, was announced. This pilot project, to be completed in 1988, was in part a test of whether a variety of housing configurations would help bring students back to university housing. Included in the Bennett Complex renovation was the remodeling and modernizing of the cafeteria. On October 21, 1988, the refurbished eating facilities were formally dedicated and named the Joe Blair Dining Center, thereby honoring the longtime food services director, who retired in early 1988. In another far-reaching action of 1987, $10.5 million in interest costs and bond payments were avoided when OSU prepaid federal government long-term, low-interest loans at a deep discount. Bond issues for Stout, Scott, Parker and Wentz, Brumley Apartments, a portion of Willham North, plus a part of the Colvin Center, were paid off early. Although not an immediate solution to the Residential Life Department's financial woes, the liquidation of these obligations would help in the years ahead.[78]

As the near-epic struggles to turn the housing program around progressed, it was almost ironic that the program continued to receive

1980 REDSKIN

In 1979, OSU's housing program received the National Association of College and University Residence Halls "Silver Anniversary Award" signifying that it was the most oustanding in the United States for a quarter century. Residence Halls Association President Gary Jones proudly displays the award.

recognition for outstanding achievements by outside organizations. In January 1988 the Residence Halls Association could trace its origins back forty years. Through all of the decades the students could take pride in their contributions to student life. In 1987 the RHA had been proclaimed the "Outstanding System of the Year" for the third time in a decade by the National Association of College and University Residence Halls (NACURH). On May 25, 1979, OSU's housing program won NACURH's "Silver Anniversary Award," acknowledging the system as the most outstanding in the nation for a quarter century. In 1981, 1984, and again in 1985, OSU was honored as "School of the Year" by the Southwest Association of College and University Residence Halls. The National Association of College and University Food Services recognized OSU as "outstanding" in three of the four years between 1981 and 1984.[79]

During the 1980s the professional staff of the Colvin Center fared better than their student services "cousins" in the Residential Life Department. Riding the crest of the wave of the nation's compulsion toward wellness and physical fitness, Leisure Services contended with delightful problems. Intramural participation rates were among the highest in the nation with 82 percent and 48 percent of the on-campus males and females taking part in one or more of twenty-four activities. Lights had been added to the intramural fields, essential when over 500 flag-football teams need to complete a schedule. The walls of the Colvin Center's weight room had to be removed to accommodate the volume of male and female users. Kent E. Bunker, intramural department chairperson, cautioned those few on a "macho ego trip" that intramural "bullies" would not be tolerated.[80] Likewise, verbal abuse and fights would lead to suspension. Obviously, along with healthy exercise, competition continued to be important.

The United States Department of Agriculture deeded Lake Carl Blackwell and the surrounding land to Oklahoma State on December 13, 1954. Two decades later Leisure Services was making excellent use of this resource. The sailing and aquatic clubs headquartered in the lake's old south side restaurant, and the clubs constructed a one-thousand-square-foot dock from donated materials. In 1981 student services had requested and received the assignment of administering Camp Redlands, a northside wooded 120-acre tract with pre-World War II buildings. Improvements and plans for the area envisioned using the camp's facilities for leadership development, conferences and retreats, camping and environmental experiences, counseling outreach programs, and leisure science classes. Kirk E. Wimberley and Dorothy Searcy, among others, enhanced the area by building a "ropes course." A series of physical and mental tasks forced participants to explore team cooperation, leadership styles, and personal attributes, sometimes resulting in exciting growth opportunities. By 1987 the OSU Ropes Course had hosted thousands of campus

The OSU Ropes Course at Camp Redlands presents participants a series of physical and mental tasks which leads to exploration of cooperation, leadership, and personal attributes.

students as well as others from across the United States. This Camp Redlands-based program also gained a strong reputation for excellence and was copied as other ropes courses were built throughout the United States.[81]

Leisure Services commanded a leadership role when the Oklahoma Special Olympics state-wide games were brought to Stillwater and the campus in 1985. In 1987 Mac L. McCrory secured $15,000 from OSU's Board of Regents to start a "Faculty-Staff Wellness Program."[82] The university had elected "to invest in our most important asset, our people."[83] The preventative health program attracted 400 pilot program volunteers in less than two months. Buoyed by this response, Leisure Services, with leadership from James H. Rogers, began pursuing private funds for the development of a campus-wide wellness program for students, which would be second to none. Support for Wimberley, Rogers, and McCrory came from George H. Oberle, head of the School of Health, Physical Education, and Leisure, Mary L. Frye and Charles F. Schelsky, both assistant directors of Leisure Services, and Ada Van Whitley, recreation coordinator.[84]

About the time that the staff of Leisure Services had started their march toward brighter horizons, the new director of the Student Union was setting his sights on returning the building to its original 1951 condition. The task would be a large one. The three-decade-old Student Union had worn well as the "flagship of the nation's unions." It had always been a complex operation; with a $9 million annual budget the Student Union continued to serve as a "hotel, food service, a comfort center, a university center and a community center."[85] But like everything else that was 92 percent self-supporting in Oklahoma's economy, by 1985 the union was facing a $5.5 million budget deficit and a pinch to maintain services after reducing its work force by thirty-three full-time equivalent people. In addition, the Student Union of the 1980s had grown old from aging and heavy use. The desire to return the union to a level of earlier grandeur could not be faulted.[86]

The soft-spoken and capable Winston G. Shindell had been the union's director for ten years. During his tenure the Department of Student Activities was shifted to his administrative leadership, and the Student Activities Center was opened in the basement of the Student Union. OSU's 260 organizations and the professionals in student activities, including Manager Jan M. Carlson, moved to the renovated facilities in the spring of 1980. Under Shindell $2.5 million worth of improvements were made. The cafeteria was re-opened as the Food Mart in fall 1979, and names such as "Yum Yum Tree," "Uncle Sam's," and the "Pastry Pantry" became jargon on campus. "The Nook," "1600 Place," and attractive new fronts in the first floor merchandising area were additional features. However, much of the money went to replace outdated equipment.[87] When Shindell departed on November 30, 1981, President Boger praised the fifteen-year student services veteran by saying he "has built one of the outstanding programs here. I'm confident he'll do very well for the University of Indiana."[88]

Replacing Shindell was his colleague and friend Thomas M. Keys, a twelve-year ally of OSU students and a former assistant dean of students and assistant in the Office of the Vice President for Academic Affairs and Research. Dr. Keys, excited about having the opportunity to administer the Student Union, became the director on January 18, 1982. The new director took up where his predecessor left off. In February 1986 the union celebrated its thirty-fifth birthday and the completion of a $1.5 million renovation of the hotel and bookstore. A five-year plan for rearranging floor space, including the possible addition of a franchised fast food chain was in place. The $30 million "heart of the campus" still relied heavily on an active Student Union Activities Board, which promoted a seven-foot tall pink bird mascot and the annual Christmas "Madrigal Dinner Concert," which by the time of its fourteenth production in 1988 was known state-wide.[89]

Within the Student Union's five-year plan for space utilization was the concept of placing similar functions in "zones" by floors within the building. This idea was moved forward in July 1984 when University Placement (now with the word "services" dropped from the office's title) moved to the third floor of the union. Director Don R. Briggs, who had been appointed to his position on July 1, 1978, worked enthusiastically

In 1986, the "heart of the campus"—the Student Union—underwent renovation in the hotel and bookstore areas. Enjoying the elegant new hotel lobby are (*left to right*) Allen Reding, a longtime Student Union administrator; Carol Bormann, interior decorator for OSU Architectural Services; and Tom Keys, the Student Union director.

to improve the operation's facilities and image. Dr. Briggs had replaced eighteen-year retiring director Hal N. Buchanan who had completed a distinguished career in placement as well as serving as the first president of the Oklahoma College and University Placement Association and the Southwest Placement Association. Buchanan's longtime assistant director Marian Dark retired on June 30, 1980, and was replaced by Linda L. L'Hote, who had been a placement counselor since 1976. In the same year Robert L. Jamison was employed in the area of teacher placement.[90]

The new facilities and staff of University Placement evoked new services to the benefit of both students and prospective employers. In July 1979 the area was given the responsibility of coordinating campus interviews for all areas of the university. In January 1981 the first annual Placement Emphasis Week was held as an activity to encourage graduates to place priority on the search for a position. Summer Recreation Placement Day, Journalism and Broadcasting Placement Day, and the annual Teacher Placement Day, which became a two-day event, all began between 1982 and 1986. A total process, including career planning, development, and professional employment after graduation, became the primary mission of University Placement during the 1980s. In the single academic year of 1983-1984, placement personnel assisted 2,035 students and alumni through one or more of eight sub-services, includ-

Don R. Briggs, the director of University Placement, emphasizes the total placement process— career planning, development, and professional employment.

ing campus interviews, job placement lists, the career library, resume service, job search counseling, and the development of placement credentials.[91]

In any organization, large or small, the joys and awards, illnesses and pain, births and deaths, and resignations and retirements among colleagues and friends are shared. This was especially the case among the people who comprised student services. Through the late seventies and eighties many people lent their energies to lasting achievements or held a special place in the division. Their experiences represented life itself, yet each contributed to students and a better campus.

Mercedier C. Cunningham, assistant director of student activities since 1972, died in July 1981, leaving a legacy of which one individual at the time rightfully said, "Students who came in contact with her were enriched."[92] In 1975 Bettye Stratton retired after working in the Student Union for twenty years. Union Director Shindell reflected that Mrs. Stratton "had the unique quality of making you feel better for having passed her way."[93] In 1978 longtime director of campus student entertainers Ashley H. Alexander Sr. retired to his Perry farm, where he continued to carry on an outreach ministry to the old and ill.[94] George B. Gathers gave up an eighteen-year Stillwater medical practice when he joined the OSU Hospital and Clinic's staff in 1970. Dr. Gathers, in private practice a surgeon and specialist in gynecology and obstetrics, probably was not disappointed. Concerning his new student-oriented practice he believed that it would not be boring.[95] "I'll be seeing everything from warts to clobbered athletes," predicted the personable doctor.[96] Eventually he became assistant director; he retired in 1987.

A man who took a job at the Student Union because he needed work of any kind spent thirty-two years in the same position. Winsel L. Bilyeu retired in 1986 as manager of the Student Union Hotel, a place that provided him the opportunity to meet Presidents Ronald Reagan and Harry Truman, Bob Hope, and Vice President Hubert H. Humphrey. Some people decided to leave mid-career. Terry H. Henderson, counseling services assistant director, departed in 1985 after fifteen years of touching the lives of thousands of students at the counseling center or on the ropes course. By 1987 Assistant Director of Residential Life Judith A. (Judy) Quisenberry had served twenty-three years in campus food services. In 1982 the National Association of College and University Food Services recognized her for "professionalism in performance and unselfish devotion to NACUFS." Thelma Lea Bauman retired in 1985 after nearly twenty years of housekeeping service in residence halls—most of them in Iba Hall. The Glencoe native left hoping that everyone had seen her as "thankful for her job."[97] Dawn Pittman, a young woman, but with eleven years of work behind her in the Student Union's Food Mart, received recognition in the 1984 Redskin. At the time Ms. Pittman, who estimated that she knew about a thousand people, reflected: "If there are new students, I show them how to get around . . . It's their cafeteria and they're here to enjoy their meal."[98]

President Reagan appointed Donald L. Cooper, physician and director of the OSU Hospital and Clinic to the President's Council on Physical Fitness and Sports in 1981. Physicians Elnora Miller and Alice F. Gambill were two additional physicians that had extended service with students. In 1987 Dr. Gambill was promoted to the position of health services assistant director when Dr. Gathers retired. Sherry C. Maxwell headed the hospital's mental health clinic through the 1980s. In 1987, Allen B. Reding, administrative assistant in the union, won the title of jack-of-all-trades, having held the greatest number of responsibilities in one building in all of student services over the years. Sadly, Pat Hofler, assistant vice president of student services, and Rex Demaree, assistant director in the Residential Life Department, planned retirements in January 1988. Meanwhile, longtime food services professional Joe Blair continued to strive for the best for students in food and dining facilities until his spring 1988 retirement. Kent Sampson persisted in communicating with students and working with what was available to improve the residence halls. As Oklahoma State neared its centennial year, Victoria E. McLaurin passed the fifteen-year anniversary of holding down one of

In 1988, longtime food services professional Joe Blair retired after a career of accepting only the best for students in food and dining facilities. In recognition of his accomplishments with University Food Services, the cafeteria in Bennett Hall was named in his honor.

those unsung, but vitally important positions, as senior unit assistant in the counseling services.[99]

Although Oklahoma State was an exception to the trend, nationally Greek social organizations lost much of their popularity in the late 1960s and early 1970s. But then there was a resurgence of interest. By 1983 national officials were reporting a steady growth in the number of campus chapters and in membership. Fourteen of 2,427 national sororities and 24 of 5,000 national fraternities surrounded the Stillwater campus in 1985. Greek life had come a long way since the turn of the century when Oklahoma A. and M. College students were asked to sign a pledge promising not to join the so-called secret societies. As the middle of the eighties passed, about 1,400 men and 900 women—approximately 10 percent of the total enrollment—continued to find enduring friendships in the thriving Greek houses. "Bigs" and "grandbigs," "functions" and "study hours," formal dinners and being stripped and thrown in Theta Pond persisted as deeply entrenched traditions.[100]

OSU's social fraternities and sororities, historically among the best in the nation, confronted and moved forward on problems that were deeply rooted, both in Stillwater and from coast to coast. James G. Jordan, coordinator of Greek life, and Marilon Morgan, student program coordinator in student activities, played critical roles as important changes were made during this period. Vice President Beer, Union Director Keys, and Student Activities Manager Carlson—the three administrators ultimately responsible for Greek-related policy—were also centrally involved. By the early fall of 1980 the Interfraternity Council (IFC) and Panhellenic Council added non-discrimination statements to their codes of governance. On November 11, 1985, the IFC officially prohibited the use of alcoholic beverages in conjunction with rush activities. "Dry rush" became the rule, and to their credit, IFC handed violating chapters stiff penalties. An even more elusive problem, that of hazing, was attacked when a "Men's and Women's Fraternity Hazing Code" became law on May 13, 1987. Although none of these enactments guaranteed that isolated incidents would not occur, they did make clear that neither the Greek system nor the university would condone continuance of these practices.[101]

Amidst the sweeping changes of policy and a period of rapid inflation and strained budgets, the usual trials, tribulations, and achievements of daily Greek life went on. Among sororities Alpha Xi Delta was lost, and Delta Zeta was forced to recolonize; but Phi Mu, after a stormy beginning, was installed on October 26, 1979. Alpha Tau Omega, one of the Big Three national fraternities, helped counter the losses. In 1984 Alpha Tau Omega was one of the first OSU fraternities to eliminate hazing when it replaced "Hell Week" with a "Help Week." Acacia, Sigma

And they're off! Coeds try their luck at winding their tricycles through the muck and mud of the Phi Psi 500.

Phi Epsilon, and Phi Kappa Psi all survived troubled days, reorganized, and grew stronger during the late 1970s and early 1980s. The Acacias remodeled their house, and a new half-million-dollar chapter home helped the Sigma Phi Epsilon chapter revitalize. Out of the turmoil the treacherous tricycle race, the "Phi Psi 500," grew more popular.[102]

Phi Kappa Theta, in July 1980, and Phi Delta Theta, in June 1983, lost chapter homes to fires. The face of "fraternity row" changed in 1981 when Sigma Chi constructed a new house, and Sigma Alpha Epsilon tore down its "beloved annex." In 1986 Delta Tau Delta opened a new wing, making the chapter house's capacity the largest one of that fraternity in the nation. The Phi Mus left apartment living in 1981, when the organization moved to the vacated Alpha Xi Delta house.[103]

Every organization has an annual anniversary. Some of the more notable among Oklahoma State's fraternities and sororities included the oldest of Greek chapters, the Lambda Chi Alpha fraternity, which boasted seventy years longevity as a national chapter on September 15, 1987. Beta Theta Pi, known for domination of intramural sports and a singing tradition, celebrated its sixty-fifth birthday as a national at OSU in 1988. FarmHouse continued to excel at its fiftieth anniversary in 1978, having won three consecutive "Outstanding FarmHouse Chapter in the Nation," an award given once every two years. In 1987 Kappa Kappa Gamma marked their fortieth anniversary, the Gamma Phis reached age twenty-five in 1982, and Triangle was twenty in 1984.[104] Delta Sigma Theta marked its fifteenth birthday in 1986 by moving into its own sorority house at 1508 West Admiral, noting that members now felt like they were "a part of the Oklahoma State University campus."[105]

When reduced to basics, everything comes down to people. Among Greeks many events involving people were significant. There were the horrible losses of Greek students Merle George, Randall Logan, Levin Wilson, and Mary Cheryl Mannering in the tragic 1977-1978 academic year. By 1987 Myrtle Sheets retired after sixteen years as housemother at Delta Upsilon fraternity. In 1983 Beryl Graham retired from a similar position at Beta Theta Pi after sixteen years of continuous service to over 500 students. Sally Hedrick, Phi Gamma Deltas' "housemom" for five years, was still going strong in May 1987 after seventeen years of continuous work with five different chapters. Glennie Townsend, housemother at Kappa Delta and the newly re-elected president of Eta Delta Gamma (the association of Oklahoma State University house directors), in May 1987 admitted that being a houseparent—or the newly instituted term of house director—took some adjustment.[106] "If only I could take a shower without interruption . . . ," Mrs. Townsend reflected. Eleanor Fehring, housemother at Pi Kappa Phi, added, "I just run this house with my heart."[107] As it has probably been for all time, the best houseparent shifted gears easily, moving from roles of administrator, host, confidante, and nurse with ease.

There were many enduring traditions that seemed to make for a 1980s collegiate environment, Oklahoma State-style. The 1986 homecoming was the sixty-sixth edition, drawing a record crowd of over 22,000 to the walkaround of house decorations as well as 15,000 attendees to the parade. The academic year continued to be spiced with special weeks including: RHA Week, Greek Week, Black Heritage Week, Native American Week, Hispanic Cultural Week, and the International Student Organization's International Week. Blue Key's Parent's Day in the fall and Mortar Board's spring Mom's Weekend traditionally enriched campus activity. The fifty-eighth "Varsity Revue" and twentieth annual "Freshman Follies" remained their usual successes.[108]

The long-running "lab" for aspiring journalists, the *Daily O'Collegian*, churned out 15,000 newspapers, five days a week to be delivered to 125 places on or near campus in the early morning. Despite the seeming constant criticism, the absence of the *O'Colly* caused a void in thousands of students' daily routine that was noticed. In 1985 a question was raised, but resolved, regarding whether the name of the Oklahoma State yearbook was derogatory to American Indians; thus the annual carried on the near eight-decade tradition of being called the *Redskin*. Much like their predecessors, *Redskin* editors continued trying to explain what their experience involved.[109] The 1982 annual's staff complained: "Everyone wants in on the action. The Greeks want everything; the people in the Residence Halls want anything; and the off-campus people don't care . . . while the *Redskin* tries to please everyone, it simply isn't possible. We do the best we can do."[110]

While many things remained unchanged, from one student generation to the next other things did change. The Off-Campus Student Association (OCSA) continued to grow as it promoted and pushed for a voice for off-campus dwellers' on-campus interests. Renter's Fair, bringing together in one place students and renters, and Spring Fling, an annual event at Stillwater's Boomer Lake, represented two OCSA events. The growing heterogeneity of students was reflected in the growth in size and influence of the Returning Student Organization (RSO). Through the 1980s Marie L. Basler, student activities program coordinator, helped to boost the efforts of both the OCSA and the RSO.[111]

Although OSU has the lowest campus crime rate of any Big Eight institution, a barometer of the times was the students themselves who focused on campus safety. By the early 1980s a series of emergency telephones with blue lights atop the poles networked across campus. Any emergency would receive a rapid response from campus security twenty-four hours a day when an individual simply picked up one of these phones. In 1984 a campus escort service began operation. The Campus and Area Resident Escort Service (CARE) provided after dark safety by a screened and trained volunteer with only a simple telephone request. In the fall semester alone of the first year of escort service operation, 700 people were escorted from places such as the library to their residence hall or car.[112]

Between 1982 and 1986 the number of Oklahoma State students that voted in Student Government Association elections had dropped from 17 percent to 4 percent. One observer posed the theory that the "intimacy of SGA to the students is important; I don't think there is any, and apparently, neither did ninety-six percent of the students here."[113] The speaker was the SGA advisor, Jan Carlson. For whatever reasons, apathy, or a cycle of student involvement that seemed to drift through student bodies periodically, was a chronic problem at the decade's midpoint. Yet SGA continued to promote and implement essential services for their constituency. CARE and the blue-lighted emergency telephones had ties to SGA. SGA money was vital to the improved situation for handicapped students. The student activity fee allocation process to student organizations, which distributed an all too little amount of about $130,000 in 1987, was an SGA function. The student's primary voice to administration was simply in a period when issues that interested large numbers of students did not exist. Interest in politics that the students might understand correlated directly to issues that people really cared about. However, if history does repeat itself the SGA will eventually return to center stage.[114]

In the 1980s students at OSU and elsewhere placed little importance on organizations like the Student Government Association. They were too busy dressing themselves in pre-professional armor, the dominant tools being hitting the books, getting high grades, and subsequently securing a well paying position. Their focus was on the job market, the future of the economy, and the push toward personal success. Protests and issues for most students were beyond their frame of reference. For colleges and universities the end of the "baby boom" meant the start of a trend toward fewer enrolling traditional eighteen to twenty-four year old students. Planning was underway to accommodate part-time students better, who by 1993 are expected to constitute close to half of all students enrolled in the nation. The trend represented more bad news for student government. Historically, older returning students took little interest in the traditional undergraduate extracurriculum.[115]

Adding to the dilemmas of transitions and uncertainties John Naisbitt in his popular 1982 book entitled *Megatrends* described the 1980s as "the time of the parenthesis, the time between eras."[116] The years were an interval in history where dramatic changes were in progress and many questions about the future could not yet be answered. The period was marked by the transformation of an industrial society to an information society. The future would be created on the basis of brain power rather than physical power, according to Naisbitt. After sixteen

The more things change—the more things stay the same. Despite the uncertainties of the future, the same eager enthusiasm radiates from each new class of students that enters OSU. As this group of Alpha participants seems to suggest, the future bodes excitement!

straight years of declining Scholastic Aptitude Test (SAT) scores by American high school students, futurists and educators feared that the nation was moving toward a scientific and technological disaster. Meantime the nation's largest corporations had tried to offset the educational deficits of their employees by reluctantly entering the education business. A powerful anomaly was developing. At the very time when the United States was moving toward a more literacy-intensive society, public and higher education was apparently graduating a less capable future citizenry.[117] Naisbitt's conclusion was that for "the first time in American history the generation moving into adulthood is less skilled than its parents."[118]

There can be little doubt that the nation and its institutions of higher education, as well as the student's relationships and expectations of them, had once again changed dramatically in only a decade. As a result educational systems at all levels were flooded with new expectations and demands. Some of these expectations would be impossible to meet. These were years in which it became clear that colleges and universities would have to become more selective in allocating their limited resources. Excellence in everything was impossible. It was far better to have quality activities in fewer areas than to market institutional mediocrity to prospective students, parents, and legislators who annually enacted university budgets. For many institutions this was a new way of thinking.

On July 26, 1987, most members of the Oklahoma State University "family" were surprised to read in the *Stillwater NewsPress* that President Boger had announced to the board of regents his intention to step down from his consuming position on June 30, 1988. His administration represented the third longest tenure among Oklahoma State's presidents.[119]

Because of President Boger's decision it would be left to a new president, and this individual's closest advisors, to identify what shape Oklahoma State University would take in the future. From those decisions OSU's Office of the Vice President for Student Services would continue to play its part. At the time people willing to risk making a prediction were suggesting that the future would offer things never before possible. It would be an exciting time for higher education. As Naisbitt suggested "the time between eras is uncertain, it is a great and yeasty time, filled with opportunity. If we can learn to make uncertainty our friend, we can achieve much more than in stable eras."[120]

From the uncertainties and turbulence of the late 1980s both the nation and Oklahoma State University should emerge restructured, yet stronger. To some the present, constituted by the 1980s, seemed a jumble. For those who were willing to give up clinging to the past, it was promised the future would be clearer—and very exciting.

# Endnotes

1. Washington, D. C. *Chronicle of Higher Education*, 4 September 1985, pp. 1-3.

2. "Analysis of University Quality Indicators," Faculty Council Minutes, 17 March 1987, Appendix V, p. 6, and "Student Retention Committee Report," April 1983, pp. 1-2, in Faculty Council Records, Special Collections, Edmon Low Library, Oklahoma State University, Stillwater, Oklahoma; Ted Pfeifer to Robin Lacy, 16 February 1987, Student Services Collection, Special Collections, Edmon Low Library; Dr. L. L. Boger, "Student Retention A Major University-Wide Priority," *Oklahoma State University Outreach*, vol. 55, no. 2 (Winter 1983), p. 39; Oklahoma State University *Daily O'Collegian*, 17 October 1980, p. 1, 10 April 1982, p. 4, 25 February 1987, p. 1, 11 June 1987, p. 1.

3. J. R. Morris, "The Most Poorly Funded System of Higher Education In America," manuscript [June 1987], p. 1, and L. L. Boger to OSU Faculty and Staff, 19 February 1986, Student Services Collection. For further information on Oklahoma's difficulties in funding public higher education between 1960 and 1987 see *Stillwater NewsPress*, 19 May 1987, p. 1; "New Report Shows Oklahoma is 50th In Tax Support for Higher Education," *Oklahoma State Alumnus Magazine*, vol. 8, no. 9 (November 1967), p. 29; *1985 Redskin*, p. 215, Oklahoma State University Yearbook; *Daily O'Collegian*, 10 February 1987, p. 1, 14 February 1986, p. 5.

4. *1982 Redskin*, p. 55; Morris, pp. 3-4.

5. *Daily O'Collegian*, 7 April 1987, p. 4. This was a reprinted editorial from the *Tulsa Tribune*.

6. *1981 Redskin*, p. 202; *Daily O'Collegian*, 11 February 1984, p. 9.

7. Ralph Hamilton, "Lawrence Boger Is Named OSU President," *Oklahoma State University Outreach*, vol. 18, no. 3 (June-July 1977), p. 4.

8. *Daily O'Collegian*, 22 March 1977, p. 1, 28 July 1977, p. 1, 30 August 1977, p. 4.

9. *1985 Redskin*, p. 202.

10. *1981 Redskin*, p. 202.

11. *Daily O'Collegian*, 14 December 1977, p. 13; "Facts About OSU," *Oklahoma State University Outreach*, vol. 51, no. 1 (September 1979), pp. 57-58; *1985 Redskin*, p. 202.

12. *1985 Redskin*, p. 202.

13. *1985 Redskin*, p. 202; *Department Profile 1986-1987*, Oklahoma State University Office of Institutional Research (Stillwater: Oklahoma State University, December 1986), p. 1; *Stillwater NewsPress*, 7 July 1987, p. 7.

14. *Daily O'Collegian*, 10 December 1983, p. 3, 7 May 1987, p. 2; "Facts About OSU," p. 58.

15. *Daily O'Collegian*, 10 December 1983, p. 3.

16. *Chronicle of Higher Education*, 4 September 1985, pp. 30-31.

17. *Chronicle of Higher Education*, 4 September 1985, p. 31; *1985 Redskin*, p. 192.

18. *1985 Redskin*, p. 192.

19. Melinda G. Spencer to OSU Faculty, 21 April 1987, Student Services Collection.

20. *1985 Redskin*, p. 192.

21. *1983 Redskin*, p. 28; Jerald G. Bachman and Lloyd D. Johnston, "The Freshmen 1979," *Psychology Today*, vol. 13, no. 9 (September 1979), pp. 79, 87; *Chronicle of Higher Education*, 4 September 1985, pp. 30-31.

22. *1985 Redskin*, p. 8.

23. Bachman and Johnston, p. 79; *Chronicle of Higher Education*, 4 September 1985, p. 32.

24. *1983 Redskin*, p. 28.

25. *Chronicle of Higher Education*, 4 September 1985, p. 1.

26. *Chronicle of Higher Education*, 4 September 1985, pp. 30-31.

27. "Student Affairs Committee Report," Faculty Council Minutes, 13 January 1987, p. 3, Faculty Council Records; *Daily O'Collegian*, 8 April 1982, p. 1; Elaine Burgess to OSU Faculty and Staff, "Campus Report on International Student Statistics, Fall 1986," January 1987, p. 1, Student Services Collection.

28. "Student Affairs Committee Report," Faculty Council Minutes, 13 January 1987, p. 3, Faculty Council Records.

29. *1986 Redskin*, p. 47; *Daily O'Collegian*, 16 April 1985, pp. 1, 3, 5 June 1987, p. 1; Author's personal communication with anonymous student, 15 May 1987.

30. *Daily O'Collegian*, 2 December 1986, p. 1, 23 September 1983, p. 1, 21 June 1983, pp. 1, 12, 23 June 1983, pp. 1, 8, 24 June 1983, pp. 1-2, 28 June 1983, pp. 1, 5, 1 July 1983, p. 1, 19 September 1985, pp. 1, 14, 19 September 1986, p. 6, 23 September 1986, p. 3, 2 October 1981, p. 16, 10 April 1985, p. 15; *Chronicle of Higher Education*, 4 September 1985, p. 32.

31. *Daily O'Collegian*, 4 October 1986, pp. 5-6, 5 March 1982, pp. 1, 12, 4 March 1981, p. 1, 4 October 1986, pp. 4, 6, 3 September 1980, p. 2, 21 June 1985, p. 4, 5 June 1980, p. 4, 4 September 1984, pp. 1-2; *1985 Redskin*, p. 28; *1984 Redskin*, p. 429; *1986 Redskin*, p. 32.

32. *1979 Redskin*, p. 42; *Daily O'Collegian*, 19 August 1985, p. 4.

33. *Daily O'Collegian*, 19 August 1985, p. 4.

34. *Daily O'Collegian*, 4 April 1986, p. 9, 27 September 1980, p. 12, 7 February 1981, p. 12, 19 February 1987, p. 1, 30 April 1982, p. 2; *1985 Redskin*, pp. 27, 33; *1986 Redskin*, p. 40.

35. *Daily O'Collegian*, 15 April 1978, p. 3, 20 September 1980, p. 4, 20 July 1984, p. 5, 12 February 1983, p. 10, 25 February 1983, p. 1; *1985 Redskin*, p. 33; *1980 Redskin*, pp. 20, 47; *1982 Redskin*, p. 500; Bachman and Johnston, p. 79.

36. *Daily O'Collegian*, 14 October 1980, p. 4, 3 December 1980, p. 16, 13 October 1982, p. 1.

37. *Daily O'Collegian*, 11 February 1982, p. 1, 23 September 1981, pp. 1, 16, 8 October 1982, p. 7, 11 April 1985, p. 1, 8 November 1986, pp. 2, 4-6, 12; *1986 Redskin*, p. 44.

38. *Daily O'Collegian*, 14 February 1987, pp. 4-5, 3 December 1983, p. 3; *1986 Redskin*, p. 44; Pamela A. Miller, "Oklahoma State University Acquired Immunodeficiency Guidelines and Educational Strategies," July 1986, pp. 1-9, and Ronald Beer to Student Services Division Heads, 10 October 1986, in Student Services Collection.

39. *1986 Redskin*, p. 44.

40. *Daily O'Collegian*, 23 October 1986, p. 20, 24 February 1987, p. 1, 21 July 1987, p. 1, 16 April 1987, p. 9, 11 February 1987, p. 1, 24 March 1987, p. 7, 16 April 1987, p. 9.

41. *1979 Redskin*, p. 336; *1980 Redskin*, p. 32; *1986 Redskin*, p. 13; *Chronicle of Higher Education*, 15 April 1987, pp. 36-37; *Daily O'Collegian*, 21 June 1985, p. 1, 1 February 1986, p. 4.

42. Martha L. Jordan, "Student Services and Students," in Donald W. Robinson, chairman, *Oklahoma State University/North Central Association Self Study 1985* (Stillwater: Oklahoma State University, January 1985), Chapter 4, p. 4.

43. Jordan, "Student Services and Students," p. 25.

44. Jordan, "Student Services and Students," pp. 1-2.

45. *People 1978-1979: Oklahoma State University Student-Faculty Directory* (Fall 1978), p. 15; Jordan, "Student Services and Students," p. 1.

46. Shannon Wingrove, "Paid For By Bonds," *Oklahoma State University Outreach*, vol. 19, no. 2 (March-April 1978), p. 17.

47. Jordan, "Student Services and Students," p. 14; Oklahoma State University *OSU Today*, February 1985, pp. 6, 10.

48. *Daily O'Collegian*, 18 April 1979, p. 1, 17 November 1979, p. 1, 9 February 1980, p. 3; *1985 Redskin*, p. 205; "New VP Excited About OSU," *Oklahoma State University Outreach*, vol. 51, no. 3 (February 1980), p. 8.

49. *1983 Redskin*, p. 214.

50. *Daily O'Collegian*, 22 February 1980, p. 15.

51. *Daily O'Collegian*, 26 March 1987, p. 8.

52. *Daily O'Collegian*, 22 January 1981, p. 8.

53. *Daily O'Collegian*, 26 March 1987, p. 8.

54. Jordan, "Student Services and Students," p. 15; *Daily O'Collegian*, 19 August 1985, p. 1, 28 September 1967, p. 1, 4 February 1967, p. 2.

55. Ronald S. Beer, "Student Growth Emphasized During the Centennial Decade," *Oklahoma State University Outreach*, vol. 56, no. 3 (Spring 1985), p. 92.

56. Beer, "Student Growth Emphasized During the Centennial Decade," p. 92; "Students Selected For Leadership Council," *Oklahoma State Alumnus Magazine*, vol. 8, no. 5 (May 1967), p. 26.

57. Jordan, "Student Services and Students," p. 15.

58. Jordan, "Student Services and Students," p. 25.

59. *Daily O'Collegian*, 1 September 1981, p. 20, 19 September 1980, p. 8, 13 October 1981, pp. 1, 16, 14 October 1981, pp. 1-2, 24 October 1981, pp. 1, 16, 3 November 1981, p. 1, 9 September 1982, p. 1, 30 September 1982, p. 1, 10 January 1984, pp. 1-2, 2 April 1987, p. 2, 22 March 1983, p. 10.

60. *Daily O'Collegian*, 9 February 1980, p. 3.

61. Jordan, "Student Services and Students," p. 4.

62. Jordan, "Student Services and Students," p. 4.

63. Norman F. Moore to General Staff, 18 September 1978, Student Services Collection.

64. "Associate Dean of Student Affairs Annual Report for 1978-1979" (July 1979), p. 1, Student Services Collection; *Daily O'Collegian*, 16 January 1979, p. 12, 26 June 1979, p. 1, 3 July 1979, p. 2; Author's personal communication with Rex T. Finnegan, Fall 1979; *Oklahoma State* University *News*, 18 December 1978, p. 2.

65. Center for Management and Organization, "Organization Review of the Office of Financial Aid" (March 1981), pp. 4-9, Student Services Collection; *Daily O'Collegian*, 5 June 1981, p. 1.

66. Jordan, "Student Services and Students," pp. 7-8; *Daily O'Collegian*, 25 November 1980, p. 1, 3 February 1983, p. 1; Carol Ann Schmitz, "A Follow-Up Study of Residents Who Voluntarily Withdrew From Oklahoma State University" (Master of Science thesis, Oklahoma State University, 1981), pp. 50-51; *1983 Redskin*, p. 225; *OSU Today*, February 1985, p. 1.

67. *Daily O'Collegian*, 3 December 1985, p. 2, 20 January 1984, p. 19, 1 October 1981, pp. 1, 16, 12 November 1983, p. 4.

68. *Dedication: 1984-1985 Residence Halls Association Floor President's Manual* (Spring 1984), p. 1, Student Services Collection; *1985 Redskin*, p. 207; *Daily O'Collegian*, 29 August 1984, p. 14.

69. *Daily O'Collegian*, 21 November 1984, p. 5.

70. *Daily O'Collegian*, 8 May 1986, p. 3, 15 July 1985, p. 2, 13 February 1986, p. 15.

71. *1986-1987 Oklahoma State University Student Directory* (Fall 1986), p. 21; *Daily O'Collegian*, 24 September 1986, p. 10.

72. *Stillwater NewsPress*, 16 March 1986, p. 12A, 18 March 1986, p. 13, 21 July 1987, pp. 1, 3; *Daily O'Collegian*, 21 January 1987, p. 1, 18 September 1986, p. 13, 19 September 1986, p. 1, 15 April 1986, p. 1; *1985 Redskin*, p. 108.

73. *Stillwater NewsPress*, 16 March 1986, p. 12A; *Daily O'Collegian*, 28 March 1984, p. 2, 3 April 1986, p. 4, 20 March 1985, p. 11, 4 October 1985, p. 5, 22 October 1986, p. 6.

74. *Stillwater NewsPress*, 15 March 1987, p. 1; *Daily O'Collegian*, 2 October 1986, p. 2, 28 April 1984, p. 5, 27 March 1987, p. 9; "Student Senate Resolution No. 25," Oklahoma State University Student Senate Record, 25 March 1987, pp. 1-2, Student Services Collection.

75. *Daily O'Collegian*, 12 January 1984, p. 3, 19 April 1983, p. 1, 24 August 1983, p. 17, 3 May 1983, p. 5; *1984 Redskin*, p. 35.

76. *Daily O'Collegian*, 26 April 1983, p. 5.

77. *Daily O'Collegian*, 17 February 1984, p. 5, 18 February 1984, pp. 1, 5, 17, 1 March 1984, p. 2, 20 February 1985, pp. 1, 3, 21 March 1985, p. 1, 24 April 1986, p. 3; *1986 Redskin*, p. 112.

78. *Daily O'Collegian*, 17 April 1984, p. 2, 26 October 1985, p. 1, 5 November 1983, p. 3; Beer, "Student Growth Emphasized During the Centennial Decade," p. 89; Jordan, "Student Services and Students," p. 20; *Stillwater NewsPress*, 19 March 1987, p. 3, 21 July 1987, pp. 1, 3, 20 October 1988, p. 9; *1985 Redskin*, p. 106.

79. Patrick M. Murphy to Diane T. Weber, 27 March 1987, Student Services Collection; *Daily O'Collegian*, 9 April 1980, p. 2, 9 April 1982, p. 4, 30 September 1982, p. 2, 24 July 1979, p. 1; *1982 Redskin*, p. 121; *1980 Redskin*, p. 90; *For The Record*, Oklahoma State University Residence Halls Association Newsletter, vol. 6, no. 10 (20 February 1986), p. 4; Beer, "Student Growth Emphasized During the Centennial Decade," p. 92.

80. *Daily O'Collegian*, 22 March 1985, p. 1, 4 September 1986, p. 12; Beer, "Student Growth Emphasized During the Centennial Decade," p. 89.

81. "Lake Carl Blackwell Deeded to the College," *Oklahoma A. and M. College Magazine*, vol. 26, no. 6 (February 1955), pp. 24-25; *1983 Redskin*, p. 23; Minutes, University Counseling Services Staff Meeting, 26 January 1979, p. 1, Student Services Collection; Beer, "Student Growth Emphasized During the Centennial Decade," p. 89.

82. *OSU Today*, February 1986, p. 6; *Daily O'Collegian*, 2 April 1987, p. 1; *Stillwater NewsPress*, 27 May 1987, p. 10.

83. *Daily O'Collegian,* 2 April 1987, p. 1.

84. *1986-1987 Oklahoma State University Student Directory*, pp. 14-15; Author interview with George H. Oberle, 25 November 1987, Stillwater, Oklahoma.

85. *Daily O'Collegian*, 12 February 1982, p. 4, 31 January 1985, p. 19.

86. *Daily O'Collegian*, 31 January 1985, p. 19.

87. *Daily O'Collegian*, 26 March 1980, p. 3, 2 September 1978, p. 1, 8 July 1977, pp. 1-2, 19 April 1978, p. 2, 16 November 1979, p. 9, 4 November 1978, p. 1, 10 December 1977, p. 1, 29 October 1977, p. 1, 16 December 1978, p. 1, 21 September 1979, p. 3, 5 November 1981, pp. 1, 20; *1981 Redskin*, p. 344; *1982 Redskin*, p. 303.

88. *Daily O'Collegian*, 22 October 1981, pp. 1, 16.

89. *Celebrating the Thirty-Fifth Year of the Student Union*, banquet program (8 February 1986), pp. 1-4, Student Services Collection; *Daily O'Collegian*, 9 July 1985, p. 1, 16 January 1987, p. 10, 17 September 1985, p. 3, 11 February 1986, p. 4, 4 March 1983, p. 4, 7 September 1982, p. 7, 10 December 1977, p. 5, 29 November 1978, p. 2, 6 December 1979, p. 11; Jana Boler, "The Student Union . . . Adds Some Centennial Luster," *Oklahoma State University Outreach*, vol. 58, no. 2 (Winter 1987), pp. 12-15; Cathy Criner, "'Heart of Campus' Celebrates 35th Anniversary," *Oklahoma State University Outreach*, vol. 57, no. 3 (Spring 1986), p. 12; *OSU Today*, February 1986, p. 3; *Stillwater NewsPress*, 19 November 1987, pp. 1B-3B, 26 October 1986, p. 10, 7 February 1986, pp. 30-31.

90. "Placement Was His Profession," *Oklahoma State University Outreach*, vol. 19, no. 4 (August-September 1978), p. 7; *Daily O'Collegian*, 30 June 1977, p. 11; Robert Jamison, "A Brief History of University Placement at Oklahoma State University," unpublished manuscript, (7 June 1986), pp. 1-2, Student Services Collection.

91. Jamison, "A Brief History of University Placement at Oklahoma State University," pp. 2-4; *Daily O'Collegian*, 21 April 1987, p. 10, 16 January 1987, p. 16, 28 January 1986, p. 5; Jordan, "Student Services and Students," p. 11.

92. *Daily O'Collegian*, 17 July 1981, p. 1.

93. *Daily O'Collegian*, 8 April 1981, p. 5.

94. *1981 Redskin*, p. 331.

95. *Daily O'Collegian*, 30 October 1970, p. 2; "Dr. George Gathers Joins OSU Staff," *Oklahoma State Alumnus Magazine*, vol. 12, no. 1 (January 1971), p. 24.

96. *Daily O'Collegian*, 30 October 1970, p. 2.

97. *Daily O'Collegian*, 25 April 1986, p. 10, 6 July 1982, p. 2, 15 October 1985, p. 1.

98. *1984 Redskin*, p. 421.

99. *Daily O'Collegian*, 20 June 1980, pp. 1, 7, 21 October 1982, p. 13, 13 October 1982, p. 13, 9 December 1981, p. 1.

100. *Chronicle of Higher Education*, 4 September 1985, p. 32; Jordan, "Student Services and Students," p. 23; *1984 Redskin*, p. 74; *1985 Redskin*, p. 128; *1986 Redskin*, p. 137.

101. Jim Jordan to Jan Carlson, 25 September 1980, Diann Wilson to Jan Carlson, 6 October 1980, Jim Jordan to Tom Keys, 7 February 1986, "Bill to Initiate a 'Dry Rush' Program Into the I.F.C. of Oklahoma State University," Interfraternity Council Bill No. 194, November 1985, p. 1, Ronald Beer to Tom Keys, 20 May 1987, Ronald Beer to Student Services Division Heads, 13 February 1987, and Thomas M. Keys, "Oklahoma State University Men's and Women's Fraternity Hazing Code," 13 May 1987, pp. 1-8, in Student Services Collection; *Daily O'Collegian*, 20 April 1979, pp. 1, 4, 16 November 1985, p. 1, 10 April 1986, p. 1, 21 January 1986, p. 5, 27 January 1987, pp. 1-2, 28 April 1979, p. 1, 28 January 1987, p. 4, 24 February 1986, p. 4, 28 January 1982, p. 1, 20 September 1978, p. 4; *1986 Redskin*, p. 172; *1985 Redskin*, pp. 135, 159; *1982 Redskin*, p. 502.

102. *Daily O'Collegian*, 11 October 1978, p. 2, 24 August 1986, p. 1; *1985 Redskin*, pp. 135, 158; *1980 Redskin*, p. 108; *1986 Redskin*, p. 160.

103. *1981 Redskin*, pp. 114-115, 179; *1982 Redskin*, p. 130; *1986 Redskin*, p. 158; *Daily O'Collegian*, 3 December 1986, p. 6.

104. *Daily O'Collegian*, 11 September 1982, p. 2, 27 March 1981, p. 7, 1 October 1986, p. 16; *1979 Redskin*, pp. 88, 110, 118, 122; *1985 Redskin*, p. 169.

105. *Daily O'Collegian*, 17 April 1986, p. 10.

106. *1978 Redskin*, p. 535; *1979 Redskin*, p. 72; *Daily O'Collegian*, 22 April 1987, p. 10, 5 May 1983, p. 3; *Stillwater NewsPress*, 3 May 1987, p. 12C.

107. *Stillwater NewsPress*, 3 May 1987, p. 12C.

108. "Homecoming '86 . . . The Biggest and Best in OSU History!" *Oklahoma State University Outreach*, vol. 58, no. 2 (Winter 1987), p. 29; *Stillwater NewsPress*, 10 April 1987, pp. 2B, 10B, 12B; *1986 Redskin*, p. 17; *1979 Redskin*, pp. 32, 314, 318; *1986 Redskin*, p. 56; *Daily O'Collegian*, 8 April 1986, p. 6, 7 September 1984, p. 2, 30 September 1980, p. 5, 27 March 1986, p. 3, 11 February 1986, p. 16, 10 February 1979, p. 4.

109. *1982 Redskin*, pp. 389, 392; *Daily O'Collegian*, 25 October 1985, p. 4.

110. *1982 Redskin*, p. 392.

111. *Daily O'Collegian*, 6 November 1982, p. 1, 28 February 1981, p. 2, 20 March 1986, p. 18, 12 February 1986, p. 8, 19 February 1985, p. 1; *1981 Redskin*, p. 67; *1982 Redskin*, p. 362.

112. *Daily O'Collegian*, 30 April 1986, p. 10, 16 January 1981, p. 3, 27 September 1983, p. 5, 7 November 1985, p. 12, 1 February 1984, p. 19, 7 November 1985, p. 12, 26 February 1981, p. 11.

113. *Daily O'Collegian*, 20 March 1986, p. 1.

114. *Daily O'Collegian*, 30 October 1982, p. 4, 28 August 1986, p. 1, 24 April 1987, p. 1.

115. *Chronicle of Higher Education*, 4 September 1985, pp. 32, 36.

116. John Naisbitt, *Megatrends* (New York, NY: Warner Books, 1982), p. 249.

117. Naisbitt, pp. 31-34.

118. Naisbitt, p. 33.

119. *Stillwater NewsPress*, 26 July 1987, pp. 1, 3.

120. Naisbitt, p. 252.

# 11 Future Images and Dreams

Since the beginning of the nation, the importance of higher education has been a continuing foundation. It was so essential an idea that the framers of the United States Constitution debated the wisdom of establishing a national university to be organized and funded by Congress. Among the proponents of a federal system of post-secondary education at the secretive Constitutional Convention were George Washington, James Madison, and Charles Pinckney. In the sweltering heat and humidity of Philadelphia in 1787 convention delegates argued the merits of a national university on at least three different occasions. In the end a federal institution of higher education was voted down on the premise that Congress itself would have sufficient latitude without making such an action a Constitutional mandate.[1]

It is interesting to speculate about the shape such a concept would have taken if a university had been guaranteed by the Constitution. At least as interesting is the reality that history has rewarded the wisdom of the delegates to the Constitutional Convention, as well as subsequent Congresses, to defer the leadership for the country's colleges and universities to other forces. Their trust with such a vital issue has been validated.

Today over 3,300 institutions of higher education, public and private, large and small, dot the nation from coast to coast. Collectively they are the envy of the world. Yet because they serve both the nation and larger world, institutions of higher education must continue to change if they are to survive. Colleges and universities do not operate within a vacuum. As though in a matrix, larger social changes inevitably impact upon higher education. Reflecting a changing society and a critical need to prepare for the future, education returned to the top of the nation's agenda as Oklahoma State University neared its centennial year. The middle 1980s will be known as a time when government, business, school boards, parents, and the public all focused interests on improving education. In 1987, the bicentennial year of the Constitution, America's educational systems were being forced to adjust to an uncertain future again.[2]

To these ends numerous national and state reports generated a near overwhelming list of recommendations to improve all levels of education. Among the more noteworthy of these studies were "A Nation at Risk," a 1983 report from the National Commission on Excellence in Education. Others, dating to 1986, included "Tomorrow's Teachers," prepared by the Holmes Group; "A Nation Prepared," developed by the Carnegie Forum on Education and the Economy; and "A Time For Results," prepared by the National Governor's Association. In Oklahoma, a 1986 report called "Oklahoma's Secret Crisis" and a 1987 pro-

The growing, diversified, intersecting economies of the nations around the world coupled with the uncertainties of politics in many parts of the globe are concerns of the 1980s. Expo International, an annual campus extravaganza sponsored by the International Student Organization, helps move world understanding forward. And, of course, no Expo would be complete without the Malaysian lion dance.

posal by Smith L. Holt, dean of OSU's College of Arts and Sciences, added further to this unique period in history.[3]

Each of these reports contained positive aspects about what would be necessary to survive the future. However, most were tied to the needs of the immediate years. This limitation is perhaps not surprising. The authors were largely individuals who had lived through the rapid technological changes of the prior twenty-five years. They were aware of how quickly science could outpace most people's imagination. Experience had also clearly demonstrated how world events could be equally unpredictable. In the late 1980s most educational planners were accustomed to thinking in terms of one year federal and state budget cycles and a presidential election every four years. At best, looking further ahead seemed risky and difficult.

Of many possible scenarios, it was likely that at the midpoint of the twenty-first century, the nation's average life expectancy would be 100. In this depiction of the future, healthy aging would be the norm. Physical old age, which sixty to seventy years earlier could begin at age fifty or sixty, would not come for many citizens until after age seventy-five. Future planners in education would be forced to respond to this revolution in longevity.[4]

The changing demographics of the nation, highlighted by an aging society, presented complex and fundamental questions which would have to be faced. What does a university teach a young person to prepare them for a lifetime that could easily be a hundred years in length? Will the pace of life, which requires constant change, growth, and being informed, result in education becoming a recurrent activity throughout life? With longevity will people, even in advanced age, simply want to learn for the joy and stimulation that it provides? Even more fundamentally, will colleges and universities be able to transform themselves sufficiently to continue their role of leadership in educating the nation's people?

In 1987 institutions of higher education were generally ill prepared for the coming revolution. Among other problems attitudes toward aging and the value of experience were far too negative. There were few mechanisms in place to assist people desiring to change careers after age fifty. Even worse, there were no systematic ways to help finance career changes or even retraining for further gainful employment among older citizens. Career counselors primarily focused their skills on students in their twenties or younger. A positive, but still meager trend had started toward teaching the concept of the closely linked relationship between mind and body and subsequent physical health. People were just beginning to understand concepts related to wellness and healthy aging.[5]

There could be no doubt that the society in the future would be different. In response, colleges and universities also would be forced to change and adapt. But life has always required human beings to translate their images and dreams into action. By chance, exactly two hundred years from the month of the signing of the United States Constitution in Philadelphia, Oklahoma State University's top administrators in student services came together in a room in the Student Union to share their ideas about the future—their images and dreams. While acknowledging that predicting twenty-five years or more ahead could be risky, even foolhardy, they undertook their task with enthusiasm. They spoke of higher education in general and Oklahoma State University in particular. Their prophesies ranged from the conservative to the outlandish— or so it seemed.

Joining Vice President for Student Services Ronald S. Beer on September 30, 1987, were: Assistant Vice President for Student Services Pat Hofler; Charles W. Bruce, director of the Department of Financial Aid; Thomas M. Keys, director of the OSU Student Union; Don R. Briggs, director of University Placement; Donald L. Cooper, director of Student Health Services; Patrick M. Murphy, director of University Counseling Services; and Robert W. Huss, director of the Residential Life Department, including on-campus residence halls, University Apartments, food services, and Student Services Maintenance. George H. Oberle, director of the School of Health, Physical Education and Leisure, was unable to participate in the session.

As the discussion proceeded, a general consensus was reached that Oklahoma State University's students and campus would be quite different by the year 2000. General student enrollment would be level. The institution's focus would be on junior-senior undergraduate upper division programs and graduate level study. For many reasons, education will become a continuing activity effecting the entire life span. In fact, by 1985 this trend was in its early stages. Elderhostel, founded in 1975 as an educational program for people over sixty, spread to more than eight hundred campuses, including OSU. Over 100,000 people were annually attending Elderhostel offerings by the mid-1980s. The matter of providing continuing educational opportunities for millions of "healthy aging" citizens would provide institutions one of its greatest opportunities in the twenty-first century.[6]

Another key to the continuing viability for Oklahoma State will be its ability to respond to social changes. Primary among these changes is the developing demographics of the nation's racial minority groups. Hispanics constituted the fastest growing minority group. At some point in the next century Hispanics could become the largest minority, perhaps becoming the majority of citizens in many localities of the nation. Although there was still time for change to the better, these situations were not a scenario for civic order or racial harmony. Obtaining an ade-

Elderhostel, an educational program for people over sixty, promotes an interest in lifelong learning as well as healthy aging. This Elderhostel group gathers on the steps of Old Central. OSU professors Ed Arquitt (*front row, left*), Michael Smith (*third row, left*), and George Carney (*fourth row, left*) served as part of the teaching faculty.

quate education, including the investment of money to guarantee equal access to higher education for all minority groups, was seen as the only way to forestall the risk of a nation with a permanent lower class. If the response is positive, the campus of the future will be increasingly heterogeneous, with vast increases in the numbers of Hispanics, blacks, and other ethnic minority groups.[7]

Student services will, by necessity, be altered in response to the changes and needs of future students. Assistant Vice President Hofler summarized: "Every organization has a birth, a period of growth, and eventually a decline. By the end of the century student services will be in decline."[8] Although Vice President Beer and others took exception to Hofler's "demise theory," all present agreed that some areas would grow, while others would be fundamentally changed.

Most of the predicted variances would have a relationship to factors beyond the direct control of student services, both internal and external. Services that will survive will do so only because of their ability to demonstrate competence and a strong relationship with the land-grant missions of education, research, and extension suggested Residential Life Director Huss. Financial Aid Director Bruce and Health Services

Director Cooper postulated that their programs would be increasingly altered by a further encroachment of the federal government. The state of Oklahoma will only appropriate tax dollars for direct educational purposes in the future suggested Student Union Director Keys. Keys then continued that revenue-generating auxiliary enterprises, such as the union, may have to help support formerly state-funded activities such as counseling, placement, financial aid, and some student activities, if they are to continue. Keys predicted, "The days of doing necessary things for students cheaper than private enterprise will be gone."[9]

At least one generalization surfaced. Student services will exist to a new century, albeit perhaps under a new organization, composed of people with different titles, and with relationships far different than currently exist. One example, discussed in depth, centered upon university-owned and operated student housing and food services. These auxiliary enterprises were born decades ago out of a fundamental need, in an absence of help from the private sector. In recent years private entrepreneurs have increasingly gained a larger share of the business of housing and feeding students. According to the division heads of student services, unless dramatic changes are made to individualize campus housing, including the liberalizing of restricting rules and regulations, the private sector will eventually be the primary, if not exclusive, landlord for students. Oklahoma State might even lease campus land upon which gallerias, or living clusters, would be built. These future campus living centers would provide apartments, a variety of restaurants, shops, recreational facilities, and other amenities, limited only by one's imagination.

While university-owned student housing and food services may become extinct, pragmatism will dictate the survival of the Student Union. Despite the nagging complaints of "unfair competition" and the continuing huge task of generating its own revenue, there will always be a need for a campus center. Human nature requires that there be a comfortable, convenient place to meet other people and interact. The future union will be more holistic, offering a place to recreate, relax, attend meetings and classes, and debate issues. In the 1980s the trend toward unions becoming incorporated entities, and thereby separated from traditional campus governance, has assured the survival of these operations on other campuses. Other unions have been taken over by private contractors and run as independent businesses. OSU's Student Union will be faced with these same alternatives in the near future. Nevertheless, the original $10 million investment, now grown to over $30 million, will survive these knotty problems and continue as the "heart of the campus."

Outside influences will largely determine the future direction of campus student health services. Since little else can be achieved in the

The 1987 Student Senate enacted a student wellness fee to help facilitate implementation of a campus wellness program. This architectural rendering shows the future wellness center which will be constructed just west of the Colvin Center.

presence of illness, Dr. Cooper talked from the assumption that medical and health promotion services will continue to the future. However, technology and government will govern much of what will evolve. The connection between mind and body, where mind serves as healer, will become a fundamental principle of the medical arts. In the future, health care will move to self- care, prevention, or wellness care. Campus hospitals may well become satellites in a pyramid configuration leading to even larger regional medical centers, all run as a national health care system. Most physicians will be on a salary, few will have a private medical practice.

On-campus student health clinics may be primarily administered by nurse practitioners. Where once nine or ten physicians plied their skills, there may be just one or two. In this future health care facility there will be no beds for in-patient care. Students will input their symptoms into a computer which will in turn diagnose the problem. The computer will then direct the student directly to the pharmacy for a prescription, to a specific place for the start of treatment, or perhaps even to a physician. In this scenario the government, not campus administrators, will determine the policies including services offered, salaries, and staffing configurations. Following objections by some of his colleagues, Dr. Cooper factually stated: "The people of this country want nationalized medical care. It will eventually become reality. A national network will naturally include campus hospitals and clinics."[10]

Dr. Briggs was far less sure of what the future of placement services would become. This director reassured that assisting graduating students and alumni through a process of self-assessment would continue. Likewise, doing employer and employee marketing research, while facilitating position placement, would also continue. Certainly technology, specifically computers, would play a major role. In the near future, service users will be able to gather data from afar. The need to come to an office to look at paper materials will no longer exist. Interviews between parties will be done electronically; recruiter visits for on-campus interviews will be optional. All of this will be complex to organize and administer. Compounding the problems will be the fact that most jobs will be with smaller companies, rather than with *Fortune 500* corporations.

Like Dr. Briggs, Counseling Services Director Murphy shared only tentative conjectures on the next century. At Oklahoma State physical and mental health services will merge to add impetus to a holistic, preventative support network for students. Educating students in matters of nutrition, exercise, and health maintenance, including stress reduction and positive lifestyle choices, will be of the utmost priority for a wide mix of professionals. Because technology will not easily replace another caring human being (especially one who is skilled in psychology, student development, and behavior related to academic success), some configuration of professionals skilled in wellness promotion will be available to students.[11] Where once campus-based counseling services were seen at some institutions as a luxury, the future heterogeneous student body will require more rather than less of these services. Further, professionals will not only need to know about late adolescence, but they will also expand their base to the entire continuum of life. There will some day be an eighty-five year old wanting to discuss a college major and a married couple of fifty years wanting to enrich their relationship by talking to a professional campus helper.

Historically Oklahoma State's placement services and career counseling services evolved separately. Yet both remain integral allies. Each of these activities fall on a continuum and, in reality, represent an ongoing process. Having a meaningful purpose is so essential to life itself that career counseling and placement services, perhaps with an entirely different configuration, will someday be combined and reconstituted at Oklahoma State University. Such a change would not be radical. Rather, it would simply mirror the needs of an aging larger society. In this theory human dignity would be recognized throughout life. Helpful services would be available to everyone, regardless of age or any other potential barrier.

In one of the more interesting future portraits Financial Aid Director Bruce predicted huge growth for his area of supervision. By the year 2000 and beyond federal, state, and private sources will still be combining to give financial access to higher education to most students. The cost of an education will continue to rise. Demand, as always, will outdistance supply. Financial aid professionals will spend much of their time counseling and teaching people about consumerism, budgeting, and financial decision-making. Electronic data processing and other automation will reduce the current mountains of paperwork in financial aid. This will free staff to serve more students individually and directly. Government "red tape" and control will continue. In Oklahoma, state involvement in financial aid programs will increase. Student financial aid was the one area among all of the services now provided students that would grow both in magnitude as well as criticalness. In closing, Dr. Bruce also added that he was confident that by the year 2050 the financial aid department would be moved from its current cramped quarters in Hanner Hall, thus mitigating a longstanding problem.

Vice President Beer then framed an overview, perhaps a summary, for all of those seated about the table. In this future Oklahoma State books and documents will reach every student by computer. Some student services will grow in importance while others may "go out of business." Still others will continue, but take a new shape. Families will remain central in whatever happens. Institutional planners will have to contend with a smaller proportion of the larger society being traditionally college-aged seventeen to twenty-two year olds. If there is to be institutional growth, it must come from increasing the offerings to people in other age brackets. Further, serious thought must be given the question of financing an education, since the prospects of incurring large debts before a career has even started is already beginning to intimidate otherwise capable students from enrolling or from completing a course of study in higher education.

Dr. Bruce agreed with Dr. Beer and then elaborated. His comments reminded that the problem of costs go beyond simple dollars to changing attitudes. He continued that few Oklahoma families see a total financial picture. More typically money decisions are made from semester to semester or from year to year. Rather than a short term perspective, the $20,000 to $25,000 cost of an education could easily be an eighty- or ninety-year investment. Higher educational institutions in Oklahoma must work hard to turn this kind of short-sighted thinking around.

An additional trend is the proposal to have parents prepay, or pay in advance, for their child's college studies. Such plans are currently in place in a scattering of states. Oklahoma is now studying the concept. Prepaid college expense savings plans feature guaranteed college cost levels and tax assistance or other incentives. Director Bruce then flatly conjectured that they were mostly a "bad idea whose time had come."[12] In the financial aid director's opinion they do little to solve

As OSU readies to celebrate its Centennial birthday and looks toward the future in the twenty-first century, the institution is under the guidance of President John R. Campbell. At the 1988 Alpha picnic, the new chief administrator enjoys a relaxing visit with some students.

more fundamental problems. These schemes simply shift the financial burden back heavily to individual, mostly middle class, families. Families from lower socioeconomic groups are afforded even less opportunity with prepaid plans. If these issues were not enough, skyrocketing costs in higher education continue unabated. Dr. Bruce added that if the current policies are not altered, attendance at institutions of higher education could be open to just the wealthiest people.

At this particular gathering the conversation closed stoically. Despite a century and more of accumulated wisdom in higher education student personnel services, many questions and issues had surfaced, but few, if any, answers followed. Although problems were foreseen, solutions would remain for tomorrow and perhaps even be left to those who follow in some distant future. Such is the nature of projecting and predicting future images and dreams.

As the student services leaders left the room, the atmosphere seemed somber, certainly reflective, perhaps even thoughtful. This gathering to forecast the future had underscored a consensus belief that there would be an Oklahoma State University in the twenty-first century. However, it was also as certain that the institution would be much different. Attempting to grasp the magnitude of the changes for the future Oklahoma State fully had been an elusive task. The departing student services directors had just finished reinforcing that contention.

It was then somehow reassuring to think back to OSU's beginnings and recall one of the basic reasons for its founding. This tenet was stated succinctly more than fifty years ago by humanist philosopher Charles Francis Potter when he penned a spinoff of the Golden Rule. Potter suggested as a rule for individuals and their institutions to "help others that they can help themselves and others."[13] In that room on that late September day in 1987 it came to mind that the virtues represented by Potter's words had permeated Oklahoma A. and M. College's beginning and continue today at Oklahoma State University.

At that moment in time it seemed that as long as OSU continues to teach students to help themselves and others, it seemed of little consequence what the institution will be called, what shape it will take, or whom it enrolls. It matters even less about how the work is done or even who does it. In the next century it will only be important that historians, sociologists, and anthropologists can agree that this generation surmounted the many unknowns and improved the world for subsequent generations and that Oklahoma State University played a vital role in that larger conclusion.

Of course, future students will continue some form of their extracurriculum. There is no doubt that every learner will still have needs that reach beyond the realm of the classroom. Comforting are the thoughts that within this continuing environment there will assuredly be a place,

With all of the quandaries about what the future may bring today's students, perhaps this young man has the best philosophy!

as well as an important purpose, for future professionals with the same collective qualities that were embodied within student services throughout most of the first century of Oklahoma State University's proud history.

In the twenty-first century the possibilities are exciting that OSU will be different yet still the same. The institution has continued as a family, a community of educators and learners. It still teaches all who come to study there to care, to solidify personal positive values, to reach out to others, and eventually to improve the circumstances for all humankind. Reassuring is the possibility that in the next century all of those who look forward will see clearly that the institution has forever remained true to this simple, yet most fundamental, reason for its beginning and magnificent endurance. Oklahoma State University, into its second century and beyond, will continue to "help others that they can help themselves and others."[14]

This history of the Oklahoma State University student life and services has attempted to tell the story of past and current students—their deeds and misdeeds, their interests and enterprises, and their considerable individual and collective influences upon the history of OSU. Accordingly, it would seem remiss to conclude without some reflection upon this book's primary characters—students.

Through one hundred years there is clear evidence that the students have made a major impact on what, how, and why things are done as they are today. In many ways Oklahoma State University has responded to the needs and sometimes demands of its students. Not surprisingly, at one time or another they have manifested human nature's full range of behavior in an effort to get what they have wanted or seen as right. History shows that students can be warm and wonderful. They can be a powerful agent of change and a source of honor and pride. They can also be troublesome, paradoxical, perplexing, and even embarrassing. Regardless, although the campus and the issues change, the students can be credited with having always toiled for an unending cause—a greater, stronger Oklahoma State University.

Perhaps a legacy of confidence in the university's future, an indomitable student spirit, has enveloped the OSU campus since the first students enrolled in 1891. This is a phenomenon which is quite indescribable. This spirit evokes pride, determination, and optimism. It can be characterized as a resiliency, confidence beyond experience, and no matter the chronological age, a certain youthfulness. This spirit frequently lay at the root of grudging institutional change and confrontations over rules and regulations.

This spirit is seen in the roar of the student section at a Cowboy football game. The *Redskin* chronicles this feeling with each passing year. It can be found each fall as the new freshmen come to campus for the first time. And, who could escape it at a Howdy Dance, Varsity Revue, or homecoming. So long as there are students, this spirit will survive.

As Oklahoma State University celebrates its centennial year and moves to the twenty-first century, it faces many perplexing issues. Only some relate to an increasingly pluralistic society, excellence and access, stability and change, finances, and even its very mission within Oklahoma's larger system of higher education. Yet, with all of the uncertainties there are certain known strengths to be built upon. The education of students has been the singular primary purpose of Oklahoma State University in the past, and this fact will not change in the next century.

## Endnotes

1. Catherine Drinker Bowen, *Miracle At Philadelphia* (Boston, MA: Little, Brown and Company, 1966), p. 346.
2. Thomas H. Hohenshil, "The Educational Reform Movement: What Does It Mean For Counseling?" *Journal of Counseling and Development,* vol. 66, no. 1 (September 1987), p. 57.
3. Hohenshil, p. 57; *Stillwater NewsPress,* 13 September 1987, p. 6A.
4. D. Lydia Bronte, "Our Aging Society: A Challenge For The Future," *Research Dialogues,* no. 14 (July 1987), pp. 1-9.
5. Bronte, pp. 1-11.
6. Bronte, p. 12; Author interview with George H. Oberle, 25 November 1987, Stillwater, Oklahoma.
7. Bronte, p. 9.
8. Pat Hofler, Future of Student Services Meeting, 30 September 1987, Oklahoma State University, Stillwater, Oklahoma.
9. Thomas M. Keys, Future of Student Services Meeting, 30 September 1987.
10. Donald L. Cooper, Future of Student Services Meeting, 30 September 1987.
11. One trend toward the future moved ahead on October 14, 1987 when the OSU Student Senate enacted a recommendation for a twenty cent per credit hour fee to help fund a campus-wide student wellness program. The assessment would generate an estimated $900,000 a year. This money would partially fund a new building to house programs in health assessment, lifestyle modification, research, and education. Among the larger student body there was widespread misunderstanding of the wellness idea and concern for still another rise in student activity fees. See Oklahoma State University *Daily O'Collegian,* 12 October 1987, p. 1, 15 October 1987, p. 1, 22 October 1987, pp. 4-5; James H. Rogers, "OSU Wellness Center Proposal, School of Health, Physical Education and Leisure, Draft 3" (September 1987), pp. 1-17, Student Services Collection, Special Collections, Edmon Low Library, Oklahoma State University, Stillwater, Oklahoma; Oberle interview.
12. Charles W. Bruce, Future of Student Services Meeting, 30 September 1987.
13. Wallace P. Rusterholtz, "Humanist Transcendence," *Religious Humanism,* vol. 22, no. 2 (Spring 1987), p. 74.
14. Rusterholtz, p. 74.

# Appendix

## Longtime Student Services Personnel
(Three or More Years of Service)*

Charles R. "Chuck" Aanenson (International Student Advisor, 1976-1979)

Shaila R. Aery (Assistant Head Resident, Stout Hall, 1968-1969; Head Resident, Stout Hall, 1969-1970; Assistant Director for Women, Single Student Housing, 1970-1973; Director, Program Development, Vice President for Student Services Office, 1973-1975; Coordinator, Freshmen Programs and Services, 1975-1976)

Iris Geraldine Akins (Registered Nurse, 1965-1968)

Ashley H. Alexander (Senior Manager, Student Entertainers, 1956-1973; Director, Student Entertainers, 1973-1978)

Harvey W. Anderson (Psychiatrist, 1965-1968)

M. M. "Bud" Andrews (Food Manager, Student Union, 1966-1975)

Verlin L. Anthony (Head Resident, Parker Hall, 1968-1969; Director, Scott-Parker-Wentz Complex, 1969-1972)

Helen I. Ashcraft (Registered Nurse, 1967-1971 and 1976-1986)

Gerald W. "Jerry" Autin (Coordinator, Willham Complex, University Food Services, 1972-1974; Assistant to Director, University Food Services, 1974-1976; Assistant Director of Personnel, University Food Services, 1976-1977)

William D. "Bill" Baker (Clinical Counselor, 1980-1983, University Counseling Services; Senior Clinical Counselor, University Counseling Services, 1983-1985)

Tim Baldwin (Physician, 1973-1984)

Carole J. Ballard (Assistant Head Resident, Willard Hall, 1981-1983; Head Resident, Willard Hall, 1983-1987)

Mary C. Barnes (Assistant Director, University Food Services, 1946-1964; Food Purchasing Agent, University Food Services, 1964-1971)

Grace M. Barreau (Registered Nurse, 1971-1976)

Michael J. Barton (Assistant Head Resident, Willham South Hall, 1977-1978; Head Resident, Scott Hall, 1978-1981)

Marie L. Basler (Student Program Coordinator, Office of Student Activities, 1982-present)

Ruby N. Basler (Registered Nurse, 1971-1978; Director of Nursing, 1978-1985; Registered Nurse, 1985-present)

Rita J. Baucom (Staff Assistant, Construction and Renovations, 1977-1978; Supervising Secretary, Construction and Renovations, 1978-1982, Warehouse Supervisor, Student Services Maintenance, 1982-present)

Ronald S. Beer (Vice President for Student Services, 1980-present)

Katherine L. Berckman (Registered Nurse, 1970-1975)

Janet J. Best (Assistant Head Resident, Murray Hall, 1982-1984; Head Resident, Murray Hall, 1984-1985)

Margaret C. Betts (Assistant Head Resident, Drummond Hall, 1982-1983; Head Resident, Willham North Hall, 1983-1985; Resident Life Specialist, 1985-1986; Information Services Coordinator, Single Student Housing, 1986-1987)

Patty K. Bible, (Supervisor, Colvin Physical Education Center and Intramural Programs, 1975-1987; Administrative Associate, Colvin Physical Education Center and Intramural Programs, 1987-present)

Ann E. Biles (Brumley Resident Manager, 1964-1968)

Winsel L. Bilyeu (Assistant Director and Manager, Union Club, Student Union, 1954-1986)

Raymond E. Bivert (Director, Student Loans, Financial Aid, 1955-1968)

Freeman F. "Joe" Blair (Student Supervisor, Student Union, 1955-1956; Manager, University Food Services, 1956-1966; Director, University Food Services, 1966-1987)

Norvel G. "J. B." Blankenship (Assistant to Bookstore Manager, 1966-1968; Assistant Bookstore Manager, 1968-1972; Bookstore Supply Supervisor, 1972-1982)

Dane E. Blubaugh (Construction Superintendent, Construction and Renovations, 1982-1988; Superintendent, Student Services Maintenance, 1988-present)

John F. Bolene (Consulting Physician, 1966-present)

W. D. Bolene (Consulting Physician, 1962-1984)

William K. "Kirk" Bonner (Head Resident, Kerr Hall, 1978-1980; Head Resident, Parker Hall, 1980-1981)

Arnold R. Bourne (Head Resident, Stout Hall, 1978-1979; Head Resident, East Bennett Hall, 1979-1982)

Jean F. Bowles (Registered Nurse, 1977-1980)

Vivian S. Bowles (Dietitian, Cordell Hall, University Food Services, 1952-1965; Dietitian, University Hospital and Clinic, 1965-1977)

F. Louise Bradley (Supervisor, Stout Hall, University Food Services, 1967-1970)

Deloris A. Brannon (Registered Nurse, 1978-1983)

Don R. Briggs (Counselor, University Placement, 1971-1976; Director, University Placement, 1978-present)

Richard D. Brown (Manager, Cordell Hall, University Food Services, 1965-1967; Manager, Willard Hall, University Food Services, 1968-1969; Manager, Kerr-Drummond Complex, University Food Services, 1970-1974; Manager, Central Bakery, University Food Services, 1974-1978; Manager, Willard Hall, University Food Services, 1978-1980)

Rosalie M. Broyles (Psychologist, 1971-1976)

Charles W. Bruce (Director, Financial Aid, 1981-present)

Jackie W. Brugh (Registered Nurse, 1970-1973)

Muhrizah D. Brunken (Program Specialist, International Student Services, 1980-1984; Student Program Coordinator, Office of Student Activities, 1988-present)

Hal N. Buchanan (Director, University Placement, 1960-1978)

Kent E. Bunker (Assistant Intramural Director, Colvin Physical Education Center and Intramural Programs, 1970-1973; Intramural Director, 1973-present)

Elaine P. Burgess (Coordinator, International Student Services, 1984-present)

Manuel D. "Manny" Bustamante (Counselor, Minority Programs and Services, 1983-1988)

Velma G. Butler (Laboratory Technician, University Hospital and Clinic, 1969-1982)

King W. Cacy Jr. (Assistant Dean, Student Affairs, 1956-1959; Director, Student Activities, 1959-1966; Director, Scholarships and Men's Employment, 1966-1969; Coordinator, Special Services, 1972-1973; Associate Director, Financial Aid, 1969-1972 and 1973-1983; Counselor, Financial Aid, 1983-1985)

Pauline E. Campbell (Head Resident, Willard Hall, 1966-1971; Head Resident, Brumley Apartments, 1971-1972)

Michael D. Canamore (Food Production Manager, Scott-Parker-Wentz Complex, University Food Services, 1978-1980; Coordinator, Scott-Parker-Wentz Complex, University Food Services, 1980-1982)

Bonita C. Card (Personnel Coordinator, Student Union, 1981-1988)

James M. Carley (Physician, 1972-1977)

I. A. "Ted" Carlisle (Catering Manager, Student Union, 1959-1970; Public Relations, Student Union, 1970-1973; Sales Supervisor, Student Union, 1973-1976)

Jan M. Carlson (Director, Student Activities, 1975-1981, Manager, Student Activities, 1981-present)

Judy Carroll (Licensed Practical Nurse, 1976-1980)

Nolen T. Cathey (Manager, Lake Carl Blackwell, 1966-1975)

Anita J. Cawley (McElroy Supervisor, University Food Services, 1982-1983; Supervisor, Willham Complex, University Food Services, 1983-1984; Supervisor, Kerr-Drummond Complex, 1984-1985)

Ermal V. Chapman (Food Services Supervisor, Student Union, 1979-present)

Eloy A. Chavez (Student Program Coordinator, Office of Student Activities, 1981-1985)

Nancy R. Childress (Graduate Assistant, Office of the Vice President for Student Services, 1983-1985; Special Programs Coordinator, Office of the Vice President for Student Services, 1985-1986)

Robert B. Clark (Director, Financial Aid, 1968-1981)

Mary J. "Jan" Riggs Cloyde (Assistant for Programs and Promotions, Student Union, 1972-1975)

Betty Coggins (Head Resident, Cordell Hall, 1975-1978)

Brenda G. Coleman (Office Administrator, Office of the Vice President for Student Services, 1977-1988)

Sandra L. Coltharp (Head Resident, Wentz Hall, 1981-1986; Coordinator, Disciplinary Program, Single Student Housing, 1986-1987; Director, Willham North Hall, 1987-present)

Valerie Colvin (Director, Women's Intramural Programs, 1929-1969)

Nellie Mabel Connarro (Licensed Practical Nurse, 1965-1971)

Thomas L. Conrady (Head Resident, Scott Hall, 1969-1970; Head Resident, Willham North Hall, 1970-1971; Area Coordinator, Willham Complex, 1971-1974; Assistant Director, Single Student Housing, 1974-1975)

Barbara Lawson Contardi (Purchasing Agent, Student Union, 1971-1972; Manager, Student Union Catering, 1972-present)

Donald L. Cooper (Director, University Hospital and Clinic and Physician, 1960-present)

Alma A. Corser (Textbooks Manager, 1967-1969; Assistant Bookstore Manager, 1969-1971)

Pete G. Coser (Counselor, Minority Programs and Services, 1985-present)

James Creech (Cordell Assistant Head Resident, 1977-1978; Cordell Head Resident, 1978-1980)

Robert M. "Bob" Culton (Manager, Kerr-Drummond Complex, University Food Services, 1967-1968; Assistant Manager, Kerr-Drummond Complex, University Food Services, 1968-1970; Manager, Cordell Hall, University Food Services, 1970-1973; Assistant Manager, Willham Complex, University Food Services, 1973-1978; Manager, Willham Complex, University Food Services, 1978-1981)

Janet Cunningham (Registered Nurse, 1981-1987)

Mercedier C. Cunningham (Assistant Dean of Student Activities, 1972-1973; Assistant Director of Student Activities, 1973-1981)

Robert N. Curry (Senior Clinical Counselor, University Counseling Services, 1985-present)

Marian Dark (Assistant Director, University Placement, 1966-1980)

Gary Davidson (Counselor, Financial Aid, 1984-present)

Carol L. Davis (Coordinator, Bennett Complex, University Food Supervisor, 1979-1981; Supervisor, Scott-Parker-Wentz Complex, University Food Services, 1981-1983)

Harlen M. "Mac" Delozier (Assistant Supervisor, Concessions and Vending, 1956-1958; Manager, Concessions and Vending, 1958-1977)

James R. "Rex" Demaree (Assistant Maintenance Superintendent, 1969-1970; Superintendent, Single Student Housing, 1970-1982; Assistant Director, Construction and Renovation, 1982-1987)

J. M. "Mike" DeYong (Assistant Head Resident, East Bennett Hall, 1980-1981; Head Resident, Stout Hall, 1981-1982; Head Resident, East Bennett Hall, 1982-1983)

Russell E. Dill (Manager, Laundry, 1964-1973)

Shirley A. Dillard (Licensed Practical Nurse, 1974-1979)

Judy Disch (Marketing Associate, Student Union, 1984-1987)

Marshall W. "Buck" Dollarhide (Director, Kerr-Drummond Complex, 1969-1971; Reservations Manager, Single Student Housing, 1971-1972; Assistant Director for Business, Single Student Housing, 1972-1973, Associate Director, Single Student Housing, 1973-1974)

Jo F. Dorris (Director, Student Activities, 1971-1975; Associate Dean of Student Affairs, 1975-1977)

Barbara A. Driskel (Medical Technologist, University Hospital and Clinic, 1981-present)

Bonnie L. Dudley (Supervising Secretary, Office of Student Activities, 1978-present)

Georgia Lee Ebersole (Resident Manager, Thatcher Hall, 1963-1965; Resident Manager, Scott Hall, 1965-1967; Head Resident, Murray Hall, 1967-1969)

Claire D. Echols (Counselor, Financial Aid, 1983-1987)

Ann Edwards (Head Resident, Willham North Hall, 1974-1977)

Carolyn Francis Elledge (Office Manager, University Placement, 1967-1971)

Ina Ellington (Assistant Purchasing Agent, University Food Services, 1969-1973)

Ralph R. Elswick (Assistant Manager, Vending, 1969-1977)

Ruby L. Eshelman (Head Resident, North Murray Hall, 1967-1971)

Carolyn A. Fair (Coordinator, Willard Hall, University Food Services, 1981-1985; Senior Coordinator, Kerr-Drummond Complex, University Food Services, 1985-1987; Manager, Residence Halls West, University Food Services, 1987-present)

Sherry K. Fairchild (Food Services Coordinator, Student Union, 1983-1986)

Jay W. Fennel (Assistant Manager, Food Services, Student Union, 1984-1985; Manager, Food Services, Student Union, 1985-present)

Nancy L. Finley (Registered Nurse, 1984-present)

Judith K. "Dee" Finnegan (Research Technician, Financial Aid, 1976-1977 and 1978-1981; Counselor, Financial Aid, 1981-present)

Rex T. Finnegan (Counselor, University Counseling Services, 1967-1969; Director, University Counseling Services, 1969-1979; Senior Clinical Counselor, University Counseling Services, 1979-present)

James R. Fleming (Coordinator, College Work-Study, 1965-1966; Director, College Work-Study, 1966-1968; Director, Work-Study and Men's Employment, 1968-1970; Assistant Director, Financial Aid, 1970-1975)

Arla Jean Fowler (Secretary, Food Units, 1959-1960; Assistant Supervisor, University Food Services, 1960-1962; Supervisor, Bennett Hall, University Food Services, 1962-1964; McElroy Supervisor, University Food Services, 1964-1966; McElroy Manager, University Food Services, 1966-1969)

M. L. Francis (Bookstore Manager, 1966-1969)

Bert A. Franks (Head Resident, Kerr Hall, 1981-1983; Head Resident, Willham South Hall, 1983-1985)

Leon C. Freed (Consulting Physician, 1947-1984)

Edith B. Friedle (Registered Nurse, 1960-1986)

Mary L. Frye (Director, Recreation for Women, Colvin Physical Education Center and Intramural Programs, 1968-1976; Director, Campus Recreation and Sports Clubs, Colvin Physical Education Center and Intramural Programs, 1976-1988)

Laurence B. "Larry" Fulgenzi (Psychologist, 1972-1983)

Kathy Furlong (Assistant Head Resident, Wentz Hall, 1974-1975; Head Resident, Cordell Hall, 1975-1976; Head Resident, West Bennett Hall, 1975-1977; Program Coordinator, Residence Life, 1978-1980; Coordinator, Residence Life, 1980-1982)

Alice F. Gambill (Physician, 1979-1988; Assistant Director, University Hospital and Clinic, 1988-present)

Gary J. Garaffolo (Assistant Director, Financial Aid, 1983-present)

Nancy J. Garfield (Career Counselor, University Counseling Services, 1975-1978)

Loretta F. Garrison (Accounts Clerk, Student Union, 1977-1980; Accounting Supervisor, Student Union, 1980-present)

George B. Gathers Jr. (Physician, 1970-1978; Assistant Director, University Hospital and Clinic, 1978-1987)

Ladoris Evelyn Gay (Licensed Practical Nurse, 1966-1970)

Ople M. Gazaway (Student Store Clerk, 1977-1979; Student Store Supervisor, 1979-1986)

Kerry A. Geffert (Counselor, International Student Services, 1981-1984)

Paul Giessen (Assistant Head Resident, Cordell Hall 1974-1976; Head Resident, Parker Hall, 1976-1980; Head Resident, Willham South Hall, 1980-1981)

Gordon B. Gilbert (Director, Men's Intramural Programs, 1940-1973)

Ralph H. Glazner (Head Resident, Willham South Hall, 1977-1980)

Jim E. Goforth (Foreman, Married Student Housing and Student Services Maintenance, 1967-1987)

Thelma A. Golbeck (Accountant and Administrative Assistant, Financial Aid, 1970-1978; Financial Assistant, Financial Aid, 1978-1983)

Sidney J. "Sid" Gonsoulin (Assistant Recreation Director, Colvin Physical Education Center and Intramural Programs, 1973-1976; Chair, Campus Recreation, Colvin Physical Education Center and Intramural Programs, 1976-1978)

Larry Gregory (Recreation Program Assistant, Colvin Physical Education Center and Intramural Programs, 1971-1976)

Lisa L. Grubbs (Career Counselor, University Counseling Services, 1984-1986; Senior Clinical Counselor, University Counseling Services, 1986-1988)

Orin Joseph Hake (Physician, 1974-present)

Wilma J. Hall (Supervisor, Scott-Parker-Wentz Complex, University Food Supervisor, 1982-1985)

Rama Lea Hamble (Registered Nurse, 1968-1986)

Marcia W. Hansen (Manager, Bennett Complex, University Food Services, 1980-1982; Coordinator, Kerr-Drummond Complex, University Food Services, 1982-1983; Coordinator, Willham Complex, 1983-1985)

Molly Harris (Assistant Head Resident, Willard Hall, 1974-1975; Head Resident, Drummond Hall, 1975-1978)

George A. Harrison (Chief of Maintenance, Student Union, 1969-1985; Building Operations Manager, Student Union, 1985-present)

Patricia A. Harrison (Counselor, University Placement, 1985-present)

Elfrieda K. Harvey (Registered Nurse, 1964-1972)

E. H. Harwell (Manager, Student Services Maintenance, 1959-1966; Superintendent, Single Student Housing, 1966-1969)

Stephen P. Haseley (Counselor, International Student Services, 1985-present)

Brenda J. Haskins (Manager, Willham Complex, 1979-1983)

Helen M. Haun (Registered Nurse, 1975-1987)

Russell C. Hays (Bookstore Clerk, 1978-1982; Bookstore Purchasing Specialist, 1982-1987)

Betty J. Hazelbaker (Collections Officer, Financial Aid, 1969-1972; Administrative Services Officer, Financial Aid, 1972-1974; Assistant Director, Administrative Services, Financial Aid, 1974-1979)

DiAnne K. Hembree (Assistant Head Resident, Wentz Hall, 1978-1979; Head Resident, Murray Hall, 1979-1981; Head Resident, West Bennett Hall, 1981-1982)

David B. Henderson (Associate Dean, Student Affairs 1977-1980)

Terry H. Henderson (Counselor, University Counseling Services, 1970-1973; Coordinator, Special Services, 1973-1979; Assistant Director, University Counseling Services, 1978-1985)

Robert N. "Bob" Hendrick (Assistant Head Resident, Stout Hall, 1978-1979; Head Resident, Stout Hall, 1979-1981; Head Resident, Willham South Hall, 1981-1982; Program Coordinator, Residence Life, 1982-1983; Assistant Coordinator, Residential Life, 1983-1985; Coordinator, Residential Life, 1985-1986)

Regina D. Henry (Unit Assistant, International Student Services, 1981-1986; Program Specialist, International Student Services, 1986-present)

Marsha Herman-Betzen (Scheduling and Meetings Manager, Student Union, 1981-1985)

John R. Herndon (Inventory Supervisor, Single Student Housing, 1970-1973; Property Manager, Single Student Housing, 1973-1978)

Abe L. Hesser (Assistant to Director, Student Union, 1950-1951; Assistant Director, Student Union, 1951-1953; Director, Student Union, 1953-1963; Director, Student Union, Housing and Food Service, 1963-1965; Director, Auxiliary Enterprises, 1965-1968; Vice President for Student Services, 1968-1971)

Lance Hinkle (Bookstore Clerk, 1982-1984; Textbook Specialist, 1984-1986; Assistant Manager, Bookstore, 1986-present)

Floyd B. Hoelting (Head Resident, Kerr Hall, 1969-1970; Director, Willham Complex, 1970-1971; Assistant Director for Men, Single Student Housing, 1971-1972)

Pat Hofler (Accountant, Auxiliary Enterprises, 1951-1962; Assistant Director, Housing and Food Service, 1962-1966; Assistant Business Manager, 1968-1971; Assistant Vice President for Student Services, 1971-1979 and 1980-1988; Interim Vice President for Student Services, 1979-1980)

Suzanne Holland (Head Resident, North Murray Hall, 1971-1972; Area Coordinator, Single Student Housing, 1972-1975; Assistant Director, Single Student Housing, 1975-1978; Director, Program Development, Office of Vice President for Student Services, 1978-1980)

Hazel Eva Honeywell (Registered Nurse, 1965-1971)

Johnnie M. Hopkins (Office Manager, Financial Aid, 1969-1972 and 1973-1974; Scholarship Officer, Financial Aid, 1972-1973)

Susan E. "Sue" Hosack (Counselor, Financial Aid, 1982-1985; Senior Counselor, Financial Aid, 1985-1987)

Samuel G. Houston (Games Room Manager, Student Union, 1968-1973)

Thomas R. Howard Jr. (Physician, 1980-1987)
Doward L. Hudlow Sr. (Assistant Director, Financial Aid, 1979-1982)

J. C. Hunt (Head Resident, East Bennett Hall, 1967-1968; Director, Bennett Complex, 1968-1971)

William E. "Bill" Hunter (Assistant to Director, Student Union, 1958-1960; Bookstore Manager, 1960-1986)

Linda J. Hyman (Senior Coordinator, Bennett Complex, University Food Services, 1985-1986; Senior Coordinator, Willham Complex, University Food Services, 1986-1987; Senior Coordinator, Residence Halls West, University Food Services, 1987-present)

Karen L. Irey (Assistant Dean, Student Affairs, 1969-1972)

David B. Jackson (Manager, Laboratory and X-ray, 1967-present)

Frances L. Jackson (Administrative Assistant, University Hospital and Clinic, 1967-1982; Senior Administrative Assistant, 1982-1985)

W. Lynn Jackson (Head Resident, East Bennett, 1966-1967; Assistant Director for Men, Single Student Housing, 1967-1970; Director, Single Student Housing, 1970-1985)

Bert H. Jacobson (Head Resident, Iba Hall, 1977-1980)

Emil E. Jafek (Assistant Chief of Maintenance, Student Union, 1950-1962; Chief of Maintenance, Student Union, 1962-1968; Assistant Director, Student Services Maintenance, 1968-1982)

David R. James (Manager, Cordell Hall, University Food Services, 1967-1968; Manager, Kerr-Drummond Complex, University Food Services, Manager, 1968-1970 and 1975-1979; Coordinator, Scott-Parker-Wentz Complex, University Food Services, 1970-1973 and 1974-1975; Coordinator, Willham Complex, University Food Services, 1973-1974; Manager, Cordell Hall, University Food Services, 1979-1981)

Robert L. "Bob" Jamison (Counselor, University Placement, 1980-present)

Paul A. Jenkins (Physician, 1967-1971)

Bonnie C. Joerschke (Counselor, Financial Aid, 1984-1987; Senior Counselor, Financial Aid, 1987-present)

Floy S. Johnson (Supervisor, Scott-Parker-Wentz Complex, 1967-1968, University Food Services; Supervisor, Cordell Hall, University Food Services, 1968-1970; McElroy Manager, University Food Services, 1970-1981)

Glenn Johnson (Assistant to Director, Financial Aid, 1971-1978; Loan Officer, Financial Aid, 1978-1981)

Beth E. Jones (Assistant Director, University Food Services, 1982-1985)

Ruth C. Jones (Counselor, Minority Programs and Services, 1975-1978)

Dianne Jones-Freeman (Counselor, University Counseling Services, 1973-1978)

James G. Jordan (Student Program Coordinator, Office of Student Activities, 1975-1983; Greek Life Coordinator, Office of Student Activities, 1983-present)

Martha L. Jordan (Career Counselor, University Counseling Services, 1978-1985; Assistant Director, University Counseling Services, 1985-present)

Mary Ann Kelly (Counselor, International Student Services, 1985-present)

Colby M. Kennedy (Supervisor, Scott-Parker-Wentz Complex, University Food Services, 1966-1967; Supervisor, Murray Hall, University Food Services, 1967-1969)

Patrick B. "Pat" Kennedy (Assistant Director, Financial Aid, 1984-present)

Kay W. Keys (Assistant Dean, Student Affairs, 1970-1974)

Thomas M. Keys (Assistant Dean, Student Affairs, 1969-1975; Director, Program Development, Office of Vice President for Student Services, 1975-1978; Director, Student Union, 1982-present)

Stephen M. King (Recreation Program Specialist, Colvin Physical Education Center and Intramural Programs, 1979-present)

Walter P. "Paul" Kinnamon (Maintenance Supervisor, Student Union, 1967-1968; Decorating and Housekeeping Supervisor, Student Union, 1968-1984)

Marvin Klufa (Assistant Intramural Director, Colvin Physical Education Center and Intramural Programs, 1982-1987)

Geraldine D. Knight (Registered Nurse, 1965-1986)

Karla L. Knoepfli (Assistant Head Resident, Willham North Hall, 1982-1983; Head Resident, Drummond Hall, 1983-1985)

Bernice A. Kroll (Administrative Secretary, Office of the Dean of Student Affairs, 1966-1975)

Robin H. Lacy (Coordinator, Freshman Programs and Services, Office of the Vice President for Student Services, 1976-1982)

Pamela F. Land (Assistant Head Resident, Wentz Hall, 1980-1981; Head Resident, Murray Hall, 1981-1983)

Dianna L. Langdon (Supervisor, Financial Aid, 1982-1985)

Charles E. Larsen (Director, University Counseling Services, 1965-1968)

Katherine E. Larson (Registered Nurse, 1978-present)

Helene A. Laster (Registered Nurse, 1969-1979)

Pauline J. Leonard (Manager, Student Store, Student Union, 1966-1977)

Linda L'Hote (Office Manager, University Placement, 1972-1976; Counselor, University Placement, 1976-1980; Assistant Director, University Placement, 1980-1987)

Lovell T. Loughridge (Foreman, Construction and Renovations, 1977-1978; Maintenance Supervisor, Construction and Renovations, 1978-1982)

Nancy E. Luce (Loan Officer, Financial Aid, 1974-1981; Senior Counselor, Financial Aid, 1981-1982)

Violet C. "Vie" Macklin (Fountains Manager, Student Union, 1966-1974; Food Services Supervisor, Student Union, 1974-1980)

Lee M. Marsh (Counselor, University Counseling Services, 1965-1968; Psychologist, University Hospital and Clinic, 1968-1974)

Dale Maxwell (Psychiatrist, 1971-1983)

Sherry C. Maxwell (Psychologist, 1977-1983; Manager, Mental Health Clinic, 1983-present)

John D. Mayes (Loan Officer, Financial Aid, 1977-1980)

Melinda A. "Mel" McCracken (Assistant Head Resident, Willham North Hall, 1981-1982; Head Resident, Willham North Hall, 1982-1983; Head Resident, Murray Hall, 1983-1984)

Frank E. McFarland (Dean of Student Affairs, 1961-1968)

William E. McFarland (Assistant Director, Financial Aid, 1975-1980)

Thomas "Tom" McKee, (Assistant Director, Recreation for Men, Colvin Physical Education Center and Intramural Programs, 1969-1970; Director, Recreation for Men, Colvin Physical Education Center and Intramural Programs, 1970-1976)

Ann T. McKennis (Registered Nurse, 1977-1984)

Tom J. McKinley (Assistant Head Resident, Willham South Hall, 1981-1984)

Victoria E. McLaurin (Unit Assistant, University Counseling Services, 1977-1987; Senior Unit Assistant, University Counseling Services, 1987-present)

Richard C. "Dick" McRee (Facilities Assistant, Colvin Physical Education Center and Intramural Programs, 1980-present)

J. V. "Mac" McReynolds (Storeroom Clerk, Student Union, 1951-1977)

Heather M. Meacham (Resident Manager, Thatcher Hall, 1965-1966; Assistant Director for Women, Single Student Housing, 1966-1968)

Joshua K. Mihesuah (Counselor, Minority Programs and Services, 1981-1985)

Elnora G. Miller (Physician, 1966-1987)

James M. Miller (Assistant Director, Auxiliary Enterprises, 1954-1955; Dean of Men and Associate Dean, 1955-1968)

Jean L. Miller (Licensed Practical Nurse, 1976-1985)

Johnny Miller (Assistant Head Resident, Stout Hall, 1975-1976; Head Resident, Stout Hall, 1976-1978)

Pamela A. Miller (Clinical Counselor, Personal Counseling Unit, University Counseling Services, 1978-1985; Coordinator, Personal Counseling Unit, University Counseling Services, 1985-present)

Betty J. Mize (Games Room Cashier, Student Union, 1969-1973; Games Room Manager, Student Union, 1973-1984)

Mary F. Montague (Registered Nurse, 1952-1983)

Beulah B. Moore (Office Supervisor, Office of the Vice President for Student Services, 1964-1971; Bookkeeper, Office of the Vice President for Student Services, 1971-1977)

Norman F. Moore (Program Consulant, Student Union, 1959-1960; Assistant to Director, Student Union, 1960-1961; Conference Coordinator, Student Union, 1961-1963; Associate Director, Student Union, 1963-1966; Director, Student Union, 1969-1971; Vice President for Student Services, 1971-1979)

Marilon Morgan (Coordinator, Student Programs, Office of Student Activities, 1982-present)

Mary Glenda Morris (Head Counselor, Stout, 1965-1966; Assistant Dean of Women, 1967-1969)

Robert C. "R. C." Morrison (Assistant Director, Allied Arts, 1972-1974; Assistant Director, Office of Student Activities, 1974-1978)

Patrick M. Murphy (Complex Director, Scott-Parker-Wentz, 1967-1968; Residence Hall Program Director, 1968-1970; Counselor, University Counseling Services, 1971-1972; Assistant Director, University Counseling Services, 1972-1977; Interim Director, University Counseling Services, 1977-1978; Coordinator, Special Services, 1978-1979; Director, University Counseling Services, 1979-present)

Philip J. Murphy (Counselor, University Counseling Services, 1972-1975)

Grace E. Newbold (Supervisor, Cordell Hall, University Food Services, 1966-1967; Supervisor, Willard Hall, University Food Services, 1967-1969)

Huc X. Nghiem (Physician, 1978-present)

George H. Oberle (Director, Colvin Physical Education Center and Intramural Programs, 1976-present)

Joann M. O'Donnell (Registered Nurse, 1984-present)

Thelma Olmstead (Cashier, Student Union, 1969-1972; Textbook Supervisor, 1972-1985; Bookstore Data Control Technician, 1985-1987)

Steven M. Olson (Counselor, International Student Services, 1980-1985)

Vita Josephine Padrone (Registered Nurse, 1965-1968)

Louella (Lou) Palmer (Counselor, Minority Programs and Services, 1975-1979)

Zelma F. Patchin (Dean of Women, 1951-1969; Associate Dean, Student Affairs, 1969-1975)

Naomi O. "Oleta" Pattillo (Assistant Dietitian, Food Units, 1949-1950; Dietitian, Cordell Hall, 1950-1952; Dietitian, Willard Hall, 1952-1968; Manager, Stout Hall, University Food Services, 1968-1969; Assistant Director, University Food Services, 1970-1980)

Lunora Payne (Secretary, International Student Advisement, 1966-1970; Administrative Secretary, Student Affairs, 1970-1976)

David C. Peshke (Recreation Program Assistant and Director of Sports Clubs, Colvin Physical Education Center and Intramural Programs, 1973-1976)

Beverly A. Pickard (Registered Nurse, 1968-1975)

Marilyn C. Pierce (Registered Nurse, 1975-1986; Supervisor, Medical Records, University Hospital and Clinic, 1986-present)

Mark Pisarra (Assistant Director, Financial Aid, Scholarships, 1974-1978)

Deborah A. Pitts (Head Resident, Willard Hall, 1978-1980; Counselor, Minority Programs and Services, 1980-1983)

William E. Porter (Assistant Dean, Student Affairs, 1974-1980)

George Portman (Head Resident, Parker Hall, 1966-1967; Head Resident, Drummond Hall, 1967-1968; Director, Kerr-Drummond Complex, 1968-1969)

Charles H. Pritchard (Head Resident, Cordell Hall, 1968-1971)

Nyla S. Ptomey (Head Resident, Murray Hall, 1977-1979; Head Resident, Willham South Hall, 1979-1980; Head Resident, Willham North Hall, 1980-1981)

Nora L. Pugh (Counselor, Minority Programs and Services, 1984-1988)

Judith A. "Judy" Quisenberry (Accounts Clerk, University Food Services, 1973-1975; Administrative Assistant, University Food Services, 1975-1984; Assistant Director, University Food Services, 1984-present)

A. K. Rahman (Coffee Shop Manager, Student Union, 1969-1972; Food Services Supervisor, Student Union, 1972-1973; State Room Manager, Student Union, 1973-1976)

Bertha M. Raper (Bookstore Supervisor, 1977-1986)

Allen B. Reding (Assistant to Director, Student Union, 1959-1961; Manager, Coffee Shop, Student Union, 1961-1962; Assistant to Director, Student Union, 1964-1965; Food Manager, Student Union, 1965-1966; Conference Coordinator, Student Union, 1966-1968; Program Consultant, Student Union, 1968-1971; Assistant Director for Programs, Student Union, 1971-1982; Assistant Director Building Services, Student Union, 1982-1985; Administrative Assistant, 1985-present)

Mary M. Reece (Supervisor, Cordell Hall, University Food Services, 1982-1984; Supervisor, Willham Complex, University Food Services, 1984-1985)

Lorena S. Reed (Registered Nurse, 1964-1966; Assistant Director of Nursing, 1966-1969)

Kathleen I. Rehbein (Licensed Practical Nurse, 1976-1985)

Alice R. Richardson (Accounting Supervisor, Student Union, 1975-1980; Business Office Manager, Student Union, 1980-present)

Joyce E. Robbins (Secretary to Vice President, Office of the Vice President for Student Services, 1966-1972; Executive Secretary, Office of the Vice President for Student Services, 1972-1976)

Gane N. Roberts (Head Resident, Scott Hall, 1982-1985)

James O. Robinson (Bookstore Receiving Clerk, 1969-1970; Assistant to Bookstore Manager, 1970-1977; Bookstore Assistant Manager, 1977-present)

Robert L. Rogers (Collections Officer, Financial Aid, 1969-1970; Student Loan Officer, Financial Aid, 1970-1974)

Jill M. Rohrbacker (Assistant Head Resident, Murray Hall, 1979-1980; Head Resident, Cordell Hall, 1980-1982; Assistant Coordinator, Residence Life, 1982-1983; Program Coordinator, Residential Life, 1983-1986; Coordinator, Residence Halls West, 1986-present)

Rochelle Rita Romano (Registered Nurse, 1966-1969)

Rebecca A. Romenesko (Assistant Dean, Student Affairs, 1972-1977)

Hazel E. Rouk (Supervisor, University Placement, 1977-1983)

Gerald E. Ruttman (Associate Director, Student Union, 1966-1967; Director, Student Union, 1967-1969)

William E. "Bill" Ryan III (Manager, University Food Services, 1982-present)

Ray A. Sadler (Engineer, Married Student Housing and Student Services Maintenance, 1968-1971; Supervisor, Married Student Housing and Student Services Maintenance, 1971-1987)

B. Kent Sampson (Head Resident, Murray Hall, 1970-1971; Program Coordinator, Single Student Housing, 1971-1972; Assistant Director, Single Student Housing, 1972-1977; Associate Director, Single Student Housing, 1977-1985; Interim Director, Single Student Housing, 1985-1986; Assistant Director, Single Student Housing, 1986-present)

M. Gene Satterfield (Accountant, Auxiliary Enterprises, 1960-1968)

Charles F. "Chuck" Schelsky (Director, Recreation for Men, Colvin Physical Education Center and Intramural Programs, 1968-1970; Director, Colvin Physical Education Center, 1970-1976; Assistant Director, Colvin Physical Education Center, 1976-present)

Robert G. Schmalfeld (Dean of Student Affairs, 1968-1981)

Carol A. Schmitz (Head Resident, Drummond Hall, 1978-1981)

Phyllis L. Schroeder (Head Resident, Drummond Hall, 1969-1971; Administrative Assistant, Single Student Housing, 1971-1972; Student Life Coordinator, Single Student Housing, 1972-1973; Area Coordinator, Willham Complex, 1973-1976; Assistant to Director, Administrative Services, Single Student Housing, 1976-1986; Assistant Director, Single Student Housing, 1986-1988)

Dorothy Searcy (Assistant, Recreation Programs, Colvin Physical Education Center and Intramural Programs, 1976-1979)

Wana L. Self (Registered Nurse, 1974-1982)

Virginia S. Shackleford (Accounting Manager, Student Union, 1972-1975)

Gladys A. Share (Director of Nursing and Registered Nurse, 1950-1979)

Cecelia A. "CeCe" Sharum (Assistant Head Resident, West Bennett Hall, 1978-1979; Head Resident, Wentz Hall, 1979-1981)

Jan Sheets (Head Resident, Single Women's Apartments, 1965-1967; Head Resident, Willham Complex, 1967-1968)

Kenneth M. Shell (Custodial Supervisor, Construction and Renovations, Single Student Housing, 1968-1985)

Randall W. Shelton (Senior Coordinator, Willham Complex, University Food Services, 1981-1985; Purchasing Specialist, University Food Services, 1985-1986; Manager, Willham Complex, University Food Services, 1986-1987)

Winston G. Shindell (Director, Student Activities, 1966-1971; Director, Student Union, 1971-1982)

Howard J. Shipp Jr. (Counselor, University Counseling Services, 1972-1980; Interim Assistant Dean of Student Affairs, 1980-1981; Coordinator, Minority Programs and Services, 1981-present)

Gary L. Silker (Counselor, University Counseling Services, 1975-1980)

Mary K. "Molly" Simmering (Program Specialist, University Counseling Services, 1980-1983)

Julianne C. "Julie" Simpson (Program Specialist, International Student Services, 1977-1979; International Student Advisor, 1979-1983)

Warren D. "Dale" Sloan (Manager, Bennett Complex, University Food Services, 1967-1972; Manager, Meat Supply, University Food Services, 1972-1974; Manager, Willham Complex, University Food Services, 1974-1980; McElroy Manager, University Food Services, 1981-1984; Manager, Bennett Complex, University Food Services, 1984-1985)

Margaret J. Smith (Registered Nurse, 1974-present)

Peggy A. Smith (Coordinator, Bennett Complex, University Food Services, 1980-1985)

Mary H. Smurl (Registered Nurse, 1969-1973)

Roger L. Sneed (Manager, Willard Hall, University Food Services, 1971-1972; Coordinator, Bennett Complex, University Food Services, 1972-1974)

Melinda G. "Mendi" Spencer (Program Manager, Student Union, 1984-1988)

Woody Spies (Head Resident, Kerr Hall, 1973-1974; Head Resident, Bennett Complex, 1974-1976)

Don R. Stafford (Assistant Dean of Men, 1965-1968)

Gerald M. Steelman (Physician, 1966-1980)

David E. "Dave" Stoddart (Area Coordinator, Kerr-Drummond Complex, 1974-1978; Assistant Director for Operations, Single Student Housing, 1978-1986; Assistant Director, Residential Life, 1986-present)

Nona J. Stone (Supervisor, Kerr-Drummond Complex, University Food Services, 1982-1984; Coordinator, Scott-Parker-Wentz Complex, University Food Services, 1984-1986; Coordinator, Willham Complex, 1986-1987; Senior Coordinator, Bennett Complex, 1987-present)

Bettye G. Stratton (Program Consultant, Student Union, 1966-1968; Food and Room Reservations Manager, Student Union, 1968-1971)

Stephen M. "Mike" Stroud (Assistant Head Resident, Iba Hall, 1978-1983)

Patricia A. Sumpter (Medical Technologist, University Hospital and Clinic, 1977-1984)

Joan L. Swander (Assistant Food Coordinator, Student Union, 1981-1984)

Trannie D. Taffs (Games Room Clerk, Student Union, 1977-1984, Games Room Manager, Student Union, 1984-1986)

Lillian E. "Esther" Tarkington (Secretary, Auxiliary Enterprises, 1968-1973; Staff Assistant, Financial Aid, 1973-1980; Supervisor, Financial Aid, 1980-1981; Coordinator, Financial Aid, 1981-1985)

Lucy A. "Annette" Tate (Registered Nurse, 1982-present)

Julie A. Teubner (Registered Nurse, 1978-1983)

Fayetta C. "Faye" Tevebaugh (Staff Assistant, Financial Aid, 1969-1981; Supervisor, Financial Aid, 1981-1982)

Bill E. Thomas (Head, Accounting Office, Student Union, 1967-1971)

Danny Thomas (Head Resident, Iba Hall, 1973-1976)

Barry E. Thompson (Head Resident, East Bennett Hall, 1977-1978; Coordinator, Residential Life, 1978-1980)

Rhonda M. Thompson (Registered Nurse, 1982-present)

Janet L. Timmons (Supervisor, University Placement, 1984-1987)

Christine G. "Chris" Tinker (Cafeteria Food Manager, Student Union, 1965-1967; Food Production Manager, Student Union, 1967-1977; Manager, Bennett Hall, University Food Services, 1977-1978; Manager, Kerr-Drummond, University Food Services, 1978-1985; Coordinator, Kerr-Drummond Complex, University Food Services, 1985-1987; Manager, Residence Halls West, University Food Services, 1987-present)

Rebecca J. Tomlinson (Registered Nurse, 1977-present)

Robert C. Tout (Assistant Director, University Hospital and Clinic and Physician, 1964-1978)

Suzy L. Tower (Assistant Head Resident, West Bennett Hall, 1981-1982; Head Resident, West Bennett Hall, 1982-1983; Head Resident, Drummond Hall, 1983-1984)

Darrel K. Troxel (Assistant to Dean of Students, Student Affairs, 1952-1953; Assistant Dean of Men, 1953-1968; Dean of Men, 1968-1969; Associate Dean, Student Affairs, 1969-1970)

Duane P. Truex (Assistant Director, Allied Arts, 1969-1972)

Alma E. Tucker (Manager, Financial Aid, 1969-1973; Staff Assistant, Financial Aid, 1973-1982)

Bruce D. Twenhofel (Assistant for Programs and Promotion, Student Union, 1975-1978)

Delores R. Viers (Night Hostess, Willard Hall, 1960-1961; Head Resident, Murray Hall, 1961-1968)

Margaret E. "Peg" Vitek (Student Conduct Officer, Office of Student Conduct, 1985-present)

Naomi E. Vongunten (Dietitian, Stout Hall, University Food Services, 1971-1972; Manager, Bennett Complex, University Food Services, 1972-1978; Coordinator, Bennett Complex, University Food Services, 1978-1985)

William "Bill" Wallace (Recreation Program Specialist, Colvin Physical Education Center and Intramural Programs, 1979-1982)

James A. Waltermire (Physician, 1975-1987)

Albin P. Warner (Director, Colvin Physical Education Center and Intramural Programs, 1964-1973)

Calvin R. Warren (Upholsterer, Student Union, 1958-1967; Upholsterer, Student Services Maintenance, 1967-1987)

Gladys V. Wass (Administrative Secretary, Financial Aid, 1968-1972; Administrative Assistant, Financial Aid, 1972-1974)

Paula N. Waters (Counselor, University Placement, 1981-1985)

Elfreda K. Wells (Assistant Receptionist, University Hospital and Clinic, 1966-1970; Head Receptionist, University Hospital and Clinic, 1970-1985)

Clyde West (Maintenance Supervisor, Veteran's Village, 1947-1957; Supervisor, Married Student Housing and Student Services Maintenance, 1957-1967; Superintendent, Married Student Housing and Student Services Maintenance, 1967-1972; Administrative Assistant, Married Student Housing and Student Services Maintenance, 1972-1976)

Marsha J. "Jo Ann" West (Assistant Head Resident, Wentz Hall, 1978-1979; Head Resident, Willard Hall, 1979-1982; Head Resident, Drummond Hall, 1982-1983)

H. Janice Whaling (Head Resident, Brumley Apartments, 1970-1971; Head Resident, Stout Hall, 1971-1972; Area Coordinator, Kerr-Drummond Complex, 1972-1973)

Levell L. "Bud" Wheeler (Food Services Manager, Student Union, 1982-1985)

Dennis L. White (Pool Manager, Colvin Physical Education Center and Intramural Programs, 1970-1978; Assistant Facilities Coordinator, Colvin Physical Education Center and Intramural Programs, 1978-present)

Gwen Whitenack (Registered Nurse, 1976-1987)

Ada Van Whitley (Director, Women's Intramural Programs, 1961-1976, Colvin Physical Education Center and Intramural Programs; Coordinator, Recreation Department, Colvin Physical Education Center and Intramural Programs, 1976-1988)

Louis T. "Lou" Wilcoxin (Head Resident, Scott Hall, 1973-1974; Head Resident, Kerr Hall, 1974-1978)

Winona E. Wilhm (Insurance Clerk, University Hospital and Clinic, 1966-1978; Senior Accounts Clerk, University Hospital and Clinic, 1978-1985; Administrative Associate, University Hospital and Clinic, 1985-present)

Richard M. Williams (Director, Married Student Housing and Student Services Maintenance, 1967-1985)

John H. Wills (Manager, Student Union Cafeteria, 1966-1968; Manager, Scott-Parker-Wentz Complex, University Food Services, 1968-1970; Assistant Purchasing Agent, University Food Services, 1970-1972; Assistant Director of Purchasing, University Food Services, 1972-1974)

Donna M. Wilson (Supervisor, Bennett Complex, University Food Services, 1982-1984; Supervisor, Iba Hall, University Food Services, 1984-1985)

Geraldine G. Wilson (Registered Nurse, 1971-1984)

W. Douglas "Doug" Wilson (International Student Advisor, 1970-1976)

Dianne L. Wimberley (Loan Officer, Financial Aid, 1980-1982; Assistant Director, Financial Aid, 1982-1983)

Kirk E. Wimberley (Assistant, Intramural Programs, Colvin Physical Education Center and Intramural Programs, 1976-1977; Chair, Sports Activities, Colvin Physical Education Center and Intramural Programs, 1977-1983; Coordinator, Outdoor Adventure and Camp Redlands, Colvin Phyical Education Center and Intramural Programs, 1983-present)

Lewis F. Wolfe (Manager, Single Student Housing, 1962-1966; Director, Single Student Housing, 1966-1970)

Carolyn J. Wollard (Registered Nurse, 1978-1982)

Randal L. Woltemath (Night Building Manager, Student Union, 1981-1984)

Mel G. Wright (Head Resident, Scott Hall, 1968-1969; Director, Willham Complex, 1969-1970; Assistant Director, Single Student Housing, 1970-1971)

* The author wishes to express a heartfelt thank you to the many people who over the past century have contributed so much to the various programs and services provided for students. Although no program can be successful without a firm foundation, the author chose only to list those staff members at OSU when the Office of the Vice President for Student Services opened in 1968. In addition, only those with at least three years of service were included. The author regrets the omission of any person from this list.

# Bibliography

In addition to the specific items listed, other sources include innumerable articles, letters, memos, programs, brochures, notes, minutes, reports, speeches, vitas, informal interviews and conversations, and other miscellaneous sources of information.

## ARTICLES

"A. and M. To Have $450,000 Girls' Dormitory." *Oklahoma A. and M. College Magazine*, vol. 5, no. 4 (January 1934), p. 7.

"Abbie Hoffman's Appearance." *Oklahoma State Alumnus Magazine*, vol. 12, no. 6 (June-July 1971), p. 17.

"Abe Hesser Accepts IACU Presidency." *Oklahoma State Alumnus Magazine*, vol. 3, no. 5 (May 1962), p. 28.

"Aching Tooth No Excuse." *Oklahoma A. and M. College Magazine*, vol. 2, no. 1 (September 1930), p. 11.

"Aggie Day - Queen Kidnapped; Four Expelled." *Oklahoma A. and M. College Magazine*, vol. 2, no. 9 (May 1931), p. 266.

Agnew, Theodore L. "Survival, Stability, Maturity." *Oklahoma State Alumnus Magazine*, vol. 10, no. 5 (May 1969), pp. 16-18.

"Albin P. Warner, Head of HPER Department, Dies." *Oklahoma State Alumnus Magazine*, vol. 14, no. 8 (November 1973), p. 26.

"ALPHA '73 Helping Students." *Oklahoma State Alumnus Magazine*, vol. 14, no. 9 (December 1973), pp. 12-13.

"Alumni Mecca . . . Student Union." *Oklahoma A. and M. College Magazine*, vol. 22, no. 6 (February 1951), pp. 12-14.

"Angelo C. Scott, Fifth President." *Oklahoma A. and M. College Magazine*, vol. 20, no. 6 (March 1949), pp. 18-19.

"Apollo 11." *Oklahoma State Alumnus Magazine*, vol. 10, no. 8 (November 1969), p. 9.

"The Army and Navy Must Eat." *Oklahoma A. and M. College Magazine*, vol. 15, no 4 (November 1943), pp. 5, 15.

"Auxiliary Enterprises At Oklahoma A. & M." *Oklahoma A. and M. College Magazine*, vol. 25, no. 2 (October 1953), pp. 8-9.

Bachman, Jerald G. and Johnston, Lloyd D. "The Freshmen, 1979." *Psychology Today*, vol. 13, no. 9 (September 1979), pp. 79-80, 82, 84, 86-87.

"Basic Hope For Peace." *Oklahoma A. and M. College Magazine*, vol. 23, no. 6 (February 1952), p. 34.

Beer, Ronald S. "Student Growth Emphasized During the Centennial Decade." *Oklahoma State University Outreach*, vol. 56, no. 3 (Spring 1985), pp. 88-89, 92.

"Behind the Change in Name." *Oklahoma State Alumnus Magazine*, vol. 2, no. 4 (March 1961), pp. 5-7.

Bentley, Nell Dent. "Thoughts on Visiting the Campus." *Oklahoma A. and M. College Magazine*, vol. 17, no 4 (January 1945), p. 3.

Boger, L. L. "Student Retention a Major University-wide Priority." *Oklahoma State University Outreach*, vol. 55, no. 2 (Winter 1983), p. 39.

Boler, Jana. "The Student Union . . . Adds Some Centennial Luster." *Oklahoma State University Outreach*, vol. 58, no. 2 (Winter 1987), pp. 12-15.

Bost, Jessie Thatcher. "The Dawning of the Twentieth Century." *Oklahoma State University Outreach*, vol. 16, no. 6 (June-July 1975), pp. 16-17.

Botkin, Mary Jo. "School Opens With Rush and Lines." *Oklahoma A. and M. College Magazine*, vol. 18, no. 1 (October 1946), pp. 3-4.

Bowers, George W. "Early Military Training." *Oklahoma A. and M. College Magazine*, vol. 1, no. 7 (March 1930), p. 4.

"Brewer Recalls Other Aggie Building Booms." *Oklahoma A. and M. College Magazine*, vol. 20, no. 5 (February 1949), p. 19.

Bronte, D. Lydia. "Our Aging Society: A Challenge For the Future." *Research Dialogues*, no. 14 (July 1987).

Brower, Fountain. "Tiger Tavern." *Oklahoma A. and M. College Magazine*, vol. 3, no. 2 (November 1931), p. 9.

"CALL Center." *Oklahoma State University Outreach*, vol. 18, no. 1 (January-February 1977), pp. 12-13.

"Campus Briefs." *Oklahoma State Alumnus Magazine*, vol. 8, no. 9 (December 1967), p. 4.

"Career of Service." *Oklahoma A. and M. College Magazine*, vol. 22, no. 10 (June 1951), pp. 42-43.

"Caskey Heads OSU Counseling Services." *Oklahoma State Alumnus Magazine*, vol. 4, no. 11 (December 1963), p. 19.

Castleman, Jack. "Historical 1953 at A. & M." *Oklahoma A. and M. College Magazine*, vol. 25, no. 5 (January 1954), pp. 5-7.

"The 'Catching Up' Process." *Oklahoma State Alumnus Magazine*, vol. 4, no. 3 (March 1963), pp. 42-43.

"Celebration of 25 Years Service to OSU." *Oklahoma State University Outreach*, vol. 17, no. 1 (January 1976), pp. 18-19.

"Changing Mode of Transportation." *Oklahoma State Alumnus Magazine*, vol. 13, no. 1 (January 1972), p. 3.

"The Changing University Scene." *Oklahoma State Alumnus Magazine*, vol. 11, no. 7 (September-October 1970), pp. 4, 8.

Chapman, B. B. "First Faculty Set Standards." *Oklahoma A. and M. College Magazine*, vol. 15, no 5 (December 1943), pp. 3-4, 12, 14-15.

"Chi Omega's Give Clock to Campus." *Oklahoma State Alumnus Magazine*, vol. 11, no. 3 (March 1970), p. 19.

"College Paper Discloses Class History." *Oklahoma A. and M. College Magazine*, vol. 1, no. 6 (February 1930), pp. 27, 31.

"Concern for Handicapped Students." *Oklahoma State Alumnus Magazine*, vol. 9, no. 8 (November 1968), p. 14.

Criner, Cathy. "'Heart of Campus' Celebrates 35th Anniversary." *Oklahoma State University Outreach*, vol. 57, no. 3 (Spring 1986), pp. 12-13.

Criner, Cathy. "Varsity Revue - Best Known Tradition." *Oklahoma State University Outreach*, vol. 57, no. 3 (Spring 1986), p. 16.

Cross, Hays. "Veterans View Five Decades." *Oklahoma A. and M. College Magazine*, vol. 12, no. 6 (March 1941), pp. 4-5, 15.

"Dean of Student Affairs." *Oklahoma State Alumnus Magazine*, vol. 10, no. 2 (February 1969), p. 28.

"Dr. George Gathers Joins OSU Staff." *Oklahoma State Alumnus Magazine*, vol. 12, no. 1 (January 1971), p. 24.

Dolde, Emma Swope. "Alumni Writes Impressions." *Oklahoma A. and M. College Magazine*, vol. 10, no. 1 (October 1938), pp. 5, 11, 15.

Donnell, Guy R. "Ah! . . . That was Life." *Oklahoma State University Outreach*, vol. 17, no. 2 (March 1976), pp. 12-13.

"Duties are Many and Varied." *Oklahoma State Alumnus Magazine*, vol. 13, no. 2 (February 1972), p. 8.

"Ed Morrison Dies From Heart Attack." *Oklahoma State Alumnus Magazine*, vol. 2, no. 10 (November 1961), p. 18.

"Educational Crossroads of Many Languages." *Oklahoma State University Magazine*, vol. 1, no. 5 (November 1957), pp. 28-29.

Emerson, Bonnie E. "Democracy in Action on Campus." *Oklahoma A. and M. College Magazine*, vol. 9, no. 9 (April 1944), pp. 3, 8-9, 14.

"Envoys of Academic Excellence." *Oklahoma State Alumnus Magazine*, vol. 2, no. 2 (February 1961), pp. 10-12.

Eyler, Frank. "A. and M. Students Well Housed." *Oklahoma A. and M. College Magazine*, vol. 11, no. 8 (May 1940), p. 7.

"Facts About OSU." *Oklahoma State University Outreach*, vol. 51, no. 1 (September 1979), pp. 57-58.

"Facts and Figures, A & M Style." *Oklahoma A. and M. College Magazine*, vol. 24, no. 1 (September 1952), p. 10.

"Fiftieth Anniversary Observed." *Oklahoma A. and M. College Magazine*, vol. 13, no. 4 (January 1942), pp. 2-3, 10, 15.

"Financial Aids: Helping Pay The Bills." *Oklahoma State University Outreach*, vol. 16, no. 4 (Spring 1975), pp. 22-23.

"Flags Fly Over International Mall." *Oklahoma State Alumnus Magazine*, vol. 13, no. 8 (November 1972), p. 26.

"Focus on Viet Nam." *Oklahoma State Alumnus Magazine*, vol. 7, no. 4 (April 1966), pp. 9-12.

"Fraternities Offer Social Opportunities." *Oklahoma A. and M. College Magazine*, vol. 22, no. 6 (February 1951), p. 15.

Frazier, Chester J. "Veterans Village Comes of Age." *Oklahoma A. and M. College Magazine*, vol. 20, no. 1 (October 1948), pp. 4-5.

Freudenberger, Helen. "Records and Reminiscences." *Oklahoma A. and M. College Magazine*, vol. 8, no. 4 (January 1937), pp. 5, 13.

"Funeral Services Held for First Women Graduate." *Oklahoma State Alumnus Magazine*, vol. 4, no. 4 (April 1963), p. 15.

Girod, Raymond. "It's Your Move Now." *Oklahoma A. and M. College Magazine*, vol. 24, no. 6 (February 1953), pp. 26-27.

Goddard, Mary. "It's . . . Older Than Oklahoma and Still in Daily Use." *Oklahoma A. and M. College Magazine*, vol. 23, no. 9 (May 1952), pp. 4-5.

Gonzales, Carolyn. "OSU's Sixth Decade: A World War Brings Sudden Maturity." *Oklahoma State University Outreach*, vol. 57, no. 2 (Winter 1985), pp. 2-11.

Gonzales, Nestor. "Not a Sacrifice, But a Privilege." *Oklahoma State University Outreach*, vol. 54, no. 1 (September 1982), pp. 10-11.

"Ground Breaking for Health Center." *Oklahoma State University Outreach*, vol. 15, no. 9 (December 1974), p. 14.

Hamilton, Ralph. "Lawrence Boger Is Named OSU President." *Oklahoma State University Outreach*, vol. 18, no. 3 (June-July 1977), pp. 3-4.

Hart, Gordon. "Fifty Years of Yearbook Memories." *Oklahoma State University Magazine*, vol. 2, no. 11 (May 1959), pp. 8-11.

Hastings, James K. "Oklahoma Agricultural and Mechanical College and Old Central." *Chronicles of Oklahoma*, vol. 27, no. 1 (Spring 1950), pp. 81-84.

"He Carries A Torch For A & M." *Oklahoma A. and M. College Magazine*, vol. 23, no. 6 (February 1952), pp. 32-33.

"Historic 79th Commencement." *Oklahoma State University Outreach*, vol. 15, no. 6 (June-July 1974), p. 3.

Hohenshil, Thomas H. "The Educational Reform Movement: What Does It Mean For Counseling." *Journal of Counseling and Development*, vol. 66, no. 1 (September 1987), pp. 57-58.

"Homecoming '86 . . . the Biggest and Best in OSU History!" *Oklahoma State University Outreach*, vol. 58, no. 2 (Winter 1987), p. 28.

House, R. Morton. "The Class of 1903 At Oklahoma A. & M. College." *Chronicles of Oklahoma*, vol. 44, no. 4 (Winter 1966-1967), pp. 391-408.

House, R. Morton. "Working Our Way Through College." *Chronicles of Oklahoma*, vol. 42, no. 2 (Summer 1964), pp. 36-54.

"Humorous, Healthy, and Exciting." *Oklahoma State Alumnus Magazine*, vol. 5, no. 10 (November 1964), pp. 12-13.

"In Memoriam." *Oklahoma State Alumnus Magazine*, vol. 5, no. 1 (January 1964), p. 6.

"Increased Numbers and Stability." *Oklahoma A. and M. College Magazine*, vol. 6, no. 1 (October 1934), p. 2.

"International Appreciation." *Oklahoma State Alumnus Magazine*, vol. 12, no. 3 (March 1971), p. 5.

"The International Mall." *Oklahoma State Alumnus Magazine*, vol. 9, no. 8 (November 1968), p. 5.

"The Intramural Program." *Oklahoma A. and M. College Magazine*, vol. 18, no. 9 (June 1947), p. 10.

"'The Iron Man' Trophy is Again Awarded to OSU." *Oklahoma State Alumnus Magazine*, vol. 4, no. 1 (January 1963), p. 11.

"James R. Fleming Dies in Tulsa." *Oklahoma State University Outreach*, vol. 16, no. 5 (May 1975), p. 22.

Jarrell, Alfred Edwin. "A First Aggie Grad Gives His 1950 Report." *Oklahoma A. and M. College Magazine*, vol. 22, no. 2 (October 1950), pp. 28-29.

Jarrell, Alfred Edwin. "The Founding of Oklahoma A. and M. College: A Memoir." *Chronicles of Oklahoma*, vol. 34, no. 3 (Autumn 1956), pp. 315-325.

Jarrell, Alfred Edwin. "Now There Are None." *Oklahoma State University Magazine*, vol. 2, no. 12 (June 1959), p. 13.

"Jessie Thatcher Bost Honored." *Oklahoma A. and M. College Magazine*, vol. 17, no. 9 (June 1946), pp. 5-6.

"Joe Blair." *Oklahoma State University Outreach*, vol. 18, no. 1 (January-February 1977), pp. 6-7.

"Joe Blair—He Feeds Thousands." *Oklahoma State Alumnus Magazine*, vol. 14, no. 9 (December 1973), pp. 6-8.

Johnson, Evanell. "Fun After Class." *Oklahoma A. and M. College Magazine*, vol. 21, no 7 (March 1950), pp. 44-45.

Jones, Olin W. "A Little Rough, Yes . . . ." *Oklahoma A. and M. College Magazine*, vol. 1, no. 7 (March 1930), p. 12.

Jones, Olin W. "Aggieland's First Collegiates." *Oklahoma A. and M. College Magazine*, vol. 1, no. 6 (February 1930), pp. 2, 24.

"Kappa Delta's Celebrate 50th Anniversary." *Oklahoma State Alumnus Magazine*, vol. 10, no. 5 (May 1969), p. 31.

Knoblock, Fred. "Memories of Williams Hall." *Oklahoma State Alumnus Magazine*, vol. 10, no. 7 (September-October 1969), pp. 12-13.

Knox, Dave. "New Dormitory Under Construction." *Oklahoma A. and M. College Magazine*, vol. 5, no. 6 (March 1934), pp. 5, 15.

"Kontinental Kapers." *Oklahoma State University Magazine*, vol. 2, no. 8 (February 1959), p. 30.

"Kudos and Criticisms." *Oklahoma State Alumnus Magazine,* vol. 7, no. 7 (September-October 1966), p. 28.

Lahman, W. L. "Orange and Black Had Stormy Beginning." *Oklahoma A. and M. College Magazine*, vol. 19, no. 1 (October 1947), p. 11.

"Lake Carl Blackwell Deeded to the College." *Oklahoma A. and M. College Magazine*, vol. 26, no. 6 (February 1955), pp. 24-25.

"Land of Opportunity For Working Students." *Oklahoma A. and M. College Magazine*, vol. 23, no. 7 (March 1952), p. 5.

"Larsen Appointed Director of OSU Counseling Services." *Oklahoma State Alumnus Magazine*, vol. 6, no 7 (September-October 1965), p. 61.

Looper, Don. "Aggieviews." *Oklahoma A. and M. College Magazine*, vol. 18, no. 1 (October 1946), p. 5.

Looper, Don. "News of the Campus." *Oklahoma A. and M. College Magazine*, vol. 19, no. 1 (October 1947), p. 18.

Martin, A. Frank. "Yesterday's Entertainers—Today," *Oklahoma A. and M. College Magazine*, vol. 16, no. 8 (March 1944), pp. 3, 8-9, 13.

"May First Marks Use of New College Infirmary.' *Oklahoma A. and M. College Magazine*, vol. 1, no. 8 (April 1930), p. 9.

"Meet the New Dean of Students." *Oklahoma State Alumnus Magazine*, vol. 2, no. 8 (September 1961), p. 42.

Miller, Freeman E. "Exit the Bandit—Enter the College!" *Oklahoma A. and M. College Magazine*, vol. 1, no. 5 (January 1930), pp. 4, 24-25.

"Miss Julia E. Stout, Former Dean, Died." *Oklahoma State Alumnus Magazine*, vol. 10, no. 5 (May 1969), p. 28.

"Modern Student Housing." *Oklahoma A. and M. College Magazine*, vol. 26, no. 7 (March 1955), pp. 10-11.

"Mortar Board Installed." *Oklahoma A. and M. College Magazine*, vol. 12, no. 4 (January 1941), p. 6.

"Multipurpose, Year-round Housing." *Oklahoma State Alumnus Magazine*, vol. 3, no. 2 (February 1962), pp. 6-7.

"Name of Oklahoma A & M Changed to Oklahoma State University." *Oklahoma A. and M. College Magazine*, vol. 28, no. 10 (June 1957), p. 5.

"The Nation's Outstanding IFC." *Oklahoma State Alumnus Magazine*, vol. 3, no. 5 (May 1962), p. 13.

Neal, Barney. "Aggieland's Rifle Teams!" *Oklahoma A. and M. College Magazine*, vol. 20, no. 6 (March 1949), pp. 2-3.

Nettleton, Kay. "OSU's Fifth Decade: Growing Up During Hard Times." *Oklahoma State University Outreach*, vol. 56, no. 2 (Winter 1984), pp. 3-8, 10-12.

Nettleton, Kay. "OSU's Fourth Decade: Adolescence During the Roaring 20s." *Oklahoma State University Outreach*, vol. 55, no. 2 (Winter 1983), pp. 2-12.

Nettleton, Kay. "OSU's Third Decade: Victorian Innocence Ends With a World War." *Oklahoma State University Outreach*, vol. 54, no. 12 (December 1982), pp. 3-11.

Nettleton, Kay. "Wes Watkins." *Oklahoma State University Outreach*, vol. 53, no. 3 (Spring 1982), p. 29.

"New Report Shows Oklahoma Is 50th In Tax Support For Higher Education." *Oklahoma State Alumnus Magazine*, vol. 8, no. 9 (November 1967), p. 29.

"New Sorority Chapter Is Chartered." *Oklahoma State Alumnus Magazine*, vol. 12, no. 6 (June-July 1971), p. 27.

"New Student Health Center." *Oklahoma State Alumnus Magazine*, vol. 14, no. 6 (June-July 1973), p. 12.

"New Students Are Introduced To University Activity." *Oklahoma State University Outreach*, vol. 15, no. 8 (November 1974), pp. 8-9.

"New VP Excited About OSU." *Oklahoma State University Outreach*, vol. 51, no. 3 (February 1980), p. 8.

"'09 Class Plans Spring Reunion." *Oklahoma A. and M. College Magazine*, vol. 20, no. 4 (January 1949), pp. 6-7.

"No Substitute for Work." *Oklahoma A. and M. College Magazine*, vol. 25, no. 4 (December 1953), pp. 6-8.

"North Central Association Report." *Oklahoma A. and M. College Magazine*, vol. 24, no. 9 (May 1953), pp. 24-26.

"On The Campus." *Oklahoma A. and M. College Magazine*, vol. 2, no. 5 (January 1931), p. 150.

"OSU's Black Heritage Week." *Oklahoma State Alumnus Magazine*, vol. 10, no. 4 (April 1969), pp. 42-43.

"OSU's New Physical Education Center." *Oklahoma State Alumnus Magazine*, vol. 9, no. 2 (February 1968), p. 2.

"OSU Placement Bureau Director Retires." *Oklahoma State University Magazine*, vol. 2, no. 6 (December 1958), p. 20.

"The Passing of an OSU Patriarch." *Oklahoma State Alumnus Magazine*, vol. 11, no. 5 (May 1970), p. 30.

"Placement Was His Profession." *Oklahoma State University Outreach*, vol. 19, no. 4 (August-September 1978), p. 7.

"Plaque Honors Shepherd Sisters." *Oklahoma State University Outreach*, vol. 16, no. 4 (April 1975), p. 34.

"Potts Sets A Good Table." *Oklahoma A. and M. College Magazine*, vol. 19, no. 2 (November 1947), p. 7.

Powell, Jerry. "The Student." *Oklahoma State Alumnus Magazine*, vol. 3, no. 4 (April 1962), p. 29.

"Problems, Problems, Problems!" *Oklahoma State Alumnus Magazine*, vol. 9, no. 4 (April 1968), pp. 13-15.

Ray, Jack. "Is A. and M. Tradition Bound?" *Oklahoma A. and M. College Magazine*, vol. 10, no. 8 (May 1939), pp. 3, 12, 15.

Rector, F. L. "Battle for Better Health." *Oklahoma A. and M. College Magazine*, vol. 28, no. 9 (May 1957), pp. 28-29.

Reynolds, Jim. "Tests Help Solve Problems." *Oklahoma A. and M. College Magazine*, vol. 19, no. 6 (March 1948), pp. 2-3.

Rives, Bob. "It Is 'Strictly Academic'." *Oklahoma A. and M. College Magazine*, vol. 26, no. 7 (March 1955), pp. 20-21.

Rogers, Murl. "An Outstanding Scholarship Program." *Oklahoma A. and M. College Magazine*, vol. 26, no. 12 (August 1955), p. 29.

Rulon, Philip Reed. "Angelo Scott: Leader in Higher Education, Oklahoma Territory." *Chronicles of Oklahoma*, vol. 47, no. 1 (Spring 1969), pp. 494-514.

Rulon, Philip Reed. "The Campus Cadets: A History of Collegiate Military Training, 1891-1951." *Chronicles of Oklahoma*, vol. 52, no. 1 (Spring 1979), pp. 67-90.

Rusterholtz, Wallace P. "Humanist Transcendence." *Religious Humanism*, vol. 22, no. 2 (Spring 1987), pp. 71-76.

"Schelsky is NIA President-elect." *Oklahoma State Alumnus Magazine*, vol. 14, no. 5 (May 1973), p. 11.

Schneider, Pete. "Student Leaders Seek Larger Role." *Oklahoma State Alumnus Magazine*, vol. 8, no. 7 (September-October 1967), pp. 12-13.

"Seeking A Solution for Mass Instruction." *Oklahoma State Alumnus Magazine*, vol. 3, no. 5 (May 1962), p. 15.

"A 75-Year Heritage." *Oklahoma State Alumnus Magazine*, vol. 6, no. 7 (September-October 1965), pp. 8-13.

"Sexpo '68." *Oklahoma State Alumnus Magazine*, vol. 10, no. 1 (February 1969), p. 4.

Shull, Warren E. "A University Without Peer." *Oklahoma State Alumnus Magazine*, vol. 7, no. 2 (February 1966), pp. 8-13.

Smith, Robert E. "The Ceramics Factory At Oklahoma State University." *Chronicles of Oklahoma*, vol. 50, no. 2 (Summer 1972), pp. 205-218.

Snipes, Larry. "Abe Hesser—An Interview." *Oklahoma State Alumnus Magazine*, vol. 10, no. 3 (March 1969), pp. 10-13.

"Some Recent Appointments." *Oklahoma State Alumnus Magazine*, vol. 12, no. 8 (November 1971), p. 13.

"Sorority's Gift Keeps Time for Campus." *Oklahoma State Alumnus Magazine*, vol. 11, no. 6 (September-October 1970), p. 27.

"Speakers Policy Is Amended." *Oklahoma State Alumnus Magazine*, vol. 12, no. 2 (February 1971), pp. 13-14.

Stout, Joe A., Jr. "The Will Rogers Project." *Chronicles of Oklahoma*, vol. 50, no. 3 (Fall 1973), pp. 356-358.

"Student Activities Director." *Oklahoma State Alumnus Magazine*, vol. 13, no. 2 (February 1972), p. 9.

"Student Industries Are Enlarged." *Oklahoma A. and M. College Magazine*, vol. 1, no. 10 (Summer 1930), p. 7.

"Student Religious Life At A & M." *Oklahoma A. and M. College Magazine*, vol. 25, no. 3 (November 1953), pp. 16-17.

"Student Union Opens." *Oklahoma A. and M. College Magazine*, vol. 22, no. 2 (October 1950), p. 5.

"Student Union Talk." *Oklahoma A. and M. College Magazine*, vol. 8, no. 4 (October 1936), p. 3.

"Students Selected for Leadership Council." *Oklahoma State Alumnus Magazine*, vol. 8, no. 5 (May 1967), p. 26.

"Tent City." *Oklahoma A. and M. College Magazine*, vol. 8, no. 9 (May 1937), p. 10.

"They Host Political Personalities." *Oklahoma State Alumnus Magazine*, vol. 8, no. 5 (May 1967), pp. 12-13.

"Thirty Years Ago." *Oklahoma A. and M. College Magazine*, vol. 1, no. 6 (February 1930), p. 14.

Thompson, H. E. "1892—A. and M. College—1930." *Oklahoma A. and M. College Magazine*, vol. 1, no. 8 (April 1930), pp. 4, 20.

Thompson, Laurence. "Poor Boy Gets A Break." *Oklahoma A. and M. College Magazine*, vol. 1, no. 1 (September 1929), p. 19.

Thompson, Laurence. "When Aggieland Was Fairyland." *Oklahoma A. and M. College Magazine*, vol. 1, no. 4 (December 1929), pp. 8, 26.

"To Help Them Adopt." *Oklahoma State Alumnus Magazine*, vol. 5, no. 9 (October 1964), p. 16.

"The Union: Introducing New Director, New Features." *Oklahoma State Alumnus Magazine*, vol. 10, no. 9 (December 1969), pp. 12-14.

"Values: How Do the Classes of 1943 and 1978 Compare?" *Oklahoma State University Outreach*, vol. 19, no. 3 (June-July 1978), p. 7.

"Why Those Students Are Protesting." *Time*, vol. 91, no. 18 (3 May 1968), pp. 24-25.

Wile, Otis. "Bricks, Stone, Dreams, and Travail." *Oklahoma State Alumnus Magazine*, vol. 6, no. 1 (January 1965), pp. 6-11.

Willham, Oliver S. "OSU Faces a Financial Crossroad." *Oklahoma State Alumnus Magazine*, vol. 4, no. 3 (March 1963), pp. 7-8.

Wingrove, Shannon. "Paid For By Bonds." *Oklahoma State University Outreach*, vol. 19, no. 2 (March-April 1978), p. 17.

"Zelma Patchin Retires After 24 Years on OSU Faculty." *Oklahoma State Alumnus Magazine*, vol. 16, no. 6 (June-July 1975), p. 22.


## BOOKS

Bowen, Catherine Drinker. *Miracle At Philadelphia*. Boston, MA: Little, Brown and Company, 1966.

Cable, Mary. *American Manners and Morals*. New York, NY: American Heritage Publishing, 1969.

Cunningham, Robert E. *Stillwater: Where Oklahoma Began*. Stillwater, OK: Arts and Humanities Council of Stillwater, Oklahoma, 1969.

Cunningham, Robert E. *Stillwater: Through the Years*. Stillwater, OK: Arts and Humanities Council of Stillwater, Oklahoma, 1974.

Dusch, Willa Adams. *The Sigma Literary Society, 1893-1897: A Chapter in the History of the Oklahoma A. and M. College*. Edited by Berlin B. Chapman. Stillwater: Oklahoma A. and M. College, 1951.

Gibson, Arrell Morgan. *Oklahoma: A History of Five Centuries*. Norman: University of Oklahoma Press, 1981.

Gill, Jerry Leon. *The Great Adventure: Oklahoma State University and International Education*. Stillwater: Oklahoma State University Press, 1978.

Hobbs, Dan S. *Oklahoma Demographics: Myths and Realities*. Oklahoma City, OK: Oklahoma State Regents For Higher Education, 1986.

Kamm, Robert B. *They're No. One! A People-Oriented Approach to Higher Education Administration*. Oklahoma City, OK: Western Heritage Books, 1980.

Miller, Freeman. *The Founding of Oklahoma Agricultural and Mechanical College*. Stillwater, OK: Hinkel and Sons, 1928.

Murphy, Patrick M. *Handicapped Students at Oklahoma State*. Stillwater: Oklahoma State University, 1982.

Naisbitt, John. *Megatrends*. New York, NY: Warner Books, 1982.

*Oklahoma A. and M. College Catalog and Announcements, 1891-1957*.

Oklahoma A. and M. College Freshman Handbook *Aggie Angles, 1950-1957*.

*Oklahoma A. and M. College Student Handbook*, 1909-1957.

*Oklahoma State University Catalog, 1958-1986*.

Oklahoma State University *Faculty Handbook*, 1973.

Oklahoma State University *Student-Faculty Directory*, 1950-1987.

*Oklahoma State University Student Handbook*, 1958-1978.

*Redskin*. Oklahoma State University Yearbook, 1910-1987.

Robinson, Donald W., chair. *Oklahoma State University—North Central Association Self-Study Report*. Stillwater: Oklahoma State University, 1986.

Rudolph, Frederick. *The American College and University*. New York, NY: Vintage Books, 1962.

Rulon, Philip Reed. *Oklahoma State University—Since 1890*. Stillwater: Oklahoma State University Press, 1975.

Scott, Angelo C. *The Story of an Administration of the Oklahoma Agricultural and Mechanical College* [Stillwater: Oklahoma Agricultural and Mechanical College, 1942].

Sumner, Jenny, editor. *Rush 1987—Picture Yourself Greek*. Stillwater: Oklahoma State University Panhellenic Council, 1987.


## COLLECTIONS

Oklahoma State University, Alumni Association, Stillwater, Oklahoma:
    Files.

Oklahoma State University, Edmon Low Library, Special Collections, Stillwater, Oklahoma:

Weldon Barnes Collection.

Board of Regents for the Oklahoma Agricultural and Mechanical Colleges Minutes.

Berlin B. Chapman Collection.

Theo Lowry Collection.

Paul Miller Papers.

Oklahoma Agricultural and Mechanical College Faculty. "Minutes of the First Faculty, March 17, 1892, to June 2, 1899." Typed manuscript in two volumes.

Oklahoma State Board of Agriculture Minutes.

Oklahoma State University Faculty Council Records.

Oklahoma State University President's Papers.

Oklahoma State University Vertical Files.

Record Book Committee, compiler. "Selections from the Record Book of the Oklahoma Agricultural and Mechanical College, 1891-1941. Compiled on the Occasion of the Fiftieth Anniversary of the Founding of the College." Volumes 1-2.

Angelo C. Scott Collection.

"Sigma Literary Society Minutes—February 8, 1895 to November 28, 1896." Manuscript Book.

Student Services Collection.

"Webster Literary Society—October 16, 1893 to October 3, 1896." Manuscript Book.

Oliver S. Willham Collection.


## DISSERTATIONS AND THESES

Anderson, Vera Kathryn Stevenson. "A History of the *Daily O'Collegian*, Student Newspaper of the Oklahoma A. and M. College: 1924-1934." Master of Science thesis, Oklahoma State University, 1975.

Azeltine, Ray Blanchard. "Determining Factors of a College Education." Master of Science thesis, Oklahoma Agricultural and Mechanical College, 1933.

Daniel, Margaret Louise. "The Social Attitudes of College Students." Master of Science thesis, Oklahoma Agricultural and Mechanical College, 1933.

Gill, Jerry Leon. "Oklahoma State University and the Great Adventure in International Education, 1951-1976." Doctor of Philosophy dissertation, Oklahoma State University, 1976.

Holmberg, Sharon Mae. "Valerie Colvin: Pioneer Physical Educator in Oklahoma." Doctor of Education dissertation, Oklahoma State University, 1958.

Johnson, Ronald Lee. "Black Student Attitudes: A Study in Alienation at Oklahoma State University." Master of Science thesis, Oklahoma State University, 1975.

Kephart, John H. "A Pictorial History of Oklahoma A. and M. College, 1891-1941." Master of Science thesis, Oklahoma Agricultural and Mechanical College, 1942.

King, Donald Neal. "A Comparative and Descriptive Study of Married Students at Oklahoma State University." Doctor of Education dissertation, Oklahoma State University, 1970.

Klock, Roger Ranch. "A Profile Analysis of Reader Interest in *The Daily O'Collegian* at Oklahoma State University." Master of Science thesis, Oklahoma State University, 1975.

Layman, Barbara Jean. "Perceptions of College Environment at Oklahoma State University By Incoming Freshman Students." Doctor of Education dissertation, Oklahoma State University, 1975.

McFarland, William Edward. "A History of Student Financial Assistance Programs at Oklahoma State University, 1891-1978, With An Emphasis on the Creation and Administration of the Lew Wentz Foundation." Doctor of Philosophy dissertation, Oklahoma State University, 1979.

Schmitz, Carol Ann. "A Follow-Up Study of Residents Who Voluntarily Withdrew From Oklahoma State University." Master of Science thesis, Oklahoma State University, 1981.

Stout, Mary Louise. "A History and Survey of the Health Services to the Student Body of the Oklahoma Agricultural and Mechanical College Over the years 1928-1937." Master of Science thesis, Oklahoma Agricultural and Mechanical College, 1938.

Wilson, W. Douglas. "Social Relationship of International Students Attending Oklahoma State University." Doctor of Education dissertation, Oklahoma State University, 1975.

## INTERVIEWS

Author interview with Ronald S. Beer, Don R. Briggs, Charles W. Bruce, Donald L. Cooper, Pat Hofler, Robert W. Huss, and Thomas M. Keys, 30 September 1987, Stillwater, Oklahoma.

Author interview with George H. Oberle, 25 November 1987, Stillwater, Oklahoma.

Kathryn M. Greenlee interview with Raymond E. Bivert, 12 February 1986, Stillwater, Oklahoma.

## NEWSPAPERS

Oklahoma A. and M. College *Home Base News*. 1947.

Oklahoma A. and M. College *New Education*. 1910-1915.

Oklahoma A. and M. College *Village Times*. 1946-1950.

Oklahoma City *Daily Oklahoman*. 1970, 1973, 1974.

*Oklahoma State* University *News*. 1970, 1978.

*OSU Today*. 1985-1987.

Oklahoma State University Student Newspapers:

 *Oklahoma A. and M. College Mirror*. 1895-1898.

 *College Paper*. 1899-1907.

 *Brown and Blue*. 1908.

 *Orange and Black*. 1908-1924.

 *O'Collegian*. 1924-1927.

 *Daily O'Collegian*. 1927-1988.

*Stillwater Eagle-Gazette*. 1894.

*Stillwater NewsPress*. 1970, 1981-1988.

*Tulsa Tribune*. 1967.

*Tulsa World*. 1967-1971.

Washington, D.C. *Chronicle of Higher Education*. 1985-1987.

# Index

American College Personnel Association: 278.
American College Testing (ACT): 370.
Anderson, Ethelyn J. C.: 261.
Anderson, Harvey W.: 262.
Andre, Reed: 209.
Andrews, M. M. "Bud": 185, 334.
Andrews, Richard: 327.
Andrews, Sue: 185, 334.
Angle, Shirley: 187.
Apathy Club: 343.
*Apollo XI*: 289.
Arcade Restaurant: 35.
Armory Building: 69-70, 157.
Armstrong, Louis: 184.
Armstrong, Neil A.: 289.
Armstrong, Neill: 183.
Armstrong, P. Joe: 292.
Arndt, David: 183.
Arquitt, Ed.: 405.
Association for Concerns of Disabled Collegiates: 346, 348, 392. *See also* Double "O" Club.
Association of College Unions-International: 205, 206, 241, 244.
Association of Women Students (AWS): 79, 162, 191, 228, 229-230, 237, 250, 288, 294, 342, 343. *See also* Women's Self-Government Association.
Athletics: 22, 45-46, 68-70, 113, 157, 158-159, 164, 165, 183, 189, 220, 223, 225, 226, 236, 246, 297, 298, 338, 360, 371, 375, 382, 413.
Atomic bomb: 186, 212.
Automobiles: 57, 58, 59, 118-119, 146, 161, 177, 178, 186, 189, 223-224, 236, 340, 349.
Autry, Barbara: 237.
Auxiliary Enterprises: 15, 190, 212, 239-240, 288, 311, 329, 372.
Awis, Joe: 330.
Aycock, T. M.: 158.

## B

Baily, William H.: 105.
Baker, Boyd "Pappy": 187, 209, 243.
Baker, Ethel: 154.
Baker, Jimmy: 185.
Baker, J. N.: 254.
Baker, Verndia: 154.
Bands: 60, 62, 66, 67, 113, 162-163, 184-185, 206, 212.
Banks, Ben: 98, 99.
Barker, Robert J.: 24, 26, 31, 42.
Barnes, Esta Lee: 225.
Barnes, Mary C.: 249, 332.
Bartlett, Dewey: 282, 293, 296.

Basic Educational Opportunity Grant (BEOG): 322.
Basketball: 69, 96, 123, 158, 159, 199, 200, 297, 298, 338.
Basler, Marie L.: 393.
Basore, Bennett L.: 189, 199.
Bates Brothers: 368.
Batkin, Sammy: 176.
Batson, Alonzo: 297.
Battiste, Willie: 344.
Bauman, Thelma Lea: 388.
Beatles: 235, 362.
Beauty pageants: 59, 75, 115, 162, 164, 229.
Beck, Dana: 294.
Beer, Ronald S.: 373-374, 375, 377, 390, 404, 405, 409.
Behring, Byron: 243.
Bell, Lee: 291.
Bell, Margie: 294.
Bellmon, Henry: 238, 245.
Bennett, Bon Bick: 365.
Bennett Hall: 187, 192, 194, 195, 245, 246, 247, 331, 368, 380, 382.
Bennett, Henry G.: 94, 118, 123, 125, 126, 135-138, 144, 149, 150, 157, 167, 168, 175, 176, 180, 182, 189, 191, 192, 199, 200, 206, 208, 209, 211-212, 221, 324.
Bennett, Margaret: 194.
Bennett, Tom: 342.
Benson, Gene: 250.
Bentley, Nell Dent: 77.
Bergegrun, Katherine: 152.
Berger, Melvin: 181.
Berlin, Irving: 58.
Berrigan, Philip: 286.
Beta Phi: 122.
Beta Sigma Psi: 341.
Beta Theta Pi: 123, 340, 391, 392. *See also* Delta Sigma.
Beyer, Gladys: 249.
Bicycles: 57, 61, 193, 349, 368.
Bilyeu, Winsel: 242, 334, 388.
Bird, Bob: 284.
Bird Brand Brooms: 142, 143.
Bird, Sandra L.: 374.
Birdwell, Harry: 294.
Bi-State Mental Health Association: 336.
Bivert, Raymond E.: 116, 257, 258, 323.
Black, Bob: 156.
Black Heritage Commission: 344.
Black Heritage Week: 344, 392.
Black student boycott: 296-298.
Black students: 49, 222-223, 238, 266, 289, 295, 296-298, 303, 321, 341, 344, 405.
Blacksmithing: 51, 157.
Blackwell, Carl P.: 85.

Blair, F. Joe: 331, 380, 382, 389.
Block and Bridle: 228.
Blue Key: 162, 392.
Board of Publications: 116, 117.
Board of Regents: 3, 192, 206, 236, 246,
   249, 264, 277, 278, 280, 282, 284-285,
   288, 290, 293, 294, 295, 304, 311, 317,
   381, 382, 385, 395. *See also* Oklahoma
   State Board of Agriculture.
Bocock, Tillman I.: 223.
Boger, Lawrence L.: 349, 359, 360, 362,
   365, 372, 374, 386, 395.
Bolend, Floyd J.: 50.
Bond, Julian: 300.
Bookstore: 94, 110-112, 157, 208, 210,
   242, 254, 333, 386.
Boost Alcohol Consciousness Concerning
   the Health of University Students
   (BACCHUS): 367.
Bormann, Carol: 386.
Bost, Armon: 304.
Bost, Henry A.: 31, 52.
Botkin, Sam: 233, 255.
Bowers, George W.: 25, 39, 52.
Bowers, Royal H.: 256, 257.
Boyer, Carolyn: 250.
Boyles, Delmer: 288.
Boyles, Walter: 249.
Breedlove, Clarence H.: 118.
Brewer, E. E.: 109.
Brezhnev, Leonid I.: 266.
Briggs, Don R.: 386, 387, 404, 407-408.
Bright, Johnny: 223.
Brobst, Harry K.: 256.
Brock's Frat Shop: 185.
Bronker, Mildred Lucille: 182.
Bronker, Mr. and Mrs. Gladden: 182.
Brooks, Margaret: 285.
Brooks, Robert: 40.
Brown, Donald: 223.
Brown, Donald N.: 345.
Brown, John J.: 61.
Brown, Robert J.: 181.
Bruce, Charles W.: 377, 404, 405,
   408-410.
Brumbaugh, Norma: 85.
Brumley Apartments: 245, 246, 382.
Brumley, Ben: 245.
Bruner, J. O.: 202.
Bruton, Bill: 194.
Buchanan, Hal N.: 260, 287.
Buck, Bob: 298.
Bullen, Alan C.: 282.
Bullen, B. C.: 64-65.
Bullock, George: 139.
Bullock, Louis: 280, 292, 293.
Bunker, Kent E.: 338, 383.
Bureau of Indian Affairs: 345.
Bureau of Tests & Measurements: 150, 256.

Burgess, Elaine P.: 376, 379.
Burkey, Phyllis: 187.
Burner, Jacob Oliver: 261.
"Burnin' Black" Choir: 344.
Bursar: 361.
Burton, L. W.: 139.
Business Manager: 190, 240.
Bustamante, Manuel D.: 379.
Butler, Kathy: 332, 343.
Butts, Jim: 253.
Byrd, Clifton J.: 181.

# C

Cabinet making shop: 142.
Cacy Jr., King W.: 254, 256, 319, 323,
   378.
CALL Center: 313.
Cambridge University: 115.
Camp Redlands: 296, 384-385.
Camp, W. E.: 80, 81.
Campbell, A.: 31.
Campbell, Irene: 104.
Campbell, John R.: 410.
Campbell, O. K.: 190, 191, 254.
Campus and Area Resident Escort Service
   (CARE): 393.
Campus Chest: 189.
Campus Club: 101-102.
Canfield, Robert B.: 249.
Cantwell, J. W.: 77, 79, 82, 84, 111.
Career Counseling Services: 13, 149, 256,
   313, 319, 363, 365, 376, 378, 387, 403,
   408.
Carlson, Jan M.: 318, 319, 375, 376, 385,
   390, 393.
Carman, Lee: 187.
Carmichael, Stokely: 376.
Carnegie, Andrew: 58.
Carney, George: 405.
Case, Herman M.: 223.
Caskey, Owen L.: 256, 257.
Cass, Maude: 79.
Castleman, Jack: 250.
Caudell, Andrew N.: 31, 39, 52.
Caves, Doug: 288.
Ceramics factory: 142-143.
*Challenger* Space Shuttle: 370.
Chambers, Boyd: 230.
Chambers, Roger: 347.
Chapel: 29, 30, 40-41, 63.
Chapel, Nimrod: 289.
Chapman, B. B.: 168.
Chapman, Carol: 346.
Chase, Joy: 250.
Cheating: 65, 187, 234, 366-367.
Chemistry Club: 47.
Cherokee Outlet: 50.
Chi Omega: 123, 197, 251, 340.

Childers, C. C.: 170.
Childress, Nancy R.: 374.
Christmas: 115, 265, 326, 386.
Civil disobedience: 275-277, 289, 290-292, 293, 394, 295, 303.
Civil rights: 275-276, 281-284, 286, 289-292, 320, 341, 344.
Civil War: 8, 10, 12, 13, 14.
Clark, Edward F.: 22, 27, 30.
Clark, Joseph J.: 180.
Clark, Robert B.: 318, 320, 323, 377.
Class fight: 63, 68, 72-74, 81, 119.
Classroom tents: 138.
Clayton, Jimmy: 206.
Clemens, Ed: 169.
Cleverdon, Lawrence Albert: 103.
Coed prom: 183.
Coffee Shop: 185.
Coffman, H.: 31, 32.
College Building. See Old Central.
College Cafeteria: 98-99, 109, 157, 194, 254. See also Tiger Tavern.
College Courts: 239.
College Entrance Examination Board (CEEB): 320-321.
College Farm: 36.
College of Education: 109, 259.
College Paper: 60, 61, 80.
Collegiate atmosphere: 6, 7, 23, 34-35, 44-45, 47, 63.
Collier, Joe: 186.
Colonial colleges: 6, 7, 8, 10.
Columbia University: 124, 158, 220, 254, 276.
Colvin Center: 15, 263-265, 313, 335, 337, 338-339, 372, 376, 382, 383, 407.
Colvin Center Annex: 337, 338.
Colvin, Valerie: 158, 198, 199, 200, 263, 264-265.
Combs, A.: 31.
Commencement: 5, 63, 71, 113.
Communism: 212, 220, 233, 257, 265, 266, 282.
Community Hospitality Committee: 325-326, 327.
Computers: 368, 377, 407, 408, 409.
Connell, J. H.: 63, 109.
Connell, Val J.: 182.
Conscientious objectors: 300.
Contardi, Barbara: 334.
Converse, Mabel: 154.
Convert, Bob: 184.
Cook, Thelma: 298.
Cooper, Donald L.: 260, 261, 262, 336, 389, 404, 406, 407.
Cooper, Thomas "Zack": 290, 292, 332.
Cordell Hall: 154-156, 157, 158, 178, 195, 248, 249, 331, 332, 380, 381-382.
Cordell, Harry: 154.

Coser, Pete G.: 376.
Cosmopolitan Club: 115-116. See also International Relations Club.
Counseling Services: 15, 239, 256, 289, 311, 319-320, 372, 377, 378-379, 404, 406, 408.
Cow Chips: 348.
Coy, Chad: 348.
Crook, Janice: 230.
Crossdale, Caroline: 105.
Crouse, Paul G.: 72, 74.
Crutchfield Hall: 83, 92, 95-96, 99, 101, 103.
Crutchfield, William Walter: 82, 83.
Cunningham, Clarence M.: 291-292.
Cunningham, Mercedier C.: 388.
Curnow, Dorothea: 261.
Curriculum: 38-39, 134, 147, 149, 163, 177, 212, 240, 284, 289, 357, 394.
Curtis, C. David: 361.

## D

Dad McGrew's: 100.
Dahms, Ken: 286.
Daily O'Collegian: 47, 118, 162-164, 165, 182-183, 187, 188, 195, 197, 199, 200, 205-206, 212, 223, 230, 231, 244, 251, 259, 282, 283, 285, 287, 288, 290, 299, 301, 304, 316-317, 343, 349, 370, 392.
Dancing: 58, 77-78, 122, 148, 162, 177, 183, 185, 186, 189, 197, 198, 199, 206, 208, 223, 234, 235, 340, 369.
Dark, Marian: 260, 387.
Darnell, Lewis J.: 42.
Dartmouth College: 8.
Davis, Nancy: 222.
"Dead Week": 225, 238.
Dean of Men: 12, 94, 124, 125, 144, 190, 203, 251-252, 254, 311, 318.
Dean of Student Affairs: 222, 240, 241, 292, 311, 313, 315, 329, 377.
Dean of Students: 15, 186, 188, 190, 233, 238, 241, 253, 288, 296.
Dean of Women: 12, 93, 94, 100-101, 122, 124, 125, 144, 145-148,161, 190, 203, 229, 234, 251-252, 311, 318, 342.
Debating clubs: 10, 46-47, 83-84, 115.
DeBlaker, Karleen Anderson: 212.
Debs, Eugene V.: 78.
Delta Chi: 197, 251, 341.
Delta Delta Delta: 250, 340, 341.
Delta Sigma: 81, 122. See also Beta Theta Pi.
Delta Sigma Theta: 340, 341, 391.
Delta Tau Delta: 197, 251, 296, 341, 391.
Delta Upsilon: 250, 341, 392.
Delta Zeta: 140, 197, 340, 390.
Demaree, Rex: 333, 380, 389.

Demerits: 29, 30, 42, 43-44, 50, 63-64, 67, 77, 102.
DeMille, Cecil B.: 115.
Dentist: 151, 152, 201, 202.
Department of Financial Aid: 15, 258, 298, 311, 313, 320-324, 372, 377-378, 404, 406, 408-410.
Department of Special Services: 314, 318, 377.
Department of Student Activities: 314, 318-319, 334, 377, 385, 388.
Depression: 127, 133-134, 137, 140-144, 150, 160, 170, 181.
Dermer, Richard: 367.
Dewey, John: 220.
Dickman, Marcia M.: 376.
Discipline: 15, 27-34, 43-44, 63-65, 78, 118, 145, 190, 221, 222, 224, 238, 253, 256, 284, 289, 292, 293, 296, 303, 315, 378.
Discrimination: 289, 295, 324, 345, 390.
Division of Student Affairs: 93, 157, 222, 238, 239, 241, 242, 253-256, 257, 259, 313, 314-329, 334, 341, 372, 376-377.
Division of Student Services: 15, 93, 94, 144-160, 240, 309-314, 350, 382, 404, 410.
Dolde, Emma Swope: 28.
Dollar, Robert J.: 256.
Dollarhide, Pamela: 347.
Domestic Science. *See* Home Economics.
Dormitories. *See* Residence Halls.
Dorris, Jo F.: 319.
Dossett, James: 298.
Double "O" Club: 226, 344. *See also* Association for Concerns of Disabled Collegiates.
Douglas Cup: 68.
Doze, Gary: 232.
Draper, Dan: 238.
Drug Analysis Center: 317.
Drugs: 284, 301, 316-317, 350, 367, 374.
Drummond, Frederick "Gent": 246.
Drummond Hall: 125, 246, 382.
Duck, Frank E.: 7.
Duck, John W.: 105.
Duesler, Floyd: 292.
Duff, Alice Moreland: 343.
Durham, Ginger: 235.
Dusch, Willa Adams: 23, 24.
Dysart, Minnie: 25.

# E

*Earthquake* humor magazine: 119.
Eating disorders: 366.
Eaton, Everett H.: 361.
Eaton, Frank: 225.
Edgley, Charles K.: 362-363.

Edmon Low Library: 220, 234, 289, 295, 327.
Elderhostel: 404, 405.
Ellis, Flora May: 158, 199, 263.
Emerson, Bonnie E.: 79, 187, 189.
Emerson, Ralph Waldo: 160.
"Emphasis People": 267.
Employment Bureau: 143, 203.
Enrollment: 124, 134, 135, 137, 138-139, 149, 150, 164, 175, 183, 189, 199, 203, 212, 220, 221, 241, 245, 256, 276, 279, 319, 345, 357, 358, 360, 365, 394.
Equal Rights Amendment: 302, 370, 371.
Equality: 229-230, 284, 294-295, 303, 312, 321, 338, 342, 344-348, 349.
Eskimo Joe's: 367.
Etchinson, Vesta: 147, 209, 242.
Evans, Al: 250.
Evans, Margaret: 94.
Evans, Ruth: 122.
Everett, Freda: 200.
Ewing, Bob: 250.
Examinations: 29, 30, 34, 40, 65, 70-71, 146, 163, 187, 225, 236.
Expenses: 35-37, 84, 96, 104, 105, 134, 140, 150, 192, 195, 203, 221, 245, 247, 320-321, 333, 358, 371, 380, 408.

# F

Faculty: 3, 12, 15, 21, 24-27, 29, 60, 95, 103, 111, 115, 144, 185-186, 187, 206, 221, 223, 236, 238, 282, 283, 285, 289, 300, 343, 350, 365, 371.
Faculty Council: 284, 287-288, 310.
Farmer, James: 286.
FarmHouse: 140, 197, 252, 340, 391.
Faulkner, Delois: 229.
Federal Rehabilitation Act of 1973: 346.
Fee waivers: 106, 108.
Fehring, Eleanor: 392.
Fenimore, Bob: 183, 185.
Fenton, Mike: 244.
Ferguson, Mark: 250.
Fields, John: 45.
Finnegan, Rex T.: 318, 319, 320, 376, 377.
Fleming, James R.: 322, 323.
Fleming, Jan: 250.
Flinn, H. H. "Rosie": 252.
Flivver Derby: 161.
Floyd, Leroy: 189.
Flying Aggies: 233.
Flynt, Elmo: 120.
Food Services: 95, 96, 98-99, 102, 157-158, 192, 194-196, 203, 206, 208-209, 220, 239, 244, 245, 247, 313, 331-332, 349, 372, 376, 379, 389, 406.
Food Services Center: 331, 335.

Hatch Act: 9.
Havenstrite, Al: 243.
Hawkins, Glenn B.: 327.
Hawkins, Jean: 265.
Hays, George P.: 180.
Hays, Grace: 230.
Hays, Richard: 230, 231.
Hazelrigg, Hal: 196.
Hazing: 64, 71-74, 79, 124, 164, 185, 252, 339, 390.
Hazley, Orlando: 223.
Health Services: 13, 15, 94, 95, 102-105, 150-152, 201-203, 239, 260-262, 311, 336-337. *See also* University Hospital and Clinic.
Hedrick, Sally: 392.
Hefley, Betty: 250.
Hell Week: 124, 390.
Hellhounds: 115.
Henderson, David: 318.
Henderson, Terry H.: 318, 319, 320, 388.
Henry, Donnetta: 341.
Hesser, Abe L.: 209-210, 222, 240, 241, 244, 254, 293, 311-312, 317, 334.
Hicks, Stanley: 329.
Hill, Helen Thacker: 256.
Hiniker, N. L.: 201.
Hispanic students: 321, 346, 379, 404, 405.
Hodges, Joe: 292.
Hoelting, Floyd: 331.
Hoffman, Abbie: 292, 293, 294.
Hofler, Pat: 240, 311, 373, 389, 404, 405.
Hollis, Wardell: 341.
Holmes, Larry: 342.
Holt, Smith L.: 402-403.
Holter, George L.: 27, 30, 42, 50.
Homecoming: 75, 139-140, 183, 189, 197, 212, 225, 235, 238, 250, 331, 392, 413.
Home Economics: 95, 98, 109, 119, 191, 220, 223, 376.
Home Economics Club: 75.
Honors system: 40, 65.
Hope, Bob: 227, 388.
Hopkins, Randy: 292.
House, R. Morton: 36.
Houska, Joe: 69.
Houston, Launa: 347.
Howard, Peggy: 187, 188.
Howard, Samuel: 223.
"Howdy" activities: 119, 183, 185, 206, 212, 226, 235, 238, 243, 318, 413.
Hull, Ray M.: 119.
Humor magazines: 11, 120, 161, 165-166, 187, 231-233.
Humphrey, Hubert H.: 300, 388.
Hunter, Bill: 334.
Hunter, Ella Effie: 52.

Hurley, Patrick J.: 180.
Hurst, Raymond: 114, 115.
Huss, Robert W.: 379, 380, 404, 405.
Hutto, Maggie: 24, 25, 26.
Hutto, W. W.: 27, 30, 31.

# I

Iba Hall: 246, 380, 382, 388.
Iba, Henry P.: 246.
Independent Men's Residence Council: 194, 249. *See also* Men's Residence Halls Association.
Independent Party: 188, 197.
Indian Heritage Week: 346, 392.
Indian students: 52, 205, 289, 321, 344-346, 392.
Infectious diseases: 34, 151, 152, 262.
Infirmary: 104, 150-152, 201-203.
*In loco parentis*: 15, 26, 63, 118, 190, 283, 295, 309-310.
Insane Liberation: 348.
Integration: 222-223, 266, 284, 289.
Interfraternity Council: 117, 122, 123, 140, 196, 197, 206, 251-252, 265, 294, 339-342, 367, 390.
International Food Manufacturers Association: 331.
International Mall: 327-328.
International Relations Club: 115, 325, 326. *See also* Cosmopolitan Club.
International Student Advisor: 14, 236, 327-328.
International Student Organization: 328, 392, 402.
International Student Services: 376, 379.
International students: 14, 51, 116, 162, 190, 192, 211, 236, 238, 279, 289, 324-329, 342, 365, 366, 380, 392, 402.
Intramural programs: 11, 13, 45-46, 68-69, 94, 123, 138, 158-159, 183, 189, 193, 197, 198-200, 202, 240, 249, 262-264, 337, 383-385, 391.
Iranian hostage crisis: 370.
"Iron Man" award: 252-253.
Ittanaha: 162, 344, 345. *See also* Native American Student Association.

# J

Jackson, Frances: 336, 379.
Jackson, Kenneth: 298.
Jackson, Ralph: 185, 225.
Jackson, Velma: 185, 225.
Jackson, W. Lynn: 290, 329, 330, 379.
Jacobson, Bob: 187.
Jafek, Emil: 333.
James, John E.: 225.
Jamison, Jeff: 347.
Jamison, Robert L.: 387.
Jarrell, Alfred Edwin: 7, 28, 42, 45.

Johnson, Bruce: 210.
Johnson, Glenn: 298.
Johnson, Harry E.: 79, 110.
Johnson, Jeanne B.: 261.
Johnson, Lyndon B.: 266, 277, 320.
Johnson, Ronald Lee: 297.
Jones, C. V.: 50.
Jones, Ewing: 164.
Jones, Herman: 341.
Jones, Jenkin Lloyd: 278.
Jones, Linda: 244.
Jones, Olin: 68.
Jones, Stephen: 294.
Jordan, James G.: 390.
Jordan, Martha L.: 376, 379.
Junior-Senior Banquet: 71, 79.
Junior-Senior Prom: 184, 189, 227-228, 235, 243.

## K

Kalivoda, Ted: 327.
Kamm, Robert B.: 265, 277-278, 279, 280-281, 282, 283, 284, 285, 287, 290, 293-294, 296, 297, 298, 302, 303-304, 309-310, 312, 314, 350, 374.
Kappa Alpha Psi: 341.
Kappa Alpha Theta: 123, 196, 197, 340.
Kappa Delta: 123, 197, 251, 340, 392.
Kappa Kappa Gamma: 197, 340, 391.
Kappa Nu: 140.
Kappa Sigma: 118, 250, 251, 340.
Katz, Jacob: 108.
Kelley, Robert: 181.
Kelly, John: 181.
Kelly, John G.: 201.
Kennedy, John F.: 265, 266, 362.
Kennedy, Robert F.: 276, 287, 362.
Kent, Mrs. F. C.: 93, 94, 95.
Kent State University: 291, 292, 293, 298, 301, 302-303, 362, 374.
Kerr Hall: 125, 246.
Kerr, Robert S.: 246.
Kevin, Jim: 263, 338.
Keys, Charlie: 206.
Keys, Thomas M.: 318, 376, 386, 390, 404, 406.
Khruschev, Nikita: 266.
Kietzman, Bob: 230.
Killingsworth, Louizon: 194.
King Jr., Martin Luther: 266, 276, 287, 289, 362.
Kinnamon, Paul: 334.
Knapp, Bradford: 104, 107, 109, 110, 116, 117, 118, 119, 125, 135.
Knox, Joe: 166.
Korea: 220.
Kosygin, Aleksei: 266.
Kurland, Robert: 183, 185.
Kuznekoff, Paul: 290-291, 292, 293.

## L

Lackey, Bill: 250.
Lahman, Wilbur: 80.
Lahoma Club: 106, 205.
Lake Carl Blackwell: 239, 296, 384.
Lambda Chi Alpha: 123, 179, 196, 251, 339-340, 391.
Land Boarding House: 37, 38.
Land-Grant Movement: 5, 9, 17, 22, 127, 135, 175, 220, 278, 359, 405.
Land, J. T.: 38.
Langston University: 223, 344.
Larason, Anne: 222.
Larsen, Charles E.: 319.
Latimer, Maud: 146, 153, 193.
Latimer, Patrice: 341, 343.
Lawson, Curtis: 344.
Lawson, David E.: 233.
Leake, Bob: 242.
Leary, Timothy: 284, 285.
Leisure Services: 13, 155, 175, 181, 182, 199, 206, 235, 243, 311, 332, 337-339, 372, 376, 383-385.
Lemon, Glen: 230.
Leonard, David: 209.
Lerd, Terry: 230.
Lester, Charley: 225.
Levin, Mrs. Alfred: 325, 326.
Lewis, Ervin G.: 7.
Lewis, Frank: 251.
Lewis, Lowery L.: 45, 66.
Lewis Stadium: 192.
L'Hote, Linda L.: 387.
Lindbergh, Charles: 115.
Lindsey, Ray: 80.
Literary societies: 10, 45, 46-47.
*Little Man on Campus* comic: 234, 235.
Logan, Randall: 392.
Long, Harry: 165, 166.
Lovelady, Lucille: 242.
Lowry, Fern: 79, 85.
Lucas, Tom: 279, 284, 286.
Luckadoo, Tim: 380.
Luper, Clara: 296, 344.
Luther, Tama Ruth: 256.
Lyceum series: 78.

## M

MacVicar, Robert: 240.
Madison, James: 401.
Madrid, Viola: 346.
Madrigal Dinner Concert: 386.
Magruder, A. C.: 26, 32, 39.
Magruder Medals: 27, 39.
Mailer, Norman: 276.
Malcolm X: 289.
Mannering, Mary Cheryl: 392.
March, John: 176.
Marcuse, Herbert: 276.

National Association of College and University Residence Halls: 250, 332, 383.
National Association of Student Personnel Administrators: 367, 374.
National Association of Women Deans and Counselors: 191.
National Defense Education Act: 257.
National Interfraternity Conference: 252, 253.
National Intramural Association: 338.
National Student Association: 266, 286.
National Youth Administration: 140, 143.
Native American Student Association: 345, 346, 392. See also Ittanaha.
Neal, J. C.: 26, 32, 39, 50.
Neal, Kate: 7, 39.
Nelson, Lila: 68.
Nelson, Margaret F.: 345.
Newbold, Grace: 332.
Nixon, Richard M.: 300, 301-302.
North Central Association: 221, 239, 278, 371, 372, 373, 375.
North Murray Hall: 153, 159, 192, 198, 331.
Nuclear power: 186, 220, 265, 363, 370, 371.

O

OAMC Service Flag: 113-114.
Oberle, George H.: 337, 338, 385, 404.
O'Bryan, Tony: 334.
O'Collegian: 116.
Off-campus housing: 13, 92, 99, 102, 122, 145, 148, 186, 190, 192, 224, 236, 241, 247, 253, 256, 283, 343.
Off-Campus Student Association: 343, 375, 393.
Oglesby, R. R.: 188, 191, 254, 325.
Oklahoma: 358, 359, 409-410, 413.
Oklahoma A. and M. College Mirror: 47, 48.
Oklahoma City: 10, 210.
Oklahoma College and University Placement Association: 387.
Oklahoma Legislature: 221, 225, 238, 282, 286, 292, 293, 302, 358, 370.
Oklahoma State Board of Agriculture: 82, 92, 93, 109, 122, 125, 138, 154, 160, 192. See also Board of Regents.
Oklahoma Student Loans: 322.
Old Central: 3, 4, 32, 36, 40, 42, 47, 50, 52, 59, 74, 110, 160.
Oldham, Beverly: 292, 349.
Olmstead, Thelma: 334.
Olsen, Forest: 202.
Omega Kappa Nu: 140.
Omega Literary Society: 47, 83.
Omicron Nu: 107.

Open house policy. See Visitation policy.
Orange and Black: 65, 80, 85, 110, 113.
Oretoopa Halls: 192, 195, 212.
Orientation: 16, 126, 145, 149, 190, 204, 229, 239, 253, 256, 313, 325, 326, 327, 349.
Orr, M. G.: 192.
Osterhout, Ron: 235.
OSU Development Foundation: 242.
Otey, M. J.: 108.
Overmiller, Wanda Lee: 154.
Owens, Wallace: 344.
Oxford, Sue: 347.

P

Pace, Elbert: 231.
Paden, Clarence: 116.
Page, LeAnn: 374.
Pallard, Jim: 243.
Panhandle A. and M. College: 240, 256.
Panhellenic Council: 117, 122, 123, 139, 197, 206, 251, 252, 285, 295, 339, 340-342, 367, 390.
Panty raids: 221, 222, 238.
Parcher, Vernon: 204.
Parent's Day: 162, 392.
Parker, Elsie: 24, 25-26.
Parker, Eva: 105.
Parker Hall: 125, 245, 246, 382.
Parker, Quanah: 245.
Pastorate movement: 10.
Patchin Award: 341, 342.
Patchin Panel: 342, 343.
Patchin, Zelma F.: 191, 251-252, 255, 342.
Patterson, H. P.: 109.
Pattillo, Naomi Oleta: 249, 331.
Payne County: 9, 10, 21-22, 230.
Peck, C. P.: 110-111.
Peck, H. L.: 110-111.
Peck, O. T.: 110-111.
Peck's Lodge: 67, 72, 79, 110-111.
Pemberton, Ina: 99.
Pender, Patricia Jo: 233.
Pente: 368.
Pep organizations: 71, 115, 189, 212.
Peppers Pep Club: 115.
Personnel point-of-view: 16, 239.
Peshke, David: 338.
Phi Delta Theta: 197, 198, 250, 251, 341, 391.
Phi Gamma Delta: 250, 341, 392.
Phi Kappa Delta: 122.
Phi Kappa Psi: 341, 391.
Phi Kappa Tau: 197, 251, 341.
Phi Kappa Theta: 140, 340, 391.
Phi Mu: 390, 391.
Phi Omega Phi: 140.

Philomathean Literary Society: 47, 71, 80, 83-84.
Physical education: 13, 43, 157, 158, 198, 264, 338, 404.
Physically disabled students: 318, 320, 344, 346, 382, 393.
Pi Beta Phi: 123, 124, 169, 197, 251, 340.
Pi Kappa Alpha: 140, 179, 340.
Pi Kappa Phi: 296, 341, 392.
Pigg, Carl: 61.
Pigg, Howard: 61.
Pinckney, Charles: 401.
"Pistol Pete": 225, 334.
Pittman, Dawn: 388-389.
Placement Services: 14, 16, 95, 109, 157, 159-160, 258-260, 311, 334, 407-409. *See also* University Placement.
*Playboy* magazine: 367, 369.
Point Four Program: 211, 234, 327.
Politics in Oklahoma: 26, 27, 32, 48, 49, 62, 110, 126, 135, 137-138, 150, 221, 238, 281.
Pope, Virginia: 154.
Porter, E. Melvin: 296, 344.
Potts, Henry Clay: 177, 194, 247.
Potts, Vernie: 155.
Pow-wow: 346.
Practicum: 35, 39.
Prairie Playhouse: 60.
Preparatory Department: 21-22, 37, 59, 135.
President's Commission on Campus Unrest: 277.
President's Leadership Council: 374-375.
Prohibition: 133, 161.
Prosser, Ethel: 191, 192-193.
Pruett, Haskell "Doc": 137, 235, 236.
Public display of affection: 303.
Pugh, Nora L.: 376.
Purdy, Daisy I.: 157.

## Q

Quality Craft Hooked Rugs: 142, 143.
Querry, Samuel R.: 47.
Quirk, Mike: 367.
Quisenberry, Judith A.: 331, 380, 388.

## R

Rachel, Frank: 194.
Racism: 296, 298, 324, 345.
Rakey, Meta: 240.
Reagan, Ronald W.: 358, 362, 388, 389.
"Record Book": 168.
Rector, F. L.: 81.
Reding, Allen B.: 334, 386, 389.
Redo, Jerry: 298.
*Redskin*: 66, 75, 80-81, 113, 115, 165, 179, 187, 188, 223, 230-231, 304, 314-315, 342, 343, 363, 388, 413.

Reed, Alyce: 184.
Reed, Gertrude: 192.
Registrar: 12, 177, 238.
Registration: 66, 150, 164-165, 175, 189, 203, 212.
Reid, Cheryl: 294.
Religious Emphasis Week: 10, 162, 167, 190, 233, 238, 282.
Religious guidance: 10, 15, 40, 82-83, 119, 162, 167, 233, 238, 288.
Renfrow, William C.: 3.
Renter's Association: 343, 393.
Representative Party: 188, 197.
Reserve Officers Training Corp (ROTC): 66, 162, 169, 176-177, 291, 292, 298, 299, 300, 331. *See also* Military Department.
Residence Halls: 12, 13, 38, 93, 95-98, 99-100, 152-156, 178, 186, 190, 191-194, 196, 223, 224, 238, 239, 240, 241, 244-247, 256, 289, 294-295, 296, 303, 311, 316, 329-331, 332, 335, 344, 379-383.
Residence Halls Association: 101, 191, 194, 290-291, 294, 295, 304, 329, 332, 343, 367, 375, 381, 382, 383.
Residence halls student government: 99, 101-102, 155, 249, 332, 343. *See also* Residence Halls Association.
Residence Halls Week: 250, 332, 392.
Resident assistants: 147, 190, 191, 319, 379.
Residential Life Department: 15, 372, 379-380, 382, 389, 404.
Returning Student Organization: 393.
Reynold's Stadium: 369.
Richards, W. S.: 81.
Richardson, Alice: 334.
Rickenbacker, Eddie: 227.
Ricker, Kenneth: 325.
"Ride 'Em Cowboys": 212.
Rife, Audris: 249.
Rifle Club: 78.
Rigg, R. R.: 202, 261.
Robinson, Joe: 210, 242.
Robinson, Joe L.: 79.
Robinson, John: 298.
Roger, Elmer B.: 150.
Rogers, James H.: 385.
Rogers, Murl: 156.
Rogers, Will: 115, 133, 162.
Roney, Lynn: 285.
Roosevelt, Franklin D.: 133, 144, 169.
Roosevelt, Theodore: 57.
Rooters' Club: 71.
Ropes course: 384-385, 388.
Rothlisberger, C. J.: 253.
Rubin, Jerry: 294.
Rulon, Philip Reed: 34.

Ruttman, Gerald E.: 334.

## S

Sammy Robertson Orchestra: 185.
Sampson, B. Kent: 318, 329, 330, 376, 380, 389.
Sandburg, Carl: 115.
Santa Fe Railroad: 35, 67.
Schelsky, Charles F.: 337, 338, 385.
Schlesinger, George B.: 261.
Schmalfeld, Robert G.: 317-318, 377.
Schmidt, Loraine: 202.
Schneider, Gil: 193.
Schneider, Pete: 230.
Scholarships: 106, 108, 146, 203, 205, 230, 253, 257, 258, 320, 375.
Scholastic Aptitude Test (SAT): 395.
Schroeder, Phyllis L.: 329, 330, 376, 380.
Schuler, Susan: 235.
Schull, R. J.: 136, 150-152.
Scott, Abbott C.: 261.
Scott, Angelo C.: 40, 51, 59-60, 62, 68, 80, 137, 245.
Scott Hall: 125, 245, 246, 382.
Scrivner, Russell: 231.
Scroggs, Schiller: 136-137, 139, 141, 165, 199.
Searcy, Dorothy: 384.
Security: 223, 361, 371, 393.
Segregation: 212, 220, 222-223, 238, 252, 217, 298.
Selassie, Haile: 243.
Seldon, Leila: 341.
Select Farm Products: 142.
Self-Help Industries: 140-143.
Selph, Duncan Hyder: 103.
Selph, Layla: 85.
Senior thesis: 39.
Seretean Center: 185.
Serviceman's Readjustment Act: 204-205.
Shadiq, Parveen: 328.
Shadiq, Shehzad: 328.
Shaklin, Donald W.: 169.
Sheets, Myrtle: 392.
Shell, Kenneth M.: 329.
Shepherd Foundation: 322.
Sherrod, H. B.: 152.
Shiever, Vi: 242.
Shindell, Winston G.: 243-244, 314, 318, 319, 334, 385-386.
Shipp Jr., Howard: 298, 299, 318, 319, 320, 376, 379.
Shirley, Ron: 250.
Shoate, Glen: 344.
Sigma Alpha Epsilon: 140, 250, 252, 340, 391.
Sigma Chi: 251, 340, 391.

Sigma Delta Chi: 230.
Sigma Literary Society: 23, 24, 26, 46, 47.
Sigma Mu Sigma: 140.
Sigma Nu: 118, 169, 179, 251, 252, 340.
Sigma Phi Epsilon: 196, 240, 340, 391.
Sigma Tau: 123.
Simmons, Charles Dudley: 103, 104.
Simons, Myron: 250.
Single Student Housing: 313, 329-331, 335, 372, 379.
Skaggs, Walter: 181.
Slack Boarding House: 38.
Stattery, Rem: 253.
Slowpokes: 226.
Smelser, Gene: 189.
Smith, Bill: 225.
Smith, Darrell: 347.
Smith, Emma: 7, 18.
Smith, Jeff: 31, 32.
Smith, Margaret E.: 154.
Smith, Michael M.: 405.
Smith, Richard B.: 301.
Smoking: 59, 161, 206, 316, 348, 368. *See also* tobacco.
Snider, Beulah: 115.
Soloman, Leonard: 182.
Sororities: 93, 120, 122, 147, 186, 190, 197-198, 250-253, 339-342, 349, 390-392.
Soutar, I. G.: 103.
Southeastern State College: 125, 136.
Southwest Association of College and University Housing Officers: 379, 383.
Soviet Union: 257, 265, 370.
Speaker's policy: 281, 282, 284-285, 286, 287-288, 292, 293, 295.
Special Olympics: 385.
Spring Sing: 339.
Spurgeon, Van D.: 266.
*Sputnik*: 257.
Stadium Hall: 192.
Staff, Connie: 230.
Stallings, Moselle W.: 255, 259.
Stallings, Susan C.: 381.
Stanley, Floyd: 304.
Star Crescent Literary Society: 46.
Stearns, Betty: 155.
Stephens, Julia Lee: 255.
Stephens, Naomi: 334.
Stevens, John A.: 182, 333.
Stiles, G. W.: 81.
Stillwater: 3, 10, 29, 163, 170, 175, 198, 227, 233, 238, 241, 244, 252, 323, 337, 365, 367, 374.
Stillwater's Congregational Church: 21, 22.
Stith, Gary: 292.
Stoddart, David E.: 329, 330, 380.
Stone, Stella: 155.
Stone, Walker: 118.

Stout Hall: 191, 192, 194, 222, 245, 247, 343, 382.
Stout, Julia E.: 124-125, 136, 145, 146-148, 190, 191, 225.
Strack, Charlie: 119.
Stratton, Bettye: 242, 388.
Streaking: 314-315, 367.
Streck, Bill: 286.
Strickler, Georgia Ann: 187, 188.
Struthers, James R.: 288.
Stubbs, Gerald T.: 259.
Student activities: 7, 24, 78-86, 101-102, 113-124, 139, 145, 157,160-167, 183-186, 190, 191, 209, 221-222, 223, 226-238, 240, 253-254, 256, 311, 312, 342-348, 392-393, 406.
Student Affairs Building: 157, 194, 254.
Student assistants. *See* Resident assistants.
Student Association: 63, 79, 110, 125, 166, 183, 187, 189, 209, 238, 242, 279, 284, 285, 286, 288, 292, 293, 294, 303, 317, 341, 342-343. *See also* Student Government Association.
Student Bill of Rights: 284.
Student Conduct Office: 361.
Student development: 15, 313, 372, 408.
Student elections: 63, 79, 113, 166-167, 188, 189, 197, 393.
Student employment: 82, 95, 96, 98, 105, 106, 109, 134, 139, 140-142, 143, 147, 184, 203-205, 206, 210, 240, 253, 255, 256, 257, 258, 276.
Student Entertainers: 190, 204, 255, 265, 314, 388.
Student fees: 105, 152, 164, 165, 189, 201, 202, 203, 206, 221, 235-236, 261, 264, 312, 336, 338, 360, 375, 393.
Student financial aid: 14, 94, 105-109, 140-144, 176, 203-205, 239, 253, 257-258, 289, 320-324, 360, 361, 371, 408-409.
Student fire department: 62, 92.
Student Government Association: 343, 367, 374, 375, 381, 382, 393. *See also* Student Association.
Student guidance: 146, 147, 148, 149, 153, 189-190, 194, 225-226, 238, 253, 310.
Student housing: 37-38, 93, 95-102, 152-156, 180-182, 186, 191-194, 196, 223, 241, 244-247, 253, 283, 284, 372, 406.
Student lawsuits: 292, 293, 294-295, 303.
Student loans: 106-108, 143-144, 204-205, 236, 253, 255, 256, 257, 258, 320.
Student newspapers: 11, 34, 116, 125, 162-164, 182, 187.
Student orations: 39, 63, 71, 84.

Student organizations: 24, 78-86, 101-102, 162-164, 177, 186-189, 191, 193-194, 205, 220, 223, 224, 236-238, 284, 314, 318, 342-348.
Student personnel: 16, 144, 190, 238, 239, 240, 254, 255, 267, 278, 309, 313, 318, 350, 372, 376, 410.
Student retention: 150, 241, 313, 357.
Student rules and regulations: 12, 26, 78, 94, 99, 100, 102, 103-104, 118, 145, 156-157, 164, 166, 186, 189, 190, 224-225, 229, 241, 245, 249, 276, 279, 280, 284, 292, 295, 296, 303, 312, 314, 350, 361, 381, 406.
Student Senate: 79, 110, 113, 115, 116, 117, 120, 164, 166-167, 185, 187, 188, 189, 192, 199, 206, 222, 227, 228, 230, 236-238, 240, 250, 258. 263, 266, 280, 283, 285, 286, 288, 290, 295, 317, 325, 326, 336.
Student sexual behavior: 116, 118, 225-226, 234, 249, 262, 288, 290, 349, 350, 368-370.
Student Union: 15, 16, 94, 109-110, 125, 167, 192, 205-211, 212, 220, 222, 226, 228, 232, 234, 238, 239, 240, 241-244, 254, 260, 289, 295, 311, 312, 319, 331, 333-335, 344, 348, 371, 372, 377, 380, 385-386, 388, 404, 406.
Student Union Activities Board (SUAB): 209, 241, 242-244, 334, 386.
Students for a Democratic Society: 267, 300, 301.
Study habits: 70-71, 99, 149, 150, 313, 319, 376, 378.
Study hours: 63, 78, 99, 146, 156, 241.
Sutherland, A. L.: 40.
Swaffar, Bob: 280, 285.
Swim's Hall: 102, 161.
Sylvester, Al: 230.

# T

Taft, William Howard: 115.
Talmage, Judy: 244.
Tarver, "Red": 84-85.
Tate, Ralph: 182, 183.
Tate, Tom: 237.
Tau Kappa Epsilon: 197.
Taylor, Arthur: 209.
Taylor, Mark: 346.
Taylor, Steve: 346.
Television: 119, 210, 211, 234, 276, 289, 370.
Temple, Cathy: 209.
Terrill, Don: 232.
Textbooks: 22, 35, 37, 111-112, 113, 164, 242, 244.
Thatcher Hall: 96-98, 153-154, 331.
Thatcher, Jessie O.: 18, 25, 39, 52, 96.

Theatre: 11.
Theta Beta Pi: 117, 118.
Theta Chi: 197.
Theta Nu Epsilon (TNE): 117-118, 188-189, 238.
Theta Pond: 74, 125, 154, 202, 212, 226, 235, 251, 315, 390.
Theta Sigma Phi: 230.
Thomas, Jim: 232.
Thomas, L. C.: 186.
Thomas, Lowell: 115.
Thompson, Anthony: 346.
Thompson, J. O.: 202.
Thomson, Joseph O.: 261.
Thornberry, Joe: 68.
Tibbetts, Chester A.: 209, 210, 244.
Tiger Round Up: 75. *See also* Harvest Carnival.
Tiger Tavern: 142, 157. *See also* College Cafeteria.
Timberlake, Dave: 253.
Tinker, Christine G.: 334.
Tobacco: 63, 99, 152, 161, 368. *See also* Smoking.
Today's Americans Protesting Executive Secrecy (TAPES): 302.
Tohee, Bill: 346.
Tolson, Melvin: 344.
Tomlinson, Arlie L.: 144.
Tout, Robert C.: 336.
Townsend, Glennie: 392.
Triangle: 250, 341, 391.
Troxel Award: 341.
Troxel, Darrel K.: 251, 253, 254, 325, 341-342.
Truman, Harry S.: 211, 227, 243, 388.
Tucker, Don: 209.
Tug-of-war: 63, 72, 74-75.
Tulsa: 10, 210.
Twenty-Five Year Campus Plan: 126, 135, 167, 175, 202, 208.
Tyhurst, June: 290.

# U

Union Club Hotel: 209, 242, 244, 386, 388.
United States Congress: 8, 238, 257, 322, 401.
United States Constitution: 8, 401, 402, 404.
University Apartments: 379. *See also* Married Student Housing.
University Center at Tulsa: 365.
University Hospital and Clinic: 15, 104-105, 150-152, 189, 201-203, 235, 260-262, 313, 331, 335-337, 372, 379, 388, 389, 404, 406-407. *See also* Health Services.

University of California at Berkeley: 220, 276.
University of Chicago: 124, 162.
University of Georgia: 9-10, 379.
University Placement: 334, 386-388, 404, 406. *See also* Placement Services.

# V

Valencia-Weber, Gloria: 346.
Van Bebber, Herman: 250.
Van Horn's College Drug: 185.
Varney, Bill J.: 242.
Varsitonians: 184, 206.
Varsity Review: 162, 163, 185, 230, 343, 392, 413.
Vee, Carmen: 363.
Vennerberg, Vaughn: 314.
Veterans: 180-183, 186, 198, 202, 204-205.
Veteran's Village: 17, 180-182, 190, 191-192, 202, 212, 245, 333.
Vice President for Student Services: 232, 239, 240, 242, 288, 290, 293, 311-314, 371, 373, 404.
Vickers, Grace: 104, 201, 261.
Vietnam: 220, 266, 267, 283, 291, 292, 298, 302, 320, 349.
Vincent, Dan: 195.
Visitation policy: 101, 249, 290-291, 295, 312, 381.

# W

Wahnee, Blanche: 345.
Wainwright, Nina: 154.
Walkouts: 185-186, 189, 190, 221, 222, 238.
Walkup, Hoyt: 233.
War Records Committee: 180.
Ward, Lee: 223.
Ward, Mike: 316.
Warner, Albin P.: 263, 338.
Warner, Tony: 332.
Washington, Booker T.: 57.
Washington, George: 401.
Watkins, Dave: 363.
Watkins, Wesley: 238.
Watt, Velma: 64.
Waugh, Frank A.: 25, 26, 27.
WAVES: 177.
Webb, Roger: 253.
Weber, Roxie A.: 201, 202, 256, 260-261, 336-337.
Webster Debating Society: 46.
Welch, Linda: 342.
Wellness: 202, 349, 368, 383, 403, 407, 408.
Wentz Foundation: 108, 175, 205, 257. 322.
Wentz Hall: 125, 245, 246, 382.

Wentz, Lew H.: 17, 107-108, 205, 245.
Wentz Scholars: 205, 257.
Wentz Student Loan Program: 107-108, 143, 205, 257.
Wertz, B. L.: 231.
West, Clyde: 333.
West, Elizabeth: 290.
West, Margaret: 153.
West, Martha Jean: 169.
West, Mr. and Mrs. Leonard: 181.
West Sixth Dormitory: 192.
Western Week: 228-229.
Wheat, Willis J.: 181.
Wheeler, Marybelle: 100.
White, Brandon A.: 201, 261.
White, Josh: 223.
White, Ralph L.: 244.
Whiteaker, Rob: 243.
Whitehurst Hall: 125, 160, 199.
Whitley, Ada Van: 263, 338, 385.
Wieman, Charley: 230-231.
Wiemer, Mary Ann: 250.
Wilber, Philip A.: 135, 206, 208, 245.
Willard, Frances E.: 154.
Willard Hall: 150, 154, 156, 157, 178, 192, 194, 222, 247, 332, 333, 380, 382.
Willham, Oliver S.: 197, 219, 220, 221, 223, 224, 235, 236-237, 239, 240, 246, 247, 255, 258, 260, 263, 265, 266, 267, 279, 311, 325.
Willham Residence Complex: 125, 246, 382.
Williams, Benjamin Franklin: 60.
Williams, Catherine: 194.
Williams Hall: 36, 60.
Williams, Margaret: 344.
Williams, Richard M.: 333, 379.
Williams, R. L.: 67.
Williams, Sonny: 196.
Wilp, Diana: 244.
Wilson, Eddie: 346.
Wilson, Levin: 392.
Wilson, Lou: 187, 188.

Wilson, W. Douglas: 327, 328.
Wilson, Woodrow: 58, 112.
Wimberley, Kirk E.: 384, 385.
Wise, Blanche: 39.
Wolfe, Lewis F.: 329.
Women's Athletic Association: 76, 85, 115, 158-159, 199, 200, 263.
Women's Building. *See* Gardiner Hall.
Women's Christian Temperance Union: 77, 154, 161.
Women's hours: 224, 229, 249, 294-295, 303.
Women's intramural programs: 158-159, 338.
Women's Residence Halls Association: 191, 194, 249, 250, 295, 329. *See also* Grand Council.
Women's Self-Government Association: 162. *See also* Association of Women Students.
Woods, Katherine Condon: 252.
Work-Study Program: 320, 322, 323.
World War I: 63, 98, 110, 112-115, 122-123, 242.
World War II: 167, 168-170, 175-180, 187, 194, 198, 203, 212, 220, 249, 340.
Wright, Phil: 304.
Wright, Ron: 243.
Wuestenburg, Doris: 230.

## XYZ

Yates, Debbie: 346.
Yeakel, S. Victor: 261.
Y-Hut: 185, 224, 326.
Young, Kay: 343.
Young Men's Christian Association: 10, 61, 63, 70, 81-83, 94, 95, 106, 113, 139, 167, 203, 233, 374.
Young Women's Christian Association: 10, 61, 76, 81-82, 85, 106, 113, 147, 167, 169, 177, 233, 254, 255.
Yo-Yos: 160-161.
Zeta Tau Alpha: 197, 251, 340.

A History of
Oklahoma State University
Student Life and Services

is a specially designed volume of the Centennial Histories Series.

The text was composed on a personal computer, transmitted by telecommunications to the OSU mainframe computer, and typeset by a computerized typesetting system. Three typefaces were used in the composition. The text is composed in 10 point Melliza with 2 points extra leading added for legibility. Chapter headings are 24 point Omega. All supplemental information contained in the endnotes, charts, picture captions, appendices, bibliography, and index are set in either 8 or 9 point Triumvirate Lite.

The book is printed on a high-quality, coated paper to ensure faithful reproduction of historical photographs and documents. Smyth-sewn and bound with a durable coated nonwoven cover material, the cover has been screen-printed with flat black ink.

The Centennial Histories Committee expresses sincere appreciation to the progressive men and women of the past and present who created and recorded the dynamic, moving history of Oklahoma State University, the story of a land-grant university fulfilling its mission to teach, to research, and to extend itself to the community and the world.